Struts: The Complete Reference, Second Edition

About the Author

James Holmes is a leading Java Web development authority. He is a committer on the Struts project, and the creator of the most popular Struts development tool, Struts Console. Additionally, Oracle Magazine named him "Java Developer of the Year" in 2002 for his work with the Struts framework and Oracle JDeveloper. Holmes is the author of the first edition of *Struts: The Complete Reference* and the co-author of *JavaServer Faces: The Complete Reference* and *The Art of Java.*

About the Technical Editor

Wendy Smoak is a Sr. Systems Analyst at Arizona State University, and a member of the Apache Software Foundation. She can be reached at wsmoak@apache.org.

About the Editor

Herbert Schildt is a leading authority on the C, C++, Java, and C# languages, and is a master Windows programmer. His programming books have sold more than 3.5 million copies worldwide and have been translated into all major foreign languages. He is author of numerous bestsellers, including *Java: A Beginner's Guide*, *Java: The Complete Reference*, *C++: A Beginner's Guide*, *C++: The Complete Reference*, *C: The Complete Reference*, and *C#: The Complete Reference*, and the co-author of *The Art of Java*. Schildt holds both graduate and undergraduate degrees from the University of Illinois. He can be reached at his consulting office at (217) 586-4683. His Web site is **www.HerbSchildt.com**.

Struts: The Complete Reference Second Edition

James Holmes

New York Chicago San Francisco
Lisbon London Madrid Mexico City
Milan New Delhi San Juan
Seoul Singapore Sydney Toronto

The McGraw-Hill Companies

McGraw-Hill books are available at special quantity discounts to use as premiums and sales promotions, or for use in corporate training programs. For more information, please write to the Director of Special Sales, Professional Publishing, McGraw-Hill, Two Penn Plaza, New York, NY 10121-2298. Or contact your local bookstore.

Struts: The Complete Reference, Second Edition

1234567890 DOC DOC 019876

ISBN-13: 978-0-07-226386-2
ISBN-10: 0-07-226386-5

Sponsoring Editor
Wendy Rinaldi

Editorial Supervisor
Jody McKenzie

Project Editor
Carolyn Welch

Acquisitions Coordinator
Mandy Canales

Editor
Herbert Schildt

Technical Editor
Wendy Smoak

Contributing Editor
Bill Siggelkow

Copy Editor
Bob Campbell

Proofreader
Carolyn Welch

Indexer
Claire Splan

Production Supervisor
George Anderson

Composition
Apollo Publishing Services

Illustration
Apollo Publishing Services

Art Director, Cover
Jeff Weeks

Cover Designer
Pattie Lee

**To my mother, who once chided me
for spending so much time in front of the computer,
but has stood behind me steadfast
and given me the platform
from which to flourish.**

Contents at a Glance

Part I The Struts Framework

1 An Introduction to Struts 3
2 Building a Simple Struts Application 11
3 The Model Layer 41
4 The View Layer 47
5 The Controller Layer 65
6 Validator 89
7 Tiles 131
8 Declarative Exception Handling 161
9 Struts Modules 173

Part II Applying Struts

10 Internationalizing Struts Applications 187
11 Securing Struts Applications 201
12 Testing Struts Applications 225

Part III The Struts Tag Libraries

13 The HTML Tag Library 251
14 The Bean Tag Library 311
15 The Logic Tag Library 333
16 The Nested Tag Library 373
17 Using JSTL with Struts 381

Part IV Struts Configuration Files

18 The Struts Configuration File 399
19 The Tiles Configuration File 419
20 The Validator Configuration Files 429

Part V Struts Extensions

21 Struts Scripting 447
22 The Struts-Faces Integration Library 457
23 Using AJAX with Struts 485

Part VI Appendixes

A Struts Console Quick Reference 497
B Third-Party Struts Extensions 515

Index 517

Contents

Acknowledgments xxi

Part I The Struts Framework

1 An Introduction to Struts 3
A Brief History of Web Application Development 3
Two Development Models 5
Model 1 Architecture Overview 5
Model 2 Architecture Overview 5
A Closer Look at the Model-View-Controller Architecture 6
Model Components 6
View Components 6
Controller Components 6
Enter Struts 7
The Evolution of Struts 7
Struts Is Open Source 8
Basic Components of Struts 8
Base Framework 9
JSP Tag Libraries 9
Tiles Plugin 9
Validator Plugin 9
Acquiring Struts 10
What You Get (Binary) 10
What You Get (Source) 10
Getting Started with Struts 10

2 Building a Simple Struts Application 11
Application Overview 11
The Mini HR Application Files 11
index.jsp 13
search.jsp 15
SearchForm.java 21
SearchAction.java 23
EmployeeSearchService.java 25
Employee.java 27
web.xml 28
struts-config.xml 29
MessageResources.properties 32

Compiling, Packaging, and Running the Application 32
Downloading and Installing Struts and Tomcat 33
Compiling the Application 33
Packaging the Application 35
Running the Application 35
Understanding the Flow of Execution 38

3 The Model Layer 41
What Is the Model? 41
Model Layer Breakdown 41
Struts and the Model 42
Using BeanUtils to Transfer Data to Model Classes 42
Reviewing the Model Layer of the Mini HR Application 44

4 The View Layer 47
Struts and the View Layer 47
JSP Pages 48
Form Beans 48
JSP Tag Libraries 57
Resource Bundles 58
Reviewing the View Layer of the Mini HR Application 60
Alternative View Technologies 64

5 The Controller Layer 65
Struts and the Controller Layer 65
The ActionServlet Class 66
The Request Processing Engine 67
Jakarta Commons Chain-Based Request Processing 68
RequestProcessor Class-Based Processing 69
The Action Class 71
Retrieving Values from Form Beans 71
Customizing the Response from an Action 73
Struts' Built-in Actions 73
The ActionForward Class 85
Reviewing the Controller Layer of the Mini HR Application 86

6 Validator 89
Validator Overview 89
Using Validator 90
Enabling the Validator Plugin 90
Creating Form Beans 91
Configuring validator-rules.xml 94
Configuring the Application Resource Bundle File 95
Configuring validation.xml 97

Using Validator's Included Validations 102
Enabling Client-Side Validations 116
Creating Custom Validations 119
Creating a Validation Method 119
Adding a New Validation Rule 121
Adding New Validation Definitions 123
Adding Messages to the MessageResources.properties File 124
Internationalizing Validations 124
Adding Validator to the Mini HR Application 126
Change SearchForm to Extend ValidatorForm 126
Create a validation.xml File 127
Add the Validator Plugin to the struts-config.xml File 128
Add Validation Error Messages to the MessageResources.properties File 129
Compile, Package, and Run the Updated Application 129

7 Tiles **131**
Tiles Overview 133
Using Tiles 133
Enabling the Tiles Plugin 133
Creating Tiles Definitions 134
Creating Layout JSPs and Using the Tiles Tag Library 138
Creating Content JSPs 138
Using the Tiles Definitions 139
Handling Relative URLS with Tiles 140
Internationalizing Tiles 140
Using the Tiles Tag Library 143
The Tiles Tag Library Tags 143
The add Tag 145
The definition Tag 146
The getAsString Tag 147
The importAttribute Tag 147
The initComponentDefinitions Tag 148
The insert Tag 148
The put Tag 150
The putList Tag 151
The useAttribute Tag 152
Adding Tiles to the Mini HR Application 153
Create Layout JSPs 153
Update Existing JSPs to Work with Layouts 155
Create a tiles-defs.xml Tiles Configuration File 157
Update the struts-config.xml Struts Configuration File 158
Repackage and Run the Updated Application 160

8 **Declarative Exception Handling** **161**
Configuring Struts' Exception Handler 161
Exception Handling for Committed Responses 162
Creating a Custom Exception Handler 163
Create a New Exception Handler Class 164
Add New Exception Handler Definitions to the Application's Struts Configuration File 166
Adding Declarative Exception Handling to the Mini HR Application 166
Create an Application Exception Class 167
Update SearchAction to Throw an Application Exception 167
Set Up an Exception Handler in the struts-config.xml Configuration File 168
Create an Exception Handler JSP 170
Add an Exception Error Message to the MessageResources.properties File 170
Recompile, Repackage, and Run the Updated Application 171

9 **Struts Modules** **173**
Using Modules 174
Creating a Struts Configuration File for Each Module 174
Configuring the web.xml Deployment Descriptor for Modules 175
Configuring Links to Access Module-Specific JSPs 176
Using Validator with Modules 177
Using Tiles with Modules 177
Converting the Mini HR Application to Use Modules 178
Set Up Module Directories and Files 179
Create a Struts Configuration File for Each Module 180
Update the Application's web.xml Deployment Descriptor File 181
Update the index.jsp File to Link to Each of the Modules 183
Repackage and Run the Updated Application 183

Part II Applying Struts

10 **Internationalizing Struts Applications** **187**
Understanding Java's Internationalization Support 187
The java.util.Locale Class 188
The java.util.ResourceBundle Class 189
The java.text.MessageFormat Class 190
Understanding Struts' Internationalization Support 190
Locale 191
Message Resources 191
Struts' Tag Library Support for Internationalization 193
Internationalizing the Mini HR Application 194
Add Entries for All Application Text to the MessageResources.properties Resource Bundle File 195

Create a Spanish Version of the MessageResources.properties File ... 195
Update JSPs to Retrieve All Application Text from the MessageResources.properties File ... 196
Repackage and Run the Updated Application ... 198

11 Securing Struts Applications ... 201
Levels of Security ... 201
Providing Secure Communications ... 201
Authentication and Authorization ... 202
Role-Based Access Control ... 202
Container- vs. Application-Managed Security ... 202
Using Container-Managed Security ... 204
Login Configurations ... 205
Container-Managed Secure Transport ... 210
Application-Managed Security ... 211
Creating a Security Service ... 211
Integrating Struts with SSL ... 221

12 Testing Struts Applications ... 225
Types of Testing ... 225
Unit Testing ... 225
Functional Testing ... 226
System Testing ... 226
Unit Testing Struts Applications ... 226
Testing the Model ... 227
Testing Controller Behavior ... 230
Testing the View ... 238
Use-Case-Driven Testing ... 240
Creating Test Cases ... 241
Using Canoo WebTest ... 242
Testing Application Performance ... 245

Part III The Struts Tag Libraries

13 The HTML Tag Library ... 251
Understanding Variables and Scope in JSP Pages ... 251
Using the HTML Tag Library ... 252
The HTML Tag Library Tags ... 253
The base Tag ... 255
The button Tag ... 256
The cancel Tag ... 257
The checkbox Tag ... 259
The errors Tag ... 260
The file Tag ... 262

The form Tag 264
The frame Tag 266
The hidden Tag 270
The html Tag 271
The image Tag 272
The img Tag 274
The javascript Tag 278
The link Tag 280
The messages Tag 283
The multibox Tag 285
The option Tag 287
The options Tag 287
The optionsCollection Tag 289
The password Tag 290
The radio Tag 292
The reset Tag 294
The rewrite Tag 296
The select Tag 299
The submit Tag 301
The text Tag 302
The textarea Tag 304
The xhtml Tag 307
Common Tag Attributes 307

14 The Bean Tag Library 311
Understanding Variables and Scope in JSPs 311
Using the Bean Tag Library 312
The Bean Tag Library Tags 313
The cookie Tag 314
The define Tag 316
The header Tag 318
The include Tag 320
The message Tag 321
The page Tag 323
The parameter Tag 324
The resource Tag 326
The size Tag 327
The struts Tag 329
The write Tag 331

15 The Logic Tag Library 333
Understanding Variables and Scope in JSPs 333
Using the Logic Tag Library 334
The Logic Tag Library Tags 335
The empty Tag 337

- The equal Tag ... 338
- The forward Tag ... 340
- The greaterEqual Tag ... 341
- The greaterThan Tag ... 343
- The iterate Tag ... 345
- The lessEqual Tag ... 348
- The lessThan Tag ... 350
- The match Tag ... 352
- The messagesNotPresent Tag ... 355
- The messagesPresent Tag ... 356
- The notEmpty Tag ... 356
- The notEqual Tag ... 357
- The notMatch Tag ... 360
- The notPresent Tag ... 362
- The present Tag ... 365
- The redirect Tag ... 367

16 The Nested Tag Library ... 373
- Understanding Object Nesting in Struts ... 373
- Using the Nested Tag Library ... 374
- The Nested Tag Library Tags ... 375
  - The nest Tag ... 377
  - The root Tag ... 378
  - The writeNesting Tag ... 379

17 Using JSTL with Struts ... 381
- JSTL Overview ... 381
  - The JSTL Expression Language ... 382
  - The JSTL Tag Libraries ... 385
- Using JSTL with Struts ... 387
  - JSTL Replacement Examples ... 389
  - Using the Struts EL Tag Libraries ... 392
  - The Struts EL Tag Library Tags ... 393

Part IV Struts Configuration Files

18 The Struts Configuration File ... 399
- Understanding XML DTDs ... 399
- Configuring the web.xml Deployment Descriptor ... 400
- The Struts Configuration File Tags ... 401
  - The action Tag ... 402
  - The action-mappings Tag ... 405
  - The controller Tag ... 405
  - The exception Tag ... 408
  - The form-bean Tag ... 409

The form-beans Tag 410
The form-property Tag 411
The forward Tag 412
The global-exceptions Tag 413
The global-forwards Tag 413
The message-resources Tag 414
The plug-in Tag 415
The set-property Tag 416
The struts-config Tag 416
Metadata Tags 417
Editing Struts Configuration Files with Struts Console 417

19 The Tiles Configuration File 419
Understanding XML DTDs 419
Enabling the Tiles Plugin 420
The Tiles Configuration File Tags 421
The add Tag 422
The bean Tag 422
The definition Tag 423
The item Tag 424
The put Tag 425
The putList Tag 425
The set-property Tag 426
The tiles-definitions Tag 427
Metadata Tags 427
Editing Tiles Configuration Files with Struts Console 428

20 The Validator Configuration Files 429
Two Configuration Files 429
Understanding XML DTDs 430
Enabling the Validator Plugin 430
The Validator Configuration File Tags 431
The arg Tag 432
The constant Tag 433
The constant-name Tag 434
The constant-value Tag 434
The field Tag 434
The form Tag 435
The form-validation Tag 436
The formset Tag 436
The global Tag 438
The javascript Tag 438
The msg Tag 439
The validator Tag 440

The var Tag 441
The var-jstype Tag 442
The var-name Tag 442
The var-value Tag 443
Editing Validator Configuration Files with Struts Console 443

Part V Struts Extensions

21 Struts Scripting 447
Bean Scripting Framework Overview 447
Struts Scripting Overview 448
Using Struts Scripting 448
Adding the Struts Scripting .jar Files and Properties File to the Application 449
Creating Script-Based Actions 450
Configuring Script-Based Actions in the Application's Struts Configuration File 450
Predefined Scripting Variables 451
Using Struts Scripting with the Mini HR Application 453
Add the Struts Scripting .jar Files and Properties File to the Application 454
Convert SearchAction to a Groovy Script 454
Configure the struts-config.xml File 455
Repackage and Run the Updated Application 456

22 The Struts-Faces Integration Library 457
JSF Overview 457
Struts-Faces Library Overview 457
Supported Versions of Struts 458
Supported Versions of JSF 458
Using the Struts-Faces Library 458
Adding the Required .jar Files to the Application 459
Adding a Servlet Definition for the JSF Controller Servlet to the web.xml File 459
Configuring Struts to Use a Custom Struts-Faces Request Processor 460
Using the Struts-Faces and JSF Tag Library Tags to Create JSF-Based User Interfaces 460
Configuring Forward and Action Definitions in the Application's Struts Configuration File 461
Known Limitations 461
The Struts-Faces Tag Library Tags 462
The base Tag 463
The commandLink Tag 464

The errors Tag 467
The form Tag 469
The html Tag 470
The javascript Tag 471
The loadMessages Tag 473
The message Tag 474
The stylesheet Tag 476
The write Tag 476
Using the Struts-Faces Library with the Mini HR Application 477
Add a JSF Implementation's and JSTL .jar Files to the Application 478
Add a Servlet Definition for the JSF Controller Servlet to the web.xml File 478
Configure the struts-config.xml File 480
Update Existing JSPs to Use the Struts-Faces and JSF Tag Library Tags 481
Repackage and Run the Updated Application 483

23 Using AJAX with Struts 485
AJAX Overview 485
Integrating AJAX with the Mini HR Application 486
Add getEmployeeCount( ) to EmployeeSearchService 486
Create a CountAction Class 487
Configure the CountAction Class in the struts-config.xml File 488
Update search.jsp to Use AJAX 489
Recompile, Repackage, and Run the Updated Application 492

Part VI Appendixes

A Struts Console Quick Reference 497
Supported Configuration Files 498
Acquiring and Installing Struts Console 500
Using Struts Console as a Stand-Alone Application 500
Using Struts Console Inside Borland JBuilder 501
Using Struts Console Inside Eclipse 503
Using Struts Console Inside IBM Rational Application Developer for WebSphere 505
Using Struts Console Inside IntelliJ IDEA 507
Using Struts Console Inside NetBeans and Sun Java Studio 509
Using Struts Console Inside Oracle JDeveloper 511
Configuring the Struts Console Output Options 513

B Third-Party Struts Extensions 515
Strecks 515
SSLEXT 515

Struts Menu 516
displaytag 516
stxx 516
formdef 516
Struts Layout 516
Struts Console 516

Index 517

Acknowledgments

Writing this book has been the effort of not one, but many. It would not have been possible without the help and support from several people. I'd like to thank everyone at McGraw-Hill. In particular, I want to thank Wendy Rinaldi for giving me the opportunity to write this book and for introducing me to and giving me the opportunity to work with Herb Schildt, whom I'd also like to thank. Not only has Herb been the editor on this book, providing me with endless insight and wisdom, he has become a great friend and a mentor.

Special thanks also go to Bill Siggelkow for providing the initial drafts of Chapters 11 and 12, Wendy Smoak for tech editing the second edition of the book, and James Mitchell for tech editing the first edition. Their efforts are sincerely appreciated.

PART I

The Struts Framework

CHAPTER 1
An Introduction to Struts

CHAPTER 2
Building a Simple Struts Application

CHAPTER 3
The Model Layer

CHAPTER 4
The View Layer

CHAPTER 5
The Controller Layer

CHAPTER 6
Validator

CHAPTER 7
Tiles

CHAPTER 8
Declarative Exception Handling

CHAPTER 9
Struts Modules

1

CHAPTER

An Introduction to Struts

Struts is the premier framework for building Java-based Web applications. Using the Model-View-Controller (MVC) design pattern, Struts solves many of the problems associated with developing high-performance, business-oriented Web applications that use Java servlets and JavaServer Pages. At the outset, it is important to understand that Struts is more than just a programming convenience. Struts has fundamentally reshaped the way that Web developers think about and structure a Web application. It is a technology that no Web developer can afford to ignore.

This chapter presents an overview of Struts, including the historical forces that drove its creation, the problems that it solves, and the importance of the Model-View-Controller architecture. The topics introduced here are examined in detail by subsequent chapters.

A Brief History of Web Application Development

In order to fully understand and appreciate the need for and value of Struts, it's necessary to shed some light on how Web application development has evolved over the past several years. Initially the Internet was used primarily by the academic and military communities for sharing research information, most of which was in the form of static documents. Thus, originally, the Internet was mostly a mechanism for sharing files.

In 1995 the commercialization of the Internet began and there was an explosion of content made available on the Web. Similar to the research content that was being shared on the Web, the early commercial content principally consisted of text mixed with simple graphics. Hyperlinks were used to connect the content together. Although hyperlinks enabled the user to move from page to page, each page was still a static document that did not support other forms of user interaction. It wasn't long, though, before businesses wanted to be able to offer dynamic content that offered the user a richer, more interactive experience.

Before continuing, it will be helpful to explain precisely what is meant by *dynamic content.* In short, dynamic content is data that is specifically targeted for a particular user. For example, a user may want to check the price and availability of some item in an online store. The user enters the item name in an HTML form and the server supplies the response. The response is generated on the fly based on the request, and is thus dynamic content.

To fill the dynamic-content void, Web server software began to support the use of CGI scripts for creating applications that could run on a Web server and generate dynamic content back to a browser. CGI, or *Common Gateway Interface,* allowed Web servers to accept a request and execute a server-side program that would perform some action and then generate output on standard out. Web server software would then read that output and send it back to the requesting browser. Initially, many of these CGI scripts were written in Perl or other Unix-based scripting languages. Over time, though, as the applications being built to run as CGI scripts grew in complexity, more application-oriented languages like C and C++ were being used to create larger, more robust applications. With the advent of HTML forms, CGI scripts also were able to receive data from the browser and process it. As most readers know, HTML forms allow data entry on a Web page. That data could be sent to a CGI script on the server and then manipulated, stored, or otherwise processed.

Around the same time that CGI-based application development was becoming popular on the server side, the Java programming language was introduced, with an initial focus on applets. Applets gave the Web developer the ability to add rich, dynamic functionality to Web pages. Because Java offered the promise of "write once and run anywhere" programs, any browser that supported Java could run the applets. For the first time, developers could easily include dynamic content on a Web page.

For the same reasons that Java began to blossom on the client side with applets, Java also began to make inroads on the server side with the advent of servlet technology in 1997. Servlets solved many of the shortcomings of CGI, such as portability and efficiency, and offered a Java-based solution for the Web application paradigm. Servlets are portable across operating systems and can run on any server that has a Java Virtual Machine (JVM) and servlet container. Thus, they also benefit from Java's "write once, run anywhere" philosophy. Servlets have a more efficient execution model than CGIs because they are multithreaded instead of requiring a new process for each request. Servlets also have access to Java's vast libraries, including the JDBC APIs.

After servlets were introduced, Sun released the *JavaServer Pages (JSP)* technology as an extension to the servlet technology. JSPs take the reverse approach from servlets to building Web applications by having Java code intermingled in an HTML-based page. When a request is made to the server for a JSP, the Java servlet container checks if the JSP has already been compiled into a servlet. If it has, it proceeds to execute the servlet. If the JSP has not yet been compiled into a servlet, the server container converts the JSP code into a Java source file and then compiles that source so that subsequent requests to the JSP will find the servlet already compiled and ready to execute.

The nice thing about this approach is that changes to the JSP HTML can be made without having to manually recompile the code. The server container manages the compilation and will recognize that the HTML in the JSP has changed and recompile the JSP into a servlet for you. JSPs solve the problem of presentation code (HTML) being embedded in servlets, which made development cumbersome because HTML authors had to wade through Java code to edit HTML (not a good separation of responsibilities). In contrast, HTML developers can work on JSPs directly without interfering with Java code.

As the preceding discussion shows, many of the changes in Web-based development that have occurred over the past several years have been driven by the desire to efficiently include dynamic content in a Web page. Streamlining the use of dynamic content has been, and remains, one of the more important issues associated with the Internet and the applications that use it. As you will see, Struts is part of the solution to the dynamic-content problem.

Two Development Models

When Sun introduced JSP technology, it provided a development road map for working with it and defined two models for building JSP-based Web applications. The two models are known as *Model 1* and *Model 2* and they prescribe different approaches to designing JSP-based Web applications. Model 1, the simpler of the two, was the primary solution implemented when JSPs were first introduced. However, over time, Model 2 has been accepted as the best way for building JSP-based Web applications and, as you'll see, is the inspiration for MVC-based Web frameworks like Struts. Following is an overview of both architectures.

Model 1 Architecture Overview

The Model 1 architecture is very simple, as you can see in Figure 1-1. A request is made to a JSP or servlet and then that JSP or servlet handles all responsibilities for the request, including processing the request, validating data, handling the business logic, and generating a response. Although conceptually simple, this architecture is not conducive to large-scale application development because, inevitably, a great deal of functionality is duplicated in each JSP. Also, the Model 1 architecture unnecessarily ties together the business logic and presentation logic of the application. Combining business logic with presentation logic makes it hard to introduce a new "view" or access point in an application. For example, in addition to an HTML interface, you might want to include a Wireless Markup Language (WML) interface for wireless access. In this case, using Model 1 will unnecessarily require the duplication of the business logic with each instance of the presentation code.

Model 2 Architecture Overview

Model 2, or as it is most commonly referred to today, *Model-View-Controller (MVC),* solves many of the inherent problems with the original Model 1 design by providing a clear separation of application responsibilities (see Figure 1-2). In the MVC architecture, a central servlet, known as the *Controller,* receives all requests for the application. The Controller then processes the request and works with the *Model* to prepare any data needed by the *View* (which is usually a JSP) and forwards the data to a JSP. The JSP then uses the data prepared by the Controller to generate a response to the browser. In this architecture, the business and presentation logic are separated from each other. Having the separation of business and presentation code accommodates multiple interfaces to the application, be they Web, wireless, or GUI (Swing). Additionally, this separation provides excellent reuse of code.

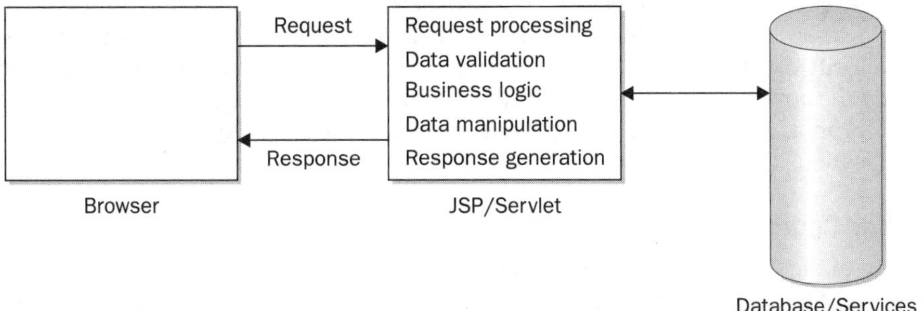

FIGURE 1-1 Model 1 architecture

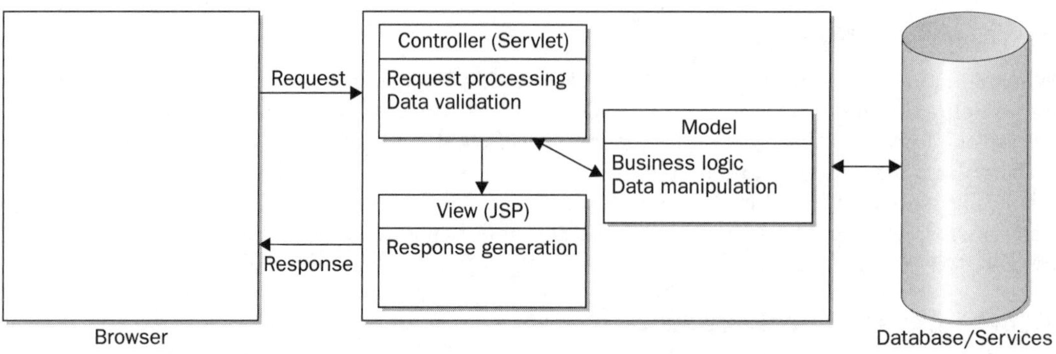

Figure 1-2 Model 2 architecture

A Closer Look at the Model-View-Controller Architecture

Because an understanding of the Model-View-Controller architecture is crucial to understanding Struts, this section takes a closer look at each of its parts. As a point of interest, MVC is based on an older graphical user interface (GUI) design pattern that has been around for some time, with its origins in the Smalltalk world. Many of the same forces behind MVC for GUI development apply nicely to Web development.

Model Components

In the MVC architecture, model components provide an interface to the data and/or services used by an application. This way, controller components don't unnecessarily embed code for manipulating an application's data. Instead, they communicate with the model components that perform the data access and manipulation. Thus, the model component provides the business logic. Model components come in many different forms and can be as simple as a basic Java bean or as intricate as Enterprise JavaBeans (EJBs) or Web services.

View Components

View components are used in the MVC architecture to generate the response to the browser. Thus, a view component provides what the user sees. Oftentimes the view components are simple JSPs or HTML pages. However, you can just as easily use WML, a templating engine such as Velocity or FreeMarker, XML with XSLT, or another view technology altogether for this part of the architecture. This is one of the main design advantages of MVC. You can use any view technology that you'd like without impacting the Model (or business) layer of your application.

Controller Components

At the core of the MVC architecture are the controller components. The Controller is typically a servlet that receives requests for the application and manages the flow of data between the Model layer and the View layer. Thus, it controls the way that the Model and View layers interact. The Controller often uses helper classes for delegating control over specific requests or processes.

Enter Struts

Although the Model-View-Controller architecture is a powerful means of organizing code, developing such code can be a painstaking process. This is where Struts comes in. Struts is a Web application framework that streamlines the building of Web applications based on the MVC design principles. But what does that mean? Is Struts an MVC Web application that you just add on to or extend? Is Struts just some libraries? Actually, Struts is a little bit of both. Struts provides the foundation, or *framework*, for building an MVC-oriented application along with libraries and utilities for making MVC development faster and easier.

You could create a new Controller servlet every time you wanted to use the MVC design pattern in your Web application. Additionally, you'd need to create the management/flow logic for getting data to and from the Model and then routing requests to the View. You'd also need to define interfaces for interacting with your Model objects and all the utility code that goes along with using the MVC design pattern. However, instead of going through this process each time you create a new application, you can use Struts. Struts provides the basic structure and outline for building that application, freeing you to concentrate on building the business logic in the application and not the "plumbing."

To better understand the benefits of Struts, consider the following analogy. If you were to create a GUI application in Java, you wouldn't write a text field widget and a drop-down widget yourself. You would use Java's Swing API that already has standardized, fully functional code that provides these controls. Not only are the Swing controls ready-to-use, but they are also understood by all Java programmers. Struts provides the same type of advantages: Struts supplies a standard way of implementing an MVC application, the Struts code is tried and true, and the techniques required to use Struts are well known and documented.

In addition to providing the foundation for MVC applications, Struts provides rich extension points so that your application can be customized as you see fit. This extensibility has led to several third-party extensions being made available for Struts, such as libraries for handling application workflow, libraries for working with view technologies other than JSP, and so on. There is a brief overview of many of these popular third-party Struts extensions in Appendix B.

The Evolution of Struts

Struts was originally created by Craig R. McClanahan and then donated to the Jakarta project of the Apache Software Foundation (ASF) in May 2000. In June 2001, Struts 1.0 was released. Since then, many people have contributed both source code and documentation to the project and Struts has become the de facto standard for building Web applications in Java and has been embraced throughout the Java community. Struts 1.1 was released in June 2003 and included a substantial amount of new functionality, including the addition of Tiles, Validator, declarative exception handling, and much more. Later, in December 2004, Struts 1.2 was released with several minor updates to the framework. Struts 1.3, released in 2006, introduced the largest change to the framework since the 1.1 release: the move to a *chain of responsibility (COR)*-based request processing engine. The latest release of Struts at the time of this writing is 1.3.5, and that is the release covered in this book.

Today, Struts is continuing to evolve. There are now two distinct major versions of Struts: Struts 1 and Struts 2. Struts 1 is the mature, widely adopted, documented, and supported version of Struts. It is the version of Struts in use now and it is the version of Struts discussed in this book. Struts 2 is a completely new version of Struts based on the merger of Struts and

WebWork, another popular open source Java Web application framework. At the time of this writing, Struts 2 is under development and does not have a specific release date. For this reason, Struts 2 is not discussed further in this book. Going forward, Struts 1 and Struts 2 will both be actively developed and maintained as separate subprojects of the Struts project.

Another event has punctuated Struts' evolution: its graduation to a top-level Apache project. Struts is no longer a subproject of the Jakarta Project. This is an important change because it affords Struts more autonomy and gives it the ability to have its own subprojects.

Struts Is Open Source

When Craig McClanahan donated Struts to the Apache Jakarta project, it became *open source software.* This means that anyone can download the source for Struts and modify that code as he or she sees fit. Of course, such changes affect only that developer. The standard code provided by ASF remains unaltered.

Over time, additional developers were added to the Struts project and were authorized to make changes to the code. These people are known as *committers,* since they have commit access to the source control repository for Struts. A limited number of people have this access, and each picks an area of interest and works on that part of the project that he or she is interested in.

A key advantage of open source is that it enables rapid development and maintenance cycles. For example, in an open source project, bugs can be fixed in a timely fashion. For ASF projects, bugs are handled by the committers, but anyone can fix a bug and provide a patch that the committers will then evaluate and "commit" if they deem it appropriate. Furthermore, anyone can contribute code to a project that incorporates changes and/or enhancements. Such submissions are also evaluated by the committers. In the case of Struts, contributions from members of the Struts community have played a significant role in the evolution of the project over the years.

Support for Struts comes in three forms. First is the API and usage documentation that comes with Struts. Second, Struts has a very active mailing list where you can get support for virtually any question. Third, several third-party consulting companies specialize in Struts support and development. Being open source, Struts is completely free of charge and allows you to make changes to it without any consequence so long as you abide by and preserve the ASF license.

NOTE *Information for signing up to be a member of the Struts users mailing list can be found on the Struts Web site at http://struts.apache.org/.*

Basic Components of Struts

The Struts framework is a rich collection of Java libraries and can be broken down into the following major pieces:

- Base framework
- JSP tag libraries
- Tiles plugin
- Validator plugin

A brief description of each follows.

NOTE *In addition to the core pieces of the framework, the Struts project has an area known as the "Sandbox" where new code and ideas can be vetted. Code from the Sandbox is not packaged with Struts distributions but is available for download from the Sandbox section of the Struts Web site.*

Base Framework

The base framework provides the core MVC functionality and consists of the building blocks for your application. At the foundation of the base framework is the Controller servlet: **ActionServlet**. The rest of the base framework is composed of base classes that your application will extend and several utility classes. Most prominent among the base classes are the **Action** and **ActionForm** classes. These two classes are used extensively in all Struts applications. **Action** classes are used by **ActionServlet** to process specific requests. **ActionForm** classes are used to capture data from HTML forms and to be a conduit of data back to the View layer for page generation.

JSP Tag Libraries

Struts comes packaged with several JSP tag libraries for assisting with programming the View logic in JSPs. JSP tag libraries enable JSP authors to use HTML-like tags to represent functionality that is defined by a Java class.

Following is a listing of the libraries and their purpose:

- **HTML** Used to generate HTML forms that interact with the Struts APIs.
- **Bean** Used to work with Java bean objects in JSPs, such as accessing bean values.
- **Logic** Used to cleanly implement simple conditional logic in JSPs.
- **Nested** Used to simplify access to arbitrary levels of nested objects from the HTML, Bean, and Logic tags.

Tiles Plugin

Struts comes packaged with the Tiles framework. Tiles is a rich JSP templating framework that facilitates the reuse of presentation (HTML) code. With Tiles, JSP pages can be broken up into individual "tiles" or pieces and then glued together to create one cohesive page. Similar to the design principles that the core Struts framework is built on, Tiles provides excellent reuse of View code. As of Struts 1.1, Tiles is part of and packaged with the core Struts download. Prior to Struts 1.1, Tiles was a third-party extension but has since been contributed to the Struts project and is now more tightly integrated. Tiles has been well adopted in the Java Web development community and is being used outside of Struts with other Java Web frameworks. Because of this popularity, at the time of this writing an effort is underway to separate Tiles into its own project. This will allow Tiles to continue to evolve independently of Struts. Of course, Struts will still have seamless integration with Tiles.

Validator Plugin

Struts comes packaged, as of version 1.1, with the Jakarta Commons Validator framework for performing data validation. Validator provides a rich framework for performing data validation on both the server side and the client side (browser). Each validation is configured in an outside XML file so that validations can easily be added to and removed from an application declaratively versus being hard-coded into the application. Similar to Tiles, prior to Struts 1.1, Validator was a third-party extension, but it has since been included in the project and is more tightly integrated.

Acquiring Struts

Struts is available free of charge and can be downloaded from the Apache Struts site at http://struts.apache.org/. Because Struts is open source, you have a couple of options when downloading the Struts framework software. You can download the software in binary, precompiled form or you can download the source code for compiling on your own. For most cases, the binary distribution will suffice; however, if you want to make changes to the Struts source code, the source distribution is available.

If you choose to download a binary distribution of Struts, you have a couple of options. You can download a released version of the code, which has been rigorously tested and certified as being of good quality, or you can download a nightly build of the code, which is less stable and not intended for production use. Opting to use a nightly build allows you to get access to the latest enhancements and bug fixes that have been made to the Struts framework ahead of an official release. However, it's important to point out again that nightly builds have no guarantee on quality because adding a new feature to Struts could potentially break another feature that has been stable for some time.

Similar to downloading a binary distribution of Struts, if you choose to download a source distribution, you have a couple of options. You can download the source for an officially released version of Struts or you can choose to get the "latest and greatest" version of the Struts source code directly from the Struts Subversion source control repository. Just as with the binary distribution, choosing to download the latest Struts source code can get you the newest enhancements and bug fixes to the software, but it may also have new bugs.

What You Get (Binary)

Since Struts is a Web application framework and not a stand-alone application, Struts distributions principally consist of the Struts API libraries and their associated files, such as Document Type Definitions (DTDs) for XML configuration files and JSP Tag Library Descriptor (TLD) files. Additionally, Struts comes with several sample Web applications that illustrate how to use the Struts framework. One of the sample Web applications, **struts-blank-[strutsversion #].war** (e.g., **struts-blank-1.3.5.war**), is typically used for new Struts applications because it provides a basic template for a Struts application, including all the necessary **.jar** files, and so on. Struts distributions also come with a sample Web application, **struts-mailreader-[struts version #].war** (e.g., **struts-mailreader-1.3.5.war**), that illustrates the basic structure of a Struts application.

What You Get (Source)

Similar to the binary distribution, the source distribution consists of the Struts API libraries and sample Web applications. The major difference, however, is that all of the code for the libraries and sample applications is in source form. This is particularly useful for projects where the source code may need to be changed or where you may want access to the source code for debugging an application and so on.

Getting Started with Struts

Now that the theoretical foundation for Struts has been covered, it is time to move on to actually writing Struts code. The next chapter walks through an example Struts application. Before then, you will need to choose one of the two Struts distribution options just discussed and download it at: http://struts.apache.org/downloads.html.

2

CHAPTER

Building a Simple Struts Application

Now that you've reviewed the history of Web application development and the fundamentals of the Struts framework, it's time to move beyond theory and into practice. As you will see, a Struts application is a composite of several interrelated parts. The goal of this chapter is to give you a general understanding of these parts and show how they work together to form a complete program. To accomplish that goal, this chapter develops a simple application that highlights each component of a Struts application. In the process, several key elements of Struts are introduced. Once you understand how this simple Struts application works, you will be able to easily understand other Struts programs because all share a common architecture. Subsequent chapters discuss in detail the many concepts introduced here.

Application Overview

The sample application in this chapter deviates from the stereotypical "Hello World" program found in many programming books. Instead, a bit more sophisticated example is needed to illustrate the components of Struts and the process required to build a Struts-based application. The example that we will use is a simple human resources (HR) application called Mini HR. Creating a full-blown HR application is a large undertaking that requires several pieces of functionality, from employee management to benefits management, so the sample application in this chapter will support only one common subset of functionality: Employee Search.

The Mini HR Application Files

All Struts applications consist of several files, which contain the various parts of a Struts program. Some are Java source files, but others contain JSP and XML. A resource bundle properties file is also required. Because of the relatively large number of files required by a Struts application, we will begin by examining the files required by Mini HR. The same general types of files will be needed by just about any Struts application.

The following table lists each file required by Mini HR and its purpose.

File	Description
index.jsp	Contains the JSP that is used as a gateway page for the Mini HR application and provides a link to the Employee Search page.
search.jsp	Contains the JSP that is used for performing employee searches and displaying the search results.
SearchForm.java	Contains the class that captures and transfers data to and from the Search page. This is a View class.
SearchAction.java	Contains the class code that processes requests from the Search page. This is a Controller class.
EmployeeSearchService.java	Contains the class that encapsulates the business logic and data access involved in searching for employees. This is a Model class.
Employee.java	Contains the class that represents an employee and encapsulates all of an employee's data. This is a Model class.
web.xml	Contains the XML that is used to configure the servlet container properties for the Mini HR Java Web application.
struts-config.xml	Contains the XML that is used to configure the Struts framework for this application.
MessageResources.properties	Contains properties that are used to externalize application strings, labels, and messages so that they can be changed without having to recompile the application. This file is also used for internationalizing the application.

The following sections examine each of the Mini HR application files in detail, and in many cases line by line. First, though, it's necessary to explain where each file should be placed in a directory hierarchy. Because this application (and all other Struts applications) will be deployed to a servlet container, the application files have to be arranged in the standard Web Archive (**.war**) format, which is simply a Java Archive (**.jar**) file with a different extension (**.war**). The Web Archive format also specifies a few key requirements for the **.jar** file:

- There must be a directory at the root level of the archive named **WEB-INF**. At run time this is a protected directory, and thus any files beneath it will be inaccessible to direct access by browsers.
- There must be a Web application deployment descriptor file named **web.xml** beneath the **WEB-INF** directory. This file will be explained later in this chapter, in the section "web.xml".
- Any libraries (**.jar** files) needed by the application should be under a directory called **lib** located beneath the **WEB-INF** directory.
- Any class files or resources needed by the application, which are not already packaged in a **.jar** file, should be under a directory called **classes** located beneath the **WEB-INF** directory.

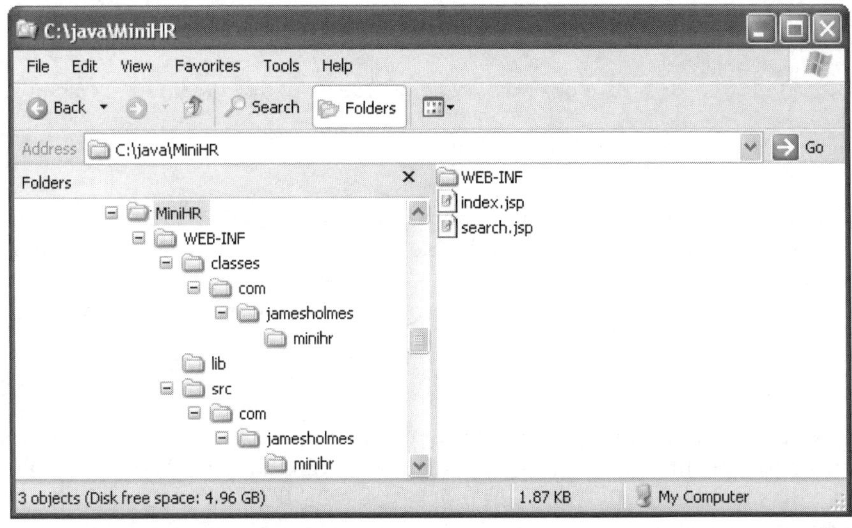

FIGURE 2-1 The c:\java\MiniHR directory layout

PART I

For the Mini HR application, you will create a directory called **MiniHR**. In principle, you can place this directory anywhere, but to follow along with this example, put it at **c:\java**. You'll use the **c:\java\MiniHR** directory as the root of your Web application so that you can easily create a Web Archive file later. Following is the layout of the **c:\java\MiniHR** directory, shown in Figure 2-1, and the location of each file examined in this section. You will need to place the files in this exact structure.

```
c:\java\MiniHR\index.jsp
c:\java\MiniHR\search.jsp
c:\java\MiniHR\WEB-INF\web.xml
c:\java\MiniHR\WEB-INF\struts-config.xml
c:\java\MiniHR\WEB-INF\classes\com\jamesholmes\minihr\MessageResources.properties
c:\java\MiniHR\WEB-INF\lib
c:\java\MiniHR\WEB-INF\src\com\jamesholmes\minihr\Employee.java
c:\java\MiniHR\WEB-INF\src\com\jamesholmes\minihr\EmployeeSearchService.java
c:\java\MiniHR\WEB-INF\src\com\jamesholmes\minihr\SearchAction.java
c:\java\MiniHR\WEB-INF\src\com\jamesholmes\minihr\SearchForm.java
```

index.jsp

The **index.jsp** file, shown here, is a very simple JSP that is used to render Mini HR's opening screen:

```
<%@ taglib uri="http://struts.apache.org/tags-html" prefix="html" %>

<html>
<head>
<title>ABC, Inc. Human Resources Portal</title>
</head>
<body>

<font size="+1">ABC, Inc. Human Resources Portal</font><br>
```

```
<hr width="100%" noshade="true">

&#149; Add an Employee<br>
&#149; <html:link forward="search">Search for Employees</html:link><br>

</body>
</html>
```

You'll notice that **index.jsp** consists mostly of standard HTML, with the exception of the JSP tag library definition at the top of the file and the "Search for Employees" link. The **index.jsp** file uses the Struts HTML Tag Library to render the Search link. Before you can use the HTML Tag Library, you have to "import" it into the JSP with the following line at the top of the JSP:

```
<%@ taglib uri="http://struts.apache.org/tags-html" prefix="html" %>
```

This line associates the tag library descriptor with a URI of **http://struts.apache.org/tags-html** with a prefix of "html". That way, any time a tag from the Struts HTML Tag Library is used, it will be prefixed with "html". In **index.jsp's** case, the **link** tag is used with the following line:

```
<html:link forward="search">Search for Employees</html:link>
```

Of course, if you wanted to use another prefix for the tag library, you could do so by updating the **prefix** attribute of the tag library import on the first line of the file.

The HTML Tag Library's **link** tag is used for rendering an HTML link, such as http://www.jamesholmes.com/. The **link** tag goes beyond basic HTML, though, by allowing you to access link, or *forward* definitions (Struts terminology), from the Struts configuration file (e.g., **struts-config.xml**), which is covered later in this chapter, in the section "struts-config.xml". In this case, the tag looks for a forward definition named "search" defined in the **struts-config.xml** file to use for the link being generated. If you skip ahead to the "struts-config.xml" section of this chapter, you'll see that the forward definition is as follows:

```
<!-- Global Forwards Configuration -->
<global-forwards>
  <forward name="search" path="/search.jsp"/>
</global-forwards>
```

Forward definitions allow you to declaratively configure the location to which a link points instead of hard-coding that information into your JSP or application. As you'll see in Chapter 5, forward definitions are used throughout Struts to direct the flow of an application from the Struts configuration file.

The following is the source code generated after **index.jsp** has been requested in the browser. Notice that the Search page link has been converted into a standard HTML link.

```
<html>
<head>
<title>ABC, Inc. Human Resources Portal</title>
</head>
<body>
```

```
<font size="+1">ABC, Inc. Human Resources Portal</font><br>

<hr width="100%" noshade="true">

&#149; Add an Employee<br>
&#149; <a href="/MiniHR/search.jsp">Search for Employees</a><br>

</body>
</html>
```

Here is how **index.jsp** looks in the browser.

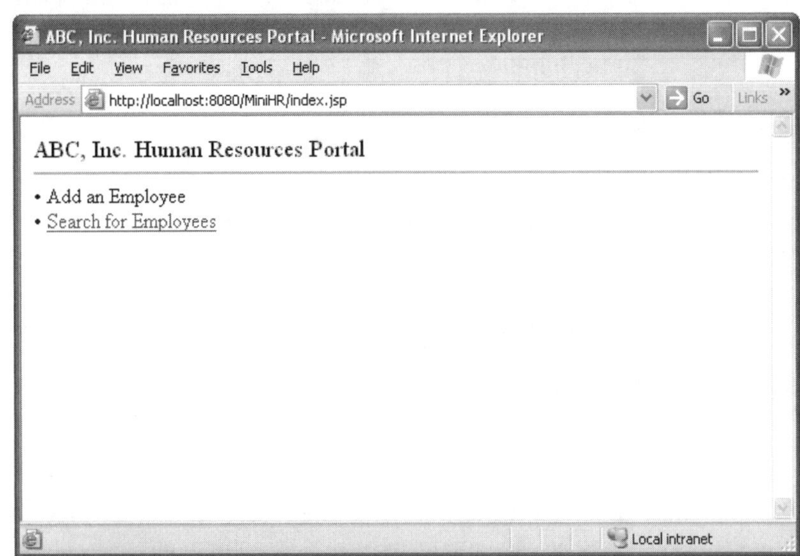

search.jsp

The **search.jsp** file is responsible for the bulk of the Employee Search functionality in the Mini HR application. When the Employee Search link is selected from the **index.jsp** page, **search.jsp** is executed. This initial request for **search.jsp** renders the basic Employee Search screen shown here:

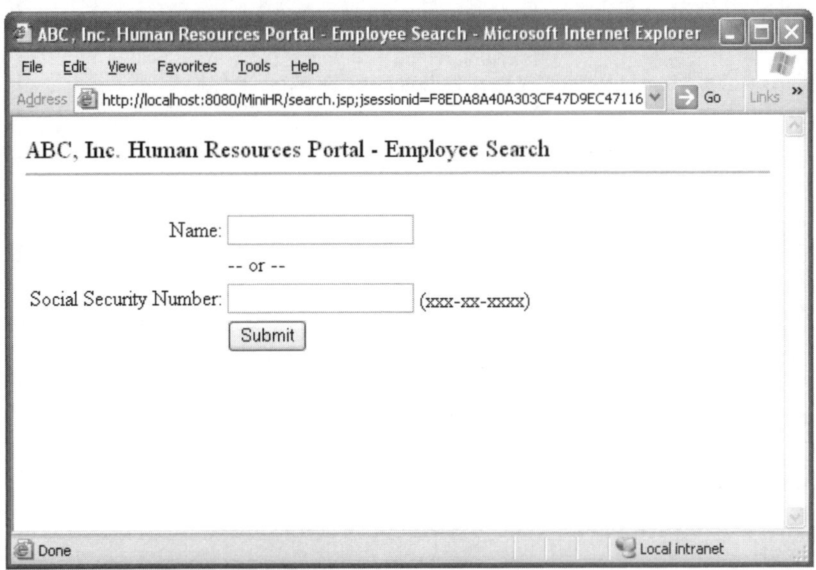

Each time a search is performed, the Struts Controller Servlet is executed and eventually **search.jsp** is executed to handle the rendering of the Employee Search screen, with the search results, as shown here:

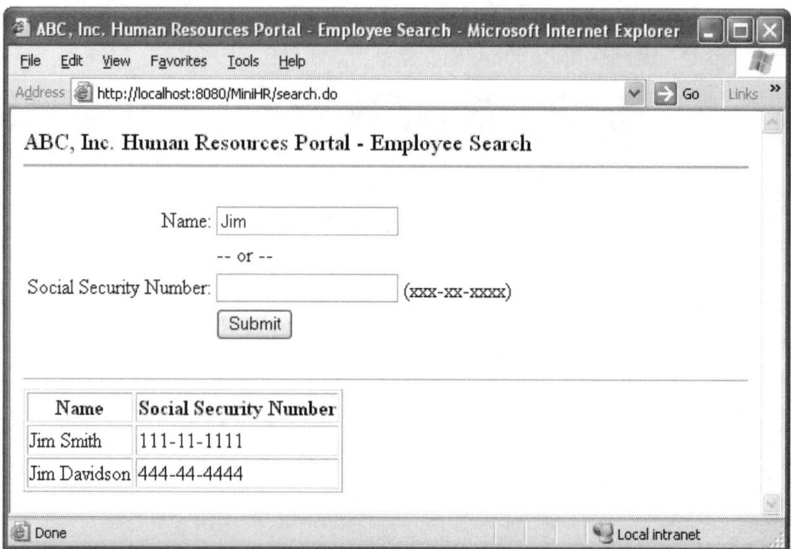

Similarly, if there are any errors with the search criteria when the search is submitted, **search.jsp** is executed to report the errors, as shown here:

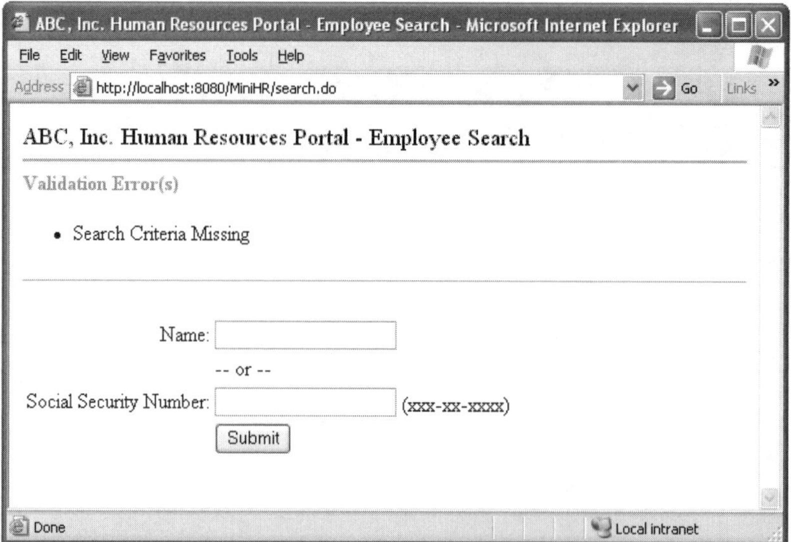

The contents of **search.jsp** are

```
<%@ taglib uri="http://struts.apache.org/tags-bean" prefix="bean" %>
<%@ taglib uri="http://struts.apache.org/tags-html" prefix="html" %>
<%@ taglib uri="http://struts.apache.org/tags-logic" prefix="logic" %>
```

```
<html>
<head>
<title>ABC, Inc. Human Resources Portal - Employee Search</title>
</head>
<body>

<font size="+1">
ABC, Inc. Human Resources Portal - Employee Search
</font><br>
<hr width="100%" noshade="true">

<html:errors/>

<html:form action="/search">

<table>
<tr>
<td align="right"><bean:message key="label.search.name"/>:</td>
<td><html:text property="name"/></td>
</tr>
<tr>
<td></td>
<td>-- or --</td>
</tr>
<tr>
<td align="right"><bean:message key="label.search.ssNum"/>:</td>
<td><html:text property="ssNum"/> (xxx-xx-xxxx)</td>
</tr>
<tr>
<td></td>
<td><html:submit/></td>
</tr>
</table>

</html:form>

<logic:present name="searchForm" property="results">

<hr width="100%" size="1" noshade="true">

<bean:size id="size" name="searchForm" property="results"/>
<logic:equal name="size" value="0">
<center><font color="red"><cTypeface:Bold>No Employees Found</b></font></center>
</logic:equal>

<logic:greaterThan name="size" value="0">
<table border="1">
<tr>
<th>Name</th>
<th>Social Security Number</th>
</tr>
<logic:iterate id="result" name="searchForm" property="results">
<tr>
<td><bean:write name="result" property="name"/></td>
<td><bean:write name="result" property="ssNum"/></td>
</tr>
</logic:iterate>
```

```
</table>
</logic:greaterThan>

</logic:present>

</body>
</html>
```

Because of its size and importance, we will examine it closely, line by line.

Similar to **index.jsp**, **search.jsp** begins by declaring the JSP tag libraries that will be used by the JSP:

```
<%@ taglib uri="http://struts.apache.org/tags-bean" prefix="bean" %>
<%@ taglib uri="http://struts.apache.org/tags-html" prefix="html" %>
<%@ taglib uri="http://struts.apache.org/tags-logic" prefix="logic" %>
```

In addition to the HTML Tag Library used by **index.jsp**, **search.jsp** uses the Struts Bean and Logic libraries. These additional tag libraries contain utility tags for working with Java beans and using conditional logic in a page, respectively.

The next several lines consist of basic HTML tags:

```
<html>
<head>
<title>ABC, Inc. Human Resources Portal - Employee Search</title>
</head>
<body>

<font size="+1">
ABC, Inc. Human Resources Portal - Employee Search
</font><br>
<hr width="100%" noshade="true">
```

Immediately following this basic HTML is this **errors** tag definition:

```
<html:errors/>
```

Recall that **search.jsp** is used to render any errors that occur while validating that the search criteria are sound. The HTML Tag Library's **errors** tag will emit any errors that are passed to the JSP from the **SearchForm** object. This is covered in more detail in the section "SearchForm.java" in this chapter.

The next several lines of **search.jsp** are responsible for rendering the HTML for the search form:

```
<html:form action="/search">

<table>
<tr>
<td align="right"><bean:message key="label.search.name"/>:</td>
<td><html:text property="name"/></td>
</tr>
<tr>
<td></td>
<td>-- or --</td>
</tr>
<tr>
```

```
<td align="right"><bean:message key="label.search.ssNum"/>:</td>
<td><html:text property="ssNum"/> (xxx-xx-xxxx)</td>
</tr>
<tr>
<td></td>
<td><html:submit/></td>
</tr>
</table>

</html:form>
```

Before discussing the specifics of the search form, let's review the use of the Bean Tag Library in this snippet. This snippet uses the library's **message** tag, as shown here:

```
<td align="right"><bean:message key="label.search.name"/>:</td>
```

The **message** tag allows externalized messages from the **MessageResources.properties** resource bundle file to be inserted into the JSP at run time. The **message** tag simply looks up the key passed to it in **MessageResources.properties** and returns the corresponding message from the file. This feature is especially useful to internationalize a page and to allow easy updating of messages outside the JSP. *Internationalization* is the process of providing content specific to a language, locale, or region. For instance, internationalization would be to create both English and Spanish versions of the same JSP.

NOTE *The acronym I18N is sometimes used in place of the word internationalization, because it is such a long word to type. I18N represents the first letter i, followed by 18 characters, and then the final letter n.*

Now, it's time to examine the form. The Struts HTML Tag Library has a tag for each of the standard HTML form tags, such as

<form>

<input type="text">

<input type="checkbox">

<input type="radio">

<select>

and so on. Instead of using the standard HTML tags, you'll use the HTML Tag Library's equivalent tag, which ties the form to Struts. For example, the **text** tag (**<html:text>**) renders an **<input type="text" ...>** tag. The **text** tag goes one step further, though, by allowing a property to be associated with the tag, as shown here:

```
<td><html:text property="name"/></td>
```

The property "name" here corresponds to the field named **name** in the **SearchForm** object. That way, when the tag is executed, it places the value of the **name** field in the HTML at run time. Thus, if the **name** field had a value of "James Holmes" at run time, the output from the tag would look like this:

```
<td><input type="text" name="name" value="James Holmes"></td>
```

At the beginning of this snippet, the HTML Tag Library's **form** tag is used to render a standard HTML **<form>** tag. Notice, however, that it specifies an **action** parameter of "/search" as shown here:

```
<html:form action="/search">
```

The **action** parameter associates an **Action** object mapping from the Struts configuration file with the form. That way, when the form is submitted, the processing will be handled by the specified **Action** object.

The final section of the **search.jsp** file contains the logic and tags for rendering search results:

```
<logic:present name="searchForm" property="results">

<hr width="100%" size="1" noshade="true">

<bean:size id="size" name="searchForm" property="results"/>
<logic:equal name="size" value="0">
<center><font color="red"><cTypeface:Bold>No Employees Found</b></font></center>
</logic:equal>

<logic:greaterThan name="size" value="0">
<table border="1">
<tr>
<th>Name</th>
<th>Social Security Number</th>
</tr>
<logic:iterate id="result" name="searchForm" property="results">
<tr>
<td><bean:write name="result" property="name"/></td>
<td><bean:write name="result" property="ssNum"/></td>
</tr>
</logic:iterate>
</table>
</logic:greaterThan>

</logic:present>
```

The beginning of this snippet uses the Struts Logic Tag Library for implementing conditional logic in a JSP. The Logic Library's **present** tag checks an object to see if a particular property is present. In this case, the **logic** tag checks to see if the **results** field of the **SearchForm** has been set. If so, then all of the HTML and JSP tags inside the **<logic:present>** tag will be executed. Otherwise, they will be ignored.

The rest of the tags in this snippet are responsible for rendering the search results. First, the Bean Library's **size** tag gets the size of the **results ArrayList** from the **SearchForm** object. Next, the size is checked to see if it is 0 using the Logic Library's **equal** tag. If the size is 0, then a "No Employees Found" message will be rendered. Otherwise, each of the employees returned from the search will be displayed. The Logic Library's **iterate** tag is used to iterate over each of the search results. Each search result is assigned to a variable named **result** by the **iterate** tag. Inside the **iterate** tag the Bean Library's **write** tag is used to access the **result** variable's **name** and **ssNum** fields.

SearchForm.java

The **SearchForm** class, shown next, is a View class that is used to capture and transfer data to and from the Employee Search page. When the HTML form on the Search page is submitted, the Struts **ActionServlet** will populate this class with the data from the form. Notice that there will be a one-to-one mapping between fields on the page and fields in the class with getter and setter methods. Struts uses encapsulation and Java's reflection mechanism to call the method corresponding to each field from a page. Additionally, when **SearchAction** (the Controller class for the Search page) executes, it will populate this object with the search results so that they can be transferred back to the Search page.

```
package com.jamesholmes.minihr;

import java.util.List;

import javax.servlet.http.HttpServletRequest;

import org.apache.struts.action.ActionErrors;
import org.apache.struts.action.ActionForm;
import org.apache.struts.action.ActionMapping;
import org.apache.struts.action.ActionMessage;

public class SearchForm extends ActionForm
{
  private String name = null;
  private String ssNum = null;
  private List results = null;

  public void setName(String name) {
    this.name = name;
  }

  public String getName() {
    return name;
  }

  public void setSsNum(String ssNum) {
    this.ssNum = ssNum;
  }

  public String getSsNum() {
    return ssNum;
  }

  public void setResults(List results) {
    this.results = results;
  }

  public List getResults() {
    return results;
  }

  // Reset form fields.
```

```
public void reset(ActionMapping mapping, HttpServletRequest request)
{
  name = null;
  ssNum = null;
  results = null;
}

// Validate form data.
public ActionErrors validate(ActionMapping mapping,
  HttpServletRequest request)
{
  ActionErrors errors = new ActionErrors();

  boolean nameEntered = false;
  boolean ssNumEntered = false;

  // Determine if name has been entered.
  if (name != null && name.length() > 0) {
    nameEntered = true;
  }

  // Determine if social security number has been entered.
  if (ssNum != null && ssNum.length() > 0) {
    ssNumEntered = true;
  }

  /* Validate that either name or social security number
     has been entered. */
  if (!nameEntered && !ssNumEntered) {
    errors.add(null,
      new ActionMessage("error.search.criteria.missing"));
  }

  /* Validate format of social security number if
     it has been entered. */
  if (ssNumEntered && !isValidSsNum(ssNum.trim())) {
    errors.add("ssNum",
      new ActionMessage("error.search.ssNum.invalid"));
  }

  return errors;
}

// Validate format of social security number.
private static boolean isValidSsNum(String ssNum) {
  if (ssNum.length() < 11) {
    return false;
  }

  for (int i = 0; i < 11; i++) {
    if (i == 3 || i == 6) {
      if (ssNum.charAt(i) != '-') {
        return false;
      }
```

```
      } else if ("0123456789".indexOf(ssNum.charAt(i)) == -1) {
        return false;
      }
    }

    return true;
  }
}
```

ActionForm subclasses, including **SearchForm**, are basic Java beans with a couple of extra Struts-specific methods: **reset**( ) and **validate**( ). The **reset**( ) method is used to clear out, or "reset," an **ActionForm**'s data after it has been used for a request. When using session-based Form Beans, Struts reuses **ActionForm** instances instead of creating new ones for each request. The **reset( )** method is necessary to ensure that data from different requests is not mixed. Typically, this method is used to just set class fields back to their initial states, as is the case with **SearchForm**. However, as you'll see in Chapter 4, this method can be used to perform other necessary logic for resetting an **ActionForm** object.

The **validate( )** method of **ActionForm** is called to perform basic validations on the data being transferred from an HTML form. In **SearchForm**'s case, the **validate( )** method first confirms that a name and a social security number have been entered. If a social security number has been entered, **SearchForm** goes one step further and validates the format of the social security number with the **isValidSsNum( )** method. The **isValidSsNum( )** method simply ensures that an 11-character string was entered and that it conforms to the following format: three digits, hyphen, two digits, hyphen, four digits (e.g., 111-22-3333). Note that business-level validations, such as looking up a social security number in a database to make sure it is valid, are considered business logic and should be in a Model-layer class. The validations in an **ActionForm** are meant to be very basic, such as just confirming that data was entered, and should not be used for performing any real business logic.

You'll notice that the **validate( )** method returns an **ActionErrors** object and the validations inside the method populate an **ActionErrors** object if any validations fail. The **ActionErrors** object is used to transfer validation error messages to the screen. Remember from the discussion of **search.jsp** that the HTML Tag Library's **errors** tag will emit any errors in a JSP if they are present. Following is the snippet from **search.jsp**:

```
<html:errors/>
```

Here in the **ActionForm** class, you simply place the keys for messages into the **ActionErrors** object, such as "error.search.criteria.missing". The **errors** tag will use these keys to load the appropriate messages from the **MessageResources.properties** resource bundle file, discussed in the section of the same name later in this chapter.

SearchAction.java

The **SearchAction** class, shown next, is a Controller class that processes requests from the Search page:

```
package com.jamesholmes.minihr;

import java.util.ArrayList;

import javax.servlet.http.HttpServletRequest;
import javax.servlet.http.HttpServletResponse;
```

```
import org.apache.struts.action.Action;
import org.apache.struts.action.ActionForm;
import org.apache.struts.action.ActionForward;
import org.apache.struts.action.ActionMapping;

public final class SearchAction extends Action
{
  public ActionForward execute(ActionMapping mapping,
    ActionForm form,
    HttpServletRequest request,
    HttpServletResponse response)
    throws Exception
  {
    EmployeeSearchService service = new EmployeeSearchService();
    ArrayList results;

    SearchForm searchForm = (SearchForm) form;

    // Perform employee search based on the criteria entered.
    String name = searchForm.getName();
    if (name != null && name.trim().length() > 0) {
      results = service.searchByName(name);
    } else {
      results = service.searchBySsNum(searchForm.getSsNum().trim());
    }

    // Place search results in SearchForm for access by JSP.
    searchForm.setResults(results);

    // Forward control to this Action's input page.
    return mapping.getInputForward();
  }
}
```

Remember from the discussion of **search.jsp** that the HTML form on the page is set to post its data to the "/search" action. The **strut-config.xml** file maps the search action to this class so that when **ActionServlet** (Controller) receives a post from the Search page, it delegates processing for the post to this **Action** subclass. This mapping is shown here:

```
<!-- Action Mappings Configuration -->
<action-mappings>
  <action path="/search"
          type="com.jamesholmes.minihr.SearchAction"
          name="searchForm"
          scope="request"
          validate="true"
          input="/search.jsp">
  </action>
</action-mappings>
```

Struts **Action** subclasses manage the processing of specific requests. You can think of them as mini-servlets assigned to manage discrete Controller tasks. For instance, in the preceding example, **SearchAction** is responsible for processing employee search requests and acts as a liaison between the Model (**EmployeeSearchService**) and the View (**search.jsp**).

SearchAction begins by overriding the **Action** class' **execute( )** method. The **execute( )** method is the single point of entry for an **Action** class by the Struts **ActionServlet**. You'll notice that this method takes an **HttpServletRequest** object and an **HttpServletResponse** object as parameters, similar to a servlet's **service( )**, **doGet( )**, and **doPost( )** methods. Additionally, **execute( )** takes a reference to the **ActionForm** associated with this **Action** and an **ActionMapping** object reference. The **ActionForm** reference passed to this **Action** will be an instance of **SearchForm**, as discussed in the preceding section, "SearchForm.java." The **ActionMapping** reference passed to this **Action** will contain all of the configuration settings from the **struts-config.xml** file for this **Action**.

The **execute( )** method begins by instantiating a few objects, and then the real work gets underway with a check to see what search criteria were entered by the user. Notice that the **ActionForm** object passed in is cast to its native type: **SearchForm**. Casting the object allows the **SearchForm** methods to be accessed for retrieving the search criteria. Based on the criteria entered, one of the **EmployeeSearchService** methods will be invoked to perform the employee search. If an employee name was entered, the **searchByName( )** method will be invoked. Otherwise, the **searchBySsNum( )** method will be invoked. Both search methods return an **ArrayList** containing the search results. This **results ArrayList** is then added to the **SearchForm** instance so that **search.jsp** (View) can access the data.

The **execute( )** method concludes by forwarding control to the **SearchAction** input page: **search.jsp**. The input page for an action is declared in the Struts configuration file, as shown here for **SearchAction**, and is used to allow an action to determine from which page it was called:

```
<action path="/search"
        type="com.jamesholmes.minihr.SearchAction"
        name="searchForm"
        scope="request"
        validate="true"
        input="/search.jsp">
```

EmployeeSearchService.java

EmployeeSearchService is a Model class that encapsulates the business logic and data access routines involved in searching for employees. The **SearchAction** Controller class uses this class to perform an employee search and then shuttles the resulting data to the View layer of the Mini HR application. **EmployeeSearchService** is shown here:

```
package com.jamesholmes.minihr;

import java.util.ArrayList;

public class EmployeeSearchService
{
  /* Hard-coded sample data. Normally this would come from a real data
     source such as a database. */
  private static Employee[] employees =
  {
    new Employee("Bob Davidson", "123-45-6789"),
    new Employee("Mary Williams", "987-65-4321"),
    new Employee("Jim Smith", "111-11-1111"),
    new Employee("Beverly Harris", "222-22-2222"),
```

```
    new Employee("Thomas Frank", "333-33-3333"),
    new Employee("Jim Davidson", "444-44-4444")
  };

  // Search for employees by name.
  public ArrayList searchByName(String name) {
    ArrayList resultList = new ArrayList();

    for (int i = 0; i < employees.length; i++) {
      if(employees[i].getName().toUpperCase().indexOf(name.toUpperCase())
         != -1)
      {
        resultList.add(employees[i]);
      }
    }

    return resultList;
  }

  // Search for employee by social security number.
  public ArrayList searchBySsNum(String ssNum) {
    ArrayList resultList = new ArrayList();

    for (int i = 0; i < employees.length; i++) {
      if (employees[i].getSsNum().equals(ssNum)) {
        resultList.add(employees[i]);
      }
    }

    return resultList;
  }
}
```

In order to simplify Mini HR, the **EmployeeSearchService** class will not actually communicate with a real data source, such as a database, to query employee data. Instead, **EmployeeSearchService** has some sample employee data hard-coded at the top of the class, as shown here:

```
/* Hard-coded sample data. Normally this would come from a real data
   source such as a database. */
private static Employee[] employees =
{
  new Employee("Bob Davidson", "123-45-6789"),
  new Employee("Mary Williams", "987-65-4321"),
  new Employee("Jim Smith", "111-11-1111"),
  new Employee("Beverly Harris", "222-22-2222"),
  new Employee("Thomas Frank", "333-33-3333"),
  new Employee("Jim Davidson", "444-44-4444")
};
```

The sample data consists of a few **Employee** objects. As you'll see in the next section, the **Employee** class is a simple class for encapsulating employee data.

The **searchByName( )** and **searchBySsNum( )** methods use the hard-coded data when performing a search. The **searchByName( )** method loops through each of the **Employee** objects in the **employees** array looking for any employees that match the name specified. If a match is found, it is added to the return **ArrayList** that will eventually be used by **search.jsp** to display the results. Note that the name search is case insensitive by virtue of uppercasing the **String**s before comparison. You should also note that the use of **String**'s **indexOf( )** method allows for partial matches instead of only exact matches.

Similar to the **searchByName( )** method, **searchBySsNum( )** loops through the hard-coded employee list looking for any employees that match the specified social security number. Note that **searchBySsNum( )** will capture only exact matches. Because social security numbers are unique to an individual, only one match should ever be returned for a social security number–based search.

Employee.java

The **Employee** class, shown next, is a basic class for encapsulating the data for an employee. The class is straightforward, consisting simply of setters and getters for the **Employee** class data.

```
package com.jamesholmes.minihr;

public class Employee
{
  private String name;
  private String ssNum;

  public Employee(String name, String ssNum) {
    this.name = name;
    this.ssNum = ssNum;
  }

  public void setName(String name) {
    this.name = name;
  }

  public String getName() {
    return name;
  }

  public void setSsNum(String ssNum) {
    this.ssNum = ssNum;
  }

  public String getSsNum() {
    return ssNum;
  }
}
```

This class is used by **EmployeeSearchService** for transferring employee search results data from the Model (**EmployeeSearchService**) to the View (**search.jsp**). Oftentimes, this "transfer" object is referred to as a Data Transfer Object (DTO) or Value Object (VO) and has the simple responsibility of being a data container and abstracting the Model from the View.

web.xml

The **web.xml** file, shown next, is a standard Web Archive deployment descriptor used to configure the Mini HR application. Because the file contains several configuration details, it will be reviewed section by section.

```
<?xml version="1.0"?>

<!DOCTYPE web-app PUBLIC
  "-//Sun Microsystems, Inc.//DTD Web Application 2.3//EN"
  "http://java.sun.com/dtd/web-app_2_3.dtd">

<web-app>

  <!-- Action Servlet Configuration -->
  <servlet>
    <servlet-name>action</servlet-name>
    <servlet-class>org.apache.struts.action.ActionServlet</servlet-class>
    <init-param>
      <param-name>config</param-name>
      <param-value>/WEB-INF/struts-config.xml</param-value>
    </init-param>
    <load-on-startup>1</load-on-startup>
  </servlet>

  <!-- Action Servlet Mapping -->
  <servlet-mapping>
    <servlet-name>action</servlet-name>
    <url-pattern>*.do</url-pattern>
  </servlet-mapping>

  <!-- The Welcome File List -->
  <welcome-file-list>
    <welcome-file>/index.jsp</welcome-file>
  </welcome-file-list>
</web-app>
```

The following is the first section of the **web.xml** file. It declares the Struts Controller servlet, **ActionServlet**, and configures it.

```
<!-- Action Servlet Configuration -->
<servlet>
  <servlet-name>action</servlet-name>
  <servlet-class>org.apache.struts.action.ActionServlet</servlet-class>
  <init-param>
    <param-name>config</param-name>
    <param-value>/WEB-INF/struts-config.xml</param-value>
  </init-param>
  <load-on-startup>1</load-on-startup>
</servlet>
```

This declaration starts by assigning a name to the servlet that will be used in the next section for mapping the servlet to specific application requests. After defining the servlet's name and class, the **config** initialization parameter is defined. This parameter informs the Struts **ActionServlet** where to find its central configuration file: **struts-config.xml**. Finally, the **<load-on-startup>** tag is used to specify the order in which servlets are loaded for a given Web application when the servlet container starts. The value specified with the **<load-on-startup>** tag is essentially a priority, and servlets with a higher priority (lower value) are loaded first.

The second section of the **web.xml** file causes **ActionServlet** to respond to certain URLs:

```
<!-- Action Servlet Mapping -->
<servlet-mapping>
  <servlet-name>action</servlet-name>
  <url-pattern>*.do</url-pattern>
</servlet-mapping>
```

Notice that the **<servlet-name>** tag references the same name declared in the preceding section. This associates the previous servlet declaration with this mapping. Next, the **<url-pattern>** tag is used to declare the URLs that **ActionServlet** will respond to. In this case, it is saying that **ActionServlet** will process any requests for pages that end in **.do**. So, for example, a request to

http://localhost:8080/MiniHR/page.do

or a request to

http://localhost:8080/MiniHR/dir1/dir2/page2.do

will be routed to the Struts **ActionServlet** for processing.

The final section of the **web.xml** file declares the Welcome File list that the Mini HR application will use:

```
<!-- The Welcome File List -->
<welcome-file-list>
  <welcome-file>/index.jsp</welcome-file>
</welcome-file-list>
```

The Welcome File list is a list of files that the Web server will attempt to respond with when a given request to the Web application goes unfulfilled. For example, in Mini HR's case, you can enter a URL of **http://localhost:8080/MiniHR/** and **index.jsp** will be executed, because no page has been specified in the URL. The servlet container detects this and references the Welcome File list for pages that should be tried to respond to the request. In this case, the servlet container will try to respond with a page at **/index.jsp**. If that page is unavailable, an error will be returned. Note that the Welcome File list can encompass several pages. In that case, the servlet container will iterate through the list until a file is found that can be served for the request.

struts-config.xml

The **struts-config.xml** file, shown next, is the central location for all of a Struts application's configuration settings. Recall from the previous description of the **web.xml** file that the **struts-config.xml** file is used by **ActionServlet** to configure the application. The basic configuration information is covered here, but a complete description will have to wait until you know more about Struts. (A complete discussion of configuration is found in Chapter 18.)

```
<?xml version="1.0"?>

<!DOCTYPE struts-config PUBLIC
  "-//Apache Software Foundation//DTD Struts Configuration 1.3//EN"
  "http://struts.apache.org/dtds/struts-config_1_3.dtd">

<struts-config>

  <!-- Form Beans Configuration -->
  <form-beans>
    <form-bean name="searchForm"
               type="com.jamesholmes.minihr.SearchForm"/>
  </form-beans>

  <!-- Global Forwards Configuration -->
  <global-forwards>
    <forward name="search" path="/search.jsp"/>
  </global-forwards>

  <!-- Action Mappings Configuration -->
  <action-mappings>
    <action path="/search"
            type="com.jamesholmes.minihr.SearchAction"
            name="searchForm"
            scope="request"
            validate="true"
            input="/search.jsp">
    </action>
  </action-mappings>

  <!-- Message Resources Configuration -->
  <message-resources
    parameter="com.jamesholmes.minihr.MessageResources"/>

</struts-config>
```

Struts configuration files are XML-based and should conform to the Struts Configuration Document Type Definition (DTD). The **struts-config.xml** file just shown begins by declaring its use of the Struts Configuration DTD:

```
<!DOCTYPE struts-config PUBLIC
  "-//Apache Software Foundation//DTD Struts Configuration 1.3//EN"
  "http://struts.apache.org/dtds/struts-config_1_3.dtd">
```

Next, is the Form Beans Configuration section, which is used to specify all of the **ActionForm** objects used in your Struts application. In this case, only one Form Bean is being used: **SearchForm**. The definition of the Form Bean, shown here, allows you to associate a logical name or alias of "searchForm" with the **SearchForm** object:

```
<form-bean name="searchForm"
           type="com.jamesholmes.minihr.SearchForm"/>
```

That way, your application code (i.e., JSPs, **Action** objects, and so on) will reference "searchForm" and not "com.jamesholmes.minihr.SearchForm". This allows the class definition to change without causing the code that uses the definition to change.

The next section of the file, Global Forwards Configuration, lists the forward definitions that your application will have. Forward definitions are a mechanism for assigning a logical name to the location of a page. For example, for the Mini HR application, the name "search" is assigned to the "search.jsp" page:

```
<forward name="search" path="/search.jsp"/>
```

As in the case of Form Beans, the use of forward definitions allows application code to reference an alias and not the location of pages. Note that this section of the file is dedicated to "Global" forwards, which are made available to the entire Struts application. You can also specify action-specific forwards that are nested in an **<action>** tag in the config file:

```
<action ...>
  <forward .../>
</action>
```

The topic of action-specific forward definitions is examined in Chapter 5.

After the Global Forwards Configuration section comes the Action Mappings Configuration section of the file. This section is used to define the **Action** classes used in your Struts application. Remember from the previous section on **SearchAction.java** that **Action** classes are used to handle discrete Controller tasks. Because the **SearchAction** mapping, shown here, has many settings, each is examined in detail.

```
<action path="/search"
        type="com.jamesholmes.minihr.SearchAction"
        name="searchForm"
        scope="request"
        validate="true"
        input="/search.jsp">
</action>
```

The first part of the Action Mappings Configuration section defines the path associated with this action. This path corresponds to the URL used to access your Struts application. Recall from the "web.xml" section that your application is configured to have any URLs ending in **.do** be handled by **ActionServlet**. Setting the path to "/search" for this action essentially says that a request to "/search.do" should be handled by **SearchAction**. Struts removes the **.do** from the URL (resulting in "/search") and then looks in the Struts configuration file settings for an Action Mapping that corresponds to the URL.

The next **<action>** attribute, **type**, specifies the **Action** class that should be executed when the path specified with the **path** attribute is requested. The **name** attribute corresponds to the name of a Form Bean defined in the **struts-config.xml** file. In this case, "searchForm" corresponds to the Form Bean set up earlier. Using the **name** attribute informs Struts to populate the specified Form Bean with data from the incoming request. The **Action** object will then have access to the Form Bean to access the request data.

The next two attributes, **scope** and **validate**, are related to the Form Bean defined with the **name** attribute. The **scope** attribute sets the scope for the Form Bean associated with this action. For example, use "request" for request scope or "session" for session scope. The

validate attribute is used to specify whether the Form Bean defined with the **name** attribute should have its **validate( )** method called after it has been populated with request data.

The final **<action>** attribute, **input**, is used to inform the **Action** object what page is being used to "input" data to (or execute) the Action; in this case, it is "search.jsp". Struts will forward to the page specified by the **input** attribute if validation fails.

The last section of the file, Message Resources Configuration, is used to define the location of the application resource bundle file (e.g., **MessageResources.properties**). Notice that the file is specified using Java's package mechanism: package.package.class (i.e., "com.jamesholmes.minihr.MessageResources"). This allows **ActionServlet** to load the properties file from the same place that classes are loaded. An extension of **.properties** is automatically appended to the resource bundle file name by Struts and thus should not be specified in the Struts configuration file.

MessageResources.properties

The **MessageResources.properties** file, shown next, is based on the Java Resource Bundle functionality for externalizing and internationalizing application strings, messages, and labels.

```
# Label Resources
label.search.name=Name
label.search.ssNum=Social Security Number

# Error Resources
error.search.criteria.missing=Search Criteria Missing
error.search.ssNum.invalid=Invalid Social Security Number
errors.header=<font color="red"><cTypeface:Bold>Validation Error(s)</b></font><ul>
errors.footer=</ul><hr width="100%" size="1" noshade="true">
errors.prefix=<li>
errors.suffix=</li>
```

Notice that this file is simply composed of name-value pairs, where the name is a key and the value is a message corresponding to the key. Each of the name-value pairs is then used by the Struts application whenever a string, message, or label needs to be displayed. Externalizing these strings in a separate file instead of embedding them in the application allows the strings to be changed without having to recompile the application (separation of concerns). Externalizing the strings also allows the application to support internationalization so that it can be tailored to different locales. As you'll see in Chapter 10, internationalization with Struts is straightforward and easy with the use of resource bundle properties files for strings, messages, and labels.

Compiling, Packaging, and Running the Application

Now that you have examined the sample application in detail, it's time to compile, package, and run the application. First, though, download and install the Struts and Tomcat software if you have not already done so. Tomcat is a free servlet container available for download from the Internet and will be used in the examples in this book for running Struts applications. Tomcat is also the reference implementation for the JSP and servlet specifications from Sun. Of course, you don't have to use Tomcat to run the examples, but it is the only method described by this book. So, to follow along, it is strongly suggested that you use Tomcat.

Each of the following sections is dedicated to a step of the process. First, you will set up the Struts and Tomcat software. Next, you'll compile the application. Then, you'll package the application in a standard Web Archive file. Finally, you'll see how to deploy and run the application with Tomcat.

Downloading and Installing Struts and Tomcat

As mentioned, both Struts and Tomcat are freely available for download from the Internet. Following are the Web sites for each:

- **Struts http://struts.apache.org/**
- **Tomcat http://tomcat.apache.org/**

After you have downloaded the Struts and Tomcat software distributions, you will need to choose a directory to install them to. After selecting a directory, extract the files of each distribution to that directory. For example, if you choose to install the distributions in a directory called **c:\java**, then the Struts files would be located at **c:\java\struts-1.3.5** (or similar) and Tomcat would be installed at **c:\java\apache-tomcat-5.5.17** (or similar).

Compiling the Application

The Mini HR application consists of several files; however, only the Java source code files need to be compiled before you package and run the application. Because the Java source code files use the servlet and Struts APIs, you need to add these libraries to your Java classpath. You could do this by updating your CLASSPATH environment variable. Alternatively, you can just specify the path when you compile the Mini HR application.

In addition to the files that you created and reviewed earlier in this chapter, you also need to copy the following files to the **c:\java\MiniHR\WEB-INF\lib** directory. These **.jar** files contain the Struts and associated library class files that are necessary for the Mini HR application to run once it is packaged as a **.war** file.

```
c:\java\struts-1.3.5\lib\antlr-2.7.2.jar
c:\java\struts-1.3.5\lib\bsf-2.3.0.jar
c:\java\struts-1.3.5\lib\commons-beanutils-1.7.0.jar
c:\java\struts-1.3.5\lib\commons-chain-1.1.jar
c:\java\struts-1.3.5\lib\commons-collections-2.1.jar
c:\java\struts-1.3.5\lib\commons-digester-1.6.jar
c:\java\struts-1.3.5\lib\commons-fileupload-1.1.1.jar
c:\java\struts-1.3.5\lib\commons-io-1.1.jar
c:\java\struts-1.3.5\lib\commons-logging-1.0.4.jar
c:\java\struts-1.3.5\lib\commons-validator-1.3.0.jar
c:\java\struts-1.3.5\lib\oro-2.0.8.jar
c:\java\struts-1.3.5\lib\struts-core-1.3.5.jar
c:\java\struts-1.3.5\lib\struts-el-1.3.5.jar
c:\java\struts-1.3.5\lib\struts-extras-1.3.5.jar
c:\java\struts-1.3.5\lib\struts-faces-1.3.5.jar
c:\java\struts-1.3.5\lib\struts-scripting-1.3.5.jar
c:\java\struts-1.3.5\lib\struts-taglib-1.3.5.jar
c:\java\struts-1.3.5\lib\struts-tiles-1.3.5.jar
```

NOTE *The preceding* **.jar** *files are those packaged with Struts 1.3.5 and may change over time with newer versions of Struts. If you are using a different version of Struts, you should use the* **.jar** *files included with that version of Struts.*

Assuming that you have installed Struts at **c:\java\struts-1.3.5**, installed Tomcat at **c:\java\apache-tomcat-5.5.17**, and placed the Mini HR application files at **c:\java\MiniHR**, the following command line will compile the Mini HR application when run from the **c:\java\MiniHR** directory:

```
javac -classpath WEB-INF\lib\antlr-2.7.2.jar;
                 WEB-INF\lib\bsf-2.3.0.jar;
                 WEB-INF\lib\commons-beanutils-1.7.0.jar;
                 WEB-INF\lib\commons-chain-1.1.jar;
                 WEB-INF\lib\commons-collections-2.1.jar;
                 WEB-INF\lib\commons-digester-1.6.jar;
                 WEB-INF\lib\commons-fileupload-1.1.1.jar;
                 WEB-INF\lib\commons-io-1.1.jar;
                 WEB-INF\lib\commons-logging-1.0.4.jar;
                 WEB-INF\lib\commons-validator-1.3.0.jar;
                 WEB-INF\lib\oro-2.0.8.jar;
                 WEB-INF\lib\struts-core-1.3.5.jar;
                 WEB-INF\lib\struts-el-1.3.5.jar;
                 WEB-INF\lib\struts-extras-1.3.5.jar;
                 WEB-INF\lib\struts-faces-1.3.5.jar;
                 WEB-INF\lib\struts-scripting-1.3.5.jar;
                 WEB-INF\lib\struts-taglib-1.3.5.jar;
                 WEB-INF\lib\struts-tiles-1.3.5.jar;
                 C:\java\apache-tomcat-5.5.17\common\lib\servlet-api.jar
                   WEB-INF\src\com\jamesholmes\minihr\*.java
                   -d WEB-INF\classes
```

Notice that you must specify the path to each **.jar** file explicitly. Of course, if you update CLASSPATH, this explicit specification is not needed. You should also notice that the compiled code will be placed into the **WEB-INF\classes** directory, as specified by the **-d WEB-INF\classes** section of the command line. Remember from the earlier discussion that this is the standard Web Archive directory that servlet containers will look in for compiled Web application code.

To simplify the process of building the Mini HR application in this chapter and in subsequent exercises in the book, on Windows-based systems you can place the preceding command line into a batch file named **build.bat**. The **build.bat** batch file can then be used to compile the application. All you have to do is type "build" from the command line and the **build.bat** batch file will be run. For Unix/Linux-based systems you can place the command line in a simple shell script to achieve similar build "automation."

Using Ant to Compile the Application

Manually compiling Java applications from the command line can be error prone and tedious. A popular alternative solution for compiling Java code is to use Apache Ant (http://ant.apache.org/). Ant is a Java-based build tool driven by an XML-based build file. The build file includes specific targets that correspond to steps in the build process, such as compiling classes, creating the distribution (such as a **.jar** file or **.war** file), and deploying the application. A full explanation of Ant is outside the scope of this book; however, a sample ant build file, **build.xml**, is given next for compiling the Mini HR application.

```
<project name="MiniHR" default="compile" basedir=".">
  <property name="src.dir" location="src"/>
  <property name="classes.dir" location="classes"/>
```

```
  <property name="struts.lib.dir"
        location="c:/java/struts-1.3.5/lib"/>
  <property name="tomcat.lib.dir"
        location="c:/java/apache-tomcat-5.5.17/common/lib"/>

  <target name="compile">
    <javac srcdir="${src.dir}" destdir="${classes.dir}" debug="on">
      <classpath>
        <pathelement path="${classpath}"/>
        <pathelement location="${tomcat.lib.dir}/servlet-api.jar"/>
        <fileset dir="${struts.lib.dir}">
          <include name="**/*.jar"/>
        </fileset>
      </classpath>
    </javac>
  </target>
</project>
```

To run the Ant build file, simply type "ant" from the directory where your **build.xml** file is located. By default, Ant looks for a file named **build.xml** and runs it.

Packaging the Application

Because Struts applications are standard Java EE Web applications, this application will be packaged using the standard Web Archive format. Packaging the application as a **.war** file allows the application to be easily deployed on any Java EE–compliant servlet container with ease. Because you arranged the files for the Mini HR application in the standard Web Archive directory structure, packaging them into a **.war** file is straightforward.

Following is the command line for creating a **MiniHR.war** file, assuming that you run the command from the Mini HR application directory (c:\java\MiniHR):

```
jar cf MiniHR.war *
```

After you run the command, a **MiniHR.war** file will be created and ready for deployment.

Running the Application

Once you have packaged your application, running it is as simple as placing the Web Archive file into Tomcat's **webapps** directory and then starting up Tomcat. By default, Tomcat starts up on port 8080, and thus the server can be accessed at **http://localhost:8080/**. To access the Mini HR application, point your browser to **http://localhost:8080/MiniHR/**. You'll notice that the name of your Web Archive file is used for the URL of your application. Because you packaged the Mini HR application in a file called **MiniHR.war**, **/MiniHR/** is used for the application's URL.

When you first access the **http://localhost:8080/MiniHR/** URL, **index.jsp** will be run, because it was specified as the Welcome File in the **web.xml** deployment descriptor. From the opening page, select the Search for Employees link. The Search page allows you to search for employees by name or social security number. If you do not enter any search criteria, an error message will be shown on the page. Similarly, if you enter an invalid social security number, an error message will be shown on the page after you click the Search button.

Figures 2-2 through 2-5 show Mini HR in action.

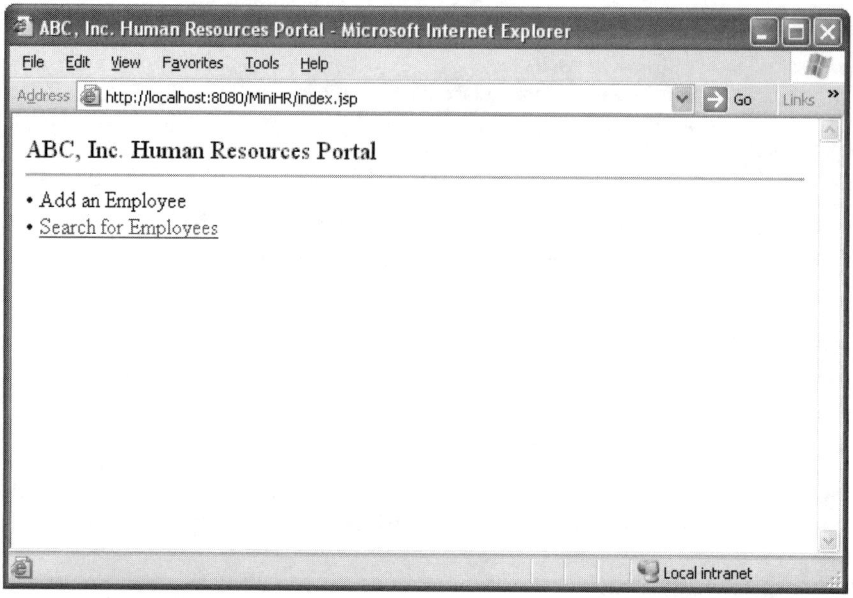

FIGURE 2-2 The opening screen

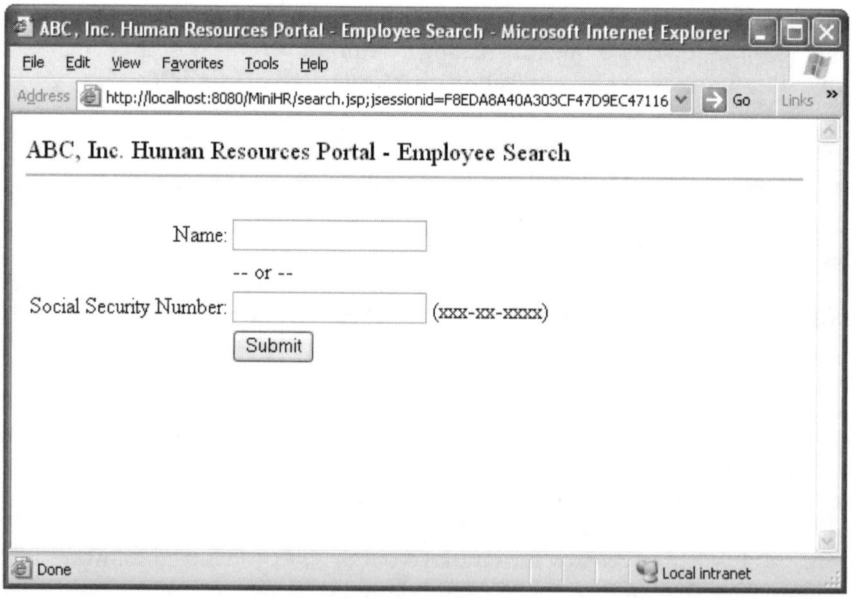

FIGURE 2-3 The Employee Search screen

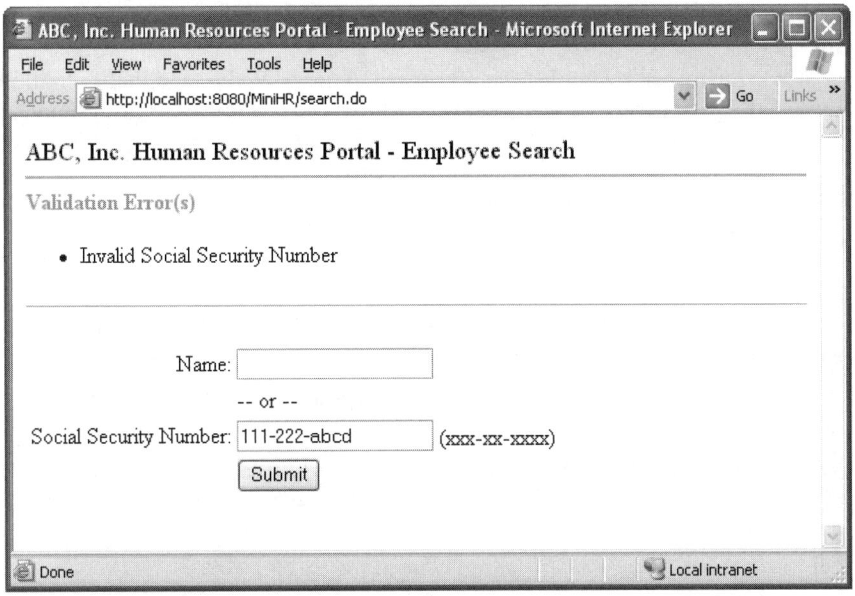

Figure 2-4 The Employee Search screen with a validation error

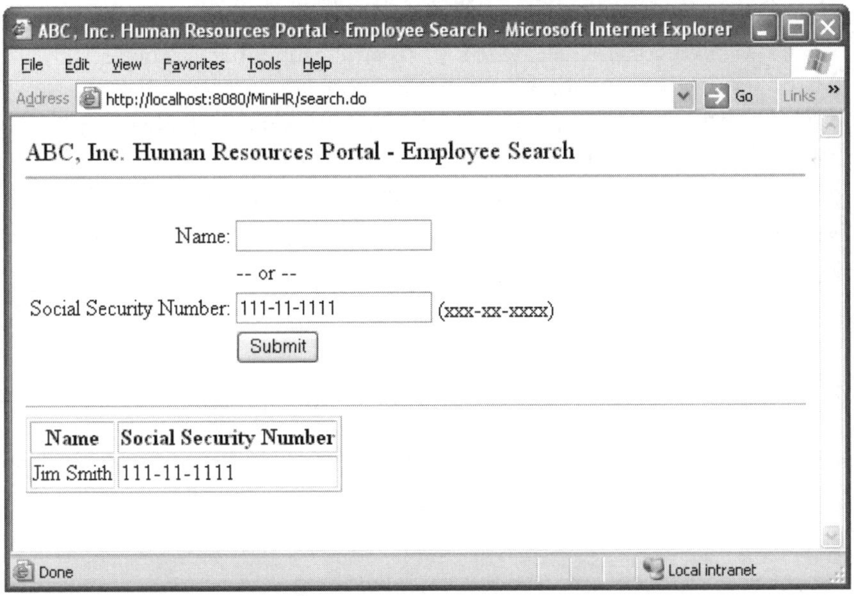

Figure 2-5 The Employee Search screen with search results

Understanding the Flow of Execution

Before leaving the Mini HR example, it is necessary to describe the way that execution takes place. As explained in Chapter 1, Struts uses the Model-View-Controller design pattern. The MVC architecture defines a specific flow of execution. An understanding of this flow of execution is crucial to an overall understanding of Struts.

For Mini HR, execution proceeds in the following way:

1. The browser makes a request to Mini HR for an employee lookup. This request is processed by **ActionServlet** (Controller).
2. **ActionServlet** populates the **SearchForm** object (View) with the search criteria entered on the **search.jsp** page.
3. **ActionServlet** delegates request-specific processing to the **SearchAction** object (Controller).
4. **SearchAction** (Controller) interfaces with the **EmployeeSearchService** object (Model) to perform the employee search. **EmployeeSearchService** returns an **ArrayList** of **Employee** objects (Model).
5. **SearchAction** (Controller) forwards control to **search.jsp** (View).
6. **search.jsp** (View) uses the **ArrayList** of **Employee** objects (Model) to generate a response to the browser.

The flow of execution for Mini HR can be generalized for any Struts application as shown here. Figure 2-6 shows the flow execution in graphic form.

1. The browser makes a request to the Struts application that is processed by **ActionServlet** (Controller).
2. **ActionServlet** (Controller) populates the **ActionForm** (View) object with HTML form data and invokes its **validate( )** method.
3. **ActionServlet** (Controller) executes the **Action** object (Controller).
4. **Action** (Controller) interfaces with model components and prepares data for view.
5. **Action** (Controller) forwards control to the JSP (View).
6. JSP (View) uses model data to generate a response to the browser.

Remember, the same basic pattern of execution applies to any Struts application.

Now that you understand the basic structure of a Struts application and how its components work together, it's time to move on to an in-depth examination of Struts. As mentioned at the start, all of the topics presented in this chapter are examined in detail in the chapters that follow.

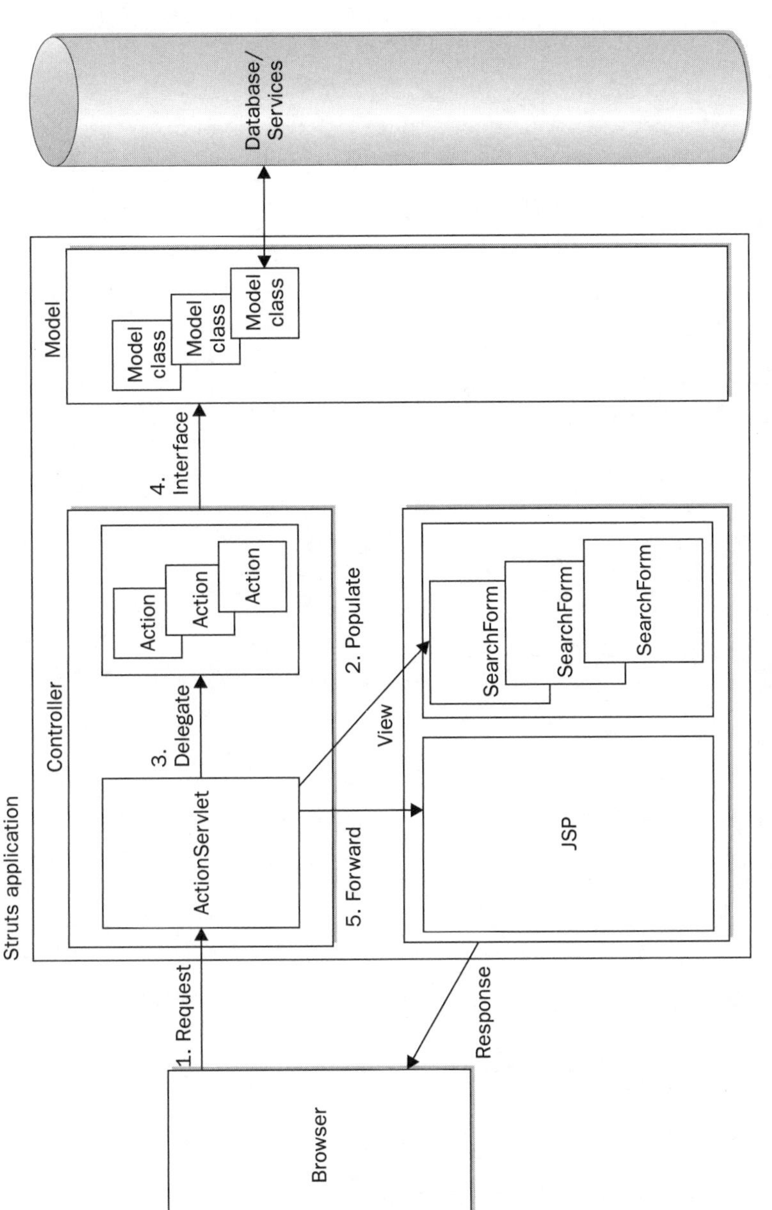

Figure 2-6 Flow of execution

CHAPTER 3

The Model Layer

As you know, Struts is a framework that is used to build applications based on the Model-View-Controller (MVC) architecture. Because the MVC organization is at the foundation of Struts, it is not possible to fully utilize Struts without a clear understanding of each part of the MVC architecture. Therefore, this and the following two chapters examine in depth the Model, View, and Controller portions of a Struts application, beginning in this chapter with the Model.

What Is the Model?

In an MVC application, the Model layer is typically the largest and most important piece. The Model is designed to house the business logic and data access code; in other words, the Model consists of the core of the application. For example, if an application computes the average sell-through rate of a product, the Model layer performs that computation. For an application that maintains a database of employees, complete with salary and tax information, the Model handles the maintenance task. Thus, it is the Model that defines what the application does. The View and Controller interact with the Model and provide a user interface to it.

The MVC architecture dictates that the Model layer should be self-contained and function independently from the View and Controller layers. That way, the core application code can be used over and over again with multiple user interfaces. For example, you could have a Web interface for the application as well as a stand-alone or wireless interface. Each interface (Web, stand-alone, and so on) would have its own code for the user interface (View) but would reuse the core application (Model) code. This is the basis for the MVC architecture: having a clean separation of responsibilities and reducing coupling between application layers.

Model Layer Breakdown

The typical Model layer of a correctly designed MVC application can be broken down into three conceptual sublayers. Each sublayer can be thought of as a component or responsibility of the Model. Figure 3-1 illustrates this breakdown.

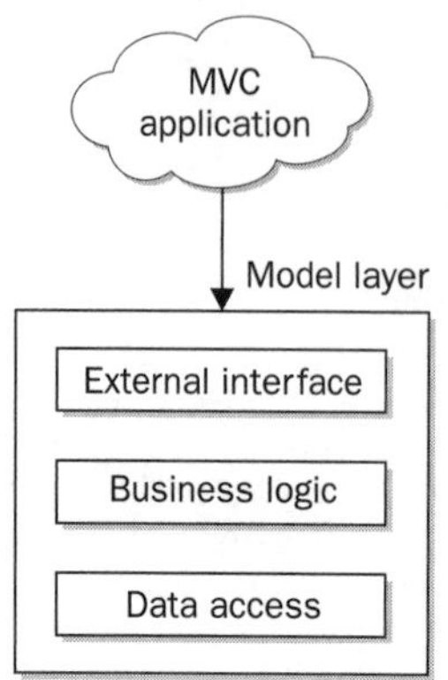

Figure 3-1 Model layer breakdown

Each sublayer does not necessarily represent a separate set of classes, but rather the Model's set of responsibilities. You may choose to house a specific function's code for all layers in one large class, or you may break down each sublayer into fine-grained objects. The level of object granularity is up to you, and what's best and/or necessary really depends on the size and complexity of your application. The following are the three sublayers:

- **External interface** Composed of code that provides an interface that external code uses to interact with the Model.
- **Business logic** Encompasses the bulk of the Model code and provides the business functionality for an application.
- **Data access** Composed of code for communicating with an application's data sources such as a database.

Struts and the Model

The Struts framework does not provide any specific features or constraints for developing the Model layer of your application. At first glance this may seem odd, or even a shortcoming, given that Struts is designed for building MVC applications. However, it's actually a key design feature of Struts and is a great benefit. By not dictating how the Model layer should be built, Struts gives your application the flexibility to use any approach or technology for building the Model layer code. Whether it be an Object-Relational Mapping (ORM) framework (e.g., Hibernate or TopLink), Enterprise JavaBeans (EJB), Java Data Objects (JDO), or the Data Access Objects (DAO) pattern, Struts will accommodate.

Because the Model defines the business logic, the Model is where Struts ends and your application code begins. Your Model code will be accessed from subclasses of the Struts **Action** object that are part of the Controller layer of the Struts framework. **Action** subclasses interact with the Model via interfaces and use its Data Transfer Objects to pass and retrieve data.

You should not place any business logic or data access code in **Action** objects. Doing so would bypass the separation of the Model and the Controller. Similarly, your Model code should not have any references to Struts code or objects. Violating this rule unnecessarily couples your core application code to Struts.

Using BeanUtils to Transfer Data to Model Classes

As stated, Model code should not have any references to Struts code to prevent from coupling your application code to Struts. This guideline can create a lot of headache for developers when accessing Model layer code. Form Beans are used to collect form data which eventually must be transferred to the Model layer code for processing. Because it is bad practice to pass a Form Bean directly to the Model layer code, you must transfer the data from the Form Bean to a Model Data Transfer Object to be transferred to the Model layer code. As you can imagine, it is cumbersome to write several "copy" statements that simply copy data from one object to the other, as shown in the following example:

```
import javax.servlet.http.HttpServletRequest;
import javax.servlet.http.HttpServletResponse;

import org.apache.struts.action.Action;
import org.apache.struts.action.ActionForm;
import org.apache.struts.action.ActionForward;
import org.apache.struts.action.ActionMapping;

public final class ExampleAction extends Action
{
  public ActionForward execute(ActionMapping mapping,
    ActionForm form,
    HttpServletRequest request,
    HttpServletResponse response)
    throws Exception
  {
    ExampleForm exampleForm = (ExampleForm) form;

    Example example = new Example();
    example.setField1(exampleForm.getField1());
    example.setField2(exampleForm.getField2());
    example.setField3(exampleForm.getField3());
    example.setField4(exampleForm.getField4());
    example.setField5(exampleForm.getField5());

    ExampleService service = new ExampleService();
    service.updateExample(example);

    return mapping.findForward("success");
  }
}
```

Instead of writing tedious, repetitive "copy" statements, you can use the Jakarta Commons BeanUtils library to copy all of the properties for you, as shown next.

```
import javax.servlet.http.HttpServletRequest;
import javax.servlet.http.HttpServletResponse;

import org.apache.commmons.beanutils.PropertyUtils;

import org.apache.struts.action.Action;
import org.apache.struts.action.ActionForm;
import org.apache.struts.action.ActionForward;
import org.apache.struts.action.ActionMapping;

public final class ExampleAction extends Action
{
  public ActionForward execute(ActionMapping mapping,
    ActionForm form,
```

```
        HttpServletRequest request,
        HttpServletResponse response)
        throws Exception
      {
        ExampleForm exampleForm = (ExampleForm) form;

        Example example = new Example();
        PropertyUtils.copyProperties(example, exampleForm);

        ExampleService service = new ExampleService();
        service.updateExample(example);

        return mapping.findForward("success");
      }
    }
```

Struts comes packaged with the Jakarta Commons BeanUtils library and makes use of it heavily in the core framework code, so you do not have to download BeanUtils separately. All you have to do is import the **org.apache.commons.beanutils.PropertyUtils** class and use its **copyProperties( )** method to transfer fields from one object to the other. The destination object is the first parameter to the **copyProperties( )** method, and the origination object is the second method parameter. The **copyProperties( )** method will automatically copy all fields from the origination object to the destination object that have the same name. For example, if the origination object has two fields named "firstName" and "lastName" respectively, the **copyProperties( )** method will attempt to find the same two fields on the destination object and call their corresponding setter methods.

NOTE *For more information on the Jakarta Commons BeanUtils project, visit the BeanUtils Web site at: http://jakarta.apache.org/commons/beanutils/. Alternatively, the FormDef extension for Struts allows you to use Model objects directly instead of creating Form Beans and transferring data between the objects. Appendix B has a brief introduction to FormDef.*

Reviewing the Model Layer of the Mini HR Application

Because Struts has little to do with the Model layer, there is little more to say about it. However, before moving on, it will be helpful to review the Model layer of the Mini HR application developed in Chapter 2. Doing so clearly illustrates how the Model code is separate from the rest of the application.

Mini HR's Model layer consists of two classes: **EmployeeSearchService** and **Employee**. The **EmployeeSearchService** class is shown next:

```
package com.jamesholmes.minihr;

import java.util.ArrayList;

public class EmployeeSearchService
{
  /* Hard-coded sample data. Normally this would come from a real data
     source such as a database. */
  private static Employee[] employees =
  {
```

```
    new Employee("Bob Davidson", "123-45-6789"),
    new Employee("Mary Williams", "987-65-4321"),
    new Employee("Jim Smith", "111-11-1111"),
    new Employee("Beverly Harris", "222-22-2222"),
    new Employee("Thomas Frank", "333-33-3333"),
    new Employee("Jim Davidson", "444-44-4444")
  };

  // Search for employees by name.
  public ArrayList searchByName(String name) {
    ArrayList resultList = new ArrayList();

    for (int i = 0; i < employees.length; i++) {
      if(employees[i].getName().toUpperCase().indexOf(name.toUpperCase())
         != -1)
      {
        resultList.add(employees[i]);
      }
    }

    return resultList;
  }

  // Search for employee by social security number.
  public ArrayList searchBySsNum(String ssNum) {
    ArrayList resultList = new ArrayList();

    for (int i = 0; i < employees.length; i++) {
      if (employees[i].getSsNum().equals(ssNum)) {
        resultList.add(employees[i]);
      }
    }

    return resultList;
  }
}
```

EmployeeSearchService fulfills all three of the model's sublayers: external interface, business logic, and data access. The external interface is defined by the methods **searchByName( )** and **searchBySsNum( )**. The business logic is contained in the implementation to those methods, which finds an employee based on either his or her name or social security number. Data access occurs each time the hard-coded **Employee** array is used.

In a small, sample application such as Mini HR, there is nothing wrong with implementing the entire Model within **EmployeeSearchService**. However, in a more complicated application, a class such as this would normally be used as only the external interface to the Model. In this approach, it would house only skeletal **searchByName( )** and **searchBySsNum( )** methods, which would pass through (or *delegate*) requests to the business logic sublayer where their actual implementation would exist. For example, the business logic sublayer code could be implemented in a class named **EmployeeSearchImpl**. Furthermore, **EmployeeSearchImpl** would then communicate with data access sublayer classes to actually query employee data from a database or such, rather than containing the data access code itself.

The **Employee** class, shown next, is a *domain* object used to represent an entity in the model. In this scenario it is used as a conduit for transferring data to and from the Model. As such, it can be thought of as being part of the Model layer.

```
package com.jamesholmes.minihr;

public class Employee
{
  private String name;
  private String ssNum;

  public Employee(String name, String ssNum) {
    this.name = name;
    this.ssNum = ssNum;
  }

  public void setName(String name) {
    this.name = name;
  }

  public String getName() {
    return name;
  }

  public void setSsNum(String ssNum) {
    this.ssNum = ssNum;
  }

  public String getSsNum() {
    return ssNum;
  }
}
```

Typically, an object of this type is referred to as a Data Transfer Object (DTO) or Value Object (VO) and is part of the external interface sublayer. The Model uses DTOs to send data back through its external interface and to accept data through its external interface. You can think of these classes as interfaces themselves because they specify the format and packaging of the data expected by the Model.

CHAPTER 4

The View Layer

In an MVC application, the View layer provides an interface to your application, be it for users with a browser or for another application using something like Web services. Basically the View layer is the conduit for getting data in and out of the application. It does not contain business logic, such as calculating interest for a banking application or storing items in a shopping cart for an online catalog. The View layer also does not contain any code for persisting data to or retrieving data from a data source. Rather, it is the Model layer that manages business logic and data access. The View layer simply concentrates on the interface.

Keeping the Model and View layers separate from one another allows an application's interface to change independent of the Model layer and vice versa. This separation also allows the application to have multiple interfaces (or views). For instance, an application could have a Web interface and a wireless interface. In this case, each interface is separate, but both use the same Model layer code without the Model layer being tied to either interface or either interface having to know about the other interface.

Struts and the View Layer

Struts provides a rich set of functionality and features for developing the View layer of MVC applications. There are several forms that the View layer of a Struts application can take. It can be HTML/JSP (the most common case) or it can be XML/XSLT, Velocity, Swing, or whatever your application requires. This is the power of Struts and MVC. Because HTML/JSP is the typical View technology used for Java-based Web applications, Struts provides the most functionality and features for developing your application this way. The remainder of this chapter focuses on Struts' support for creating the View layer using HTML/JSP.

Struts' HTML/JSP View layer support can be broken down into the following major components:

- JSP pages
- Form Beans
- JSP tag libraries
- Resource bundles

Each of these components is examined in detail in this chapter, but first it is helpful to understand how they fit together in the View layer.

JSP pages are at the center of the View components; they contain the HTML that is sent to browsers for users to see and they contain JSP library tags. The library tags are used to retrieve data from Form Beans and to generate HTML forms that, when submitted, will populate Form Beans. Additionally, library tags are used to retrieve content from resource bundles. Together, all of the Struts View layer components are used to generate HTML that browsers render. This is what the user sees.

On the back side, the View layer populates Form Beans with data coming from the HTML interface. The Controller layer then takes the Form Beans and manages getting their data and putting it into the Model layer. Additionally, the Controller layer takes data from the Model layer and populates Form Beans so that the data can be presented in the View layer.

The following sections explain each of these major View components in detail.

JSP Pages

JSPs are the centerpiece of the Struts View layer. They contain the static HTML and JSP library tags that generate dynamic HTML. Together the static and dynamically generated HTML gets sent to the user's browser for rendering. That is, the JSPs contain the code for the user interface with which a user interacts.

JSPs in Struts applications are like JSPs in any other Java-based Web application. However, to adhere to the MVC paradigm, the JSPs should not contain any code for performing business logic or code for directly accessing data sources. Instead, the JSPs are intended to be used solely for displaying data and capturing data. Struts provides a set of tag libraries that supports displaying data and creating HTML forms that capture data. Additionally, the tags support displaying content stored in resource bundles. Therefore, JSPs (coupled with Form Beans) provide the bulk of the Struts View layer. The JSP tag libraries glue those two together and the resource bundles provide a means of content management.

Form Beans

Form Beans provide the conduit for transferring data between the View and Controller layers of Struts applications. When HTML forms are submitted to a Struts application, Struts takes the incoming form data and uses it to populate the form's corresponding Form Bean. The Struts Controller layer then uses the Form Beans to access data that must be sent to the Model layer. On the flip side, the Controller layer populates Form Beans with Model layer data so that it can be displayed with the View layer. Essentially, Form Beans are simple data containers. They either contain data from an HTML form that is headed to the Model via the Controller or contain data from the Model headed to the View via the Controller.

Form Beans are basic Java beans with getter and setter methods for each of their properties, allowing their data to be set and retrieved easily. The **org.apache.struts.action.ActionForm** class is the base abstract class that all Form Beans must descend from (be it directly or via a subclass). Because Form Beans are simple data containers, they are principally composed of fields, and getter and setter methods for those fields. Business logic and data access code should not be placed in these classes. That code goes in Model layer classes. The only other methods that should be in these classes are helper methods or methods that override **ActionForm**'s base **reset( )** and **validate( )** methods.

NOTE *Form Beans are based on the JavaBeans specification and must have proper getter and setter methods for each field in order for introspection by the Struts framework to function properly. For more information on the JavaBeans specification visit: http://java.sun.com/products/javabeans/.*

The **ActionForm** class has a **reset( )** method and a **validate( )** method that are intended to be overridden by subclasses where necessary. The **reset( )** method is a hook that Struts calls before the Form Bean is populated from an application request (e.g., HTML form submission). The **validate( )** method is a hook that Struts calls after the Form Bean has been populated from an application request. Both of these methods are described in detail later in this section.

Following is an example Form Bean:

```
import org.apache.struts.action.ActionForm;

public class EmployeeForm extends ActionForm
{
  private String firstName;
  private String lastName;
  private String department;

  public void setFirstName(String firstName) {
    this.firstName = firstName;
  }

  public String getFirstName() {
    return firstName;
  }

  public void setLastName(String lastName) {
    this.lastName = lastName;
  }

  public String getLastName() {
    return lastName;
  }

  public void setDepartment(String department) {
    this.department = department;
  }

  public String getDepartment() {
    return department;
  }
}
```

Form Bean properties can be of any object type, be it a built-in class like **String**, **Integer**, or **Boolean** or a complex application-specific class such as an **Address** object that has fields for street address, city, state, and ZIP. Struts uses reflection to populate the Form Beans and can traverse nested object hierarchies to any level so long as the getter and setter methods are public. For example, if your Form Bean had an **Address** object field named **address**, to access the **city** field on the **Address** object the Form Bean would need a public **getAddress( )** method that returned an **Address** object. The **Address** object would need a public **getCity( )** method that would return a **String**. Properties that are themselves objects with properties are known as *nested properties*. Nested properties is the name given to properties that represent an object hierarchy.

Often, it's best to have Form Bean fields be **Strings** instead of other types. For example, instead of having an **Integer**-type field for storing a number, it's best to use a **String**-type field. This is because all HTML form data comes in the form of strings. If a letter rather than a number is entered in a numeric field, it's better to store the value in a **String** so that the original data can be returned to the form for correcting. If instead the data is stored in a **Long**, when Struts attempts to convert the string value to a number, it will throw a **NumberFormatException** if the value is a letter. Then, when the form is redisplayed showing the invalid data, it will show 0 instead of the originally entered value, because letters cannot be stored in numeric-type fields.

NOTE *Although Struts best practices dictate that all Form Bean fields should be of type* **String**, *the simplicity of using types that more naturally match the data sometimes prevails. For this scenario, the Struts* **ActionServlet** *has an initialization parameter,* **convertNull**, *that informs Struts to default to null for Java wrapper type classes (e.g., null instead of 0 for numeric types).*

Configuring Form Beans

To use Form Beans, you have to configure them in the Struts configuration file. Following is a basic Form Bean definition:

```
<!-- Form Beans Configuration -->
<form-beans>
  <form-bean name="searchForm"
             type="com.jamesholmes.minihr.SearchForm"/>
</form-beans>
```

Form Bean definitions specify a logical name and the class type for a Form Bean. Once defined, Form Beans are associated with actions by action mapping definitions, as shown next:

```
<!-- Action Mappings Configuration -->
<action-mappings>
  <action path="/search"
          type="com.jamesholmes.minihr.SearchAction"
          name="searchForm"
          scope="request"
          validate="true"
          input="/search.jsp">
  </action>
</action-mappings>
```

Actions specify their associated Form Bean with the **name** attribute of the **action** tag, as shown in the preceding snippet. The value specified for the **name** attribute is the logical name of a Form Bean defined with the **form-bean** tag. The **action** tag also has a **scope** attribute to specify the scope that the Form Bean will be stored in and a **validate** attribute to specify whether the Form Bean's **validate( )** method should be invoked after the Form Bean is populated. The **input** attribute of the **action** tag is typically used to specify a path that Struts should forward to if the **validate( )** method generates any errors.

The reset( ) Method

As previously stated, the abstract **ActionForm** class has a **reset( )** method that subclasses can override. The **reset( )** method is a hook that gets called before a Form Bean is populated with request data from an HTML form. This method hook was designed to account for a shortcoming in the way the HTML specification dictates that browsers should handle check boxes. Browsers send the value of a check box only if it is checked when the HTML form is submitted. For example, consider an HTML form with a check box for whether or not a file is read-only:

```
<input type="checkbox" name="readonly" value="true">
```

When the form containing this check box is submitted, the value of "true" is sent to the server only if the check box is checked. If the check box is not checked, no value is sent.

For most cases, this behavior is fine; however, it is problematic when Form Bean **boolean** properties have a default value of "true." For example, consider the read-only file scenario again. If your application has a Form Bean with a read-only property set to true and the Form Bean is used to populate a form with default settings, the read-only property will set the read-only check box's state to checked when it is rendered. If a user decides to uncheck the check box and then submits the form, no value will be sent to the server to indicate that the check box has been unchecked (i.e., set to false). By using the **reset( )** method, this can be solved by setting all properties tied to check boxes to false before the Form Bean is populated. Following is an example implementation of a Form Bean with a **reset( )** method that accounts for unchecked check boxes:

```
import org.apache.struts.action.ActionForm;

public class FileForm extends ActionForm
{
  private boolean readOnly;

  public void setReadOnly(boolean readOnly) {
    this.readOnly = readOnly;
  }

  public boolean getReadOnly() {
    return readOnly;
  }

  public void reset() {
    readOnly = false;
  }
}
```

The **reset( )** method in this example class ensures that the **readOnly** property is set to false before the form is populated. Having the **reset( )** method hook is equivalent to having the HTML form actually send a value for unchecked check boxes.

A side benefit of the **reset( )** method hook is that it offers a convenient place to reset data between requests when using Form Beans that are stored in session scope. When Form Beans are stored in session scope, they persist across multiple requests. This solution is most often used for wizard-style process flows. Sometimes it's necessary to reset data between requests, and the **reset( )** method provides a convenient place for doing this.

The validate( ) Method

In addition to the **reset( )** method hook, the **ActionForm** class provides a **validate( )** method hook that can be overridden by subclasses to perform validations on incoming form data.

The **validate( )** method hook gets called after a Form Bean has been populated with incoming form data. Following is the method signature for the **validate( )** method:

```
public ActionErrors validate(ActionMapping mapping,
                             HttpServletRequest request)
```

Notice that the **validate( )** method has a return type of **ActionErrors**. The **org.apache.struts.action.ActionErrors** class is a Struts class that is used for storing validation errors that have occurred in the **validate( )** method. If all validations in the **validate( )** method pass, a return value of null indicates to Struts that no errors occurred.

NOTE *Data validations can be performed in the* **execute( )** *method of action classes; however, having them in Form Beans allows them to be reused across multiple actions where more than one action uses the same Form Bean. Having the validation code in each action would be redundant.*

Following is an example Form Bean with a **validate( )** method:

```
import javax.servlet.http.HttpServletRequest;

import org.apache.struts.action.ActionErrors;
import org.apache.struts.action.ActionForm;
import org.apache.struts.action.ActionMapping;
import org.apache.struts.action.ActionMessage;

public class NameForm extends ActionForm
{
  private String name;

  public void setName(String name) {
    this.name = name;
  }

  public String getName() {
    return name;
  }

  public ActionErrors validate(ActionMapping mapping,
    HttpServletRequest request)
  {
    if (name == null || name.length() < 1) {
      ActionErrors errors = new ActionErrors();
      errors.add("name",
        new ActionMessage("error.name.required"));
      return errors;
    }

    return null;
  }
}
```

This example Form Bean has one field, **name**, that is validated in the **validate( )** method. The **validate( )** method checks whether or not the **name** field is empty. If it is empty, it returns an error indicating that fact. The **ActionErrors** object is basically a collection class for storing

org.apache.struts.action.ActionMessage instances. Each validation inside the **validate( )** method creates an **ActionMessage** instance that gets stored in the **ActionErrors** object. The **ActionMessage** class takes a key to an error message stored in the application resource bundle. Struts uses the key to look up the corresponding error message. Furthermore, the **ActionMessage** class has constructors that take additional arguments that contain replacement values for the error message associated with the specified key.

Struts also has a built-in Validator framework that greatly simplifies performing data validations. The Validator framework allows you to declaratively configure in an XML file the validations that should be applied to Form Beans. For more information on the Validator framework, see Chapter 6.

NOTE *The* **validate( )** *method will be called unless the Action Mapping has been configured with "validate=false" in the Struts configuration file.*

The Lifecycle of Form Beans

Form Beans have a defined lifecycle in Struts applications. To fully understand how Form Beans work, it's necessary to understand this lifecycle. The Form Bean lifecycle is shown in Figure 4-1.

Following is an explanation of the Form Bean lifecycle. When a request is received by the Struts controller servlet, Struts maps the request to an action class that is delegated to process the request. If the action being delegated to has an associated Form Bean, Struts attempts to look up the specified Form Bean in request or session scope, based on how the action is configured in the Struts configuration file. If an instance of the Form Bean is not found in the specified scope, an instance is created and placed in the specified scope. Next, Struts calls the **reset( )** method on the Form Bean so that any processing is executed that needs to occur before the Form Bean is populated. After that, Struts populates the Form

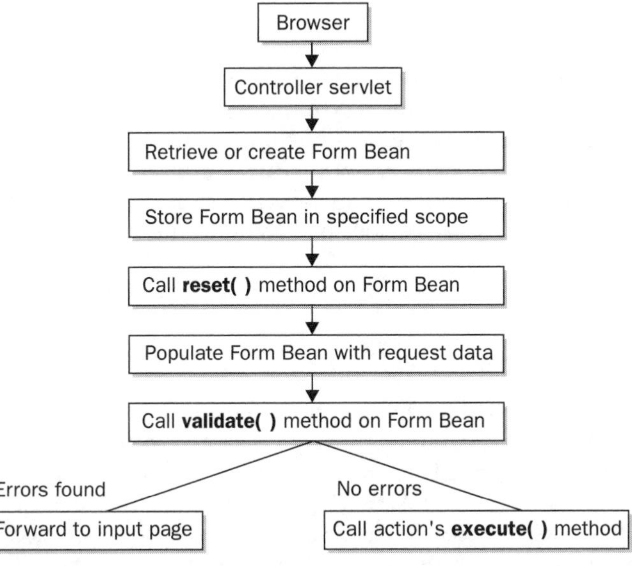

FIGURE 4-1 The Form Bean lifecycle

Bean with data from the incoming request. Next, the Form Bean's **validate( )** method is called. The next step in the process is based on the return value from the **validate( )** method. If the **validate( )** method records any errors and subsequently returns a non-null **ActionErrors** object, Struts forwards back to the action's input page. If, however, the return value from the **validate( )** method is null, Struts continues processing the request by calling the action's **execute( )** method.

Dynamic Form Beans

A useful addition to the 1.1 release of Struts was the introduction of Dynamic Form Beans. Dynamic Form Beans are an extension of Form Beans that allows you to specify their properties inside the Struts configuration file instead of having to create a concrete class, with a getter and setter method for each property. The concept of Dynamic Form Beans originated because many developers found it tedious to create for every page a Form Bean that had a getter method and a setter method for each of the fields on the page's HTML form. Using Dynamic Form Beans allows the properties to be specified in a Struts configuration file. To change a property, simply update the configuration file. No code has to be recompiled.

The following snippet illustrates how Dynamic Form Beans are configured in the Struts configuration file:

```
<!-- Form Beans Configuration -->
<form-beans>
  <form-bean name="employeeForm"
             type="org.apache.struts.action.DynaActionForm">
    <form-property name="firstName"
                   type="java.lang.String"/>
    <form-property name="lastName"
                   type="java.lang.String"/>
    <form-property name="department"
                   type="java.lang.String"/>
  </form-bean>
</form-beans>
```

Dynamic Form Beans are declared in the same way as standard Form Beans, by using the **form-bean** tag. The difference is that the type of the Form Bean specified with the **form-bean** tag's **type** attribute must be **org.apache.struts.action.DynaActionForm** or a subclass thereof. Additionally, the properties for Dynamic Form Beans are specified by nesting **form-property** tags beneath the **form-bean** tag. Each property specifies its name and class type. Furthermore, an initial value for the property can be specified using the **form-property** tag's **initial** attribute, as shown next:

```
<form-property name="department"
               type="java.lang.String"
               initial="Engineering"/>
```

If an initial value is not supplied for a property, Struts sets the initial value using Java's initialization conventions. That is, numbers are set to zero, objects are set to null, and so on.

Because you declare Dynamic Form Beans in the Struts configuration file instead of creating concrete classes that extend **ActionForm**, you do not define **reset( )** or **validate( )** methods for the Dynamic Form Beans. The **reset( )** method is no longer necessary for setting default values because the **initial** attribute on the **form-property** tag achieves the same effect. The **DynaActionForm** class's implementation of the **reset( )** method resets all properties to their initial value when it is called. You can either code the functionality of the **validate( )** method inside action classes or use the Validator framework for validation. These two options eliminate the need to create a **validate( )** method on the Form Bean. If, however, you have a special case where you need to have an implementation of the **reset( )** and/or **validate( )** method for your Dynamic Form Bean, you can subclass **DynaActionForm** and create the methods there. Simply specify your **DynaActionForm** subclass as the type of the Form Bean in the Struts configuration file to use it.

While Dynamic Form Beans shift the declaration of Form Beans and their fields from concrete classes to the Struts configuration file, an argument can be made that they don't save that much time. You still have to explicitly define each field for the Form Beans in the Struts configuration file. Thus you are really only getting the benefit of not having to recompile classes each time a change is made to the definition of a Form Bean. To further reduce the amount of overheard required in creating Form Beans, you can use what's known as a *Lazy DynaBean.* Lazy DynaBeans come to Struts by way of the Jakarta Commons BeanUtils project that Struts uses throughout the framework for bean manipulation. As of Struts 1.2.4, you can simply declare a name for a Form Bean in the Struts configuration file and specify its type as **org.apache.commons.beanutils.LazyDynaBean** and no other configuration is needed. The Lazy DynaBean will accommodate any form properties sent to it from an HTML Form. That is, no fields need to be explicitly declared for the Form Bean. An example of configuring a Lazy DynaBean is shown here:

```
<form-beans>
  <form-bean name="employeeForm"
             type="org.apache.commons.beanutils.LazyDynaBean"/>
</form-beans>
```

As you can see, it is very simple and fast to set up a Lazy DynaBean, saving much of the time traditionally spent in explicitly declaring the fields a Form Bean has.

Indexed and Mapped Properties

Using simple properties and nested properties on Form Beans will satisfy most requirements; however, there are scenarios where it is necessary to use a collection as a property. For example, when creating a form that has a variable number of fields, a collection must be used to capture the field data because the exact number of fields is not known in advance. Collection properties are also useful for transferring and displaying a variable-length list of data returned from the Model layer of an application. Struts supports two types of collection properties: indexed properties (e.g., arrays and **java.util.List** descendants such as **ArrayList**) and mapped properties (e.g., **java.util.Map** descendants such as **HashMap**).

Indexed properties are those properties that are backed by an indexed collection, such as arrays, **ArrayLists**, etc. To use an indexed property, you must set up the proper type of getter and setter methods in your Form Bean, as shown here:

```
import org.apache.struts.action.ActionForm;

public class EmployeeForm extends ActionForm
{
  private String[] departments =
    {"Accounting", "Sales", "Marketing", "IT'};

  public String getDepartments(int index) {
    return departments[index];
  }
```

```
  public void setDepartments(int index, String value) {
    departments[index] = value;
  }
}
```

This example uses an array-based indexed property called **departments**. Notice that the **getDepartments( )** and **setDepartments( )** methods take an **index** argument to specify the index in the array for the value that should be gotten or set. **java.util.List**-based indexed properties only require you to create a getter method, as shown next:

```
import java.util.ArrayList;
import java.util.List;
import org.apache.struts.action.ActionForm;

public class EmployeeForm extends ActionForm
{
  private ArrayList departments = new ArrayList();

  public EmployeeForm() {
    departments.add("Accounting");
    departments.add("Sales");
    departments.add("Marketing");
    departments.add("IT");
  }

  public List getDepartments() {
    return departments;
  }
}
```

Struts takes care of calling the getter and setter methods for indexed properties with the proper index when capturing data from a form or when populating a form. The following example illustrates how to reference an indexed property using the Struts tag libraries:

```
<html:form>
  <html:text property="departments[0]"/>
</html:form>
```

Notice that an index is specified for the **departments** field using **[ ]** notation. When this hypothetical form is submitted, an index of 0 and the value entered in the control will be used to populate the proper element in the collection. While this example illustrates how to reference a specific element in an indexed property, the real power of indexed properties is realized when a loop is used so that individual element indexes don't have to be specified. The following example illustrates how to use a loop to iterate over an indexed property's elements.

```
<html:form>
  <logic:iterate name="employeeForm" property="departments"
                 id="department" indexId="index">
    <html:text property="<%="departments[" + index + "]"%>"/>
  </logic:iterate>
</html:form>
```

A variable number of text input fields will be generated. If the **departments** property has 10 elements, 10 text input fields will be generated; if **departments** has no elements, no text input fields will be generated.

Mapped properties work much the same way that indexed properties do—only they are backed by **java.util.Map** descendants instead of arrays or **java.util.List** descendants. The syntax for referencing elements in a map differs as well. Instead of using **[ ]** notation to specify an index, **( )** notation is used to specify a key in the map. An example Form Bean with a mapped property is shown here.

```
import java.util.HashMap;
import java.util.Map;
import org.apache.struts.action.ActionForm;

public class EmployeeForm extends ActionForm
{
  private HashMap departments = new HashMap();

  public EmployeeForm() {
    departments.put("dep1", "Accounting");
    departments.put("dep2", "Sales");
    departments.put("dep3", "Marketing");
    departments.put("dep4", "IT");
  }

  public Object getDepartments(String key) {
    return departments.get(key);
  }

  public void setDepartments(String key, Object value) {
    departments.put(key, value);
  }
}
```

The **getDepartments( )** and **setDepartments( )** methods take a key argument to specify the key in the map for the value that should be gotten or set. Referencing mapped properties is similar to referencing indexed properties, as shown here:

```
<html:form>
  <html:text property="departments(dep1)"/>
</html:form>
```

NOTE *Indexed and mapped properties can be both nested and contain nested properties, just as any other type of property can be.*

JSP Tag Libraries

Struts comes packaged with a set of its own custom JSP tag libraries that aid in the development of JSPs. The tag libraries are fundamental building blocks in Struts applications because they provide a convenient mechanism for creating HTML forms whose data will be captured in Form Beans and for displaying data stored in Form Beans. Additionally, the Struts tag libraries provide several utility tags to accomplish things such as conditional logic, iterating over collections, and so on. However, with the advent of the JSP Standard Tag Library (JSTL), many of the utility tags have been superceded. (Using JSTL with Struts is covered in Chapter 17.)

Following is a list of the Struts tag libraries and their purpose:

- **HTML** Used to generate HTML forms that interact with the Struts APIs.
- **Bean** Used to work with Java bean objects in JSPs, such as to access bean values.
- **Logic** Used to cleanly implement simple conditional logic in JSPs.
- **Nested** Used to simplify access to arbitrary levels of nested objects from the HTML, Bean, and Logic tags.

Later in this book, each of these libraries has an entire chapter dedicated to its use, but this section provides a brief introduction to using the tag libraries, focusing on the core Struts JSP tag library, the HTML Tag Library, as an example. This library is used to generate HTML forms that, when submitted, populate Form Beans. Additionally, the HTML Tag Library tags can create HTML forms populated with data from Form Beans. To use the HTML Tag Library in a Struts application, your application's JSPs must declare their use of the library with a JSP **taglib** directive:

```
<%@ taglib uri="http://struts.apache.org/tags-html" prefix="html" %>
```

Notice that the **prefix** attribute is set to "html". This attribute can be set to whatever you want; however, "html" is the accepted default for the HTML Tag Library. The **prefix** attribute declares the prefix that each tag must have when it is used in the JSP, as shown here:

```
<html:form action="/logon">
```

Because "html" was defined as the prefix, the **form** tag was used as shown. However, if you chose to use a prefix of "strutshtml", the tag would be used the following way:

```
<strutshtml:form action="/logon">
```

NOTE *Modern application servers use the* **uri** *attribute of the* **taglib** *directive to automatically resolve the location of the tag library descriptor file. Older application servers that support only JSP version 1.1 and/or version 1.0 require that tag libraries be registered in the* **web.xml** *file so that they can be resolved, as shown here:*

```
<taglib>
  <taglib-uri>http://struts.apache.org/tags-html</taglib-uri>
  <taglib-location>/WEB-INF/tlds/struts-html.tld</taglib-location>
</taglib>
```

Resource Bundles

Resource bundles allow Java applications to be easily internationalized by having application content placed into bundles. This content can then be read by the application at run time. Therefore, instead of having content hard-coded in the application, the application reads its content from the bundle. A side benefit of using resource bundles to store application content (whether for internationalization or not) is that the content can be changed without having to recompile the application. Additionally, bundles serve as a central repository for content that is common to multiple uses (i.e., multiple applications). Having content in a central repository reduces unnecessary duplication.

Struts has built-in support for working with Java's resource bundle mechanism. Having this support allows the Struts framework to seamlessly support application internationalization as well as have a mechanism for externalizing content so that it can be easily changed without having to modify JSPs or application code. Struts uses resource bundle resources throughout the framework. For example, resource bundle resources can be accessed from JSPs to populate them with content. Similarly, action objects can access content stored in resource bundles to do such things as generate error or informational messages that get displayed on screen. The Struts Form Bean validation mechanism is also tied to resource bundles for managing error messages. Actually, there are several uses for resource bundles throughout Struts.

The rest of this section explains how to create a resource bundle properties file and configure Struts to use it. An example of accessing resource bundle content from a JSP is also shown. Later chapters provide specific information about how to use resource bundles in the context of those chapters' topics.

Using resource bundles in Struts is as easy as creating a properties file to store the resources in, and then configuring Struts to use the properties file. Once this is done, accessing the resources is straightforward. Following is a very simple resource bundle properties file containing a few properties:

```
page.title=Employee Search
link.employeeSearch=Search for Employees
link.addEmployee=Add a New Employee
```

Resource bundle properties files simply contain key/value pairs. The resources are accessed by their key. The standard name for the resource bundle properties file in Struts is **MessageResources.properties**. In order for Struts to be able to load this file, it must be stored on your application's classpath. For example, it could be stored in the **/WEB-INF/classes** directory.

The following snippet configures the resource bundle with Struts:

```
<!-- Message Resources Configuration -->
<message-resources
  parameter="com.jamesholmes.minihr.MessageResources"/>
```

The **parameter** attribute of the **message-resources** tag specifies the fully qualified name of the resource bundle properties file minus the **.properties** file extension. In this example, a file named **MessageResources.properties** would be stored in the **/WEB-INF/classes/com/jamesholmes/minihr** directory.

Once a properties file has been created and configured in the Struts configuration file, the resources in the bundle can be accessed from several places in the Struts framework. The most common place is in JSPs. The following snippet illustrates how to use the Bean Tag Library's **message** tag to load a message from the resource bundle:

```
<%@ taglib uri="http://struts.apache.org/tags-bean" prefix="bean" %>

<html>
<head>
<title><bean:message key="page.title"/></title>
</head>
<body>

...
```

The value specified with the **message** tag's **key** attribute is the key for a message in the resource bundle. At run time, Struts retrieves the message and places it in the JSP.

NOTE *Detailed information on resource bundles and internationalizing Struts applications is found in Chapter 10.*

Reviewing the View Layer of the Mini HR Application

To solidify your understanding of the View layer of Struts applications, it will be helpful to review the View layer of the Mini HR application developed in Chapter 2. Doing so clearly illustrates the core components involved in creating the View layer.

Mini HR's View layer consists of a Form Bean, two JSPs, and a resource bundle properties file. The **SearchForm** Form Bean is shown next:

```
package com.jamesholmes.minihr;

import java.util.List;

import javax.servlet.http.HttpServletRequest;

import org.apache.struts.action.ActionErrors;
import org.apache.struts.action.ActionForm;
import org.apache.struts.action.ActionMapping;
import org.apache.struts.action.ActionMessage;

public class SearchForm extends ActionForm
{
  private String name = null;
  private String ssNum = null;
  private List results = null;

  public void setName(String name) {
    this.name = name;
  }

  public String getName() {
    return name;
  }

  public void setSsNum(String ssNum) {
    this.ssNum = ssNum;
  }

  public String getSsNum() {
    return ssNum;
  }

  public void setResults(List results) {
    this.results = results;
  }

  public List getResults() {
    return results;
  }

  // Reset form fields.
  public void reset(ActionMapping mapping, HttpServletRequest request)
```

```
{
  name = null;
  ssNum = null;
  results = null;
}

// Validate form data.
public ActionErrors validate(ActionMapping mapping,
  HttpServletRequest request)
{
  ActionErrors errors = new ActionErrors();

  boolean nameEntered = false;
  boolean ssNumEntered = false;

  // Determine if name has been entered.
  if (name != null && name.length() > 0) {
    nameEntered = true;
  }

  // Determine if social security number has been entered.
  if (ssNum != null && ssNum.length() > 0) {
    ssNumEntered = true;
  }

  /* Validate that either name or social security number
     has been entered. */
  if (!nameEntered && !ssNumEntered) {
    errors.add(null,
      new ActionMessage("error.search.criteria.missing"));
  }

  /* Validate format of social security number if
     it has been entered. */
  if (ssNumEntered && !isValidSsNum(ssNum.trim())) {
    errors.add("ssNum",
      new ActionMessage("error.search.ssNum.invalid"));
  }

  return errors;
}

// Validate format of social security number.
private static boolean isValidSsNum(String ssNum) {
  if (ssNum.length() < 11) {
    return false;
  }

  for (int i = 0; i < 11; i++) {
    if (i == 3 || i == 6) {
      if (ssNum.charAt(i) != '-') {
        return false;
      }
    } else if ("0123456789".indexOf(ssNum.charAt(i)) == -1) {
      return false;
```

```
        }
      }

      return true;
    }
}
```

The **SearchForm** class is a basic Form Bean with a few properties and implementations for the **reset( )** and **validate( )** method hooks. Mini HR uses this Form Bean to capture search criteria from the search page using the **name** and **ssNum** fields. The **results** field is used to transfer search results back to the search page after a search has been performed.

The **index.jsp** page, shown next, is a simple JSP used as an example menu page for linking to Mini HR's functions:

```
<%@ taglib uri="http://struts.apache.org/tags-html" prefix="html" %>

<html>
<head>
<title>ABC, Inc. Human Resources Portal</title>
</head>
<body>

<font size="+1">ABC, Inc. Human Resources Portal</font><br>
<hr width="100%" noshade="true">

&#149; Add an Employee<br>
&#149; <html:link forward="search">Search for Employees</html:link><br>

</body>
</html>
```

This page is the opening page for the Mini HR application and provides a link to the Mini HR search page.

The **search.jsp** page shown here provides the core interface to the Mini HR search functionality. It serves as the search criteria page as well as the search results page.

```
<%@ taglib uri="http://struts.apache.org/tags-bean" prefix="bean" %>
<%@ taglib uri="http://struts.apache.org/tags-html" prefix="html" %>
<%@ taglib uri="http://struts.apache.org/tags-logic" prefix="logic" %>

<html>
<head>
<title>ABC, Inc. Human Resources Portal - Employee Search</title>
</head>
<body>

<font size="+1">
ABC, Inc. Human Resources Portal - Employee Search
</font><br>
<hr width="100%" noshade="true">

<html:errors/>

<html:form action="/search">
```

```
<table>
<tr>
<td align="right"><bean:message key="label.search.name"/>:</td>
<td><html:text property="name"/></td>
</tr>
<tr>
<td></td>
<td>-- or --</td>
</tr>
<tr>
<td align="right"><bean:message key="label.search.ssNum"/>:</td>
<td><html:text property="ssNum"/> (xxx-xx-xxxx)</td>
</tr>
<tr>
<td></td>
<td><html:submit/></td>
</tr>
</table>

</html:form>

<logic:present name="searchForm" property="results">

<hr width="100%" size="1" noshade="true">

<bean:size id="size" name="searchForm" property="results"/>
<logic:equal name="size" value="0">
<center><font color="red"><cTypeface:Bold>No Employees Found</b></font></center>
</logic:equal>

<logic:greaterThan name="size" value="0">
<table border="1">
<tr>
<th>Name</th>
<th>Social Security Number</th>
</tr>
<logic:iterate id="result" name="searchForm" property="results">
<tr>
<td><bean:write name="result" property="name"/></td>
<td><bean:write name="result" property="ssNum"/></td>
</tr>
</logic:iterate>
</table>
</logic:greaterThan>

</logic:present>

</body>
</html>
```

This page uses Struts tag library tags to determine whether or not it is being executed before or after a search has been submitted. If the page is being displayed before a search, it simply displays the search criteria form. However, if the page is being displayed after a search, it displays the search criteria form in addition to the search results.

The **MessageResources.properties** resource bundle file, shown next, is used by the **SearchForm** Form Bean and the JSPs to retrieve externalized content from a central repository:

```
# Label Resources
label.search.name=Name
label.search.ssNum=Social Security Number

# Error Resources
error.search.criteria.missing=Search Criteria Missing
error.search.ssNum.invalid=Invalid Social Security Number
errors.header=<font color="red"><cTypeface:Bold>Validation Error(s)</b></font><ul>
errors.footer=</ul><hr width="100%" size="1" noshade="true">
errors.prefix=<li>
errors.suffix=</li>
```

The **SearchForm** Form Bean uses this file to store validation error messages. The JSPs use this file to store field labels. Together they are able to leverage Struts' built-in resource bundle mechanism for externalizing content. Doing so allows for easy updates to the content and provides a simple interface for internationalizing the content if necessary.

Alternative View Technologies

Before concluding this chapter, it's important to point out again that Struts is an extensible Web framework that allows you to use any technology you desire to develop the View layer of your Struts application. While this chapter has focused primarily on the built-in JSP-related support, there are several alternatives available. The following table lists a few of the options and a brief description, including a URL for each option.

Technology	Description and URL
Cocoon	The Apache Cocoon project is an XML-based Web application publishing engine for generating, transforming, processing, and outputting data. Don Brown created a Struts plugin, Cocoon Plugin, which integrates the Cocoon framework with the Struts framework. http://struts.sourceforge.net/struts-cocoon/
stxx	Struts for transforming XML with XSL (stxx) is a third-party extension of the Struts framework that supports using XSLT (XML Style Language Templates) for the View layer. http://stxx.sourceforge.net/
Swing	Java's Swing library can be used to create rich GUI front ends for Struts applications. The following article illustrates how to do this. http://javaboutique.internet.com/tutorials/Swing/
Velocity	The Jakarta Velocity project is a Java-based templating engine that can be used as an alternative to JSPs. VelocityStruts is a Velocity subproject that integrates Velocity with the Struts framework. http://jakarta.apache.org/velocity/tools/struts/

CHAPTER 5

The Controller Layer

The Controller layer of an MVC application is responsible for creating the abstraction between the Model and View layers. That is, the Controller layer acts as a liaison between the Model and View layers, separating one from the other. This abstraction is the foundation of the MVC design pattern. Recall that the Model contains the application's core, including the business logic and data access code, and the View contains the interface to the application. The Controller layer stands between these two layers, allowing them to change independently of one another. With this architecture, the Model (or core application code) is not limited to a singular use. This is a key advantage of MVC.

In MVC Web applications, the Controller layer serves as the central point of access to the application. All requests to an MVC Web application flow through the controller. By doing so, the Controller layer provides processing common to all requests, such as security, caching, logging, and so on. Most importantly, though, having all requests flow through the Controller allows the Controller to have complete autonomy over how requests are mapped to business processing and how the proper View is selected, based on the outcome of the business processing.

Struts and the Controller Layer

Struts provides a robust Controller layer implementation that has been designed from the ground up to be extensible. At its core is the Controller servlet, **ActionServlet**, which is responsible for initializing a Struts application's configuration from the Struts configuration file and for receiving all incoming requests to the application. Upon receiving a request, **ActionServlet** delegates its processing to the Struts request processing engine. The request processing engine processes all aspects of the request, including selecting the Form Bean associated with the request, populating the Form Bean with data, validating the Form Bean, and then selecting the correct **Action** class to execute for the request. The **Action** class is where the Struts framework ends and your application code begins. **Action** classes provide the glue between the View and Model layers and return instances of the **ActionForward** class to direct the Controller which View to display. Figure 5-1 illustrates the Controller layer lifecycle.

The following sections explain each of the major Controller layer components in detail.

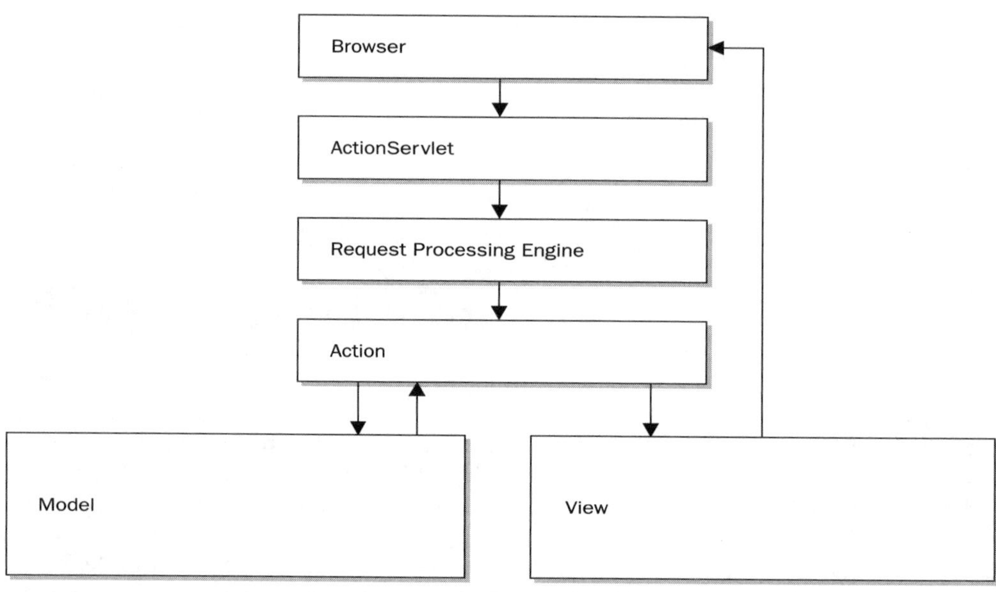

Figure 5-1 The Controller layer lifecycle

The ActionServlet Class

The **ActionServlet** class is the main controller class that receives all incoming HTTP requests for the application. Additionally, **ActionServlet** is responsible for initializing the Struts framework for your application. Like any other servlet, **ActionServlet** must be configured in your application's Web application deployment descriptor: **web.xml**. The configuration settings in **web.xml** specify how to map requests to your Web application to the **ActionServlet**. There are two ways that **ActionServlet** can be configured to receive requests in **web.xml**. First, **ActionServlet** can be configured using path mapping, as shown here:

```
<?xml version="1.0"?>

<!DOCTYPE web-app PUBLIC
  "-//Sun Microsystems, Inc.//DTD Web Application 2.3//EN"
  "http://java.sun.com/dtd/web-app_2_3.dtd">

<web-app>

  <!-- Action Servlet Configuration -->
  <servlet>
    <servlet-name>action</servlet-name>
    <servlet-class>org.apache.struts.action.ActionServlet</servlet-class>
    <init-param>
      <param-name>config</param-name>
      <param-value>/WEB-INF/struts-config.xml</param-value>
    </init-param>
    <load-on-startup>1</load-on-startup>
  </servlet>
```

```
  <!-- Action Servlet Mapping -->
  <servlet-mapping>
    <servlet-name>action</servlet-name>
    <url-pattern>/do/*</url-pattern>
  </servlet-mapping>

</web-app>
```

Path mapping routes to **ActionServlet** all requests that match a specified path. The default path is **/do/***, as shown in the preceding **web.xml** file; however, you can use any path that you like.

The second way to map requests to **ActionServlet** is to use extension mapping, as shown next:

```
<?xml version="1.0"?>

<!DOCTYPE web-app PUBLIC
  "-//Sun Microsystems, Inc.//DTD Web Application 2.3//EN"
  "http://java.sun.com/dtd/web-app_2_3.dtd">

<web-app>

  <!-- Action Servlet Configuration -->
  <servlet>
    <servlet-name>action</servlet-name>
    <servlet-class>org.apache.struts.action.ActionServlet</servlet-class>
    <init-param>
      <param-name>config</param-name>
      <param-value>/WEB-INF/struts-config.xml</param-value>
    </init-param>
    <load-on-startup>1</load-on-startup>
  </servlet>

  <!-- Action Servlet Mapping -->
  <servlet-mapping>
    <servlet-name>action</servlet-name>
    <url-pattern>*.do</url-pattern>
  </servlet-mapping>

</web-app>
```

Extension mapping maps to **ActionServlet** all requests with the specified extension. The default extension to use is **.do**; however, you can use any extension you like.

NOTE *Extension mapping is required if you are using Struts' module feature. For more information on modules, see Chapter 9.*

The Request Processing Engine

Struts uses its request processing engine to perform the processing for all requests received by the **ActionServlet**. The request processing engine takes each request and breaks its processing down into several small tasks. This approach allows each individual part of the request processing cycle to be customized.

In version 1.3, a new request processing engine was introduced that is built on top of the Jakarta Commons Chain library (http://jakarta.apache.org/commons/chain/). Previous versions of Struts performed all of the request processing in a single class named **org.apache.struts.action.RequestProcessor**. Both of these request processing methods are described separately in the following sections.

Jakarta Commons Chain-Based Request Processing

The **RequestProcessor** class-based processing originally used in Struts (and described in the following eponymously named section) provided a nice abstraction for each part of the request processing cycle; however, it had its limitations. The principal limitation was that customization of the request processing cycle required subclassing the **RequestProcessor** class. This subclassing precluded multiple independent customizations to be created and used together because there was not a way to tie the assorted customizations back together. Because of this, Commons Chain is now being utilized by Struts to further abstract the processing of requests and solve the problem of having multiple customizations.

The Commons Chain library provides an implementation of the *Chain of Responsibility (COR)* pattern described in the seminal **Design Patterns** book by the *Gang of Four.* The COR pattern models a computation as a series of *commands* that are combined into a *chain.* Chains represent the entire computation, while commands represent discrete pieces of the computation. Each command in a chain is executed in succession until all commands in the chain have been executed or until a command returns a flag indicating that execution is complete for the chain. This pattern of processing is essentially what was implemented in the Struts **RequestProcessor** class. However, the **RequestProcessor** class did not provide a mechanism for introducing new commands into (or removing commands from) its chain. Additionally, the list of steps and the order of the steps of processing in the **RequestProcessor** class is hard-coded and cannot be changed without subclassing **RequestProcessor**. Commons Chain allows commands to be easily added or removed by abstracting the definition of chains into an XML configuration file.

In converting to Commons Chain, each of the processing methods of the **RequestProcessor** class was moved to its own command class and all of the commands were wired together into a chain. The chain definition is stored in the default Struts Chain configuration file, **chain-config.xml**, that is stored in the Struts Core **.jar** file (e.g., **struts-core-1.3.5.jar**) in the **org\apache\struts\chain** directory. To add or remove commands from the default chain configuration, the Chain configuration file must be modified. Because the Chain configuration file is stored in the Struts Core **.jar** file, it is cumbersome to update that file. Instead, a new Chain configuration file should be created. The default Chain configuration file can be used as a template and then any changes can be made. Once the new Chain configuration file is created, Struts must be configured to use it as shown in the following example:

```
<servlet>
  <servlet-name>action</servlet-name>
  <servlet-class>org.apache.struts.action.ActionServlet</servlet-class>
  <init-param>
    <param-name>config</param-name>
    <param-value>/WEB-INF/struts-config.xml</param-value>
  </init-param>
  <init-param>
    <param-name>chainConfig</param-name>
```

```
    <param-value>/WEB-INF/chain-config.xml</param-value>
  </init-param>
  <load-on-startup>1</load-on-startup>
</servlet>
```


Like the Struts configuration file, the Chain configuration file is specified with an initialization parameter to the Struts **ActionServlet**. The initialization parameter is named **chainConfig** and its value is the path to the Chain configuration file.

RequestProcessor Class-Based Processing

As stated, in versions of Struts prior to version 1.3, the **RequestProcessor** class was used to handle all request processing. The **RequestProcessor** class uses a separate method to carry out each request processing task. Each of the separate methods is aptly named with a prefix of *process*; for example, **processMultipart( )** and **processPath( )**.

Table 5-1 lists and describes briefly each of the **process*( )** methods from the **RequestProcessor** class (in the order they are executed).

Method	Description
processMultipart( )	Wraps multipart requests with a special wrapper class.
processPath( )	Determines the path that will be used to select an action to which processing is delegated.
processLocale( )	Saves the user's locale in session scope.
processContent( )	Sets the default content type for the response.
processNoCache( )	Sets no-cache HTTP headers for the response if necessary.
processPreprocess( )	Provides a hook for subclasses to override. It is used to tell the request processor whether or not to continue processing the request after this method has been called.
processCachedMessages( )	Removes cached **ActionMessage** objects from the session so that they are available only for one request.
processMapping( )	Selects the action mapping to use for the request.
processRoles( )	Checks if the current user has a role that is allowed to access the requested resource.
processActionForm( )	Creates a new Form Bean or retrieves one from the session for the request.
processPopulate( )	Populates the Form Bean returned from **processActionForm( )** with data from the incoming request.
processValidate( )	Invokes the **validate( )** method on the Form Bean returned from **processActionForm( )** if necessary.
processForward( )	Processes the forward for the action mapping matching the current request path, if the matching mapping is specified to be a forward.

Table 5-1 The process*( ) Methods of the RequestProcessor Class

Method	Description
processInclude( )	Processes the include for the action mapping matching the current request path, if the matching mapping is specified to be an include.
processActionCreate( )	Creates or recycles an existing action to process the current request.
processActionPerform( )	Invokes the **execute( )** method on the action returned from **processActionCreate( )**.
processForwardConfig( )	Forwards to the forward returned from **processActionPerform( )**.

TABLE 5-1 The process*( ) Methods of the RequestProcessor Class *(continued)*

By having each phase of the request processing cycle take place in a separate method, request processing can easily be customized. Simply create a custom request processor that extends the base **RequestProcessor** class and override the methods that need to be customized. For example, a custom request processor can apply a logged-in security check before any action is executed. The **RequestProcessor** class provides the **processPreprocess( )** method hook expressly for this. The **processPreprocess( )** method is called before actions are executed. The following example shows how to do this:

```
package com.jamesholmes.minihr;

import javax.servlet.http.HttpServletRequest;
import javax.servlet.http.HttpServletResponse;

import org.apache.struts.action.RequestProcessor;

public class LoggedInRequestProcessor extends RequestProcessor
{
  protected boolean processPreprocess(
    HttpServletRequest request,
    HttpServletResponse response)
  {
    // Check if user is logged in.
    // If so return true to continue processing,
    // otherwise return false to not continue processing.
    return (true);
  }
}
```

To use a custom request processor, you have to configure Struts to use it in the Struts configuration file:

```
<controller processorClass="com.jamesholmes.minihr.LoggedInRequestProcessor"/>
```

NOTE *When using the Struts module feature, each module has its own request processor. Thus, if you want to apply a custom request processor to all modules, you must configure it in each module's Struts configuration file.*

The Action Class

The **Action** class is where the Struts framework ends and your application code begins. As previously mentioned, **Action** classes provide the glue between the View and Model layers and are responsible for processing specific requests. **Action** classes are intended to transfer data from the View layer to a specific business process in the Model layer, and then to return data from the business process to the View layer. Business logic should not be embedded in actions, because that violates the principles of MVC.

Each action is mapped to a path in the Struts configuration file. When a request with the specified path is made to the **ActionServlet**, the action is invoked to process the request. The following snippet illustrates how to configure an action in the Struts configuration file:

```
<action-mappings>
  <action path="/UpdateUser"
          type="com.jamesholmes.example.UpdateUserAction"/>
</action-mappings>
```

Which URL is used to access the action depends on how **ActionServlet** is configured in **web.xml**. If **ActionServlet** is configured to use path mapping, the action defined in the preceding example is accessed as **http://localhost:8080/MiniHR/do/UpdateUser**, assuming a server of **localhost** running on port **8080** and an application deployed as **MiniHR**. If extension mapping were used to configure **ActionServlet**, the URL would be **http://localhost:8080/MiniHR/UpdateUser.do**.

When an action is called to process a request, its **execute( )** method is invoked. The **execute( )** method is analogous to the **service( )** method in servlets. It handles all processing. Following is an example **Action** subclass and its **execute( )** method:

```
import javax.servlet.http.HttpServletRequest;
import javax.servlet.http.HttpServletResponse;

import org.apache.struts.action.Action;
import org.apache.struts.action.ActionForm;
import org.apache.struts.action.ActionForward;
import org.apache.struts.action.ActionMapping;

public class UpdateUserAction extends Action
{
  public ActionForward execute(ActionMapping mapping,
    ActionForm form,
    HttpServletRequest request,
    HttpServletResponse response)
    throws Exception
  {
    // Perform request processing here.
  }
}
```

Retrieving Values from Form Beans

Action classes are the principal location for transferring data from the View layer to the Model layer and vice versa. Form Beans are used to encapsulate the data being transferred to and from the View layer and are passed to the **execute( )** method of **Action** classes. **Action** classes then retrieve values from the Form Bean and transfer the values to the Model Layer.

Form Beans should not be transferred directly to the Model layer because it creates an artificial dependency on Struts. Because of this, it is important to understand how to retrieve the data stored in Form Beans. Each of the different types of Form Beans has a different mechanism for retrieving the values stored in the Form Bean and is explained here.

Standard Form Beans that subclass **org.apache.struts.action.ActionForm** have basic getter and setter methods that are called directly to retrieve the values from the Form Bean as shown here:

```
public ActionForward execute(ActionMapping mapping,
  ActionForm form,
  HttpServletRequest request,
  HttpServletResponse response)
  throws Exception
{
  SearchForm searchForm = (SearchForm) form;

  String name = searchForm.getName();
  String ssNum = searchForm.getSsNum();
}
```

Notice that the incoming Form Bean must be cast to its proper type before calling any getter or setter methods.

The following code sample illustrates how to access the properties of a dynamic Form Bean. Dynamic Form Beans do not have concrete getter and setter methods. Instead their values are retrieved by passing the name of a field to the **get( )** method of the **DynaActionForm** class.

```
public ActionForward execute(ActionMapping mapping,
  ActionForm form,
  HttpServletRequest request,
  HttpServletResponse response)
  throws Exception
{
  DynaActionForm searchForm = (DynaActionForm) form;

  String name = (String) searchForm.get("name");
  String ssNum = (String) searchForm.get("ssNum");
}
```

The **DynaActionForm get( )** method has a return type of **Object** thus fields must be cast to their proper type when being retrieved.

Lazy DynaBeans operate identically to Dynamic Form Beans: simply pass the name of the field being retrieved to the **get( )** method of the **LazyDynaBean** class.

```
public ActionForward execute(ActionMapping mapping,
  ActionForm form,
  HttpServletRequest request,
  HttpServletResponse response)
  throws Exception
{
  LazyDynaBean searchForm = (LazyDynaBean) form;

  String name = (String) searchForm.get("name");
  String ssNum = (String) searchForm.get("ssNum");
}
```

Customizing the Response from an Action

By default, an **ActionForward** should be returned from the **execute( )** method of actions to direct the controller on which view should be displayed. The controller takes care of routing to the proper JSP and the JSP generates the response to the browser. There are scenarios, however, where it is necessary to customize the response generated from an action. File downloads are an example of this. Instead of forwarding to a JSP to render a page, an action can interface directly with the HTTP response and transmit the file being downloaded. To do this, an action simply has to use the **HttpServletResponse** object passed to **Action** classes' execute **method( )**. Additionally the action must return **null** from the **execute( )** method to indicate to the Struts Controller that no further processing is required. Following is an example file download action:

```
import javax.servlet.http.HttpServletRequest;
import javax.servlet.http.HttpServletResponse;

import org.apache.struts.action.Action;
import org.apache.struts.action.ActionForm;
import org.apache.struts.action.ActionForward;
import org.apache.struts.action.ActionMapping;

public class DownloadAction extends Action
{
  public ActionForward execute(ActionMapping mapping,
    ActionForm form,
    HttpServletRequest request,
    HttpServletResponse response)
    throws Exception
  {
    // Perform file download processing here.

    return null;
  }
}
```

Notice that **null** is returned from the **Action** class instead of an **ActionForward**. This is a critical detail when taking control of the HTTP response directly from within the **Action** class.

Struts' Built-in Actions

Struts comes packaged with several built-in utility actions that provide functionality that is useful to many applications. Table 5-2 lists each of the built-in actions and their purpose.

The following sections describe each of the built-in actions in detail.

The DispatchAction Class

The **org.apache.struts.actions.DispatchAction** class provides a mechanism for modularizing a set of related functions into a single action, thus eliminating the need to create separate, independent actions for each function. For example, consider a set of related functions for adding a user, updating a user, and removing a user. Instead of creating an **AddUserAction** class, an **UpdateUserAction** class, and a **RemoveUserAction** class, by extending **DispatchAction**, you can create one **UserAction** class that has three methods: **add( )**, **update( )**, and **remove( )**. At run time, **DispatchAction** manages routing requests to the appropriate method in its subclass. **DispatchAction** determines which method to call based on the value of a request parameter that is passed to it from the incoming request.

Action	Description
DispatchAction	Provides a mechanism for modularizing a set of related functions into a single action, thus eliminating the need to create separate, independent actions for each function.
DownloadAction	Provides a mechanism for easing the creation of file download actions.
EventDispatchAction	Provides a mechanism for modularizing a set of related functions into a single action, thus eliminating the need to create separate, independent actions for each function.
ForwardAction	Provides a mechanism for forwarding to a specified URL.
IncludeAction	Provides a mechanism for including the contents of a specified URL.
LocaleAction	Provides a mechanism for setting a user's locale and then forwarding to a specified page.
LookupDispatchAction	Provides a mechanism for modularizing a set of related functions into a single action, thus eliminating the need to create separate, independent actions for each function.
MappingDispatchAction	Provides a mechanism for modularizing a set of related functions into a single action, thus eliminating the need to create separate, independent actions for each function.
SwitchAction	Provides a mechanism for switching between modules in a modularized Struts application.

TABLE 5-2 Struts' Built-in Utility Actions

To use **DispatchAction**, you must create a subclass from it and provide a set of methods that will be called to process requests. Additionally, you have to set up for the action an action mapping that specifies the name of a request parameter that will be used to select which method should be called for each request. Following is an example **UserAction** class that extends **DispatchAction**:

```
package com.jamesholmes.minihr;

import javax.servlet.http.HttpServletRequest;
import javax.servlet.http.HttpServletResponse;

import org.apache.struts.action.ActionForm;
import org.apache.struts.action.ActionForward;
import org.apache.struts.action.ActionMapping;
import org.apache.struts.actions.DispatchAction;

public class UserAction extends DispatchAction
{
  public ActionForward add(ActionMapping mapping,
    ActionForm form,
    HttpServletRequest request,
    HttpServletResponse response)
    throws Exception
  {
```

```
    // Add user.
    ...

    return mapping.findForward("success");
  }

  public ActionForward update(ActionMapping mapping,
    ActionForm form,
    HttpServletRequest request,
    HttpServletResponse response)
    throws Exception
  {
    // Update user.
    ...

    return mapping.findForward("success");
  }

  public ActionForward remove(ActionMapping mapping,
    ActionForm form,
    HttpServletRequest request,
    HttpServletResponse response)
    throws Exception
  {
    // Remove user.
    ...

    return mapping.findForward("success");
  }
}
```

Notice that this class does not provide an implementation for the **execute( )** method the way typical **Action** classes do. This is because **DispatchAction** provides to you an implementation of this method that manages delegating to the individual methods. In order for your **DispatchAction** subclass to work, you must create in the Struts configuration file an action mapping that specifies the name of a request parameter that will be used to select the method that will be called for specific requests. Following is a sample snippet that illustrates how to do this:

```
<action-mappings>
  <action path="/User"
          type="com.jamesholmes.minihr.UserAction"
     parameter="function"/>
</action-mappings>
```

The value specified with the **parameter** attribute of the **action** tag will be used as the name of a request parameter that will contain the name of a method to invoke for handling the request. Given the preceding mapping of **/User** to **UserAction**, the following URL will invoke the **add( )** method (assuming the application was run on your **localhost** at port **8080** and the application was deployed as **/MiniHR/**):

http://localhost:8080/MiniHR/User.do?function=add

To invoke the **remove( )** method, use the following URL:

http://localhost:8080/MiniHR/User.do?function=remove

The DownloadAction Class

The **org.apache.struts.actions.DownloadAction** class provides a mechanism for easing the creation of file download actions. Instead of creating an action from scratch with all of the required infrastructure code for downloading files, the **DownloadAction** class can be extended. **DownloadAction** provides all of the infrastructure code in a simple, reusable package. **DownloadAction** subclasses must include a **getStreamInfo( )** method that returns a **StreamInfo** instance with details about the file to download.

```
package com.jamesholmes.minihr;

import java.io.File;

import javax.servlet.http.HttpServletRequest;
import javax.servlet.http.HttpServletResponse;

import org.apache.struts.action.ActionForm;
import org.apache.struts.action.ActionForward;
import org.apache.struts.action.ActionMapping;
import org.apache.struts.actions.DownloadAction;

public class ReportDownloadAction extends DownloadAction
{
  protected StreamInfo getStreamInfo(ActionMapping mapping,
    ActionForm form,
    HttpServletRequest request,
    HttpServletResponse response)
    throws Exception
  {
    String contentType = "application/vnd.ms-excel";
    File file = new File("/dir1/dir2/report.xls");

    return new FileStreamInfo(contentType, file);
  }
}
```

When the **DownloadAction** subclass, such as **ReportDownloadAction** in the preceding example, is invoked, it will stream the file specified in the **getStreamInfo( )** method back to the browser.

The EventDispatchAction Class

The **org.apache.struts.actions.EventDispatchAction** class is a subclass of **DispatchAction** and provides a mechanism for modularizing a set of related functions into a single action, thus eliminating the need to create separate, independent actions for each function. For example, consider a set of related functions for adding a user, updating a user, and removing a user. Instead of creating an **AddUserAction** class, an **UpdateUserAction** class, and a **RemoveUserAction** class, by extending **EventDispatchAction**, you can create one **UserAction** class that has three methods: **add( )**, **update( )**, and **remove( )**. At run time, **EventDispatchAction** manages routing requests to the appropriate method in its subclass. **EventDispatchAction** determines which method to call based on the presence of a request parameter that is passed to it from the incoming request.

To use **EventDispatchAction**, you must create a subclass from it and provide a set of methods that will be called to process requests. Additionally, you have to set up for the action an action mapping that specifies the names of request parameters that will be used to select which method should be called for each request. Following is an example **UserAction** class that extends **EventDispatchAction**:

```
package com.jamesholmes.minihr;

import javax.servlet.http.HttpServletRequest;
import javax.servlet.http.HttpServletResponse;

import org.apache.struts.action.ActionForm;
import org.apache.struts.action.ActionForward;
import org.apache.struts.action.ActionMapping;
import org.apache.struts.actions.EventDispatchAction;

public class UserAction extends EventDispatchAction
{
  public ActionForward add(ActionMapping mapping,
    ActionForm form,
    HttpServletRequest request,
    HttpServletResponse response)
    throws Exception
  {
    // Add user.
    ...

    return mapping.findForward("success");
  }

  public ActionForward update(ActionMapping mapping,
    ActionForm form,
    HttpServletRequest request,
    HttpServletResponse response)
    throws Exception
  {
    // Update user.
    ...

    return mapping.findForward("success");
  }

  public ActionForward remove(ActionMapping mapping,
    ActionForm form,
    HttpServletRequest request,
    HttpServletResponse response)
    throws Exception
  {
    // Remove user.
    ...

    return mapping.findForward("success");
  }
}
```

Notice that this class does not provide an implementation for the **execute( )** method the way typical **Action** classes do. This is because **EventDispatchAction** provides to you an implementation of this method that manages delegating to the individual methods. In order for your **EventDispatchAction** subclass to work, you must create in the Struts configuration file an action mapping that specifies the names of request parameters that will be used to select the method that will be called for specific requests. Following is a sample snippet that illustrates how to do this:

```
<action-mappings>
  <action path="/User"
          type="com.jamesholmes.minihr.UserAction"
     parameter="add,update,delete=remove,default=add"/>
</action-mappings>
```

The value specified with the **parameter** attribute of the **action** tag specifies a comma-delimited list of method names to dispatch to if a request parameter of the same name is present in the request. In the preceding example, the **add( )** method will be invoked for handling the request if an "add" request parameter is sent to the action. The value of the "add" request parameter is disregarded; only the presence of the request parameter is needed. The **remove( )** method will be invoked if a request parameter named "delete" is sent. The **remove( )** method, instead of a **delete( )** method, is invoked because of an alias of "delete". Method aliases are specified using *alias=method* notation, where *alias* is the name of the alias for a method and *method* is the name of the method to invoke. A default method can be specified by using an alias with the name of "default" as shown in the preceding example. Default aliases are used for scenarios where no request parameter matches the method names specified with the **action** tag's **parameter** attribute.

Given the preceding mapping of **/User** to **UserAction**, the following URL will invoke the **add( )** method (assuming the application was run on your **localhost** at port **8080** and the application was deployed as **/MiniHR/**):

http://localhost:8080/MiniHR/User.do?add.x=103

To invoke the **remove( )** method, use the following URL:

http://localhost:8080/MiniHR/User.do?remove=true

The ForwardAction Class

The **org.apache.struts.actions.ForwardAction** class provides a mechanism for forwarding to a specified URL. As explained earlier, in an MVC Web application, all requests to the application are supposed to flow through the Controller servlet. This ensures that the Controller layer of the application has an opportunity to prepare any resources that may be needed to handle the request (i.e., selecting the correct module and so on). **ForwardAction** is provided as a simple utility action that can be used for scenarios in which you simply want to link to a JSP page. Of course, linking directly to the JSP would be a violation of the MVC principles because all requests are supposed to be routed through the Controller. **ForwardAction** can be used to create links to JSPs so that you don't have to create an action whose only responsibility is to forward a request every time you want to link to a JSP. With **ForwardAction**, you simply create an action mapping in the Struts configuration file and specify the location to which the action will forward.

To use **ForwardAction**, simply create action mapping entries in the Struts configuration file, as shown next:

```
<action-mappings>
  <action path="/menu"
          type="org.apache.struts.actions.ForwardAction"
     parameter="/menu.jsp/>
</action-mappings>
```

For each page to which you want to link, you must create an action mapping. Each action mapping uses **ForwardAction**, but each specifies a different path for the action. The **parameter** attribute specifies the URL that will be forwarded to when the specified path is accessed.

An alternative solution to using **ForwardAction** is to use the **forward** attribute of the **action** tag in the Struts configuration file, as shown here:

```
<action-mappings>
  <action path="/menu"
       forward="/menu.jsp"/>
</action-mappings>
```

These two approaches effectively yield the same results.

The IncludeAction Class

The **org.apache.struts.actions.IncludeAction** class provides a mechanism for including the contents of a specified URL. This action behaves similarly to **ForwardAction**, but instead of forwarding to the specified URL, the specified URL is included. This action is useful when you want to include the contents of one page in another.

Using **IncludeAction** is quite easy. Just create action mapping entries in the Struts configuration file:

```
<action-mappings>
  <action path="/menu"
          type="org.apache.struts.actions.IncludeAction"
     parameter="/menu.jsp/>
</action-mappings>
```

For each page you want to include, you must create an action mapping. Each action mapping uses **IncludeAction**, but specifies a different path for the action. The **parameter** attribute specifies the URL that will be included when the specified path is accessed.

An alternative solution to using **IncludeAction** is to use the **include** attribute of the **action** tag in the Struts configuration file, as shown here:

```
<action-mappings>
  <action path="/menu"
       include="/menu.jsp"/>
</action-mappings>
```

These two approaches effectively yield the same results.

The LocaleAction Class

The **org.apache.struts.actions.LocaleAction** class provides a mechanism for setting a user's locale and then forwarding to a specified page. This action provides a convenient mechanism for changing a user's locale. For example, consider a site that is offered in English and Spanish versions. **LocaleAction** can be used to offer users a way to switch between the two languages without having to change their browser settings. With **LocaleAction** you simply create an action mapping and then link to the action, specifying request parameters for which locale to switch to and a page to forward after the locale has been switched.

To use **LocaleAction**, you must create an action mapping entry for it in the Struts configuration file and then link to the action, specifying locale information and a page to forward to after the locale has been set. Following is an example of how to configure **LocaleAction** in the Struts configuration file:

```
<action-mappings>
  <action path="/SwitchLocale"
          type="org.apache.struts.actions.LocaleAction"/>
</action-mappings>
```

Once configured in the Struts configuration file, **LocaleAction** can be put to use. Simply create a link to the action and specify the locale settings that will be set and a page to forward to. Locale settings are specified with two request parameters: **language** and **country**. The page to forward to after setting the locale is specified with the **page** request parameter. The following URL illustrates how to use the request parameters:

http://localhost:8080/MiniHR/SwitchLocale.do?country=MX&language=es&page=/Menu.do

This example URL sets the country to **MX** (Mexico) and the language to **es** (Spanish). The **/Menu.do** page will be forwarded to after the new locale has been set.

The LookupDispatchAction Class

The **org.apache.struts.actions.LookupDispatchAction** class is a subclass of **DispatchAction** and provides a mechanism for modularizing a set of related functions into a single action, thus eliminating the need to create separate, independent actions for each function. For example, consider a set of related functions for adding a user, updating a user, and removing a user. Instead of creating an **AddUserAction** class, an **UpdateUserAction** class, and a **RemoveUserAction** class, by extending **LookupDispatchAction**, you can create one **UserAction** class that has three methods: **add( )**, **update( )**, and **remove( )**.

At run time, **LookupDispatchAction** manages routing requests to the appropriate method in its subclass. **LookupDispatchAction** determines which method to route to based on the value of a request parameter being passed to it from the incoming request. **LookupDispatchAction** uses the value of the request parameter to reverse-map to a property in the Struts resource bundle file (e.g., **MessageResources.properties**). That is, the value of the request parameter is compared against the values of properties in the resource bundle until a match is found. The key for the matching property is then used as a key to another map that maps to a method in your **LookupDispatchAction** subclass that will be executed.

To use **LookupDispatchAction**, you must create a subclass from it and provide a set of methods that will be called to process requests. The subclass must also include a **getKeyMethodMap( )** method that maps methods in the class to keys in the Struts resource bundle file. Additionally, you have to set up for the action an action mapping that specifies the name of a request parameter that will be used to select which method will be called for each request. Following is an example **UserAction** class that extends **LookupDispatchAction**:

```
package com.jamesholmes.minihr;

import javax.servlet.http.HttpServletRequest;
```

```
import javax.servlet.http.HttpServletResponse;

import org.apache.struts.action.ActionForm;
import org.apache.struts.action.ActionForward;
import org.apache.struts.action.ActionMapping;
import org.apache.struts.actions.LookupDispatchAction;

public class UserAction extends LookupDispatchAction
{
  protected Map getKeyMethodMap()
  {
    HashMap map = new HashMap();
    map.put("button.add", "add");
    map.put("button.update", "update");
    map.put("button.remove", "remove");

    return map;
  }

  public ActionForward add(ActionMapping mapping,
    ActionForm form,
    HttpServletRequest request,
    HttpServletResponse response)
    throws Exception
  {
    // Add user.
    ...

    return mapping.findForward("success");
  }

  public ActionForward update(ActionMapping mapping,
    ActionForm form,
    HttpServletRequest request,
    HttpServletResponse response)
    throws Exception
  {
    // Update user.
    ...

    return mapping.finwForward("success");
  }

  public ActionForward remove(ActionMapping mapping,
    ActionForm form,
    HttpServletRequest request,
    HttpServletResponse response)
    throws Exception
  {
    // Remove user.
    ...

    return mapping.findForward("success");
  }
}
```

Notice that this class does not provide an implementation for the **execute( )** method as other **Action** classes do. This is because **LookupDispatchAction** provides to you an implementation of this method that manages delegating to the individual methods. Notice also the implementation of the **getKeyMethodMap( )** method. This method is required by **LookupDispatchAction** subclasses and is used to map the names of keys in the Struts resource bundle file to methods in the class. The keys' values in the bundle file are used to match against the value of the incoming request parameter specified by the **parameter** attribute of the **action** tag in the Struts configuration file.

In order for your **LookupDispatchAction** subclass to work, you must create in the Struts configuration file an action mapping that specifies the name of a request parameter that will be used to select the method that will be called for a specific request. Following is a sample snippet that illustrates how to do this:

```
<action-mappings>
  <action path="/User"
          type="com.jamesholmes.minihr.UserAction"
     parameter="function"/>
</action-mappings>
```

The value specified with the **parameter** attribute of the **action** tag will be used as the name of a request parameter that will contain the value of a key in the Struts resource bundle shown here:

```
button.add=Add User
button.update=Update User
button.remove=Remove User
```

LookupDispatchAction will use the value of the incoming request parameter to perform a reverse lookup for a key in the resource bundle. The matching key is then mapped to the appropriate method to execute based on the key-to-method mapping specified by the **getKeyMethodMap( )** method.

Given the preceding mapping of **/User** to **UserAction**, the following URL will invoke the **add( )** method (assuming the application was run on your **localhost** at port **8080** and the application was deployed as **/MiniHR/**):

http://localhost:8080/MiniHR/User.do?function=Add%20User

To invoke the **remove( )** method, use the following URL:

http://localhost:8080/MiniHR/User.do?function=Remove%20User

The MappingDispatchAction Class

The **org.apache.struts.actions.MappingDispatchAction** class is a subclass of **DispatchAction** and provides a mechanism for modularizing a set of related functions into a single action, eliminating the need to create separate, independent actions for each function. For example, consider a set of related functions for adding a user, updating a user, and removing a user. Instead of creating an **AddUserAction** class, an **UpdateUserAction** class, and a **RemoveUserAction** class, by extending **MappingDispatch Action**, you can create one **UserAction** class that has three methods: **add( )**, **update( )**, and **remove( )**. At run time, **MappingDispatchAction** manages routing requests to the appropriate method in its subclass. **MappingDispatchAction** determines which method to route based on the value of a parameter being passed to it from an action mapping in the Struts configuration file.

To use **MappingDispatchAction**, you must create a subclass from it and provide a set of methods that will be called to process requests. Additionally, you must set up action mappings that specify which method will be called for each request. Following is an example **UserAction** class that extends **MappingDispatchAction**:

```
package com.jamesholmes.minihr;

import javax.servlet.http.HttpServletRequest;
import javax.servlet.http.HttpServletResponse;

import org.apache.struts.action.ActionForm;
import org.apache.struts.action.ActionForward;
import org.apache.struts.action.ActionMapping;
import org.apache.struts.actions.MappingDispatchAction;

public class UserAction extends MappingDispatchAction
{
  public ActionForward add(ActionMapping mapping,
    ActionForm form,
    HttpServletRequest request,
    HttpServletResponse response)
    throws Exception
  {
    // Add user.
    ...

    return mapping.findForward("success");
  }

  public ActionForward update(ActionMapping mapping,
    ActionForm form,
    HttpServletRequest request,
    HttpServletResponse response)
    throws Exception
  {
    // Update user.
    ...

    return mapping.findForward("success");
  }

  public ActionForward remove(ActionMapping mapping,
    ActionForm form,
    HttpServletRequest request,
    HttpServletResponse response)
    throws Exception
  {
    // Remove user.
    ...

    return mapping.findForward("success");
  }
}
```

Notice that this class does not provide an implementation for the **execute( )** method as other **Action** classes do. This is because **MappingDispatchAction** provides to you an implementation of this method that manages delegating to the individual function methods.

In order for your **MappingDispatchAction** subclass to work, you must create in the Struts configuration file action mappings that specify the method that will be called for specific requests. Following is a sample snippet that illustrates how to do this:

```
<action-mappings>
  <action path="/AddUser"
          type="com.jamesholmes.minihr.UserAction"
     parameter="add"/>
  <action path="/UpdateUser"
          type="com.jamesholmes.minihr.UserAction"
     parameter="update"/>
  <action path="/RemoveUser"
          type="com.jamesholmes.minihr.UserAction"
     parameter="remove"/>
</action-mappings>
```

Notice that each action mapping uses the **UserAction** class, but specifies a different path for the action. Each of the unique paths will be processed by the same action, but a different method will be called based on the value specified with the **parameter** attribute. The value specified with the **parameter** attribute must match the name of a method in your **MappingDispatchAction** subclass.

The SwitchAction Class

The **org.apache.struts.actions.SwitchAction** class provides a mechanism for switching between modules in a modularized Struts application. As you'll see in Chapter 9, Struts enables you to modularize your Struts application. Each module has its own set of configuration data as well as its own request processor. **SwitchAction** works similarly to **ForwardAction**, except that before forwarding to a specified resource, the action changes the currently selected module. This is useful for forwarding to JSPs outside of the current module.

NOTE *Detailed information on using the Struts modules feature is found in Chapter 9.*

To use **SwitchAction**, you must create an action mapping entry for it in the Struts configuration file and then link to the action, specifying the module to switch to and a page to forward to after the module has been switched. Following is an example of how to configure **SwitchAction** in the Struts configuration file:

```
<action-mappings>
  <action path="/SwitchModule"
          type="org.apache.struts.actions.SwitchAction"/>
</action-mappings>
```

Once configured in the Struts configuration file, **SwitchAction** can be put to use. Simply create a link to the action and specify the module to switch to and a page to forward to afterward. The module to switch to is specified with the **prefix** parameter and the page to forward to afterward is specified with the **page** parameter. The following URL illustrates how to use the request parameters:

http://localhost:8080/MiniHR/SwitchModule.do?prefix=/Corporate&page=/Menu.do

This example URL switches to the **/Corporate** module, and the **/Menu.do** page will be forwarded to after the module has been switched.

The ActionForward Class

The **ActionForward** class encapsulates a *forward*. Forwards were introduced in Chapter 2, but this section takes a closer look at them because they are used by the **ActionForward** class.

Struts provides the forward as an alternative to hard-coding URLs inside your application. Forwards allow you to define logical names for URLs and then to use the names to reference the URLs. If you reference a URL by its logical name instead of referencing it directly, when the URL changes, you don't have to update each reference to the URL. For example, with forwards you can define a forward for a search page with a logical name of "search" that points to the **/search.jsp** page. Instead of hard-coding the search page's **/search.jsp** URL throughout your application, you use the forward's logical name. If the location of the search page changes, you need to make only one change to the forward definition and all places in the application that point to that forward will receive the change. Essentially, forwards are URL aliases. They abstract URLs and shield you from changes. The application knows only the alias. Where the alias points does not matter.

Forwards are defined declaratively in the Struts configuration file. There are two types of forwards that can be defined, a global forward and an action-specific forward. Global forwards are available throughout an application, whereas action-specific forwards are available only to their respective action. Following is an example of how to define a global forward in the Struts configuration file:

```
<global-forwards>
  <forward name="searchPage" path="/search.jsp"/>
</global-forwards>
```

Action-specific forwards are defined by nesting the **forward** tag inside an **action** tag, as shown next:

```
<action-mappings>
  <action path="/updateUser"
          type="com.jamesholmes.minihr.UpdateUserAction">
    <forward name="success" path="/updateSuccess.jsp"/>
  </action>
</action-mappings>
```

Struts' **ActionForward** class encapsulates a forward inside an application. For example, the **Action** class's **execute( )** method has a return type of **ActionForward**. After an action executes, it must return an **ActionForward** or null (to indicate processing is complete). **ActionForward**s returned from actions are used to forward to the View layer. The following snippet illustrates how the **ActionForward** class is used in an action:

```
package com.jamesholmes.minihr;

import javax.servlet.http.HttpServletRequest;
import javax.servlet.http.HttpServletResponse;

import org.apache.struts.action.Action;
import org.apache.struts.action.ActionForm;
```

```
import org.apache.struts.action.ActionForward;
import org.apache.struts.action.ActionMapping;

public class UpdateUserAction extends Action
{
  public ActionForward execute(ActionMapping mapping,
    ActionForm form,
    HttpServletRequest request,
    HttpServletResponse response)
    throws Exception
  {
    // Perform action processing.

    return new ActionForward("updateSuccess");
  }
}
```

The value passed to the **ActionForward** class's constructor corresponds to the logical name of a forward defined in the Struts configuration file.

Reviewing the Controller Layer of the Mini HR Application

To solidify your understanding of the Controller layer of Struts applications, this section reviews the Controller layer of the Mini HR application developed in Chapter 2. Doing so clearly illustrates the core components involved in creating the Controller layer.

Mini HR's Controller layer consists of a single class: **SearchAction**. The **SearchAction** class, shown next, is responsible for processing requests from the **search.jsp** page:

```
package com.jamesholmes.minihr;

import java.util.ArrayList;

import javax.servlet.http.HttpServletRequest;
import javax.servlet.http.HttpServletResponse;

import org.apache.struts.action.Action;
import org.apache.struts.action.ActionForm;
import org.apache.struts.action.ActionForward;
import org.apache.struts.action.ActionMapping;

public final class SearchAction extends Action
{
  public ActionForward execute(ActionMapping mapping,
    ActionForm form,
    HttpServletRequest request,
    HttpServletResponse response)
    throws Exception
  {
    EmployeeSearchService service = new EmployeeSearchService();
    ArrayList results;

    SearchForm searchForm = (SearchForm) form;
```

```
    // Perform employee search based on what criteria was entered.
    String name = searchForm.getName();
    if (name != null && name.trim().length() > 0) {
      results = service.searchByName(name);
    } else {
      results = service.searchBySsNum(searchForm.getSsNum().trim());
    }

    // Place search results in SearchForm for access by JSP.
    searchForm.setResults(results);

    // Forward control to this Action's input page.
    return mapping.getInputForward();
  }
}
```

When a search is initiated, the Struts **ActionServlet** Controller servlet delegates processing to this **Action** class. This class acts as the liaison between the Model layer and the View layer. Based on the search criteria entered from the View layer, **SearchAction** determines which search method to invoke on the **EmployeeSearchService** Model class and passes in the data from the View layer. **EmployeeSearchService** returns the results of the search and **SearchAction** manages getting the data back to the View layer.

CHAPTER 6

Validator

One of the major benefits of using the Struts framework is its built-in interface for performing data validations on incoming form data. As discussed in Chapter 4, upon submitting an HTML form, Struts captures the form data and uses it to populate one of your application's **ActionForm** subclasses (Form Beans) assigned to the form. The Form Bean's **validate( )** method is then called to perform any necessary validation of the incoming data. If any validations fail, the HTML form is redisplayed so that the invalid data can be corrected. Otherwise, processing continues. This simple interface alleviates much of the headache associated with handling data validation, allowing you to focus on validation code and not the mechanics of capturing data and redisplaying incomplete or invalid data.

Struts' built-in validation interface, however, still has its shortcomings. Often, for example, validation code is heavily duplicated throughout an application because many fields require the same validation logic. Any change in the validation logic for similar fields requires code changes in several places, as well as recompilation of the affected code. To solve this problem and to enhance Struts' validation interface, David Winterfeldt created the Validator framework as a third-party add-on to Struts. Validator was later integrated into the core Struts code base and has since been detached from Struts and is now a stand-alone Jakarta Commons project (http://jakarta.apache.org/commons/validator/) that can be used with or without Struts. Although Validator is an independent framework again, Struts still comes packaged with it and it is seamlessly integrated.

The Validator framework comes prepackaged with several validation routines, making the transition from hard-coded validation logic painless. Instead of coding validation logic in each Form Bean's **validate( )** method, with Validator you use an XML configuration file to declare the validations that should be applied to each Form Bean. If you need a validation not provided by Validator, you can plug your own custom validations into Validator. Additionally, Validator supports both server-side and client-side (JavaScript) validations whereas Form Beans only provide a server-side validation interface.

Validator Overview

Before getting into the details of using the Validator framework, it's necessary to give an overview of how Validator works. Recall that without Validator, you have to code all of your form data validations into the **validate( )** methods of your Form Bean objects. Each

Form Bean field that you want to perform a validation on requires you to code logic to do so. Additionally, you have to write code that will store error messages for validations that fail. With Validator, you don't have to write any code in your Form Beans for validations or storing error messages. Instead, your Form Beans extend one of Validator's **ActionForm** subclasses that provide this functionality for you.

The Validator framework is set up as a pluggable system of validation routines that can be applied to Form Beans. Each validation routine is simply a Java method that is responsible for performing a specific type of validation and can either pass or fail. By default, Validator comes packaged with several useful validation routines that will satisfy most validation scenarios. However, if you need a validation that is not provided by the framework, you can create your own custom validation routine and plug it into the framework.

Validator uses two XML configuration files to tell it which validation routines should be "installed" and how they should be applied for a given application, respectively. The first configuration file, **validator-rules.xml**, declares the validation routines that are plugged into the framework and assigns logical names to each of the validations. Additionally, the **validator-rules.xml** file is used to define client-side JavaScript code (or the location of client-side JavaScript code) for each validation routine. If configured to do so, Validator will emit this JavaScript code to the browser so that validations are performed on the client side as well as the server side. The second configuration file, **validation.xml**, defines which validation routines are applied to which Form Beans. The definitions in this file use the logical names of Form Beans from the Struts configuration file (e.g., **struts-config.xml**) along with the logical names of validation routines from the **validator-rules.xml** file to tie the two together.

NOTE *It's important to point out that while traditionally the* **validator-rules.xml** *file stores validation routine definitions and the* **validation.xml** *file applies validation routines to Form Beans, both configuration files are governed by the same DTD. Thus their contents could technically be combined into one file.*

Using Validator

Using the Validator framework involves enabling the Validator plugin, configuring Validator's two configuration files, and creating Form Beans that extend Validator's **ActionForm** subclasses. The following sections explain how to configure and use the Validator in detail.

NOTE *Detailed information on configuring the Validator XML configuration files is found in Chapter 20.*

Enabling the Validator Plugin

Although the Validator framework comes packaged with Struts, by default Validator is not enabled. In order to enable and use Validator, you have to add to your application's Struts configuration file the following definition for the **plug-in** tag:

```
<!-- Validator Configuration -->
<plug-in className="org.apache.struts.validator.ValidatorPlugIn">
  <set-property property="pathnames"
                   value="/org/apache/struts/validator/validator-rules.xml,
                          /WEB-INF/validation.xml"/>
</plug-in>
```

This definition causes Struts to load and initialize the Validator plugin for your application. Upon initialization, the plugin loads the comma-delimited list of Validator configuration files specified by the **pathnames** property. Each configuration file's path must be specified by using a Web application–relative path or by using a path to a file on the classpath of the server, as shown in the preceding example. The **validator-rules.xml** file shown in the preceding example happens to be stored in the core Struts **.jar** file, and thus it is accessible via the classpath.

Note that your application's Struts configuration file must conform to the Struts Configuration DTD, which specifies the order in which elements are to appear in the file. Because of this, you must place the Validator **plug-in** tag definition in the proper place in the file. The easiest way to ensure that you are properly ordering elements in the file is to use a tool like Struts Console that automatically formats your configuration file so that it conforms to the DTD.

Creating Form Beans

In order to use Validator, your application's Form Beans must subclass one of Validator's **ActionForm** subclasses instead of **ActionForm** itself. Validator's **ActionForm** subclasses provide an implementation for **ActionForm**'s **reset( )** and **validate( )** methods that hook into the Validator framework. Instead of hard-coding validations into the **validate( )** method, as you would normally do, you simply omit the method altogether because Validator provides the validation code for you.

Parallel to the core functionality provided by Struts, Validator gives you two options to choose from when creating Form Beans. The first option is to create a concrete Form Bean object like the one shown here:

```
package com.jamesholmes.minihr;

import org.apache.struts.validator.ValidatorForm;

public class LogonForm extends ValidatorForm {
  private String username;
  private String password;

  public String getUsername() {
    return username;
  }

  public void setUsername(String username) {
    this.username = username;
  }

  public String getPassword() {
    return password;
  }

  public void setPassword(String password) {
    this.password = password;
  }
}
```

This class is similar to one that you would create if you were not using Validator; however, this class extends **ValidatorForm** instead of **ActionForm**. This class also does not provide an implementation for **ActionForm**'s empty **reset( )** and **validate( )** methods, because **ValidatorForm** does.

You configure this Form Bean in the Struts configuration file the same way you would a regular Form Bean, as shown here:

```
<form-beans>
  <form-bean name="logonForm"
             type="com.jamesholmes.minihr.LogonForm"/>
</form-beans>
```

The logical name given to the Form Bean with the **form-bean** tag's **name** attribute is the name that you will use when defining validations in the **validation.xml** file, as shown here:

```
<!DOCTYPE form-validation PUBLIC
          "-//Apache Software Foundation//DTD Commons
           Validator Rules Configuration 1.3.0//EN"
          "http://jakarta.apache.org/commons/dtds/validator_1_3_0.dtd">

<form-validation>
  <formset>
    <form name="logonForm">
      <field property="username" depends="required">
        <arg position="0" key="prompt.username"/>
      </field>
    </form>
  </formset>
</form-validation>
```

Validator uses the value of the **form** tag's **name** attribute to match validation definitions to the name of the Form Bean to which they are applied.

The second option you can choose when creating your Form Bean is to define a Dynamic Form Bean in the Struts configuration file, as shown here:

```
<form-beans>
  <form-bean name="logonForm"
             type="org.apache.struts.validator.DynaValidatorForm">
    <form-property name="username" type="java.lang.String"/>
    <form-property name="password" type="java.lang.String"/>
  </form-bean>
</form-beans>
```

Dynamic Form Beans do not require you to create concrete Form Bean objects; instead, you define the properties that your Form Bean will have and their types, and Struts will dynamically create the Form Bean for you. Validator allows you to use this concept just as you would with core Struts. The only difference for Validator is that you specify that your Form Bean is of type **org.apache.struts.validator.DynaValidatorForm** instead of **org.apache .struts.action.DynaActionForm**.

Identical to the way concrete Form Beans work with Validator, the logical name given to Dynamic Form Beans is the name that you will use when defining validations in the **validation.xml** file. Validator uses the matching names to tie the validations to the Form Bean.

In addition to the two standard options for creating Form Beans, Validator provides an advanced feature for tying multiple validation definitions to one Form Bean definition.

When using **ValidatorForm**- or **DynaValidatorForm**-based Form Beans, Validator uses the logical name for the Form Bean from the Struts configuration file to map the Form Bean to validation definitions in the **validation.xml** file. This mechanism is ideal for most cases; however, there are scenarios where Form Beans are shared among multiple actions. One action may use all the Form Bean's fields, and another action may use only a subset of the fields. Because validation definitions are tied to the Form Bean, the action that uses only a subset of the fields has no way of bypassing validations for the unused fields. When the Form Bean is validated, it will generate error messages for the unused fields because Validator has no way of knowing not to validate the unused fields; it simply sees them as missing or invalid.

To solve this problem, Validator provides two additional **ActionForm** subclasses that allow you to tie validations to actions instead of Form Beans. That way you can specify which validations to apply to the Form Bean based on which action is using the Form Bean. For concrete Form Beans, you subclass **org.apache.struts.validator.ValidatorActionForm**, as shown here:

```
public class AddressForm extends ValidatorActionForm {
  ...
}
```

For Dynamic Form Beans, you specify a type of **org.apache.struts.validator.DynaValidatorActionForm** for your Form Bean definition in the Struts configuration file:

```
<form-bean name="addressForm"
           type="org.apache.struts.validator.DynaValidatorActionForm">
  ...
</form-bean>
```

Inside your **validation.xml** file, you map a set of validations to an action path instead of to a Form Bean name. Here's why: if you have two actions defined, such as Create Address and Edit Address, which use the same Form Bean, then each will have a unique action path. This situation is shown here:

```
<action-mappings>
  <action path="/createAddress"
          type="com.jamesholmes.minihr.CreateAddressAction"
          name="addressForm"/>
  <action path="/editAddress"
          type="com.jamesholmes.minihr.EditAddressAction"
          name="addressForm"/>
</action-mappings>
```

The following **validation.xml** file snippet shows two sets of validations that are intended for the same Form Bean but are distinguished by different action paths:

```
<formset>
  <form name="/createAddress">
    <field property="city" depends="required">
      <arg position="0" key="prompt.city"/>
    </field>
  </form>
  <form name="/editAddress">
```

```
    <field property="state" depends="required">
      <arg position="0" key="prompt.state"/>
    </field>
  </form>
</formset>
```

Because your Form Bean subclasses either **ValidatorActionForm** or **DynaValidatorActionForm**, Validator knows to use an action path to find validations instead of the Form Bean's logical name.

Using Validator in Conjunction with the Form Bean's reset( ) and validate( ) Methods

As described, Validator's **ActionForm** subclasses take care of the processing that is normally placed in the **reset( )** and **validate( )** methods of a Form Bean. Thus, you typically do not have an implementation of these two methods in your Form Beans when using Validator. However, it is occasionally necessary to augment the automatic processing provided by Validator with your own custom validations or data resets. To do this, you must override the **reset( )** and/or **validate( )** methods provided by the Validator Form Bean classes and call **super.reset( )** and **super.validate( )** respectively before adding any custom processing to the methods. An example of this is shown next:

```
public void reset(ActionMapping mapping,
                  HttpServletRequest request) {
  super.reset(mapping, request);

  // Custom reset code goes here.
}

public ActionErrors validate(ActionMapping mapping,
                             HttpServletRequest request) {
  ActionErrors errors = super.validate(mapping, request);
  if (errors == null) {
    errors = new ActionErrors();
  }

  // Custom validation code goes here.

  return errors;
}
```

Notice that the call to **super.validate( )** in the **validate( )** method returns an **ActionErrors** instance. Errors generated from custom validations should be added to that **ActionErrors** instance and that instance should be used as the method's return value.

Configuring validator-rules.xml

The Validator framework is set up as a pluggable system whereby each of its validation routines is simply a Java method that is plugged into the system to perform a specific validation. The **validator-rules.xml** file is used to declaratively plug in the validation routines that Validator will use for performing validations. Struts comes packaged with a preconfigured copy of this file in the Struts core **.jar** file (e.g., **struts-core-1.3.5.jar**). Under most circumstances, you will use this preconfigured copy and will not ever need to modify it. Modification to the file would require extracting it from the core **.jar** file, making changes to the file and then repackaging the core **.jar** file with the modified file. As you can imagine, that is cumbersome and should only be done if absolutely necessary. Otherwise you can simply add validation routine definitions to the **validation.xml** file as explained in the section "Creating Custom Validations."

Following is a sample **validator-rules.xml** file that illustrates how validation routines are plugged into Validator:

```
<!DOCTYPE form-validation PUBLIC
          "-//Apache Software Foundation//DTD Commons
           Validator Rules Configuration 1.3.0//EN"
          "http://jakarta.apache.org/commons/dtds/validator_1_3_0.dtd">

<form-validation>
  <global>
    <validator name="minlength"
          classname="org.apache.struts.validator.FieldChecks"
             method="validateMinLength"
       methodParams="java.lang.Object,
                     org.apache.commons.validator.ValidatorAction,
                     org.apache.commons.validator.Field,
                     org.apache.struts.action.ActionMessages,
                     org.apache.commons.validator.Validator,
                     javax.servlet.http.HttpServletRequest"
                msg="errors.minlength"
         jsFunction="org.apache.commons.validator.javascript.validateMinLength"/>
  </global>
</form-validation>
```

Each validation routine in the **validator-rules.xml** file has its own definition that is declared with a **validator** tag. The **validator** tag is used to assign a logical name to the routine, with the **name** attribute, and to specify the class and method for the routine. The logical name given to the routine will be used to refer to the routine by other routines in this file as well as by validation definitions in the **validation.xml** file.

Notice that the **validator** tag specifies a **msg** attribute. The **msg** attribute specifies a key for a message in the application resource bundle file that will be used as the error message when the validation fails. Notice also that the **validator** tag specifies a **jsFunction** attribute. The **jsFunction** attribute is used to define the path to a file that contains client-side JavaScript code for the validation routine. The JavaScript code performs the same validation on the client side as is performed on the server side.

NOTE *In lieu of using the* **jsFunction** *attribute of the* **validator** *tag to declare the file in which the routine's client-side JavaScript code is housed, you can nest a* **javascript** *tag beneath the* **validator** *tag to specify the JavaScript code for a validation routine.*

Configuring the Application Resource Bundle File

Validator uses the Struts Resource Bundle mechanism for externalizing error messages. Instead of having hard-coded error messages in the framework, Validator allows you to specify a key to a message in the application resource bundle file (e.g., **MessageResources.properties**) that is returned if a validation fails. Each validation routine in the **validator-rules.xml** file specifies an error message key with the **validator** tag's **msg** attribute, as shown here:

```
<validator name="minlength"
      classname="org.apache.struts.validator.FieldChecks"
```

```
        method="validateMinLength"
  methodParams="java.lang.Object,
                org.apache.commons.validator.ValidatorAction,
                org.apache.commons.validator.Field,
                org.apache.struts.action.ActionMessages,
                org.apache.commons.validator.Validator,
                javax.servlet.http.HttpServletRequest"
           msg="errors.minlength"
    jsfunction="org.apache.commons.validator.javascript.validateMinLength"/>
```

If the validation fails when it is run, the message corresponding to the key specified by the **msg** attribute will be returned.

The following snippet shows the default set of validation error messages from the **MessageResources.properties** file that comes prepackaged with the Struts example applications. Each message key corresponds to those specified by the validation routines in the **validator-rules.xml** file that also comes prepackaged with the Struts example applications:

```
# Error messages for Validator framework validations
errors.required={0} is required.
errors.minlength={0} cannot be less than {1} characters.
errors.maxlength={0} cannot be greater than {1} characters.
errors.invalid={0} is invalid.
errors.byte={0} must be a byte.
errors.short={0} must be a short.
errors.integer={0} must be an integer.
errors.long={0} must be a long.
errors.float={0} must be a float.
errors.double={0} must be a double.
errors.date={0} is not a date.
errors.range={0} is not in the range {1} through {2}.
errors.creditcard={0} is not a valid credit card number.
errors.email={0} is an invalid e-mail address.
errors.url={0} is an invalid URL.
```

Notice that each message has placeholders in the form of {0}, {1}, or {2}. At run time, the placeholders will be substituted for another value, such as the name of the field being validated. This feature is known as *parametric replacement* and is especially useful in allowing you to create generic validation error messages that can be reused for several different fields of the same type.

Take for example the **required** validation's error message, **errors.required**:

```
errors.required={0} is required.
```

When you use the **required** validation in the **validation.xml** file, you have to define the value that should be used to substitute {0} in the error message:

```
<form name="auctionForm">
  <field property="bid" depends="required">
    <arg position="0" key="prompt.bid"/>
  </field>
</form>
```

Error messages can have multiple placeholders: {0} – {N}. These placeholders are specified using the **arg** tag. In the preceding example, the **arg** tag specifies the value that will replace the {0} placeholder. This tag's **key** attribute specifies a message key from the application resource bundle file, such as the one shown next, whose value will be used as the replacement for the placeholder:

```
prompt.bid=Auction Bid
```

Using a message key for the placeholder value frees you from having to hard-code the replacement value over and over in the **validation.xml** file. However, if you don't want to use the Resource Bundle key/value mechanism to specify placeholder values, you can explicitly specify the placeholder value by using the following syntax for the **arg** tag:

```
<arg position="0" key="Auction Bid" resource="false"/>
```

In this example, the **resource** attribute is set to *false*, instructing Validator that the value specified with the **key** attribute should be taken as the literal placeholder value and not as a key for a message in the application resource bundle file.

Configuring validation.xml

The **validation.xml** file is used to declare sets of validations that should be applied to Form Beans. Each Form Bean that you want to validate has its own definition in this file. Inside that definition specify the validations that you want to apply to the Form Bean's fields. Following is a sample **validation.xml** file that illustrates how validations are defined:

```
<!DOCTYPE form-validation PUBLIC
          "-//Apache Software Foundation//DTD Commons
           Validator Rules Configuration 1.3.0//EN"
          "http://jakarta.apache.org/commons/dtds/validator_1_3_0.dtd">

<form-validation>
  <formset>
    <form name="logonForm">
      <field property="username" depends="required">
        <arg position="0" key="prompt.username"/>
      </field>
      <field property="password" depends="required">
        <arg position="0" key="prompt.password"/>
      </field>
    </form>
  </formset>
</form-validation>
```

The first element in the **validation.xml** file is the **<form-validation>** element. This element is the master element for the file and is defined only once. Inside the **<form-validation>** element you define **<form-set>** elements that encapsulate multiple **<form>** elements. Generally, you will define only one **<form-set>** element in your file; however, you would use a separate one for each locale if you were internationalizing validations. Internationalizing validations is covered later in this chapter.

Each <form> element uses the **name** attribute to associate a name with the set of field validations it encompasses. Validator uses this logical name to map the validations to a Form Bean defined in the Struts configuration file. Based on the type of Form Bean being validated, Validator will attempt to match the name either against a Form Bean's logical name or against an action's path. Inside the **<form>** element, **<field>** elements are used to define the validations that will be applied to specified Form Bean fields. The **<field>** element's **property** attribute corresponds to the name of a field in the specified Form Bean. The **depends** attribute specifies the logical names of validation routines from the **validator-rules.xml** file that should be applied to the field. The validations specified with the **depends** attribute will be performed in the order specified and they all must pass.

Working with Configurable Validations

Each of the prepackaged validations provided by Validator requires configuring before it will function properly. There are two types of configuration constructs that validations can use: error message parametric replacement definitions and variable definitions. Error message parametric replacement definitions are defined with the **arg** tag and specify values for placeholders in the error message associated with a validation. Before an error message is generated for a failed validation, the message's placeholders are replaced with the values specified with **arg** tags. Variable definitions are defined with the **var** tag and specify validation-specific configuration settings. Validations use the configuration settings specified with **var** tags to guide their behavior.

Following is an example of how to use the **arg** tag to specify a parametric replacement value for a validation's error message:

```
<field property="password" depends="required, minlength">
  <arg position="0" key="prompt.password"/>
</field>
```

The **position** attribute of the **arg** tag is used to specify which parameter will be replaced with the given value. For example, position "0" is used to replace "{0}" in a message, position "1" is used to replace "{1}" and so on. An example error message with a replacement placeholder is shown here:

```
errors.required={0} is required.
```

The **key** attribute of the **arg** tag specifies a key for a value in the application resource bundle file that will be used to populate the validation's error message. Alternatively, you can set the **resource** attribute of the **arg** tag to "false" to indicate that the value specified with the **key** attribute should be taken as the literal replacement value instead of as the key for a value in the resource bundle. An example of specifying a literal replacement value is shown next:

```
<field property="password" depends="required, minlength">
  <arg position="0" key="Password" resource="false"/>
</field>
```

The value "Password" will be used to replace the "{0}" in the validations' error messages.

Each validation applied to a field via the **depends** attribute of the **field** tag will use the same parametric replacement values specified with **arg** tags unless an **arg** tag explicitly specifies the validation it is to be used for with the **name** attribute, as shown next:

```
<field property="password" depends="required, minlength">
  <arg position="0" name="required" key="prompt.passwordReq"/>
```

```
  <arg position="0" name="minlength" key="prompt.passwordMin"/>
</field>
```

The **name** attribute specifies the name of a specific validation that the parametric replacement value is for.

Next is an example of how to use the **var** tag to specify a configuration setting for a validation:

```
<field property="socialSecurityNum" depends="required, mask">
  <arg position="0" key="label.sampleForm.socialSecurityNum"/>
  <var>
    <var-name>mask</var-name>
    <var-value>^\d{3}-\d{2}-\d{4}$</var-value>
  </var>
</field>
```

Inside the **var** tag you must nest **var-name** and **var-value** tags to specify the name and value of a configuration setting, respectively. The names of acceptable configuration settings specified with the **var-name** tag are validation-specific and can be found in the sections dedicated to each validation later in this chapter. With some validations it is useful to use the value set for a variable with the **var-value** tag as the value for a parametric replacement in the error message. For example, the **minlength** validation's error message has a placeholder for minimum length. Instead of specifying the minimum length twice, once for the error message and once for the validation configuration setting, you can use the value of the configuration setting as the value for the placeholder. The example shown next illustrates how to do this:

```
<field property="password" depends="required, minlength">
  <arg position="0" key="label.sampleForm.password"/>
  <arg position="1" key="${var:minlength}" resource="false"/>
  <var>
    <var-name>minlength</var-name>
    <var-value>4</var-value>
  </var>
</field>
```

Notice that the second **arg** tag's **key** attribute is set to "${var:minlength}" and the **resource** attribute is set to "false". Recall that setting the **resource** attribute to false indicates that the value specified with the **key** attribute is to be taken as a literal value instead of as a key from the application resource bundle file. The "${var:minlength}" value of the **key** attribute indicates that the literal value should be the value of the **minlength** variable defined with the **var** tag.

Extending a Set of Validations

As of Commons Validator version 1.2, Validator has a feature for extending form definitions. This powerful mechanism is analogous to inheritance in Java and makes setting up similar forms very simple. For example, if you have a registration form with several fields and you need to define another form that has all of the same fields as the registration form plus a few additional fields, you can simply extend the registration form and add only the additional fields to the second form's definition. Following is an example of how this is done:

```
<form-validation>
  <formset>
    <form name="registrationForm">
```

```
      <field property="name" depends="required">
        <arg position="0" key="prompt.name"/>
      </field>
      <field property="address" depends="required">
        <arg position="0" key="prompt.address"/>
      </field>
    </form>
    <form name="businessRegistrationForm" extends="registrationForm">
      <field property="suite" depends="required">
        <arg position="0" key="prompt.suite"/>
      </field>
    </form>
  </formset>
</form-validation>
```

Notice in the example that the form definition for the **businessRegistrationForm** uses the **form** tag's **extends** attribute to specify another form that the form extends. All of the validation configuration details from the **registrationForm** form definition will be added to the **businessRegistrationForm** form defintion. Again, as with Java's inheritance feature, you can have any number of levels of extension.

Creating Validations for Indexed Properties

As mentioned in Chapter 4, indexed properties are a powerful and convenient mechanism for working with lists of objects on form beans. Validator provides built-in support for validating indexed properties via the **indexedListProperty** attribute of the **field** tag, as shown here:

```
<form name="registrationForm">
  <field property="firstName"
      indexedListProperty="customer" depends="required">
    <arg position="0" key="prompt.firstName"/>
  </field>
  <field property="lastName"
      indexedListProperty="customer" depends="required">
    <arg position="0" key="prompt.lastName"/>
  </field>
</form>
```

In this example, the **registrationForm** has a **customer** indexed property, as specified with the **indexedListProperty** attribute of the **field** tag. Validator will loop over each object in the **customer** indexed property and validate the field specified with the **property** attribute. This scenario assumes that the property specified with the **indexedListProperty** attribute is a collection of objects and the field specified with the **property** attribute has getter and setter methods on the individual objects in the collection.

Validations That Span Multiple Pages

Web applications often use wizard-like page flows to break up large monolithic forms into multiple pages to reduce the amount of information that must be entered on a single page. In that scenario, it is commonplace to use one Form Bean to store the data collected across all of the pages. At the end of the wizard page flow an action will process all of the collected data at once. The problem with that scenario, validation-wise, is that validations are specified per form in the **validation.xml** file and not all validations should be run against the form on each page. For example, the fields on page 2 shouldn't be validated on page 1 because they have not been entered yet. Any validations for page 2 that are run before page 2 is reached will fail. This is the case for each successive page in the wizard page flow. Validator has a feature to handle this situation so that validations are run only at the appropriate times.

In order to limit when validations are run for a form that spans multiple pages, the **field** tag has a **page** attribute that is used to specify a page number, as shown next:

```
<form name="registrationForm">
  <field property="name" page="1" depends="required">
    <arg position="0" key="prompt.name"/>
  </field>
  <field property="address" page="1" depends="required">
    <arg position="0" key="prompt.address"/>
  </field>
  <field property="username" page="2" depends="required">
    <arg position="0" key="prompt.username"/>
  </field>
  <field property="password" page="2" depends="required">
    <arg position="0" key="prompt.password"/>
  </field>
</form>
```

The page number specified with the **field** tag's **page** attribute corresponds to the value of a field on the associated form bean that must be set in the JSP page:

```
<html:hidden property="page" value="1"/>
```

The page property is already on the Validator **ActionForm** subclasses, so you don't need to add it to your Form Beans.

Each page must use the HTML Tag Library's **hidden** tag to specify a unique value for the **page** property. When validations are run, Validator compares the page value from the form with the page value set on the **field** tag with the **page** attribute. If the values are less than or equal to one another, the validations for the given field are run. Otherwise, the field's validations are skipped. Note that if you need to apply any custom reset logic on your Form Bean's fields using the **reset( )** method, you can use the **page** property, as shown here:

```
public void reset(ActionMapping mapping,
                  HttpServletRequest request) {
  super.reset(mapping, request);

  // Custom reset code goes here.
  if (page == 1) {
    // Reset page 1 properties.
  }
  else if (page == 2) {
    // Reset page 2 properties.
  }
}
```

As mentioned, the **page** property is a protected member of the Validator **ActionForm** subclasses, and thus it is available to Form Beans that extend those subclasses.

Using Validator's Included Validations

Validator, by default, includes several basic validation routines that you can use to solve most validation scenarios. As mentioned, Struts comes packaged with a preconfigured **validator-rules.xml** file that defines these routines. Table 6-1 lists each of the preconfigured validations by logical name and states its purpose. The following sections describe each of the preconfigured validations listed in the table, and usage examples are given.

Name	Description
byte	Determines whether the field being validated contains a value that can be converted to a Java **byte** primitive type.
byteLocale	Determines whether the field being validated contains a value that can be converted to a Java **byte** primitive type using the number formatting conventions of the current user's locale.
creditCard	Determines whether the field being validated contains a valid credit card number from one of the four major credit card companies (American Express, Discover, MasterCard, or Visa).
date	Determines whether the field being validated contains a value that can be converted to a **java.util.Date** type using the **java.text.SimpleDateFormat** class.
double	Determines whether the field being validated contains a value that can be converted to a Java **double** primitive type.
doubleRange	Determines whether the field being validated contains a Java **double** primitive type value that falls within the specified range.
email	Determines whether the field being validated contains a value that is a properly formatted e-mail address.
float	Determines whether the field being validated contains a value that can be converted to a Java **float** primitive type.
floatLocale	Determines whether the field being validated contains a value that can be converted to a Java **float** primitive type using the number formatting conventions of the current user's locale.
floatRange	Determines whether the field being validated contains a Java **float** primitive type value that falls within the specified range.
integer	Determines whether the field being validated contains a value that can be converted to a Java **int** primitive type.
integerLocale	Determines whether the field being validated contains a value that can be converted to a Java **int** primitive type using the number formatting conventions of the current user's locale.
intRange	Determines whether the field being validated contains a Java **int** primitive type value that falls within the specified range.
long	Determines whether the field being validated contains a value that can be converted to a Java **long** primitive type.

Table 6-1 Validator's Preconfigured Validations

Name	Description
longLocale	Determines whether the field being validated contains a value that can be converted to a Java **long** primitive type using the number formatting conventions of the current user's locale.
longRange	Determines whether the field being validated contains a Java **long** primitive type value that falls within the specified range.
mask	Determines whether the field being validated contains a value that is properly formatted according to a specified regular expression.
maxlength	Determines whether the field being validated contains a value whose character length is less than the specified maximum length.
minlength	Determines whether the field being validated contains a value whose character length is more than the specified minimum length.
required	Determines whether the field being validated contains a value other than white space (i.e., space, tab, and newline characters).
requiredif	Deprecated. Originally used for creating conditional validations. Use the **validwhen** validation instead.
short	Determines whether the field being validated contains a value that can be converted to a Java **short** primitive type.
shortLocale	Determines whether the field being validated contains a value that can be converted to a Java **short** primitive type using the number formatting conventions of the current user's locale.
url	Determines whether the field being validated contains a value that is a properly formatted URL.
validwhen	Determines whether the field being validated is required based on a specified test condition.

TABLE 6-1 Validator's Preconfigured Validations *(continued)*

The byte Validation

The **byte** validation is used to determine whether the field being validated contains a value that can be converted to a Java **byte** primitive type. If the conversion succeeds, the validation passes. The following snippet illustrates how to configure a **byte** validation in a Validator configuration file:

```
<field property="testByte" depends="required, byte">
  <arg position="0" key="label.sampleForm.testByte"/>
</field>
```

Configuring the **byte** validation is straightforward: you specify it in the list of validations for the given field with the **depends** attribute of the **field** tag. You must also use an **arg** tag to specify the key for a value in the application resource bundle file or a literal value that will be used to populate the **byte** validation's error message.

The **byte** validation is set up in the preconfigured **validator-rules.xml** file to use the **errors.byte** entry in the resource bundle file for its error message. The default **errors.byte** entry is shown next:

```
errors.byte={0} must be a byte.
```

The byteLocale Validation

The **byteLocale** validation is used to determine whether the field being validated contains a value that can be converted to a Java **byte** primitive type using the number formatting conventions of the current user's locale. If the conversion succeeds, the validation passes. This validation works identically to the **byte** validation except that it uses the user's locale to constrain the values that will be valid. The following snippet illustrates how to configure a **byteLocale** validation in a Validator configuration file:

```
<field property="testByte" depends="required, byteLocale">
  <arg position="0" key="label.sampleForm.testByte"/>
</field>
```

Configuring the **byteLocale** validation is straightforward: you specify it in the list of validations for the given field with the **depends** attribute of the **field** tag. You must also use an **arg** tag to specify the key for a value in the application resource bundle file or a literal value that will be used to populate the **byteLocale** validation's error message.

The **byteLocale** validation is set up in the preconfigured **validator-rules.xml** file to use the **errors.byte** entry in the resource bundle file for its error message. The default **errors.byte** entry is shown next:

```
errors.byte={0} must be a byte.
```

The creditCard Validation

The **creditCard** validation is used to determine whether the field being validated contains a valid credit card number from one of the four major credit card companies (American Express, Discover, MasterCard, or Visa). If the credit card number passes a checksum routine, the validation passes. The following snippet illustrates how to configure a **creditCard** validation in a Validator configuration file:

```
<field property="cardNumber" depends="required, creditCard">
  <arg position="0" key="label.sampleForm.cardNumber"/>
</field>
```

Configuring the **creditCard** validation is straightforward: you specify it in the list of validations for the given field with the **depends** attribute of the **field** tag. You must also use an **arg** tag to specify the key for a value in the application resource bundle file or a literal value that will be used to populate the **creditCard** validation's error message.

The **creditCard** validation is set up in the preconfigured **validator-rules.xml** file to use the **errors.creditcard** entry in the resource bundle file for its error message. The default **errors.creditcard** entry is shown next:

```
errors.creditcard={0} is an invalid credit card number.
```

The date Validation

The **date** validation is used to determine whether the field being validated contains a value that can be converted to a **java.util.Date** type using the **java.text.SimpleDateFormat** class.

If the conversion succeeds, the validation passes. The following snippet illustrates how to configure a **date** validation in a Validator configuration file:

```
<field property="birthDate" depends="required, date">
  <arg position="0" key="label.sampleForm.birthDate"/>
  <var>
    <var-name>datePattern</var-name>
    <var-value>MM/dd/yyyy</var-value>
  </var>
</field>
```

or

```
<field property="birthDate" depends="required, date">
  <arg position="0" key="label.sampleForm.birthDate"/>
  <var>
    <var-name>datePatternStrict</var-name>
    <var-value>MM/dd/yyyy</var-value>
  </var>
</field>
```

To configure the **date** validation, you specify it in the list of validations for the given field with the **depends** attribute of the **field** tag. You must use an **arg** tag to specify the key for a value in the application resource bundle file or a literal value that will be used to populate the **date** validation's error message. Additionally, you must use the **var** tag to define a **datePattern** or **datePatternStrict** variable. The **datePattern** variable is used by the **date** validation to specify the pattern that dates must have in order to pass the validation. The **datePatternStrict** variable works the same way as the **datePattern** variable except that it requires that dates adhere strictly to the pattern by matching the pattern's length. For example, a date value of "6/12/2006" would not match the pattern of "MM/dd/yyyy" with the **datePatternStrict** variable because it wasn't "06/12/2006" (notice the leading zero on the day). The abbreviated date would, however, match with the **datePattern** variable. The **datePattern** and **datePatternStrict** variables accept any pattern accepted by the **java.text.SimpleDateFormat** class.

The **date** validation is set up in the preconfigured **validator-rules.xml** file to use the **errors.date** entry in the resource bundle file for its error message. The default **errors.date** entry is shown next:

```
errors.date={0} is not a date.
```

The double Validation

The **double** validation is used to determine whether the field being validated contains a value that can be converted to a Java **double** primitive type. If the conversion succeeds, the validation passes. The following snippet illustrates how to configure a **double** validation in a Validator configuration file:

```
<field property="orderTotal" depends="required, double">
  <arg position="0" key="label.sampleForm.orderTotal"/>
</field>
```

Configuring the **double** validation is straightforward: you specify it in the list of validations for the given field with the **depends** attribute of the **field** tag. You must also use an **arg** tag to specify the key for a value in the application resource bundle file or a literal value that will be used to populate the **double** validation's error message.

The **double** validation is set up in the preconfigured **validator-rules.xml** file to use the **errors.double** entry in the resource bundle file for its error message. The default **errors.double** entry is shown next:

```
errors.double={0} must be a double.
```

The doubleRange Validation

The **doubleRange** validation is used to determine whether the field being validated contains a Java **double** primitive type value that falls within the specified range. If the value is within the specified range, the validation passes. The following snippet illustrates how to configure a **doubleRange** validation in a Validator configuration file:

```
<field property="orderTotal" depends="required, doubleRange">
  <arg position="0" key="label.sampleForm.orderTotal"/>
  <arg position="1" key="${var:min}" resource="false"/>
  <arg position="2" key="${var:max}" resource="false"/>
  <var>
    <var-name>min</var-name>
    <var-value>100</var-value>
  </var>
  <var>
    <var-name>max</var-name>
    <var-value>1000</var-value>
  </var>
</field>
```

To configure the **doubleRange** validation, you specify it in the list of validations for the given field with the **depends** attribute of the **field** tag. You must use **arg** tags to specify the keys for values in the application resource bundle file or literal values that will be used to populate the **doubleRange** validation's error message. Additionally, you must use **var** tags to define **min** and **max** variables. The **min** and **max** variables are used by the **doubleRange** validation to specify the minimum and maximum values for the range, respectively. Notice that the **arg** tags' keys are set to **$var:min** and **$var:max**. The **min** and **max** values specified with the **var** tags will be used to populate the error message, respectively.

The **doubleRange** validation is set up in the preconfigured **validator-rules.xml** file to use the **errors.range** entry in the resource bundle file for its error message. The default **errors.range** entry is shown next:

```
errors.range={0} is not in the range {1} through {2}.
```

The email Validation

The **email** validation is used to determine whether the field being validated contains a value that is a properly formatted e-mail address. If the format is correct, the validation passes. The following snippet illustrates how to configure an **email** validation in a Validator configuration file:

```
<field property="emailAddress" depends="required, email">
  <arg position="0" key="label.sampleForm.emailAddress"/>
</field>
```

Configuring the **email** validation is straightforward: you specify it in the list of validations for the given field with the **depends** attribute of the **field** tag. You must also use an **arg** tag to specify the key for a value in the application resource bundle file or a literal value that will be used to populate the **email** validation's error message.

The **email** validation is set up in the preconfigured **validator-rules.xml** file to use the **errors.email** entry in the resource bundle file for its error message. The default **errors.email** entry is shown next:

```
errors.email={0} is an invalid e-mail address.
```

The float Validation

The **float** validation is used to determine whether the field being validated contains a value that can be converted to a Java **float** primitive type. If the conversion succeeds, the validation passes. The following snippet illustrates how to configure a **float** validation in a Validator configuration file:

```
<field property="orderTotal" depends="required, float">
  <arg position="0" key="label.sampleForm.orderTotal"/>
</field>
```

Configuring the **float** validation is straightforward: you specify it in the list of validations for the given field with the **depends** attribute of the **field** tag. You must also use an **arg** tag to specify the key for a value in the application resource bundle file or a literal value that will be used to populate the **float** validation's error message.

The **float** validation is set up in the preconfigured **validator-rules.xml** file to use the **errors.float** entry in the resource bundle file for its error message. The default **errors.float** entry is shown next:

```
errors.float={0} must be a float.
```

The floatLocale Validation

The **floatLocale** validation is used to determine whether the field being validated contains a value that can be converted to a Java **float** primitive type using the number formatting conventions of the current user's locale. If the conversion succeeds, the validation passes. This validation works identically to the **float** validation except that it uses the user's locale to constrain the values that will be valid. The following snippet illustrates how to configure a **floatLocale** validation in a Validator configuration file:

```
<field property="orderTotal" depends="required, floatLocale">
  <arg position="0" key="label.sampleForm.orderTotal"/>
</field>
```

Configuring the **floatLocale** validation is straightforward: you specify it in the list of validations for the given field with the **depends** attribute of the **field** tag. You must also use an **arg** tag to specify the key for a value in the application resource bundle file or a literal value that will be used to populate the **floatLocale** validation's error message.

The **floatLocale** validation is set up in the preconfigured **validator-rules.xml** file to use the **errors.float** entry in the resource bundle file for its error message. The default **errors.float** entry is shown next:

```
errors.float={0} must be a float.
```

The floatRange Validation

The **floatRange** validation is used to determine whether the field being validated contains a Java **float** primitive type value that falls within the specified range. If the value is within the range, the validation passes. The following snippet illustrates how to configure a **floatRange** validation in a Validator configuration file:

```
<field property="orderTotal" depends="required, floatRange">
  <arg position="0" key="label.sampleForm.orderTotal"/>
  <arg position="1" key="${var:min}" resource="false"/>
  <arg position="2" key="${var:max}" resource="false"/>
  <var>
    <var-name>min</var-name>
    <var-value>100</var-value>
  </var>
  <var>
    <var-name>max</var-name>
    <var-value>1000</var-value>
  </var>
</field>
```

To configure the **floatRange** validation, you specify it in the list of validations for the given field with the **depends** attribute of the **field** tag. You must use **arg** tags to specify the keys for values in the application resource bundle file or literal values that will be used to populate the **floatRange** validation's error message. Additionally, you must use **var** tags to define **min** and **max** variables. The **min** and **max** variables are used by the **floatRange** validation to specify the minimum and maximum values for the range, respectively. Notice that the **arg** tags' keys are set to **$var:min** and **$var:max**. The **min** and **max** values specified with the **var** tags will be used to populate the error message, respectively.

The **floatRange** validation is set up in the preconfigured **validator-rules.xml** file to use the **errors.range** entry in the resource bundle file for its error message. The default **errors.range** entry is shown next:

```
errors.range={0} is not in the range {1} through {2}.
```

The integer Validation

The **integer** validation is used to determine whether the field being validated contains a value that can be converted to a Java **int** primitive type. If the conversion succeeds, the validation passes. The following snippet illustrates how to configure an **integer** validation in a Validator configuration file:

```
<field property="productCount" depends="required, integer">
  <arg position="0" key="label.sampleForm.productCount"/>
</field>
```

Configuring the **integer** validation is straightforward: you specify it in the list of validations for the given field with the **depends** attribute of the **field** tag. You must also use an **arg** tag to specify the key for a value in the application resource bundle file or a literal value that will be used to populate the **integer** validation's error message.

The **integer** validation is set up in the preconfigured **validator-rules.xml** file to use the **errors.integer** entry in the resource bundle file for its error message. The default **errors.integer** entry is shown next:

```
errors.integer={0} must be an integer.
```

The integerLocale Validation

The **integerLocale** validation is used to determine whether the field being validated contains a value that can be converted to a Java **int** primitive type using the number formatting conventions of the current user's locale. If the conversion succeeds, the validation passes. This validation works identically to the **integer** validation except that it uses the user's locale to constrain the values that will be valid. The following snippet illustrates how to configure an **integerLocale** validation in a Validator configuration file:

```
<field property="productCount" depends="required, integerLocale">
  <arg position="0" key="label.sampleForm.productCount"/>
</field>
```

Configuring the **integerLocale** validation is straightforward: you specify it in the list of validations for the given field with the **depends** attribute of the **field** tag. You must also use an **arg** tag to specify the key for a value in the application resource bundle file or a literal value that will be used to populate the **integerLocale** validation's error message.

The **integerLocale** validation is set up in the preconfigured **validator-rules.xml** file to use the **errors.integer** entry in the resource bundle file for its error message. The default **errors.integer** entry is shown next:

```
errors.integer={0} must be an integer.
```

The intRange Validation

The **intRange** validation is used to determine whether the field being validated contains a Java **int** primitive type value that falls within the specified range. If the value is within the range, the validation passes. The following snippet illustrates how to configure an **intRange** validation in a Validator configuration file:

```
<field property="orderTotal" depends="required, intRange">
  <arg position="0" key="label.sampleForm.orderTotal"/>
  <arg position="1" key="${var:min}" resource="false"/>
  <arg position="2" key="${var:max}" resource="false"/>
  <var>
    <var-name>min</var-name>
    <var-value>100</var-value>
  </var>
  <var>
    <var-name>max</var-name>
    <var-value>1000</var-value>
  </var>
</field>
```

To configure the **intRange** validation, you specify it in the list of validations for the given field with the **depends** attribute of the **field** tag. You must use **arg** tags to specify the keys for values in the application resource bundle file or literal values that will be used to populate the **intRange** validation's error message. Additionally, you must use **var** tags to define **min** and **max** variables. The **min** and **max** variables are used by the **intRange** validation to specify the minimum and maximum values for the range, respectively. Notice that the **arg** tags' keys are set to **$var:min** and **$var:max**. The **min** and **max** values specified with the **var** tags will be used to populate the error message, respectively.

The **intRange** validation is set up in the preconfigured **validator-rules.xml** file to use the **errors.range** entry in the resource bundle file for its error message. The default **errors.range** entry is shown next:

```
errors.range={0} is not in the range {1} through {2}.
```

The long Validation

The **long** validation is used to determine whether the field being validated contains a value that can be converted to a Java **long** primitive type. If the conversion succeeds, the validation passes. The following snippet illustrates how to configure a **long** validation in a Validator configuration file:

```
<field property="productCount" depends="required, long">
  <arg position="0" key="label.sampleForm.productCount"/>
</field>
```

Configuring the **long** validation is straightforward: you specify it in the list of validations for the given field with the **depends** attribute of the **field** tag. You must also use an **arg** tag to specify the key for a value in the application resource bundle file or a literal value that will be used to populate the **long** validation's error message.

The **long** validation is set up in the preconfigured **validator-rules.xml** file to use the **errors.long** entry in the resource bundle file for its error message. The default **errors.long** entry is shown next:

```
errors.long={0} must be a long.
```

The longLocale Validation

The **longLocale** validation is used to determine whether the field being validated contains a value that can be converted to a Java **long** primitive type using the number formatting conventions of the current user's locale. If the conversion succeeds, the validation passes. This validation works identically to the **long** validation except that it uses the user's locale to constrain the values that will be valid. The following snippet illustrates how to configure a **longLocale** validation in a Validator configuration file:

```
<field property="productCount" depends="required, longLocale">
  <arg position="0" key="label.sampleForm.productCount"/>
</field>
```

Configuring the **longLocale** validation is straightforward: you specify it in the list of validations for the given field with the **depends** attribute of the **field** tag. You must also use an **arg** tag to specify the key for a value in the application resource bundle file or a literal value that will be used to populate the **longLocale** validation's error message.

The **longLocale** validation is set up in the preconfigured **validator-rules.xml** file to use the **errors.long** entry in the resource bundle file for its error message. The default **errors.long** entry is shown next:

```
errors.long={0} must be a long.
```

The longRange Validation

The **longRange** validation is used to determine whether the field being validated contains a Java **long** primitive type value that falls within the specified range. If the value is within the range, the validation passes. The following snippet illustrates how to configure a **longRange** validation in a Validator configuration file:

```
<field property="orderTotal" depends="required, longRange">
  <arg position="0" key="label.sampleForm.orderTotal"/>
  <arg position="1" key="${var:min}" resource="false"/>
  <arg position="2" key="${var:max}" resource="false"/>
  <var>
    <var-name>min</var-name>
    <var-value>100</var-value>
  </var>
  <var>
    <var-name>max</var-name>
    <var-value>1000</var-value>
  </var>
</field>
```

To configure the **longRange** validation, you specify it in the list of validations for the given field with the **depends** attribute of the **field** tag. You must use **arg** tags to specify the keys for values in the application resource bundle file or literal values that will be used to populate the **longRange** validation's error message. Additionally, you must use **var** tags to define **min** and **max** variables. The **min** and **max** variables are used by the **longRange** validation to specify the minimum and maximum values for the range, respectively. Notice that the **arg** tags' keys are set to **$var:min** and **$var:max**. The **min** and **max** values specified with the **var** tags will be used to populate the error message, respectively.

The **longRange** validation is set up in the preconfigured **validator-rules.xml** file to use the **errors.range** entry in the resource bundle file for its error message. The default **errors. range** entry is shown next:

```
errors.range={0} is not in the range {1} through {2}.
```

The mask Validation

The **mask** validation is used to determine whether the field being validated contains a value that is properly formatted according to a specified regular expression. If the value's format matches the regular expression, the validation passes. The following snippet illustrates how to configure a **mask** validation in a Validator configuration file:

```
<field property="socialSecurityNum" depends="required, mask">
  <arg position="0" key="label.sampleForm.socialSecurityNum"/>
  <var>
    <var-name>mask</var-name>
    <var-value>^\d{3}-\d{2}-\d{4}$</var-value>
  </var>
</field>
```

To configure the **mask** validation, you specify it in the list of validations for the given field with the **depends** attribute of the **field** tag. You must use an **arg** tag to specify the key for a value in the application resource bundle file or a literal value that will be used to populate the **mask** validation's error message. Additionally, you must use the **var** tag to define a **mask** variable. The **mask** variable is used by the **mask** validation to specify a regular expression to which values must conform in order to be deemed valid.

NOTE *Regular expressions are a powerful tool for text analysis and manipulation; however, they constitute a large, and at times complex, topic. Therefore, a discussion of regular expressions is outside the scope of this book.*

The **mask** validation is set up in the preconfigured **validator-rules.xml** file to use the **errors.invalid** entry in the resource bundle file for its error message. The default **errors.invalid** entry is shown next:

```
errors.invalid={0} is invalid.
```

The maxlength Validation

The **maxlength** validation is used to determine whether the field being validated contains a value whose character length is less than the specified maximum length. If the value contains fewer characters than the specified maximum, the validation passes. The following snippet illustrates how to configure a **maxlength** validation in a Validator configuration file:

```
<field property="password" depends="required, maxlength">
  <arg position="0" key="label.sampleForm.password"/>
  <arg position="1" key="${var:maxlength}" resource="false"/>
  <var>
    <var-name>maxlength</var-name>
    <var-value>8</var-value>
  </var>
</field>
```

To configure the **maxlength** validation, you specify it in the list of validations for the given field with the **depends** attribute of the **field** tag. You must use **arg** tags to specify the keys for values in the application resource bundle file or literal values that will be used to populate the **maxlength** validation's error message. Additionally, you must use the **var** tag to define a **maxlength** variable. The **maxlength** variable is used by the **maxlength** validation to specify the maximum character length that values can have. Notice that the **arg** tag's key is set to **$var:maxlength**. The **maxlength** value specified with the **var** tag will be used to populate the error message.

The **maxlength** validation is set up in the preconfigured **validator-rules.xml** file to use the **errors.maxlength** entry in the resource bundle file for its error message. The default **errors.maxlength** entry is shown next:

```
errors.maxlength={0} can not be greater than {1} characters.
```

The minlength Validation

The **minlength** validation is used to determine whether the field being validated contains a value whose character length is more than the specified minimum length. If the value contains more characters than the specified minimum, the validation passes. The following snippet illustrates how to configure a **minlength** validation in a Validator configuration file:

```
<field property="password" depends="required, minlength">
  <arg position="0" key="label.sampleForm.password"/>
  <arg position="1" key="${var:minlength}" resource="false"/>
  <var>
    <var-name>minlength</var-name>
    <var-value>4</var-value>
```

```
  </var>
</field>
```

To configure the **minlength** validation, you specify it in the list of validations for the given field with the **depends** attribute of the **field** tag. You must use **arg** tags to specify the keys for values in the application resource bundle file or literal values that will be used to populate the **minlength** validation's error message. Additionally, you must use the **var** tag to define a **minlength** variable. The **minlength** variable is used by the **minlength** validation to specify the minimum character length that values can have. Notice that the **arg** tag's key is set to **$var:minlength**. The **minlength** value specified with the **var** tag will be used to populate the error message.

The **minlength** validation is set up in the preconfigured **validator-rules.xml** file to use the **errors.minlength** entry in the resource bundle file for its error message. The default **errors.minlength** entry is shown next:

```
errors.minlength={0} can not be less than {1} characters.
```

The required Validation

The **required** validation is used to determine whether the field being validated contains a value other than white space (i.e., space, tab, and newline characters). If a non–white space value is present, the validation passes. The following snippet illustrates how to configure a **required** validation in a Validator configuration file:

```
<field property="name" depends="required">
  <arg position="0" key="label.sampleForm.name"/>
</field>
```

Configuring the **required** validation is straightforward: you specify it in the list of validations for the given field with the **depends** attribute of the **field** tag. You must also use an **arg** tag to specify the key for a value in the application resource bundle file or a literal value that will be used to populate the **required** validation's error message.

The **required** validation is set up in the preconfigured **validator-rules.xml** file to use the **errors.required** entry in the resource bundle file for its error message. The default **errors.required** entry is shown next:

```
errors.required={0} is required.
```

The short Validation

The **short** validation is used to determine whether the field being validated contains a value that can be converted to a Java **short** primitive type. If the conversion succeeds, the validation passes. The following snippet illustrates how to configure a **short** validation in a Validator configuration file:

```
<field property="productCount" depends="required, short">
  <arg position="0" key="label.sampleForm.productCount"/>
</field>
```

Configuring the **short** validation is straightforward: you specify it in the list of validations for the given field with the **depends** attribute of the **field** tag. You must also use an **arg** tag to specify the key for a value in the application resource bundle file or a literal value that will be used to populate the **short** validation's error message.

The **short** validation is set up in the preconfigured **validator-rules.xml** file to use the **errors.short** entry in the resource bundle file for its error message. The default **errors.short** entry is shown next:

```
errors.short={0} must be a short.
```

The shortLocale Validation

The **shortLocale** validation is used to determine whether the field being validated contains a value that can be converted to a Java **short** primitive type using the number formatting conventions of the current user's locale. If the conversion succeeds, the validation passes. This validation works identically to the **short** validation except that it uses the user's locale to constrain the values that will be valid. The following snippet illustrates how to configure a **shortLocale** validation in a Validator configuration file:

```
<field property="productCount" depends="required, shortLocale">
  <arg position="0" key="label.sampleForm.productCount"/>
</field>
```

Configuring the **shortLocale** validation is straightforward: you specify it in the list of validations for the given field with the **depends** attribute of the **field** tag. You must also use an **arg** tag to specify the key for a value in the application resource bundle file or a literal value that will be used to populate the **shortLocale** validation's error message.

The **shortLocale** validation is set up in the preconfigured **validator-rules.xml** file to use the **errors.short** entry in the resource bundle file for its error message. The default **errors.short** entry is shown next:

```
errors.short={0} must be a short.
```

The url Validation

The **url** validation is used to determine whether the field being validated contains a value that is a properly formatted URL. If the format is correct, the validation passes. The following snippet illustrates how to configure a **url** validation in a Validator configuration file:

```
<field property="websiteUrl" depends="required, url">
  <arg position="0" key="label.sampleForm.websiteUrl"/>
</field>
```

To configure the **url** validation, you specify it in the list of validations for the given field with the **depends** attribute of the **field** tag. You must use an **arg** tag to specify the key for a value in the application resource bundle file or a literal value that will be used to populate the **url** validation's error message. Additionally, you can use **var** tags to define four optional variables: **allowallschemes**, **allow2slashes**, **nofragments**, and **schemes**.

The **allowallschemes** and **schemes** variables are used to specify which URL schemes are acceptable when the **url** validation is determining if a URL is valid or not. The **schemes** variable allows you to specify a list of schemes the URL must have in order to pass the validation, as shown here:

```
<field property="websiteUrl" depends="required, url">
  <arg position="0" key="label.sampleForm.websiteUrl"/>
  <var>
```

```
    <var-name>schemes</var-name>
    <var-value>http,https</var-value>
  </var>
</field>
```

In this example, only URLs having the "http" or "https" schemes will be valid (e.g., http://domain.com or https://domain.com). A URL with an "ftp" scheme (e.g., ftp://domain.com) would be invalid. The **allowallschemes** variable, shown next, accepts *true* or *false* to specify whether the **url** validation will accept any scheme. This variable defaults to false.

```
<field property="websiteUrl" depends="required, url">
  <arg position="0" key="label.sampleForm.websiteUrl"/>
  <var>
    <var-name>allowallschemes</var-name>
    <var-value>true</var-value>
  </var>
</field>
```

Note that the **allowallschemes** variable overrides the **schemes** variable if both are specified.

The **allow2slashes** variable accepts *true* or *false* to specify whether double slash (/) characters are allowed in the path of URLs (e.g., http://domain.com/dir1//page.html). This variable defaults to *false*. The **nofragments** variable accepts *true* or *false* to specify whether URL fragments (i.e., anchors) are allowed to be a part of acceptable URLs. This variable defaults to *false* meaning that fragments are allowed (e.g., http://domain.com/page.html#fragment).

The **url** validation is set up in the preconfigured **validator-rules.xml** file to use the **errors.url** entry in the resource bundle file for its error message. The default **errors.url** entry is shown next:

```
errors.url={0} is an invalid URL.
```

The validwhen Validation

The **validwhen** validation is used to determine whether the field being validated is required based on a specified test condition. If the test condition succeeds, the validation passes. The following snippet illustrates how to configure a **validwhen** validation in a Validator configuration file:

```
<field property="emailConfirm" depends="validwhen">
  <arg position="0" key="label.sampleForm.emailConfirm"/>
  <var>
    <var-name>test</var-name>
    <var-value>((email == null) or (*this* != null))</var-value>
  </var>
</field>
```

To configure the **validwhen** validation, you specify it in the list of validations for the given field with the **depends** attribute of the **field** tag. You must use an **arg** tag to specify the key for a value in the application resource bundle file or a literal value that will be used to populate the **validwhen** validation's error message. Additionally, you must use the **var** tag to define a **test** variable. The **test** variable is used by the **validwhen** validation to specify a test condition that must pass in order for the validation to succeed.

The test condition specified with the **test** variable is designed to allow for dependent validations to be defined. Dependent validations are validations where one field's validity is based on the value of another field. For example, an email confirmation field may be required only if a related email field has a value. There is no way to define this interdependent requirement with the standard **required** validation. With the **validwhen** validation, however, you can create a validation dependency from one field to another, as was shown in the previous configuration example.

The **test** variable's test condition is a Boolean expression that must evaluate to true in order for the validation to succeed. Following is the list of rules governing the syntax for creating test conditions:

- Form fields are referenced by their logical name (e.g., name, email, etc.).
- The field for which the validation is being performed is referenced as ***this***.
- **null** is used to indicate null or an empty string.
- Literal string values must be single- or double-quoted.
- Literal integer values can be specified using decimal, hex, or octal formats.
- All comparisons must be enclosed in parentheses.
- A maximum of two comparisons can be made in one condition using **and** or **or**.
- A numeric comparison is performed for conditions that have two numerical values; otherwise, a string comparison is performed.

The **validwhen** validation is set up in the preconfigured **validator-rules.xml** file to use the **errors.required** entry in the resource bundle file for its error message. The default **errors.required** entry is shown next:

```
errors.required={0} is required.
```

Enabling Client-Side Validations

In addition to providing a framework for simplifying server-side form data validations, Validator provides an easy-to-use mechanism for performing client-side validations. Each validation routine defined in the **validator-rules.xml** file optionally specifies JavaScript code that can be run in the browser (client side) to perform the same validations that take place on the server side. When run on the client side, the validations will not allow the form to be submitted until they have all passed. Validations that fail will trigger error dialog windows that specify the fields and the type of validation that failed. Figure 6-1 shows a sample error dialog triggered from a failed validation.

Figure 6-1 Validator's client-side JavaScript error dialog

To enable client-side validation, you have to place the HTML Tag Library's **javascript** tag in each JSP for which you want client-side validation performed, as shown here:

```
<html:javascript formName="logonForm"/>
```

The **javascript** tag outputs the JavaScript code necessary to run all of a form's configured validations on the client-side. Note that the **javascript** tag requires that you use the **formName** attribute to specify the name of a **<form>** definition from the **validation.xml** file, as shown here, for which you want validations performed:

```
<form name="logonForm">
  <field property="username" depends="required">
    <arg position="0" key="prompt.username"/>
  </field>
  <field property="password" depends="required">
    <arg position="0" key="prompt.password"/>
  </field>
</form>
```

All the validations that you have specified for the **<form>** definition to run on the server side will be run on the client side.

After adding the **javascript** tag to your page, you must update the HTML Tag Library's **form** tag to have an **onsubmit** attribute. The **onsubmit** attribute is used to specify JavaScript code that is executed when the form is submitted.

In addition to outputting all of the JavaScript code for the validation routines, the **javascript** tag generates a master JavaScript validation method that is used to invoke all of the configured validations for the form. This master method must be called from the **onsubmit** attribute of the **form** tag. Following is an example of how to specify the **onsubmit** attribute for Validator's client-side validations:

```
<html:form action="/Logon" onsubmit="return validateLogonForm(this);">
```

The master validation method generated by the **javascript** tag is named based on concatenating "validate" with the name of the form name specified with the **formName** attribute of the **javascript** tag. For example, a form named "searchForm" will have a generated method named "validateSearchForm".

NOTE *The* **method** *attribute of the* **javascript** *tag can be used to specify an alternate method name for the master method that Validator generates. This is useful in scenarios where the auto-generated method name conflicts with other JavaScript method names in your application.*

Understanding the Client-Side Validation Process

Validator's client-side validations are performed in a specific order and, as previously mentioned, trigger error dialog windows upon failure. It's important to understand the sequence in which validations are performed in order to understand when error dialogs are triggered. Validator's client-side JavaScript processes validations based on the order they are specified in the **validation.xml** file for a form. Validator proceeds field-by-field processing the validations, but there is one important detail about how the validations are processed.

Once a validation is run for a field, for example, the **required** validation, all fields that are to be validated using that validation are run at that time. That is, instead of running a validation each time it is specified in the order it is specified, it is run once for all fields that specify it and then the next validation is processed.

Validator stops processing validations and triggers an error dialog window if any fields being validated by a particular validation fail. This behavior can sometimes be frustrating for users of an application who submit a form that has several validations on it. If multiple validations fail, the user will be prompted only for the first validation that fails. The user can then fix the field(s) with errors and submit the form again. If the validation that failed the first time passes and another validation fails, another error dialog will be displayed. This back-and-forth process of alerting the user of which fields failed validation and then resubmitting the form again for another run of the validations can be cumbersome for the user. The basic problem is that Validator stops processing validations and displays an error dialog for only the first validation that fails. This is the default behavior. However, Validator supports an option for processing all validations, whether they fail or not, and then displaying error dialogs for each validation that failed after all validations have been processed. To enable this option, you have to update the Validator **<plug-in>** definition in the Struts configuration file, as shown next:

```
<!-- Validator Configuration -->
<plug-in className="org.apache.struts.validator.ValidatorPlugIn">
  <set-property property="pathnames"
                value="/org/apache/struts/validator/validator-rules.xml,
                       /WEB-INF/validation.xml"/>
  <set-property property="stopOnFirstError" value="false"/>
</plug-in>
```

The **stopOnFirstError** property has to be set to false in order to have Validator process all validations and then display error dialogs for each failed validation. Each validation that fails will have its own error dialog listing each of the fields that failed that particular validation.

Creating a Common Client-Side Validations JSP

The HTML Tag Library's **javascript** tag outputs the JavaScript code for all validation routines independent of whether they are used or not. For example, even if a form on a page has only two fields and makes use of only the **required** validation for those fields, the **javascript** tag outputs the JavaScript code for the **required** validation and all other validations configured in the **validator-rules.xml** file. This can add a large amount of unnecessary page download overhead to each page making use of client-side validations.

To get around all of the validations being inserted into each page, you can create a common client-side validations JSP that will house the JavaScript for all validations. Each page that makes use of client-side validation will link to the common page, instead of embedding the validations inline. This approach allows the browser to cache the common validations page, thus eliminating the unnecessary overheard of downloading the validation code for every request of each page. To make use of a common validations JSP, you must first create the common JSP, as shown next:

```
<%@ page contentType="application/x-javascript" language="java" %>
<%@ taglib uri="http://struts.apache.org/tags-html" prefix="html" %>

<html:javascript dynamicJavascript="false" staticJavascript="true"/>
```

This page is typically named **staticJavascript.jsp**; however, the name is entirely up to you. Notice that this page uses the **javascript** tag with the **dynamicJavascript** and **staticJavascript** attributes set to false and true, respectively. This instructs the **javascript** tag to output only the JavaScript code for the validation routines and not the code that invokes the routines for the fields of a form. The JavaScript code that invokes the routines is dynamic and must be housed in each of the individual JSPs utilizing client-side validation. Following is the snippet that must be placed in each of the individual JSPs utilizing client-side validation.

```
<html:javascript formName="LogonForm"
        dynamicJavascript="true"
         staticJavascript="false"/>
<script language="JavaScript" src="staticJavascript.jsp"></script>
```

Notice that the **javascript** tag's **dynamicJavascript** and **staticJavascript** attributes are set to true and false respectively in the individual pages; this is the opposite of how they are set in the **staticJavascript.jsp** page. In addition to using the **javascript** tag to emit the dynamic JavaScript code, you must use a **script** tag to link to the common validations JSP.

Creating Custom Validations

Validator comes packaged with several useful validations that will suit most situations; however, your application may require a specific validation that is not provided by the framework. For this situation, Validator provides a simple interface for creating your own custom validations that can easily be plugged into the framework. Following is a list of the steps you need to take to create your own custom validation:

1. Create a new validation method.
2. Add a new validation rule to the **validation.xml** file.
3. Add new validation definitions to the **validation.xml** file.
4. Add messages to the **MessageResources.properties** file.

The following sections walk through each step of the process in detail, enabling you to create a custom validation based on the Social Security Number validation used in the example Mini HR application in Chapter 2. Remember that the Social Security Number validation in Chapter 2 was defined inside of the **SearchForm** Form Bean class. Creating a custom validation for social security numbers enables the validation code to be reused and to be used declaratively instead of being hard-coded in each Form Bean that wants to use it.

Creating a Validation Method

The first step in creating a custom validation is to create a validation method that can be called by the Validator framework. Typically, all of an application's methods for custom validations are grouped into a class of their own, as is the case for the example in this section. However, you can place the method in any class. Your validation method needs to have the following signature:

```
public static boolean validateSsNum(java.lang.Object,
  org.apache.commons.validator.ValidatorAction,
  org.apache.commons.validator.Field,
  org.apache.struts.action.ActionMessages,
  org.apache.commons.validator.Validator,
  javax.servlet.http.HttpServletRequest);
```

Argument	Description
java.lang.Object	The Form Bean object (downcast to **Object**) contains the field to be validated.
org.apache.commons.validator.ValidatorAction	The **ValidatorAction** object encapsulates the **<validator>** definition from the **validator-rules.xml** file for this validation routine.
org.apache.commons.validator.Field	The **Field** object encapsulates the **<field>** definition from the **validation.xml** file for the field that is currently being validated.
org.apache.struts.action.ActionMessages	The **ActionMessages** object stores validation error messages for the field that is currently being validated.
org.apache.commons.validator.Validator	The **Validator** object encapsulates the current Validator instance and is used to access other field values.
javax.servlet.http.HttpServletRequest	The **HttpServletRequest** object encapsulates the current HTTP request.

TABLE 6-2 The Validation Method Arguments

Of course, the name of your method will vary, but its arguments should match the types shown in the preceding example. Table 6-2 explains each of the validation method's arguments.

Following is the custom validation code for validating social security numbers. Notice that the **validateSsNum( )** method conforms to the proper method signature for custom validations.

```
package com.jamesholmes.minihr;

import javax.servlet.http.HttpServletRequest;
import org.apache.commons.validator.Field;
import org.apache.commons.validator.Validator;
import org.apache.commons.validator.ValidatorAction;
import org.apache.commons.validator.ValidatorUtil;
import org.apache.struts.action.ActionMessages;
import org.apache.struts.validator.Resources;

public class MiniHrValidator
{
  public static boolean validateSsNum(Object bean,
    ValidatorAction action,
    Field field,
    ActionMessages errors,
    Validator validator,
    HttpServletRequest request)
  {
    String value =
      ValidatorUtil.getValueAsString(bean, field.getProperty());
```

```
    if (value == null || value.length() < 11) {
      errors.add(field.getKey(),
        Resources.getActionMessage(validator, request, action, field));
      return false;
    }

    for (int i = 0; i < 11; i++) {
      if (i == 3 || i == 6) {
        if (value.charAt(i) != '-') {
          errors.add(field.getKey(),
            Resources.getActionMessage(validator, request, action, field));
          return false;
        }
      } else if ("0123456789".indexOf(value.charAt(i)) == -1) {
        errors.add(field.getKey(),
          Resources.getActionMessage(validator, request, action, field));
        return false;
      }
    }

    return true;
  }
}
```

The **validateSsNum( )** method begins by retrieving the value for the field being validated. The value is retrieved by determining the field's name with a call to **field. getProperty( )** and then looking up that field in the Form Bean with a call to **ValidatorUtil. getValueAsString( )**. The **getValueAsString( )** method matches the name of the field with the name of one of the Form Bean fields and then gets that field's value. The rest of the **validateSsNum( )** method performs the actual validation logic. If the validation fails for any reason, an error message will be stored in the **errors ActionMessages** object.

Adding a New Validation Rule

After the custom validation code has been created, a new validation rule needs to be added to the **validation.xml** file. As discussed earlier in this chapter, validation rules "plug" validation methods into the Validator. Once defined in **validation.xml**, as shown here, the validation rule can be referenced by a **field** tag's **depends** attribute:

```
<validator name="ssNum"
      classname="com.jamesholmes.minihr.MiniHrValidator"
         method="validateSsNum"
   methodParams="java.lang.Object,
                 org.apache.commons.validator.ValidatorAction,
                 org.apache.commons.validator.Field,
                 org.apache.struts.action.ActionMessages,
                 org.apache.commons.validator.Validator,
                 javax.servlet.http.HttpServletRequest"
            msg="errors.ssNum">
  <javascript>
    <![CDATA[
    function validateSsNum(form) {
      var isValid = true;
      var focusField = null;
```

```
        var i = 0;
        var fields = new Array();
        var oSsNum = eval('new ' + jcv_retriveFormName(form) + '_ssNum()');

        for (var x in oSsNum) {
          if (!jcv_verifyArrayElement(x, oSsNum[x])) {
            continue;
          }

          var field = form[oSsNum[x][0]];
          if (!jcv_isFieldPresent(field)) {
            continue;
          }

          if ((field.type == 'hidden' ||
               field.type == 'password' ||
               field.type == 'text' ||
               field.type == 'textarea') &&
              (field.value.length > 0))
          {
            var value = field.value;
            var isRightFormat = true;

            if (value.length != 11) {
              isRightFormat = false;
            }

            for (var n = 0; n < 11; n++) {
              if (n == 3 || n == 6) {
                if (value.substring(n, n+1) != '-') {
                  isRightFormat = false;
                }
              } else if ("0123456789".indexOf(
                            value.substring(n, n+1)) == -1) {
                  isRightFormat = false;
              }
            }

            if (!isRightFormat) {
              if (i == 0) {
                focusField = field;
              }
              fields[i++] = oSsNum[x][1];
              isValid = false;
            }
          }
        }
        if (fields.length > 0) {
          jcv_handleErrors(fields, focusField);
        }
        return isValid;
      }
      ]]>
    </javascript>
  </validator>
```

As you can see, the validation rule applies a name to the validation with the **name** attribute; specifies the class in which the validation method is housed with the **classname** attribute; and specifies the validation method's arguments with the **methodParams** attribute. The **msg** attribute specifies a key that will be used to look up an error message in the application's resource bundle file (e.g., **MessageResources.properties**) if the validation fails. Note that the name applied with the **name** attribute is the logical name for the rule and will be used to apply the rule to definitions in the **validation.xml** file.

The preceding custom validation rule also defines JavaScript code, inside the opening and closing **<javascript>** elements, which will be used if client-side validation is enabled when using the rule. The JavaScript code simply performs the same validation on the client side as is performed on the server side. If the JavaScript validation fails, it will alert the user and prevent the HTML form from being submitted.

Note that validation rules must be placed in a **<global>** element in the **validation.xml** file, as shown here:

```
<form-validation>
  <global>
    <validator name="ssNum" .../>
    ...
    ...
  </global>
</form-validation>
```

Of course, the order of the **<validator>** elements underneath the **<global>** element is arbitrary, so you can place the new **ssNum** validation rule anywhere.

Adding New Validation Definitions

Once you have defined your custom validation rule in the **validation.xml** file, you can make use of it by referencing its logical name in the **validation.xml** file:

```
<!DOCTYPE form-validation PUBLIC
          "-//Apache Software Foundation//DTD Commons
           Validator Rules Configuration 1.3.0//EN"
          "http://jakarta.apache.org/commons/dtds/validator_1_3_0.dtd">

<form-validation>
  <formset>
    <form name="searchForm">
      <field property="ssNum" depends="required,ssNum">
        <arg position="0" key="prompt.ssNum"/>
      </field>
    </form>
  </formset>
</form-validation>
```

In the preceding validation definition, each of the comma-delimited values of the **field** tag's **depends** attribute corresponds to the logical name of a validation rule defined in the **validation-rules.xml** file. The use of **ssNum** instructs Validator to use the custom Social Security Number validation. Each time you want to use the new Social Security Number validation, you simply have to add its logical name to the **depends** attribute of a **field** tag.

Adding Messages to the MessageResources.properties File

The final step in creating a custom validation is to add messages to the **MessageResources.properties** file:

```
prompt.ssNum=Social Security Number
errors.ssNum={0} is not a valid Social Security Number
```

Remember that the **errors.ssNum** message key was specified by the **msg** attribute of the **validator** tag for the custom validation rule in the **validation.xml** file. The key's corresponding message will be used if the validation fails. The **prompt.ssNum** message key was specified by the **arg** tag of the validation definition in the **validation.xml** file. Its corresponding message will be used as the parametric replacement for the **errors.ssNum** message's {0} parameter. Thus, if the Social Security Number custom validation fails, the following error message will be generated by substituting the **prompt.ssNum** message for {0} in the **errors.ssNum** message:

```
Social Security Number is not a valid Social Security Number
```

Internationalizing Validations

Similar to other areas of Struts, Validator fully supports internationalization. Remember that internationalization is the process of tailoring content to a specific locale or region. In Validator's case, internationalization means tailoring validation error messages to a specific locale and/or tailoring actual validation routines to a specific locale. This way, the U.S. and French versions of a Web site can each have their own language-specific validation error messages. Similarly, internationalization enables the U.S. and French versions of a Web site to validate entries in monetary fields differently. The U.S. version requires commas to separate dollar values and a period to demarcate cents (i.e., 123,456.78), whereas the French (Euro monetary system) version requires periods to separate dollar amounts and a comma to demarcate cents (i.e., 123.456,78).

Tailoring validation error messages to a specific locale is built into Struts by way of its Resource Bundle mechanism for externalizing application strings, messages, and labels. You simply create a resource bundle file for each locale you want to support. Each locale-specific resource bundle file will have a locale identifier at the end of the filename that denotes which locale it is for, such as **MessageResources_ja.properties** for Japan.

NOTE *For detailed information on internationalizing a Struts application, see Chapter 10.*

Thus, when Validator goes to load an error message, it will use the locale object that Struts stores in the session (or from the request if Struts is configured that way) to determine which resource bundle file to load the message from. Remember that each validation rule in the **validator-rules.xml** file specifies a key for a validation error message stored in the application's resource bundle files. This key is the same across each locale's resource bundle file, thus allowing Validator to load the appropriate message based on only a locale and a key.

Tailoring validation routines to specific locales is similar to tailoring error messages; you have to define validation definitions in the **validation.xml** file for each locale. The **validation.xml** file contains a **form-validation** tag that contains one or more **formset** tags, which in turn contain one or more **form** tags, and so on:

```
<!DOCTYPE form-validation PUBLIC
          "-//Apache Software Foundation//DTD Commons
            Validator Rules Configuration 1.3.0//EN"
          "http://jakarta.apache.org/commons/dtds/validator_1_3_0.dtd">

<form-validation>
  <formset>
    <form name="auctionForm">
      <field property="bid" depends="mask">
        <var>
          <var-name>mask</var-name>
          <var-value>^\d{1,3}(,?\d{3})*\.?(\d{1,2})?$</var-value>
        </var>
      </field>
    </form>
  </formset>
</form-validation>
```

The **form-set** tag takes optional attributes, **country**, **language**, and **variant**, to tailor its nested forms to a specific locale. In the preceding example, all locales use the same currency validation to validate the "bid" property, because none of the **country**, **language**, or **variant** attributes was specified for the **form-set** tag.

In order to have a generic currency validation for all users of the Web site and a Euro-specific currency validation for users from France, you'd create an additional **form-set** definition specifically for the French users, as shown here:

```
<!DOCTYPE form-validation PUBLIC
          "-//Apache Software Foundation//DTD Commons
            Validator Rules Configuration 1.3.0//EN"
          "http://jakarta.apache.org/commons/dtds/validator_1_3_0.dtd">

<form-validation>
  <formset>
    <form name="auctionForm">
      <field property="bid" depends="required,mask">
        <var>
          <var-name>mask</var-name>
          <var-value>^\d{1,3}(,?\d{3})*\.?(\d{1,2})?$</var-value>
        </var>
      </field>
    </form>
  </formset>
  <formset country="fr">
    <form name="auctionForm">
      <field property="bid" depends="required,mask">
        <var>
          <var-name>mask</var-name>
          <var-value>^\d{1,3}(\.?\d{3})*,?(\d{1,2})?$</var-value>
        </var>
      </field>
    </form>
  </formset>
</form-validation>
```

In this listing, the second **<formset>** definition specifies a **country** attribute set to "fr". That instructs Validator to use the enclosed validation definitions for users with a French locale. Notice that the bid validation in the second **<formset>** definition is different from the first definition, as the period and comma are transposed in the mask value. Thus, the first **<formset>** definition validates that bids are in U.S. currency format and the second definition validates that bids are in Euro currency format.

A powerful feature of using internationalized **<formset>** definitions is that you can define only the validations that are locale-specific, and all other validations are taken from the default **<formset>** definition.

Adding Validator to the Mini HR Application

Now that you've seen the benefits of using the Validator framework and how it works, you are ready to revisit the Mini HR application and replace the hard-coded validation logic with Validator. Following is the list of steps involved in adding the Validator to the Mini HR application:

1. Change **SearchForm** to extend **ValidatorForm**.
2. Create a **validation.xml** file.
3. Add the Validator plugin to the **struts-config.xml** file.
4. Add Validation error messages to the **MessageResources.properties** file.
5. Recompile, repackage, and run the updated application.

The following sections walk through each step of the process in detail.

Change SearchForm to Extend ValidatorForm

The first step in converting the Mini HR application to use Validator is to change **SearchForm** to extend Validator's **ValidatorForm** class instead of extending Struts' basic **ActionForm** class. Recall that **ValidatorForm** extends **ActionForm** and provides an implementation for its **reset( )** and **validate( )** methods that hook into the Validator framework; thus, those methods should be removed from the **SearchForm** class. Additionally, the **isValidSsNum( )** method should be removed from the **SearchForm** class because its functionality is being replaced by Validator as well.

Following is the updated **SearchForm.java** file:

```
package com.jamesholmes.minihr;

import java.util.List;
import org.apache.struts.validator.ValidatorForm;

public class SearchForm extends ValidatorForm
{
  private String name = null;
  private String ssNum = null;
  private List results = null;

  public void setName(String name) {
    this.name = name;
  }
```

```
  public String getName() {
    return name;
  }

  public void setSsNum(String ssNum) {
    this.ssNum = ssNum;
  }

  public String getSsNum() {
    return ssNum;
  }

  public void setResults(List results) {
    this.results = results;
  }

  public List getResults() {
    return results;
  }
}
```

Notice that this file no longer has the **reset( )**, **validate( )**, and **validateSsNum( )** methods and that the class been updated to extend **ValidatorForm**.

Create a validation.xml File

After removing the hard-coded validation logic from **SearchForm**, you must create a **validation.xml** file. This file will inform Validator which validations from the **validator-rules .xml** file should be applied to **SearchForm**. Following is a basic **validation.xml** file that validates that social security numbers have the proper format if entered:

```
<!DOCTYPE form-validation PUBLIC
          "-//Apache Software Foundation//DTD Commons
            Validator Rules Configuration 1.3.0//EN"
          "http://jakarta.apache.org/commons/dtds/validator_1_3_0.dtd">

<form-validation>
  <formset>
    <form name="searchForm">
      <field property="ssNum" depends="mask">
        <arg position="0" key="label.search.ssNum"/>
        <var>
          <var-name>mask</var-name>
          <var-value>^\d{3}-\d{2}-\d{4}$</var-value>
        </var>
      </field>
    </form>
  </formset>
</form-validation>
```

Notice that this file does not contain any validation definitions to ensure that either a name or a social security number was entered, the way the original hard-coded logic did. This is because such logic is complicated to implement with Validator and thus should be implemented using Struts' basic validation mechanism.

Add the Validator Plugin to the struts-config.xml File

After setting up Validator's configuration file, the following snippet must be added to the Struts configuration file to cause Struts to load the Validator plugin:

```
<!-- Validator Configuration -->
<plug-in className="org.apache.struts.validator.ValidatorPlugIn">
  <set-property property="pathnames"
              value="/org/apache/struts/validator/validator-rules.xml,
                     /WEB-INF/validation.xml"/>
</plug-in>
```

Notice that each of the configuration files is specified with the **set-property** tag. The following snippet lists the updated Struts configuration file for Mini HR in its entirety:

```
<!DOCTYPE struts-config PUBLIC
  "-//Apache Software Foundation//DTD Struts Configuration 1.3//EN"
  "http://struts.apache.org/dtds/struts-config_1_3.dtd">

<struts-config>

  <!-- Form Beans Configuration -->
  <form-beans>
    <form-bean name="searchForm"
               type="com.jamesholmes.minihr.SearchForm"/>
  </form-beans>

  <!-- Global Forwards Configuration -->
  <global-forwards>
    <forward name="search" path="/search.jsp"/>
  </global-forwards>

  <!-- Action Mappings Configuration -->
  <action-mappings>
    <action path="/search"
            type="com.jamesholmes.minihr.SearchAction"
            name="searchForm"
            scope="request"
            validate="true"
            input="/search.jsp">
    </action>
  </action-mappings>

  <!-- Message Resources Configuration -->
  <message-resources
    parameter="com.jamesholmes.minihr.MessageResources"/>

  <!-- Validator Configuration -->
  <plug-in className="org.apache.struts.validator.ValidatorPlugIn">
    <set-property property="pathnames"
                value="/org/apache/struts/validator/validator-rules.xml,
                       /WEB-INF/validation.xml"/>
  </plug-in>

</struts-config>
```

Add Validation Error Messages to the MessageResources.properties File

Recall from earlier in this chapter that each validation routine defined in the **validator-rules.xml** file declares a key for an error message in Struts' resource bundle file: **MessageResources.properties**. At run time, Validator uses the keys to look up error messages to return when validations fail. Because you are using the **mask** validation defined in the **validator-rules.xml** file, you must add the following error message for its declared key to the **MessageResources.properties** file:

```
errors.invalid={0} is not valid
```

The following code shows the updated **MessageResources.properties** file in its entirety:

```
# Label Resources
label.search.name=Name
label.search.ssNum=Social Security Number

# Error Resources
error.search.criteria.missing=Search Criteria Missing
error.search.ssNum.invalid=Invalid Social Security Number
errors.header=<font color="red"><cTypeface:Bold>Validation Error(s)</b></font><ul>
errors.footer=</ul><hr width="100%" size="1" noshade="true">
errors.prefix=<li>
errors.suffix=</li>

errors.invalid={0} is not valid
```

Compile, Package, and Run the Updated Application

Because you removed the **reset( )**, **validate( )**, and **validateSsNum( )** methods from **SearchForm** and changed it to extend **ValidatorForm** instead of **ActionForm**, you need to recompile and repackage the Mini HR application before you run it. Assuming that you've made modifications to the original Mini HR application and it was set up in the **c:\java\MiniHR** directory (as described in Chapter 2), you can run the **build.bat** batch file or the **build.xml** Ant script file to recompile the application.

After recompiling Mini HR, you need to repackage it using the following command line:

```
jar cf MiniHR.war *
```

This command should also be run from the directory where you have set up the Mini HR application (e.g., **c:\java\MiniHR**).

Similar to the way you ran Mini HR the first time, you now need to place the new **MiniHR.war** file that you just created into Tomcat's **webapps** directory, delete the **webapps/MiniHR** directory, and start Tomcat. As before, to access the Mini HR application, point your browser to **http://localhost:8080/MiniHR/**. Once you have the updated Mini HR running, try entering valid and invalid social security numbers. As you will see, they are now verified using the new Validator code.

CHAPTER 7

Tiles

Two of the foremost principles that underpin the Struts framework are the *separation of concerns* and *reuse*. These principles can be seen at work throughout the framework. For example, the separation of business logic into a Model layer applies separation of concerns, and the use of a configuration file for declarative coupling of components applies reuse. These principles are not, however, unique to the server side (Model and Controller) of applications.

Client-side (View) development has also been evolving to support the principles of separation of concerns and reuse. For example, cascading style sheets (CSS) allows common style elements to be defined in an external file that can be *sourced in* (that is, its contents included) by several pages. That way, each page does not have to define the same styles over and over. Instead, the pages simply use the common definitions defined in a style sheet. If a style needs to be changed, that change can be made in one file rather than in each page individually. This reduces the amount of time and overhead needed to make global changes, and reduces errors. This is the essence of reuse.

JSP technology supports a similar feature for reuse called *includes*. JSP includes allow other files (JSPs or otherwise) to be sourced in to a JSP, either at compile time or dynamically at run time. This feature is useful for abstracting common sections of pages, such as headers, footers, and menus, into reusable chunks that can be used by several files. If a change needs to be made to a common section, the change can be made once and each of the pages that includes that section will automatically receive the updates.

JSP includes offer both convenience and time savings. They are, however, somewhat limited insofar as the potential for a great deal of duplication still exists. Each JSP that sources in common sections duplicates the include definitions. If the names of one or more files being included change, each of the files including them would have to be updated. For example, assume that you have a set of JSPs called **a.jsp**, **b.jsp**, **c.jsp**, and **d.jsp** that all include **header.jsp**. If you rename **header.jsp** to **mainHeader.jsp**, then you would have to update **a.jsp**, **b.jsp**, **c.jsp**, and **d.jsp** to include **mainHeader.jsp** instead of **header.jsp**. This can be tedious, time consuming, and error prone. To solve this problem, and to enhance Struts, David Geary created the Template Tag Library for Struts that was based on the Composite View design pattern. Later Cedric Dumoulin created the Tiles framework as an enhancement to the Template Tag Library's functionality and as a third-party add-on to Struts. Tiles has since been integrated into the core Struts code base and has been packaged with Struts since version 1.1.

NOTE *Tiles has been well adopted in the Java Web development community and is being used outside of Struts with other Java Web frameworks. Because of this popularity, at the time of this writing an effort is underway to separate Tiles into its own project. This will allow Tiles to continue to evolve independently of Struts. Of course, Struts will still have seamless integration with Tiles.*

Tiles expands the concept of reuse via includes by allowing you to define *layouts* (also known as *templates*) and then specify how the layouts are populated with content. To understand the value of Tiles, first consider how the JSP include paradigm works. Each JSP specifies its layout and explicitly populates that layout through includes. Most JSP layouts are identical, sourcing in the same files in the same places and then having a section of unique content, which is usually body content. Thus, there is significant duplication. Tiles takes the reverse approach.

With Tiles, you define a master layout JSP that specifies each of the includes that fill in the layout and then you define which content should fill in the layout in an external configuration file. The same layout can be used over and over by simply specifying different filler content for the layout in the configuration file.

For example, consider a typical Web site layout that has a header at the top of the page, a menu on the left, body content in the middle, and a footer on the bottom, as shown in Figure 7-1. If you were to implement this page using only JSP includes, each JSP that has this layout would have to explicitly include the header, menu, and footer sections of the page, and the body content would be in the JSP itself. Essentially, the only unique part of the page is the body content.

Alternatively, if you were to implement this layout with Tiles, you'd create one JSP that includes the header, menu, and footer and then dynamically include the body based on a parameter passed to the layout that indicates which JSP to use for the body content. This Tiles layout could then be reused for as many pages as you'd like, and the only thing your content JSPs would have to contain is the body content that goes in the middle of the page. Tiles takes care of wrapping the body content JSP with the layout. As you can see, Tiles significantly enhances JSP development and allows for an even greater amount of reuse than JSP includes offer.

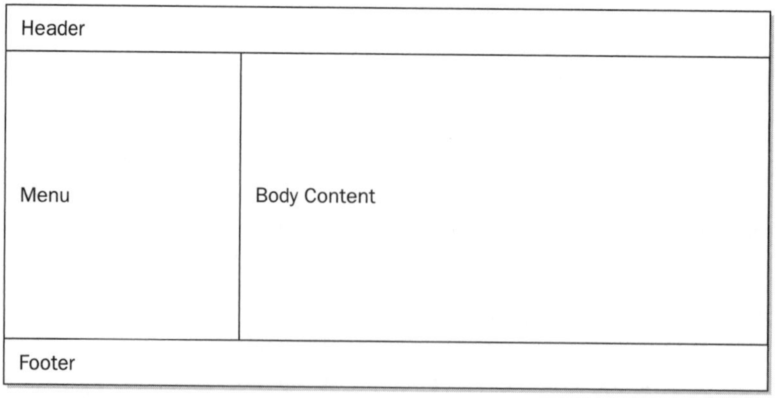

FIGURE 7-1 Typical Web site layout

Tiles Overview

Before getting into the details of using the Tiles framework, it's necessary to give an overview of how Tiles works. Tiles allows you to exploit the concept of JSP includes by providing a framework for defining and dynamically populating page layouts. Each page layout is simply a JSP that defines a template frame (or outline) with placeholders for where content should go. At run time, Tiles replaces the placeholders with their associated content, creating a complete page and unique instance of the layout. To accomplish this, Tiles uses its concepts of *definitions* and *attributes.*

A Tiles definition creates a piece of content that Tiles can insert into a JSP using that definition's name. Each definition consists of a name (or identifier), a layout JSP, and a set of attributes associated with the definition. Once defined, a definition can be included in a page or, as is most often the case, be used as the target of a Struts forward. In both cases, when the definition is encountered, Tiles passes to the layout JSP specified by the definition the set of attributes that were declared for that definition. An attribute value can be the path to a JSP, a literal string, or a list of either.

To facilitate the use of definitions and attributes, Tiles uses an XML configuration file (typically named **tiles-defs.xml**) for storing their definitions. Tiles also provides a JSP tag library for defining definitions and attributes. Additionally, the Tiles Tag Library is used for inserting attributes into JSPs.

Using Tiles

Using the Tiles framework involves these five steps:

1. Enable the Tiles plugin.
2. Create Tiles definitions.
3. Create layout JSPs and use the Tiles Tag Library.
4. Create content JSPs to fill in the layout JSPs.
5. Use the Tiles definitions.

The following sections explain how to configure and use Tiles in detail.

Enabling the Tiles Plugin

Although Tiles comes packaged with Struts, by default Tiles is not enabled. To enable and use Tiles, you have to add the following **<plug-in>** definition to your application's Struts configuration file (e.g., **struts-config.xml**) file:

```
<!-- Tiles Configuration -->
<plug-in className="org.apache.struts.tiles.TilesPlugin">
  <set-property property="definitions-config"
                   value="/WEB-INF/tiles-defs.xml"/>
</plug-in>
```

This definition causes Struts to load and initialize the Tiles plugin for your application. Upon initialization, the plugin loads the comma-delimited list of Tiles configuration files specified by the **definitions-config** property. Each configuration file's path should be specified using a Web application-relative path, as shown in the preceding example.

Note that your application's Struts configuration file must conform to the Struts Configuration DTD, which specifies the order in which elements are to appear in the file. Because of this, you must place the Tiles **<plug-in>** definition in the proper place in the file. The easiest way to ensure that you are properly ordering elements in the file is to use a tool like Struts Console that automatically formats your configuration file so that it conforms to the DTD.

In version 1.3 Struts moved away from using the **RequestProcessor** for customized request processing to using a Jakarta Commons Chain-based solution. As a result of this change, Tiles no longer extends the base Struts **RequestProcessor** to implement its functionality. Instead Tiles now uses a custom chain command and custom chain configuration file with the custom command enabled to handle its processing. For Struts versions 1.3 and later, you must configure the Struts **ActionServlet** definition in the **web.xml** file to use a Tiles-specific chain configuration file. Following is an example of the necessary servlet configuration with the additional configuration details in bold:

```
<servlet>
  <servlet-name>action</servlet-name>
  <servlet-class>org.apache.struts.action.ActionServlet</servlet-class>
  <init-param>
    <param-name>config</param-name>
    <param-value>/WEB-INF/struts-config.xml</param-value>
  </init-param>
  <init-param>
    <param-name>chainConfig</param-name>
    <param-value>org/apache/struts/tiles/chain-config.xml</param-value>
  </init-param>
  <load-on-startup>1</load-on-startup>
</servlet>
```

This will cause Struts to load the Tiles-specific **chain-config.xml** file from the Tiles **.jar** file (e.g., **struts-tiles-1.3.5.jar**).

Creating Tiles Definitions

There are two ways that you can create Tiles definitions and specify their attributes for your application. First, you can define them in a Tiles XML configuration file. Second, you can define them inside JSPs using the Tiles Tag Library. Each approach is described here, along with information on extending definitions, and information on how to use definitions as attribute values.

XML Configuration File-Based Definitions and Attributes

The first, and most often used, way that you can define Tiles definitions and attributes is by placing them in an XML configuration file typically named **tiles-defs.xml**. Of course, you can use another name for the file, but that is the standard name. Upon application startup, Tiles loads this file and places its definitions into memory. Following is a basic example of how to define a definition in a Tiles configuration file:

```
<?xml version="1.0"?>

<!DOCTYPE tiles-definitions PUBLIC
  "-//Apache Software Foundation//DTD Tiles Configuration 1.3//EN"
```

```
  "http://struts.apache.org/dtds/tiles-config_1_3.dtd">

<tiles-definitions>
  <definition name="search.page" path="/mainLayout.jsp">
    <put name="header" value="/header.jsp"/>
    <put name="body"   value="/search.jsp"/>
    <put name="footer" value="/footer.jsp" />
  </definition>
</tiles-definitions>
```

Each definition in the **tiles-defs.xml** file has its own definition that is declared with a **definition** tag. The **definition** tag assigns a logical name to the definition, with the **name** attribute, and specifies the path to a layout JSP for the definition, with the **path** attribute. The logical name given to the definition will be used to refer to the definition inside JSPs and the Struts configuration file. Nested inside the **definition** tag, **put** tags are used to specify the definition's list of attributes.

NOTE *Detailed information on the Tiles configuration file is found in Chapter 19.*

JSP-Based Definitions and Attributes

The second way that you can define a Tiles definition and its attributes is by specifying them with Tiles Tag Library tags inside JSPs. Following is a basic definition defined in a JSP:

```
<%@ taglib uri="http://struts.apache.org/tags-tiles" prefix="tiles" %>

<tiles:definition id="search.page" template="/mainLayout.jsp" >
  <tiles:put name="header" value="/header.jsp" />
  <tiles:put name="body"   value="/search.jsp" />
  <tiles:put name="footer" value="/footer.jsp" />
</tiles:definition>
```

This definition will be stored in a page scope JSP variable named **search.page** (as specified by the **id** attribute of the **definition** tag) so that it can be accessed from other tags. To use this JSP-based definition, you must use the Tiles **insert** tag, as shown next:

```
<tiles:insert beanName="search.page" flush="true"/>
```

Because the **definition** tag stores the definition in a JSP scripting variable, you must use the **beanName** attribute of the **insert** tag to specify the definition. This differs from the way in which you would insert a definition defined in a Tiles configuration file.

The idea behind defining Tiles definitions inside JSPs is that you can define several definitions in a "layout configuration" JSP and then include that JSP in every JSP that uses the definitions. Thus, a layout configuration JSP is similar in purpose to a Tiles configuration file.

Extending Definitions

A powerful and often-used feature of definitions is the ability to have one definition extend another. This functionality is similar to the way inheritance works in Java. When defining a definition, you can specify that the definition extends another definition, instead of specifying a layout JSP for the definition. The child definition inherits the layout JSP and attributes of the parent and can override any of the parent attributes as well as add its own attributes.

For example, you may want to have a master layout definition for your site that all other definitions extend from. The master definition can specify values for the attributes that are common across all pages. The child definitions can then specify values for just the attributes that are unique to that page. Additionally, child definitions can override any of the master definitions' common attribute values when necessary, such as for a page that needs a unique header or footer. Following is an example Tiles configuration file that illustrates a few definition-extending scenarios:

```
<?xml version="1.0"?>

<!DOCTYPE tiles-definitions PUBLIC
  "-//Apache Software Foundation//DTD Tiles Configuration 1.3//EN"
  "http://struts.apache.org/dtds/tiles-config_1_3.dtd">

<tiles-definitions>

  <!-- Main Layout -->
  <definition name="main.layout" path="/mainLayout.jsp">
    <put name="title"  value=""/>
    <put name="header" value="/header.jsp"/>
    <put name="menu"   value="/menu.jsp"/>
    <put name="body"   value=""/>
    <put name="footer" value="/footer.jsp" />
  </definition>

  <!-- Search Page -->
  <definition name="search.page" extends="main.layout">
    <put name="title"  value="Search Page"/>
    <put name="body"   value="/search.jsp"/>
  </definition>

  <!-- Employee Layout -->
  <definition name="employee.layout" extends="main.layout">
    <put name="menu"  value="/employee/menu.jsp"/>
  </definition>

  <!-- Employee Edit Page -->
  <definition name="employeeEdit.page" extends="employee.layout">
    <put name="title"  value="Employee Edit Page"/>
    <put name="body"   value="/employee/edit.jsp"/>
  </definition>

</tiles-definitions>
```

As stated, this file contains a few different extension scenarios. First, the file declares the main layout from which the other definitions will extend. This layout specifies values for the attributes that will be common across most pages. However, it purposely leaves the page-specific attributes' values blank, because they will be overridden by extending definitions. The first extending definition, **search.page**, extends the main layout definition and provides values for the **title** and **body** attributes. The rest of the attributes that are necessary to fill in the main layout will be inherited from the main layout definition. At run time, when the **search.page** definition is used, Tiles will use the **mainLayout.jsp** file and populate it with content from the child and parent definitions, as appropriate.

The second definition-extension scenario represented in the preceding configuration file creates a specific layout by extending the generic main layout and customizing it. The **employee.layout** definition extends the main layout and overrides the **menu** attribute's value to create a new employee-specific layout. Note that the **menu** attribute points to an employee-specific menu JSP. The **employeeEdit.page** definition extends the **employee.layout** layout definition. This final definition, like the **search.page** definition, specifies values for the **title** and **body** attributes. The rest of the attribute values that are necessary to populate the layout JSP are inherited from the parent definition.

Note that Tiles supports an essentially unlimited number of definition extensions. Thus, you could create a generic master definition followed by several more specific definitions that extend it. Then, you could add yet another level of definitions that extend the extended definitions to create even more specific page definitions. This is a very powerful feature and is the key advantage that Tiles has over JSP includes.

Using Tiles Definitions as Attribute Values

Another feature of the Tiles framework is the ability to use definitions as the value for an attribute. This feature allows pages to be constructed in a hierarchical fashion. For instance, you can define a master layout that has a **menu** attribute and, instead of specifying the URL to a JSP as the value for the attribute, specify the name of another definition. A sample configuration file for this scenario is shown next:

```
<?xml version="1.0"?>

<!DOCTYPE tiles-definitions PUBLIC
  "-//Apache Software Foundation//DTD Tiles Configuration 1.3//EN"
  "http://struts.apache.org/dtds/tiles-config_1_3.dtd">

<tiles-definitions>

  <!-- Menu Layout -->
  <definition name="menu.layout" paths="/menu/layout.jsp">
    <put name="menuItem1" value="/meanu/menuItem1.jsp"/>
    <put name="menuItem2" value="/meanu/menuItem2.jsp"/>
    <put name="menuItem3" value="/meanu/menuItem3.jsp"/>
  </definition>

  <!-- Main Layout -->
  <definition name="main.layout" path="/mainLayout.jsp">
    <put name="title"  value=""/>
    <put name="header" value="/header.jsp"/>
    <put name="menu"   value="menu.layout"/>
    <put name="body"   value=""/>
    <put name="footer" value="/footer.jsp" />
  </definition>

  <!-- Search Page -->
  <definition name="search.page" extends="main.layout">
    <put name="title"  value="Search Page"/>
    <put name="body"   value="/search.jsp"/>
  </definition>

</tiles-definitions>
```

In this scenario, the **main.layout** definition has a **menu** attribute whose value points to the name of another definition, **menu.layout**. Tiles intelligently determines the type of value each attribute has and processes its content accordingly. Thus, if an attribute is set to a JSP, then Tiles will use a JSP. If the attribute is set to the name of a definition, Tiles will recognize that and use the definition. This feature allows you to create sophisticated layouts that maximize content reuse.

Creating Layout JSPs and Using the Tiles Tag Library

Creating layout JSPs with the Tiles Tag Library is similar to the way you would go about creating JSPs that leverage JSP's include mechanism. Simply place your layout page's HTML in the JSP and then use Tiles Tag Library tags to source in content. The HTML creates a template (or wire frame) for a page and the Tiles tags act as placeholders for content that will be inserted into the template at run time. Following is a basic layout JSP that illustrates how this works:

```
<%@ taglib uri="http://struts.apache.org/tags-tiles" prefix="tiles" %>

<html>
<head>
<title><tiles:getAsString name="title"/></title>
</head>
<body>

<tiles:insert attribute="header"/>

<table>
<tr>
<td width="20%"><tiles:insert attribute="menu"/></td>
<td width="80%"><tiles:insert attribute="body"/></td>
</tr>
</table>

<tiles:insert attribute="footer"/>

</body>
</html>
```

At run time, when a definition uses this layout, it will make a set of attributes available to the page to be inserted with the Tiles Tag Library's **insert** tag.

NOTE *A complete overview of the Tiles Tag Library is given later in this chapter, beginning in the section "Using the Tiles Tag Library."*

Creating Content JSPs

Content JSPs are used to fill in the placeholders created by layouts. These JSPs simply contain the HTML necessary to fill in a specific section of a layout. You create these JSPs the same way you would create JSPs that are used for includes. You don't, however, specifically source in any of these JSPs into the layout JSPs, as you would if you were using includes. Instead, layout JSPs use Tiles tags to insert attributes whose values point to these content JSPs.

Using the Tiles Definitions

Once you have created Tiles layout JSPs and have defined definitions that use them, you can put the definitions to use. There are two different ways to use definitions: you can insert a definition's content into a JSP, or you can use definitions as the targets of Struts forwards.

The following example illustrates how to insert a Tiles definition into a JSP:

```
<%@ taglib uri="http://struts.apache.org/tags-tiles" prefix="tiles" %>

<html>
<head>
<title>Employee Search</title>
</head>
<body>

<font size="+1">ABC, Inc. Human Resources Portal</font><br>
<hr width="100%" noshade="true">

<tiles:insert definition="search.page"/>

<hr width="100%" noshade="true">

</body>
</html>
```

As you can see, to insert a definition, you just use the Tiles Tag Library's **insert** tag. The content specified by the definition will be processed and inserted in its final state (i.e., all levels of layouts will be collapsed into one). This way of using definitions is very powerful because you can insert definitions that comprise a page's whole content, as shown next. Or you could insert definitions that are only intended to fill a portion of a page with content, as was shown in the first example.

```
<%@ taglib uri="http://struts.apache.org/tags-tiles" prefix="tiles" %>

<tiles:insert definition="search.page"/>
```

The second way to use Tiles definitions is to have them be used as the target of Struts forwards. This way works by having the names of definitions be used as forwards. Instead of a forward pointing to a JSP or another URL, it points to the name of a Tiles definition. At run time, when the Tiles plugin is enabled, Tiles intercepts all requests being made through the Struts controller servlet. Tiles does this by inserting itself into the Struts request processing engine. If Tiles sees a forward whose value is the name of a definition, it will handle the request and return the contents of the definition. Following is an example of how to define a forward in the Struts configuration file that uses a Tiles definition:

```
<global-forwards>
  <forward name="search" path="search.page"/>
</global-forwards>
```

Notice that the **path** attribute specifies the name of a Tiles definition. Tiles will recognize this and handle processing for this forward.

Handling Relative URLS with Tiles

Many page elements such as images, style sheets, and hyperlinks are referred to using *relative URLs* when developing web applications. Relative URLs are those URLs that are relative to their context (e.g., **/rel-dir/image.jpg**) instead of being fully qualified (e.g., http://abc.com/appname/rel-dir/image.jpg). Relative URLs can be very useful during development, as they remove the direct reference to a specific domain name and application context, allowing the pages using them to be portable. The problem with relative URLs, though, occurs when a page using a relative URL to a certain path gets moved to somewhere that path is no longer applicable. This scenario is quite common when working with Tiles because there are common include pages and page-specific resources.

To solve the problem of relative URL portability, you can use the **rewrite** tag from the Struts HTML Tag Library. The **rewrite** tag ensures that relative URLs are prefixed with the proper application context path. Following are a couple of examples of using the rewrite tag for this purpose:

```
<img src="<html:rewrite page='/images/logo.jpg'/>">

<link rel="stylesheet" type="text/css"
    href="<html:rewrite page='/css/master.css'/>">
```

Internationalizing Tiles

Similar to other areas of Struts, Tiles fully supports internationalization. Remember that internationalization is the process of tailoring content to a specific locale or region. For Tiles, internationalization means tailoring Tiles definitions and attributes to a specific locale. That way, the U.S. and French versions of a Web site can each have their own language-specific definitions and attributes, for example.

Although Tiles' internationalization support is similar to the core internationalization support in Struts, it's intended to allow you to provide locale-specific layout differences, not to internationalize text or messages. That should be done with the core Struts internationalization features. Tiles internationalization support is for such things as the differences in the size of internationalized images or the length of internationalized text. For example, using Tiles' internationalization support, you can define one version of a definition that handles the appropriate sizing for images and text for the United States and a second version designed for France, which accommodates the larger images and longer text necessary for the French content. Tiles simply provides the mechanism to define the layout appropriately for each locale.

NOTE *Internationalizing text and images should be left to the core Struts internationalization functionality.*

To tailor Tiles definitions and attributes to a specific locale, you have to create a Tiles XML configuration file for each locale. Each locale-specific configuration file is distinguished by its filename using the same naming scheme that is used for Java Resource Bundles. Thus, to create English and French versions of a set of definitions and their attributes, you would create a file named **tiles-defs_en.xml** for the English version and a file named **tiles-defs_fr.xml** for the French version. The suffix portion of each filename contains the language code for the locale that the file is intended for. At run time, Tiles uses the locale object that

Struts stores in the session (or from the request if Struts is configured that way) to determine which configuration file it should use definitions from to process the current request. Each configuration file should have the same definitions with the same attributes. All of the names of definitions and attributes must be the same (that is, line up) in each file. The values of the definitions and attributes, however, will be specific to the locale of the particular file.

Parallel to the way Java Resource Bundles function, Tiles will attempt to find definitions and attributes for the current request's locale in a configuration file specific to that locale. If the definitions and attributes are not found in the locale-specific configuration file, Tiles will attempt to load them from the default configuration file whose filename does not contain any locale information (e.g., **tiles-defs.xml**). This is especially helpful when you want to tailor only a few definitions to a specific locale. To accomplish this, create a default configuration file (**tiles-defs.xml**) that contains all the "master" Tiles definitions and attributes. Then, create locale-specific configuration files (e.g., **tiles-defs_fr.xml** or **tiles-defs_es.xml**) that override definitions in the default configuration file. You can choose to override as few or as many definitions as you like. At run time, if Tiles cannot find a locale-specific version of a definition, it will automatically use the definition from the default configuration file.

To illustrate how Tiles' internationalization supports works, let's step through an example scenario. Assume that you have a Web site that is available in English (default), French, and Spanish versions. This requires three Tiles configuration files.

The first file, **tiles-defs.xml**, which is shown next, houses the master Tiles definitions for the Web site. Because the default language for the site is English, the English definitions will reside in this file and serve as the default definitions for the other languages when the other languages are not overriding the definitions in this file.

```
<?xml version="1.0"?>

<!DOCTYPE tiles-definitions PUBLIC
  "-//Apache Software Foundation//DTD Tiles Configuration 1.3//EN"
  "http://struts.apache.org/dtds/tiles-config_1_3.dtd">

<tiles-definitions>

  <!-- Search Page -->
  <definition name="search.page" path="/mainLayout.jsp">
    <put name="header" value="/header.jsp"/>
    <put name="body"   value="/search.jsp"/>
    <put name="footer" value="/footer.jsp" />
  </definition>

  <!-- View Employee Page -->
  <definition name="viewEmployee.page" path="/mainLayout.jsp"">
    <put name="header" value="/header.jsp"/>
    <put name="body"   value="/viewEmployee.jsp"/>
    <put name="footer" value="/footer.jsp" />
  </definition>

</tiles-definitions>
```

This configuration file contains two basic page definitions that utilize the same page layout and simply provide different values for the **body** attribute.

The second file, **tiles-defs_fr.xml**, provides French-specific definitions and attributes:

```
<?xml version="1.0"?>

<!DOCTYPE tiles-definitions PUBLIC
  "-//Apache Software Foundation//DTD Tiles Configuration 1.3//EN"
  "http://struts.apache.org/dtds/tiles-config_1_3.dtd">

<tiles-definitions>

  <!-- Search Page -->
  <definition name="search.page" path="/mainLayout_fr.jsp">
    <put name="header" value="/header_fr.jsp"/>
    <put name="body"   value="/search_fr.jsp"/>
    <put name="footer" value="/footer_fr.jsp" />
  </definition>

  <!-- View Employee Page -->
  <definition name="viewEmployee.page" path="/mainLayout_fr.jsp"">
    <put name="header" value="/header_fr.jsp"/>
    <put name="body"   value="/viewEmployee_fr.jsp"/>
    <put name="footer" value="/footer_fr.jsp" />
  </definition>

</tiles-definitions>
```

The definitions in this file mirror those of the default configuration file, with the exception that the values for the definitions and attributes are different. The definition and attribute names are the same so that they match up with those in the default file. Notice that the values for the definition paths are set to a JSP named **mainLayout_fr.jsp**. That is a French-specific version of **mainLayout.jsp**. If the layout JSP itself did not need to change to accommodate the French version, you would leave the path set to **/mainLayout.jsp** and specify only French-specific versions of the attributes inside the definitions. It's up to you to determine how much customization you need or want for each locale.

The third file, **tiles-defs_es.xml**, includes the Spanish-specific definitions and attributes. This file, shown next, includes only a Spanish-specific version of the **search.page** definition.

```
<?xml version="1.0"?>

<!DOCTYPE tiles-definitions PUBLIC
  "-//Apache Software Foundation//DTD Tiles Configuration 1.3//EN"
  "http://struts.apache.org/dtds/tiles-config_1_3.dtd">

<tiles-definitions>

  <!-- Search Page -->
  <definition name="search.page" path="/es/mainLayout.jsp">
    <put name="header" value="/es/header.jsp"/>
    <put name="body"   value="/es/search.jsp"/>
    <put name="footer" value="/es/footer.jsp" />
  </definition>

</tiles-definitions>
```

Because this file contains only a Spanish version of the **search.page** definition, if a request is made for the Spanish version of the **viewEmployee.page** definition, Tiles will (after not finding it in **tiles-defs_es.xml**) look for it in the default configuration file, **tiles-defs.xml**. Notice that the attributes in this file point to JSPs underneath an **es** directory. There are many ways you can organize your application's content to support internationalization. This example places the locale-specific files in a directory dedicated to that locale. The French configuration file points to files whose locale is part of the filename. Which approach you take to organizing content is up to you.

NOTE *Detailed information on internationalizing a Struts application is found in Chapter 10.*

Using the Tiles Tag Library

The Tiles Tag Library provides a set of tags that you can use to create Tiles-based page layouts. Also, as mentioned earlier in this chapter, with the Tiles tags, you can define Tiles definitions inside JSPs instead of (or in addition to) defining them in a Tiles XML configuration file.

To use the Tiles Tag Library in a Struts application, your application's JSPs must declare their use of the library with a JSP **taglib** directive:

```
<%@ taglib uri="http://struts.apache.org/tags-tiles" prefix="tiles" %>
```

Notice that the **prefix** attribute is set to **tiles**. This attribute can be set to whatever you want; however, **tiles** is the accepted default for the Tiles Tag Library. The **prefix** attribute declares the prefix that each tag must have when it is used in the JSP, as shown here:

```
<tiles:insert attribute="header"/>
```

Because **tiles** was defined as the prefix, the **insert** tag was used as shown. However, if you were to choose to use a prefix of **strutstiles**, the tag would be used as follows:

```
<strutstiles:insert attribute="header"/>
```

NOTE *Modern application servers use the* **uri** *attribute of the* **taglib** *directive to automatically resolve the location of the tag library descriptor file. Older application servers that support only JSP version 1.1 and/or version 1.0 require that tag libraries be registered in the* **web.xml** *file so that they can be resolved, as shown here:*

```
<taglib>
  <taglib-uri>http://struts.apache.org/tags-tiles</taglib-uri>
  <taglib-location>/WEB-INF/tlds/struts-tiles.tld</taglib-location>
</taglib>
```

The Tiles Tag Library Tags

Table 7-1 lists each of the tags in the Tiles Tag Library and provides a short description of each tag's purpose. The remainder of this section discusses each tag in detail, including a complete description of the tag, a table listing each of the tag's attributes, and a usage example for the tag. In the tables that describe each tag's attributes, pay special attention to the Accepts JSP Expression and Required columns.

Tag	Description
add	Defines an entry for a list created with the **putList** tag.
definition	Defines a tile (which is a region within a page) and stores it in a JSP scripting variable.
get	Deprecated. Originally for compatibility with the now-defunct Template Tag Library. Use the **insert** tag instead.
getAsString	Renders the value of a Tiles attribute to the JSP's output stream.
importAttribute	Stores the values of all defined Tiles attributes in JSP scripting variables.
initComponentDefinitions	Initializes the Tiles definition factory with definitions from a Tiles XML configuration file.
insert	Inserts a Tiles definition or attribute into a JSP page.
put	Defines an attribute for a definition.
putList	Defines a list attribute (of **java.util.List** type) containing an ordered collection of individual attributes.
useAttribute	Stores the value of a Tiles attribute in a JSP scripting variable.

Table 7-1 The Tiles Tag Library Tags

The Required column simply denotes whether the given attribute is required when using the tag. In addition to the required column denoting whether an attribute is required, the rows for required attributes are highlighted in gray so that you can determine at a glance which attributes are required.

If an attribute is required and you do not specify it when using the tag, the tag will throw a **javax.servlet.jsp.JspException** at run time. Note that you can declare an error page in your JSP with a **page** directive to capture any **JspException**s that might be thrown, as shown here:

```
<%@ page errorPage="error.jsp" %>
```

If an exception occurs, the page specified by the **errorPage** attribute will be internally redirected to display an error page.

The Accepts JSP Expression column denotes whether or not the given attribute's value can be specified with a JSP expression. If a JSP expression is used to specify an attribute value, the expression must comprise the complete value, quote (") to quote ("), as shown here.
Correct:

```
<tiles:put name="<%=title%>">
```

Incorrect:

```
<tiles:put name="<%=title%>-title">
```

Notice in the incorrect example that "-title" is used as part of the value for the **name** attribute following the expression. This is invalid because there are extra characters between the end of the expression and the ending quote.

A corrected version of the incorrect example follows:

```
<tiles:put name="<%=title + "-title"%>"/>
```

The concatenation of "-title" is now part of the expression and the expression comprises the complete value for the attribute.

The add Tag

The **add** tag is used to define an entry for a list created with the **putList** tag. There are two ways that the value for the entry can be specified. The value can be specified with the **value** attribute, or the value can be placed between opening and closing **add** tags, as shown next:

```
<tiles:add>value goes here</tiles:add>
```

Attributes

Attribute	Description	Accepts JSP Expression	Required
beanName	Specifies the name of an object whose value will be used for this entry. If the **property** attribute is also specified, one of the fields of the object defined by this attribute will have its getter method called to return the object whose value will be used for this entry.	Yes	No
beanProperty	Specifies the field of the object specified by the **name** attribute whose value will be used for this entry.	Yes	No
beanScope	Specifies the scope (*application, page, request,* or *session*) to look in for the object specified by the **name** attribute. If not specified, each scope will be searched, in this order: page, request, session, and then application.	No	No
content	Deprecated. Originally for compatibility with the now-defunct Template Tag Library. Use the **value** attribute instead.	Yes	No
direct	Deprecated. Originally for compatibility with the now-defunct Template Tag Library. Use the **type** attribute set to "string" instead.	No	No
role	Specifies the role the currently authenticated user must have for this entry to be added to the enclosing list. If the user is not in the specified role, the entry will not be added to the list.	Yes	No
type	Specifies the type (*string, page,* or *definition*) of the value. If present, it indicates how the value specified with the **value** attribute is treated.	No	No
value	Specifies the value for this entry.	No	No

Example Usage

The following example illustrates the basic usage of the **add** tag:

```
<tiles:insert page="/mainLayout.jsp">
  <tiles:putList name="menu">
    <tiles:add value="Home"/>
    <tiles:add value="Products"/>
    <tiles:add value="Search"/>
  </tiles:putList>
</tiles:insert>
```

Each **add** definition is added to the enclosing list in the order specified.

The definition Tag

The **definition** tag is used to define a tile (which is a region within a page) and store it in a JSP scripting variable. Additionally, this tag allows you to specify the scope in which the JSP scripting variable should be placed. Once this definition is defined, it can be inserted into JSPs by using the **insert** tag.

Attributes

Attribute	Description	Accepts JSP Expression	Required
extends	Specifies the name of another definition that this definition extends.	Yes	No
id	Specifies the name of the JSP variable that will hold this definition.	No	Yes
page	Specifies the URL for the tile.	Yes	No
role	Specifies the role the currently authenticated user must have for this definition to be created. If the user is not in the specified role, the definition will not be created.	Yes	No
scope	Specifies the scope (*application, page, request,* or *session*) in which the JSP scripting variable defined by the **id** attribute will be stored. If not specified, the JSP scripting variable will be stored in page scope.	No	No
template	Deprecated. Originally for compatibility with the now-defunct Template Tag Library. Use the **page** attribute instead.	Yes	No

Example Usage

The following example illustrates the basic usage of the **definition** tag:

```
<tiles:definition name="mainLayout"
                  page="/layouts/main.jsp">
  <tiles:put name="header" value="/layouts/header.jsp"/>
  <tiles:put name="footer" value="/layouts/footer.jsp"/>
</tilesdefinition>
```

Each of the attributes nested underneath the **definition** tag can be accessed by the JSP specified with the **page** attribute.

The getAsString Tag

The **getAsString** tag is used to render the value of a Tiles attribute to the JSP's output stream.

Attributes

Attribute	Description	Accepts JSP Expression	Required
ignore	Accepts *true* or *false* to specify whether this tag should return without error if the specified Tiles attribute does not exist. Defaults to *false*, which will cause a run-time exception to be thrown if the attribute does not exist.	Yes	No
name	Specifies the name of a Tiles attribute whose value should be rendered.	Yes	Yes
role	Specifies the role the currently authenticated user must have for the specified Tiles attribute to be rendered.	Yes	No

Example Usage

The following example illustrates how to use the **getAsString** tag:

```
<tiles:getAsString name="title"/>
```

This example renders the value of the **title** attribute to the JSP's output stream.

The importAttribute Tag

The **importAttribute** tag is used to store the values of all defined Tiles attributes in JSP scripting variables. Additionally, this tag allows you to specify the scope in which the JSP scripting variables should be placed. This tag functions similarly to the **useAttribute** tag in that it can store the value of a specific attribute in a JSP scripting variable. However, it differs in that it can import all attributes at once and that it does not have an **id** attribute to specify the name of the JSP scripting variable in which values will be stored.

Attributes

Attribute	Description	Accepts JSP Expression	Required
ignore	Accepts *true* or *false* to specify whether this tag should return without error if the specified Tiles attribute does not exist. Defaults to *false*, which will cause a run-time exception to be thrown if the attribute does not exist.	Yes	No
name	Specifies the name of a Tiles attribute that should be imported.	Yes	No

Attribute	Description	Accepts JSP Expression	Required
scope	Specifies the scope (*application, page, request,* or *session*) that attribute values should be stored in. If not specified, JSP scripting variables will be stored in page scope.	No	No

Example Usage

The following example illustrates how to use the **importAttribute** tag:

```
<tiles:importAttribute/>
```

This example stores the values of all defined Tiles attributes in JSP scripting variables. Alternatively, you could import just one attribute by specifying its name with the **name** attribute, as shown here:

```
<tiles:importAttribute name="title"/>
```

The initComponentDefinitions Tag

The **initComponentDefinitions** tag is used to initialize the Tiles definition factory with definitions from a Tiles XML configuration file. This tag was created when Tiles was initially a third-party add-on to Struts. At that time, Tiles required you to use a special subclass of **ActionServlet** to initialize the definition factory. Alternatively, you could use this tag to initialize the factory. However, now that Tiles has been integrated into the core of Struts, this tag is no longer relevant. The Tiles plugin takes care of initializing the definition factory now.

Attributes

Attribute	Description	Accepts JSP Expression	Required
classname	Specifies the fully qualified class name of the Tiles definition factory to use.	No	No
file	Specifies the Tiles configuration file containing the definitions for the factory.	No	Yes

Example Usage

The following example illustrates how to use the **initComponentDefinitions** tag:

```
<tiles:initComponentDefinitions file="tiles-defs.xml"/>
```

As you can see, using this tag is straightforward.

The insert Tag

The **insert** tag is used to insert a Tiles definition or attribute into a JSP page. Additionally, this tag can be used to create and insert a definition at the same time by specifying a layout JSP with the **page** attribute and optionally nesting **put** tags inside this tag.

Attributes

Attribute	Description	Accepts JSP Expression	Required
attribute	Specifies the name of an attribute to insert.	No	No
beanName	Specifies the name of an object whose value will be inserted into the JSP. If the **property** attribute is also specified, one of the fields of the object defined by this attribute will have its getter method called to return the object whose value will be inserted into the JSP.	Yes	No
beanProperty	Specifies the field of the object specified by the **name** attribute whose value will be inserted into the JSP.	Yes	No
beanScope	Specifies the scope (*application, page, request,* or *session*) to look in for the object specified by the **name** attribute. If not specified, each scope will be searched, in this order: page, request, session, and then application.	No	No
component	Deprecated. Use the **page** attribute instead.	Yes	No
controllerClass	Specifies the fully qualified class name of a controller object that is executed before this definition is inserted.	Yes	No
controllerUrl	Specifies the URL for a controller that is executed before this definition is inserted.	Yes	No
definition	Specifies the name of a definition to insert.	Yes	No
flush	Accepts *true* or *false* to specify whether the JSP's output stream should be flushed before this definition is inserted. Defaults to *false.*	*No*	*No*
ignore	Accepts *true* or *false* to specify whether this tag should return without error if the specified Tiles attribute does not exist. Defaults to *false,* which will cause a run-time exception to be thrown if the attribute does not exist.	Yes	No
name	Specifies the name of an entity (definition or attribute) to insert.	Yes	No
page	Specifies the URL to a page to insert into the JSP.	Yes	No
role	Specifies the role the currently authenticated user must have for the specified attribute to be inserted. If the user is not in the specified role, the attribute will not be inserted.	Yes	No
template	Deprecated. Originally for compatibility with the now-defunct Template Tag Library. Use the **page** attribute instead.	Yes	No

Example Usage

The following example illustrates the basic usage of the **insert** tag:

```
<tiles:insert attribute="header"/>
```

This example inserts an attribute named "header" into a JSP.

To insert a definition, you use the **definition** attribute, as shown next:

```
<tiles:insert definition="tabLayout"/>
```

This example inserts an entire definition into a JSP.

As mentioned, you can also use the **insert** tag to create and insert a definition:

```
<tiles:insert page="/layouts/tabLayout.jsp">
  <tiles:put name="header" value="/tabHeader.jsp"/>
  <tiles:put name="body" value="/search.jsp"/>
  <tiles:put name="footer" value="/tabFooter.jsp"/>
</tiles:insert>
```

This type of insertion is useful for declaring the attributes that get passed to a layout JSP from inside the JSP instead of in a Tiles configuration file.

The put Tag

The **put** tag is used to define an attribute for a definition. There are two ways that the value for the attribute can be specified. The value can be specified with the **value** attribute, or the value can be placed between opening and closing **put** tags, as shown next:

```
<tiles:put name="header">value goes here</tiles:put>
```

Attributes

Attribute	Description	Accepts JSP Expression	Required
beanName	Specifies the name of an object whose value will be used for this attribute. If the **property** attribute is also specified, one of the fields of the object defined by this attribute will have its getter method called to return the object whose value will be used for this attribute.	Yes	No
beanProperty	Specifies the field of the object specified by the **name** attribute whose value will be used for this attribute.	Yes	No
beanScope	Specifies the scope (*application, page, request,* or *session*) to look in for the object specified by the **name** attribute. If not specified, each scope will be searched, in this order: page, request, session, and then application.	No	No
content	Deprecated. Originally for compatibility with the now-defunct Template Tag Library. Use the **value** attribute instead.	Yes	No

Attribute	Description	Accepts JSP Expression	Required
direct	Deprecated. Originally for compatibility with the now-defunct Template Tag Library. Use the **value** attribute instead.	No	No
name	Specifies the name for the attribute.	No	No
role	Specifies the role the currently authenticated user must have for this attribute to be created. If the user is not in the role, this attribute will not be created.	Yes	No
type	Specifies the type (*string, page,* or *definition*) of the value. If present, it indicates how the value specified with the **value** attribute is treated.	No	No
value	Specifies the value for the attribute.	Yes	No

Example Usage

The following example illustrates the basic usage of the **put** tag:

```
<tiles:definition name="mainLayout"
                  page="/layouts/main.jsp">
  <tiles:put name="header" value="/layouts/header.jsp"/>
  <tiles:put name="footer" value="/layouts/footer.jsp"/>
</tiles:definition>
```

Defining attributes with the **put** tag is as simple as specifying their names and values.

The putList Tag

The **putList** tag is used to define a list attribute (of **java.util.List** type) containing an ordered collection of individual attributes. The elements of the list are set by nesting instances of the **add** tag or instances of this tag. This tag must be nested inside either the **definition** tag or the **insert** tag.

Attribute

Attribute	Description	Accepts JSP Expression	Required
name	Specifies the name of the attribute.	No	Yes

Example Usage

The following example illustrates how to use the **putList** tag:

```
<tiles:insert page="/mainLayout.jsp">
  <tiles:putList name="menu">
    <tiles:add value="Home"/>
    <tiles:add value="Products"/>
    <tiles:add value="Search"/>
  </tiles:putList>
</tiles:insert>
```

This example creates a **java.util.List**-based Tiles attribute named **menu** containing the values specified with the nested **add** tags.

You can also create hierarchical structures with the **putList** tag by nesting instances of the **putList** tag inside itself, as shown next:

```
<tiles:putList name="menu">
  <tiles:add value="Home"/>
  <tiles:putList name="Products">
    <tiles:add value="Products Menu Item 1"/>
    <tiles:add value="Products Menu Item 2"/>
  </tiles:putList>
  <tiles:add value="Search"/>
</tiles:putList>
```

Tiles allows you to nest the **putList** tags to any level for whatever hierarchal structure you need.

The useAttribute Tag

The **useAttribute** tag is used to store the value of a Tiles attribute in a JSP scripting variable. Additionally, this tag allows you to specify which scope the JSP scripting variable should be placed in.

Attributes

Attribute	Description	Accepts JSP Expression	Required
classname	Deprecated. This attribute is no longer used.	No	No
id	Specifies the name of the JSP variable that will hold the specified attribute's value.	No	No
ignore	Accepts *true* or *false* to specify whether this tag should return without error if the specified Tiles attribute does not exist. Defaults to *false*, which will cause a run-time exception to be thrown if the attribute does not exist.	Yes	No
name	Specifies the name of a Tiles attribute whose value should be stored.	Yes	Yes
scope	Specifies the scope (*application, page, request,* or *session*) in which the JSP scripting variable defined by the **id** attribute will be stored. If not specified, the JSP scripting variable will be stored in page scope.	No	No

Example Usage

The following example illustrates how to use the **useAttribute** tag:

```
<tiles:useAttribute name="title"/>
```

This example stores the value of the Tiles attribute named **title** in a JSP scripting variable with the same name.

If you want to store the value in a JSP scripting variable with a different name, you must use the **id** attribute, as shown next:

```
<tiles:useAttribute id="pageTitle" name="title"/>
```

Additionally, you can specify the scope of the JSP scripting variable that the attribute value will be stored in with the **scope** attribute:

```
<tiles:useAttribute id="pageTitle" name="title" scope="session"/>
```

Adding Tiles to the Mini HR Application

Now that you've reviewed the benefits of using the Tiles framework and how it works, you are ready to update the Mini HR application to use Tiles. Following is the list of steps that you must follow to add Tiles to the Mini HR application:

1. Create layout JSPs.
2. Update existing JSPs to work with layouts.
3. Create a **tiles-defs.xml** Tiles configuration file.
4. Update the **struts-config.xml** Struts configuration file.
5. Repackage and run the updated application.

The following sections walk through each step of the process in detail.

Create Layout JSPs

This first step demonstrates how to create one layout, to illustrate the basic concepts of Tiles. This layout will be based on the structure of the application's existing pages. Following is the original **search.jsp** page that will be used to extract the common template:

```
<%@ taglib uri="http://struts.apache.org/tags-bean" prefix="bean" %>
<%@ taglib uri="http://struts.apache.org/tags-html" prefix="html" %>
<%@ taglib uri="http://struts.apache.org/tags-logic" prefix="logic" %>

<html>
<head>
<title>ABC, Inc. Human Resources Portal - Employee Search</title>
</head>
<body>

<font size="+1">
ABC, Inc. Human Resources Portal - Employee Search
</font><br>
<hr width="100%" noshade="true">

<html:errors/>

<html:form action="/search">

<table>
<tr>
<td align="right"><bean:message key="label.search.name"/>:</td>
<td><html:text property="name"/></td>
</tr>
```

```
<tr>
<td></td>
<td>-- or --</td>
</tr>
<tr>
<td align="right"><bean:message key="label.search.ssNum"/>:</td>
<td><html:text property="ssNum"/> (xxx-xx-xxxx)</td>
</tr>
<tr>
<td></td>
<td><html:submit/></td>
</tr>
</table>

</html:form>

<logic:present name="searchForm" property="results">

<hr width="100%" size="1" noshade="true">

<bean:size id="size" name="searchForm" property="results"/>
<logic:equal name="size" value="0">
<center><font color="red"><cTypeface:Bold>No Employees Found</b></font></center>
</logic:equal>

<logic:greaterThan name="size" value="0">
<table border="1">
<tr>
<th>Name</th>
<th>Social Security Number</th>
</tr>
<logic:iterate id="result" name="searchForm" property="results">
<tr>
<td><bean:write name="result" property="name"/></td>
<td><bean:write name="result" property="ssNum"/></td>
</tr>
</logic:iterate>
</table>
</logic:greaterThan>

</logic:present>

</body>
<html>
```

The body content of the page is shown in bold. This section will be different for each distinct page. The rest of the page, however, will be consistent across several pages, thus allowing for it to be abstracted into a general-purpose layout.

There are three JSP files that make up the layout: **mainLayout.jsp**, **header.jsp**, and **footer.jsp**. The **mainLayout.jsp** file is shown here:

```
<%@ taglib uri="http://struts.apache.org/tags-tiles" prefix="tiles" %>

<html>
<head>
```

```
<title><tiles:getAsString name="title"/></title>
</head>
<body>

<tiles:insert attribute="header"/>

<tiles:insert attribute="body"/>

<tiles:insert attribute="footer"/>

</body>
</html>
```

This JSP defines the layout's template and is used to source in the other layout JSPs as well as the body content that will be defined by pages utilizing the layout. The body content and other layout JSPs are sourced in with **<tiles:insert>** tags. These tags specify the names of attributes defined in the Tiles configuration file whose values are the names of the JSPs that should be inserted into the JSP at run time. Notice the use of the **<tiles:getAsString>** tag. This tag works similarly to the **<tiles:insert>** tag, but instead of using the specified attribute's value as the name of a page to include, it is used as a literal string. This is useful for defining variables that can be customized by page definitions that extend layout definitions in the Tiles configuration file.

Following are the header and footer layout JSPs.

header.jsp:

```
<font size="+1">ABC, Inc. Human Resources Portal</font><br>
<hr width="100%" noshade="true">
```

footer.jsp:

```
<hr width="100%" noshade="true">
Copyright &copy; ABC, Inc.
```

As you can see, the **header.jsp** and **footer,jsp** files are quite simple and do not contain much HTML. The content of these JSPs could have been placed directly in the **mainLayout.jsp** file instead of here and content pages would still only have to contain the body content of the page. However, breaking the pages up into smaller chunks allows for more flexibility in how layouts are used. For example, if you wanted all pages to have the standard header and footer, you wouldn't have to worry about changing anything. On the other hand, if you needed some pages to have a custom header and footer and others to use the standard ones, separating the header and footer into discrete chunks would allow you to do that. You would simply define values for the header and footer attributes at the layout level, and each page that wanted a custom header, footer, or both would override the necessary attributes with new values at the page level. This will make more sense after you see the Tiles configuration file, which is discussed shortly.

Update Existing JSPs to Work with Layouts

Once you have created the layout JSPs, the next step is to update the application's original JSPs to contain only the body content of their pages. To do this, you must remove each of the pieces of the original page that were used to craft the common layout. Following is the updated **search.jsp** page containing only body content:

```
<%@ taglib uri="http://struts.apache.org/tags-bean" prefix="bean" %>
<%@ taglib uri="http://struts.apache.org/tags-html" prefix="html" %>
<%@ taglib uri="http://struts.apache.org/tags-logic" prefix="logic" %>

<html:errors/>

<html:form action="/search">

<table>
<tr>
<td align="right"><bean:message key="label.search.name"/>:</td>
<td><html:text property="name"/></td>
</tr>
<tr>
<td></td>
<td>-- or --</td>
</tr>
<tr>
<td align="right"><bean:message key="label.search.ssNum"/>:</td>
<td><html:text property="ssNum"/> (xxx-xx-xxxx)</td>
</tr>
<tr>
<td></td>
<td><html:submit/></td>
</tr>
</table>

</html:form>

<logic:present name="searchForm" property="results">

<hr width="100%" size="1" noshade="true">

<bean:size id="size" name="searchForm" property="results"/>
<logic:equal name="size" value="0">
<center><font color="red"><cTypeface:Bold>No Employees Found</b></font></center>
</logic:equal>

<logic:greaterThan name="size" value="0">
<table border="1">
<tr>
<th>Name</th>
<th>Social Security Number</th>
</tr>
<logic:iterate id="result" name="searchForm" property="results">
<tr>
<td><bean:write name="result" property="name"/></td>
<td><bean:write name="result" property="ssNum"/></td>
</tr>
</logic:iterate>
</table>
</logic:greaterThan>

</logic:present>
```

As you can see, the updated page no longer contains the header or footer portions of the content. The search page did not have a true footer, so the content placed in the **footer.jsp** file is new. At run time, the layout JSPs will surround the contents of this updated page with the common layout content to create the complete page.

Because the **search.jsp** page contains only body content now, linking directly to it from the **index.jsp** page is no longer a valid option. Instead, the link to the search page needs to point to the Tiles definition for the search page. This is accomplished by linking to an action mapping that forwards to the Tiles definition. The updated **index.jsp** is shown next with the updated link in bold:

```
<%@ taglib uri="http://struts.apache.org/tags-html" prefix="html" %>

<html>
<head>
<title>ABC, Inc. Human Resources Portal</title>
</head>
<body>

<font size="+1">ABC, Inc. Human Resources Portal</font><br>

<hr width="100%" noshade="true">

&#149; Add an Employee<br>
&#149; <html:link action="/viewSearch">Search for Employees</html:link><br>

</body>
</html>
```

Create a tiles-defs.xml Tiles Configuration File

As mentioned, there are two ways to declare Tiles layouts: with Tiles tags in a master JSP that gets included into each of the layout JSPs or by declaring them in an XML configuration file. This example uses the configuration file option because it is the most flexible and easy to maintain approach. Following is the **tiles-defs.xml** file that declares the layouts. This file should be placed inside the Mini HR **/WEB-INF/** folder.

```
<?xml version="1.0"?>

<!DOCTYPE tiles-definitions PUBLIC
  "-//Apache Software Foundation//DTD Tiles Configuration 1.3//EN"
  "http://struts.apache.org/dtds/tiles-config_1_3.dtd">

<tiles-definitions>

  <!-- Main Layout -->
  <definition name="main.layout" path="/mainLayout.jsp">
    <put name="title"  value=""/>
    <put name="header" value="/header.jsp"/>
    <put name="body"   value=""/>
    <put name="footer" value="/footer.jsp" />
  </definition>

  <!-- Search Page -->
  <definition name="search.page" extends="main.layout">
```

```
    <put name="title"
        value="ABC, Inc. Human Resources Portal - Employee Search"/>
    <put name="body"   value="/search.jsp"/>
  </definition>

</tiles-definitions>
```

There are two Tiles definitions in this file. The first definition in the file declares a layout named **main.layout**. The **.layout** extension given to the definition's name is used to denote that it is a *layout* definition. This is not a formal naming scheme; however, it is a simple way to distinguish the types of definitions. Generally speaking, layout definitions specify the template for a page and the list of attributes whose values will be used to fill in the template. *Page* definitions extend layout definitions and provide values for the attributes defined in the extended layout. So, essentially, page definitions are instances of a layout with attributes set to the content for a specific page.

Notice that the first definition defines four attributes with **put** tags. These attributes will be available for use by the layout JSP specified by the **path** attribute. The layout JSP uses these attributes to supply it with the locations of its content. Additionally, attributes can be used to supply literal strings, as is the case with the **title** attribute. This attribute will be used by **mainLayout.jsp** to enable a dynamic title based on the value set by page definitions that extend the layout definition.

The second definition in the file declares a page definition named **search.page**. This definition extends the **main.layout** layout definition and supplies values for the attributes that don't have values in the layout definition. This definition can override any of the attributes in the layout definition if so desired; however, only the **title** and **body** attributes are overridden in this case.

Update the struts-config.xml Struts Configuration File

After you have created the Tiles configuration file, you must update Mini HR's **struts-config .xml** file to point to Tiles definitions instead of pointing directly to JSPs for each page that has been converted to use Tiles. You also must add a new action mapping that forwards to the search page for the link in the **index.jsp** page. Additionally, the Tiles plugin must be added to the file.

Without Tiles, forward and action definitions point directly to JSPs. With Tiles, they point to the page's definition in the Tiles configuration file. For example, before, the **search** action pointed directly to **search.jsp**, as shown here:

```
<action path="/search"
        type="com.jamesholmes.minihr.SearchAction"
        name="searchForm"
       scope="request"
    validate="true"
       input="/search.jsp"/>
```

However, now the action will point to the search page's Tiles definition, as shown here:

```
<action path="/search"
        type="com.jamesholmes.minihr.SearchAction"
        name="searchForm"
```

```
        scope="request"
     validate="true"
        input="search.page"/>
```

At run time, the Tiles plugin will determine if a specified page is the name of a Tiles definition or an actual path to a page. If a Tiles definition is specified, then Tiles will process the page accordingly; otherwise, normal Struts processing will take place.

Because the **search.jsp** page contains only body content now, linking directly to it from the **index.jsp** page is no longer a valid option. Instead, the link to the search page needs to point to the Tiles definition for the search page. To accomplish that, an action mapping that forwards to the Tiles definition must be added to the Struts configuration file, as shown next:

```
<action path="/viewSearch"
     forward="search.page"/>
```

This action mapping then is referenced via the HTML Tag Library's **link** tag from the **index.jsp** page.

To add the Tiles plugin to the application, you must add the following snippet to **struts-config.xml**:

```
<!-- Tiles Configuration -->
<plug-in className="org.apache.struts.tiles.TilesPlugin">
  <set-property property="definitions-config"
                   value="/WEB-INF/tiles-defs.xml"/>
</plug-in>
```

This causes Struts to load the Tiles plugin at application startup. Notice that the Tiles configuration file is specified with the **set-property** tag. You can specify multiple configuration files by providing a comma-delimited list of files.

The following code shows the updated Struts configuration file for Mini HR in its entirety. The sections that have changed or that have been added are shown in bold.

```
<?xml version="1.0"?>

<!DOCTYPE struts-config PUBLIC
  "-//Apache Software Foundation//DTD Struts Configuration 1.3//EN"
  "http://struts.apache.org/dtds/struts-config_1_3.dtd">

<struts-config>

  <!-- Form Beans Configuration -->
  <form-beans>
    <form-bean name="searchForm"
               type="com.jamesholmes.minihr.SearchForm"/>
  </form-beans>

  <!-- Action Mappings Configuration -->
  <action-mappings>
    <action path="/viewSearch"
         forward="search.page"/>

    <action path="/search"
```

```
            type="com.jamesholmes.minihr.SearchAction"
            name="searchForm"
           scope="request"
        validate="true"
           input="search.page"/>
  </action-mappings>

  <!-- Message Resources Configuration -->
  <message-resources
    parameter="com.jamesholmes.minihr.MessageResources"/>

  <!-- Tiles Configuration -->
  <plug-in className="org.apache.struts.tiles.TilesPlugin">
    <set-property property="definitions-config"
                     value="/WEB-INF/tiles-defs.xml"/>
  </plug-in>

</struts-config>
```

Repackage and Run the Updated Application

Because no Java code was modified during this process, it's not necessary to recompile the Mini HR application. However, several files have been added and a few have been modified, so the application needs to be repackaged and redeployed before it is run. Assuming you've made modifications to the original Mini HR application and it was set up in the **c:\java\MiniHR** directory (as described in Chapter 2), the following command line will repackage the application when run from **c:\java\MiniHR**:

```
jar cf MiniHR.war *
```

Similar to the way you ran Mini HR the first time, you now need to place the new **MiniHR.war** file that you just created into Tomcat's **webapps** directory, delete the **webapps/MiniHR** directory, and start Tomcat. As before, to access the Mini HR application, point your browser to **http://localhost:8080/MiniHR/**. Once you have the updated Mini HR running, everything should work as it did before. However, now you can add new pages and make global changes to the application with minimal effort.

CHAPTER 8

Declarative Exception Handling

A major part of developing Java applications is handling error conditions, and Struts applications are no exception to that rule. Like most other such applications, Struts bases its error handling around Java's exception-handling mechanism. However, as of version 1.1, Struts supports a powerful exception-handling mechanism called *declarative exception handling*. Declarative exception handling is a mechanism that lets you specify how an exception should be handled, but without having to include the handler within your application's Java code. Instead, the exception handler is declared in the Struts configuration file (e.g., **struts-config.xml**). Declarative exception handling enables you to change how exceptions are handled without having to recompile your application's code. You simply update the Struts configuration file and restart the application. This is a significant advantage.

Prior to version 1.1, exception handling in Struts applications functioned much the same way as it does in most other applications. Inside your code, you had to have several **try-catch** blocks to handle each of the exceptions that could be thrown. While this solution works and is effective, there is often a great deal of overlap between different parts (e.g., **Action** classes) of a Struts application that have to implement the same exception processing logic. For instance, if two **Action** classes interface with the same business service and that service throws a custom business exception, each class would have to implement logic to handle the exception being thrown when something goes awry. Now, imagine that you have 20 or 30 **Action** classes that use a service (or set of services) that could throw a custom business exception. There would be a great deal of exception-handling logic duplicated across those **Action** classes. Struts' declarative exception-handling mechanism allows you to create a common exception handler that can be reused by all of those actions. This centralizes all of the exception-handling logic in one place and reduces the duplication of code.

This chapter illustrates how to configure and use Struts' built-in exception handler and provides instructions for creating your own custom exception handler. Finally, this chapter steps through the process of updating the Mini HR application to take advantage of declarative exception handling.

Configuring Struts' Exception Handler

Using Struts' declarative exception-handling mechanism is very simple. All you have to do is add exception handler definitions to your application's Struts configuration file. Exception handler definitions work in much the same way as forward definitions. You can create global exception handler definitions and/or create action-specific handlers. Each exception handler definition specifies the exception that it is to handle, a key to an error message in the application resource bundle (e.g., **MessageResources.properties**), and the path to a page to forward to when the exception is caught by the handler. Following is an example global exception handler definition:

```
<global-exceptions>
  <exception
    type="com.jamesholmes.minihr.NoResultsFoundException"
     key="error.NoResultsFoundException"
    path="/exception.jsp"/>
</global-exceptions>
```

The **type** attribute specifies the fully qualified class name of the exception that the handler is for. When an exception of this type is thrown, the exception handler will take control and process the exception. The **key** attribute specifies the name of a key in the application resource bundle file that will be used to populate an **ActionMessage** object that will be passed to the page specified by the **path** attribute. The **path** attribute specifies the path to a page that will be forwarded to by the exception handler when the specified exception type is thrown. The page can then display the error message placed in the **ActionMessage** object, if so desired.

The second way that exception handlers can be defined is by nesting them inside action definitions, as shown next:

```
<!-- Action Mappings Configuration -->
<action-mappings>
  <action path="/search"
          type="com.jamesholmes.minihr.SearchAction"
          name="searchForm"
          scope="request"
          validate="true"
          input="/search.jsp">
    <exception
      type="com.jamesholmes.minihr.NoResultsFoundException"
       key="error.NoResultsFoundException"
      path="/exception.jsp"/>
  </action>
</action-mappings>
```

Action-nested exception handlers handle the specified exception only if it is thrown by the enclosing action. If the exception is thrown by another action, it will not be handled.

You don't have to modify your **Action** classes in any way to take advantage of declarative exception handling. However, if you already have **try-catch** blocks for exceptions that you want handled by the exception handler, you need to remove them so that the exception gets propagated up the chain for the exception handler to process.

Exception Handling for Committed Responses

Generally speaking, Struts' declarative exception handling mechanism was designed to handle the scenario where an exception gets thrown from an **Action** class during regular processing before a response has been generated back to the client (i.e., browser). In that scenario the response is in what's called a non-committed state. However, there are scenarios where the response has been committed (meaning that data has been sent to the response) before an exception is thrown that the exception handler must handle. This causes a problem for the default Struts exception handler. When an exception occurs, the default Struts exception handler forwards to the page specified by the **<exception>** element's **path** attribute, however, forwards cannot be performed if a response has already been committed.

As part of the Struts 1.3 release, the default exception handler was modified to manage the scenario where the response has already been committed before an exception is thrown and then handled by the handler. In that scenario, the default exception handler will now include the contents of the URL specified by the **<exception>** element's **path** attribute instead of forwarding to the URL. As part of the additional functionality for the default exception handler, two configurable properties were added to modify the behavior of the exception handler when dealing with committed responses: **INCLUDE_PATH** and **SILENT_IF_COMMITTED**.

The **INCLUDE_PATH** property is used to specify an alternate URL to use for the include in the scenario where the response has been committed. This is especially useful if the **<exception>** element's **path** attribute is a Tiles definition or similar resource that is unsuitable for an include. Following is an example of how to use the **INCLUDE_PATH** property:

```
<exception key="GlobalExceptionHandler.default"
         type="java.lang.Exception"
         path="/error.jsp">
  <set-property key="INCLUDE_PATH" value="/error-alt.jsp"/>
</exception>
```

The **SILENT_IF_COMMITTED** property is used to suppress the exception handler's default behavior of performing an include if the response has been committed. If this property is set to *true*, the exception handler will revert to its old behavior of forwarding regardless of the state of the response. The following snippet illustrates the usage of the **SILENT_IF_COMMITTED** property.

```
<exception key="GlobalExceptionHandler.default"
         type="java.lang.Exception"
         path="/error.jsp">
  <set-property key="SILENT_IF_COMMITTED" value="true"/>
</exception>
```

Creating a Custom Exception Handler

Strut's built-in exception handler will suit most exception-handling scenarios; however, your application may require a specialized exception handler. For this situation, Struts provides a simple interface for creating your own custom exception handler that can be easily plugged into the framework. Following are the two steps you need to take to create your own custom exception handler:

1. Create a new exception handler class.
2. Add new exception handler definitions to the application's Struts configuration file.

The following sections walk through each step of the process in detail, illustrating how to create a custom exception handler that can send an e-mail when an exception is caught. The example is designed to be generic so that it can be used with any type of exception and can be easily enhanced.

Create a New Exception Handler Class

The first step in creating a custom exception handler is to create an exception handler class that can be plugged into Struts. Custom exception handler classes must extend Struts' base **org.apache.struts.action.ExceptionHandler** class and override its **execute( )** method. The **execute( )** method of the **ExceptionHandler** class that gets overridden is very similar to the **execute( )** method of the **Action** class and behaves almost identically. However, **ExceptionHandler.execute( )** takes two additional arguments, **java.lang.Exception** and **org.apache.struts.config.ExceptionConfig**. Table 8-1 explains each of the **ExceptionHandler.execute( )** method's arguments.

To illustrate how to create a custom exception handler, we'll examine a sample exception handler that can be used to send an e-mail with a stack trace for the exception when the handler is triggered. Following is the example **EmailExceptionHandler** class:

```
package com.jamesholmes.minihr;

import java.io.*;
import java.util.*;
import javax.mail.*;
import javax.mail.internet.*;
import javax.servlet.*;
import javax.servlet.http.*;
import org.apache.struts.action.*;
import org.apache.struts.config.*;

public class EmailExceptionHandler extends ExceptionHandler
{
  private static final String EMAIL_SERVER = "smtp.company.com";
  private static final String EMAIL_SENDER = "sender@company.com";
  private static final String EMAIL_RECIPIENT = "receiver@company.com";
  private static final String EMAIL_SUBJECT = "Exception Thrown";

  public ActionForward execute(Exception ex,
    ExceptionConfig config, ActionMapping mapping, ActionForm form,
    HttpServletRequest request, HttpServletResponse response)
      throws ServletException
  {
    // Send email with exception.
    try {
      sendEmail(ex);
    } catch (Exception e) {
      throw new ServletException(e);
    }

    // Forward processing to the default exception handler.
    return
      super.execute(ex, config, mapping, form, request, response);
  }

  private void sendEmail(Exception ex)
    throws Exception
  {
```

```
    // Set the host SMTP address.
    Properties props = new Properties();
    props.put("mail.smtp.host", EMAIL_SERVER);

    // Get the default mail session.
    Session session = Session.getDefaultInstance(props, null);

    // Store exception stack trace as message text string.
    ByteArrayOutputStream stream = new ByteArrayOutputStream();
    ex.printStackTrace(new PrintStream(stream));
    String messageText = stream.toString();

    // Create a message.
    Message message = new MimeMessage(session);
    message.setFrom(new InternetAddress(EMAIL_SENDER));
    message.setRecipient(Message.RecipientType.TO,
      new InternetAddress(EMAIL_RECIPIENT));
    message.setSubject(EMAIL_SUBJECT);
    message.setSentDate(new Date());
    message.setText(messageText);

    // Send the message.
    Transport.send(message);
  }
}
```

Argument	Description
java.lang.Exception	The exception that has been thrown and is to be handled.
org.apache.struts.config.ExceptionConfig	The **ExceptionConfig** object encapsulates the **<exception>** definition from the Struts configuration file for this exception handler.
org.apache.struts.action.ActionMapping	The **ActionMapping** object encapsulates the **<action>** definition from the Struts configuration file for the action that threw the exception that this exception handler is configured to handle.
org.apache.struts.action.ActionForm	The **ActionForm** object encapsulates the Form Bean associated with the action that threw the exception that this exception handler is configured to handle.
javax.servlet.http.HttpServletRequest	The **HttpServletRequest** object encapsulates the current HTTP request.
javax.servlet.http.HttpServletResponse	The **HttpServletResponse** object encapsulates the current HTTP response.

Table 8-1 The **execute( )** Method Arguments

Instead of completely overriding the functionality of the base **ExceptionHandler** class, the **EmailExceptionHandler** class augments its functionality. The **EmailExceptionHandler** class takes the exception passed to it and uses the JavaMail API to send the exception's stack trace in an e-mail. After sending the e-mail, **EmailExceptionHandler** calls **super.execute( )**, which invokes the default exception handler. This example illustrates how you can jump into the exception-handling process and add processing of your own. Alternatively, you could create an exception handler that completely overrides the behavior of the base handler.

NOTE *In order for the* **EmailExceptionHandler** *to work, you must include the JavaMail API* **.jar** *files in your application's* **/WEB-INF/lib** *directory (or on the server's classpath). For more information on JavaMail, visit http://java.sun.com/products/javamail.*

Add New Exception Handler Definitions to the Application's Struts Configuration File

After you have created the custom exception handler, you put it to use by adding exception handler definitions to the application's Struts configuration file. Using a custom exception handler is not much different from using the default handler. All you have to add to the standard definition is the fully qualified class name of the handler with the **exception** tag's **handler** attribute, as shown next:

```
<exception type="com.jamesholmes.minihr.NoResultsFoundException"
       handler="com.jamesholmes.minihr.EmailExceptionHandler"
           key="error.NoResultsFoundException"
          path="/exception.jsp"/>
```

Because the **EmailExceptionHandler** handler simply extends the base handler and does not completely override it, you must specify a path, by using the **path** attribute, for the handler to forward to. However, if you were to create a custom handler that completely overrides the base handler, you would not have to specify a value for the **path** attribute unless your handler wanted to use it. The **type** and **key** attributes are required regardless of the handler you use.

Adding Declarative Exception Handling to the Mini HR Application

Now that you've seen the benefits of using declarative exception handling and how it works, you are ready to revisit the Mini HR application and add declarative exception handling to it. Following is the list of steps involved in adding declarative exception handling to the Mini HR application:

1. Create an application exception class.
2. Update **SearchAction** to throw an application exception.
3. Set up an exception handler in the **struts-config.xml** configuration file.
4. Create an exception handler JSP.
5. Add an exception error message to the **MessageResources.properties** file.
6. Recompile, repackage, and run the updated application.

The following sections walk through each step of the process in detail.

Create an Application Exception Class

The first step in updating the Mini HR application to use declarative exception handling is to create an application exception class. Application exceptions are useful for distinguishing between specific error conditions. For example, an application could have a **ConfigurationFileNotFoundException** class and use it to indicate that a configuration file was not found, instead of simply throwing the more general **java.io.FileNotFoundException**. Application exceptions are also useful for distinguishing business logic-based exceptions, as is the case for the following **NoResultsFoundException** exception, which you will add to the Mini HR application:

```
package com.jamesholmes.minihr;

public class NoResultsFoundException extends Exception
{
}
```

As you can see, this exception is very basic; it simply extends **Exception** and does not provide any other functionality. This approach uniquely identifies the exception and is useful when no additional functionality is needed beyond the base functionality provided by the **Exception** class.

Update SearchAction to Throw an Application Exception

Once you have created the application exception, **NoResultsFoundException**, you can put it to use in the **SearchAction** class. To use the exception, you'll add a check that determines whether or not any search results were returned from the **EmployeeSearchService** class. If no results are found, a **NoResultsFoundException** exception will be thrown. Following is the code that implements this logic:

```
// Throw an application exception if results were not found.
if (results.size() < 1) {
  throw new NoResultsFoundException();
}
```

When this exception is thrown, Struts will catch it and process it accordingly.

Following is the updated **SearchAction** class in its entirety:

```
package com.jamesholmes.minihr;

import java.util.ArrayList;

import javax.servlet.http.HttpServletRequest;
import javax.servlet.http.HttpServletResponse;

import org.apache.struts.action.Action;
import org.apache.struts.action.ActionForm;
import org.apache.struts.action.ActionForward;
import org.apache.struts.action.ActionMapping;

public final class SearchAction extends Action
{
  public ActionForward execute(ActionMapping mapping,
```

```
      ActionForm form,
      HttpServletRequest request,
      HttpServletResponse response)
      throws Exception
    {
      EmployeeSearchService service = new EmployeeSearchService();
      ArrayList results;

      SearchForm searchForm = (SearchForm) form;

      // Perform employee search based on the criteria entered.
      String name = searchForm.getName();
      if (name != null && name.trim().length() > 0) {
        results = service.searchByName(name);
      } else {
        results = service.searchBySsNum(searchForm.getSsNum().trim());
      }

      // Throw an application exception if results were not found.
      if (results.size() < 1) {
        throw new NoResultsFoundException();
      }

      // Place search results in SearchForm for access by JSP.
      searchForm.setResults(results);

      // Forward control to this Action's input page.
      return mapping.getInputForward();
    }
  }
```

Set Up an Exception Handler in the struts-config.xml Configuration File

After you create an application exception and put it to use in an action, you must set up an exception handler for it in the **struts-config.xml** configuration file. For Mini HR, the **NoResultsFoundException** exception will be thrown only by the **SearchAction** class; thus, you'll define the action-specific exception handler shown next rather than a global exception handler:

```
<!-- Action Mappings Configuration -->
<action-mappings>
  <action path="/search"
          type="com.jamesholmes.minihr.SearchAction"
          name="searchForm"
          scope="request"
          validate="true"
          input="/search.jsp">
    <exception
      type="com.jamesholmes.minihr.NoResultsFoundException"
       key="error.NoResultsFoundException"
      path="/exception.jsp"/>
  </action>
</action-mappings>
```

Because this exception handler is nested inside the action definition for **SearchAction**, it will only handle **NoResultsFoundException** exceptions that are thrown from that action. Alternatively, if you wanted to handle **NoResultsFoundException**s being thrown from *any* action, you would have to define a global exception handler, as shown next:

```
<global-exceptions>
  <exception
    type="com.jamesholmes.minihr.NoResultsFoundException"
     key="error.NoResultsFoundException"
    path="/exception.jsp"/>
</global-exceptions>
```

Following is the updated **struts-config.xml** configuration file in its entirety:

```
<?xml version="1.0"?>

<!DOCTYPE struts-config PUBLIC
  "-//Apache Software Foundation//DTD Struts Configuration 1.3//EN"
  "http://struts.apache.org/dtds/struts-config_1_3.dtd">

<struts-config>

  <!-- Form Beans Configuration -->
  <form-beans>
    <form-bean name="searchForm"
               type="com.jamesholmes.minihr.SearchForm"/>
  </form-beans>

  <!-- Global Forwards Configuration -->
  <global-forwards>
    <forward name="search" path="/search.jsp"/>
  </global-forwards>

  <!-- Action Mappings Configuration -->
  <action-mappings>
    <action path="/search"
            type="com.jamesholmes.minihr.SearchAction"
            name="searchForm"
            scope="request"
            validate="true"
            input="/search.jsp">
      <exception
        type="com.jamesholmes.minihr.NoResultsFoundException"
         key="error.NoResultsFoundException"
        path="/exception.jsp"/>
    </action>
  </action-mappings>

  <!-- Message Resources Configuration -->
  <message-resources
    parameter="com.jamesholmes.minihr.ApplicationResources"/>

</struts-config>
```

Create an Exception Handler JSP

When using exception handlers, you have to specify the URL to the page that will be forwarded to if the specified exception is caught by the handler. Following is the **exception.jsp** file specified for the **NoResultsFoundException** exception in the **struts-config.xml** file:

```
<%@ taglib uri="http://struts.apache.org/tags-html" prefix="html" %>

<html>
<head>
<title>ABC, Inc. Human Resources Portal</title>
</head>
<body>

<font size="+1">ABC, Inc. Human Resources Portal</font><br>
<hr width="100%" noshade="true">

<html:errors/>

</body>
</html>
```

As stated earlier in this chapter, when an exception is processed by Struts' built-in exception handler, it creates an **ActionMessage** object and stores it in request or session scope so that it can be accessed by the page being forwarded to. This page uses the **errors** tag from the HTML Tag Library to output the error message.

One other point: Although this JSP is intended to be used by the exception handler for **NoResultsFoundException**, it is generic enough that you could use it as a general-purpose exception handler page.

Add an Exception Error Message to the MessageResources.properties File

Recall from earlier in this chapter that each exception handler defined in the Struts configuration file declares a key for an error message in the application's resource bundle file (e.g., **MessageResources.properties**). At run time, the key is used to look up an error message to pass to the exception handler page when the exception handler is triggered. Following is the error message that you must add to the MiniHR **MessageResources.properties** file for the exception handler that was defined in the **struts-config.xml** file:

```
# Exception Error Resources
error.NoResultsFoundException=No Search Results Found
```

The following code shows the updated **MessageResources.properties** file in its entirety:

```
# Label Resources
label.search.name=Name
label.search.ssNum=Social Security Number

# Error Resources
error.search.criteria.missing=Search Criteria Missing
error.search.ssNum.invalid=Invalid Social Security Number
errors.header=<font color="red"><cTypeface:Bold>Error(s)</b></font><ul>
errors.footer=</ul><hr width="100%" size="1" noshade="true">
errors.prefix=<li>
```

```
errors.suffix=</li>

# Exception Error Resources
error.NoResultsFoundException=No Search Results Found
```

Recompile, Repackage, and Run the Updated Application

Because you created a new application exception class and updated the **SearchAction** class, you must recompile and repackage the Mini HR application before you run it. Assuming that you've made modifications to the original Mini HR application and it was set up in the **c:\java\MiniHR** directory (as described in Chapter 2), you can run the **build.bat** batch file or the **build.xml** Ant script file to recompile the application.

After recompiling Mini HR, you need to repackage it using the following command line:

```
jar cf MiniHR.war *
```

This command must also be run from the directory where you have set up the Mini HR application (e.g., **c:\java\MiniHR**).

Similar to the way you ran Mini HR the first time, you now need to place the new **MiniHR.war** file that you just created into Tomcat's **webapps** directory, delete the **webapps/MiniHR** directory, and start Tomcat. As before, access the Mini HR application at **http://localhost:8080/MiniHR/**. Once you have the updated Mini HR application running, try entering a name or social security number that will not be found when searched for. When this happens, the **SearchAction** class will throw the **NoResultsFoundException** exception and then the **exception.jsp** page will be displayed, as shown in Figure 8-1.

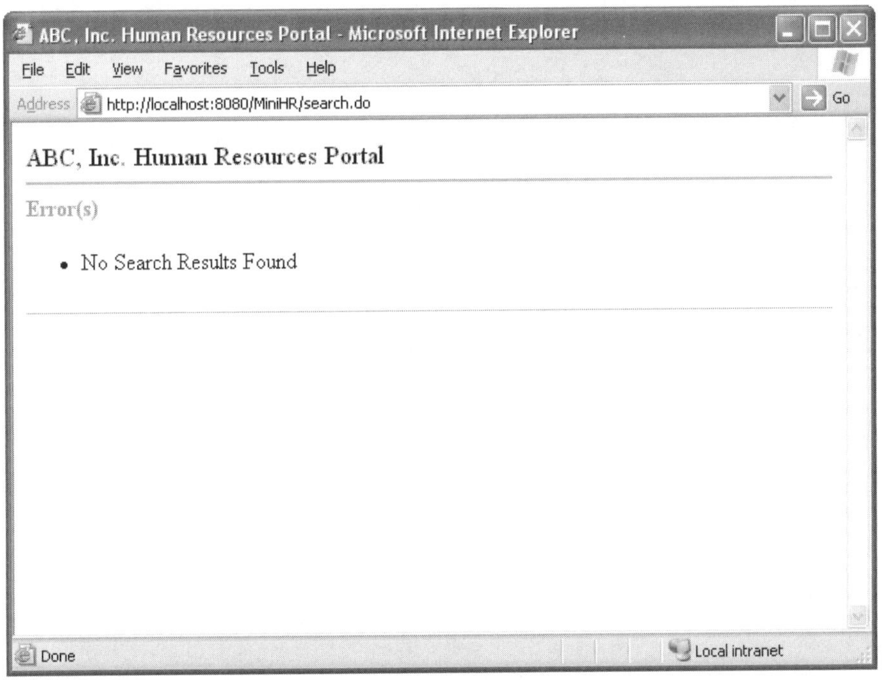

FIGURE 8-1 The exception error page

CHAPTER 9

Struts Modules

During the 1.1 release cycle of Struts, a significant number of new features were added to the framework. Each of these features greatly improved the framework, and each is important in its own right. However, one feature stands out because of its profound impact on the framework: support for *modules*.

Support for modules solves a problem commonly encountered when using earlier versions of Struts. In all versions of Struts, including version 1.3, the only supported configuration is mapping a single instance of the Struts **ActionServlet** to a single URL. That is, in your application's **web.xml** file, you should have exactly one **<servlet>** and one **<servlet-mapping>** element for the Struts **ActionServlet**. This is because the **ActionServlet** stores several details of the framework's configuration in variables within the Web application scope, which is the scope shared by all parts of the application. Thus, attempting to run multiple instances of the **ActionServlet** in the same Web application causes a problem, because the data associated with one instance overwrites the data associated with another instance. Prior to version 1.1 and its introduction of modules, this was a major limitation of Struts, because your entire application's configuration had to reside in a single Struts configuration file. For large applications, where the configuration file gets very large and several developers are involved, that proved to be a problematic point of contention.

Today, you still can have only one instance of **ActionServlet** for the same reasons as before; however, you can *simulate* the functionality of having multiple instances by subdividing your application into discreet units by using modules. Each module has its own Struts configuration file, its own set of actions and forwards, a separate URL namespace, and so on. Essentially, modules are like mini-Struts applications inside a master Struts application and are analogous to the way Web applications reside in a servlet container. Each module has its own URL namespace, just as Web applications do. Modules also solve the problems of parallel development that are commonly experienced when using versions of Struts prior to 1.1.

Before moving on, it is necessary to mention another feature added by Struts 1.1 that, in some cases, offers an alternative to modules: support for multiple configuration files. Although added in the same release (1.1) as modules, multiple configuration files can be used independently, without having to convert your application for use with modules. Support for multiple configuration files alleviates some of the problems associated with large, team-based development with Struts. However, multiple configuration files do not partition your Struts application the way that modules do. When using multiple configuration files, the information in the files is combined to create one large set of configuration data. This can cause a problem, however. For example, if you define an action with a certain name in one file and another configuration file defines another action with the same name, the configuration file last read will override the first file's data. Basically, last one in wins. Modules do not have this problem, because Struts stores each module's configuration data separately. Thus, modules offer the best solution when you need the functionality of multiple instances of **ActionServlet**.

NOTE *For more information on configuring the use of multiple Struts configuration files, see Chapter 18.*

This chapter describes how to set up and use modules in your application, including details on how to use Tiles and Validator with modules. It also shows how to apply modules to the Mini HR application.

Using Modules

As stated, using modules allows you to partition your Struts application into discrete functional areas, almost like having wholly separate applications. Each module has its own Struts configuration file, actions, forwards, and JSPs, allowing it to function independently of other modules. Using modules in a Struts application involves these three steps:

1. Create a Struts configuration file for each module.
2. Configure the **web.xml** deployment descriptor for modules.
3. Configure links to access module-specific JSPs.

The following sections explain how to configure and use modules in detail.

Creating a Struts Configuration File for Each Module

In order to separate each module's configuration details, you must create a separate Struts configuration file for each module. Having a separate configuration file for each module allows all of a module's actions, forwards, and so on to be grouped into one module-specific file that is independent of other modules' configuration data. You configure actions, forwards, and so on inside the file, just as you would with a non-modularized application. The only difference with module configuration files is in the way the Tiles and Validator plugin definitions are set up, which is described later in this chapter.

The typical naming convention for module configuration files is **struts-config-*module*.xml**, where ***module*** is the name of the module that the file is for. Note, however, that there are no restrictions on the names of module configuration files and thus any name can be used as long as it is unique. Alternatively, if your application is using Tiles and/or Validator, you may want to create a module-specific directory under **/WEB-INF/** for each module to store its configuration files. For example, if your application is using modules, Tiles, and Validator, you could arrange the files as shown next:

```
/WEB-INF/moduleA/struts-config.xml
/WEB-INF/moduleA/tiles-defs.xml
/WEB-INF/moduleA/validation.xml
/WEB-INF/moduleB/struts-config.xml
/WEB-INF/moduleB/tiles-defs.xml
/WEB-INF/moduleB/validation.xml
```

With this arrangement you wouldn't have to use the module name in the names of the configuration files, because they are under a module-specific directory.

NOTE *Detailed information on the Struts configuration file is found in Chapter 18.*

Configuring the web.xml Deployment Descriptor for Modules

Each module's Struts configuration file has to be specified in the **web.xml** deployment descriptor, just as is done for non-modularized Struts applications; however, the way they are configured is slightly different. Recall that with a non-modularized application, you specify the path to the Struts configuration file with the **config** initialization parameter for the **ActionServlet** controller servlet, as shown next:

```
<!-- Action Servlet Configuration -->
<servlet>
  <servlet-name>action</servlet-name>
  <servlet-class>org.apache.struts.action.ActionServlet</servlet-class>
  <init-param>
    <param-name>config</param-name>
    <param-value>/WEB-INF/struts-config.xml</param-value>
  </init-param>
  <load-on-startup>1</load-on-startup>
</servlet>
```

The **config** parameter is set to the location of your application's Struts configuration file.

To specify module configuration files, you need an initialization parameter for each module and it must be named **config/*moduleName***, where ***moduleName*** is the name you want to assign to the module. For example, to specify two modules named **moduleA** and **moduleB**, your **ActionServlet** definition must look like this:

```
<!-- Action Servlet Configuration -->
<servlet>
  <servlet-name>action</servlet-name>
  <servlet-class>org.apache.struts.action.ActionServlet</servlet-class>
  <init-param>
    <param-name>config/moduleA</param-name>
    <param-value>/WEB-INF/struts-config-moduleA.xml</param-value>
  </init-param>
  <init-param>
    <param-name>config/moduleB</param-name>
    <param-value>/WEB-INF/struts-config-moduleB.xml</param-value>
  </init-param>
  <load-on-startup>1</load-on-startup>
</servlet>
```

In this file, two configuration files are specified: **struts-config-moduleA.xml** and **struts-config-moduleB.xml**.

The name given to the module through the **param-name** tag is known as the *module prefix* and is very important. Struts uses the module prefix to distinguish and route requests to the module. The module name becomes part of the URL that must be used to access the module's actions.

It is important to understand that all of a module's action paths are relative to the module. For example, the modularized version of the Mini HR application developed later in this chapter is deployed at **/MiniHR/** on the server (i.e., **http://localhost:8080/MiniHR/**). It has a module named **employee**, which has an action mapped to **/search**. Therefore, the URL to access the action is **/MiniHR/employee/search.do**. Figure 9-1 shows a breakdown of what each piece of the URL is.

When using modules, the standard **config** parameter (that is, the one without any module name appended to it) is used to specify a configuration file for a *default* module. The default module has no module prefix, so any URL whose path does not include a module name will be routed to the default module. Thus, using the Mini HR example developed later in this chapter, if a request were made to **/MiniHR/admin/viewAppUsers.do**, Struts would execute the action mapped to **/admin/viewAppUsers** in the default module's configuration file, because the URL does not contain a module prefix.

NOTE *A side effect of using modules is that you cannot use path mapping (e.g.,* **/do/*** *) for the* **ActionServlet** *controller servlet. Instead, you must use extension mapping (e.g.,* ***.do** *) because Struts uses the URL path to determine which module a request is being made for; using path mapping would interfere with that mechanism. For more information on setting up* **ActionServlet***'s mapping, refer to Chapter 5.*

Configuring Links to Access Module-Specific JSPs

Modules fundamentally change the way JSPs are linked to and accessed in a Struts application. Recall that in non-modularized Struts applications, you link to and access JSPs just as you would in any Web application. With modules, the rules change because Struts requires that URLs that are used to access a module must have a module prefix that designates which module is being accessed. This is necessary to enable Struts to select the correct module configuration data to use for each request.

When using modules, Struts needs some way to know how to select the correct module configuration data to use for a JSP. Here's why: When you access JSPs, the request for the JSP does not go through the Struts controller servlet, as requests for actions do. Because of this, Struts does not have the opportunity to select the correct module configuration data to use for the JSP. Thus, if the JSP is using any Struts tag library tags that reference a Struts action, Struts will not know how to determine what action the JSP is trying to reference, because no module has been selected.

To solve this problem, all requests for module JSPs must be routed through the Struts controller servlet. Struts provides a built-in action called **org.apache.struts.actions.SwitchAction** to help with this. **SwitchAction** allows you to create module-specific JSP links that preserve the module name so that Struts can properly select the right module configuration data. **SwitchAction** does this by taking a module name and a JSP as request parameters. When executed, it takes care of selecting the module specified and then forwarding to the specified JSP. This way, the module configuration data is set up for the JSP. To use **SwitchAction**, you must add an action definition for it in your Struts configuration file. Typically this is

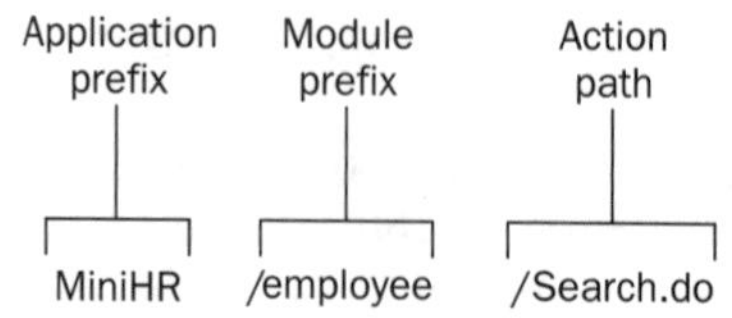

FIGURE 9-1 The module URL breakdown

added to the default module configuration file, but you can add it to module-specific configuration files, too. Following is a sample **SwitchAction** definition:

```
<action path="/switchMod"
        type="org.apache.struts.actions.SwitchAction"/>
```

You can put this definition to use with the following example link:

```
<html:link action="/switchMod?prefix=/moduleA&page=/main.jsp">
ModuleA main JSP
</html:link>
```

This example usage creates a link that will route the Struts request processor to the JSP at **/moduleA/main.jsp** and select the configuration data for **moduleA**.

Using Validator with Modules

Using Validator with modules works the same way as it does with a non-modularized application. You simply add the Validator plugin to each module's Struts configuration file. Doing so allows each module to specify its own module-specific Validator configuration file, as shown next:

```
<!-- Validator Configuration -->
<plug-in className="org.apache.struts.validator.ValidatorPlugIn">
  <set-property property="pathnames"
                value="/org/apache/struts/validator/validator-rules.xml,
                       /WEB-INF/validation-moduleA.xml"/>
</plug-in>
```

In this example, the first configuration file specified with the **pathnames** property is the **validator-rules.xml** file. Recall from Chapter 6 that this file is used to declaratively plug in the validation routines that Validator will use to perform validations. Because validation routines are typically the same across all modules, you do not need a **validator-rules.xml** file for each module. Instead, you simply point each module's Validator plugin to the one common file. However, using modules does allow you to specify a unique **validation.xml** configuration file for each module.

The second configuration file specified with the **pathnames** property is the module-specific Validator configuration file. This file should include all of the validation definitions specific to the given module.

Using Tiles with Modules

Like Validator, in order to use Tiles with modules, you have to add the Tiles plugin to each module's Struts configuration file that you want to use Tiles with. For example, if your application has two modules, **moduleA** and **moduleB**, you have to add a Tiles plugin definition to **moduleA**'s Struts configuration file and a definition to **moduleB**'s Struts configuration file. This is necessary so that each module's Tiles configuration file can be specified. In versions of Struts prior to 1.3, this was also necessary because Struts uses a separate request processor for each module, and the Tiles plugin added its own custom request processor that extended the base Struts request processor (per module). If you didn't add the Tiles plugin to each module's Struts configuration file, not all modules would have the Tiles request processor that was necessary for processing forwards to Tiles definitions.

Following is the standard Tiles plugin definition that you would have in your Struts configuration file for a non-modularized Struts application:

```
<!-- Tiles Configuration -->
<plug-in className="org.apache.struts.tiles.TilesPlugin">
  <set-property property="definitions-config"
                   value="/WEB-INF/tiles-defs.xml"/>
</plug-in>
```

You would use this exact same definition in each Module's Struts configuration file for a modularized application. Of course, the name of the Tiles configuration file specified with the **definitions-config** property would change with each module, unless they all shared the same configuration file.

If you want each of your modules to have its own Tiles configuration file and don't want each module's Tiles definitions to be shared across modules, you can indicate this intent with the Tiles plugin **moduleAware** parameter. Following is a sample Tiles plugin definition for the Struts configuration file that illustrates this:

```
<!-- Tiles Configuration -->
<plug-in className="org.apache.struts.tiles.TilesPlugin">
  <set-property property="definitions-config"
                   value="/WEB-INF/tiles-defs.xml"/>
  <set-property property="moduleAware" value="true"/>
</plug-in>
```

By default, Tiles stores each module's configuration file settings in the same internal configuration structure. Thus, **moduleA** can see all of the Tiles definitions from **moduleB**'s Tiles configuration file and vice versa. Tiles does this by default to save memory in case each module uses the same configuration file. However, in most cases each module has its own module-specific definitions that other modules shouldn't be able to access. For this scenario, you set the **moduleAware** property to true. This informs Tiles to create a separate configuration structure for each module's Tiles definitions.

As explained earlier, module prefixes apply only to actions. Thus, any URLs to JSPs specified in your Tiles configuration files are not relative to a module prefix but rather are relative to the root of the application, just as they are in non-modularized Struts applications.

Converting the Mini HR Application to Use Modules

Now that you've seen the benefits of using Strut's module mechanism and how it works, you are ready to update the Mini HR application to use modules. Here are the steps that you will follow:

1. Set up module directories and files.
2. Create a Struts configuration file for each module.
3. Update the application's **web.xml** deployment descriptor file.
4. Update the **index.jsp** file to link to each of the modules.
5. Repackage and run the updated application.

The following sections walk you through each step of the process in detail.

Set Up Module Directories and Files

The first step in updating the Mini HR application is to set up a directory for each module that will store its JSPs. This example will have two modules, an **employee** module and a **reports** module. The **employee** module will contain functionality previously existing in Mini HR. The **reports** module adds new functionality. You need to create a directory for each of these modules beneath the main Mini HR application directory (e.g., **c:\java\MiniHR**). Thus, you will have the following directories:

```
c:\java\MiniHR\employee
c:\java\MiniHR\reports
```

After you have created the directories, you need to put the corresponding JSPs into them. Because the original Mini HR application already has **employee** functionality, you can simply move the employee search JSP (**search.jsp**) from the root application directory (e.g., **c:\java\MiniHR**) to the new **employee** module directory you just created. The **reports** module contains new functionality, which is provided by the **menu.jsp** file, shown here. Store this file in the **reports** module directory.

```
<html>
<head>
<title>ABC, Inc. Human Resources Portal - Reports Menu</title>
</head>
<body>

<font size="+1">
ABC, Inc. Human Resources Portal - Reports Menu
</font><br>
<hr width="100%" noshade="true">

&#149; New Employee Report<br>
&#149; 5-Year Employee Report<br>
&#149; 10-Year Employee Report<br>
&#149; 20-Year Employee Report<br>

</body>
<html>
```

After you move the **search.jsp** file and create the **menu.jsp** file, your main application directory should look like this:

```
C:\java\MiniHR\employee\search.jsp
c:\java\MiniHR\reports\menu.jsp
c:\java\MiniHR\index.jsp
```

Before moving on, a short, but important, digression is in order. The general idea behind the directory structure just described can be extended to configuration files, if you like. For example, you could create a directory for each module beneath **/WEB-INF/** that would hold the module's Struts, Tiles, and Validator configuration files. Following is an example directory layout illustrating this:

```
MiniHR/WEB-INF/moduleA/struts-config.xml
MiniHR/WEB-INF/moduleA/tiles-defs.xml
MiniHR/WEB-INF/moduleA/validation.xml
```

```
MiniHR/WEB-INF/moduleB/struts-config.xml
MiniHR/WEB-INF/moduleB/tiles-defs.xml
MiniHR/WEB-INF/moduleB/validation.xml
```

Create a Struts Configuration File for Each Module

After you have set up the module directories and files, the next step is to create a Struts configuration file for each of the modules. The application's current **struts-config.xml** file will be used as the configuration file for the **employee** module and thus must be renamed to **struts-config-employee.xml**. Following is the renamed and updated **struts-config-employee.xml** file:

```
<?xml version="1.0"?>

<!DOCTYPE struts-config PUBLIC
  "-//Apache Software Foundation//DTD Struts Configuration 1.3//EN"
  "http://struts.apache.org/dtds/struts-config_1_3.dtd">

<struts-config>

  <!-- Form Beans Configuration -->
  <form-beans>
    <form-bean name="searchForm"
               type="com.jamesholmes.minihr.SearchForm"/>
  </form-beans>

  <!-- Action Mappings Configuration -->
  <action-mappings>
    <action path="/viewSearch" forward="/search.jsp"/>
    <action path="/search"
            type="com.jamesholmes.minihr.SearchAction"
            name="searchForm"
            scope="request"
            validate="true"
            input="/search.jsp">
    </action>
  </action-mappings>

  <!-- Message Resources Configuration -->
  <message-resources
    parameter="com.jamesholmes.minihr.MessageResources"/>

</struts-config>
```

In addition to being renamed, this file has also been updated. Notice that the Global Forwards Configuration section has been removed and the **/viewSearch** action has been added.

As mentioned earlier in this chapter, Struts incorporates the concept of a default module. The default module's configuration file is named **struts-config.xml** and is shown next:

```
<?xml version="1.0"?>

<!DOCTYPE struts-config PUBLIC
  "-//Apache Software Foundation//DTD Struts Configuration 1.3//EN"
  "http://struts.apache.org/dtds/struts-config_1_3.dtd">

<struts-config>
```

```
  <!-- Global Forwards Configuration -->
  <global-forwards>
    <forward name="viewSearch" path="/employee/viewSearch.do"/>
  </global-forwards>

  <!-- Message Resources Configuration -->
  <message-resources
    parameter="com.jamesholmes.minihr.MessageResources"/>

</struts-config>
```

You will need to create this new file and place it under the **/WEB-INF/** directory (e.g., **c:\java\MiniHR\WEB-INF**). This configuration file simply has a forward pointing to the Search page that is used by **index.jsp** for its "Search for Employees" link.

The **reports** module's configuration file, **struts-config-reports.xml**, is shown next:

```
<?xml version="1.0"?>

<!DOCTYPE struts-config PUBLIC
  "-//Apache Software Foundation//DTD Struts Configuration 1.3//EN"
  "http://struts.apache.org/dtds/struts-config_1_3.dtd">

<struts-config>

  <!-- Action Mappings Configuration -->
  <action-mappings>
    <action path="/viewMenu" forward="/menu.jsp"/>
  </action-mappings>

  <!-- Message Resources Configuration -->
  <message-resources
    parameter="com.jamesholmes.minihr.MessageResources"/>

</struts-config>
```

You will also need to create this new file and place it under the **/WEB-INF/** directory (e.g., **c:\java\MiniHR\WEB-INF**). This configuration file simply has a forward action pointing to the Reports Menu page that is used by **index.jsp** for its Reports Menu link.

Update the Application's web.xml Deployment Descriptor File

Once you have created the Struts configuration files for each module, you must update Mini HR's **web.xml** deployment descriptor file. Each module's configuration file will be passed to the Struts **ActionServlet** controller servlet as an initialization parameter, as shown next:

```
<!-- Action Servlet Configuration -->
<servlet>
  <servlet-name>action</servlet-name>
  <servlet-class>org.apache.struts.action.ActionServlet</servlet-class>
  <init-param>
    <param-name>config</param-name>
    <param-value>/WEB-INF/struts-config.xml</param-value>
  </init-param>
  <init-param>
    <param-name>config/employee</param-name>
```

```
    <param-value>/WEB-INF/struts-config-employee.xml</param-value>
  </init-param>
  <init-param>
    <param-name>config/reports</param-name>
    <param-value>/WEB-INF/struts-config-reports.xml</param-value>
  </init-param>
  <load-on-startup>1</load-on-startup>
</servlet>
```

Each initialization parameter specifies a name and a value for the parameter with the **param-name** and **param-value** tags, respectively. The default module's configuration file is specified with a parameter named **config**. Each of the module-specific configuration files is specified with a parameter named **config/*moduleName***, where ***moduleName*** is the name of the module the configuration file is for.

Following is the updated **web.xml** file in its entirety:

```
<?xml version="1.0"?>

<!DOCTYPE web-app PUBLIC
  "-//Sun Microsystems, Inc.//DTD Web Application 2.3//EN"
  "http://java.sun.com/dtd/web-app_2_3.dtd">

<web-app>

  <!-- Action Servlet Configuration -->
  <servlet>
    <servlet-name>action</servlet-name>
    <servlet-class>org.apache.struts.action.ActionServlet</servlet-class>
    <init-param>
      <param-name>config</param-name>
      <param-value>/WEB-INF/struts-config.xml</param-value>
    </init-param>
    <init-param>
      <param-name>config/employee</param-name>
      <param-value>/WEB-INF/struts-config-employee.xml</param-value>
    </init-param>
    <init-param>
      <param-name>config/reports</param-name>
      <param-value>/WEB-INF/struts-config-reports.xml</param-value>
    </init-param>
    <load-on-startup>1</load-on-startup>
  </servlet>

  <!-- Action Servlet Mapping -->
  <servlet-mapping>
    <servlet-name>action</servlet-name>
    <url-pattern>*.do</url-pattern>
  </servlet-mapping>

  <!-- The Welcome File List -->
  <welcome-file-list>
```

```
    <welcome-file>/index.jsp</welcome-file>
  </welcome-file-list>

</web-app>
```

Update the index.jsp File to Link to Each of the Modules

Now that each module has been configured, you must update the **index.jsp** file to link to the two modules. First, update the link to the search page as shown here:

```
&#149; <html:link forward="viewSearch">Search for Employees</html:link><br><br>
```

Next you have to add a link to the new reports module:

```
&#149; <html:link action="/reports/viewMenu">Reports Menu</html:link><br>
```

Following is the updated **index.jsp** file in its entirety:

```
<%@ taglib uri="http://struts.apache.org/tags-html" prefix="html" %>

<html>
<head>
<title>ABC, Inc. Human Resources Portal</title>
</head>
<body>

<font size="+1">ABC, Inc. Human Resources Portal</font><br>

<hr width="100%" noshade="true">

&#149; Add an Employee<br>
&#149; <html:link forward="viewSearch">Search for Employees</html:
link><br><br>

&#149; <html:link action="/reports/viewMenu">Reports Menu</html:link><br>

</body>
</html>
```

Repackage and Run the Updated Application

Because no Java source code files had to be modified to update the Mini HR application to use modules, you do not have to recompile the application. All you have to do is repackage the application and redeploy it before running it again. Assuming that you have made modifications to the original Mini HR application and it was set up in the **c:\java\MiniHR** directory (as described in Chapter 2), the following command line will repackage the application:

```
jar cf MiniHR.war *
```

This command should be run from the directory where you have set up the Mini HR application (e.g., **c:\java\MiniHR**).

Similar to the way you ran Mini HR the first time, you now need to place the new **MiniHR.war** file that you just created into Tomcat's **webapps** directory, delete the **webapps/MiniHR** directory, and start Tomcat. As before, to access the Mini HR application, point your browser to **http://localhost:8080/MiniHR/**. Once you have the updated Mini HR application running, you will see the screen shown in Figure 9-2.

Clicking the Search for Employees link takes you to the same employee search page that you were taken to by clicking the same link in the original application. The Reports Menu link takes you to the new **menu.jsp** page created for the **reports** module.

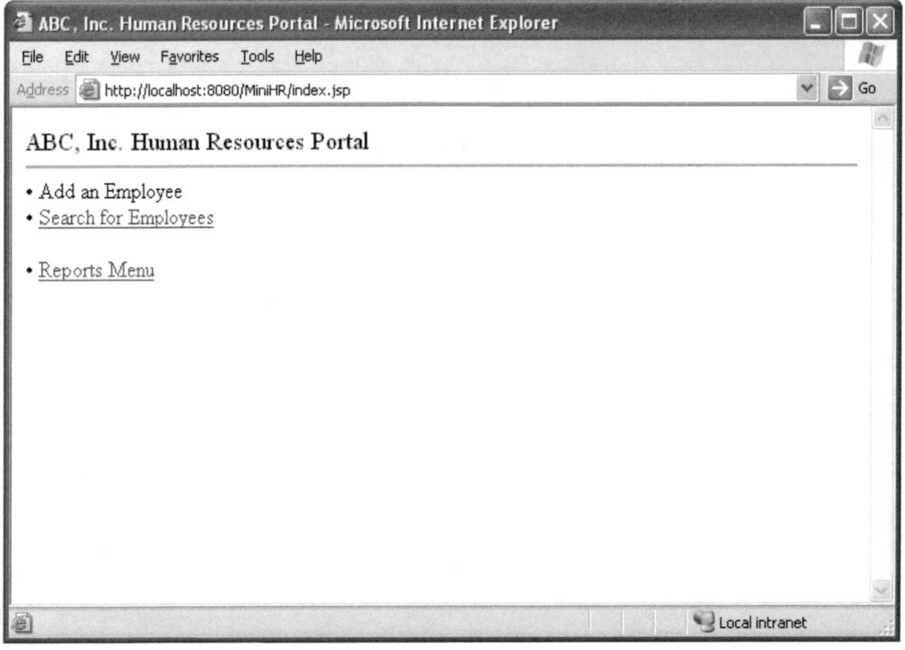

FIGURE 9-2 The opening Mini HR application screen

PART II

Applying Struts

CHAPTER 10
Internationalizing Struts Applications

CHAPTER 11
Securing Struts Applications

CHAPTER 12
Testing Struts Applications

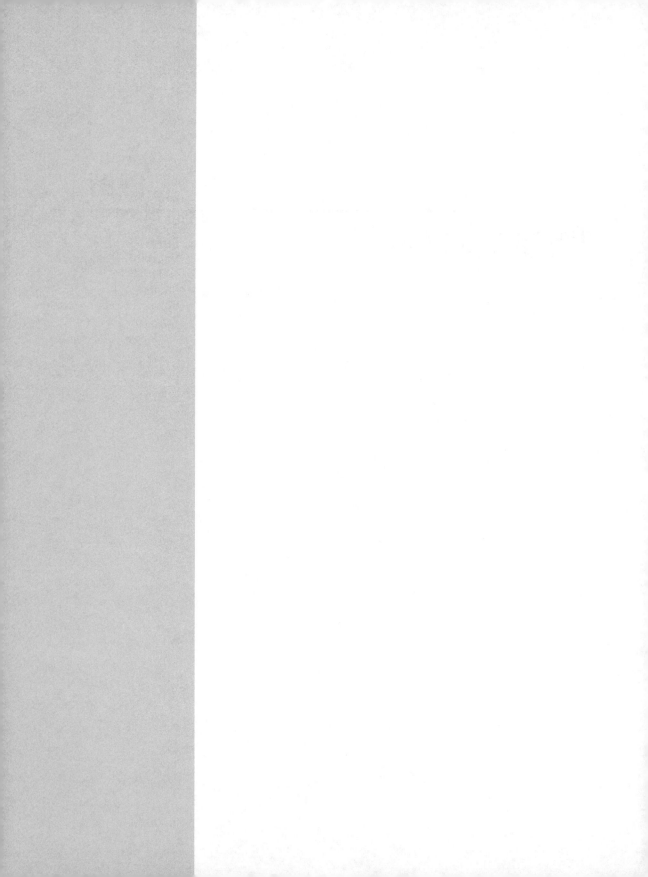

10

CHAPTER

Internationalizing Struts Applications

The Internet has created a global, electronic shopping mall. Whereas businesses once catered only to customers in their same geographic region, today business is transacted with customers worldwide. A product of this globalization is the need for software that can adapt to the conventions and languages used by customers in different countries. To achieve this, applications must be internationalized. *Internationalization*, also known as *I18N*, encompasses tailoring content specific to locales based on their different languages, currencies, and formatting conventions.

NOTE *The acronym I18N is sometimes used in place of the word internationalization, because it is such a long word to type. I18N represents the first letter i, followed by 18 characters, and then the final letter n.*

From the beginning, Java was designed with internationalization in mind. For example, it offers support for Unicode character sets and provides built-in classes that manage locale-specific content. Struts builds upon Java's support, making development of internationalized Struts applications straightforward. This chapter presents an overview of Java's built-in internationalization support and then explains how Struts' internationalization builds upon it.

Understanding Java's Internationalization Support

Java's built-in internationalization support is centered on three main classes. The following table lists each class and its description.

Class	Description
java.util.Locale	Encapsulates the language, country, and variant for a specific locale.
java.util.ResourceBundle	Encapsulates locale-specific resources.
java.text.MessageFormat	Provides methods for creating locale-specific formatted messages.

The following three sections provide a brief introduction to each class.

The java.util.Locale Class

At the core of Java's internationalization API is the **Locale** class. The **Locale** class encapsulates the language, country, and variant for a specific locale. That is, the **Locale** class is used to uniquely represent a specific locale. All other locale-oriented classes use instances of this class to tailor their behavior and output to a specific locale.

When you create a **Locale** object, you specify the locale's language; language and country; or language, country, and variant. Thus, **Locale** lets you represent as specific a locale as needed. The constructors for the **Locale** class are shown here:

```
Locale(String language)
Locale(String language, String country)
Locale(String language, String country, String variant)
```

The following snippet illustrates each of these uses in order:

```
Locale locale1 = new Locale("en");
Locale locale2 = new Locale("en", "US");
Locale locale3 = new Locale("en", "US", "WIN");
```

The first example creates an English language–specific locale; the second example creates a United States English language–specific locale; and the third example creates a United States English language Windows–specific locale. The more attributes you specify, the more specific the locale is. For example, if you create a Spanish language **Locale** object, as shown next, it will serve all users whose language is Spanish, independent of what country they are from:

```
Locale spanishLocale = new Locale("es");
```

Alternatively, to create a Spanish language locale specific to Mexico, you can use this declaration:

```
Locale mexicoSpanishLocale = new Locale("es", "MX");
```

Using combinations of language, country, and variant together narrows the scope of **Locale** objects.

The **Locale** object's **language** argument must be specified using a valid two-letter ISO-639 language code (e.g., "en" for English or "es" for Spanish). The **country** argument must be specified using a valid uppercase two-letter ISO-3166 country code (e.g., "US" for United States or "CA" for Canada"). The **variant** argument is for a vendor- or browser-specific code (e.g., "WIN" for Windows or "MAC" for Macintosh). For a listing of each of the ISO language and country codes, visit their respective specification Web sites:

http://www.unicode.org/unicode/onlinedat/languages.html

http://www.unicode.org/unicode/onlinedat/countries.html

Here are a couple of important notes about **Locale** objects that you should know. First, **Locale** objects are immutable; thus, once you have created an instance, you cannot change any of its attributes (i.e., language, country, or variant). Because of this, if you need to change a locale for some reason, you must create a new locale instance. Second, the **Locale** class provides several static locale constants as a convenience. For example, **Locale.US** and **Locale.FRANCE** are country code constants and **Locale.ENGLISH** and **Locale.FRENCH** are language code constants. Following is an example use of the constants:

```
Locale us = Locale.US;
Locale french = Locale.FRENCH;
```

The java.util.ResourceBundle Class

The **ResourceBundle** class encapsulates locale-specific resources for an application. Essentially, the **ResourceBundle** class is a central repository that applications use to hold resources. Applications simply provide the name of a resource and a locale, and the bundle returns the application resource for the specified locale. The resource names are the same across all locales, enabling an application to know only the name of a resource and how it should be handled. For example, assume that a label is displayed beside a field on an HTML form. Using a resource bundle, an application can obtain the text for the label by requesting the label from the resource bundle by name. When requesting the label, the application passes a locale that specifies what version of the label's text to obtain, such as English or Spanish. The resource bundle returns to the application the proper version of the text, which it can then display beside the field. The application does not need to have separate logic for each translation. It just needs to know how to get the text and display it. This is the premise and power of internationalization.

Resource bundles most often contain locale-specific text (e.g., error messages, field and button labels, and so on) for applications, but can also be used to manage any locale-specific resources. The **ResourceBundle** class provides the core interface for working with resource bundles, but it is not intended to be used directly, because it is an abstract class. Java provides two subclasses of **ResourceBundle**: **java.util.ListResourceBundle** and **java.util.PropertyResourceBundle**. The **ListResourceBundle** class is an abstract class that provides a mechanism for using lists to store resources; because it's abstract you must provide a concrete subclass implementation to make use of it. The **PropertyResourceBundle** class is a concrete subclass that provides a mechanism for using properties files to store resources. This class is the most commonly used for working with resource bundles in Java and is the default mechanism used by the **ResourceBundle** class's static **getBundle( )** methods.

Because the **PropertyResourceBundle** class is the default (and the most commonly used) implementation, it's important to know how it works. The **PropertyResourceBundle** class provides an interface to access resources stored in properties files. Internally, it uses the **java.util.Properties** class. The **PropertyResourceBundle** class requires that resource bundle properties files be named using a special scheme, which takes the following format:

bundlename_language_country_variant.properties

For example, if you had a bundle named MessageResources for the English language in the United States for the Windows platform, the properties file would be **MessageResources_en_US_WIN.properties**. Of course, not all locale components are required, so the name for a simple English file would be **MessageResources_en.properties**. Resource bundles also support the concept of a default resource bundle, which in this case is simply **MessageResources.properties**.

The default resource bundle is used when there is not a bundle for a locale or if a locale-specific bundle does not have an entry for a certain resource. For example, if you have a French bundle and it does not contain an entry for a requested resource, the **ResourceBundle** classes will attempt to find an entry for that resource in the default bundle. Typically, applications use the default bundle to store the English version of resources and then create language-specific bundles for other languages. However, if a language-specific bundle does not have an entry for a resource, the English version will be used from the default bundle.

The java.text.MessageFormat Class

The **MessageFormat** class provides methods for creating locale-specific formatted messages. As you saw in the preceding section, resource bundles can be used to retrieve locale-specific static messages from properties files. Although that is quite useful, there will be times when a message needs to be constructed dynamically, at run time. The **MessageFormat** class provides the means for creating locale-specific dynamic messages. To understand what dynamic messages are, it helps to first review properties file–based static messages. An example snippet from a properties file is shown next:

```
error.firstName.required=First Name is required.
error.lastName.required=Last Name is required.
```

This snippet shows two properties whose values are very similar. The main difference between them is simply the subject of what is required. Using this model, a property would have to be created for every required field, with each property being almost identical to the next. Thus, significant duplication would exist.

With the **MessageFormat** class, you can create a dynamic message to solve the problem of duplication. Instead of creating a separate static property for each required field, you create one dynamic property that can be used to generate specific messages. Following is an example of a dynamic message:

```
error.required={0} is required.
```

This property specifies a placeholder with **{0}**. The **MessageFormat** class takes a dynamic message and a list of substitution data and replaces the dynamic message's placeholders with the substitution data. To illustrate how this works, consider the following example code:

```
ResourceBundle bundle = ResourceBundle.getBundle("MessageResources");
String requiredMessage = bundle.getString("error.required");

String[] substituteData1 = {"First Name"};
String firstNameMessage =
  MessageFormat.format(requiredMessage, substituteData1);

String[] substituteData2 = {"Last Name"};
String lastNameMessage =
  MessageFormat.format(requiredMessage, substituteData2);
```

In this example, the dynamic message is used twice, with different substitution data to create unique messages. This is a powerful and often used technique in internationalized applications. Of course, the **MessageFormat** class accepts a locale in its constructor so that dynamic messages can be tailored to specific locales.

Understanding Struts' Internationalization Support

Now that you have reviewed Java's built-in support for internationalization, you are ready to see how internationalization works in Struts. Struts is similar to Java in that internationalization support was a base requirement and not an afterthought. Struts was designed from the ground up to provide strong support for internationalizing an application. This is one of its most valuable features. For the most part, Struts' internationalization support is built on top of Java's. However, Struts uses some of its own facilities for internationalization where necessary.

Like Java, Struts' internationalization support is centered on the **Locale** class and resource bundles. However, Struts differs in that it uses its own custom set of classes for managing and accessing resource bundles. The Struts **org.apache.struts.util.MessageResources** class and its descendant class, **org.apache.struts.util.PropertyMessageResources**, provide functionality parallel to the **ResourceBundle** and **PropertyResourceBundle** classes built into Java. Struts uses these custom classes to manage resource bundles because the built-in Java classes are not serializable. Because Struts applications can be deployed in distributed (i.e., clustered) application server environments, Struts requires that any objects it manages be serializable (that is, they must implement the **java.io.Serializable** interface). Because Java's **ResourceBundle** classes are not serializable, Struts has created its own classes that duplicate their functionality and are serializable.

The following three sections cover the specifics of how internationalization works in Struts, starting with an overview of how Struts handles locale, followed by an overview of Struts' message resources, and concluding with a section on how Struts' tag libraries support internationalization.

Locale

Like other Java applications, Struts applications use **Locale** objects to store users' locale settings and to customize content based on those settings. Struts determines a user's locale from the HTTP requests made to the application. When making a request to a Web server, browsers pass along an HTTP header (**Accept-Language**) that indicates the user's locale. Java's **javax.servlet.http.HttpServletRequest** request object makes this locale setting available to servlets via a **getLocale( )** method, which returns a **Locale** object containing the settings from the request.

When a user first accesses a Struts application, Struts captures the user's locale and stores it in the user's session. Storing the locale in the session allows it to be easily accessed throughout the Struts framework from one convenient place. A side benefit of placing the **Locale** object in a user's session (instead of simply requesting it each time from a request) is that applications can update the locale settings for a user independent of the browser settings. For example, assume that a user accesses an application from a browser with English set as its locale. You can change the user's locale (say to French) without making the user change the browser settings by simply placing another **Locale** object into the user's session. Struts would then operate based on the new locale because Struts determines locale settings from the object stored in the session, not the settings passed in on each request.

Conversely, sometimes it's necessary to override Struts' default behavior of storing locale settings in the session. For example, your application may want to always use the locale settings specified in the request. That way if the user changes his or her browser settings, Struts will pick up the change. To do this, you have to configure Struts not to store locales in the session by setting the **controller** element's **locale** attribute to **false** in your application's Struts configuration file, as shown here:

```
<controller locale="false"/>
```

Message Resources

As you saw in the example application in Chapter 2, message resources are a fundamental building block in Struts applications whether you're intending to internationalize your application or not. Struts uses message resources as a means of dynamically inserting text into JSPs as well as for storing error messages that get returned from data validations. By using message resources in this way, it's easy to internationalize an application, whether it is an initial requirement for your application or an enhancement. You simply store all of your application's text in resource bundles. Then, when it comes time to internationalize the application, all you have to do is create locale-specific versions of the resource bundle. Struts transparently handles selecting the right resource bundle from which to obtain resources based on the user's locale.

To use message resources, you must create a properties file for your resources to be stored in. The standard name that Struts applications use for this file is **MessageResources .properties**; however, you can use any filename with an extension of **.properties**. Like Java's built-in **PropertyResourceBundle** class, **PropertyMessageResources** requires that locale-specific versions of the file specify the locale information in the filename. For example, to create a French version of the **MessageResources.properties** file, you would create a file named **MessageResources_fr.properties**. Also in parallel with Java's version, **PropertyMessageResources** will attempt to load resources for a locale from the corresponding locale-specific resource bundle. If the resource bundle does not exist or the resource does not exist in the bundle, Struts will attempt to load the resource from the default resource bundle.

Once you have created a properties file, it has to be placed somewhere on your application's classpath (i.e., somewhere beneath the **/WEB-INF/classes/** directory or inside a **.jar** file underneath the **/WEB-INF/lib** directory). This is necessary because Struts uses Java's class loader to load the properties file. This is very important. If the file is not on your application's classpath, Struts will not be able to access the file. Next, you have to configure Struts to know where the file is located. This is done by placing a **message-resources** element in your application's Struts configuration file, as shown next:

```
<!-- Message Resources Configuration -->
<message-resources
  parameter="com.jamesholmes.minihr.MessageResources"/>
```

The **parameter** attribute of the **message-resources** element informs Struts of the location of your application's resource bundle. Notice that the directory of the file is specified using Java's package notation with dots. Thus, the resource bundle in the preceding example is in a directory named **com/jamesholmes/minihr** that is somewhere on the classpath, and the resource bundle filename is **MessageResources**. Struts automatically appends **.properties** to the filename specified with the **parameter** attribute. If you mistakenly specify the **.properties** extension, Struts will not be able to locate your file.

You can define multiple resource bundles in the Struts configuration files by using multiple **message-resources** elements. Each additional resource bundle beyond the main, default bundle has to specify a logical bundle name using the **key** attribute, as shown next:

```
<!-- Message Resources Configuration -->
<message-resources
  parameter="com.jamesholmes.minihr.MessageResources"/>
<message-resources
        key="alternate"
  parameter="com.jamesholmes.minihr.AlternateResources"/>
```

The main resource bundle does not specify a logical name because it is the default bundle. Additional bundles have to specify a logical name so that they can be explicitly referenced by name by the application.

After you have created a resource bundle and configured Struts to use it, you can make use of it in your application a couple ways. First, you can dynamically insert text into JSPs by using the Bean Tag Library's **message** tag, as shown here:

```
...
<head>
<title><bean:message key="searchPage.title"/></title>
</head>
...
```

This example dynamically inserts the value of the **searchPage.title** resource into the JSP at run time. Second, you can return a set of messages from an action to a JSP by using Struts' **ActionMessages** class.

NOTE *When your application first accesses a resource bundle, Struts loads the bundle into memory and caches it so that it can be quickly accessed again. Because of this, if you modify your resource bundles while your application is running, you will have to restart your application server before you can see the changes.*

Struts' Tag Library Support for Internationalization

Several of the Struts tag library tags support internationalization by way of allowing certain attributes' values to be specified as keys to properties in a message resources bundle. At run time, Struts uses the keys to look up a corresponding value and then uses the value for the given attribute. The following table lists each of the tags and their attributes that support internationalization.

Library	Tag	Attribute
Bean	message	key
Bean	write	formatKey
HTML	button	altKey
HTML	button	titleKey
HTML	cancel	altKey
HTML	cancel	titleKey
HTML	checkbox	altKey
HTML	checkbox	titleKey
HTML	file	altKey
HTML	file	titleKey
HTML	frame	titleKey
HTML	hidden	altKey
HTML	hidden	titleKey
HTML	image	altKey
HTML	image	pageKey
HTML	image	srcKey

PART II

Library	Tag	Attribute
HTML	image	titleKey
HTML	img	altKey
HTML	img	pageKey
HTML	img	srcKey
HTML	img	titleKey
HTML	link	titleKey
HTML	messages	footer
HTML	messages	header
HTML	multibox	altKey
HTML	multibox	titleKey
HTML	option	key
HTML	password	altKey
HTML	password	titleKey
HTML	radio	altKey
HTML	radio	titleKey
HTML	reset	altKey
HTML	reset	titleKey
HTML	select	altKey
HTML	select	titleKey
HTML	submit	altKey
HTML	submit	titleKey
HTML	text	altKey
HTML	text	titleKey
HTML	textarea	altKey
HTML	textarea	titleKey

NOTE *Many of the Struts tags have a* **bundle** *attribute that allows you to specify the name of a bundle from which values are loaded. That way you're not limited to putting all of your internationalized properties into a single resource bundle.*

Internationalizing the Mini HR Application

Now that you've seen how Struts' internationalization support works, you are ready to revisit the Mini HR application and update it to support internationalization. Following is the list of steps involved in adding internationalization support to Mini HR:

1. Add entries for all application text to the **MessageResources.properties** resource bundle file.

2. Create a Spanish version of the **MessageResources.properties** file.
3. Update JSPs to retrieve all application text from the **MessageResources.properties** file.
4. Repackage and run the updated application.

The following sections walk through each step of the process in detail.

Add Entries for All Application Text to the MessageResources.properties Resource Bundle File

The first step in updating Mini HR to support internationalization is to add entries for all application text to the **MessageResources.properties** resource bundle file. As you'll see, having all application text in this file allows it to be easily translated into other languages. The **MessageResources.properties** file from the original Mini HR application in Chapter 2 already contains some of the application's text; however, all text needs to be placed in this file for internationalization to work.

Following is the updated **MessageResources.properties** file in its entirety:

```
# Title Resources
title.application=ABC, Inc. Human Resources Portal
title.employee.search=Employee Search

# Link Resources
link.employee.add=Add an Employee
link.employee.search=Search for Employees

# Label Resources
label.search.name=Name
label.search.ssNum=Social Security Number
label.submit=Submit

# Error Resources
error.search.criteria.missing=Search Criteria Missing
error.search.ssNum.invalid=Invalid Social Security Number
error.search.not.found=No Employees Found
errors.header=<font color="red"><cTypeface:Bold>Validation Error(s)</b></
font><ul>
errors.footer=</ul><hr width="100%" size="1" noshade="true">
errors.prefix=<li>
errors.suffix=</li>
```

Notice that there are several new entries. All of the text from the JSPs has been moved into this file so that the application can have both English and Spanish versions.

Create a Spanish Version of the MessageResources.properties File

Once entries for all of the application text have been put in the **MessageResources.properties** file, you have to create a Spanish version of the file to support Spanish users. Do this by creating the **MessageResources_es.properties** file, shown here:

```
# Title Resources
title.application=ABC, Inc. Recursos Humanos Porta
title.employee.search=Búsqueda Del Empleado
```

```
# Link Resources
link.employee.add=Agregue a empleado
link.employee.search=Búsqueda para los empleados

# Label Resources
label.search.name=Nombre
label.search.ssNum=Número De la Seguridad Social
label.submit=Someter

# Error Resources
error.search.criteria.missing=El Faltar De los Criterios De la Búsqueda
error.search.ssNum.invalid=Número Inválido De la Seguridad Social
error.search.not.found=Ningunos Empleados Encontraron
errors.header=<font color="red"><cTypeface:Bold>Error De la Validación(s)</b></
font><ul>
errors.footer=</ul><hr width="100%" size="1" noshade="true">
errors.suffix=<li>
errors.prefix=</li>
```

Notice that this file's name is only slightly different from **MessageResources.properties** in that it has **_es** appended to the **MessageResources** part of the original filename. The **_es** denotes which locale the file is for—in this case, the Spanish language. You could, of course, include a country code along with the language code to make the file specific to a certain country/language combination. This file contains all the same entries as the **MessageResources.properties** file, but the property values are in Spanish. The property names are universal across all locales' files. That's how applications reference the text.

NOTE *The translations in this section were performed using Google's translation service and are for demonstration purposes only.*

Update JSPs to Retrieve All Application Text from the MessageResources.properties File

After you have updated **MessageResources.properties** and created a **MessageResources_es.properties** file, you have to update Mini HR's JSPs. The original JSPs have a mix of hard-coded text and text that is dynamically inserted into the page from the **MessageResources.properties** file. In order to support internationalization, all of the hard-coded text has to be moved into the **MessageResources.properties** file so that it can be obtained dynamically, based on locale. Following are the updated JSPs, **index.jsp** and **search.jsp**, with all the hard-coded text replaced with **<bean:message>** tags that dynamically insert the text into the pages.

index.jsp:

```
<%@ taglib uri="http://struts.apache.org/tags-bean" prefix="bean" %>
<%@ taglib uri="http://struts.apache.org/tags-html" prefix="html" %>

<html>
<head>
<title><bean:message key="title.application"/></title>
</head>
<body>
```

```
<font size="+1"><bean:message key="title.application"/></font><br>

<hr width="100%" noshade="true">

&#149; <bean:message key="link.employee.add"/><br>
&#149; <html:link forward="search">
<bean:message key="link.employee.search"/></html:link><br>

</body>
</html>
```

search.jsp:

```
<%@ taglib uri="http://struts.apache.org/tags-bean" prefix="bean" %>
<%@ taglib uri="http://struts.apache.org/tags-html" prefix="html" %>
<%@ taglib uri="http://struts.apache.org/tags-logic" prefix="logic" %>

<html>
<head>
<title>
<bean:message key="title.application"/> -
<bean:message key="title.employee.search"/>
</title>
</head>
<body>

<font size="+1">
<bean:message key="title.application"/> -
<bean:message key="title.employee.search"/>
</font><br>
<hr width="100%" noshade="true">

<html:errors/>

<html:form action="/search">

<table>
<tr>
<td align="right"><bean:message key="label.search.name"/>:</td>
<td><html:text property="name"/></td>
</tr>
<tr>
<td></td>
<td>-- or --</td>
</tr>
<tr>
<td align="right"><bean:message key="label.search.ssNum"/>:</td>
<td><html:text property="ssNum"/> (xxx-xx-xxxx)</td>
</tr>
<tr>
<td></td>
<td><html:submit><bean:message key="label.submit"/></html:submit></td>
</tr>
</table>
```

PART II

```
</html:form>

<logic:present name="searchForm" property="results">

<hr width="100%" size="1" noshade="true">

<bean:size id="size" name="searchForm" property="results"/>
<logic:equal name="size" value="0">
<center><font color="red"><b>
<bean:message key="error.search.not.found"/>
</b></font></center>
</logic:equal>

<logic:greaterThan name="size" value="0">
<table border="1">
<tr>
<th><bean:message key="label.search.name"/></th>
<th><bean:message key="label.search.ssNum"/></th>
</tr>
<logic:iterate id="result" name="searchForm" property="results">
<tr>
<td><bean:write name="result" property="name"/></td>
<td><bean:write name="result" property="ssNum"/></td>
</tr>
</logic:iterate>
</table>
</logic:greaterThan>

</logic:present>

</body>
<html>
```

Note that the Bean Tag Library definition had to be added to **index.jsp** so that it could use the **<bean:message>** tag to source in text.

Repackage and Run the Updated Application

Because no Java source code files had to be modified to update the Mini HR application to support internationalization, you do not have to recompile the application. All you have to do is repackage the application and redeploy it before running it again. Assuming that you've made modifications to the original Mini HR application and it was set up in the **c:\java\MiniHR** directory (as described in Chapter 2), the following command line will repackage the application:

```
jar cf MiniHR.war *
```

This command should be run from the directory where you have set up the Mini HR application (e.g., **c:\java\MiniHR**).

To test the Spanish version of the application, you have to change your browser's language settings to Spanish. Following are the instructions for doing this with Microsoft Internet Explorer 6:

1. Open Internet Explorer's Internet Options dialog box by selecting Tools | Internet Options.
2. Click the Languages button on the General tab of the Internet Options dialog box.
3. Click the Add button in the Language Preference dialog box.

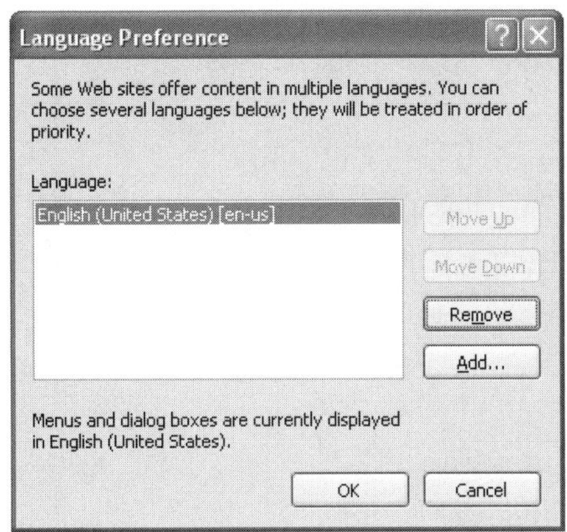

4. Add the Spanish (United States) [es-us] language preference by selecting it in the list, as shown here, and then clicking OK.

5. Select the Spanish (United States) [es-us] language preference and click Move Up so that it is the first preference in the list, like this.

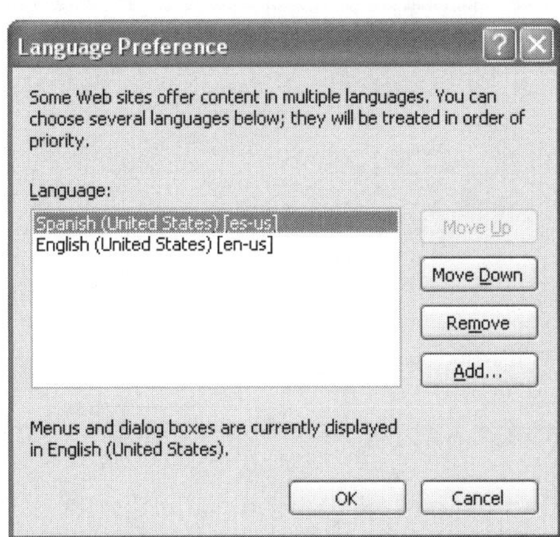

Once you have added the Spanish language setting for your browser, you need to place the new **MiniHR.war** file that you just created into Tomcat's **webapps** directory, delete the **webapps/MiniHR** directory, and start Tomcat. As before, to access the Mini HR application, point your browser to **http://localhost:8080/MiniHR/**. When you run the updated Mini HR application with your browser set to Spanish, it should detect that you are accessing it from a Spanish-language browser and automatically serve the Spanish version of the application. Figure 10-1 shows the search page in Spanish.

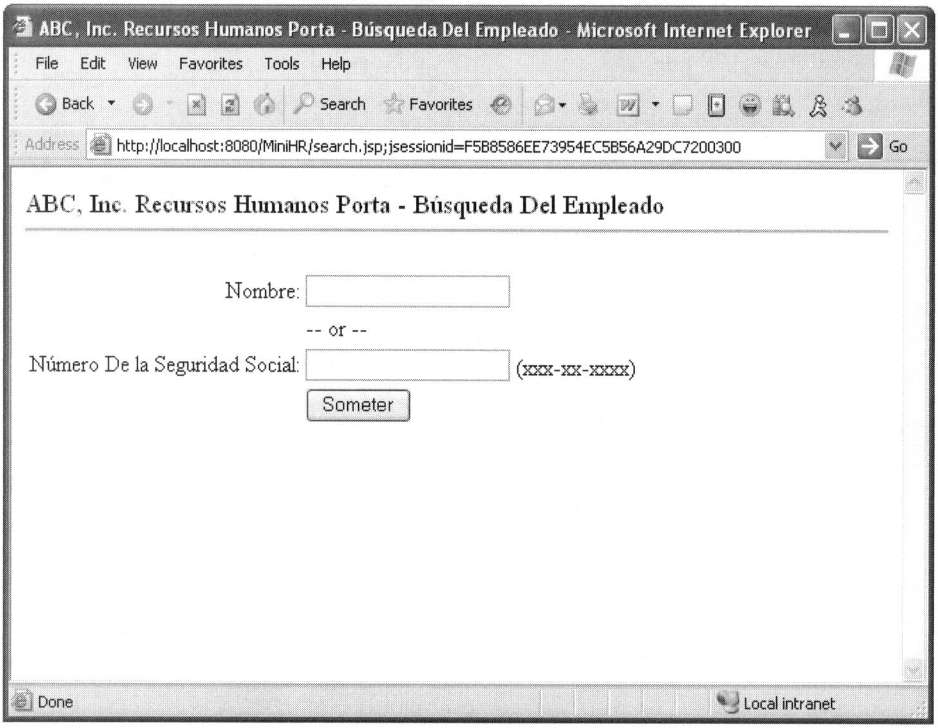

Figure 10-1 The Spanish version of the search page

11

CHAPTER

Securing Struts Applications

Most Web applications require certain aspects of the system to be secured in some manner. Security requirements are often specified at both the system and functional levels. System requirements may dictate, for example, that entry of sensitive information should be performed over a secure HTTP connection (HTTPS). On a higher level, functional requirements may dictate that only users with administrative privileges can access certain pages and menu items. From a developer's perspective, the critical task is to identify which of the requirements can be satisfied using standard security mechanisms, and which requirements require a customized security solution. Quite often, security requirements dictate some sort of customization. In some cases, you can use a combination of standard security mechanisms and customization to achieve the desired security policy.

Levels of Security

Security is a fairly broad topic and may encompass everything from encryption to personalization, depending on how "security" is defined. This chapter focuses on the levels of security that you can implement to secure your Struts applications, beginning in this section with an overview of the various security levels. That is followed by sections that look in depth at using container-managed security and application-managed security, the two primary ways to secure your Struts applications.

- Transport-level security using HTTPS
- Authentication and authorization
- Role-based access control
- Container-managed security
- Application-managed security

Some aspects of personalization—specifically, some techniques for hiding or displaying content based on a user's authorization—will also be covered.

Providing Secure Communications

Data can be securely transmitted by using HTTP over Secure Socket Layer (referred to as HTTPS). HTTPS secures data by encrypting the protocol at the transport level. In other words, the entire HTTP conversation between the client browser and the Web server is encrypted. Struts applications, like most Web applications, can send data over HTTPS without modification.

HTTPS does impact performance, however. There is an order of magnitude of performance penalty when using HTTPS. To reduce the impact on performance, it is common for applications to switch the protocol between HTTP and HTTPS. The typical scenario uses the HTTPS protocol for application login and submission of sensitive data. Once the data has been transmitted, the protocol is switched back to HTTP. While on the surface this seems like a good approach, it leaves open a serious security hole whereby the user's session can be hijacked. Sensitive user information, such as a credit card number, may be stored in that session. A network snoop could use the session ID to spoof a valid user session. Due to this risk, container-managed security does not support protocol switching. However, if you need protocol switching and can accept the security risks, there are mechanisms for doing so that integrate with Struts, as you will see in "Integrating Struts with SSL," later in this chapter.

Authentication and Authorization

Authentication is the process of proving to an application that you are who you say you are. For Web applications, this process is most commonly associated with entering a username and password. If you are registered as a user of the application and you provide a valid password, the application allows access to privileged features of the application. In contrast, if you cannot provide valid credentials, you are allowed access only to the public areas of the site. In fact, many Web applications may only allow authenticated access—with the only public page being the login screen. Authentication can be provided through custom coding for the application, or by using container-managed security services.

Authorization is how the application determines which aspects of the Web application you are allowed to access. Generally speaking, determining a user's authorization requires the user to first be authenticated. At that point, application-provided or container-managed security can be used to determine a user's authorization.

Role-Based Access Control

Role-based access control (RBAC) is a common scheme for implementing authorization. Users are assigned roles through a container-specific means. When a user is authenticated, the user's roles are associated with the HTTP request. Given this information, access to certain pages or user interface components can be allowed or disallowed based on the user's roles. In most cases, a user is allowed to have multiple roles. However, roles are typically flat; that is, there is no hierarchical relationship between roles.

Container- vs. Application-Managed Security

Servlet containers provide security as specified by the servlet specification. Container-managed security allows the developer to declaratively specify how authentication is to be performed and how authorization is to be granted. Container-managed security provides an easy, unobtrusive way of adding security to an application. This mechanism of implementing security provides the following benefits:

- It is declarative. Authentication and authorization are specified in the **web.xml** file. Container-specific details, such as the security realm, typically are configured in server-specific XML configuration files.
- It supports multiple authentication schemes, such as password authentication, FORM-based authentication, authentication using encrypted passwords, and authentication using client-side digital certificates.
- Using container-specific security realms, user data can be provided by a variety of stores, including flat files, relational databases, and Lightweight Directory Access Protocol (LDAP) servers.
- Redirects are handled automatically. In other words, the container determines when a user is accessing a protected URL, prompts for user credentials, and, if authenticated, redirects to the requested page. This is a powerful mechanism, particularly for applications that publish links to protected pages in e-mail communications.

Containers are, however, somewhat limiting because of the following:

- The implementation of container-managed security varies by container. An application using container-managed security generally requires modification at some level when ported from one application server to another.
- The login flow does not allow easy custom processing of login requests. In other words, additional processing cannot be performed in the authentication process.
- Authorization can only use a flat, role-based approach. Access to Web pages cannot be granted based on multiple factors, for example, a managerial level and a department number.
- FORM-based login forces a workflow that uses a separate page for login. This limits the flexibility of the application.
- Container-managed authentication requires changes to the application server's configuration that may not be allowed in a hosted environment.

These limitations can be overcome by using application-managed security. However, using application-managed security means that custom code must be designed and written. The decision of which approach to take should be driven by the requirements. While container-managed security is simpler to implement, it does restrict the flexibility of your security policy. One container's security implementation may be different from another's, making your application less portable. Also, container-managed security limits you to a specific login workflow that may not be what you want for your application.

Application-managed security, on the other hand, allows you to implement your security policy as needed at the price of requiring more custom code. Struts mitigates this problem by allowing for customized role processing via a chain command (or a custom request processor in versions of Struts prior to 1.3). Also, servlet filters can be used to apply across-the-board security policies. Cookies can be used to persist user login information between sessions. In addition, there are Struts extensions that permit finer-grained control of the use of HTTPS.

One last point: there is a somewhat hybrid approach that allows programmatic access to the methods that are usually only available when using container-managed security. This interesting mechanism will be covered later in the chapter, in the section "Using Servlet Filters for Security."

Using Container-Managed Security

To explain how to use container-managed security, this section describes how you would apply container-managed security to the Mini HR application, introduced in Chapter 2, to fulfill a particular security requirement. Assume that Mini HR resides on ABC, Inc.'s corporate intranet. The application allows anyone to access the employee search. However, only *administrators* can add or remove employees from the database. If someone attempts to perform an administrator function, that user is prompted to input a username and password. If the password is valid, and the user is an administrator, the application will display the requested page.

Although this security requirement can be completely fulfilled without making any modifications to Java code or JSP pages, as you will see, it is often better to group URLs under role-specific path prefixes. Therefore, you must change the location of **add.jsp** and **add.do** to **/admin/add.jsp** and **/admin/add.do**, respectively. This also means that you need to change the **index.jsp** page and the **struts-config.xml** file. Making these changes may seem burdensome, but it will make implementing security easier. Following are the additions needed to **web.xml** to implement container-managed security:

```
<web-app>
    [... snipped ...]
    <security-constraint>
        <web-resource-collection>
            <web-resource-name>AdminPages</web-resource-name>
            <description>Administrator-only pages</description>
            <url-pattern>/admin/*</url-pattern>
        </web-resource-collection>
        <auth-constraint>
            <role-name>administrator</role-name>
        </auth-constraint>
    </security-constraint>
    <login-config>
        <auth-method>BASIC</auth-method>
        <realm-name>MiniHRRealm</realm-name>
    </login-config>
    <security-role>
        <description>HR Administrator</description>
        <role-name>administrator</role-name>
    </security-role>
</web-app>
```

The three XML elements (**security-constraint**, **login-config**, and **security-role**) that were added define the security requirements. The **security-constraint** element associates a collection of pages with a role. The pages are identified using URL patterns. If a user attempts to access a page that matches one of the patterns and the user has the associated role, then the user is allowed access. If the user has not yet been authenticated, the user is prompted to log in according to the settings of the **login-config** element. If the user authenticates and has the *administrator* role, then the user is redirected to the requested page.

Before discussing the login configurations, a quick detour is necessary to describe URL patterns. These patterns, also known as *URL mappings,* are dictated by the Java servlet specification. Four types of patterns are searched, in the following order:

- **Explicit mapping** No wildcards are used (e.g., **/add.jsp** or **/admin/remove.do**).
- **Path prefix mapping** Contains a **/**, then a path prefix, then a **/***. This mapping can be used to specify an entire subbranch of your Web application (e.g., **/admin/*** or **/search/company/***).
- **Extension mapping** Contains ***.** followed by an extension. This mapping can be used to specify all files of a certain type (e.g., ***.jsp**). It is also often used to map Struts actions (e.g., ***.do**).
- **Default mapping /** Matches all URLs for the Web application. This mapping matches any URL of the Web application. Any URL beginning with the context path of the Web application will match this pattern.

As you can see, these patterns are not very flexible. You cannot, for example, specify a pattern of **/add.***. If you did not place the administrative URLs under a specific path prefix, you would have to explicitly list each constrained URL. From a security perspective, partitioning your application using role-based paths makes securing the application much easier. Even if you are not using container-managed security, this approach has benefits, as you will discover later, in the section "Using Servlet Filters for Security."

If you decide to use Struts modules, then you have already established some partitioning for your application. Each module will be in its own path off the context root. Organizing modules by role is a reasonable approach—therefore, the use of Struts modules generally will make implementing your security policy easier.

Login Configurations

The **login-config** element indicates the type of authentication to be performed and where the user information can be found. A Web application can have only one login configuration. The **auth-method** nested element indicates the type of authentication and accepts the values listed and described in the following table.

Authentication	Description
BASIC	The browser pops up a dialog box that allows the user to enter a username and password. The username and password are encoded using the Base-64 algorithm and sent to the server. The Base-64 algorithm is a common Web encoding scheme that is often used to encode e-mail attachments and so on.
FORM	Allows for a custom form to be specified. The form must contain a **j_username** field for the username and a **j_password** field for the password. The form must submit to **j_security_check**. The username and password are Base-64 encoded.
DIGEST	Similar to BASIC authentication except that the username and password are encrypted into a message digest value. This configuration may not be supported by all browsers.
CLIENT-CERT	The client is required to provide a digital certificate for authentication. This is the most secure configuration. However, it also is the most costly. Certificates for production use must be purchased from a certificate authority.

In addition to specifying the type of login, the login configuration may also specify a security realm. A *security realm* is essentially the store from which a Web application retrieves and verifies user credentials. In addition, a realm provides a mechanism for specifying the roles that users may have. For the login configuration, no details of the realm can be provided other than the realm name. That name refers, either directly or indirectly, to a container-specific security realm implementation.

DIGEST authentication provides the same basic user experience as BASIC. However, because DIGEST authentication may not be supported by all browsers, it is not discussed further here. There are ways of encrypting the user credentials without requiring DIGEST. CLIENT-CERT requires the user to have a digital certificate. This chapter discusses only BASIC and FORM-based login because these are the authentication methods that are encountered in most situations.

BASIC Login

The simplest way to get started with container-managed security is to use BASIC authentication, which involves the use of the security realm. The security realm serves as a reference to container-specific security storage. The mechanism for associating this logical realm to the concrete realm varies by container. Typically, realms can be based on flat files (for example, property files or XML files), a relational database, or an LDAP server. Some containers, such as JBoss, provide a mapping between a realm and a Java Authentication and Authorization Service (JAAS) implementation.

For simplicity, the security realm for ABC, Inc., will be implemented using the Tomcat **UserDatabase** realm. By its default configuration, Tomcat supports this realm for all applications. The realm retrieves usernames, passwords, roles, and role assignments from the **tomcat-users.xml** file.

You will add three users to the system to test the functionality—two of the users will be assigned the administrator role. The third user will be defined using a nonadministrator role. This third user is defined for testing and illustrative purposes. Add the following four elements (in bold) to the **<TOMCAT_HOME>/conf/tomcat_users.xml** file:

```
<tomcat-users>
  <role name="administrator"/>
  <user name="bsiggelkow" password="thatsme" roles="administrator"/>
  <user name="jholmes"  password="maindude" roles="administrator"/>
  <user name="gburdell"   password="gotech" roles="employee"/>
</tomcat-users>
```

Now, deploy this new version of the Mini HR application. You need to restart Tomcat to enable the new functionality. Then, browse to the welcome page, **index.jsp**. You should see no differences here. Next, click the Add an Employee link. Your browser will display a dialog box similar to that shown in Figure 11-1.

Entering a valid username and password of a user with the administrator role displays the requested page. If the user does not have the administrator role but is otherwise valid, an HTTP status of 403 (Forbidden) is the response. Likewise, if you click Cancel, an HTTP status of 401 (Unauthorized) is returned. If a matching username and password are not found, then the dialog box simply redisplays.

Once a user has been authenticated, the Web application can glean useful user data from the HTTP request. The two methods of interest are **getUserPrincipal( )**, which can be used to acquire the username, and **isUserInRole( )**, which can be used to determine if a user has

FIGURE 11-1 Browser-provided authentication dialog box

a specified role. These methods can be used in the **Action** classes to perform such things as the following:

- Load the user's profile and store it in the session.
- Render a specific response or redirect to a certain URL based on the user's role.

In addition to the programmatic uses of this data, Struts applications can also use this information to do the following:

- Allow role-based access to **Action** classes configured in the Struts configuration file.
- Dynamically hide or display presentation components (links, buttons, menus, etc.) based on the user's role using the Logic Tag Library's **<logic:present>** and **<logic: notPresent>** tags.

The first two programmatic uses are available to any JSP/servlet-based application. The Struts-specific uses, however, warrant more discussion.

Action mappings in the Struts configuration file have an optional **roles** attribute, which accepts a comma-separated list of roles. If a user has any one of those roles, the user can access the action. Otherwise, access is denied. This attribute provides a much more natural way of granting/denying access than using the URL patterns. Note, however, that using the action mappings only restricts access to URLs served through the Struts controller (e.g., ***.do**). It does not restrict access to JSP pages or static HTML pages. The following snippet from a Struts configuration file shows the use of the **roles** attribute:

```
<action path="/add"
        type="com.jamesholmes.minihr.AddAction"
        name="addForm"
        scope="request"
        validate="true"
        input="/add.jsp"
        roles="administrator">
</action>
```

If your Web application places the JSP pages under the **WEB-INF** folder (which makes them protected resources) and *all* requests are handled by the Struts controller, the **roles** attribute can be used to completely control access to Web resources.

NOTE *The* **WEB-INF** *folder is a protected folder whose files cannot be accessed directly via a browser. Thus, placing JSPs underneath this folder makes them inaccessible directly via a browser; however, the JSPs can be forwarded to using a servlet such as the Struts* **ActionServlet**. *Another method for protecting JSPs from direct access is to use a* **<security-constraint>** *definition in the* **web.xml** *file setup with a role to which no user is assigned.*

As mentioned, the rendering of portions of a JSP page can be based on role using the Logic Tag Library tags. Considering the main page, it might be worthwhile to display the Add an Employee link only if the user is an administrator. Such a page might look something like the following:

```
<ul>
<logic:present role="administrator"/>
  <li><html:link forward="add">Add an Employee</html:link></li>
</logic:present>
  <li><html:link forward="search">Search for Employees</html:link></li>
</ul>
```

However, this approach leads to a common problem with container-managed security. You want to show the link only if the user is an administrator, but you don't know if the user is an administrator unless the user selects the link and is authenticated. There are several alternatives that you can use to solve this problem. One alternative is to force all users to log in—obviously leading to disgruntled users if the login does not add value. Another alternative is to provide a means for a user to proactively log in.

The proactive login behavior can still be accomplished by using container-managed security—albeit through some trickery. What you will do is create a link on the main page (**index.jsp**) to a security-constrained JSP page (**/admin/admin_login.jsp**). This page will simply redirect back to the main page. Since it will be a protected page, the user will be forced to log in.

The **admin_login.jsp** page is as simple as the following:

```
<%@ taglib uri="http://struts.apache.org/tags-logic" prefix="logic" %>
<logic:redirect page="/index.jsp"/>
```

The **<logic:redirect>** tag results in an HTTP redirect response. The **page** attribute of the tag indicates where to redirect the response. In this example, this will result in a redirect to the main page of the application. Since this page is put under the **/admin** path, no changes are necessary to the security constraint in the **web.xml** file.

The user experience now is as follows:

1. When the index page is first displayed, the user does not see the Add an Employee link but can log in.
2. Upon login, the index is redisplayed, this time displaying the administrative link.
3. Upon selecting this link, the user does not have to reauthenticate.

FORM-Based Login

FORM-based login is another variant of a container-managed login configuration. With FORM-based login, you supply a Web page (either a JSP or static HTML page) that contains the login form and a page to display if an error occurs. This provides a much more consistent look and feel for your application. The behavior of FORM-based login when a user is trying to access protected resources is similar to the behavior of BASIC login. To implement FORM-based login, you supply a Web page that has a form for login that must follow specific guidelines. The form must submit two parameters with the names **j_username** and **j_password**, holding the username and password respectively, to the **j_security_check** URL. Optionally, you can also specify a Web page that will be displayed if a login error occurs. Here's the **login_form.html** page:

```
<html>
<head>
<title>ABC, Inc. Human Resources Portal</title>
</head>
<body>
  <font size="+1">ABC, Inc. Human Resources Portal Login</font><br>
  <hr width="100%" noshade="true">
  <form action="j_security_check">
    Username: <input type="text" name="j_username"/><br/>
    Password: <input type="password" name="j_password"/><br/>
    <input type="submit" value="Login"/>
  </form>
</body>
</html>
```

Next, change the **login-config** element of **web.xml** to use FORM-based authentication:

```
<login-config>
  <auth-method>FORM</auth-method>
  <realm-name>MiniHRRealm</realm-name>
  <form-login-config>
    <form-login-page>/login_form.html</form-login-page>
    <form-error-page>/login_error.html</form-error-page>
  </form-login-config>
</login-config>
```

Now, instead of displaying the standard dialog box, the browser displays the new page (albeit a little bland in this case). Once authenticated, the user is taken back to the **index.jsp** page, where the hidden link is now displayed.

A natural progression of these modifications is to place the login form on the main index page, thereby reducing an extra mouse click and page display. This approach is quite common in Web applications. Often, the main pages of applications have a login form on the welcome page. The main page provides lots of information to anyone. When you log in, however, the user experience becomes personalized for you. However, if you move the login form to the Mini HR **index.jsp** page, you will find that it will not work. When you submit your username and password, an error will occur. Tomcat generates the following error: "HTTP Status 400 – Invalid direct reference to form login page."

Tomcat raises this error because the login page can only be managed by the container. Access by a user to a protected page is the only mechanism that should trigger display of the login page. In the container-managed authentication workflow, once a user is authenticated, the client is then redirected to the requested protected page. If the user browses directly to the login page, the protected resource to redirect to is undefined. In other words, if the user were to submit the form, the container would not know where to redirect the request.

There is no good work-around for this problem. This is one of the frustrations with FORM-based authentication and container-managed security—a simple change in requirements (e.g., put the login on the main page) causes you to rethink your security implementation. However, if you and your users can live with the constraints of container-managed security, it is a great way to provide robust security with minimal coding.

Container-Managed Secure Transport

The last container-managed security service to be discussed concerns transport-level security. This service operates by declaratively specifying whether pages should be accessed using HTTPS. This is specified using the **user-data-constraint** subelement of the **security-constraint** element. Following is a sample from **web.xml**:

```
<security-constraint>
  <web-resource-collection>
    <web-resource-name>AdminPages</web-resource-name>
    <description>Administrator-only pages</description>
    <url-pattern>/admin/*</url-pattern>
  </web-resource-collection>
  <auth-constraint>
    <role-name>administrator</role-name>
  </auth-constraint>
  <user-data-constraint>
    <transport-guarantee>
      CONFIDENTIAL
    </transport-guarantee>
  </user-data-constraint>
</security-constraint>
```

The key here is the **transport-guarantee** element. The values accepted are the following:

- **NONE** No restrictions, use normal HTTP
- **INTEGRAL** Use HTTPS
- **CONFIDENTIAL** Use HTTPS

It is important to note that the use of the **user-data-constraint** subelement does *not* require specification of an authentication constraint. This means that you can define Web resources that are secure but do not require authentication. This is useful, for example, when you are using application-managed authentication but still want to use a container-managed protocol. At one time, the servlet specification did not indicate how this constraint was to be handled. Some servers would not automatically redirect to HTTPS but instead would simply report an error and leave the user dumbfounded.

Tomcat 4 does redirect to HTTPS; however, it does not always redirect back to HTTP after leaving the constrained page. Also, the behavior seems to vary by browser. Fortunately, there is a more flexible solution for Struts 1.2 (and older) applications, which is described in "Integrating Struts with SSL" later in this chapter. For the time being, you may want to experiment using Tomcat with HTTPS and setting the transport guarantee. Like other container-managed services, if you can get it to work for you without having to compromise your requirements, then it is worth pursuing.

Application-Managed Security

If container-managed security is not sufficient for your application, then you need to consider creating your own security structure. Generally, you need to address the same issues in application-managed security that are addressed in container-managed security:

- How and when do you authenticate the users?
- What determines the authorization levels?
- Is there a guest user and, if so, what privileges does that user have?
- Does the application need to support HTTPS for transmission of sensitive data?

The following sections look at several ways of handling these issues. As you read through them, you will apply your knowledge to the Mini HR application. Most of this discussion applies to Java-based Web applications in general—not just Struts-based applications.

Creating a Security Service

Using application-managed security requires different skills and knowledge than are required to use a container-managed approach. For application-managed security, you need to rely on traditional "best practices" development. For use with Mini HR, you will create a **SecurityService** interface API that will act as a façade for whatever underlying implementations exist. The definition of the interface to meet the needs of the Mini HR application is shown here:

```
package com.jamesholmes.minihr.security;

public interface SecurityService {
  public User authenticate(String username, String password)
    throws AuthenticationException;
}
```

Next is a sample implementation that uses a **HashMap** to store the user data in memory. Of course, a real implementation would retrieve this data from a persistent store such as a file system, relational database, or LDAP server.

```
package com.jamesholmes.minihr.security;

import java.util.HashMap;
import java.util.Map;

public class SecurityServiceImpl implements SecurityService {
  private Map users;
  private static final String ADMIN_ROLE = "administrator";

  public SecurityServiceImpl() {
    users = new HashMap();
    users.put("bsiggelkow",
      new User( "bsiggelkow","Bill", "Siggelkow",  "thatsme",
```

```
        new String[] {ADMIN_ROLE}));
    users.put("jholmes",
      new User( "jholmes","James", "Holmes",  "maindude",
        new String[] {ADMIN_ROLE}));
    users.put("gburdell",
      new User( "gburdell","George", "Burdell",  "gotech",
        new String[] {ADMIN_ROLE}));
  }

  public User authenticate(String username, String password)
    throws AuthenticationException
  {
    User user = (User) users.get(username);
    if (user == null)
      throw new AuthenticationException("Unknown user");
    boolean passwordIsValid = user.passwordMatch(password);
    if (!passwordIsValid)
      throw new AuthenticationException("Invalid password");
    return user;
  }
}
```

This interface provides the basic security services. The **authenticate( )** method verifies the user's password and returns an object that represents the user. For the authorization needs of the application, there are different alternatives. While it may be tempting to engineer a complete role-based infrastructure, a more pragmatic approach is to provide a mechanism to determine if a user is an administrator. Following is the object that will hold the user data:

```
package com.jamesholmes.minihr.security;

import java.io.Serializable;

public class User implements Serializable {
  private String firstName;
  private String lastName;
  private String username;
  private String password;
  private String[] roles;

  public User(String name, String fName, String lName,
    String pwd, String[] assignedRoles) {
    username = name;
    firstName = fName;
    lastName  = lName;
    password  = pwd
    roles = assignedRoles;
  }

  public String getUsername() {
    return username;
  }

  public String getFirstName() {
```

```
    return firstName;
  }

  public String getLastName() {
    return lastName;
  }

  public boolean passwordMatch(String pwd) {
    return password.equals(pwd);
  }

  public boolean hasRole(String role) {
    if (roles.length > 0) {
      for (int i=0; i<roles.length; i++) {
        if (role.equals(roles[i])) return true;
      }
    }
    return false;
  }

  public boolean isAdministrator() {
    return hasRole("administrator");
  }
}
```

Notice that some basic information that can be used for personalization, such as the user's first and last name, has been included. In addition, the **isAdministrator( )** method indicates whether or not the user is an administrator. Also, a **hasRole( )** method has been implemented that will indicate whether or not a user has been assigned a given role. This method will be useful with customized Struts role processing. To tie this custom security service into the application, you also need to create a **LoginAction** that will process the user login, as shown in the following code. A **LogoutAction** that allows a user to log out of the application is also created by the following code. A logout action typically needs to just invalidate the user's session. While you cannot force a user to log out, it is important to provide this feature, particularly if your application is accessible from a public terminal.

```
package com.jamesholmes.minihr;

import javax.servlet.http.*;
import org.apache.commons.beanutils.PropertyUtils;
import org.apache.struts.action.*;
import com.jamesholmes.minihr.security.*;

public final class LoginAction extends Action {
  public ActionForward execute(ActionMapping mapping,
    ActionForm form,
    HttpServletRequest request,
    HttpServletResponse response)
    throws Exception
  {
    HttpSession session = request.getSession();
    String username =
     (String) PropertyUtils.getSimpleProperty(form, "username");
```

PART II

```
    String password =
     (String) PropertyUtils.getSimpleProperty(form,"password");
    SecurityService service = new SecurityServiceImpl();
    User user = service.authenticate(username, password);
    session.setAttribute("User", user);
    // Forward control to this Action's success forward
    return mapping.findForward("success");
  }
}
```

First, the action gets the username and password from the login form. Then, it calls the **authenticate** method of the security service. The returned user is then stored in the session. The exception handling is performed using Struts' declarative exception handling. Back at the **index.jsp** page, you need to change it from the container-managed implementation as shown in the following example. In this case, you want to check the **administrator** bean property of the user and display the link only if the value is *true*. Note also that you must explicitly check whether the User object is in the session. This handles the case where the user has not yet been authenticated.

```
<%@ taglib uri="http://struts.apache.org/tags-html" prefix="html" %>
<%@ taglib uri="http://struts.apache.org/tags-logic" prefix="logic" %>

<html>
<head>
  <title>ABC, Inc. Human Resources Portal</title>
</head>
<body>
<font size="+1">ABC, Inc. Human Resources Portal</font><br>

<logic:notPresent name="user" scope="session">
<hr width="100%" noshade="true">
<html:form action="/login">
Username: <html:text property="username"/><br/>
Password: <html:password property="password"/><br/>
<html:submit value="Login"/>
</html:form>
<html:errors/>
</logic:notPresent>

<hr width="100%" noshade="true">
<ul>
<logic:present name="user" scope="session">
<logic:equal name="user" property="administrator" value="true">
<li><html:link forward="add">Add an Employee</html:link></li>
</logic:equal>
</logic:present>
<li><html:link forward="search">Search for Employees</html:link></li>
</ul>
</body>
</html>
```

The important modification to this index page is the use of the **<logic:present>** tag to hide or show the login form. In addition, the **<logic:equal>** tag is used to hide or show the

Add an Employee link. You are not finished, however. First, remove (or comment out) the container-managed security sections from the **web.xml** file. Then, remove the **roles** attribute from the **add.do** action mapping.

You are still not done yet. Notice that there is now nothing to prevent someone who is not an administrator from adding a new employee. Anyone can browse directly to the Add an Employee page and submit the form. In addition, although securing the **add.jsp** page is not critical, it is imperative that you secure the **AddAction** (**add.do**). What you need to do is implement the checks that were in place with container-managed security. There are several alternatives to consider.

Page/Action-Level Security Checks

You want to disallow access to the JSP page and, what is more important, to the **AddAction** (**add.do**). The JSP page can be checked by adding in logic to the JSP, similar to the **index.jsp** page, that looks for the **User** object in the session and checks whether the user is an administrator. If the user is not an administrator, a **<logic:redirect>** tag can be used to send the user back to the index page. To protect the action, the most obvious solution is to add these same checks into the **AddAction** class. If the checks fail, the user can be redirected to a page where an error could be displayed, or an exception can be thrown, or an appropriate HTTP status (e.g., 400) can be set in the response. While this solution works for one JSP and one action, it will not scale when many pages and actions are involved.

One mechanism for making this solution scale for the action is to place the authorization check in a base **Action** class. If, however, you still want to use role-based access for authorization, a better solution is to extend the Struts' request processing engine.

Extending Struts' Request Processing Engine

Struts' request processing engine can be customized by inserting new commands into the request processing chain of **ActionServlet** which was discussed in Chapter 3. Specifically, security customizations can be brought into play by replacing the default **AuthorizeAction** chain command with a custom command. **AuthorizeAction** simply extends **AbstractAuthorizeAction**, providing an implementation for its abstract **isAuthorized( )** method. The **isAuthorized( )** method determines how roles, specified for an action mapping via the **roles** attribute, are handled. Its purpose is to ensure that a user who is accessing an action with assigned roles has at least one of those roles. The method returns *true* to continue processing normally or *false* to stop processing and return an appropriate response. The default implementation uses the **HttpServletRequest.isUserInRole( )** method to determine if a user has a particular role. This can be used with container-managed security. For application-managed security, you need to override this method in a custom command that extends **AbstractAuthorizeAction**. For your implementation, you will get the **User** object from the session and then call the **User.hasRole( )** method. The custom chain command with the overridden method is shown here:

```
package com.jamesholmes.minihr.security;

public class AuthorizeAction extends AbstractAuthorizeAction {
  protected boolean isAuthorized(ActionContext context, String[] roles,
    ActionConfig mapping)
      throws Exception {
    // Is this action protected by role requirements?
    if ((roles == null) || (roles.length < 1)) {
```

```
      return (true);
    }

    // Identify the HTTP request object
    ServletActionContext servletActionContext =
      (ServletActionContext) context;
    HttpServletRequest request = servletActionContext.getRequest();

    // Check the current user against the list of required roles
    HttpSession session = request.getSession();
    User user = (User) session.getAttribute("user");
    if (user == null) {
      return false;
    }
    for (int i = 0; i < roles.length; i++) {
      if (user.hasRole(roles[i])) {
        return (true);
      }
    }

    // Default to unauthorized
    return (false);
  }

  protected String getErrorMessage(ActionContext context,
    ActionConfig actionConfig) {
    ServletActionContext servletActionContext =
      (ServletActionContext) context;

    // Retrieve internal message resources
    ActionServlet servlet = servletActionContext.getActionServlet();
    MessageResources resources = servlet.getInternal();

    return resources.getMessage("notAuthorized", actionConfig.getPath());
  }
}
```

In versions of Struts previous to 1.3, the **RequestProcessor** must be extended to customize request processing. Following is a custom request processor with the **processRoles( )** method overridden to provide custom processing:

```
package com.jamesholmes.minihr.security;

import java.io.IOException;
import javax.servlet.ServletException;
import javax.servlet.http.*;
import org.apache.struts.action.*;
import com.jamesholmes.minihr.security.User;

public class CustomRequestProcessor extends RequestProcessor {
  protected boolean processRoles(HttpServletRequest request,
    HttpServletResponse response, ActionMapping mapping)
    throws IOException, ServletException
  {
```

```
    // Is this action protected by role requirements?
    String roles[] = mapping.getRoleNames();
    if ((roles == null) || (roles.length < 1)) {
      return (true);
    }
    // Check the current user against the list of required roles
    HttpSession session = request.getSession();
    User user = (User) session.getAttribute("user");
    if (user == null) {
      return false;
    }
    for (int i = 0; i < roles.length; i++) {
      if (user.hasRole(roles[i])) {
        return (true);
      }
    }
    response.sendError(HttpServletResponse.SC_BAD_REQUEST,
                       getInternal().getMessage("notAuthorized",
                       mapping.getPath()));
    return (false);
  }
}
```

Now, you can add the **roles** attribute back to your action mapping and the action will be protected. Of course, you also need to plug the custom chain command into the chain configuration file (or for previous versions of Struts, the customized request processor into the Struts configuration file). That still leaves the somewhat nagging problem of unauthorized users gaining access to the JSP pages. One solution is to place all the JSP pages under **WEB-INF** and route all JSP page requests through the **ActionServlet** by using **ForwardActions**. This is an appealing solution, because you can then use the **roles** attribute on these actions. This does mean a fairly drastic change to the organization of a Web application and may require substantial modification of your JSP pages. However, as you will see in the following section, servlet filters can be used to implement security policies that can be applied to related Web resources.

In addition to creating a custom **AuthorizeAction** command, you can create other commands that get called earlier in the chain request processing. That is a good way to put in security checks that cannot be implemented using roles alone. In versions of Struts previous to 1.3, the **processPreprocess( )** method of the **RequestProcessor** gave this same flexibility.

Using Servlet Filters for Security

Servlet filters were introduced as part of the Servlet 2.3 specification. They provide a powerful mechanism for creating customized request and response processing that can be applied across many Web resources. You can create a filter and then map it to a collection of URLs by using the URL mapping discussed earlier in the chapter. Filters can alter a request before it arrives at its destination and, likewise, can modify the response after it leaves a destination. Filters can be applied to static HTML pages, JSP pages, Struts actions—essentially, any resource that you can specify with a URL.

You can use a filter to implement role-based access controls. The filter in effect performs the same checks that were implemented in the custom request processing code described in the previous section of this chapter. The filter determines if a user is allowed access to a given Web resource. It checks if the user has been authenticated and if the user has one of the required roles. If either of these checks fails, the filter stores an appropriate error message in the request and forwards the request to a URL. Initialization parameters are used to specify the authorization as well as the page to forward to if an error occurs. As you can see, the initialization parameters enable the creation of filter classes that can easily be reused. Here is the complete implementation for the authorization filter that Mini HR will be using:

```
package com.jamesholmes.minihr.security;

import java.io.IOException;
import javax.servlet.*;
import javax.servlet.http.*;
import org.apache.struts.Globals;
import org.apache.struts.action.*;

public class AuthorizationFilter implements Filter {
  private String[] roleNames;
  private String onErrorUrl;

  public void init(FilterConfig filterConfig)
      throws ServletException {
    String roles = filterConfig.getInitParameter("roles");
    if (roles == null || "".equals(roles)) {
      roleNames = new String[0];
    }
    else {
      roles.trim();
      roleNames = roles.split("\\s*,\\s*");
    }
    onErrorUrl = filterConfig.getInitParameter("onError");
    if (onErrorUrl == null || "".equals(onErrorUrl)) {
      onErrorUrl = "/index.jsp";
    }
  }

  public void doFilter(ServletRequest request,
                       ServletResponse response,
                       FilterChain chain)
                  throws IOException, ServletException {
    HttpServletRequest req = (HttpServletRequest) request;
    HttpServletResponse res = (HttpServletResponse) response;

    HttpSession session = req.getSession();
    User user = (User) session.getAttribute("user");
    ActionErrors errors = new ActionErrors();
    if (user == null) {
      errors.add(ActionErrors.GLOBAL_ERROR,
        new ActionMessage("error.authentication.required"));
    }
    else {
      boolean hasRole = false;
      for (int i=0; i<roleNames.length; i++) {
        if (user.hasRole(roleNames[i])) {
          hasRole = true;
          break;
```

```
        }
      }
      if (!hasRole) {
        errors.add(ActionErrors.GLOBAL_ERROR,
          new ActionMessage("error.authorization.required"));
      }
    }
    if (errors.isEmpty()) {
      chain.doFilter(request, response);
    }
    else {
      req.setAttribute(Globals.ERROR_KEY, errors);
      req.getRequestDispatcher(onErrorUrl).forward(req, res);
    }
  }

  public void destroy() {
  }
}
```

First, notice that the **AuthorizationFilter** class implements **Filter**. Thus, it must implement the **init( )**, **doFilter( )**, and **destroy( )** methods. The comma-separated list of roles and the URL of the error page to forward to are retrieved from the initialization parameters in the **init( )** method. The **doFilter( )** method first checks if there is a **User** object in the session. If not, an appropriate **ActionMessage** is created and no further checks are performed. Otherwise, it iterates through the list of roles to determine if the user has any of them. If not, an **ActionMessage** is created. If any errors were created, then a **RequestDispatcher** is created to forward to the given URL; otherwise, the **doFilter( )** method calls **chain.doFilter( )** to continue normal processing. This implementation also demonstrates the ability to integrate filters with Struts. You could have provided a more generic implementation, by calling the **sendError( )** method of the **HttpServletResponse** class with an appropriate HTTP status code (e.g., 401).

Filters are configured and deployed like servlets. In the **web.xml** file, you can specify the filter name and class, and initialization parameters. Then, associate the filter with a URL pattern in a filter mapping. The following is the snippet from the **web.xml** file that shows the necessary changes for this filter:

```
<filter>
  <filter-name>adminAccessFilter</filter-name>
  <filter-class>
    com.jamesholmes.minihr.security.AuthorizationFilter
  </filter-class>
  <init-param>
    <param-name>roles</param-name>
    <param-value>administrator</param-value>
  </init-param>
  <init-param>
    <param-name>onError</param-name>
    <param-value>/index.jsp</param-value>
  </init-param>
</filter>

<filter-mapping>
```

```
    <filter-name>adminAccessFilter</filter-name>
    <url-pattern>/admin/*</url-pattern>
</filter-mapping>
```

As you can see, the **AuthorizationFilter** is fairly generic. There is, in fact, an open-source security filter known as **SecurityFilter** (http://securityfilter.sourceforge.net) that is worth considering. This filter permits implementation of a custom security policy, yet it still allows programmatic access to role and user information (i.e., the **request.isUserInRole( )** and **request.getUserPrincipal( )** methods) that is generally only available when using container-managed authentication. It performs this magic by using wrapper classes around the **HttpServletRequest**. **SecurityFilter** is configured using a separate configuration file that is very similar to the standard **security-constraint** element of the **web.xml** file. It provides the benefits of application-managed security while still enabling standard role processing without modification. There is no need to extend the Struts request processing engine for role handling, and the **<logic:equal>** tag with the **role** attribute will also work correctly. **SecurityFilter** is implemented similarly to **AuthorizationFilter**. You will want to understand how the filter works and its limitations before migrating your application.

Like servlets and Struts actions, filters are extremely powerful. You have complete access to the Java API that can be applied as needed using URL patterns. However, to truly integrate filters with Struts, you may need to delve into Struts implementation details as was shown in the **AuthorizationFilter**.

Using Cookies

A cookie consists of name-value data that can be sent to a client's browser and then read back again at a later time. Persistent cookies are stored by the client's browser. Cookies can be read only by the same server or domain that originated them. Also, a cookie can have an expiration period. Cookies are supported by most major browsers. However, cookies are often considered a privacy risk and can be disabled by the client. A good approach is to design your Web application to use cookies to improve the user experience, but not to require or force users to allow cookies.

For application-managed security, you can use cookies to allow users automatic logins. Specifically, you can create a persistent cookie that contains the user's username and password. Then, when a user accesses the application, you can check for those cookie values. If present, the values can be used to log the user in without requiring them to fill out a login form. Using a servlet filter, or some JavaScript, you could log in a user automatically. Alternatively, you may want to just prepopulate the login form with the values from the cookie.

To illustrate the use of cookies, Mini HR will be changed to use them as follows:

1. Once a user logs in, Mini HR creates persistent cookies containing the username and password.
2. Mini HR uses the cookie support of the Struts tags to set the initial values for the login form.

For the login action, this means adding the following lines *after* the authentication check has been performed:

```
Cookie usernameCookie = new Cookie("MiniHRUsername", username);
usernameCookie.setMaxAge(60 * 60 * 24 * 30); // 30 day expiration
response.addCookie(usernameCookie);
```

```
Cookie passwordCookie = new Cookie("MiniHRPassword", password);
passwordCookie.setMaxAge(60 * 60 * 24 * 30); // 30 day expiration
response.addCookie(passwordCookie);
```

This code creates cookies for holding the username and password. Each cookie has an expiration of 30 days. Each cookie is then added to the response.

Next, use the Struts Bean Tag Library tags to retrieve the cookie values and write the values to the login form:

```
<logic:notPresent name="user" scope="session">
  <bean:cookie id="uname" name="MiniHRUsername" value=""/>
  <bean:cookie id="pword" name="MiniHRPassword" value=""/>
  <hr width="100%" noshade="true">
  <html:form action="/login">
    Username: <html:text property="username"
                value="<%=uname.getValue()%>"/><br/>
    Password: <html:password property="password"
                value="<%=pword.getValue()%>"/><br/>
    <html:submit value="Login"/>
  </html:form>
  <html:errors/>
</logic:notPresent>
```

The **cookie** tags retrieve the cookie values from the request and store them in page scope variables. These variables are then used as the initial values for the login form fields. However, this example is too simplistic for production use. Generally, using cookies without input from the user is considered overly presumptuous. A good Web application lets the user specify whether they want their user data stored as a cookie. It is also reasonable to let the user specify the length of time before the cookie expires. This type of information is easily gathered and stored by an application. Typically, this information is collected at registration time and stored as part of the user's profile.

In addition, the data sent in the cookies should be secured or encrypted. A simple encryption scheme, such as MD5 or a variant of the Secure Hash Algorithm (SHA), can be used to encrypt the cookie value when it is created. Since the server creates the cookie and is the only party to legitimately use the data, it can encrypt and decrypt the data using the algorithm of its own choosing. Alternatively, cookies can be configured to be transmitted only over HTTPS—thereby providing encryption/decryption at the transport level.

Integrating Struts with SSL

Web applications often need to allow certain operations to be performed under secure processing—that is, using HTTPS. Users have come to expect sensitive data such as their usernames, passwords, and credit card numbers to be transmitted over a secure channel. As was noted earlier, the use of HTTPS for specific URLs can be specified using a user data constraint within a security constraint in the **web.xml** file. This declarative mechanism can be used to restrict URLs to SSL (by specifying a transport guarantee of INTEGRAL or CONFIDENTIAL). However, this approach does not address all the issues when using SSL. As a container-managed service, the implementation and behavior with SSL can vary by container. If the service is not used carefully and with a full understanding of its nuances, it is easy to code an application that will only run in a specific container—even when using services that are defined via an industry-accepted specification.

Therefore, HTTPS typically is used only when passing sensitive data, and otherwise HTTP is used. This requires redirecting from nonsecure pages to secure pages and then back again. Performing this redirection requires changing the protocol scheme on a URL from **http** to **https** on each redirection. The biggest problem with needing to do this protocol switching is that absolute URLs must be hard-coded into JSP pages and **Action** classes. This quickly leads to deployment and maintenance problems that arise when server names are different between development, integration, test, and production servers. Some techniques for overcoming this problem are described shortly.

More pragmatically, programming an application to use HTTPS has other, more mundane but nevertheless equally frustrating issues. A common one is that the **https** protocol of the URL must often be hard-coded into a page. In fact, generally if you create HTML links that reference HTTPS, you must specify a fully qualified absolute URL. This makes it difficult to develop an application that is easy to migrate between deployment servers. Also, because switching the protocol requires an HTTP redirect, request attributes for the current request cannot be propagated to the secure URL. Thankfully, there is an open-source solution for handling these types of problems.

SSLEXT to the Rescue

The SSL Extension to Struts (SSLEXT) is an open-source plug-in for Struts. This software was created and is maintained by Steve Ditlinger (and others) and is hosted at SourceForge, **http://sslext.sourceforge.net**. It is the recommended approach for integrating Struts with SSL processing for Struts 1.2 and earlier. Unfortunately, at the time of this writing SSLEXT does not support Struts 1.3 because of its move to Jakarta Commons Chain for request processing. It is possible that SSLEXT will support later versions of Struts in the future, but there were not any committed timelines for that at the time of this writing.

SSLEXT's features include

- The ability to declaratively specify in the Struts configuration file whether or not an action mapping should be secure. This feature allows your application to switch protocols between actions and JSP pages.
- Extensions of the Struts JSP tags that can generate URLs that use the **https** protocol.

SSLEXT consists of a plug-in class for initialization, a custom extension to the Struts **RequestProcessor**, and a custom extension of the Struts **ActionMapping**. In addition, custom JSP tags, which extend the Struts tags, are provided for protocol-specific URL generation. SSLEXT also includes an additional JSP tag that lets you specify whether an entire JSP page is secure. SSLEXT depends on the Java Secure Socket Extension (JSSE), which is included with JDK 1.4 and later. Finally, you need to enable SSL for your application server. For Tomcat, this can be found in the *Tomcat SSL How-To* documentation.

SSLEXT works by intercepting the request in its **SecureRequestProcessor**. If the request is directed toward an action that is marked as **secure**, the **SecureRequestProcessor** generates a redirect. The redirect changes the protocol to **https** and the port to a secure port (e.g., 443 or 8443). This sounds simple enough; however, a request in a Struts application usually contains request attributes. These attributes are lost on a redirect. SSLEXT solves this problem by temporarily storing the request attributes in the session.

SSLEXT does not include a lot of documentation, but it comes with a sample application that demonstrates its use and features. To try SSLEXT, you can modify Mini HR to use it by changing the login behavior so that the **LoginAction** occurs over HTTPS. Once logged in,

SSLEXT should switch the protocol back to HTTP. To set up SSLEXT for the Mini HR application, follow these steps:

1. Copy the **sslext.jar** file into the **MiniHR\WEB-INF\lib** folder.
2. Copy the **sslext.tld** file into the **MiniHR\WEB-INF** folder.
3. Add a **taglib** declaration in the **web.xml** for the **sslext** tag library as follows:

```
<taglib>
  <taglib-uri>/WEB-INF/sslext.tld</taglib-uri>
  <taglib-location>/WEB-INF/sslext.tld</taglib-location>
</taglib>
```

Now, make the following changes to the **struts-config.xml** file:

1. Add the **type** attribute to the **action-mappings** element to specify the custom secure action mapping class as follows:

```
<action-mappings type="org.apache.struts.config.SecureActionConfig">
```

2. Add the **controller** element configured to use the **SecureRequestProcessor**. If you are already using a custom request processor, change it to extend the **SecureRequestProcessor**.

```
<controller
  processorClass="org.apache.struts.action.SecureRequestProcessor"/>
```

3. Add the **plug-in** declaration to load the SSLEXT code:

```
<plug-in className="org.apache.struts.action.SecurePlugIn">
  <set-property property="httpPort" value="8080"/>
  <set-property property="httpsPort" value="8443"/>
  <set-property property="enable" value="true"/>
  <set-property property="addSession" value="true"/>
</plug-in>
```

4. Set the **secure** property to true for the **login** action mapping by adding the following element:

```
<set-property property="secure" value="true"/>
```

5. Finally, you need to configure the **index.jsp** page to always run on **http**, not **https**. Otherwise, after you log in, the protocol will remain on **https**. Add the following **taglib** directive and custom tag to the **index.jsp** page (after the existing **taglib** directives):

```
<%@ taglib uri="/WEB-INF/tlds/sslext.tld" prefix="sslext"%>
<sslext:pageScheme secure="false"/>
```

This tag is only needed for those JSP pages that are not accessed through your actions.

Now all you need to do is rebuild and redeploy the application. When you click the login link, the protocol will switch to **https** and the port will switch to 8443. After you log in, you should be redirected back to the **index.jsp** page and the protocol and port should switch back to **http** and 8080. You should experiment with using the **<sslext:link>** tag to create links to secure actions. You will find that using SSLEXT is much easier than using the **user-data-constraint** subelement of the **web.xml** file. It gives you fine-grained control where you need it through the tags. At the same time, it leverages the Struts configuration file to enable simple declarative configuration for secure request processing.

PART II

12

CHAPTER

Testing Struts Applications

Testing, and unit testing in particular, has become a hot topic in software development in recent years. Spurred on by the advent of agile methodologies such as Extreme Programming and Scrum, developers are placing a greater emphasis on software testing. Successful iterative development hinges on having repeatable tests that can be run with every build. Because of this need, this chapter covers testing Struts applications. Before you read about how to test a Struts application, however, take a look at the types of testing that are applicable.

Types of Testing

There are different levels, or types, of testing. Each type serves different purposes. Traditionally, testing is viewed as a quality control function. However, unit testing is considered to be in the development domain. This chapter covers testing from both of these perspectives. However, the primary focus will be on the types of tests run by developers.

Unit Testing

Unit testing refers to independent testing of individual software units. In Java development, a unit is typically associated with a Java class. Unit testing is normally performed by the developer, not the quality assurance or quality control department. The goal of unit testing is to ensure that the unit under test does what it is supposed to do. More specifically, the developer specifies in a unit test what the expected output or behavior of individual methods is for a given set of inputs. Unit testing is typically associated with the *x*Unit family of software testing frameworks led by the JUnit framework.

The folks at the Cactus project (**http://jakarta.apache.org/cactus**), a testing framework covered in the section "Using Cactus for Integration Unit Testing," refer to the following three specific types of unit testing:

- **Code logic testing** The traditional view of unit testing, where the unit is completely isolated.
- **Integration unit testing** Testing of a unit that is not in isolation; that is, the unit communicates with other units.

- **Functional unit testing** An integrated unit test that verifies the output of a unit for a known input. The unit in this case is typically not a software unit per say, but an application unit (e.g., a Web page). Functional unit testing can be considered black-box integration testing.

This chapter covers several tools and techniques that assist with unit testing.

Functional Testing

Functional testing is driven by requirements and use cases and is usually performed by a quality control group. Functional tests ensure that the application performs the functions specified by the requirements. Functional tests are typically focused on verifying that the application or components of the application respond with the expected output when given known input. For Web applications, functional tests can be automated using testing tools.

System Testing

Performance is an important aspect of most applications. *System* testing is concerned with measuring and verifying the response of the system when the application is run under varying loads. System responses include such things as performance/latency, throughput, and memory consumption. At the end of this chapter, two open-source tools are presented that can measure and analyze this type of data.

Unit Testing Struts Applications

If a developer follows the best practices of Web application design—specifically, use of the Model-View-Controller (MVC) design pattern supported by Struts—most of the critical unit tests will be written for testing the model, and the Struts-specific tests will be only a small portion of the application's unit test suite. A well-designed Struts application promotes the definition of actions that delegate processing to business components and services that reside in the model. The **Action** classes are responsible only for transferring data from the View layer to the Model layer and vice versa.

The bulk of the unit tests required for a Struts application should be for the business components and services. JUnit (**http://www.junit.org**), developed by Erich Gamma and Kent Beck, is an excellent framework for unit testing these types of Java objects. This framework provides the software infrastructure for developing tests. It has become the *de facto* standard for Java unit testing. JUnit provides a base test class that is extended by the developer to create a specific unit test. The developer then writes test methods in this new test class. The test methods exercise the class to be tested and verify that the class being tested behaves as expected.

JUnit provides several features that make writing and running these tests simple. First, JUnit treats any method in the test class that begins with the word "test" as a method to run. Therefore, the developer uses that convention to name the test methods (e.g., *test*SearchByName, *test*Success). Within the test, JUnit provides methods for performing the verifications. These methods are referred to as *assertions.* An assertion simply expresses a Boolean (true/false) relationship. For example, you may assert that a value returned from a method is not null, or that the returned value has a specific value. If an assertion fails, that particular test method fails. Finally, JUnit provides several test runners that run the tests and report the test results. The following section describes how JUnit can be applied to the sample Mini HR application.

Testing the Model

The **EmployeeSearchService** class, first introduced in Chapter 2, is the primary business component of the Mini HR application. It provides methods to search for employees by name or social security number. Following is a JUnit unit test for this service. Note that the unit test can be run independently of the Web application and servlet container. Its only dependency is to the class being tested.

```
package com.jamesholmes.minihr;

import java.util.ArrayList;
import junit.framework.TestCase;

public class EmployeeSearchServiceTest extends TestCase {
  private EmployeeSearchService service;

  public EmployeeSearchServiceTest(String arg0) {
    super(arg0);
  }

  public void setUp() {
    super.setUp();
    service = new EmployeeSearchService();
  }

  public void tearDown() {
    super.tearDown();
  }

  public void testSearchByName() {
    String name = "Jim";
    ArrayList results = service.searchByName(name);
    assertEquals("Number of results", 2, results.size());
  }

  public void testSearchBySSN() {
    String ssn = "333-33-3333";
    ArrayList results = service.searchBySsNum(ssn);
    assertEquals("Number of results", 1, results.size());
    Employee e = (Employee) results.get(0);
    assertEquals("SSN", ssn, e.getSsNum());
  }

  public void testSearchByUnknownSSN() {
    String ssn = "999099-49493939";
    ArrayList results = service.searchBySsNum(ssn);
    assertEquals("Number of results", 0, results.size());
  }
}
```

First, notice that the test class is in the same package as the **EmployeeSearchService** class and uses the ***Class under test*Test** naming convention. If the test class were in a different package, only public methods could be tested. The next thing to notice is the **setUp( )** method, which is used to prepare each test. Here, this method creates the **EmployeeSearchService** object and stores a reference to it in an instance variable. As a corollary, a **tearDown( )** method can be implemented to perform any test cleanup. That would be the place, for example, to close a database connection or file resource used by the test.

A JUnit test runner actually runs the test. JUnit includes three test runner user interfaces—one based on Java AWT, one based on Java Swing, and a text-based runner that can be run from the command line. In addition, many Java IDEs provide some level of integration with JUnit. The test runner first creates a new instance of the test class. Then, for *each* test method (i.e., each method that begins with "test"), the runner calls **setUp( )**, then the test method itself, and then **tearDown( )**. This approach allows for the creation of independent, repeatable tests. Each test method should be capable of running separately, with the **setUp( )** and **tearDown( )** methods performing the initialization and cleanup.

The actual verification part of the test is encapsulated in the individual test methods. Generally speaking, there should be at least one test method for each method of the external interface of a class under test. The test method should create the input values, call the appropriate method, and then verify the results. This verification may include examining any returned values as well as checking any expected state changes. Each verification is implemented using one or more of the JUnit **assert( )** methods. For example, if a search by social security number is performed using a value for which there is no match, then an assertion can be made that the returned collection should be empty. This type of negative test is illustrated in the **EmployeeSearchServiceTest** class in the **testSearchByUnknownSSN( )** method.

To run this test, ensure that the **junit.jar** file and the application classes are on your classpath. Then, simply execute the following command:

```
java junit.swingui.TestRunner
```

This displays the JUnit graphical user interface (GUI), shown in Figure 12-1, which allows you to select the test to run. You can then run the test and view the results. If you get a green

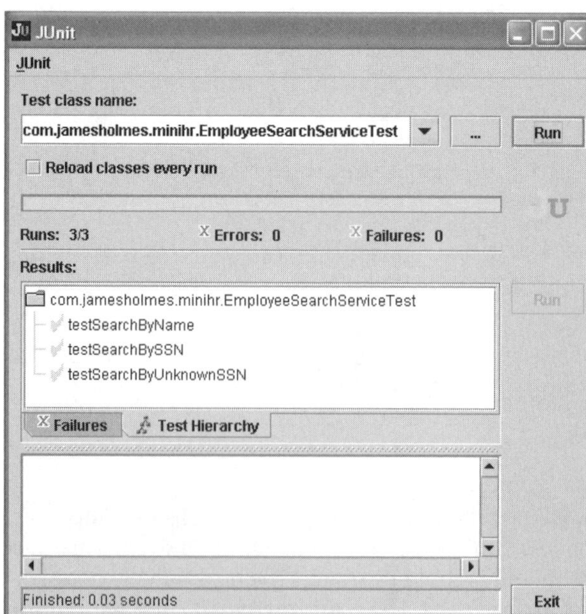

FIGURE 12-1 A successful test run using the JUnit Swing test runner

bar, then all tests succeeded. If the test fails, you can change the code to make it work—then rerun the test. Usually, you do not need to restart the JUnit Swing user interface because it incorporates a mechanism for reloading classes.

Now that you've seen how to write a unit test, you need to integrate unit testing into the build process. Testing can be added to the build cycle by including testing targets in the application's Ant build script. This chapter will not go into complete details of integrating JUnit with Ant; however, it is fairly straightforward and the Ant support for unit testing is well documented in Ant's documentation set. Following is the Ant build script, **build.xml**, that will be used and expanded throughout this chapter. The test target is the last target in this file.

```
<project name="MiniHR" default="dist" basedir=".">
  <property environment="env"/>
  <property name="build.compiler" value="javac1.4"/>
  <!-- set global properties for this build -->
  <property name="src" location="src"/>
  <property name="webinf.dir" location="web/WEB-INF"/>
  <property name="build.dir" location="build"/>
  <property name="dist.dir"  location="dist"/>
  <property name="server.dir" location="${env.CATALINA_HOME}"/>
  <property name="servlet.jar"
        location="${tomcat.dir}/common/lib/servlet.jar"/>
  <property name="test.dir" location="test"/>
  <property name="deploy.dir" location="${server.dir}/webapps"/>

  <target name="clean">
    <delete dir="${build.dir}"/>
    <delete dir="${dist.dir}"/>
  </target>

  <target name="init">
    <mkdir dir="${build.dir}"/>
    <mkdir dir="${dist.dir}"/>
  </target>

  <target name="compile" depends="init"
        description="compile the source ">
    <javac srcdir="${src}:${test.dir}/src"
           destdir="${build.dir}" debug="on">
      <classpath>
        <pathelement path="${classpath}"/>
        <pathelement location="${servlet.jar}"/>
        <fileset dir="${webinf.dir}/lib">
          <include name="**/*.jar"/>
         </fileset>
      </classpath>
    </javac>

    <copy todir="${build.dir}">
      <fileset dir="${src}">
        <include name="**/*.properties"/>
      </fileset>
    </copy>
  </target>
```

PART II

```
  <target name="dist" depends="compile">
    <war destfile="${dist.dir}/${ant.project.name}.war"
         webxml="${webinf.dir}/web.xml">
      <webinf dir="${webinf.dir}">
        <include name="struts-config.xml"/>
        <include name="validation.xml"/>
      </webinf>
      <classes dir="${build.dir}"/>
      <fileset dir="web" excludes="WEB-INF/**.*"/>
    </war>
  </target>

  <target name="deploy" depends="dist">
    <unjar src="${dist.dir}/${ant.project.name}.war"
           dest="${deploy.dir}/${ant.project.name}"/>
  </target>

  <target name="test" depends="compile">
    <mkdir dir="${test.dir}/results"/>
    <junit printsummary="yes" fork="no" haltonfailure="no"
           errorProperty="test.failed" failureProperty="test.failed">
      <formatter type="xml" />
      <classpath>
        <pathelement path="${build.dir}"/>
      </classpath>
      <batchtest todir="${test.dir}/results">
        <fileset dir="${build.dir}">
          <include name="**/*Test.class" />
        </fileset>
      </batchtest>
    </junit>
    <junitreport todir="${test.dir}/reports">
      <fileset dir="${test.dir}/results">
        <include name="TEST-*.xml"/>
      </fileset>
      <report format="frames" todir="${test.dir}/reports"/>
    </junitreport>
    <fail message="JUnit tests failed. Check reports." if="test.failed"/>
  </target>
</project>
```

The test target in the preceding build script integrates testing into the build. The **junit** task is used to run tests and generate the results. The **junitreport** task is used to accumulate and generate an HTML report from those results. These tests are run by simply typing **ant test** at a command prompt. The reports are generated into the **test/reports** directory. The generated report includes information about which tests passed, which ones failed, and the specific assertions that failed. If an exception was thrown, the stack trace is included with the report. In addition, some basic timing information is also recorded. As mentioned previously, testing the model should be the top priority when determining what aspects of the system to test first.

Testing Controller Behavior

Assuming that unit tests have been completed for the Model portion of the application, the next step is to test Controller behavior. Here the focus is on verifying the behavior of Struts actions. You want to check that an action performs as expected. This includes ensuring that the action does such things as the following:

- Receives the data it needs from the request or session
- Handles cases properly where required input is missing or invalid
- Calls the model passing the correct data
- Marshals and transforms as needed the data from the model
- Stores the data in the appropriate context or scope
- Returns the correct action response

These types of tests can be performed in a running container (i.e., a servlet engine such as Tomcat) or outside of the container in a normal client JVM. This is an important distinction. Test execution outside the container allows you to isolate the class under test from outside dependencies. When the test fails, you know that the failure is in the class under test, not a problem with the container.

In-container tests are a form of integrated unit tests. Integrated unit tests can be valuable for verifying that the class being tested will work in an actual deployed environment. Practically speaking, in-container tests are more complex to set up and run and generally take more CPU time than tests run independently of a container. On the other hand, outside-the-container tests often require creation of mock objects to stand in for container-provided software entities such as the servlet request and response objects, the servlet context, and the HTTP session.

Using StrutsTestCase

StrutsTestCase (**http://strutstestcase.sourceforge.net**) is an open-source JUnit extension that provides a framework of Java classes specifically for testing Struts actions. It provides support for unit-testing Struts actions outside of a servlet container using mock objects. These objects are provided as stand-ins for the servlet request and response, and context components such as the servlet context and the HTTP session. Test cases using the mock objects use information from your application's configuration files—specifically the **web.xml** file and the Struts configuration file (e.g., **struts-config.xml**). In addition, StrutsTestCase also supports in-container testing through integration with the Cactus framework. In-container testing will be covered in "Using Cactus for Integration Unit Testing" later in this chapter. Since StrutsTestCase extends JUnit, the tests can be run using the JUnit test-running tools. Consider a unit test for the **SearchAction** class of the sample application. This action performs the following steps:

1. Gets the entered name from the form.
2. Determines whether the search is by name (i.e., a name was entered) or by social security number.
3. Performs the search using **EmployeeSearchService**.
4. Stores the results back in the form.
5. Forwards the request back to the input page.

Here's a unit test that verifies this behavior:

```
package com.jamesholmes.minihr;
```

```
import servletunit.struts.MockStrutsTestCase;

public class SearchActionTest extends MockStrutsTestCase {
  public SearchActionTest(String testName) {
    super(testName);
  }

  public void setUp() throws Exception {
    super.setUp();
    setRequestPathInfo("/search");
  }

  public void testSearchByName() throws Exception {
    addRequestParameter("name", "Jim");
    actionPerform();
    assertNotNull("Results are null",
      ((SearchForm) getActionForm()).getResults());
    verifyInputForward();
  }
}
```

First, notice that the class inherits from **servletunit.struts.MockStrutsTestCase**, which in turn inherits from the JUnit **TestCase** (**junit.framework.TestCase**). This relationship allows access to all the assertion methods provided by JUnit. Next, in the **setUp( )** method, the parent's **setUp( )** method is called and the request path is set. Both of these steps are critical. If you override **setUp( )**, you must call **super.setUp( )**. Setting the request path ensures that the desired action is called. Notice that an extension mapping (e.g., **.do**) is not included in the request path. StrutsTestCase uses the **web.xml** file to determine which extension mapping is in use and uses that. Note also that there is no reference in the test to the **SearchAction** class itself. StrutsTestCase actually relies on the action mappings in the Struts configuration file to determine which action to call. So, in reality, you are testing not just the **SearchAction** class, but the entire action configuration.

The test method itself is relatively simple. First, a request parameter is added that represents the data that would be submitted from the HTML form on the **search.jsp** page. Next, **actionPerform( )** actually executes the action. After that, the resultant behavior is verified. Specifically, the **results** property of the **SearchForm** object is checked for null. In addition, the forward back to the input page (**search.jsp**) is verified using the **verifyInputForward( )** method.

To run this test, some changes need to be made to the **test** target of the Ant script. Since StrutsTestCase relies on the XML configuration files of the application, the parent directory of the application's **WEB-INF** directory must be on the classpath. The following three entries should be added to the **classpath** element of the **junit** task:

```
<fileset dir="${webinf.dir}/lib"/>
<pathelement location="${servlet.jar}"/>
<pathelement path="web"/>
```

The first entry adds all **.jar** files in the **WEB-INF/lib** folder. The second element adds the **servlet.jar** file. Finally, the third element specifies the directory that contains the **WEB-INF** directory.

The use of StrutsTestCase for mock testing is extremely powerful. The underlying mock implementation allows your test to focus on the specific unit being tested. In addition, the tests can be run without requiring a running container with the application deployed. If you are in an environment where the container is running on a different server, likely even a different operating system, you can still unit-test your actions on your local development computer. That being said, these unit tests do not take into account deployment issues, container dependencies, and other run-time behaviors that can only be tested with a running application. Fortunately, there is a tool that can help with this testing also.

Using Cactus for Integration Unit Testing

Some would consider *integration unit testing* a bit of an oxymoron. Typically, unit tests should be written such that they are isolated from outside dependencies. Isolating the unit test makes it much easier to identify the cause of errors when a test fails. However, there certainly is a place for integrated testing. A counter-argument can be made that an integrated unit test gives you a more realistic test. For some types of objects, say for example, Enterprise JavaBeans (EJBs), certain aspects of the objects can only be tested in the container. Container-provided services such as transactions and persistence are not easily mocked up. Another case where integration tests are invaluable is with regression testing. Deployments to different application servers and different operating systems can be verified using integrated unit tests.

Cactus was developed to provide these types of unit tests. It was originally developed to test EJBs but is equally up to the task of testing servlets, servlet filters, and JSPs. In fact, Cactus can be used to test any type of behavior that relies on a Java EE servlet container. As will be shown later in this section, Struts actions can be tested through interaction with the Struts **ActionServlet**. However, these tests do come at a cost of increased complexity and slower performance. Cactus tests are fairly easy to write, but configuration and deployment can be complex. If you are running your unit tests frequently as part of your build process, you may find that your build takes far too long. The reason Cactus tests take longer is that Cactus starts your application server every time it runs its suite of tests. A good option is to only run Cactus periodically, such as on nightly automated builds. Here are some guidelines to help you decide what type of testing to use and when:

- *Concentrate on unit tests for the model, first.* That is where most of the business logic is and that should be the focus.
- *Use StrutsTestCase with mock objects to test your **Action** classes.* Tests using mock objects can be run much faster and do not require a servlet container.
- *Use Cactus testing for those classes that rely on container-provided services.* For example, if you are using JNDI, or testing behavior based on container-managed security, you should use Cactus.

In addition, the Cactus site itself includes an even-handed comparison of mock object testing to Cactus in-container tests.

To get started with Cactus, you need to download the distribution. As of this writing, Cactus 1.7.2 was the latest release build. Cactus can run tests via integration with your IDE; however, the preferred approach is via Ant. First, you need to define the task definitions for the Ant tasks that Cactus provides:

```
<path id="cactus.classpath">
  <fileset dir="cactus/lib">
```

```
      <include name="*.jar"/>
    </fileset>
  </path>
  <taskdef resource="cactus.tasks"
    classpathref="cactus.classpath"/>
```

This defines a path containing the Cactus **.jar** files and creates the Cactus task definitions.

Next, add the Cactus classpath to the classpath of the **compile** target. Use **cactus.classpath** as the reference ID for the **path** element. As stated, Cactus tests will make the build slower; therefore, create a separate **test.cactus** target. In addition, provide a **test** wrapper target for running both test sets. The **test.cactus** target performs the following:

1. Instruments the application's **.war** file for testing by creating a new **.war** file. This process is referred to as *cactifying* the **.war** file.
2. Runs the unit tests. This is done using the *cactus* task. The **containerset** element indicates the container to run the tests against. This task extends the **junit** task. It uses the same subelements for specifying the results format and the set of tests to run.
3. Creates an HTML report of the results. This is done using the **junitreport** task that was shown previously.

Now the test case needs to be written. Cactus is an extension of JUnit. Cactus provides base classes that extend **junit.framework.TestCase**. If you have written a JUnit test, Cactus tests will be familiar. However, since Cactus runs on both the client and server, there are some additional APIs that are of use. Before delving into test code, a review of how Cactus works is in order.

One of the most important aspects of Cactus to understand is that a Cactus test runs in two JVMs. Specifically, there is a copy of the test on the client JVM, and a copy on the server JVM (that is, the JVM running the J2EE/servlet container). From Figure 12-2 you can see that Cactus provides hooks on both the server and client side. The server-side hooks are the standard JUnit fixture methods—**setUp( )** and **tearDown( )**. These methods are run, on the server, before and after execution of each **test*YourMethod*( )** method. The **begin( )** and **end( )** methods are unique to Cactus. These methods are executed on the client side—before the request is sent, and after the response is received. Since there are two copies of the test, instance variables set in the **begin( )** method are not set on the server side. Likewise, variables set in **setUp( )** and **tearDown( )** are not available in the client-side **begin( )** and **end( )** methods.

These optional methods can be used to simulate the request and interrogate the response. Think of these methods as the browser side of the test. To make things concrete, the **SearchActionTest** class, implemented before as a **MockStrutsTestCase**, is reimplemented in the following code as a Cactus **ServletTestCase**. As mentioned, Cactus does not provide a direct way of testing a Struts action, as StrutsTestCase does. Struts actions are tested indirectly by interacting with the **ActionServlet**. Here is the Cactus unit test for testing the **SearchAction** class:

```
package com.jamesholmes.minihr;

import org.apache.cactus.ServletTestCase;
import org.apache.cactus.WebRequest;
import org.apache.struts.action.ActionServlet;

public class SearchActionCactusTest extends ServletTestCase {
```

```
  private ActionServlet servlet;

  public SearchActionCactusTest(String theName) {
    super(theName);
  }

  public void setUp() throws Exception {
    servlet = new ActionServlet();
    servlet.init(config);
  }

  public void beginSuccess(WebRequest request) {
    request.setURL
    (
      null,           // server name (e.g. 'localhost:8080')
      null,           // context (e.g. '/MiniHR')
      "/search.do",   // servlet path
      null,           // extra path info
      "name=Jim"      // query string
    );
  }

  public void testSuccess() throws Exception {
    servlet.doGet(request, response);
    SearchForm form = (SearchForm) request.getAttribute("searchForm");
    assertNotNull(form.getResults());
  }

  public void tearDown() throws Exception {
    servlet.destroy();
  }
}
```


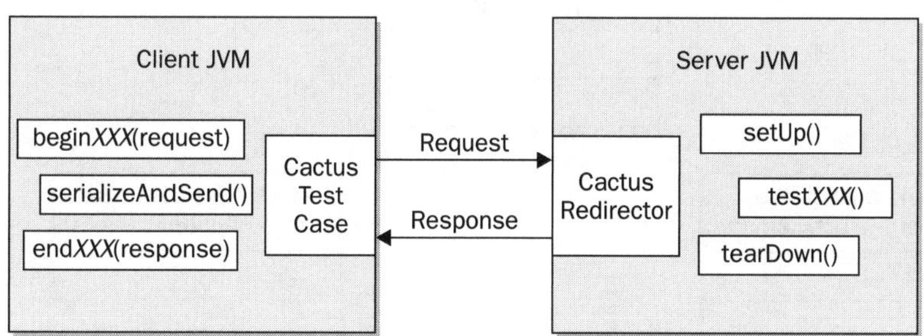

1. The **beginXXX( )** method is called to set up the Web request.

2. Cactus serializes the request and sends it (using HttpClient).

3. Redirector receives the request.

4. Redirector calls the **setUp( )** method.

5. Redirector calls the **testXXX( )** method.

6. Redirector calls the **tearDown( )** method.

7. Redirector returns the response.

8. The **endXXX( )** method is called and passed the Web response.

FIGURE 12-2 Cactus architecture

There are key differences between this test and the previous mock test. First, notice that the **setUp( )** method creates an instance of the Struts **ActionServlet** itself. Then, in the **beginSuccess( )** method, the URL of the request object is set to the page to access and the query string. The **SearchAction** class is executed indirectly by calling the **doGet( )** method of the **ActionServlet**. Essentially, the test is emulating the behavior of the container. Also notice that the request path must include the **.do** extension—Cactus knows nothing about Struts or the **ActionServlet**'s mapping. Finally, in the **testSuccess( )** method, the request is queried for the form. Note that the attribute name "searchForm" had to be hard-coded into the test. Using StrutsTestCase, this information was pulled from the Struts configuration file. Simply changing the name of the form in the Struts configuration file will break this Cactus test.

As you might suspect, these tests can become rather brittle. The tests are dependent on configuration settings that are outside the scope of the test. It would be preferable if there were a base class that could get configuration information from Struts. Fortunately, StrutsTestCase provides just that.

Using StrutsTestCase with Cactus

StrutsTestCase actually provides two base classes that can be used to create **Action** tests. **MockStrutsTestCase**, which extends the JUnit **TestCase**, has already been demonstrated. Tests that extend this class can be run outside the container. For in-container tests, StrutsTestCase includes the **CactusStrutsTestCase** base class. This class extends the Cactus **ServletTestCase**. The UML diagram in Figure 12-3 shows how these objects relate.

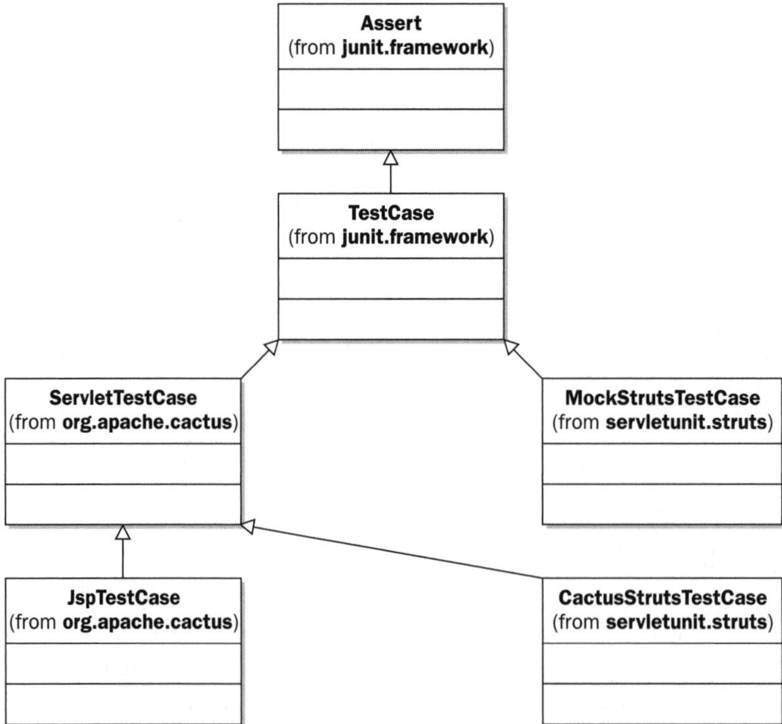

FIGURE 12-3 JUnit/StrutsTestCase/Cactus relationships

A **MockStrutsTestCase** can easily be turned into a container-driven Cactus test case by simply changing the class it extends to the **CactusStrutsTestCase**. You may find that you will want to have both forms of these tests. In fact, you could probably refactor the common test behavior (that is, the setup, assertions, and verifications) into a common class that is used by both the mock test and the in-container test. The previous StrutsTestCase can be changed to run under Cactus by simply changing it to extend from **CactusStrutsTestCase**—the rest is the same.

```
package com.jamesholmes.minihr;

import servletunit.struts.CactusStrutsTestCase;

public class SearchActionStrutsTest extends CactusStrutsTestCase {
  public SearchActionStrutsTest(String testName) {
    super(testName);
  }

  public void setUp() throws Exception {
    super.setUp();
    setRequestPathInfo("/search");
  }

  public void testSearchByName() throws Exception {
    addRequestParameter("name", "Jim");
    actionPerform();
    assertNotNull("Results are null",
      ((SearchForm) getActionForm()).getResults());
    verifyInputForward();
  }
}
```

As you can see, the code is much simpler and easier to maintain than the same test written using the Cactus framework alone. Moreover, because it extends the Cactus classes, the test can easily be run as an in-container test that more closely tests actual deployment.

Now that you know how to test actions both in and out of the container, you should consider the additional verifications that StrutsTestCase provides. Both **MockStrutsTestCase** and **CactusStrutsTestCase** extend **TestCase** and therefore offer all the standard assertion methods that are available with the JUnit API. In addition, several Struts-specific assertions are available in both of the StrutsTestCase base classes. All of these methods begin with *verify*:

- **verifyActionErrors( )** Verifies that a specific set of error messages, identified by key, were sent
- **verifyNoActionErrors( )** Verifies that no errors were sent
- **verifyActionMessages( )** Verifies that a specific set of action messages, identified by key, were sent
- **verifyNoActionMessages( )** Verifies that no action messages were sent
- **verifyForward( )** Verifies that the controller forwarded to a specified logical forward name, global or local, as specified in the Struts configuration file
- **verifyForwardPath( )** Verifies that the controller forwarded to a specified absolute path

- **verifyInputForward( )** Verifies that the controller forwarded to the path identified by the action mapping's **input** attribute
- **verifyTilesForward( )** Verifies that the controller forwarded to a specified logical forward name from the Struts configuration and a Tiles definition name from the Tiles configuration
- **verifyInputTilesForward( )** Verifies that the controller forwarded to the defined input of a specified Tiles definition

Before leaving the subject of in-container tests, it is worth mentioning that Cactus also provides a base class for testing servlet filters. This could be used, for example, to test the authorization filter used in Chapter 11.

Testing the View

Verifying that an application's presentation is correct is a critical step in software development. You are never quite sure if the view is appropriate until you put it before the customer. All too frequently, countless hours are spent building a complex system without regard to the presentation. Testing these views typically falls under the heading of functional testing and acceptance testing. However, there is important behavior that a view provides that can be unit tested. Most Struts applications leverage the rich Struts tag library in JSP pages to provide dynamic HTML rendering. The Logic Tag Library tags, for example, can be used to selectively render HTML markup in a JSP page. Such pages can be unit-tested by supplying the appropriate inputs to the page, accessing the page, and then verifying the response. The difficulty comes in two areas. First, the inputs may come from the container-managed objects such as the HTTP request, **HttpSession** or **ServletContext**. Second, the response is generally in HTML—verifying that the correct HTML was rendered involves complex parsing.

Cactus helps address the first problem, as was shown earlier in the **SearchActionCactusTest**. These tests can be run in the container and the tests have access to the container-managed context objects. For parsing HTML, HttpUnit can be used. HttpUnit (**http://httpunit.sourceforge.net**) is a Java-based open-source framework for functional testing of Web sites. It provides Java APIs for accessing all aspects of the HTTP interaction. HttpUnit refers to this as the *Web conversation.*

One aspect of Cactus that has not been demonstrated is use of the **WebResponse** object provided by the **endTest( )** method. Cactus supports two versions of this method. The first method provides access to a simple object, **org.apache.cactus.WebResponse**, which represents the HTTP response. With this object you can check the HTTP response status code and headers, check cookies, and assert actions based on the content. The content of the response is returned as a simple string. For a complex Web site, the returned content could be quite large. The other accepted version of the **endTest( )** method receives an HttpUnit **WebResponse** object, **com.meterware.httpunit.WebResponse**. Contrary to the Cactus **WebResponse**, this object provides a rich API for accessing the HTML content of the returned response. Through this integration with HttpUnit, Cactus tests can navigate through the response in an object-oriented fashion, verifying that the response contains specific HTML details such as HTML tables, links, and forms.

Consider a unit test for the security-enabled version of the **index.jsp** page. The dynamic aspects of this page are conditioned on the presence of a **User** object in the session. An additional link is rendered if the user is an administrator, enabling the administrator to add an employee. A unit test for this JSP allows for these assertions. Here is a Cactus unit test that includes a test method that performs these assertions. This test allows the JSP to be tested in isolation.

```
package com.jamesholmes.minihr;

import org.apache.cactus.JspTestCase;
import com.jamesholmes.minihr.security.User;
import com.meterware.httpunit.WebLink;
import com.meterware.httpunit.WebResponse;

public class IndexJspTest extends JspTestCase {
  public IndexJspTest(String theName) {
    super(theName);
  }

  public void testAdministratorAccess() throws Exception {
    User user = new User("bsiggelkow", "Bill", "Siggelkow", "thatsme",
                         new String[] {"administrator"});
    session.setAttribute("user", user);
    pageContext.forward("/index.jsp");
  }

  public void endAdministratorAccess(WebResponse response)
    throws Exception {
    // verify that the login form is not displayed
    assertNull("Login form should not have rendered",
      response.getFormWithName("loginForm"));

    //verify that the proper links are present
    WebLink[] links = response.getLinks();
    assertTrue("First link is admin/add.jsp",
      links[0].getURLString().startsWith("/test/admin/add.jsp"));
    assertTrue("Second link is search.jsp",
      links[1].getURLString().startsWith("/test/search.jsp"));
  }
}
```

The first thing you should notice is that the test imports the HttpUnit classes. HttpUnit is bundled with Cactus. (You may also want to get the latest HttpUnit distribution and documentation at **http://httpunit.sourceforge.net**.) Note also that the class extends **JspTestCase** instead of **ServletTestCase**. **JspTestCase**, which inherits from **ServletTestCase**, allows a JSP to be tested in isolation. The JSP page context can be accessed by the test class as needed. The test method was named to indicate that it is testing the display of the index page for a logged-in user with administrative privileges. Other conditions should also be modeled as test methods as appropriate. The first thing that the **testAdministratorAccess( )** method does is instantiate a **User** object that is assigned the **administrator** role. This object is placed in the **HttpSession** under the name by which it will be accessed on the page. The page is then rendered by forwarding to the **index.jsp** page. The implicit **PageContext** object performs the job of forwarding the request.

The actual test assertions and verifications are now performed in the **endAdministratorAccess( )** method. Remember that this method is executed in the client-side JVM after the request is processed. If a **User** object is in the session, the login form should not be displayed. The first assertion verifies this by asserting that the response does not contain a form named **loginForm**. Next, the set of links contained in the response is retrieved. Assertions are made that the first link is to the **Add an Employee** page (**/admin/add.jsp**), and that the second link is to the Search page (**search.jsp**). Initially, these assertions were written using the **assertEquals( )** method as follows:

```
assertEquals("Check first link", "/test/admin/add.jsp",
  links[0].getURLString());
```

At first glance, this appears correct; however, if you run the test using this assertion, it most likely will fail, because the servlet container may append a session identifier string to the link. In this case, the actual value of the URL was the following:

```
/test/admin/add.jsp;jsessionid=0E5EFB6F64C01749EE94E3A57BDEBD21
```

Therefore, the assertion was changed to verify that the URL *starts with* the expected result.

While the tests just demonstrated certainly are useful, they are getting more into the realm of functional testing than unit testing. HttpUnit can be used for broader functional testing—not just unit testing JSPs. HttpUnit provides full support for the entire Web conversation. The API provides methods for constructing requests, following links, and populating and submitting forms. Tests can be written using this API that mimic expected usage scenarios of the Web application. However, the amount of code to support such a test can be extensive. Also, this code can be extremely sensitive to simple changes in presentation. In the following section, a better approach for this type of functional testing is presented.

Use-Case-Driven Testing

The classical view of testing, from a quality control perspective, is use-case driven. That is, test cases are derived from use cases. For example, the following is a use case for the Mini HR "Search by Name" feature.

Precondition:

- The user has browsed to the Mini HR main page.

Primary Flow:

1. Click the Search link on the main page.
2. On the Search page, choose to Search by Name.
3. Enter all or part of an employee's name.
4. Submit the form. If a username was not entered, a validation error is displayed.
5. All employees that match the input name are displayed on the page. For each user, the employee name and social security number are listed. If no employees match, a message is displayed indicating that no matches exist.

This use case is straightforward and easy to understand. It is complete in that it specifies what must happen prior to the scenario (preconditions), all steps that the user must take, and the results of those steps.

Creating Test Cases

Specific test cases can be easily derived from this use case. A test case is generally more explicit than the use case in that it may describe specific test data to be used. In addition, alternate use-case flows are often modeled as separate test cases. The test explicitly states the steps that must be taken to test the functionality described by the use case. In addition, it explicitly states what the results should be. Think of a test case as a set of steps that you would hand to someone who is testing a certain function or feature of the application. The following are the two test cases for Search by Name—the key differences from the use case are in bold.

Test Case: Search by Name with Matches

Preconditions:

- The employee database is preloaded with test data.
- The browser location is the Mini HR main page.

Primary Flow:

1. Click the Search link on the main page.
2. **Verify that the Search page is displayed.**
3. On the Search page, choose to Search by Name.
4. **Enter "Jim" in the username field.**
5. Submit the form.
6. **Verify that the results are displayed with a table like the following:**

Jim Smith	123-45-6789
Will Jimmerson	987-65-4321

Test Case: Search by Name with No Matches

Preconditions:

- The employee database is preloaded with test data.
- **The browser location is the Mini HR main page.**

Primary Flow:

1. Click the Search link on the main page.
2. **Verify that the Search page is displayed.**
3. On the Search page, choose to Search by Name.
4. **Enter "Fred" in the username field.**
5. Submit the form.
6. **Verify that the "No Employees Found" message is displayed.**

These test cases now provide the test engineer with a *script* to follow for testing. While manual testing is important, it would also be beneficial if test cases like these could be automated. Automated testing would permit regression tests of an application anytime such testing is needed. For example, these tests would be run whenever a new version of the application was deployed to the QA server. The next section demonstrates a tool for automating these types of tests.

Using Canoo WebTest

Canoo WebTest, developed by Canoo Engineering, was designed to test Web applications. It is distributed as free open-source software. WebTest uses the Ant build utility as a test driver and HttpUnit to interact with an HTTP server. It works off an XML-based test specification. Test cases can be easily modeled using this test description. These tests are functional tests, not unit tests. The expected behavior is specified as a set of steps. These steps closely match the steps in a test case. Ant is used to execute the tests. You can create these tests in your normal Ant build script. However, it is better if they are separated out into separate files. They can always be integrated into a build, say for use by Quality Control, using Ant's **ant** task (which can execute a target of another build file). To demonstrate WebTest, a functional test for the "Search by Name" test case from the preceding section will be created.

First, download Canoo WebTest (**http://webtest.canoo.com**). Extract the distribution into a directory and create the environment variable ***WEBTESTHOME*** that refers to that directory. You can test the installation by running the ***WEBTESTHOME*\doc\samples\ installTest.xml** file with Ant as follows:

```
cd WEBTESTHOME\doc\samples
webtest -buildfile installTest.xml
```

However, this test may fail on certain systems. As suggested in the WebTest installation instructions, HtmlUnit (which is used internally by WebTest) may not handle the **file** protocol. To verify the installation, make a copy of **installTest.xml**. In the copied file, change the host, port, and protocol to valid values for your application server. For example, if you are running Tomcat locally on port 8080, you would change the **checkWebTest** element to the following:

```
<target name="checkWebTest">
  <testSpec name="check calling and parsing a local file">
    <config host="" port="8080" basepath="/" summary="false"
            verbose="true" saveresponse="false" haltonfailure="true"
            protocol="http" />
    <steps>
      <invoke stepid="get local file" url="/index.jsp" />
      <verifytitle stepid="check the title is parsed correctly"
                   text="Apache Tomcat" regex="true" />
    </steps>
  </testSpec>
</target>
```

An important item to note here is that the **checkWebTest** target is a regular Ant target. The first nested element of the **testSpec** element is **config**. This element is required. It defines the location of the application under test. **Host** defaults to **localhost** if not specified. Following the **config** element are the steps of the test specification. The steps consist of a sequential set of nested elements that define the actions that the test is to take. These steps can generally be categorized as either *action* steps or *verification* steps. Action steps include such things as accessing a URL, clicking a link or button, and typing text on a form. Verification steps are used like assertions in a JUnit unit test. They define steps that evaluate to true or false.

Once WebTest is up and running, you will want to create the test specifications for the test cases. The following test specification is used to test the two Search by Name test cases. A target is created for each test case. These test targets can be run by simply calling Ant, passing the build filename using the **–buildfile testfile.xml** (or **–f testfile.xml**) option. Likewise, if your IDE provides Ant integration (as most IDEs do), you can run the tests from your IDE in the same manner that you run an Ant build script.


```
<?xml version="1.0"?>
<!DOCTYPE project SYSTEM "WebTest.dtd"[
   <!ENTITY definition SYSTEM "includes/definition.xml">
   <!ENTITY config SYSTEM "includes/config.xml">
   <!ENTITY getSearchPage SYSTEM "includes/getSearchPage.xml">]>
<project name="MiniHR-SearchTest" basedir="." default="all">
  <property name="webtest.home" value="../../canoo"/>
  &definition;
  <target name="all" depends="nameSearchWithResults, nameSearchNoResults"/>
  <target name="nameSearchWithResults">
    <testSpec name="Perform a Search by Name">
      &config;
      <steps>
        &getSearchPage;
        <setinputfield stepid="Enter 'Jim' into Name field"
                       name="name" value="Jim"/>
        <clickbutton stepid="Submit the 'search by' form"
                     label="Submit"/>
        <verifyxpath stepid="Verify xpath 'Jim Smith'"
                    xpath="/html/body/table/tr/td[1]"
                     text="[Jj][Ii][Mm]"
                     regex="true"/>
      </steps>
    </testSpec>
  </target>
  <target name="nameSearchNoResults">
    <testSpec name="Perform a Search by Name with No Results">
      &config;
      <steps>
        &getSearchPage;
        <setinputfield stepid="Enter 'Morty' into Name field"
                       name="name" value="Morty"/>
        <clickbutton stepid="Submit the 'search by' form"
                     label="Submit"/>
        <verifytext stepid="Verify 'No Employees Found'"
                    text="No Employees Found"/>
      </steps>
    </testSpec>
  </target>
</project>
```

As you can see in the DOCTYPE declaration, this test makes extensive use of XML entities to bring in shared XML fragments. The first entity, **definition**, defines an entity that contains the task definitions for Canoo.

includes/definition.xml:

```
<taskdef file="${webtest.home}/webtestTaskdefs.properties">
  <classpath>
    <pathelement path="${webtest.home}/lib"/>
    <fileset dir="${webtest.home}" includes="**/lib/*.jar"/>
  </classpath>
</taskdef>
```

This fragment is generic to most any use of Canoo WebTest.

The second entity, **config**, is specific to the application being tested. In this case, the XML fragment defines the **config** element specifically for accessing the Mini HR application running on Tomcat.

includes/config.xml:

```
<config host="" port="8080" basepath="/MiniHR" summary="false"
  verbose="true" saveresponse="false" haltonfailure="true"
  protocol="http"/>
```

You can reuse this element for any test specification of your application.

The final entity, **getSearchPage**, is specific to this test set. It defines the steps that are necessary to get the Search page. These steps include accessing the application's main page, clicking the Search link, and then verifying that the Search page is displayed. While the steps could have been duplicated for each target, creating the entity allows reuse of this functionality for additional tests that need to get the Search page. Those tests may be added to this set of specifications or to new sets of specifications.

includes/getSearchPage.xml:

```
<invoke stepid="Get main page" url="/index.jsp"/>
<verifytitle stepid="Check that title is correct"
  text="ABC, Inc. Human Resources Portal"/>
<clicklink stepid="Click Search for Employees link"
  label="Search for Employees"/>
<verifytext stepid="Find 'Employee Search' text"
  text="Employee Search"/>
```

The first step of this fragment, **Get main page**, uses the **invoke** task to access the page of the application. The URL is relative to the settings in the **config** element. Next, the title of the displayed page is verified. Following that, the Search link is clicked. Finally, the text "Employee Search" is searched for and verified. This XML fragment is used in both of the test targets.

The test case to Search by Name uses these entities. First, the **config** entity is referenced to indicate the basic configuration. Next, the **getSearchPage** entity is used. At this point in the test, the Search page should be displayed. Next, the **setinputfield** element is used to emulate a user typing "Jim" into the **name** field. The **clickbutton** task is then used to submit the form. The last step is the most interesting. Canoo allows you to use XPath expressions to identify and verify portions of the expected response. In this case, the XPath attribute of the **verifyxpath** task refers to the first table data cell of the first row in the table. The **text** attribute indicates what the expected value should be. The **text** attribute can be either normal text to search for or a regular expression. Here, a regular expression is used to indicate that the table data cell referenced by the XPath expression should contain the text "JIM" regardless of case.

The second test target, **nameSearchNoResults**, verifies proper behavior when the search results in no matches for the entered name. This target reuses the **getSearchPage** steps. Also, it uses the simpler **verifytext** task to check if the resulting response contains the expected message—No Employees Found.

As you can see, Canoo WebTest is very powerful. Test cases map to automated test specifications in a natural and easy-to-understand fashion. The test specification tasks are well documented and can be written by nondevelopers. WebTest also provides the capability to generate test reports for a test specification. These reports, generated in XML, can then be rendered in HTML using an XSLT stylesheet. Check the Canoo WebTest samples for examples of how to utilize this functionality. Finally, the use of Ant as the underlying framework means easier integration with cross-platform build processes.

The one aspect that WebTest does not easily provide verifications for is presentation and layout. These verifications can be made using XPath; however, wholesale use of XPath to verify the presentation of a page can get extensive and difficult to maintain.

Depending on the size of your application, you may want to consider a testing tool that provides record and playback capability. Such tools are usually not open source or free; however, they are usually quite powerful and may be necessary for large sites— particularly if those sites use a lot of JavaScript and other Dynamic HTML techniques. *Selenium* (**http://www.openqa.org/selenium**), from the Open QA quality assurance project repository, is one such open-source test tool for Web applications that provides record and playback functionality.

PART II

Testing Application Performance

A final and sometimes overlooked area of testing is performance. Too often, an application is rolled out to production only to find that the performance of the application is unacceptable. For Struts applications, the first step to good performance is proper design and planning. Developers should plan for the expected number of concurrent users. Testing should be performed on a platform that is as similar as possible to the production environment. Developers are not often called on to test their applications for performance. However, tools are available that allow a developer to measure and test the performance of their application. One such tool, JUnitPerf, allows for performance tests to be run against existing JUnit tests. JUnitPerf accomplishes this by *decorating* a unit test. In other words, it wraps an existing test with a test that measures the performance of the wrapped test methods.

JUnitPerf (**http://www.clarkware.com/software/JUnitPerf.html**) was written and is maintained by Mike Clark of Clarkware Consulting. It can be downloaded and used free of charge. There are two main types of performance tests that JUnitPerf supports:

- **Timed tests** Measure the amount of time that a test takes. Assertions can be made about the maximum amount of time that the test should take. If the test takes longer than that, then the assertion fails.

- **Load tests** Allow the test writer to indicate the number of concurrent users (threads) that are running the test and optionally the number of times to execute the test.

To start, the following code defines a timed test for the simple JUnit **EmployeeSearchServiceTest** class that was created earlier, in the section "Testing the Model." Of course, the test execution should be integrated into the Ant build.

```
package com.jamesholmes.minihr;

import com.clarkware.junitperf.TimedTest;
import junit.framework.Test;
import junit.framework.TestSuite;

public class EmployeeSearchServicePerfTest {
  public static final long toleranceInMillis = 10;

  public static Test suite() {
    long maxElapsedTimeInMillis = 10 + toleranceInMillis;
    Test timedTest = new TimedTest(
       new TestSuite(EmployeeSearchServiceTest.class),
                    maxElapsedTimeInMillis);
    TestSuite suite = new TestSuite();
    suite.addTest(timedTest);
    return suite;
  }
}
```

As you can see, this class is somewhat atypical of previous unit tests in that it does not extend **TestCase**. It does, however, provide a **suite** method that returns a **Test**. This method creates a test suite of a JUnitPerf **TimedTest** by wrapping a test suite created from the original **EmployeeSearchServiceTest**. The maximum time that the test should take to run is passed in as the second parameter to the **TimedTest**. This test can be run just as any other JUnit test—that is, using the JUnit test runners, IDE/JUnit integration, or via an Ant task.

Another tool, in the open-source domain, for testing and measuring the performance of Web applications is Apache JMeter (**http://jakarta.apache.org/jmeter**). JMeter allows a developer to create and run test plans against running applications. It was originally designed for testing Web sites, so it is well suited for most Struts applications. JMeter provides a Java Swing user interface for creating and running test plans. Performance metrics are gathered and can be visualized graphically as well as in other formats.
To get started, you need to first download JMeter and install it. Follow the provided documentation to create a test plan. You can create thread groups that simulate a number of concurrent users. Then, you can specify the details of an HTTP request to test. Figure 12-4 shows an HTTP request configured to access the Search by Name feature of the Mini HR application.

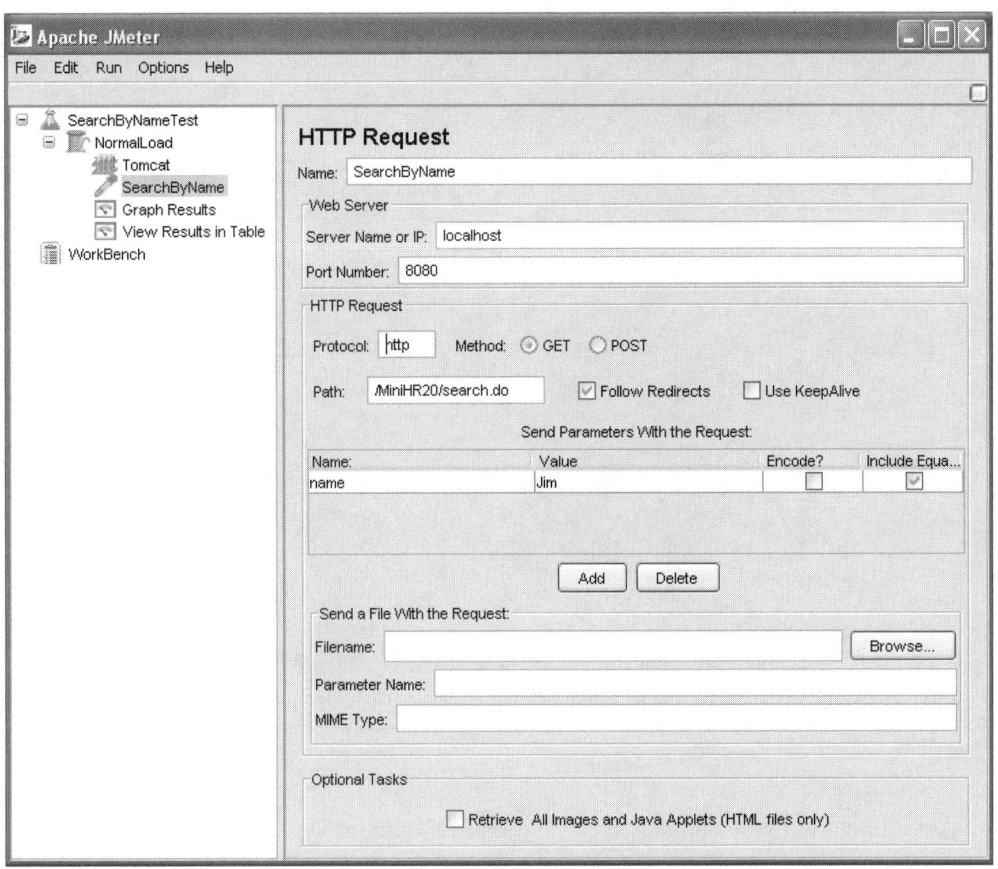

FIGURE 12-4 JMeter HTTP request

The request is configured to access the URL **http://localhost:8080/MiniHR/search.do**. In addition, request parameters can be specified. In this case, the query string **name=Jim** will be added to the request.

The test can then be run against the running server, and the results are accumulated for each result listener. Figure 12-5 shows the display using the Graph Results listener. The thread group, in this case, was configured to run with 20 concurrent users, each making 25 requests to the Search page—a total of 500 data points.

From the results, you can see that on average the search could be performed in a bit over 50 milliseconds, with some requests taking as long as 120 milliseconds. JMeter is a powerful tool and has a great deal more capabilities than described here. It is well documented and has many additional features that you may want to use.

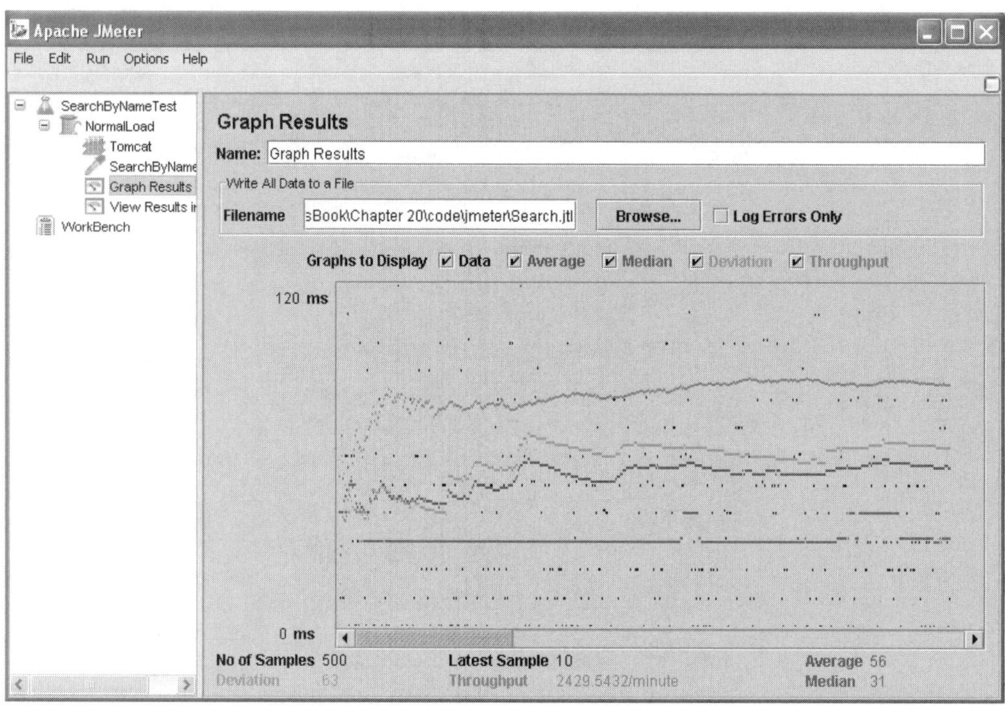

FIGURE 12-5 JMeter graph results

Performance is an area of your application that should not be overlooked—particularly if the application is targeted for high-volume, high-performance Web sites. As was shown in the preceding text, JUnitPerf and Apache JMeter can be used to test the performance of your Web application under simulated loads. These tools can be used to help identify those areas of your application that are bottlenecks. Once identified, profiling tools should be used to focus the performance analysis.

III

PART

The Struts Tag Libraries

CHAPTER 13
The HTML Tag Library

CHAPTER 14
The Bean Tag Library

CHAPTER 15
The Logic Tag Library

CHAPTER 16
The Nested Tag Library

CHAPTER 17
Using JSTL with Struts

13

CHAPTER

The HTML Tag Library

The HTML Tag Library provides a set of tags that parallels HTML's set of tags for creating forms. Instead of using HTML tags to create forms, you can use their corresponding HTML Tag Library tags to create forms that tie into the Struts framework. The tags in this library can automatically populate form controls with data from Form Beans, thereby saving you time and several lines of code. Additionally, the HTML Tag Library provides a few other tags that parallel HTML tags, such as the **base**, **frame**, and **img** tags.

Understanding Variables and Scope in JSP Pages

Before the tags in this library are discussed, it's necessary to review how variables and scope work in JSPs. First, remember that JSPs get converted into servlets and then compiled before they are executed. All of the HTML and code inside the JSP gets placed into the generated servlet's **service( )** method. Because of this, any variables that get defined inside the JSP with a scriptlet, as shown here, are local to the **service( )** method:

```
<%

String test = "test value";
%>
```

Similarly, any variables that are defined with a JSP declaration are local to the **service( )** method:

```
<%! String test = "test value"; %>
```

Also, all of the implicit JSP objects, such as **application**, **request**, and **session**, are local to the resulting servlet's **service( )** method.

JSPs and servlets also have the notion of "scope" for variables, because some variables need to persist longer than the lifespan of a page request and some variables need to be accessible outside of a servlet's **service( )** method. There are four scopes that JSP variables can be placed in: application, page, request, and session. The following table explains each scope.

Scope	Description
application	Variables placed in this scope persist for the life of an application.
page	Variables placed in this scope persist until the current JSP's **service( )** method completes. Included JSPs cannot see page scope variables from the page including them. Also, this scope is exclusive to JSPs.
request	Variables placed in this scope persist until processing for the current request is completed. This scope differs from page scope because multiple servlets may be executed during the lifespan of a request. Page scope variables persist only for the execution of one servlet.
session	Variables placed in this scope persist until the current user's session is invalidated or expires. This scope is valid only if the JSP or servlet in question is participating in a session.

Note that variables must be explicitly placed into a scope, as shown here:

```
<%
request.setAttribute("reqScopeVar", "test");
%>
```

This snippet uses JSP's implicit **request** object to place a variable into request scope. Similarly, the following snippet uses JSP's implicit **session** object to place a variable into session scope:

```
<%
session.setAttribute("sesScopeVar", "test");
%>
```

Of course, variables can also be put into each of the scopes by JSP library tags as many of the tags in the Logic Tag Library do.

Using the HTML Tag Library

To use the HTML Tag Library in a Struts application, your application's JSPs must declare their use of the library with a JSP **taglib** directive:

```
<%@ taglib uri="http://struts.apache.org/tags-html" prefix="html" %>
```

Notice that the **prefix** attribute is set to "html". This attribute can be set to whatever you want; however, "html" is the accepted default for the HTML Tag Library. The **prefix** attribute declares the prefix that each tag must have when it is used in the JSP, as shown here:

```
<html:form action="/logon">
```

Because "html" was defined as the prefix, the **form** tag was used as shown. However, if you chose to use a prefix of "strutshtml", the tag would be used the following way:

```
<strutshtml:form action="/logon">
```

NOTE *Modern application servers use the* **uri** *attribute of the* **taglib** *directive to automatically resolve the location of the tag library descriptor file. Older application servers that support only JSP version 1.1 and/or version 1.0 require that tag libraries be registered in the* **web.xml** *file so that they can be resolved, as shown here:*

```
<taglib>
  <taglib-uri>http://struts.apache.org/tags-html</taglib-uri>
  <taglib-location>/WEB-INF/tlds/struts-html.tld</taglib-location>
</taglib>
```

The HTML Tag Library Tags

The following table lists each of the tags in the HTML Tag Library and a short description of each tag's purpose.

Tag	Description
base	Generates an HTML **<base>** tag with its **href** attribute set to the absolute URL of the enclosing JSP.
button	Generates an HTML **<input type="button">** tag.
cancel	Generates an HTML **<input type="submit">** tag that, when executed, causes Struts' Cancel feature to be triggered.
checkbox	Generates an HTML **<input type="checkbox">** tag populated with data from a specified object.
errors	Displays a set of error messages stored as an **org.apache.struts.action.ActionErrors** object, a **String**, or a **String** array in any scope.
file	Generates an HTML **<input type="file">** tag populated with data from a specified object.
form	Generates an HTML **<form>** tag tied to an **Action** object and its corresponding Form Bean from the **struts-config.xml** file.
frame	Generates an HTML **<frame>** tag.
hidden	Generates an HTML **<input type="hidden">** tag populated with data from a specified object.
html	Generates an HTML **<html>** tag with language attributes set to the current user's locale.
image	Generates an HTML **<input type="image">** tag.
img	Generates an HTML **<img>** tag.
javascript	Generates client-side JavaScript validation code for validations defined in the Validator framework's **validation.xml** file.
link	Generates an HTML hyperlink **<a>** tag whose URL is composed by specifying a base URL and optionally specifying an anchor and/or query string parameters to add to the URL.
messages	Displays a set of messages stored as an **org.apache.struts.action.ActionErrors** object, an **org.apache.struts.action.ActionMessages** object, a **String**, or a **String** array in any scope.
multibox	Generates an HTML **<input type="checkbox">** tag whose checked status is based on whether a specified value matches one of the values in a specified array of values.
option	Generates an HTML **<option>** tag.

Tag	Description
options	Generates a set of HTML **<option>** tags for each element in a collection.
optionsCollection	Generates a set of HTML **<option>** tags for each element in a collection.
password	Generates an HTML **<input type="password">** tag populated with data from a specified object.
radio	Generates an HTML **<input type="radio">** tag populated with data from a specified object.
reset	Generates an HTML **<input type="reset">** tag.
rewrite	Generates a URL by specifying a base URL and optionally specifying an anchor and/or query string parameters to add to the URL.
select	Generates an HTML **<select>** tag.
submit	Generates an HTML **<input type="submit">** tag.
text	Generates an HTML **<input type="text">** tag populated with data from a specified object.
textarea	Generates an HTML **<textarea>** tag populated with data from a specified object.
xhtml	Instructs the rest of the tags in the HTML Tag Library to generate their output as XHTML instead of HTML.

The remainder of this chapter discusses each tag in detail, including a complete description of the tag, a table listing each of the tag's attributes, and a usage example for the tag. In the tables that describe each tag's attributes, pay special attention to the Required and Accepts JSP Expression columns.

The Required column simply denotes whether the given attribute is required when using the tag. In addition to the required column denoting whether an attribute is required, the rows for required attributes are highlighted in gray so that you can determine at a glance which attributes are required.

If an attribute is required and you do not specify it when using the tag, the tag will throw a **javax.servlet.jsp.JspException** at run time. Note that you can declare an error page in your JSP with a **page** directive to capture any **JspException**s that might be thrown, as shown here:

```
<%@ page errorPage="error.jsp" %>
```

If an exception occurs, the page specified by the **errorPage** attribute will be internally redirected to display an error page.

The Accepts JSP Expression column denotes whether the given attribute's value can be specified with a JSP expression. If a JSP expression is used to specify an attribute value, the expression must comprise the complete value, quote (") to quote ("), as shown here. Correct:

```
<html:checkbox property="<%=prop%>">
```

Incorrect:

```
<html:checkbox property="<%=result%>-checked">
```

Notice in the incorrect example that "-checked" is used as part of the value for the **property** attribute following the expression. This is invalid because there are extra characters between the end of the expression and the ending quote.

A corrected version of the incorrect example follows:

```
<html:checkbox property="<%=result + "-checked"%>"/>
```

The concatenation of "-checked" is now part of the expression, and the expression comprises the complete value for the attribute.

One other point: Several of the tags have a set of tag attributes in common, such as **onclick**, **onmousedown**, and **onkeypress**. Rather than repeat the description for these common attributes numerous times, they are described once, at the end of this chapter, in the section"Common Tag Attributes." The Description column in each tag's table of attributes refers you to the section "Common Tag Attributes" for any of the common tag attributes that the tag has in its set of tag attributes.

The base Tag

The **base** tag is used to generate an HTML **<base>** tag with its **href** attribute set to the absolute URL of the enclosing JSP. Note that this tag must be nested inside of an HTML **<head>** tag.

PART III

Attributes

Attribute	Description	Accepts JSP Expression	Required
ref	Specifies what the base URL will be based on. This attribute accepts two values: *page* (default) for basing the URL on the location of the enclosing JSP or *site* for basing the URL on the application's context path. Added in Struts 1.3.	Yes	No
server	Specifies the server name to use when generating the corresponding HTML tag's **href** attribute.	Yes	No
target	Same as the corresponding HTML tag's attribute with the same name. Specifies the frame or window target in which links will be opened.	Yes	No

Example Usage

The following snippet shows the basic usage of the **base** tag:

```
<html:html>
<head>
  <title></title>
  <html:base/>
</head>
```

Remember that this tag must be enclosed by opening and closing HTML **<head>** tags.

The button Tag

The **button** tag is used to generate an HTML **<input type="button">** tag. Note that this tag must be nested inside of this library's **form** tag.

Attributes

Attribute	Description	Accepts JSP Expression	Required
accesskey	See the section "Common Tag Attributes" at the end of this chapter.	Yes	No
alt	See "Common Tag Attributes."	Yes	No
altKey	See "Common Tag Attributes."	Yes	No
bundle	See "Common Tag Attributes."	Yes	No
disabled	See "Common Tag Attributes."	Yes	No
indexed	See "Common Tag Attributes."	Yes	No
onblur	See "Common Tag Attributes."	Yes	No
onchange	See "Common Tag Attributes."	Yes	No
onclick	See "Common Tag Attributes."	Yes	No
ondblclick	See "Common Tag Attributes."	Yes	No
onfocus	See "Common Tag Attributes."	Yes	No
onkeydown	See "Common Tag Attributes."	Yes	No
onkeypress	See "Common Tag Attributes."	Yes	No
onkeyup	See "Common Tag Attributes."	Yes	No
onmousedown	See "Common Tag Attributes."	Yes	No
onmousemove	See "Common Tag Attributes."	Yes	No
onmouseout	See "Common Tag Attributes."	Yes	No
onmouseover	See "Common Tag Attributes."	Yes	No
onmouseup	See "Common Tag Attributes."	Yes	No
property	Same as the corresponding HTML tag's **name** attribute. Specifies the name that will be associated with this control.	Yes	Yes
style	See "Common Tag Attributes."	Yes	No
styleClass	See "Common Tag Attributes."	Yes	No
styleId	See "Common Tag Attributes."	Yes	No
tabindex	See "Common Tag Attributes."	Yes	No
title	See "Common Tag Attributes."	Yes	No
titleKey	See "Common Tag Attributes."	Yes	No

Attribute	Description	Accepts JSP Expression	Required
value	Specifies a constant value that this control will be populated with. This value will be used for the button's label. If not specified, this tag will attempt to use its body content as the value for the button's label.	Yes	No

Example Usage

The following snippet illustrates the basic usage of the **button** tag:

```
<html:button property="direction" value="Next Page"/>
```

The value specified with the **value** attribute will be used for the button's label. Alternatively, you can specify the button's label value by nesting a string between opening and closing **button** tags, as shown here:

```
<html:button>Next Page</html:button>
```


The cancel Tag

Struts has a built-in Cancel feature that will cause it to bypass calling a Form Bean's **validate( )** method if a request parameter named "org.apache.struts.taglib.html.CANCEL" is present in an incoming request. Additionally, **Action** objects can call an **isCancelled( )** method to determine whether a request was canceled. Note that as of Struts 1.3 an **org.apache.struts.action.InvalidCancelException** will be thrown at run time if the cancel button generated by this tag is clicked and the form's associated action mapping in the Struts configuration file does not have its **cancellable** attribute set to **true**.

The **cancel** tag is used to generate an HTML **<input type="submit">** tag with its **name** attribute set to "org.apache.struts.taglib.html.CANCEL" so that, when executed, Struts' Cancel feature will be triggered. Note that this tag must be nested inside of the **form** tag.

Attributes

Attribute	Description	Accepts JSP Expression	Required
accesskey	See the section "Common Tag Attributes" at the end of this chapter.	Yes	No
alt	See "Common Tag Attributes."	Yes	No
altKey	See "Common Tag Attributes."	Yes	No
bundle	See "Common Tag Attributes."	Yes	No
disabled	See "Common Tag Attributes."	Yes	No
onblur	See "Common Tag Attributes."	Yes	No
onchange	See "Common Tag Attributes."	Yes	No
onclick	See "Common Tag Attributes."	Yes	No
ondblclick	See "Common Tag Attributes."	Yes	No

Attribute	Description	Accepts JSP Expression	Required
onfocus	See "Common Tag Attributes."	Yes	No
onkeydown	See "Common Tag Attributes."	Yes	No
onkeypress	See "Common Tag Attributes."	Yes	No
onkeyup	See "Common Tag Attributes."	Yes	No
onmousedown	See "Common Tag Attributes."	Yes	No
onmousemove	See "Common Tag Attributes."	Yes	No
onmouseout	See "Common Tag Attributes."	Yes	No
onmouseover	See "Common Tag Attributes."	Yes	No
onmouseup	See "Common Tag Attributes."	Yes	No
property	Same as the corresponding HTML tag's **name** attribute. Specifies the name that will be associated with this control. *See the Caution about this attribute following this table.*	*Yes*	*No*
style	See "Common Tag Attributes."	Yes	No
styleClass	See "Common Tag Attributes."	Yes	No
styleId	See "Common Tag Attributes."	Yes	No
tabindex	See "Common Tag Attributes."	Yes	No
title	See "Common Tag Attributes."	Yes	No
titleKey	See "Common Tag Attributes."	Yes	No
value	Specifies a constant value that this control will be populated with. This value will be used for the button's label. If not specified, this tag will attempt to use its body content as the value for the button's label.	Yes	No

CAUTION *If you set the property attribute to a value other than its default, Struts' Cancel feature will not be triggered.*

Example Usage

The following snippet illustrates the basic usage of the **cancel** tag:

```
<html:cancel value="Cancel Update"/>
```

The value specified with the **value** attribute will be used for the button's label. Alternatively, you can specify the button's label value by nesting a string between opening and closing **cancel** tags, as shown here:

```
<html:cancel>Cancel Update</html:cancel>
```

The checkbox Tag

The **checkbox** tag is used to generate an HTML **<input type="checkbox">** tag populated with data from a specified object. Note that this tag must be nested inside of this library's **form** tag. Additionally, the underlying Form Bean field associated with this control must be of primitive type **boolean** or of type **Boolean** and the Form Bean's **reset( )** method must include a statement that resets the field to **false**.

Attributes

Attribute	Description	Accepts JSP Expression	Required
accesskey	See the section "Common Tag Attributes" at the end of this chapter.	Yes	No
alt	See "Common Tag Attributes."	Yes	No
altKey	See "Common Tag Attributes."	Yes	No
bundle	See "Common Tag Attributes."	Yes	No
disabled	See "Common Tag Attributes."	Yes	No
errorKey	Specifies the name of the **org.apache.struts.util.MessageResources** object that contains the messages to be rendered. Defaults to the value stored in the **org.apache.struts.Globals.ERROR_KEY** constant.	Yes	No
errorStyle	Specifies the CSS style to apply to this control if an error exists for it.	Yes	No
errorStyleClass	Specifies the CSS class to apply to this control if an error exists for it.	Yes	No
errorStyleId	Specifies the CSS ID to apply to this control if an error exists for it.	Yes	No
indexed	See "Common Tag Attributes."	Yes	No
name	Specifies the name of an object (in any scope) whose field, specified by the **property** attribute, will be used to populate this control with data.	Yes	No
onblur	See "Common Tag Attributes."	Yes	No
onchange	See "Common Tag Attributes."	Yes	No
onclick	See "Common Tag Attributes."	Yes	No
ondblclick	See "Common Tag Attributes."	Yes	No
onfocus	See "Common Tag Attributes."	Yes	No
onkeydown	See "Common Tag Attributes."	Yes	No
onkeypress	See "Common Tag Attributes."	Yes	No
onkeyup	See "Common Tag Attributes."	Yes	No

Attribute	Description	Accepts JSP Expression	Required
onmousedown	See "Common Tag Attributes."	Yes	No
onmousemove	See "Common Tag Attributes."	Yes	No
onmouseout	See "Common Tag Attributes."	Yes	No
onmouseover	See "Common Tag Attributes."	Yes	No
onmouseup	See "Common Tag Attributes."	Yes	No
property	Specifies the value to set the corresponding HTML tag's **name** attribute to. Additionally, this attribute is used to specify the field of the object specified by the **name** attribute whose getter method will be called to return an object whose value will be used to populate this control. If no object is specified with the **name** attribute, the Form Bean object associated with the enclosing **form** tag will be used to retrieve the property specified by this attribute.	Yes	Yes
style	See "Common Tag Attributes."	Yes	No
styleClass	See "Common Tag Attributes."	Yes	No
styleId	See "Common Tag Attributes."	Yes	No
tabindex	See "Common Tag Attributes."	Yes	No
title	See "Common Tag Attributes."	Yes	No
titleKey	See "Common Tag Attributes."	Yes	No
value	Specifies a constant value that the control will be populated with.	Yes	No

Example Usage

The following snippet illustrates the basic usage of the **checkbox** tag:

```
<html:form action="/register">
Subscribe to mailing list: <html:checkbox property="subscribe"/><br>
<html:submit/>
</html:form>
```

This tag will look up the Form Bean associated with the **Action** specified by the **form** tag's **action** attribute and then call the getter method for the field specified by this tag's **property** attribute. The field's value will then be used to populate the HTML control with data.

The errors Tag

The **errors** tag is used to display a set of error messages stored as an **org.apache.struts.action.ActionErrors** object, a **String**, or a **String** array in any scope. This tag will take the stored error messages and iterate over them, displaying them in succession. Additionally, this tag uses the values for the following table of keys from the application resource bundle file (e.g., **MessageResources.properties)** to format the messages.

Key	Purpose
errors.header	Text that will be output before the list of error messages.
errors.footer	Text that will be output after the list of error messages.
errors.prefix	Text that will be output before each error message.
errors.suffix	Text that will be output after each error message.

Attributes

Attribute	Description	Accepts JSP Expression	Required
bundle	Specifies the logical name of a resource bundle that will be used when looking up message keys. The referenced resource bundle must be defined in the application's Struts configuration file.	Yes	No
footer	Specifies text that will be output after the list of error messages. If not specified, defaults to text stored under the "errors.footer" key in your application's resource bundle.	Yes	No
header	Specifies text that will be output before the list of error messages. If not specified, defaults to text stored under the "errors.header" key in your application's resource bundle.	Yes	No
locale	Specifies the key for a **java.util.Locale** instance stored as a session attribute that will be used when looking up error keys.	Yes	No
name	Specifies the key (in any scope) under which the errors to be displayed are stored. If not specified, the default **org.apache.struts.Globals.ERROR_KEY** key will be used.	Yes	No
prefix	Specifies text that will be output before each error message. If not specified, defaults to text stored under the "errors.prefix" key in your application's resource bundle.	Yes	No
property	Specifies the field for which errors will be displayed. If not specified, all errors will be displayed.	Yes	No
suffix	Specifies text that will be output after each error message. If not specified, defaults to text stored under the "errors.suffix" key in your application's resource bundle.	Yes	No

Example Usage

The following snippet illustrates the basic usage of the **errors** tag:

```
<html:errors/>
```

This example will display all the errors currently stored. If you want to limit the errors that are displayed to a specific property, you can specify that property when using the **errors** tag, as shown here:

```
<html:errors property="username"/>
```

In this case, only the errors associated with the property specified by the **property** attribute will be displayed.

The file Tag

The **file** tag is used to generate an HTML **<input type="file">** tag populated with data from a specified object. Note that this tag must be nested inside of the **form** tag. Additionally, the enclosing **form** tag must specify its HTTP method as being POST and its encoding type as being multipart/form-data, as shown here:

```
<html:form method="POST" enctype="multipart/form-data">
…
</html:form>
```

Attributes

Attribute	Description	Accepts JSP Expression	Required
accept	Same as the corresponding HTML tag's attribute with the same name. Specifies a comma-delimited list of content types that the server you submit the enclosing form to knows how to process. Browsers can use this list to limit the set of files made available for selection.	Yes	No
accesskey	See the section "Common Tag Attributes" at the end of this chapter.	Yes	No
alt	See "Common Tag Attributes."	Yes	No
altKey	See "Common Tag Attributes."	Yes	No
bundle	See "Common Tag Attributes."	Yes	No
disabled	See "Common Tag Attributes."	Yes	No
errorKey	Specifies the name of the **org.apache.struts.util.MessageResources** object that contains the messages to be rendered. Defaults to the value stored in the **org.apache.struts.Globals.ERROR_KEY** constant.	Yes	No

Attribute	Description	Accepts JSP Expression	Required
errorStyle	Specifies the CSS style to apply to this control if an error exists for it.	Yes	No
errorStyleClass	Specifies the CSS class to apply to this control if an error exists for it.	Yes	No
errorStyleId	Specifies the CSS ID to apply to this control if an error exists for it.	Yes	No
indexed	See "Common Tag Attributes."	Yes	No
maxlength	Same as the corresponding HTML tag's attribute with the same name. Specifies the maximum number of characters that this control will accept.	Yes	No
name	Specifies the name of an object (in any scope) whose field, specified by the **property** attribute, will be used to populate this control with data.	Yes	No
onblur	See "Common Tag Attributes."	Yes	No
onchange	See "Common Tag Attributes."	Yes	No
onclick	See "Common Tag Attributes."	Yes	No
ondblclick	See "Common Tag Attributes."	Yes	No
onfocus	See "Common Tag Attributes."	Yes	No
onkeydown	See "Common Tag Attributes."	Yes	No
onkeypress	See "Common Tag Attributes."	Yes	No
onkeyup	See "Common Tag Attributes."	Yes	No
onmousedown	See "Common Tag Attributes."	Yes	No
onmousemove	See "Common Tag Attributes."	Yes	No
onmouseout	See "Common Tag Attributes."	Yes	No
onmouseover	See "Common Tag Attributes."	Yes	No
onmouseup	See "Common Tag Attributes."	Yes	No
property	Specifies the value to which the corresponding HTML tag's **name** attribute is set. Additionally, this attribute is used to specify the field of the object specified by the **name** attribute whose getter method will be called to return an object whose value will be used to populate this control. If no object is specified with the **name** attribute, the Form Bean object associated with the enclosing **form** tag will be used to retrieve the property specified by this attribute.	Yes	Yes

Attribute	Description	Accepts JSP Expression	Required
size	Same as the corresponding HTML tag's attribute with the same name. Specifies the number of characters that will be visible in the control.	Yes	No
style	See "Common Tag Attributes."	Yes	No
styleClass	See "Common Tag Attributes."	Yes	No
styleId	See "Common Tag Attributes."	Yes	No
tabindex	See "Common Tag Attributes."	Yes	No
title	See "Common Tag Attributes."	Yes	No
titleKey	See "Common Tag Attributes."	Yes	No
value	Specifies a constant value that is used to populate the control.	Yes	No

Example Usage

The following snippet illustrates the basic usage of the **file** tag:

```
<html:form method="POST"
          enctype="multipart/form-data"
           action="/attachFile">
Upload File: <html:file property="uploadFile"/><br>
<html:submit/>
</html:form>
```

This tag will look up the Form Bean associated with the **Action** specified by the **form** tag's **action** attribute and then call the getter method for the field specified by this tag's **property** attribute. The field's value will then be used to populate the HTML control with data.

The form Tag

The **form** tag is used to generate an HTML **<form>** tag tied to an **Action** and its corresponding Form Bean from the Struts configuration file (e.g., **struts-config.xml**). The **Action**'s Form Bean will be used by other tags from this library to populate them with data when they are nested inside this tag.

Attributes

Attribute	Description	Accepts JSP Expression	Required
acceptCharset	Specifies the list of character encodings that the server should accept for field input data.	Yes	No
action	Specifies the logical name of an **Action**, defined in the Struts configuration file, whose path will be used to define the corresponding HTML tag's attribute with the same name. If not specified, the original URI for the request will be used.	Yes	No

Attribute	Description	Accepts JSP Expression	Required
disabled	See the section "Common Tag Attributes" at the end of this chapter.	Yes	No
enctype	Same as the corresponding HTML tag's attribute with the same name. Specifies the encoding to be used when submitting this form if the POST method is used. This must be set to "multipart/form-data" if you are using the **file** tag to upload files.	Yes	No
focus	Specifies the name of a field inside this form that initial focus will be assigned to using JavaScript.	Yes	No
focusIndex	Specifies an index to be used if the field specified with the **focus** attribute is a field array such as a radio button group.	Yes	No
method	Same as the corresponding HTML tag's attribute with the same name. Specifies the HTTP method that will be used when submitting this form (e.g., GET or POST).	Yes	No
onreset	Same as the corresponding HTML tag's attribute with the same name. Specifies the JavaScript code to execute when this form is reset.	Yes	No
onsubmit	Same as the corresponding HTML tag's attribute with the same name. Specifies the JavaScript code to execute when this form is submitted.	Yes	No
readonly	Same as the corresponding HTML tag's attribute with the same name. Accepts *true* or *false* to specify whether the form elements will be read-only, preventing them from being changed. Defaults to *false.*	*Yes*	*No*
scriptLanguage	Accepts *true* or *false* to specify whether the **language** attribute of the **<focus>** tag generated by this tag's **focus** attribute should be omitted. Note that the generated **<focus>** tag's **language** attribute is omitted regardless when the tags in this library are in XHTML mode. Defaults to *true.*	*Yes*	*No*
style	See "Common Tag Attributes."	Yes	No

PART III

Attribute	Description	Accepts JSP Expression	Required
styleClass	See "Common Tag Attributes."	Yes	No
styleId	See "Common Tag Attributes."	Yes	No
target	Same as the corresponding HTML tag's attribute with the same name. Specifies the frame or window target in which this form will be submitted.	Yes	No

Example Usage

The following snippet illustrates the basic usage of the **form** tag:

```
<html:form action="/logon">
UserName: <html:text property="username"/><br>
Password: <html:password property="password"/><br>
<html:submit/>
</html:form>
```

The Form Bean associated with the **Action** specified by the **action** attribute will be used for populating the nested HTML controls inside the opening and closing **form** tags.

If you want to use a postback form, use the **form** tag as shown here:

```
<html:form>
UserName: <html:text property="username"/><br>
Password: <html:password property="password"/><br>
<html:submit/>
</html:form>
```

In this scenario, the URI of the original request is used to populate the rendered HTML tag's **action** attribute.

The frame Tag

The **frame** tag is used to generate an HTML **<frame>** tag. The frame's URL is composed by specifying a base URL and optionally specifying an anchor and/or query string parameters to add to the URL.

There are four ways to specify the base URL:

- You can use the **action** attribute to specify the name of an **Action** from the Struts configuration file whose URL will be used.
- You can use the **forward** attribute to specify the name of a forward from the Struts configuration file whose URL will be used.
- You can use the **href** attribute to specify an absolute URL, including protocol (e.g., http://www.yahoo.com/).
- You can use the **page** attribute to specify an application-relative URL.

In addition to specifying the base URL, you have two options for specifying query string parameters to add to the base URL:

- You can use the **paramId** attribute in conjunction with the **paramName** attribute, and optionally the **paramProperty** attribute, to specify a single parameter.
- You can use the **name** attribute, either alone or in tandem with the **property** attribute, to specify a **java.util.Map** object that will be used to add several parameters.

Attributes

Attribute	Description	Accepts JSP Expression	Required
action	Specifies the name of an **Action**, from the Action Mappings section of the Struts configuration file, which contains the URL for this frame.	Yes	No
anchor	Specifies the anchor (e.g., "#bottom") to be added to the URL for this frame. This value must be specified without the leading hash (#) character.	Yes	No
bundle	See the section "Common Tag Attributes" at the end of this chapter.	Yes	No
forward	Specifies the name of a forward, from the Global Forwards Configuration section of the Struts configuration file, that contains the URL for this frame.	Yes	No
frameborder	Same as the corresponding HTML tag's attribute with the same name. Specifies the border size for this frame (0 for no border).	Yes	No
frameName	Same as the corresponding HTML tag's **name** attribute. Specifies the logical name to give the frame.	Yes	No
href	Specifies the absolute URL, including protocol (e.g., http://www.yahoo.com), for this frame.	Yes	No
longdesc	Same as the corresponding HTML tag's attribute with the same name. Specifies the URL for a long description of the frame that supplements the short description provided by the **title** attribute.	Yes	No
marginheight	Same as the corresponding HTML tag's attribute with the same name. Specifies the number of pixels that will be placed between this frame's contents and its top and bottom margins.	Yes	No

PART III

Attribute	Description	Accepts JSP Expression	Required
marginwidth	Same as the corresponding HTML tag's attribute with the same name. Specifies the number of pixels that will be placed between this frame's contents and its left and right margins.	Yes	No
module	Specifies the name of a module that contains the action mapping for the Action specified with the **action** attribute.	Yes	No
name	Specifies the name of the **java.util.Map** object whose elements are added as query string parameters to the URL for this frame. If the **property** attribute is also specified, one of the fields of the object defined by this attribute will have its getter method called to return the **java.util.Map** object whose elements are added as query string parameters to the URL for this frame.	Yes	No
noresize	Same as the corresponding HTML tag's attribute with the same name. Accepts *true* or *false* to specify whether this frame will not be resizable. Defaults to *false.*	*Yes*	*No*
page	Specifies the application-relative URL (starts with a leading slash, /) for this frame.	Yes	No
paramId	Specifies the name of a single parameter to add to the URL for this frame.	Yes	No
paramName	Specifies the name of an object whose value will be used as the value for the parameter specified with the **paramId** attribute. If the **property** attribute is also specified, one of the fields of the object defined by this attribute will have its getter method called to return an object whose value will be used as the value for the parameter specified with the **paramId** attribute.	Yes	*No*
paramProperty	Specifies the field of the object specified by the **name** attribute whose getter method will be called to return an object whose value will be used as the value for the parameter specified with the **paramId** attribute.	Yes	No

Attribute	Description	Accepts JSP Expression	Required
paramScope	Specifies the scope (application, page, request, or session) to look in for the object specified by the **paramName** attribute. If not specified, each scope will be searched, in this order: page, request, session, and then application.	Yes	No
property	Specifies the field of the object specified by the **name** attribute whose getter method will be called to return the **java.util.Map** object whose elements are added as query string parameters to the URL for this frame.	Yes	No
scope	Specifies the scope (application, page, request, or session) to look in for the object specified by the **name** attribute. If not specified, each scope will be searched, in this order: page, request, session, and then application.	Yes	No
scrolling	Same as the corresponding HTML tag's attribute with the same name. Specifies whether this frame is scrollable. Specify *yes* to have scroll bars unconditionally, *no* to never have scroll bars, or *auto* to have scroll bars automatically based on how much content is in the frame.	Yes	No
style	See "Common Tag Attributes."	Yes	No
styleClass	See "Common Tag Attributes."	Yes	No
styleId	See "Common Tag Attributes."	Yes	No
title	See "Common Tag Attributes."	Yes	No
titleKey	See "Common Tag Attributes."	Yes	No
transaction	Accepts *true* or *false* to specify whether the current transaction token is included in the URL for this frame. Defaults to *false*.	*Yes*	*No*

Example Usage

There are a few different ways to use the **frame** tag. The first way, shown here, uses the **href** attribute to specify an absolute URL for the frame:

```
<html:frame href="http://www.yahoo.com/"/>
```

The following example adds to the first example by specifying a single query string parameter to add to the base URL specified by the **href** attribute:

```
<html:frame href="http://www.yahoo.com/"
        paramId="query"
      paramName="queryObj"/>
```

This example takes the base URL specified by the **href** attribute and appends the query string parameter specified by the **paramId** and **paramName** attributes and composes a URL for the frame.

Another way to use the **frame** tag is shown here:

```
<html:frame page="/search.jsp" name="params"/>
```

This example uses the **page** attribute to specify an application-relative base URL and uses the **name** attribute to specify a **java.util.Map** object whose entries are added to the URL as query string parameters.

The hidden Tag

The **hidden** tag is used to generate an HTML **<input type="hidden">** tag populated with data from a specified object. Note that this tag must be nested inside of the **form** tag.

Attributes

Attribute	Description	Accepts JSP Expression	Required
accesskey	See the section "Common Tag Attributes" at the end of this chapter.	Yes	No
alt	See "Common Tag Attributes."	Yes	No
altKey	See "Common Tag Attributes."	Yes	No
bundle	See "Common Tag Attributes."	Yes	No
disabled	See "Common Tag Attributes."	Yes	No
indexed	See "Common Tag Attributes."	Yes	No
name	Specifies the name of an object (in any scope) whose field, specified by the **property** attribute, will be used to populate this control with data.	Yes	No
onblur	See "Common Tag Attributes."	Yes	No
onchange	See "Common Tag Attributes."	Yes	No
onclick	See "Common Tag Attributes."	Yes	No
ondblclick	See "Common Tag Attributes."	Yes	No
onfocus	See "Common Tag Attributes."	Yes	No
onkeydown	See "Common Tag Attributes."	Yes	No
onkeypress	See "Common Tag Attributes."	Yes	No
onkeyup	See "Common Tag Attributes."	Yes	No
onmousedown	See "Common Tag Attributes."	Yes	No
onmousemove	See "Common Tag Attributes."	Yes	No
onmouseout	See "Common Tag Attributes."	Yes	No
onmouseover	See "Common Tag Attributes."	Yes	No

Attribute	Description	Accepts JSP Expression	Required
onmouseup	See "Common Tag Attributes."	Yes	No
property	Specifies the value to which the corresponding HTML tag's **name** attribute is set. Additionally, this attribute is used to specify the field of the object specified by the **name** attribute whose getter method will be called to return an object whose value will be used to populate this control. If no object is specified with the **name** attribute, the Form Bean object associated with the enclosing **form** tag will be used to retrieve the property specified by this attribute.	Yes	Yes
style	See "Common Tag Attributes."	Yes	No
styleClass	See "Common Tag Attributes."	Yes	No
styleId	See "Common Tag Attributes."	Yes	No
title	See "Common Tag Attributes."	Yes	No
titleKey	See "Common Tag Attributes."	Yes	No
value	Specifies a constant value that this control will be populated with.	Yes	No
write	Accepts *true* or *false* to specify whether this control's value will also be written out to the page so that it is visible. Defaults to *false*.	*Yes*	*No*

Example Usage

The following snippet illustrates the basic usage of the **hidden** tag:

```
<html:form action="/search">
<html:hidden property="lastId"/>
<html:submit/>
</html:form>
```

This tag will look up the Form Bean associated with the **Action** specified by the **form** tag's **action** attribute and then call the getter method for the field specified by this tag's **property** attribute. The field's value will then be used to populate the HTML control with data.

The html Tag

The **html** tag is used to generate an HTML **<html>** tag with language attributes set to the current user's locale. Additionally, you can use this tag to instruct the rest of the tags in the HTML Tag Library to generate their output as XHTML instead of HTML. More information on XHTML can be found at **http://www.xhtml.org/**.

PART III

Attributes

Attribute	Description	Accepts JSP Expression	Required
lang	Accepts *true* or *false* to specify whether an attribute of the same name will be rendered on the generated <html> tag. If set to *true*, the attribute will be set to the language from the locale currently stored in the user's session. If there is not a locale stored in the session, the language will be set to that specified by the current request's "AcceptLanguage" HTTP header. Finally, if there is not an "AcceptLanguage" header value, the language will be set to server's default. Defaults to *false*.	*Yes*	*No*
xhtml	Accepts *true* or *false* to specify whether the rest of the tags in the HTML Tag Library will generate their output as XHTML instead of HTML. Defaults to *false*.	*Yes*	*No*

Example Usage

The following snippet shows the basic usage of the **html** tag:

```
<html:html/>
```

If you want the HTML Tag Library's tags to generate XHTML instead of HTML, use the **html** tag as shown here:

```
<html:html xhtml="true"/>
```

The image Tag

The **image** tag is used to generate an HTML **<input type="image">** tag. Note that this tag must be nested inside of a **form** tag.

There are two ways you can use the **image** tag, as listed here and shown later, in the section "Example Usage":

- You can use the **page** or **pageKey** attribute to specify a module-relative URL that will be used as the generated HTML tag's **src** attribute.
- You can use the **src** or **srcKey** attribute to specify a URL that will be used as the generated HTML tag's **src** attribute.

Attributes

Attribute	Description	Accepts JSP Expression	Required
accesskey	See the section "Common Tag Attributes" at the end of this chapter.	Yes	No

Attribute	Description	Accepts JSP Expression	Required
align	Same as the corresponding HTML tag's attribute with the same name. Specifies how the image will be aligned (i.e., left, right, top, bottom, and so on).	Yes	No
alt	See "Common Tag Attributes."	Yes	No
altKey	See "Common Tag Attributes."	Yes	No
border	Same as the corresponding HTML tag's attribute with the same name. Specifies the width of the border surrounding the image.	Yes	No
bundle	See "Common Tag Attributes."	Yes	No
disabled	See "Common Tag Attributes."	Yes	No
indexed	See "Common Tag Attributes."	Yes	No
locale	Specifies the key for a **java.util.Locale** instance stored as a session attribute that will be used when looking up message keys specified by other attributes of this tag (i.e., **pageKey** and **srcKey**).	Yes	No
onblur	See "Common Tag Attributes."	Yes	No
onchange	See "Common Tag Attributes."	Yes	No
onclick	See "Common Tag Attributes."	Yes	No
ondblclick	See "Common Tag Attributes."	Yes	No
onfocus	See "Common Tag Attributes."	Yes	No
onkeydown	See "Common Tag Attributes."	Yes	No
onkeypress	See "Common Tag Attributes."	Yes	No
onkeyup	See "Common Tag Attributes."	Yes	No
onmousedown	See "Common Tag Attributes."	Yes	No
onmousemove	See "Common Tag Attributes."	Yes	No
onmouseout	See "Common Tag Attributes."	Yes	No
onmouseover	See "Common Tag Attributes."	Yes	No
onmouseup	See "Common Tag Attributes."	Yes	No
page	Specifies a module-relative URL for this button's image.	Yes	No
pageKey	Specifies a key from the application resource bundle whose value will be used to set the corresponding HTML tag's **src** attribute with a module-relative URL.	Yes	No

Attribute	Description	Accepts JSP Expression	Required
property	Same as the corresponding HTML tag's **name** attribute. Specifies the name that will be associated with this control.	Yes	No
src	Same as the corresponding HTML tag's attribute with the same name. Specifies the source URL for this button's image.	Yes	No
srcKey	Specifies a key from the application resource bundle whose value will be used to set the corresponding HTML tag's **src** attribute.	Yes	No
style	See "Common Tag Attributes."	Yes	No
styleClass	See "Common Tag Attributes."	Yes	No
styleId	See "Common Tag Attributes."	Yes	No
tabindex	See "Common Tag Attributes."	Yes	No
title	See "Common Tag Attributes."	Yes	No
titleKey	See "Common Tag Attributes."	Yes	No
value	Specifies a constant value that this control will be populated with. If not specified, this tag will attempt to use its body content as the value.	Yes	No

Example Usage

As mentioned, there are two ways you can use the **image** tag. The first way, shown here, uses the **page** attribute to specify a module-relative URL for the generated HTML tag's **src** attribute:

```
<html:image page="previous.gif"/>
```

The second way to use the **image** tag is shown here:

```
<html:image src="/images/next.gif"/>
```

This example uses the **src** attribute to specify a URL for the generated HTML tag's **src** attribute. The **image** tag will be used in this way for most applications; however, if you are taking advantage of Struts' module functionality, you will use the **page** or **pageKey** attribute.

The img Tag

The **img** tag is used to generate an HTML **<img>** tag. The image's URL is composed by specifying a base URL and optionally specifying query string parameters to add to the URL.

Attributes

Attribute	Description	Accepts JSP Expression	Required
action	Specifies the name of an action, from the Action Mappings Configuration section of the Struts configuration file, that contains the base URL for the image.	Yes	No
align	Same as the corresponding HTML tag's attribute with the same name. Specifies how the image will be aligned (i.e., left, right, top, bottom, and so on).	Yes	No
alt	See the section "Common Tag Attributes" at the end of this chapter.	Yes	No
altKey	See "Common Tag Attributes."	Yes	No
border	Same as the corresponding HTML tag's attribute with the same name. Specifies the width of the border surrounding the image.	Yes	No
bundle	See "Common Tag Attributes."	Yes	No
height	Same as the corresponding HTML tag's attribute with the same name. Specifies the height of this image in pixels.	Yes	No
hspace	Same as the corresponding HTML tag's attribute with the same name. Specifies the number of pixels that will be placed between this image and text surrounding it from the top or bottom.	Yes	No
imageName	Same as the corresponding HTML tag's **name** attribute. Specifies the scriptable name for the image.	Yes	No
ismap	Same as the corresponding HTML tag's attribute with the same name. Specifies the name of a server-side image map to use to map different regions of the image to different URLs.	Yes	No
locale	Specifies the key for a **java.util.Locale** instance stored as a session attribute that will be used when looking up message keys specified by other attributes of this tag (i.e., **pageKey** and **srcKey**).	Yes	No
module	Specifies the name of a module that contains the action specified with the **action** attribute.	Yes	No
name	Specifies the name of the **java.util.Map** object whose elements are added as query string parameters to the URL for this image. If the **property** attribute is also specified, one of the fields of the object defined by this attribute will have its getter method called to return the **java.util.Map** object whose elements are added as query string parameters to the URL for this image.	Yes	No

Attribute	Description	Accepts JSP Expression	Required
onclick	See "Common Tag Attributes."	Yes	No
ondblclick	See "Common Tag Attributes."	Yes	No
onkeydown	See "Common Tag Attributes."	Yes	No
onkeypress	See "Common Tag Attributes."	Yes	No
onkeyup	See "Common Tag Attributes."	Yes	No
onmousedown	See "Common Tag Attributes."	Yes	No
onmousemove	See "Common Tag Attributes."	Yes	No
onmouseout	See "Common Tag Attributes."	Yes	No
onmouseover	See "Common Tag Attributes."	Yes	No
onmouseup	See "Common Tag Attributes."	Yes	No
page	Specifies a module-relative URL for this image.	Yes	No
pageKey	Specifies a key from the application resource bundle whose value will be used to set the corresponding HTML tag's **src** attribute with a module-relative URL.	Yes	No
paramId	Specifies the name of a single parameter to add to the URL for this image.	Yes	No
paramName	Specifies the name of an object whose value will be used as the value for the parameter specified with the **paramId** attribute. If the **property** attribute is also specified, one of the fields of the object defined by this attribute will have its getter method called to return an object whose value will be used as the value for the parameter specified with the **paramId** attribute.	Yes	No
paramProperty	Specifies the field of the object specified by the **name** attribute whose getter method will be called to return an object whose value will be used as the value for the parameter specified with the **paramId** attribute.	Yes	No
paramScope	Specifies the scope (application, page, request, or session) to look in for the object specified by the **paramName** attribute. If not specified, each scope will be searched, in this order: page, request, session, and then application.	Yes	No
property	Specifies the field of the object specified by the **name** attribute whose getter method will be called to return the **java.util.Map** object whose elements are added as query string parameters to the URL for this image.	Yes	No
scope	Specifies the scope (application, page, request, or session) to look in for the object specified by the **name** attribute. If not specified, each scope will be searched, in this order: page, request, session, and then application.	Yes	No
src	Same as the corresponding HTML tag's attribute with the same name. Specifies the source URL for this image.	Yes	No

Attribute	Description	Accepts JSP Expression	Required
srcKey	Specifies a key from the application resource bundle whose value will be used to set the corresponding HTML tag's **src** attribute.	Yes	No
style	See "Common Tag Attributes."	Yes	No
styleClass	See "Common Tag Attributes."	Yes	No
styleId	See "Common Tag Attributes."	Yes	No
title	See "Common Tag Attributes."	Yes	No
titleKey	See "Common Tag Attributes."	Yes	No
useLocalEnding	Accepts *true* or *false* to specify whether the character encoding of the URL parameters should be performed using the encoding type of the HTTP response object. If this attribute is set to *false*, the encoding type defaults to UTF-8. Defaults to *false*.	*Yes*	*No*
usemap	Same as the corresponding HTML tag's attribute with the same name. Specifies the name of a client-side image map to use for mapping different regions of the image to different URLs.	Yes	No
vspace	Same as the corresponding HTML tag's attribute with the same name. Specifies the number of pixels that will be placed between this image and text surrounding it from the left or right.	Yes	No
width	Same as the corresponding HTML tag's attribute with the same name. Specifies the width of this image in pixels.	Yes	No

Example Usage

There are a few different ways to use the **img** tag. The first way, shown here, uses the **src** attribute to specify an absolute URL for the image:

```
<html:img src="http://www.domain.com/image.gif"/>
```

The following example adds to the first example by specifying a single query string parameter to add to the base URL specified by the **src** attribute:

```
<html:img href=" http://www.domain.com/image.gif"
       paramId="image"
     paramName="imageObj"/>
```

This example takes the base URL specified by the **href** attribute and appends the query string parameter specified by the **paramId** and **paramName** attributes and composes a URL for the image.

The javascript Tag

The **javascript** tag is used to generate client-side JavaScript validation code for validations defined in the Validator framework's **validation.xml** file.

The JavaScript code generated by the **javascript** tag can be broken down into two pieces: static code and dynamic code. The static piece is composed of all the generic validation routine methods. The dynamic piece is composed of the code that is specific to a particular HTML form and that calls the static validation methods. Because the static piece of code is typically very large and is often repeated across several pages, it is advantageous to break that piece out and store it in its own file. That way it can simply be referenced by each page that makes use of it. The **javascript** tag allows you to break up the two pieces of code by specifying which code it generates with the **dynamicJavascript** and **staticJavascript** attributes.

Attributes

Attribute	Description	Accepts JSP Expression	Required
bundle	Specifies the logical name of a resource bundle that will be used when looking up message keys. The referenced resource bundle must be defined in the application's Struts configuration file.	Yes	No
cdata	Accepts *true* or *false* to specify whether the generated JavaScript code will *not* be enclosed in XML CDATA tags (i.e., **<![CDATA[ ]]>**). Note that CDATA tags are necessary to prevent JavaScript code from being parsed when used in conjunction with XHTML. Defaults to *true*.	*Yes*	*No*
dynamicJavascript	Accepts *true* or *false* to specify whether dynamic JavaScript will be generated. Defaults to *true*.	*Yes*	*No*
formName	Specifies the logical name of a Form Bean whose validation rules will be used to generate JavaScript validation code.	Yes	No
htmlComment	Accepts *true* or *false* to specify whether the generated JavaScript code will *not* be enclosed in HTML comment tags (i.e., <!- - - ->). Defaults to *true*.	*Yes*	*No*
method	Specifies an alternate JavaScript method name to be used instead of the default.	Yes	No

Attribute	Description	Accepts JSP Expression	Required
page	Specifies the logical name of a page to use to filter which validations for the specified form will be generated. This logical name matches the logical name that can be applied to individual fields in the Validator configuration file (e.g., **validation.xml**).	Yes	No
scriptLanguage	Accepts *true* or *false* to specify whether the **language** attribute of the **<script>** tag generated by this tag should be omitted. Note that the generated **<script>** tag's **language** attribute is omitted regardless when the tags in this library are in XHTML mode. Defaults to *true.*	*Yes*	*No*
src	Same as the corresponding JavaScript tag's attribute with the same name. Specifies the URL to a static JavaScript file to be included.	Yes	No
staticJavascript	Accepts *true* or *false* to specify whether static JavaScript will be generated. Defaults to *true.*	*Yes*	*No*

PART III

Example Usage

The following snippet illustrates the basic usage of the **javascript** tag:

```
<html:javascript formName="logonForm"/>
```

This example will generate JavaScript code for all the validation rules in the **validation.xml** file that are tied to the Form Bean specified by the **formName** attribute.

If you want to separate the dynamic and static pieces of the generated JavaScript code, you can use the **javascript** tag as shown next:

```
<html:javascript formName="logonForm"
        staticJavascript="false"
                     src="staticJavascript.jsp"/>
```

This usage only generates the dynamic JavaScript for the specified form. The following example generates the generic static JavaScript code:

```
<html:javascript formName="logonForm" dynamicJavascript="false"/>
```

This snippet must be placed into a separate file named **staticJavascript.jsp** to match the file name specified by the **src** attribute of the previous example.

The link Tag

The **link** tag is used to generate an HTML hyperlink **<a>** tag whose URL is composed by specifying a base URL and optionally specifying an anchor and/or query string parameters to add to the URL.

There are four ways to specify the base URL:

- You can use the **action** attribute to specify the name of an **Action** from the Struts configuration file whose URL will be used.
- You can use the **forward** attribute to specify the name of a forward from the Struts configuration file whose URL will be used.
- You can use the **href** attribute to specify an absolute URL, including protocol (e.g., http://www.yahoo.com/).
- You can use the **page** attribute to specify an application-relative URL.

In addition to specifying the base URL, you have two options for specifying query string parameters to add to the base URL:

- You can use the **paramId** attribute in conjunction with the **paramName** attribute, and optionally the **paramProperty** attribute, to specify a single parameter.
- You can use the **name** attribute, either alone or in tandem with the **property** attribute, to specify a **java.util.Map** object that will be used to add several parameters.

Attributes

Attribute	Description	Accepts JSP Expression	Required
accesskey	See the section "Common Tag Attributes" at the end of this chapter.	Yes	No
action	Specifies the name of an **Action**, from the Action Mappings section of the Struts configuration file, that contains the URL for this link.	Yes	No
anchor	Specifies the anchor (e.g., "#bottom") to be added to the URL for this link. This value must be specified without the leading hash (#) character.	Yes	No
bundle	See "Common Tag Attributes."	Yes	No
forward	Specifies the name of a forward, from the Global Forwards section of the Struts configuration file, which contains the URL for this link.	Yes	No
href	Specifies the absolute URL, including protocol (e.g., http://www.yahoo.com), for this link.	Yes	No

Attribute	Description	Accepts JSP Expression	Required
indexed	See "Common Tag Attributes."	Yes	No
indexId	Specifies the name to use for an indexed parameter if the **indexed** attribute is used. This attribute is applicable only when this tag is nested inside the Logic Tag Library's **iterate** tag.	Yes	No
linkName	Same as the corresponding HTML tag's **name** attribute. Specifies the name of a page anchor for intra-page hyperlinks.	Yes	No
module	Specifies the name of a module that contains the action specified with the **action** attribute.	Yes	No
name	Specifies the name of the **java.util.Map** object whose elements are added as query string parameters to the URL for this link. If the **property** attribute is also specified, one of the fields of the object defined by this attribute will have its getter method called to return the **java.util.Map** object whose elements are added as query string parameters to the URL for this link.	Yes	No
onblur	See "Common Tag Attributes."	Yes	No
onclick	See "Common Tag Attributes."	Yes	No
ondblclick	See "Common Tag Attributes."	Yes	No
onfocus	See "Common Tag Attributes."	Yes	No
onkeydown	See "Common Tag Attributes."	Yes	No
onkeypress	See "Common Tag Attributes."	Yes	No
onkeyup	See "Common Tag Attributes."	Yes	No
onmousedown	See "Common Tag Attributes."	Yes	No
onmousemove	See "Common Tag Attributes."	Yes	No
onmouseout	See "Common Tag Attributes."	Yes	No
onmouseover	See "Common Tag Attributes."	Yes	No
onmouseup	See "Common Tag Attributes."	Yes	No
page	Specifies the application-relative URL (starts with a leading slash, /) for this link.	Yes	No
paramId	Specifies the name of a single parameter to add to the URL for this link.	Yes	No

Attribute	Description	Accepts JSP Expression	Required
paramName	Specifies the name of an object whose value will be used as the value for the parameter specified with the **paramId** attribute. If the **property** attribute is also specified, one of the fields of the object defined by this attribute will have its getter method called to return an object whose value will be used as the value for the parameter specified with the **paramId** attribute.	Yes	No
paramProperty	Specifies the field of the object specified by the **name** attribute whose getter method will be called to return an object whose value will be used as the value for the parameter specified with the **paramId** attribute.	Yes	No
paramScope	Specifies the scope (application, page, request, or session) to look in for the object specified by the **paramName** attribute. If not specified, each scope will be searched, in this order: page, request, session, and then application.	Yes	No
property	Specifies the field of the object specified by the **name** attribute whose getter method will be called to return the **java.util.Map** object whose elements are added as query string parameters to the URL for this link.	Yes	No
scope	Specifies the scope (application, page, request, or session) to look in for the object specified by the **name** attribute. If not specified, each scope will be searched, in this order: page, request, session, and then application.	Yes	No
style	See "Common Tag Attributes."	Yes	No
styleClass	See "Common Tag Attributes."	Yes	No
styleId	See "Common Tag Attributes."	Yes	No
tabindex	See "Common Tag Attributes."	Yes	No
target	Same as the corresponding HTML tag's attribute with the same name. Specifies the frame or window target in which this link will be displayed.	Yes	No
title	See "Common Tag Attributes."	Yes	No

Attribute	Description	Accepts JSP Expression	Required
titleKey	See "Common Tag Attributes."	Yes	No
transaction	Accepts *true* or *false* to specify whether the current transaction token will be included in the URL for this link. Defaults to *false.*	*Yes*	*No*
useLocalEnding	Accepts *true* or *false* to specify whether the character encoding of the URL parameters should be performed using the encoding type of the HTTP response object. If this attribute is set to *false*, the encoding type defaults to UTF-8. Defaults to *false.*	*Yes*	*No*

Example Usage

There are a few different ways to use the **link** tag. The first way, shown here, uses the **href** attribute to specify an absolute URL for the frame:

```
<html:link href="http://www.yahoo.com/"/>
```

The following example adds to the first example by specifying a single query string parameter to add to the base URL specified by the **href** attribute:

```
<html:link href="http://www.yahoo.com/"
           paramId="query"
         paramName="queryObj"/>
```

This example takes the base URL specified by the **href** attribute and appends the query string parameter specified by the **paramId** and **paramName** attributes and composes a URL that the tag then redirects to.

Another way to use the **link** tag is shown here:

```
<html:link page="/search.jsp" name="params"/>
```

This example uses the **page** attribute to specify an application-relative base URL and uses the **name** attribute to specify a **java.util.Map** object whose entries are added to the URL as query string parameters.

The messages Tag

The **messages** tag is used to display a set of messages stored as an **org.apache.struts.action.ActionErrors** object, an **org.apache.struts.action.ActionMessages** object, a **String**, or a **String** array in any scope. Similar to the **errors** tag, this tag will take the stored messages and iterate over them; however, instead of actually outputting the messages to the JSP, this tag behaves similar to the Logic Tag Library's **iterate** tag. On each iteration it stores the current message in a page scope JSP variable.

Attributes

Attribute	Description	Accepts JSP Expression	Required
bundle	See the section "Common Tag Attributes" at the end of this chapter.	Yes	No
footer	Specifies a key from the application resource bundle whose value will be printed after the messages have been iterated through.	Yes	No
header	Specifies a key from the application resource bundle whose value will be printed before the messages have been iterated through.	Yes	No
id	Specifies the name for a page scope JSP variable that will hold a reference to the current message on each iteration.	No	Yes
locale	Specifies the key for a **java.util.Locale** instance stored as a session attribute that will be used when looking up message keys specified by other attributes of this tag (e.g., **footer** and **header**).	Yes	No
message	Accepts *true* or *false* to specify whether the messages to be displayed are stored under the **org.apache.struts.Globals.MESSAGE_KEY** key instead of the **org.apa284che.struts.Globals. ERROR_KEY** key. Defaults to *false*.	*Yes*	*No*
name	Specifies the key (in any scope) under which the messages to be displayed are stored. If not specified, the default **org.apache.struts.Globals. ERROR_KEY** key will be used.	Yes	No
property	Specifies the field for which messages will be displayed. If not specified, all messages will be displayed.	Yes	No

Example Usage

The following snippet illustrates the basic usage of the **messages** tag:

```
<html:messages id="msg">
<li><bean:write name="msg"/></li>
</html:messages>
```

This example will display all the messages currently stored. If you want to limit the messages that are displayed to a specific property, you can specify that property when using the **messages** tag, as shown here:

```
<html:messages id="msg" property="category">
<li><bean:write name="msg"/></li>
</html:messages>
```

In this case, only the messages associated with the property specified by the **property** attribute will be displayed.

The multibox Tag

The **multibox** tag is used to generate an HTML **<input type="checkbox">** tag whose checked status is based on whether a specified value matches one of the values in a specified array of values. This tag is useful when your JSP is displaying several check boxes at a time. Instead of using several instances of the **checkbox** tag, you can use this tag in conjunction with the Logic Tag Library's **iterate** tag to reduce the amount of code it takes to deal with several check boxes.

Attributes

Attribute	Description	Accepts JSP Expression	Required
accesskey	See the section "Common Tag Attributes" at the end of this chapter.	Yes	No
alt	See "Common Tag Attributes."	Yes	No
altKey	See "Common Tag Attributes."	Yes	No
bundle	See "Common Tag Attributes."	Yes	No
disabled	See "Common Tag Attributes."	Yes	No
errorKey	Specifies the name of the **org.apache.struts.util.MessageResources** object that contains the messages to be rendered. Defaults to the value stored in the **org.apache.struts.Globals.ERROR_KEY** constant.	Yes	No
errorStyle	Specifies the CSS style to apply to this control if an error exists for it.	Yes	No
errorStyleClass	Specifies the CSS class to apply to this control if an error exists for it.	Yes	No
errorStyleId	Specifies the CSS ID to apply to this control if an error exists for it.	Yes	No
name	Specifies the name of an object (in any scope) whose field, specified by the **property** attribute, will be used to populate this control with data.	Yes	No
onblur	See "Common Tag Attributes."	Yes	No
onchange	See "Common Tag Attributes."	Yes	No
onclick	See "Common Tag Attributes."	Yes	No
ondblclick	See "Common Tag Attributes."	Yes	No
onfocus	See "Common Tag Attributes."	Yes	No
onkeydown	See "Common Tag Attributes."	Yes	No

Attribute	Description	Accepts JSP Expression	Required
onkeypress	See "Common Tag Attributes."	Yes	No
onkeyup	See "Common Tag Attributes."	Yes	No
onmousedown	See "Common Tag Attributes."	Yes	No
onmousemove	See "Common Tag Attributes."	Yes	No
onmouseout	See "Common Tag Attributes."	Yes	No
onmouseover	See "Common Tag Attributes."	Yes	No
onmouseup	See "Common Tag Attributes."	Yes	No
property	Specifies the value to set the corresponding HTML tag's **name** attribute to. Additionally, this attribute is used to specify the field of the object specified by the **name** attribute whose getter method will be called to return an object whose value will be used to populate this control. If no object is specified with the **name** attribute, the Form Bean object associated with the enclosing **form** tag will be used to retrieve the property specified by this attribute.	Yes	Yes
style	See "Common Tag Attributes."	Yes	No
styleClass	See "Common Tag Attributes."	Yes	No
styleId	See "Common Tag Attributes."	Yes	No
tabindex	See "Common Tag Attributes."	Yes	No
title	See "Common Tag Attributes."	Yes	No
titleKey	See "Common Tag Attributes."	Yes	No
value	Specifies a constant value that the control will be populated with.	Yes	No

Example Usage

The following snippet illustrates the basic usage of the **multibox** tag:

```
<logic:iterate id="item" property="items">
  <html:multibox property="selectedItems">
    <bean:write name="item"/>
  </html:multibox>
  <bean:write name="item"/>
</logic:iterate>
```

In this example, the **iterate** tag loops through each of the elements in the collection specified by its **property** attribute. Each iteration of the loop uses the **multibox** tag to generate an HTML **<input type="checkbox">** tag whose checked status is based on whether the loop's current element is present in the collection specified by the property attribute of the **multibox** tag.

The option Tag

The **option** tag is used to generate an HTML **<option>** tag. Note that this tag must be nested inside of the **select** tag. If an instance of this tag's value matches the value of the Form Bean field corresponding to the enclosing **select** tag, the instance will be marked as selected.

Attributes

Attribute	Description	Accepts JSP Expression	Required
bundle	See the section "Common Tag Attributes" at the end of this chapter.	Yes	No
disabled	See "Common Tag Attributes."	Yes	No
key	Specifies a key from the application resource bundle whose value will be used to set the text that will be displayed for this option. If not specified, the text displayed for this option will be taken from this tag's body content.	Yes	No
locale	Specifies the key for a **java.util.Locale** instance stored as a session attribute that will be used when looking up the message specified by the **key** attribute.	Yes	No
style	See "Common Tag Attributes."	Yes	No
styleClass	See "Common Tag Attributes."	Yes	No
styleId	See "Common Tag Attributes."	Yes	No
value	Specifies a constant value that the control will be populated with.	Yes	Yes

Example Usage

The following snippet illustrates the basic usage of the **option** tag:

```
<html:select property="gender">
  <html:option value="male">Male</html:option>
  <html:option value="female">Female</html:option>
</html:select>
```

If the value specified by an **option** tag's **value** attribute matches the value of the Form Bean field specified by the **select** tag's property attribute, the HTML **<option>** tag will be marked as selected when it is generated.

The options Tag

The **options** tag is used to generate a set of HTML **<option>** tags for each element in a collection. Note that this tag must be nested inside of the **select** tag.

There are three ways you can specify which collection to generate options from, as listed here and shown later, in the section "Example Usage":

- You can use the **collection** attribute to specify an expression that evaluates to a collection object.

PART III

- You can use the **name** attribute to specify the name of a collection object that can be in any scope.
- You can use the **name** and **property** attributes in tandem to specify the name of an object and its field whose getter method will be called to return a collection object.

Attributes

Attribute	Description	Accepts JSP Expression	Required
collection	Specifies the name of a collection object (in any scope) whose elements will be used to create a set of options.	Yes	No
filter	Accepts *true* or *false* to specify whether option labels will *not* be filtered for sensitive HTML characters (e.g., > and <). Defaults to *true.*	*Yes*	*No*
labelName	Specifies the name of an object (in any scope) whose field, specified by the **property** attribute, will have its getter method called to return a collection object whose elements will be used as labels for the created options.	Yes	No
labelProperty	Specifies the field of the object specified by the **name** attribute whose getter method will be called to return a collection object whose elements will be used as labels for the created options. If no object is specified with the **name** attribute, the Form Bean object associated with the enclosing **form** tag will be used to retrieve the property specified by this attribute.	Yes	No
name	Specifies the name of an object (in any scope) whose field, specified by the **property** attribute, will have its getter method called to return a collection object whose elements will be used to create a set of options.	Yes	No
property	Specifies the field of the object specified by the **name** attribute whose getter method will be called to return a collection object whose elements will be used to create a set of options. If no object is specified with the **name** attribute, the Form Bean object associated with the enclosing **form** tag will be used to retrieve the property specified by this attribute.	Yes	No
style	See the section "Common Tag Attributes" at the end of this chapter.	Yes	No
styleClass	See "Common Tag Attributes."	Yes	No

Example Usage

As mentioned there are three basic ways you can use the **options** tag. The first way, shown here, uses the **collection** attribute to specify the collection from which to create options:

```
<html:select property="category">
  <html:options collection="catOptions"/>
</html:select>
```

This example assumes you have defined a collection named "category" and then uses its elements to generate a set of options.

The second way to use the **options** tag is shown here:

```
<html:select property="category">
  <html:options name="catOptions"/>
</html:select>
```

This example is very similar to the first example; however, it differs in that the collection from which to generate options is specified with the **name** attribute.

The third way to use the **options** tag is shown here:

```
<html:select property="category">
  <html:options name="cat" property="options"/>
</html:select>
```

In this example, the **name** and **property** attributes are used in tandem to specify the name of an object and its field whose getter method will be called to return a collection for which to generate options.

The optionsCollection Tag

The **optionsCollection** tag is used to generate a set of HTML **<option>** tags for each element in a collection. This tag is very similar to the **options** tag, but it differs in that it requires the objects in the specified collection to have fields for the generated options' labels and values. Note that this tag must be nested inside of the **select** tag.

Attributes

Attribute	Description	Accepts JSP Expression	Required
filter	Accepts *true* or *false* to specify whether option labels will *not* be filtered for sensitive HTML characters (e.g., > and <). Defaults to *true*.	*Yes*	*No*
label	Specifies the field of the object specified with the **name** and **property** attributes whose value will be used as the label for the generated options.	Yes	No
name	Specifies the name of an object (in any scope) whose field, specified by the **property** attribute, will have its getter method called to return a collection object whose elements will be used to create a set of options.	Yes	No

Attribute	Description	Accepts JSP Expression	Required
property	Specifies the field of the object specified by the **name** attribute whose getter method will be called to return a collection object whose elements will be used to create a set of options. If no object is specified with the **name** attribute, the Form Bean object associated with the enclosing **form** tag will be used to retrieve the property specified by this attribute.	Yes	*No*
style	See the section "Common Tag Attributes" at the end of this chapter.	Yes	No
styleClass	See "Common Tag Attributes."	Yes	No
value	Specifies the field of the object specified with the **name** and **property** attributes whose value will be used as the value for the generated options.	Yes	No

Example Usage

The following snippet illustrates the basic usage of the **optionsCollection** tag:

```
<html:select property="category">
  <html:optionsCollection name="cat" property="options"/>
</html:select>
```

In this example, the **name** and **property** attributes are used in tandem to specify the name of an object and its field whose getter method will be called to return a collection for which to generate options.

The password Tag

The **password** tag is used to generate an HTML **<input type="password">** tag populated with data from a specified object. Note that this tag must be nested inside of the **form** tag.

Attributes

Attribute	Description	Accepts JSP Expression	Required
accesskey	See the section "Common Tag Attributes" at the end of this chapter.	Yes	No
alt	See "Common Tag Attributes."	Yes	No
altKey	See "Common Tag Attributes."	Yes	No
bundle	See "Common Tag Attributes."	Yes	No
disabled	See "Common Tag Attributes."	Yes	No
errorKey	Specifies the name of the **org.apache.struts.util.MessageResources** object that contains the messages to be rendered. Defaults to the value stored in the **org.apache.struts.Globals.ERROR_KEY** constant.	Yes	No

Attribute	Description	Accepts JSP Expression	Required
errorStyle	Specifies the CSS style to apply to this control if an error exists for it.	Yes	No
errorStyleClass	Specifies the CSS class to apply to this control if an error exists for it.	Yes	No
errorStyleId	Specifies the CSS ID to apply to this control if an error exists for it.	Yes	No
indexed	See "Common Tag Attributes."	Yes	No
maxlength	Same as the corresponding HTML tag's attribute with the same name. Specifies the maximum number of characters that this control will accept.	Yes	No
name	Specifies the name of an object (in any scope) whose field, specified by the **property** attribute, will be used to populate this control with data.	Yes	No
onblur	See "Common Tag Attributes."	Yes	No
onchange	See "Common Tag Attributes."	Yes	No
onclick	See "Common Tag Attributes."	Yes	No
ondblclick	See "Common Tag Attributes."	Yes	No
onfocus	See "Common Tag Attributes."	Yes	No
onkeydown	See "Common Tag Attributes."	Yes	No
onkeypress	See "Common Tag Attributes."	Yes	No
onkeyup	See "Common Tag Attributes."	Yes	No
onmousedown	See "Common Tag Attributes."	Yes	No
onmousemove	See "Common Tag Attributes."	Yes	No
onmouseout	See "Common Tag Attributes."	Yes	No
onmouseover	See "Common Tag Attributes."	Yes	No
onmouseup	See "Common Tag Attributes."	Yes	No
property	Specifies the value to set the corresponding HTML tag's **name** attribute to. Additionally, this attribute is used to specify the field of the object specified by the **name** attribute whose getter method will be called to return an object whose value will be used to populate this control. If no object is specified with the **name** attribute, the Form Bean object associated with the enclosing **form** tag will be used to retrieve the property specified by this attribute.	Yes	Yes

Attribute	Description	Accepts JSP Expression	Required
readonly	Same as the corresponding HTML tag's attribute with the same name. Accepts *true* or *false* to specify whether the control's value will be read-only, preventing it from being changed. Defaults to *false.*	*Yes*	*No*
redisplay	Accepts *true* or *false* to specify whether the value specified with the **name** and **property** attributes or specified with the **value** attribute will *not* be used to populate this control. Defaults to *true.*	*Yes*	*No*
size	Same as the corresponding HTML tag's attribute with the same name. Specifies the number of characters that will be visible in the control.	Yes	No
style	See "Common Tag Attributes."	Yes	No
styleClass	See "Common Tag Attributes."	Yes	No
styleId	See "Common Tag Attributes."	Yes	No
tabindex	See "Common Tag Attributes."	Yes	No
title	See "Common Tag Attributes."	Yes	No
titleKey	See "Common Tag Attributes."	Yes	No
value	Specifies a constant value that the control will be populated with.	Yes	No

Example Usage

The following snippet illustrates the basic usage of the **password** tag:

```
<html:form action="/logon">
UserName: <html:text property="username"/><br>
Password: <html:password property="password"/><br>
<html:submit/>
</html:form>
```

This tag will look up the Form Bean associated with the **Action** specified by the **form** tag's **action** attribute and then call the getter method for the field specified by this tag's **property** attribute. The field's value will then be used to populate the HTML control with data.

The radio Tag

The **radio** tag is used to generate an HTML **<input type="radio">** tag populated with data from a specified object. Note that this tag must be nested inside of the **form** tag.

Attributes

Attribute	Description	Accepts JSP Expression	Required
accesskey	See the section "Common Tag Attributes" at the end of this chapter.	Yes	No
alt	See "Common Tag Attributes."	Yes	No
altKey	See "Common Tag Attributes."	Yes	No
bundle	See "Common Tag Attributes."	Yes	No
disabled	See "Common Tag Attributes."	Yes	No
errorKey	Specifies the name of the **org.apache.struts.util.MessageResources** object that contains the messages to be rendered. Defaults to the value stored in the **org.apache.struts.Globals.ERROR_KEY** constant.	Yes	No
errorStyle	Specifies the CSS style to apply to this control if an error exists for it.	Yes	No
errorStyleClass	Specifies the CSS class to apply to this control if an error exists for it.	Yes	No
errorStyleId	Specifies the CSS ID to apply to this control if an error exists for it.	Yes	No
idName	If an iterator is used to generate a series of **radio** tags, this attribute can be used to specify a name for the object exposed by the iterator. In this case, the **value** attribute is used as the name of a field on the exposed object whose getter method will be called to return the value that the **radio** tag for this iteration will be populated with.	Yes	No
indexed	See "Common Tag Attributes."	Yes	No
name	Specifies the name of an object (in any scope) whose field, specified by the **property** attribute, will be used to populate this control with data.	Yes	No
onblur	See "Common Tag Attributes."	Yes	No
onchange	See "Common Tag Attributes."	Yes	No
onclick	See "Common Tag Attributes."	Yes	No
ondblclick	See "Common Tag Attributes."	Yes	No
onfocus	See "Common Tag Attributes."	Yes	No
onkeydown	See "Common Tag Attributes."	Yes	No
onkeypress	See "Common Tag Attributes."	Yes	No

Attribute	Description	Accepts JSP Expression	Required
onkeyup	See "Common Tag Attributes."	Yes	No
onmousedown	See "Common Tag Attributes."	Yes	No
onmousemove	See "Common Tag Attributes."	Yes	No
onmouseout	See "Common Tag Attributes."	Yes	No
onmouseover	See "Common Tag Attributes."	Yes	No
onmouseup	See "Common Tag Attributes."	Yes	No
property	Specifies the value to set the corresponding HTML tag's **name** attribute to. Additionally, this attribute is used to specify the field of the object specified by the **name** attribute whose getter method will be called to return an object whose value will be used to populate this control. If no object is specified with the **name** attribute, the Form Bean object associated with the enclosing **form** tag will be used to retrieve the property specified by this attribute.	Yes	Yes
style	See "Common Tag Attributes."	Yes	No
styleClass	See "Common Tag Attributes."	Yes	No
styleId	See "Common Tag Attributes."	Yes	No
tabindex	See "Common Tag Attributes."	Yes	No
title	See "Common Tag Attributes."	Yes	No
titleKey	See "Common Tag Attributes."	Yes	No
value	Specifies a constant value that the control will be populated with.	Yes	Yes

Example Usage

The following snippet illustrates the basic usage of the **radio** tag:

```
<html:form action="/register"/>
Male: <html:radio property="gender" value="male"/><br>
Female: <html:radio property="gender" value="female"/><br>
<html:submit/>
</html:form>
```

This tag will look up the Form Bean associated with the **Action** specified by the **form** tag's **action** attribute and then call the getter method for the field specified by this tag's **property** attribute. If the field's value matches the value specified with the **value** attribute, the radio button will be selected.

The reset Tag

The **reset** tag is used to generate an HTML **<input type="reset">** tag. Note that this tag must be nested inside of the **form** tag.

Attributes

Attribute	Description	Accepts JSP Expression	Required
accesskey	See the section "Common Tag Attributes" at the end of this chapter.	Yes	No
alt	See "Common Tag Attributes."	Yes	No
altKey	See "Common Tag Attributes."	Yes	No
bundle	See "Common Tag Attributes."	Yes	No
disabled	See "Common Tag Attributes."	Yes	No
onblur	See "Common Tag Attributes."	Yes	No
onchange	See "Common Tag Attributes."	Yes	No
onclick	See "Common Tag Attributes."	Yes	No
ondblclick	See "Common Tag Attributes."	Yes	No
onfocus	See "Common Tag Attributes."	Yes	No
onkeydown	See "Common Tag Attributes."	Yes	No
onkeypress	See "Common Tag Attributes."	Yes	No
onkeyup	See "Common Tag Attributes."	Yes	No
onmousedown	See "Common Tag Attributes."	Yes	No
onmousemove	See "Common Tag Attributes."	Yes	No
onmouseout	See "Common Tag Attributes."	Yes	No
onmouseover	See "Common Tag Attributes."	Yes	No
onmouseup	See "Common Tag Attributes."	Yes	No
property	Same as the corresponding HTML tag's **name** attribute. Specifies the name that will be associated with this control.	Yes	No
style	See "Common Tag Attributes."	Yes	No
styleClass	See "Common Tag Attributes."	Yes	No
styleId	See "Common Tag Attributes."	Yes	No
tabindex	See "Common Tag Attributes."	Yes	No
title	See "Common Tag Attributes."	Yes	No
titleKey	See "Common Tag Attributes."	Yes	No
value	Specifies a constant value that this control will be populated with. This value will be used for the button's label. If not specified, this tag will attempt to use its body content as the value for the button's label.	Yes	No

PART III

Example Usage

The following snippet illustrates the basic usage of the **reset** tag:

```
<html:reset value="Reset Form"/>
```

The value specified with the **value** attribute will be used for the button's label. Alternatively, you can specify the button's label value by nesting a string between opening and closing **reset** tags, as shown here:

```
<html:reset>Reset Form</html:reset>
```

The rewrite Tag

Similar to the **link** tag, the **rewrite** tag is used to generate a URL by specifying a base URL and optionally specifying an anchor and/or query string parameters to add to the URL. However, this tag does not create an HTML **<a>** tag for the generated URL. This tag is useful for creating URLs that are used as string constants in JavaScript code.

There are four ways to specify the base URL:

- You can use the **action** attribute to specify the name of an **Action** from the Struts configuration file whose URL will be used.
- You can use the **forward** attribute to specify the name of a forward from the Struts configuration file whose URL will be used.
- You can use the **href** attribute to specify an absolute URL, including protocol (e.g., http://www.yahoo.com/).
- You can use the **page** attribute to specify an application-relative URL.

In addition to specifying the base URL, you have two options for specifying query string parameters to add to the base URL:

- You can use the **paramId** attribute in conjunction with the **paramName** attribute, and optionally the **paramProperty** attribute, to specify a single parameter.
- You can use the **name** attribute, either alone or in tandem with the **property** attribute, to specify a **java.util.Map** object that will be used to add several parameters.

Attributes

Attribute	Description	Accepts JSP Expression	Required
action	Specifies the name of an action, from the Action Mappings Configuration section of the Struts configuration file, that contains the base URL for the generated URL.	Yes	No
anchor	Specifies the anchor (e.g., "#bottom") to be added to the generated URL. This value must be specified without the leading hash (#) character.	Yes	No

Attribute	Description	Accepts JSP Expression	Required
forward	Specifies the name of a forward, from the Global Forwards Configuration section of the Struts configuration file, which contains the base URL for the generated URL.	Yes	No
href	Specifies the absolute base URL, including protocol (e.g., http://www.yahoo.com), for the generated URL.	Yes	No
module	Specifies the name of a module that contains the action specified with the **action** attribute.	Yes	No
name	Specifies the name of the **java.util.Map** object whose elements are added as query string parameters to the generated URL. If the **property** attribute is also specified, one of the fields of the object defined by this attribute will have its getter method called to return the **java.util.Map** object whose elements are added as query string parameters to the generated URL.	Yes	No
page	Specifies the application-relative base URL (starts with a leading slash, /) for the generated URL.	Yes	No
paramId	Specifies the name of a single parameter to add to the generated URL.	Yes	No
paramName	Specifies the name of an object whose value will be used as the value for the parameter specified with the **paramId** attribute. If the **property** attribute is also specified, one of the fields of the object defined by this attribute will have its getter method called to return an object whose value will be used as the value for the parameter specified with the **paramId** attribute.	Yes	No
paramProperty	Specifies the field of the object specified by the **name** attribute whose getter method will be called to return an object whose value will be used as the value for the parameter specified with the **paramId** attribute.	Yes	No
paramScope	Specifies the scope (application, page, request, or session) to look in for the object specified by the **paramName** attribute. If not specified, each scope will be searched, in this order: page, request, session, and then application.	Yes	No

Attribute	Description	Accepts JSP Expression	Required
property	Specifies the field of the object specified by the **name** attribute whose getter method will be called to return the **java.util.Map** object whose elements are added as query string parameters to the generated URL.	Yes	No
scope	Specifies the scope (application, page, request, or session) to look in for the object specified by the **name** attribute. If not specified, each scope will be searched, in this order: page, request, session, and then application.	Yes	No
transaction	Accepts *true* or *false* to specify whether the current transaction token will be included in the generated URL. Defaults to *false.*	*Yes*	*No*
useLocalEnding	Accepts *true* or *false* to specify whether the character encoding of the URL parameters should be performed using the encoding type of the HTTP response object. If this attribute is set to *false,* the encoding type defaults to UTF-8. Defaults to *false.*	*Yes*	*No*

Example Usage

There are a few different ways to use the **rewrite** tag. The first way, shown here, uses the **href** attribute to specify an absolute URL for the frame:

```
<html:rewrite href="http://www.yahoo.com/"/>
```

The following example adds to the first example by specifying a single query string parameter to add to the base URL specified by the **href** attribute:

```
<html:rewrite href="http://www.yahoo.com/"
           paramId="query"
         paramName="queryObj"/>
```

This example takes the base URL specified by the **href** attribute and appends the query string parameter specified by the **paramId** and **paramName** attributes and composes a URL that the tag then redirects to.

Another way to use the **rewrite** tag is shown here:

```
<html:rewrite page="/search.jsp" name="params"/>
```

This example uses the **page** attribute to specify an application-relative base URL and uses the **name** attribute to specify a **java.util.Map** object whose entries are added to the URL as query string parameters.

The select Tag

The **select** tag is used to generate an HTML **<select>** tag. Note that this tag must be nested inside of the **form** tag.

There are two ways you can use the **select** tag, as listed here and shown later, in the section "Example Usage":

- You can omit the **multiple** attribute so that only one selection can be made. If you take this route, the **property** attribute must evaluate to a scalar value for the nested option that is selected.
- You can assign an arbitrary value to the **multiple** attribute so that multiple selections can be made. If you take this route, the **property** attribute must evaluate to an array of scalar values for each nested option that is selected.

Attributes

Attribute	Description	Accepts JSP Expression	Required
alt	See the section "Common Tag Attributes" at the end of this chapter.	Yes	No
altKey	See "Common Tag Attributes."	Yes	No
bundle	See "Common Tag Attributes."	Yes	No
disabled	See "Common Tag Attributes."	Yes	No
errorKey	Specifies the name of the **org.apache.struts.util.MessageResources** object that contains the messages to be rendered. Defaults to the value stored in the **org.apache.struts.Globals.ERROR_KEY** constant.	Yes	No
errorStyle	Specifies the CSS style to apply to this control if an error exists for it.	Yes	No
errorStyleClass	Specifies the CSS class to apply to this control if an error exists for it.	Yes	No
errorStyleId	Specifies the CSS ID to apply to this control if an error exists for it.	Yes	No
indexed	See "Common Tag Attributes."	Yes	No
multiple	Same as the corresponding HTML tag's attribute with the same name. Accepts an arbitrary value to denote that multiple selections can be made on the control.	Yes	No
name	Specifies the name of an object (in any scope) whose field, specified by the **property** attribute, will be used to determine which nested **option** tag will be set as selected.	Yes	No
onblur	See "Common Tag Attributes."	Yes	No
onchange	See "Common Tag Attributes."	Yes	No

PART III

Attribute	Description	Accepts JSP Expression	Required
onclick	See "Common Tag Attributes."	Yes	No
ondblclick	See "Common Tag Attributes."	Yes	No
onfocus	See "Common Tag Attributes."	Yes	No
onkeydown	See "Common Tag Attributes."	Yes	No
onkeypress	See "Common Tag Attributes."	Yes	No
onkeyup	See "Common Tag Attributes."	Yes	No
onmousedown	See "Common Tag Attributes."	Yes	No
onmousemove	See "Common Tag Attributes."	Yes	No
onmouseout	See "Common Tag Attributes."	Yes	No
onmouseover	See "Common Tag Attributes."	Yes	No
onmouseup	See "Common Tag Attributes."	Yes	No
property	Specifies the value to set the corresponding HTML tag's **name** attribute to. Additionally, this attribute is used to specify the field of the object specified by the **name** attribute whose getter method will be called to return an object whose value will be used to determine which nested **option** tag will be set as selected. If no object is specified with the **name** attribute, the Form Bean object associated with the enclosing **form** tag will be used to retrieve the property specified by this attribute.	Yes	Yes
size	Same as the corresponding HTML tag's attribute with the same name. Specifies the number of options that will be visible at a time.	Yes	No
style	See "Common Tag Attributes."	Yes	No
styleClass	See "Common Tag Attributes."	Yes	No
styleId	See "Common Tag Attributes."	Yes	No
tabindex	See "Common Tag Attributes."	Yes	No
title	See "Common Tag Attributes."	Yes	No
titleKey	See "Common Tag Attributes."	Yes	No
value	Specifies the value to use when determining which nested **option** tag will be set as selected.	Yes	No

Example Usage

As mentioned, there are two ways you can use the **select** tag. The first way, shown here, omits the **multiple** attribute so that only one nested option will be selected:

```
<html:select property="gender">
  <html:option value="male">Male</html:option>
  <html:option value="female">Female</html:option>
</html:select>
```

The second way to use the **select** tag is shown here:

```
<html:select property="color" multiple="true" size="3">
  <html:option value="red">Red</html:option>
  <html:option value="green">Green</html:option>
  <html:option value="blue">Blue</html:option>
  <html:option value="black">Black</html:option>
  <html:option value="white">White</html:option>
</html:select>
```

This example uses the **multiple** attribute to denote that the object specified with the **property** attribute will be an array of values for each nested option that will be selected.

The submit Tag

The **submit** tag is used to generate an HTML **<input type="submit">** tag. Note that this tag must be nested inside of the **form** tag.

Attributes

Attribute	Description	Accepts JSP Expression	Required
accesskey	See the section "Common Tag Attributes" at the end of this chapter.	Yes	No
alt	See "Common Tag Attributes."	Yes	No
altKey	See "Common Tag Attributes."	Yes	No
bundle	See "Common Tag Attributes."	Yes	No
disabled	See "Common Tag Attributes."	Yes	No
indexed	See "Common Tag Attributes."	Yes	No
onblur	See "Common Tag Attributes."	Yes	No
onchange	See "Common Tag Attributes."	Yes	No
onclick	See "Common Tag Attributes."	Yes	No
ondblclick	See "Common Tag Attributes."	Yes	No
onfocus	See "Common Tag Attributes."	Yes	No
onkeydown	See "Common Tag Attributes."	Yes	No
onkeypress	See "Common Tag Attributes."	Yes	No
onkeyup	See "Common Tag Attributes."	Yes	No
onmousedown	See "Common Tag Attributes."	Yes	No
onmousemove	See "Common Tag Attributes."	Yes	No
onmouseout	See "Common Tag Attributes."	Yes	No

Attribute	Description	Accepts JSP Expression	Required
onmouseover	See "Common Tag Attributes."	Yes	No
onmouseup	See "Common Tag Attributes."	Yes	No
property	Same as the corresponding HTML tag's **name** attribute. Specifies the name that will be associated with this control.	Yes	No
style	See "Common Tag Attributes."	Yes	No
styleClass	See "Common Tag Attributes."	Yes	No
styleId	See "Common Tag Attributes."	Yes	No
tabindex	See "Common Tag Attributes."	Yes	No
title	See "Common Tag Attributes."	Yes	No
titleKey	See "Common Tag Attributes."	Yes	No
value	Specifies a constant value that this control will be populated with. This value will be used as the button's label.	Yes	No

Example Usage

The following snippet illustrates the basic usage of the **submit** tag:

```
<html:submit value="Add Record"/>
```

The value specified with the **value** attribute will be used for the button's label. Alternatively, you can specify the button's label value by nesting a string between opening and closing **submit** tags, as shown here:

```
<html:submit>Next Page</html:submit>
```

The text Tag

The **text** tag is used to generate an HTML **<input type="text">** tag populated with data from a specified object. Note that this tag must be nested inside of the **form** tag.

Attributes

Attribute	Description	Accepts JSP Expression	Required
accesskey	See the section "Common Tag Attributes" at the end of this chapter.	Yes	No
alt	See "Common Tag Attributes."	Yes	No
altKey	See "Common Tag Attributes."	Yes	No

Attribute	Description	Accepts JSP Expression	Required
bundle	See "Common Tag Attributes."	Yes	No
disabled	See "Common Tag Attributes."	Yes	No
errorKey	Specifies the name of the **org.apache.struts.util.MessageResources** object that contains the messages to be rendered. Defaults to the value stored in the **org.apache.struts.Globals.ERROR_KEY** constant.	Yes	No
errorStyle	Specifies the CSS style to apply to this control if an error exists for it.	Yes	No
errorStyleClass	Specifies the CSS class to apply to this control if an error exists for it.	Yes	No
errorStyleId	Specifies the CSS ID to apply to this control if an error exists for it.	Yes	No
indexed	See "Common Tag Attributes."	Yes	No
maxlength	Same as the corresponding HTML tag's attribute with the same name. Specifies the maximum number of characters that this control will accept.	Yes	No
name	Specifies the name of an object (in any scope) whose field, specified by the **property** attribute, will be used to populate this control with data.	Yes	No
onblur	See "Common Tag Attributes."	Yes	No
onchange	See "Common Tag Attributes."	Yes	No
onclick	See "Common Tag Attributes."	Yes	No
ondblclick	See "Common Tag Attributes."	Yes	No
onfocus	See "Common Tag Attributes."	Yes	No
onkeydown	See "Common Tag Attributes."	Yes	No
onkeypress	See "Common Tag Attributes."	Yes	No
onkeyup	See "Common Tag Attributes."	Yes	No
onmousedown	See "Common Tag Attributes."	Yes	No
onmousemove	See "Common Tag Attributes."	Yes	No
onmouseout	See "Common Tag Attributes."	Yes	No
onmouseover	See "Common Tag Attributes."	Yes	No
onmouseup	See "Common Tag Attributes."	Yes	No

Attribute	Description	Accepts JSP Expression	Required
property	Specifies the value to set the corresponding HTML tag's **name** attribute to. Additionally, this attribute is used to specify the field of the object specified by the **name** attribute whose getter method will be called to return an object whose value will be used to populate this control. If no object is specified with the **name** attribute, the Form Bean object associated with the enclosing **form** tag will be used to retrieve the property specified by this attribute.	Yes	Yes
readonly	Same as the corresponding HTML tag's attribute with the same name. Accepts *true* or *false* to specify whether the control's value will be read-only, preventing it from being changed. Defaults to *false.*	*Yes*	*No*
size	Same as the corresponding HTML tag's attribute with the same name. Specifies the number of characters that will be visible in the control.	Yes	No
style	See "Common Tag Attributes."	Yes	No
styleClass	See "Common Tag Attributes."	Yes	No
styleId	See "Common Tag Attributes."	Yes	No
tabindex	See "Common Tag Attributes."	Yes	No
title	See "Common Tag Attributes."	Yes	No
titleKey	See "Common Tag Attributes."	Yes	No
value	Specifies a constant value that the control will be populated with.	Yes	No

Example Usage

The following snippet illustrates the basic usage of the **text** tag:

```
<html:form action="/search">
Search Query: <html:text property="query"/><br>
<html:submit/>
</html:form>
```

This tag will look up the Form Bean associated with the **Action** specified by the **form** tag's **action** attribute and then call the getter method for the field specified by this tag's **property** attribute. The field's value will then be used to populate the HTML control with data.

The textarea Tag

The **textarea** tag is used to generate an HTML **<textarea>** tag populated with data from a specified object. Note that this tag must be nested inside of the **form** tag.

Attributes

Attribute	Description	Accepts JSP Expression	Required
accesskey	See the section "Common Tag Attributes" at the end of this chapter.	Yes	No
alt	See "Common Tag Attributes."	Yes	No
altKey	See "Common Tag Attributes."	Yes	No
bundle	See "Common Tag Attributes."	Yes	No
cols	Same as the corresponding HTML tag's attribute with the same name. Specifies the number of columns to display.	Yes	No
disabled	See "Common Tag Attributes."	Yes	No
errorKey	Specifies the name of the **org.apache.struts.util.MessageResources** object that contains the messages to be rendered. Defaults to the value stored in the **org.apache.struts.Globals.ERROR_KEY** constant.	Yes	No
errorStyle	Specifies the CSS style to apply to this control if an error exists for it.	Yes	No
errorStyleClass	Specifies the CSS class to apply to this control if an error exists for it.	Yes	No
errorStyleId	Specifies the CSS ID to apply to this control if an error exists for it.	Yes	No
indexed	See "Common Tag Attributes."	Yes	No
name	Specifies the name of an object (in any scope) whose field, specified by the **property** attribute, will be used to populate this control with data.	Yes	No
onblur	See "Common Tag Attributes."	Yes	No
onchange	See "Common Tag Attributes."	Yes	No
onclick	See "Common Tag Attributes."	Yes	No
ondblclick	See "Common Tag Attributes."	Yes	No
onfocus	See "Common Tag Attributes."	Yes	No
onkeydown	See "Common Tag Attributes."	Yes	No
onkeypress	See "Common Tag Attributes."	Yes	No
onkeyup	See "Common Tag Attributes."	Yes	No
onmousedown	See "Common Tag Attributes."	Yes	No
onmousemove	See "Common Tag Attributes."	Yes	No
onmouseout	See "Common Tag Attributes."	Yes	No
onmouseover	See "Common Tag Attributes."	Yes	No

Attribute	Description	Accepts JSP Expression	Required
onmouseup	See "Common Tag Attributes."	Yes	No
property	Specifies the value to set the corresponding HTML tag's **name** attribute to. Additionally, this attribute is used to specify the field of the object specified by the **name** attribute whose getter method will be called to return an object whose value will be used to populate this control. If no object is specified with the **name** attribute, the Form Bean object associated with the enclosing **form** tag will be used to retrieve the property specified by this attribute.	Yes	Yes
readonly	Same as the corresponding HTML tag's attribute with the same name. Accepts *true* or *false* to specify whether the control's value will be read-only, preventing it from being changed. Defaults to *false.*	*Yes*	*No*
rows	Same as the corresponding HTML tag's attribute with the same name. Specifies the number of rows to display.	Yes	No
style	See "Common Tag Attributes."	Yes	No
styleClass	See "Common Tag Attributes."	Yes	No
styleId	See "Common Tag Attributes."	Yes	No
tabindex	See "Common Tag Attributes."	Yes	No
title	See "Common Tag Attributes."	Yes	No
titleKey	See "Common Tag Attributes."	Yes	No
value	Specifies a constant value that the control will be populated with.	Yes	No

Example Usage

The following snippet illustrates the basic usage of the **textarea** tag:

```
<html:form action="/feedback">
Comments: <html:textarea property="comments"/><br>
<html:submit/>
</html:form>
```

This tag will look up the Form Bean associated with the **Action** specified by the **form** tag's **action** attribute and then call the getter method for the field specified by this tag's **property** attribute. The field's value will then be used to populate the HTML control with data.

The xhtml Tag

The **xhtml** tag causes the rest of the tags in the HTML Tag Library to generate their output as XHTML instead of HTML. For more information on XHTML, see **http://www.w3.org/TR/xhtml1/**.

Using this tag is equivalent to using this library's **html** tag with the **xhtml** attribute set to "true", as shown here:

```
<html:html xhtml="true"/>
```

Attributes

This tag does not have any attributes.

Example Usage

Using the **xhtml** tag is very simple because it has no attributes that can or need to be set. You simply just use the tag as shown here:

```
<html:xhtml/>
```

You must place this tag before using any other tags from this library; otherwise, they will not know to generate XHTML. Note thsat using this tag will not guarantee that your JSP is 100 percent XHTML compliant; you must ensure that any direct usages of HTML tags also conform.

Common Tag Attributes

As mentioned earlier, many of the tags in this library have several attributes in common. They are described in the following table.

Attribute	Description	Accepts JSP Expression	Required
accesskey	Same as the corresponding HTML tag's attribute with the same name. Specifies the keyboard key that causes this control to immediately receive focus when the key is pressed.	Yes	No
alt	Same as the corresponding HTML tag's attribute with the same name. Specifies the alternate text for this control.	Yes	No
altKey	Specifies a key from the application resource bundle whose value will be used to set the corresponding HTML tag's **alt** attribute.	Yes	No
bundle	Specifies the logical name of a resource bundle that will be used when looking up message keys specified by other attributes of this tag (e.g., **altKey**). The referenced resource bundle must be defined in the application's Struts configuration file.	Yes	No
disabled	Same as the corresponding HTML tag's attribute with the same name. Accepts *true* or *false* to specify whether the control will be disabled, preventing its use. Defaults to *false*.	*Yes*	*No*

Attribute	Description	Accepts JSP Expression	Required
indexed	Accepts *true* or *false* to specify whether the value assigned to the corresponding HTML tag's **name** attribute will have an index (e.g., "name[x].property"). This attribute is applicable only when this tag is nested inside the Logic Tag Library's **iterate** tag. Defaults to *false*.	*Yes*	*No*
onblur	Same as the corresponding HTML tag's attribute with the same name. Specifies the JavaScript code to execute when this control loses input focus.	Yes	No
onchange	Same as the corresponding HTML tag's attribute with the same name. Specifies the JavaScript code to execute when this control loses input focus and its value has changed.	Yes	No
onclick	Same as the corresponding HTML tag's attribute with the same name. Specifies the JavaScript code to execute when this control receives a mouse click.	Yes	No
ondblclick	Same as the corresponding HTML tag's attribute with the same name. Specifies the JavaScript code to execute when this control receives a mouse double-click.	Yes	No
onfocus	Same as the corresponding HTML tag's attribute with the same name. Specifies the JavaScript code to execute when this control receives input focus.	Yes	No
onkeydown	Same as the corresponding HTML tag's attribute with the same name. Specifies the JavaScript code to execute when this control has focus and a key is pressed.	Yes	No
onkeypress	Same as the corresponding HTML tag's attribute with the same name. Specifies the JavaScript code to execute when this control has focus and a key is pressed and released.	Yes	No
onkeyup	Same as the corresponding HTML tag's attribute with the same name. Specifies the JavaScript code to execute when this control has focus and a key is released.	Yes	No
onmousedown	Same as the corresponding HTML tag's attribute with the same name. Specifies the JavaScript code to execute when this control is under the mouse pointer and a mouse button is pressed.	Yes	No

Attribute	Description	Accepts JSP Expression	Required
onmousemove	Same as the corresponding HTML tag's attribute with the same name. Specifies the JavaScript code to execute when this control is under the mouse pointer and the mouse is moved.	Yes	No
onmouseout	Same as the corresponding HTML tag's attribute with the same name.Specifies the JavaScript code to execute when this control is under the mouse pointer and is then moved away from the control.	Yes	No
onmouseover	Same as the corresponding HTML tag's attribute with the same name. Specifies the JavaScript code to execute when this control is not under the mouse pointer and is then moved to the control.	Yes	No
onmouseup	Same as the corresponding HTML tag's attribute with the same name. Specifies the JavaScript code to execute when this control is under the mouse pointer and a mouse button is released.	Yes	No
style	Same as the corresponding HTML tag's attribute with the same name. Specifies the CSS style to apply to this control.	Yes	No
styleClass	Same as the corresponding HTML tag's **class** attribute. Specifies the CSS class to apply to this control.	Yes	No
styleId	Same as the corresponding HTML tag's **id** attribute. Specifies the CSS ID to apply to this control.	Yes	No
tabindex	Same as the corresponding HTML tag's attribute with the same name. Specifies the tab order for this control.	Yes	No
title	Same as the corresponding HTML tag's attribute with the same name. Specifies the title for this control.	Yes	No
titleKey	Specifies a key from the application resource bundle whose value will be used to set the corresponding HTML tag's **title** attribute.	Yes	No

14

CHAPTER

The Bean Tag Library

The Bean Tag Library is a collection of utility tags that provides convenient access for interacting with Web application objects within a JSP. Most of the tags are used to capture references to specific objects and store them in JSP scripting variables so that other tags can access the objects. The remaining tags are used to render objects to the JSP output.

NOTE *Some of the tags in this library have JSTL equivalents that should be used in lieu of these tags. See Chapter 17 for more information on using JSTL with Struts and the list of Struts tags that can be replaced with JSTL equivalents.*

Understanding Variables and Scope in JSPs

Before discussing each of the tags in this library, it's necessary to review how variables and scope work in JSPs. First, remember that JSPs get converted into servlets and then compiled before they are executed. All of the HTML and code inside the JSP gets placed into the generated servlet's **service( )** method. Because of this, any variables that get defined inside the JSP with a scriptlet, as shown here, are local to the **service( )** method:

```
<%
String test = "test value";
%>
```

Similarly, any variables that are defined with a JSP declaration are local to the **service( )** method:

```
<%! String test = "test value"; %>
```

Also, all of the implicit JSP objects, such as **application**, **request**, and **session**, are local to the resulting servlet's **service( )** method.

JSPs and servlets also have the notion of "scope" for variables, because some variables need to persist longer than the lifespan of a page request and some variables need to be accessible outside of a servlet's **service( )** method. There are four scopes that JSP variables can be placed in: application, page, request, and session. The following table explains each scope.

Scope	Description
application	Variables placed in this scope persist for the life of an application.
page	Variables placed in this scope persist until the current JSP's **service( )** method completes. Included JSPs cannot see page scope variables from the page including them. Also, this scope is exclusive to JSPs.
request	Variables placed in this scope persist until processing for the current request is completed. This scope differs from page scope because multiple servlets may be executed during the lifespan of a request. Page-scoped variables only persist for the execution of one servlet.
session	Variables placed in this scope persist until the current user's session is invalidated or expires. This scope is only valid if the JSP or servlet in question is participating in a session.

Note that variables must be explicitly placed into a scope, as shown here:

```
<%
request.setAttribute("reqScopeVar", "test");
%>
```

This snippet uses JSP's implicit **request** object to place a variable into request scope. Similarly, the following snippet uses JSP's implicit **session** object to place a variable into session scope:

```
<%
session.setAttribute("sesScopeVar", "test");
%>
```

Of course, variables can also be put into each of the scopes by JSP tag library tags, as do many of the tags in the Bean Tag Library.

Using the Bean Tag Library

To use the Bean Tag Library in your Struts application, your application's JSPs must declare their use of the library with a JSP **taglib** directive:

```
<%@ taglib uri="http://struts.apache.org/tags-bean" prefix="bean" %>
```

Notice that the **prefix** attribute is set to "bean." This attribute can be set to any value; however, "bean" is the accepted default for the Bean Library. The **prefix** attribute declares the prefix that each tag must have when it is used in the JSP, as shown here:

```
<bean:write name="result" property="ssNum"/>
```

Because "bean" was defined as the prefix, the **write** tag was used as shown. However, if you chose to use a prefix of "strutsbn", the tag would be used the following way:

```
<strutsbn:write name="result" property="ssNum"/>
```

NOTE *Modern application servers use the* **uri** *attribute of the* **taglib** *directive to automatically resolve the location of the tag library descriptor file. Older application servers that support only JSP version 1.1 and/or version 1.0 require that tag libraries be registered in the* **web.xml** *file so that they can be resolved, as shown here:*

```
<taglib>
  <taglib-uri>http://struts.apache.org/tags-bean</taglib-uri>
  <taglib-location>/WEB-INF/tlds/struts-bean.tld</taglib-location>
</taglib>
```

The Bean Tag Library Tags

The following table lists each of the tags in the Bean Tag Library and a short description of each tag's purpose.

Tag	Description
cookie	Stores a reference to an HTTP cookie (**javax.servlet.http.Cookie**) from the incoming request in a JSP scripting variable with page scope.
define	Stores a reference to a new or existing object in a JSP scripting variable.
header	Stores an HTTP header from the incoming request as a **String** object in a JSP scripting variable with page scope.
include	Performs a request to a page and stores the contents as a **String** object in a JSP scripting variable with page scope.
message	Retrieves an internationalized message from the application resource bundle and renders it to a JSP's output stream.
page	Stores one of a JSP's implicit objects in a JSP scripting variable with page scope.
parameter	Stores a parameter from the incoming request as a **String** object in a JSP scripting variable with page scope.
resource	Loads the contents of a Web application resource and stores them as a **String** object in a JSP scripting variable with page scope.
size	Stores the size (number of elements) of an array, **java.util.Collection**-based object, or **java.util.Map**-based object as a variable with page scope.
struts	Stores a reference to a Struts configuration object in a JSP scripting variable with page scope.
write	Renders the value of an object to a JSP's output stream.

Following is a dedicated section for each tag, including a complete description of the tag, a table listing each of the tag's attributes, and a usage example for the tag. In the tables that describe each tag's attributes, pay special attention to the Accepts JSP Expression and

Required columns. The Required column simply denotes whether the given attribute is required when using the tag. In addition to the required column denoting whether an attribute is required, the rows for required attributes are highlighted in gray so that you can determine at a glance which attributes are required.

If an attribute is required and you do not specify it when using the tag, the tag will throw a **javax.servlet.jsp.JspException** at run time. Note that you can declare an error page in your JSP with a **page** directive to capture any **JspExceptions** that might be thrown, as shown here:

```
<%@ page errorPage="error.jsp" %>
```

If an exception occurs, the page specified by the **errorPage** attribute will be internally redirected to display an error page.

The Accepts JSP Expression column denotes whether the given attribute's value can be specified with a JSP expression. If a JSP expression is used to specify an attribute value, the expression must comprise the complete value, quote (") to quote ("), as shown here. Correct:

```
<bean:cookie id="category" name="<%=catName%>"/>
```

Incorrect:

```
<bean:cookie id="category" name="<%=catName%>-cat"/>
```

Notice in the incorrect example that "-cat" is used as part of the value for the **name** attribute following the expression. This is invalid because there are extra characters between the end of the expression and the ending quote.

A corrected version of the incorrect example follows:

```
<bean:cookie id="category" name="<%=catName + "-cat"%>"/>
```

The concatenation of "-cat" is now part of the expression, and the expression comprises the complete value for the attribute.

The cookie Tag

The **cookie** tag is used to store a reference to an HTTP cookie (**javax.servlet.http.Cookie**) from the incoming request in a JSP scripting variable with page scope. Additionally, the **cookie** tag can be used to store multiple cookies of the same name if the **multiple** attribute is specified. For example, if the incoming request has two cookies that are both named "category", a **Cookie[ ]** array would be used to capture each cookie value and then the array would be stored in the specified JSP variable.

If the incoming request does not include a cookie with the specified **name** attribute and the **value** attribute is not specified, a **JspException** will be thrown by this tag at run time.

Attributes

Attribute	Description	Accepts JSP Expression	Required
id	Specifies the name of the JSP variable that will hold the specified HTTP cookie(s).	No	Yes
multiple	Accepts an arbitrary value to denote that multiple cookies should be stored. If specified, cookies will be stored in a **Cookie[ ]** array. If not specified and multiple cookies have the same name, the first cookie with the name specified will be stored.	Yes	No
name	Specifies the name of the HTTP cookie(s) to store in the JSP variable.	Yes	Yes
value	If the cookie specified with the **name** attribute is not found and this attribute is specified, a new **Cookie** object will be created and assigned the value of this attribute.	Yes	No

Example Usage

The following snippet shows a basic usage of the **cookie** tag:

```
<bean:cookie id="category" name="cat" value="default"/>
```

This example attempts to find a cookie named "cat" in the incoming request and store a reference to it in a variable named "category". If the cookie is not in the request, a new cookie will be created and assigned the value of "default". This new cookie will then have a reference stored to it.

After you have used the **cookie** tag to store a cookie, you can access it with the following snippet:

```
Category Cookie: <%=category.getValue()%>
```

This snippet simply uses a JSP expression to render the value of the **Cookie** object stored in the **category** variable. Additionally, because the **cookie** tag places the **category** variable in page scope, it can be accessed by other tags, as shown here:

```
Category Cookie: <bean:write name="category" property="value"/>
```

The following snippet shows an example of using the **cookie** tag for multiple cookies with the same name:

```
<bean:cookie id="category" name="cat" multiple="true"/>
```

The **multiple** attribute accepts arbitrary values; thus, you could use "true" as shown in the example, or any other value. As long as a value is present, a **Cookie[ ]** array will be used to store the cookies. To access the first cookie stored when using the **multiple** attribute, use the following snippet:

```
Category Cookie: <%=category[0].getValue()%>
```

The define Tag

The **define** tag is used to store a reference to an existing object in a JSP scripting variable. This tag can also be used to create a new object (of type **String**), whose reference will be stored in a JSP scripting variable. Additionally, the **define** tag allows you to specify what scope the object reference should be placed in.

There are four ways you can use the **define** tag, as listed here and shown later, in the section "Example Usage":

- You can use the **name** attribute to specify the name of the object to which a reference will be stored. This object can be in any scope or limited to a specific scope with the **scope** attribute.
- You can use the **name** and **property** attributes in tandem to specify the name of an object and its field whose getter method will be called to return an object to which a reference will be stored. Again, the object specified by the **name** attribute can be in any scope or limited to a specific scope with the **scope** attribute.
- You can use the **value** attribute to specify a value that will be used to create a new **String** object whose reference will be stored.
- You can place text between opening and closing **define** tags that will be used to create a new **String** object whose reference will be stored.

If none of the aforementioned ways is used to specify the object whose reference should be stored, a **JspException** will be thrown by the tag at run time.

You may have noticed that this tag is similar to JSP's "built-in" **<jsp:useBean>** tag; however, it differs markedly, as described in this list:

- The **define** tag unconditionally creates (or replaces) a scripting variable with the specified **id** attribute.
- The **define** tag can create a scripting variable from one of an object's fields, as specified with the **property** attribute.
- The **define** tag can create a scripting variable from a literal string with use of the **value** attribute.
- The **define** tag does not support nested **<jsp:setProperty>** tags.

Attributes

Attribute	Description	Accepts JSP Expression	Required
id	Specifies the name of the JSP variable that will hold the specified object reference.	No	Yes
name	Specifies the name of the object to which a reference will be stored. If the **property** attribute is also specified, one of the fields of the object defined by this attribute will have its getter method called to return the object to which a reference will be stored.	Yes	No
property	Specifies the field of the object specified by the **name** attribute, whose getter method will be called to return the object to which a reference will be stored.	Yes	No
scope	Specifies the scope (application, page, request, or session) to look in for the object specified by the **name** attribute. If not specified, each scope will be searched, in this order: page, request, session, and then application.	Yes	No
toScope	Specifies the scope (application, page, request, or session) that the specified object reference should be stored in.	Yes	No
type	Specifies the fully qualified class type (e.g., **java.lang.Integer**) of the object being stored as a scripting variable. If not specified, defaults to **java.lang.String** if you specify a **value** attribute; otherwise, defaults to **java.lang.Object**.	Yes	No
value	Specifies a value that will be used to create a new **String** object whose reference will be stored.	Yes	No

Example Usage

As mentioned, there are four ways you can use the **define** tag. The first way, shown here, uses the **name** attribute to specify the name of the object to which a reference will be stored:

```
<bean:define id="name" name="nameObj"/>
```

Of course, this example assumes you have an object in some scope with the name "nameObj". Remember that you can explicitly specify the scope of the object with the **scope** attribute.

The second way to use the **define** tag is shown here:

```
<bean:define id="name" name="nameObj" property="nameField"/>
```

In this example, the **name** and **property** attributes are used in tandem to specify the name of an object and its field whose getter method will be called to return an object to which a reference will be stored. Again, you can explicitly specify the scope of the object with the **scope** attribute.

The third way to use the **define** tag is shown here:

```
<bean:define id="name" value="James"/>
```

In this example, the **value** attribute is used to specify the value for a new **String** object whose reference will be stored.

The following is the fourth and final way to use the **define** tag:

```
<bean:define id="name">James</bean:define>
```

This example uses the nested string between the opening and closing **define** tags to specify a value for a new **String** object whose reference will be stored.

After you have used the **define** tag to store a reference to an object, you can access it with the following snippet:

```
Name: <%=name%>
```

This snippet simply uses a JSP expression to render the value of the object stored in the **name** variable. Additionally, because the **define** tag places the **name** variable into a scope, it can be accessed by other tags, as shown here:

```
Name: <bean:write name="name"/>
```

The header Tag

The **header** tag is used to store a reference to an HTTP header from the incoming request as a **String** object in a JSP scripting variable with page scope. Additionally, the **header** tag can be used to store multiple headers of the same name if the **multiple** attribute is specified. For example, if the incoming request has two headers that are both named "Accept-Language", a **String[ ]** array would be used to capture each header value and then the array would be stored in the specified JSP variable.

For more information on the HTTP protocol and its headers, visit the World Wide Web Consortium (W3C) page located at **http://www.w3.org/Protocols/HTTP/**.

If the incoming request does not include a header with the specified **name** attribute and the **value** attribute is not specified, a **JspException** will be thrown by this tag at run time.

Attributes

Attribute	Description	Accepts JSP Expression	Required
id	Specifies the name of the JSP variable that will hold the specified HTTP header(s).	No	Yes
multiple	Accepts an arbitrary value to denote that multiple headers should be stored. If specified, headers will be stored in a **String[ ]** array. If not specified and multiple headers have the same name, the first header with the name specified will be stored.	Yes	No
name	Specifies the name of the HTTP header(s) to store in the JSP variable.	Yes	Yes
value	Specifies the default value to assign to the **String** object being placed in the JSP variable if the specified header is not present in the incoming request.	Yes	No

Example Usage

The following snippet shows a basic usage of the **header** tag:

```
<bean:header id="browser" name="User-Agent" value="unknown"/>
```

This example attempts to find an HTTP header named "User-Agent" in the incoming request and store a reference to it in a variable named "browser". If the header is not in the request, a new **String** object will be created and have the value of the **value** attribute assigned to it. A reference to the **String** will then be stored.

After you have used the **header** tag to store a header, you can access it with the following snippet:

```
This page was requested using: <%=browser%>
```

This snippet simply uses a JSP expression to render the value of the **browser** variable. Additionally, because the **header** tag places the **browser** variable in page scope, it can be accessed by other tags, as shown here:

```
This page was requested using: <bean:write name="browser"/>
```

The following snippet shows an example of using the **header** tag for multiple headers with the same name:

```
<bean:header id="languages" name="Accept-Language" multiple="true"/>
```

Remember that the **multiple** attribute accepts an arbitrary value; thus, you could use "true" as shown in the example, or any other value. As long as a value is present, a **String[ ]** array will be used to store the headers. To access the first header stored when using the **multiple** attribute, use the following snippet:

```
First Language: <%=languages[0]%>
```

The include Tag

The **include** tag is used to perform a request to a page and store the contents as a **String** object in a JSP scripting variable with page scope. This tag is similar to JSP's built-in **<jsp:include>** tag; however, it differs because it stores the contents of the included page in a scripting variable instead of writing the contents to the JSP output.

There are three ways you can use the **include** tag, as listed here and shown later, in the section "Example Usage":

- You can use the **forward** attribute to specify the name of a forward, from the Global Forwards Configuration section of the Struts configuration file, which contains the URL of the page whose contents should be stored.
- You can use the **href** attribute to specify the absolute URL of the page whose contents should be stored.
- You can use the **page** attribute to specify an application-relative URL whose contents should be stored.

Attributes

Attribute	Description	Accepts JSP Expression	Required
anchor	Specifies the anchor (e.g., "#bottom") to be added to the URL for this include. This value should be specified without the leading hash (#) character.	Yes	No
forward	Specifies the name of a forward, from the Global Forwards Configuration section of the Struts configuration file, which contains the URL of the page whose contents should be stored.	Yes	No
href	Specifies the absolute URL, including the protocol, of the page whose contents should be stored (e.g., http://www.yahoo.com).	Yes	No
id	Specifies the name of the JSP variable that will hold the contents of the specified page.	No	Yes
page	Specifies the application-relative URL (starts with a leading slash, /) of the page whose contents should be stored.	Yes	No
transaction	Accepts *true* or *false* to specify whether the current transaction token will be included in the URL for this include. Defaults to *false*.	*Yes*	*No*

Example Usage

As mentioned, there are three ways you can use the **include** tag. The first way, shown here, uses the **forward** attribute to specify the name of a forward, from the Global Forwards Configuration section of the Struts configuration file, whose contents will be stored:

```
<bean:include id="searchPageContents" forward="search"/>
```

The following is the second way to use the **include** tag:

```
<bean:include id="yahooContents" href="http://www.yahoo.com/"/>
```

This example uses the **href** attribute to specify the absolute URL of a page whose contents will be stored.

The third way to use the **include** tag is shown here:

```
<bean:include id="searchPageContents" page="/search.jsp"/>
```

In this example, the **page** attribute is used to specify an application-relative URL whose contents will be stored.

The message Tag

The **message** tag is used to retrieve an internationalized message from the application resource bundle (e.g., **MessageResources.properties)** and render it to a JSP's output stream. Remember that resource bundle files in Struts applications are based on Java's Resource Bundle functionality for externalizing and internationalizing application strings, messages, and labels. Following is a sample **MessageResources.properties** file:

```
# Label Resources
label.search.name=Name
label.search.ssNum=Social Security Number

# Error Resources
error.search.criteria.missing=Search Criteria Missing
error.search.ssNum.invalid=Invalid Social Security Number
errors.header=<font color="red"><cTypeface:Bold>Validation Error(s)</b></font><ul>
errors.footer=</ul><hr width="100%" size="1" noshade="true">
errors.prefix=<li>
errors.suffix=</li>
```

As you can see, the file is made up of key/value pairs. The **message** tag simply looks up a message with a given key and returns its matching value.

NOTE *The resource bundle file must be configured in your application's Struts configuration file before it can be accessed via the* **message** *tag. See Chapter 18 for more information on the Struts configuration file.*

The **message** tag also allows you to insert content into messages at run time before they are rendered using *parametric replacement,* which is the substitution of an argument for a placeholder parameter at run time. Following is an example message that uses parametric replacement:

```
missing.field=The {0} field is missing.
```

Notice the {0} reference in the message. At run time, the {0} parameter will be replaced with another value. The **message** tag allows you to specify what the replacement values are by use of the **arg0** – **arg4** attributes. Thus, you can have up to five parametric replacements in a message with {0} – {4}.

There are three ways you can use the **message** tag, as listed here and shown later in the section "Example Usage":

- You can specify a message's key with the **key** attribute.
- You can use the **name** attribute to specify the name of the object whose value will be used as the key for the message. This object can be in any scope or limited to a specific scope with the **scope** attribute.
- You can use the **name** and **property** attributes in tandem to specify the name of an object and its field whose getter method will be called to return an object whose value will be used as the key for the message. Again, the object specified by the **name** attribute can be in any scope or limited to a specific scope with the **scope** attribute.

If the specified message does not exist, a **JspException** will be thrown by this tag at run time.

Attributes

Attribute	Description	Accepts JSP Expression	Required
arg0	First parametric replacement value as specified by {0} in the message to be rendered.	Yes	No
arg1	Second parametric replacement value as specified by {1} in the message to be rendered.	Yes	No
arg2	Third parametric replacement value as specified by {2} in the message to be rendered.	Yes	No
arg3	Fourth parametric replacement value as specified by {3} in the message to be rendered.	Yes	No
arg4	Fifth parametric replacement value as specified by {4} in the message to be rendered.	Yes	No
bundle	Specifies the name of the application-scoped **org.apache.struts.util.MessageResources** object that contains the messages to be rendered. Defaults to the value stored in the **org.apache.struts.Globals.MESSAGES_KEY** constant.	Yes	No
key	Specifies the name of the application resource bundle key whose corresponding value will be rendered.	Yes	No
locale	Specifies the name of the session-scoped **java.util.Locale** object to use for selecting which message to render. Defaults to the value stored in the **org.apache.struts.Globals.LOCALE_KEY** constant.	Yes	No

Attribute	Description	Accepts JSP Expression	Required
name	Specifies the name of the object whose value will be used as the key for the message. If the **property** attribute is also specified, one of the fields of the object defined by this attribute will have its getter method called to return the object whose value will be used as the key for the message.	Yes	No
property	Specifies the field, of the object specified by the **name** attribute, whose getter method will be called to return the object whose value will be used as the key for the message.	Yes	No
scope	Specifies the scope (application, page, request, or session) to look in for the object specified by the **name** attribute. If not specified, each scope will be searched, in this order: page, request, session, and then application.	Yes	No

Example Usage

As mentioned, there are three ways you can use the **message** tag. The first way, shown here, uses the **key** attribute to specify the key for the message that will be rendered:

```
<bean:message key="label.search.name"/>
```

The following is the second way to use the **message** tag:

```
<bean:message name="keyObj"/>
```

This example uses the **name** attribute to specify the name of an object whose value will be used as the key for the message. Remember that you can explicitly specify the scope of the object with the **scope** attribute.

The third way to use the **message** tag is shown here:

```
<bean:message name="keyObj" property="keyField"/>
```

In this example, the **name** and **property** attributes are used in tandem to specify the name of an object and its field whose getter method will be called to return an object whose value will be used as the key for the message. Again, you can explicitly specify the scope of the object with the **scope** attribute.

The page Tag

The **page** tag is used to store one of a JSP's implicit objects in a JSP scripting variable with page scope. By default, a JSP's implicit objects cannot be "seen" by JSP tag library tags because they are not stored in a scope. Remember that JSPs get converted into a servlet and then compiled into a class file before they are run. JSP implicit objects are simply local variables in a servlet's **service( )** method. For this reason, JSP tag library tags cannot "see" the objects. However, JSP tag library tags can access objects that have been stored in a scope, thus the reason for the **page** tag.

The **page** tag works with the following implicit JSP objects:

- application
- config
- request
- response
- session

One of the aforementioned objects must be specified with the **property** attribute or this tag will throw a **JspException** at run time.

Attributes

Attribute	Description	Accepts JSP Expression	Required
id	Specifies the name of the JSP variable that will hold the specified JSP implicit object.	No	Yes
property	Specifies the name of the JSP implicit object to store in the JSP variable. Must be application, config, request, response, or session.	Yes	Yes

Example Usage

The following snippet shows a basic usage of the **page** tag:

```
<bean:page id="cfg" property="config"/>
```

This example simply stores a reference to the implicit **config** object in a page scope variable named "cfg".

After you have used the **page** tag to store a JSP implicit object, you can use it with a JSP tag library tag as shown here:

```
<bean:write name="cfg" property="servletName"/>
```

Remember that the **write** tag wouldn't be able to see the implicit **config** object without the use of the **page** tag.

The parameter Tag

The **parameter** tag is used to store a parameter from the incoming request as a **String** object in a JSP scripting variable with page scope. Additionally, the **parameter** tag can be used to store multiple parameters of the same name if the **multiple** attribute is specified. For example, if the incoming request has two parameters that are both named "color", a **String[ ]** array would be used to capture each parameter value and then the array would be stored in the specified JSP variable.

If the incoming request does not include a parameter with the specified **name** attribute and the **value** attribute is not specified, a **JspException** will be thrown by this tag at run time.

Attributes

Attribute	Description	Accepts JSP Expression	Required
id	Specifies the name of the JSP variable that will hold the specified parameter(s).	No	Yes
multiple	Accepts an arbitrary value to denote that multiple parameters should be stored. If specified, parameters will be stored in a **String[ ]** array. If not specified and multiple parameters have the same name, the first parameter with the name specified will be stored.	Yes	No
name	Specifies the name of the parameter(s) to store in the JSP variable.	Yes	Yes
value	Specifies the default value to assign to the **String** object being placed in the JSP variable if the specified parameter is not present in the incoming request.	Yes	No

Example Usage

The following snippet shows a basic usage of the **parameter** tag:

```
<bean:parameter id="color" name="clr" value="none"/>
```

This example attempts to find a parameter named "clr" in the incoming request and store a reference to it in a variable named "color". If the parameter is not in the request, a new **String** object will be created and have the value of the **value** attribute assigned to it. A reference to the **String** will then be stored.

After you have used the **parameter** tag to store a parameter, you can access it with the following snippet:

```
Color Request Parameter: <%=color%>
```

This snippet simply uses a JSP expression to render the value of the **color** variable. Additionally, because the **parameter** tag places the **color** variable in page scope, it can be accessed by JSP tag library tags, as shown here:

```
Color Request Parameter: <bean:write name="color"/>
```

The following snippet shows an example of using the **parameter** tag for multiple parameters with the same name:

```
<bean:parameter id="color" name="clr" multiple="true" value="none"/>
```

Remember that the **multiple** attribute accepts an arbitrary value; thus, you could use "true" as shown in the example, or any other value. As long as a value is present, a **String[ ]** array

PART III

will be used to store the parameters. To access the first parameter stored when using the **multiple** attribute, use the following snippet:

```
First Color: <%=color[0]%>
```

The resource Tag

The **resource** tag is used to load the contents of a Web application resource and store them as a **String** object in a JSP scripting variable with page scope. Additionally, you have the option of specifying whether you simply want a **java.io.InputStream** reference for the resource instead of storing its contents in a **String**.

Web application resources are those files that are packaged as part of a Web application. For example, if your Web application is housed in a directory called **c:\java\MiniHR** and has the following files,

- c:\java\MiniHR\index.jsp
- c:\java\MiniHR\WEB-INF\struts-config.xml
- c:\java\MiniHR\WEB-INF\web.xml

you can access the **index.jsp** file as "/index.jsp." Similarly, you can access the **struts-config.xml** file as "/WEB-INF/struts-config.xml." Note that Web application resource paths are relative to the application and must begin with a leading slash (/).

A **JspException** will be thrown by the **resource** tag at run time if there is a problem loading the resource.

Attributes

Attribute	Description	Accepts JSP Expression	Required
id	Specifies the name of the JSP variable that will hold the contents of the specified resource.	No	Yes
input	Accepts an arbitrary value to denote that a **java.io.InputStream** reference for the resource should be stored in the JSP variable instead of storing the contents of the resource in a **String**.	Yes	No
name	Specifies the path of the Web application resource that will be loaded. The path must begin with a leading slash (/).	Yes	Yes

Example Usage

The following snippet shows how you could use the **resource** tag to load the contents of a **struts-config.xml** file:

```
<bean:resource id="strutsConfig" name="/WEB-INF/struts-config.xml"/>
```

After you have used the **resource** tag to load the contents of the Struts configuration file, you can access them with the following snippet:

```
Struts Config file contents: <%=strutsConfig%>
```

This snippet simply uses a JSP expression to render the value of the **String** object stored in the **strutsConfig** variable. Additionally, because the **resource** tag places the **strutsConfig** variable in page scope, it can be accessed by JSP tag library tags, as shown here:

```
Struts Config file: <bean:write name="strutsConfig"/>
```

The following snippet shows how to use the **resource** tag to obtain a **java.io.InputStream** reference for a Web application resource:

```
<bean:resource id="strutsConfig"
               input="true"
               name="/WEB-INF/struts-config.xml"/>
```

Remember that the **input** attribute accepts arbitrary values; thus, you could use "true" as shown in the example, or any other value. As long as a value is present, a **java.io.InputStream** reference will be stored in the JSP variable instead of a **String** containing the contents of the resource file.

As you can imagine, using the **resource** tag is significantly cleaner and less involved than using a scriptlet to load the contents of a Web application resource.

The size Tag

The **size** tag is used to store the size (number of elements) of an array, **java.util.Collection**-based object, or **java.util.Map**-based object as a **java.lang.Integer** in a JSP scripting variable with page scope. This tag is especially useful when used in conjunction with tags in the Logic Tag Library. For example, you could use this tag to determine the size of a collection and then use the Logic Library's **iterate** tag to iterate over each item in the collection.

There are three ways you can specify which collection's size to store, as listed here and shown later in the section "Example Usage":

- You can use the **collection** attribute to specify an expression that evaluates to a collection object.
- You can use the **name** attribute to specify the name of a collection object that can be in any scope or limited to a specific scope with the **scope** attribute.
- You can use the **name** and **property** attributes in tandem to specify the name of an object and its field whose getter method will be called to return a collection object. Again, the object specified by the **name** attribute can be in any scope or limited to a specific scope with the **scope** attribute.

Note that if none of the aforementioned ways is used to specify the collection whose size should be taken, a **JspException** will be thrown by this tag at run time.

Attributes

Attribute	Description	Accepts JSP Expression	Required
collection	Specifies an expression that evaluates to an array, **java.util.Collection**-based object, or **java.util.Map**-based object.	Yes	No
id	Specifies the name of the JSP variable that will hold the size value (**java.lang.Integer**).	No	Yes

Attribute	Description	Accepts JSP Expression	Required
name	Specifies the name of the object that contains the collection whose size will be taken. If the **property** attribute is also specified, one of the fields of the object defined by this attribute will have its getter method called to return the collection whose size will be taken.	Yes	No
property	Specifies the field, of the object specified by the **name** attribute, whose getter method will be called to return the collection whose size will be taken.	Yes	No
scope	Specifies the scope (application, page, request, or session) to look in for the object specified by the **name** attribute. If not specified, each scope will be searched, in this order: page, request, session, and then application.	Yes	No

Example Usage

As mentioned, there are three basic ways you can use the **size** tag. The first way, shown here, uses the **collection** attribute to specify which collection's size to store:

```
<%
// Example array.
String[] genders = {"male", "female"};
%>

<bean:size id="genderCount" collection="<%=genders%>"/>
```

Remember that the **collection** attribute accepts only an expression as a value. Because the **collection** attribute was used to specify the collection whose size will be taken, variables that are not in any particular scope can be accessed by the tag by way of an expression. The following two ways of using the **size** tag require the collection whose size is being taken to be in a scope.

The second way to use the **size** tag is shown here:

```
<%
// Example Collection.
ArrayList genders = new ArrayList();
genders.add("male");
genders.add("female");
pageContext.setAttribute("genders", genders);
%>

<bean:size id="genderCount" name="genders"/>
```

In this example, the **name** attribute is used to specify the name of a JSP scripting variable that has a collection in it. Remember that all scopes will be searched in succession (page then request then session then application) to find the specified object. Optionally, you can use the **scope** attribute to explicitly tell the tag which scope to look in for the collection.

The third and final way to use the **size** tag is shown here:

```
<bean:size id="genderCount" name="profile" property="genders"/>
```

This example assumes you have an object named "profile" with a field called "genders". The object's **getGenders( )** method will be called to return a collection whose size will be taken.

After you have used the **size** tag to store a collection's size, you can access it with the following snippet:

```
Gender Count: <%=genderCount%>
```

This snippet simply uses a JSP expression to render the value of the **Integer** object stored in the **genderCount** variable. Additionally, because the **size** tag places the **genderCount** variable in page scope, it can be accessed by JSP tag library tags, as shown here:

```
Gender Count: <bean:write name="genderCount"/>
```

The struts Tag

The **struts** tag is used to store a reference to a Struts configuration object in a JSP scripting variable with page scope. When the Strut **ActionServlet** initializes, it loads in Struts configuration files and creates an internal representation of the configuration settings with configuration objects. The **struts** tag provides convenient access to the three most prominent of these configuration objects: **FormBeanConfig**, **ForwardConfig**, and **ActionConfig**.

Note that one of the **formBean**, **forward**, or **mapping** attributes must be specified when using this tag or a **JspException** will be thrown at run time. Additionally, a **JspException** will be thrown at run time if the specified configuration object cannot be found.

Attributes

Attribute	Description	Accepts JSP Expression	Required
formBean	Specifies the name of a **FormBean** whose **org.apache.struts.config.FormBeanConfig** object reference will be stored in the specified JSP scripting variable.	Yes	No
forward	Specifies the name of a forward whose **org.apache.struts.config.ForwardConfig** object reference will be stored in the specified JSP scripting variable.	Yes	No
id	Specifies the name of the JSP variable that will hold the reference to the specified Struts configuration object.	No	Yes
mapping	Specifies the name of an **Action** whose **org.apache.struts.config.ActionConfig** object reference will be stored in the specified JSP scripting variable.	Yes	No

PART III

Example Usage

Before you examine the **struts** tag usage, review the following sample Struts configuration file. Each of the following examples is based on this configuration file.

```
<?xml version="1.0"?>

<!DOCTYPE struts-config PUBLIC
  "-//Apache Software Foundation//DTD Struts Configuration 1.3//EN"
  "http://struts.apache.org/dtds/struts-config_1_3.dtd">

<struts-config>

  <!-- Form Beans Configuration -->
  <form-beans>
    <form-bean name="searchForm"
               type="com.jamesholmes.minihr.SearchForm"/>
  </form-beans>

  <!-- Global Forwards Configuration -->
  <global-forwards>
    <forward name="search" path="/search.jsp"/>
  </global-forwards>

  <!-- Action Mappings Configuration -->
  <action-mappings>
    <action path="/search"
            type="com.jamesholmes.minihr.SearchAction"
            name="searchForm"
            scope="request"
            validate="true"
            input="/search.jsp">
    </action>
  </action-mappings>

  <!-- Message Resources Configuration -->
  <message-resources
    parameter="com.jamesholmes.minihr.ApplicationResources"/>

</struts-config>
```

There are three ways to use the **struts** tag. The first way, shown here, is used to store a reference to a **FormBean** configuration object:

```
<bean:struts id="cfg" formBean="searchForm"/>
```

Notice that the value used for the **formBean** attribute matches the value given to the **name** attribute of the **<form-bean>** tag in the Struts configuration file shown earlier.

The second way to use the **struts** tag, shown next, stores a reference to a forward configuration object:

```
<bean:struts id="cfg" forward="search"/>
```

Again, notice in this example that the value used for the **forward** attribute matches the value given to the **name** attribute of the **<forward>** tag in the Struts configuration file shown earlier.

The third way to use the **struts** tag stores a reference to an **Action** configuration object, as shown here:

```
<bean:struts id="cfg" mapping="/search"/>
```

As in the previous two examples, the value used for the **mapping** attribute matches the value given to the **path** attribute of the **<action>** tag in the Struts configuration file shown earlier.

Because the **struts** tag stores configuration object references in page scope, the objects can be accessed both with scriptlets and JSP tag library tags.

The write Tag

The **write** tag is used to render the value of an object to a JSP's output stream. Additionally, this tag can optionally format the value of the object before it is rendered by use of the **format** attribute.

There are two ways you can use the **write** tag, as listed here and shown later in the "Example Usage" section:

- You can use the **name** attribute to specify the name of any object to render. This object can be in any scope or limited to a specific scope with the **scope** attribute.
- You can use the **name** and **property** attributes in tandem to specify the name of an object and its field whose getter method will be called to return an object to be rendered. Again, the object specified by the **name** attribute can be in any scope or limited to a specific scope with the **scope** attribute.

Attributes

Attribute	Description	Accepts JSP Expression	Required
bundle	Specifies the name of the application-scoped **org.apache.struts.util.MessageResources** object that contains the format key/value pairs for the **formatKey** attribute.Defaults to the value stored in the **org.apache.struts.Globals.MESSAGES_KEY** constant.	Yes	No
filter	Accepts *true* or *false* to specify whether HTML-sensitive characters should be converted to their entity equivalents. For example, if this attribute is set to *true*, the less-than sign (<) would get converted to < before it is rendered. Defaults to *true*.	Yes	No
format	Specifies the format string to use to convert the value being rendered. If not specified, **write** will try to use the **formatKey** attribute to look up the format string.	Yes	No
formatKey	Specifies the key for a format string to look up in the application resource bundle.	Yes	No

Attribute	Description	Accepts JSP Expression	Required
ignore	Accepts *true* or *false* to specify whether to skip throwing a **JspException**, similar to the other tags in this library, when the object specified by the **name** attribute is not found. Defaults to *false*.	Yes	No
locale	Specifies the name of the session-scoped **java.util.Locale** object to use when formatting values with the **format** attribute. Defaults to the value stored in the **org.apache.struts .Globals. LOCALE_KEY** constant.	Yes	No
name	Specifies the name of the object that will be rendered. If the **property** attribute is also specified, one of the fields of the object defined by this attribute will have its getter method called to return the object that will be rendered.	Yes	Yes
property	Specifies the field, of the object specified by the **name** attribute, whose getter method will be called to return the object that will be rendered.	Yes	No
scope	Specifies the scope (application, page, request, or session) to look in for the object specified by the **name** attribute. If not specified, each scope will be searched, in this order: page, request, session, and then application.	Yes	No

Example Usage

As mentioned, there are two ways you can use the **write** tag. The first way, shown here, uses the **name** attribute to specify the name of an object to be rendered. Remember that you can explicitly specify the scope of the object with the **scope** attribute.

```
<bean:write name="bizObj"/>
```

The following is the second way to use the **write** tag:

```
<bean:write name="bizObj" property="bizField"/>
```

In this example, the **name** and **property** attributes are used in tandem to specify the name of an object and its field whose getter method will be called to return an object to be rendered. Again, you can explicitly specify the scope of the object with the **scope** attribute.

15

CHAPTER

The Logic Tag Library

The Logic Tag Library provides a rich set of tags for cleanly implementing simple conditional logic in JSPs. With these tags you can wrap content that will be processed only when a particular condition is true. For example, you can use the **equal** tag to wrap content that is conditionally processed based on whether two specified values are equal or not. The following snippet illustrates this:

```
<logic:equal name="resultCount" value="0">
Search returned no results.
</logic:equal>
```

If the object specified by the **name** attribute is equal to "0", as specified by the **value** attribute, then the content between the starting and ending **equal** tags will be processed. Otherwise, the content will be ignored.

Note that the Logic Library has three tags that are not used for conditional logic: the **forward** tag, the **iterate** tag, and the **redirect** tag. The **forward** tag is used to look up a forward from the Struts configuration file and redirect to it. The **iterate** tag is used to wrap content that should be processed for each element of a collection, and the **redirect** tag is used to send an HTTP redirect response to a browser, causing it to load another page.

NOTE *Many of the tags in this library have JSTL equivalents that should be used in lieu of these tags. See Chapter 17 for more information on using JSTL with Struts and the list of Struts tags that can be replaced with JSTL equivalents.*

Understanding Variables and Scope in JSPs

Before discussing each of the tags in this library, it's necessary to review how variables and scope work in JSPs. First, remember that JSPs get converted into servlets and then compiled before they are executed. All of the HTML and code inside the JSP gets placed into the generated servlet's **service( )** method. Because of this, any variables that get defined inside the JSP with a scriptlet, as shown here, are local to the **service( )** method:

```
<%
String test = "test value";
%>
```

Similarly, any variables that are defined with a JSP declaration are local to the **service( )** method:

```
<%! String test = "test value"; %>
```

Also, all of the implicit JSP objects, such as **application**, **request**, and **session**, are local to the resulting servlet's **service( )** method.

JSPs and servlets also have the notion of "scope" for variables, because some variables need to persist longer than the lifespan of a page request and some variables need to be accessible outside of a servlet's **service( )** method. There are four scopes that JSP variables can be placed in: application, page, request, and session. The following table explains each scope.

Scope	Description
application	Variables placed in this scope persist for the life of an application.
page	Variables placed in this scope persist until the current JSP's **service( )** method completes. Included JSPs cannot see page scope variables from the page including them. Also, this scope is exclusive to JSPs.
request	Variables placed in this scope persist until processing for the current request is completed. This scope differs from page scope in that multiple servlets may be executed during the lifespan of a request. Page scope variables persist only for the execution of one servlet.
session	Variables placed in this scope persist until the current user's session is invalidated or expires. This scope is valid only if the JSP or servlet in question is participating in a session.

Note that variables must be explicitly placed into a scope, as shown here:

```
<%
request.setAttribute("reqScopeVar", "test");
%>
```

This snippet uses JSP's implicit **request** object to place a variable into request scope. Similarly, the following snippet uses JSP's implicit **session** object to place a variable into session scope:

```
<%
session.setAttribute("sesScopeVar", "test");
%>
```

Of course, variables can also be put into each of the scopes by JSP tag library tags.

Using the Logic Tag Library

To use the Logic Tag Library in a Struts application, your application's JSPs must declare their use of the library with a JSP **taglib** directive:

```
<%@ taglib uri="http://struts.apache.org/tags-logic" prefix="logic" %>
```

Notice that the **prefix** attribute is set to "logic." This attribute can be set to whatever you want; however, "logic" is the accepted default for the Logic Library. The **prefix** attribute declares the prefix that each tag must have when it is used in the JSP, as shown here:

```
<logic:present name="searchForm" property="results">
```

Because "logic" was defined as the prefix, the **present** tag was used as shown. However, if you chose to use a prefix of "strutslgc", the tag would be used the following way:

```
<strutslgc:present name="searchForm" property="results">
```

NOTE *Modern application servers use the* **uri** *attribute of the* **taglib** *directive to automatically resolve the location of the tag library descriptor file. Older application servers that support only JSP version 1.1 and/or version 1.0 require that tag libraries be registered in the* **web.xml** *file so that they can be resolved, as shown here:*

```
<taglib>
  <taglib-uri>http://struts.apache.org/tags-logic</taglib-uri>
  <taglib-location>/WEB-INF/tlds/struts-logic.tld</taglib-location>
</taglib>
```


The Logic Tag Library Tags

The following table lists each of the tags in the Logic Tag Library and a short description of each tag's purpose.

Tag	Description
empty	Wraps content that is conditionally processed based on whether the specified object is **null** or contains an empty (zero-length) **String**.
equal	Wraps content that is conditionally processed based on whether a specified object's value equals a specified constant value.
forward	Looks up a forward from the Struts configuration file and processes it.
greaterEqual	Wraps content that is conditionally processed based on whether a specified object's value is greater than or equal to a specified constant value.
greaterThan	Wraps content that is conditionally processed based on whether a specified object's value is greater than a specified constant value.
iterate	Wraps content that is repeated for each element of a specified collection.
lessEqual	Wraps content that is conditionally processed based on whether a specified object's value is less than or equal to a specified constant value.
lessThan	Wraps content that is conditionally processed based on whether a specified object's value is less than a specified constant value.

Tag	Description
match	Wraps content that is conditionally processed based on whether a specified object's value contains, starts with, or ends with a specified constant value.
messagesNotPresent	Wraps content that is conditionally processed based on whether Struts' **org.apache.struts.action.ActionErrors** or **org.apache.struts.action.ActionMessages** object does *not* have any errors or messages in it, respectively.
messagesPresent	Wraps content that is conditionally processed based on whether Struts' **org.apache.struts.action.ActionErrors** or **org.apache.struts.action.ActionMessages** object has any errors or messages in it, respectively.
notEmpty	Wraps content that is conditionally processed based on whether the specified object is non-**null** and does *not* contain an empty (zero-length) **String**.
notEqual	Wraps content that is conditionally processed based on whether a specified object's value is *not* equal to a specified constant value.
notMatch	Wraps content that is conditionally processed based on whether a specified object's value does *not* contain, start with, or end with a specified constant value.
notPresent	Wraps content that is conditionally processed based on whether a specified object does *not* exist.
present	Wraps content that is conditionally processed based on whether a specified object exists.
redirect	Composes a URL to another page and then redirects to it.

The remainder of this chapter discusses each tag in detail, including a complete description of the tag, a table listing each of the tag's attributes, and a usage example for the tag. In the tables that describe each tag's attributes, pay special attention to the Required and Accepts JSP Expression columns. The Required column simply denotes whether the given attribute is required when using the tag. In addition to the required column denoting whether an attribute is required, the rows for required attributes are highlighted in gray so that you can determine at a glance which attributes are required.

If an attribute is required and you do not specify it when using the tag, the tag will throw a **javax.servlet.jsp.JspException** at run time. Note that you can declare an error page in your JSP with a **page** directive to capture any **JspException**s that might be thrown, as shown here:

```
<%@ page errorPage="error.jsp" %>
```

If an exception occurs, the page specified by the **errorPage** attribute will be internally redirected to display an error page.

The Accepts JSP Expression column denotes whether the given attribute's value can be specified with a JSP expression. If a JSP expression is used to specify an attribute value, the expression must comprise the complete value, quote (") to quote ("), as shown here.

Correct:

```
<logic:present name="<%=result%>">
```

Incorrect:

```
<logic:present name="<%=result%>-result">
```

Notice in the incorrect example that "-result" is used as part of the value for the **name** attribute following the expression. This is invalid because there are extra characters between the end of the expression and the ending quote.

A corrected version of the incorrect example follows:

```
<logic:present name="<%=result + "-result"%>"/>
```

The concatenation of "-result" is now part of the expression and the expression comprises the complete value for the attribute.

The empty Tag

The **empty** tag is used to wrap content that is conditionally processed based on whether the specified object is **null** or contains an empty (zero-length) **String**. Additionally, if the object specified implements **java.util.Collection** or **java.util.Map**, this tag will call the object's **isEmpty( )** method to determine whether the object is empty. If the object is empty, then the wrapped content will be processed.

Attributes

Attribute	Description	Accepts JSP Expression	Required
name	Specifies the name of an object to check as being empty. If the **property** attribute is also specified, one of the fields of the object defined by this attribute will have its getter method called to return an object to check as being empty.	Yes	No
property	Specifies the field of the object specified by the **name** attribute whose getter method will be called to return an object to check as being empty.	Yes	No
scope	Specifies the scope (application, page, request, or session) to look in for the object specified by the **name** attribute. If not specified, each scope will be searched, in this order: page, request, session, and then application.	Yes	No

Example Usage

There are two ways you can use the **empty** tag. The first way, shown here, uses the **name** attribute to specify the name of an object to check as being empty:

```
<logic:empty name="results">
Your search yielded no results.
</logic:empty>
```

If the **results** object is **null**, contains a zero-length string, or contains a **Collection** or **Map** with zero elements, then the content between the starting and ending **empty** tags will be processed. Remember that you can explicitly specify the scope of the object with the **scope** attribute.

The second way to use the **empty** tag is shown here:

```
<logic:empty name="bizObj" property="results">
Your search yielded no results.
</logic:empty>
```

In this example, the **name** and **property** attributes are used in tandem to specify the name of an object and its field whose getter method will be called to return an object to check as being empty. Again, you can explicitly specify the scope of the object with the **scope** attribute.

The equal Tag

The **equal** tag is used to wrap content that is conditionally processed based on whether a specified object's value equals a specified constant value. This tag works for both numeric and string comparisons.

There are five ways you can use the **equal** tag, as listed here and shown later in the section "Example Usage":

- You can use the **cookie** attribute to specify the name of an HTTP cookie from the incoming request whose value will be used for the comparison.
- You can use the **header** attribute to specify the name of an HTTP header from the incoming request whose value will be used for the comparison.
- You can use the **parameter** attribute to specify the name of a parameter from the incoming request whose value will be used for the comparison.
- You can use the **name** attribute to specify the name of an object whose value will be used for the comparison. This object can be in any scope or limited to a specific scope with the **scope** attribute.
- You can use the **name** and **property** attributes in tandem to specify the name of an object and its field whose getter method will be called to return an object whose value will be used for the comparison. Again, the object specified by the **name** attribute can be in any scope or limited to a specific scope with the **scope** attribute.

Attributes

Attribute	Description	Accepts JSP Expression	Required
cookie	Specifies the name of the HTTP cookie from the incoming request whose value is used for comparison.	Yes	No

Attribute	Description	Accepts JSP Expression	Required
header	Specifies the name of the HTTP header from the incoming request whose value is used for comparison.	Yes	No
name	Specifies the name of an object whose value is used for comparison. If the **property** attribute is also specified, one of the fields of the object defined by this attribute will have its getter method called to return an object whose value is used for comparison.	Yes	No
parameter	Specifies the name of the parameter from the incoming request whose value is used for comparison.	Yes	No
property	Specifies the field of the object specified by the **name** attribute whose getter method will be called to return an object whose value is used for comparison.	Yes	No
scope	Specifies the scope (application, page, request, or session) to look in for the object specified by the **name** attribute. If not specified, each scope will be searched, in this order: page, request, session, and then application.	Yes	No
value	Specifies the constant value to which the value, specified by other attributes of this tag, will be compared.	Yes	Yes

Example Usage

As mentioned, there are five ways you can use the **equal** tag. The first way, shown here, uses the **cookie** attribute to specify the name of an HTTP cookie from the incoming request whose value is compared against the value specified with the **value** attribute:

```
<logic:equal cookie="role" value="Manager">
User is a Manager.
</logic:equal>
```

If the cookie's value and the **value** attribute's value are equal, the content between the starting and ending **equal** tags will be processed. Otherwise, it will be ignored.

The second way to use the **equal** tag is shown here:

```
<logic:equal header="User-Agent"
              value="Mozilla/4.0 (compatible; MSIE 6.0; Windows NT 5.1)">
Browser is Internet Explorer.
</logic:equal>
```

This example compares the incoming request's User-Agent header against the **value** attribute to determine whether they are equal. If so, the content between the starting and ending **equal** tags will be processed.

The following is the third way to use the **equal** tag:

```
<logic:equal parameter="catId" value="10">
Category Id is 10.
</logic:equal>
```

This example compares a request parameter from the incoming request against the value of the **value** attribute. If the two values are equal, the content between the starting and ending **equal** tags will be processed.

The fourth way to use the **equal** tag is shown here:

```
<logic:equal name="resultCount" value="0">
Search returned no results.
</logic:equal>
```

This example compares the value of the **resultCount** object against the value of the **value** attribute. If the two values are equal, the content between the starting and ending **equal** tags will be processed. Remember that you can explicitly specify the scope of the **resultCount** object with the **scope** attribute.

The following is the fifth and final way to use the **equal** tag:

```
<logic:equal name="employee" property="name" value="Bob">
Hello, Bob!
</logic:equal>
```

In this example, the **name** and **property** attributes are used in tandem to specify the name of an object and its field whose getter method will be called to return an object whose value will be compared against that of the **value** attribute. Again, you can explicitly specify the scope of the object with the **scope** attribute.

The forward Tag

The **forward** tag is used to look up a forward from the Struts configuration file and process it. Based on the way that the forward is defined in the configuration file, this tag will either forward to the URL specified by the forward or perform a redirect to it. If the forward has its **redirect** attribute set to *true,* as shown in the following example, this tag will perform a redirect:

```
<forward name="google" path="http://www.google.com/" redirect="true"/>
```

A redirect sends a response to the user's browser instructing it to load another page. A forward, on the other hand, simply "forwards" control (on the server side) to another URL without having the browser make another request. Note that only URLs residing in the same application can be forwarded to, whereas any URL can be redirected to.

Attribute

Attribute	Description	Accepts JSP Expression	Required
name	Specifies the name of the forward to process.	Yes	Yes

Example Usage

The following snippet shows how to use the **forward** tag:

```
<logic:forward name="search"/>
```

As you can see, this tag is very straightforward. All you have to do is specify the name of the forward to process.

The greaterEqual Tag

The **greaterEqual** tag is used to wrap content that is conditionally processed based on whether a specified object's value is greater than or equal to a specified constant value. Note that this tag works for both numeric and string comparisons.

There are five ways you can use the **greaterEqual** tag, as listed here and shown later in the section "Example Usage":

- You can use the **cookie** attribute to specify the name of an HTTP cookie from the incoming request whose value will be used for the comparison.
- You can use the **header** attribute to specify the name of an HTTP header from the incoming request whose value will be used for the comparison.
- You can use the **parameter** attribute to specify the name of a parameter from the incoming request whose value will be used for the comparison.
- You can use the **name** attribute to specify the name of an object whose value will be used for the comparison. This object can be in any scope or limited to a specific scope with the **scope** attribute.
- You can use the **name** and **property** attributes in tandem to specify the name of an object and its field whose getter method will be called to return an object whose value will be used for the comparison. Again, the object specified by the **name** attribute can be in any scope or limited to a specific scope with the **scope** attribute.

Attributes

Attribute	Description	Accepts JSP Expression	Required
cookie	Specifies the name of the HTTP cookie from the incoming request whose value is used for comparison.	Yes	No

PART III

Attribute	Description	Accepts JSP Expression	Required
header	Specifies the name of the HTTP header from the incoming request whose value is used for comparison.	Yes	No
name	Specifies the name of an object whose value is used for comparison. If the **property** attribute is also specified, one of the fields of the object defined by this attribute will have its getter method called to return an object whose value is used for comparison.	Yes	No
parameter	Specifies the name of the parameter from the incoming request whose value is used for comparison.	Yes	No
property	Specifies the field of the object specified by the **name** attribute whose getter method will be called to return an object whose value is used for comparison.	Yes	No
scope	Specifies the scope (application, page, request, or session) to look in for the object specified by the **name** attribute. If not specified, each scope will be searched, in this order: page, request, session, and then application.	Yes	No
value	Specifies the constant value to which the value, specified by other attributes of this tag, will be compared.	Yes	Yes

Example Usage

As mentioned, there are five ways you can use the **greaterEqual** tag. The first way, shown here, uses the **cookie** attribute to specify the name of an HTTP cookie from the incoming request whose value is compared against the value specified with the **value** attribute:

```
<logic:greaterEqual cookie="size" value="0">
Size is valid.
</logic:greaterEqual>
```

If the cookie's value is greater than or equal to the **value** attribute's value, the content between the starting and ending **greaterEqual** tags will be processed. Otherwise, it will be ignored.

The following is the second way to use the **greaterEqual** tag:

```
<logic:greaterEqual header="Content-Length" value="100000">
Page has large amount of content.
</logic:greaterEqual>
```

This example compares the incoming request's Content-Length header against the **value** attribute to determine whether the content length is greater than or equal to 100,000. If so, the content between the starting and ending **greaterEqual** tags will be processed.

The third way to use the **greaterEqual** tag is shown here:

```
<logic:greaterEqual parameter="catId" value="10">
Category Id is greater than or equal to 10.
</logic:greaterEqual>
```

This example compares a request parameter from the incoming request against the value of the **value** attribute. If the parameter is greater than or equal to the value, the content between the starting and ending **greaterEqual** tags will be processed.

The fourth way to use the **greaterEqual** tag is shown here:

```
<logic:greaterEqual name="resultCount" value="1">
Search returned at least 1 result.
</logic:greaterEqual>
```

This example compares the value of the **resultCount** object against the value of the **value** attribute. If the **resultCount** object's value is greater than or equal to the value of the **value** attribute, the content between the starting and ending **greaterEqual** tags will be processed. Remember that you can explicitly specify the scope of the **resultCount** object with the **scope** attribute.

The following is the fifth and final way to use the **greaterEqual** tag:

```
<logic:greaterEqual name="employee" property="age" value="21">
Employee is old enough to drink.
</logic:greaterEqual>
```

In this example, the **name** and **property** attributes are used in tandem to specify the name of an object and its field whose getter method will be called to return an object whose value will be compared against that of the **value** attribute. Again, you can explicitly specify the scope of the object with the **scope** attribute.

The greaterThan Tag

The **greaterThan** tag is used to wrap content that is conditionally processed based on whether a specified object's value is greater than a specified constant value. This tag works for both numeric and string comparisons.

There are five ways you can use the **greaterThan** tag, as listed here and shown later in the section "Example Usage":

- You can use the **cookie** attribute to specify the name of an HTTP cookie from the incoming request whose value will be used for the comparison.
- You can use the **header** attribute to specify the name of an HTTP header from the incoming request whose value will be used for the comparison.
- You can use the **parameter** attribute to specify the name of a parameter from the incoming request whose value will be used for the comparison.
- You can use the **name** attribute to specify the name of an object whose value will be used for the comparison. This object can be in any scope or limited to a specific scope with the **scope** attribute.
- You can use the **name** and **property** attributes in tandem to specify the name of an object and its field whose getter method will be called to return an object whose

value will be used for the comparison. Again, the object specified by the **name** attribute can be in any scope or limited to a specific scope with the **scope** attribute.

Attributes

Attribute	Description	Accepts JSP Expression	Required
cookie	Specifies the name of the HTTP cookie from the incoming request whose value is used for comparison.	Yes	No
header	Specifies the name of the HTTP header from the incoming request whose value is used for comparison.	Yes	No
name	Specifies the name of an object whose value is used for comparison. If the **property** attribute is also specified, one of the fields of the object defined by this attribute will have its getter method called to return an object whose value is used for comparison.	Yes	No
parameter	Specifies the name of the parameter from the incoming request whose value is used for comparison.	Yes	No
property	Specifies the field of the object specified by the **name** attribute whose getter method will be called to return an object whose value is used for comparison.	Yes	No
scope	Specifies the scope (application, page, request, or session) to look in for the object specified by the **name** attribute. If not specified, each scope will be searched, in this order: page, request, session, and then application.	Yes	No
value	Specifies the constant value to which the value, specified by other attributes of this tag, will be compared.	Yes	Yes

Example Usage

As mentioned, there are five ways you can use the **greaterThan** tag. The first way, shown here, uses the **cookie** attribute to specify the name of an HTTP cookie from the incoming request whose value is compared against the value specified with the **value** attribute:

```
<logic:greaterThan cookie="size" value="0">
Size is valid.
</logic:greaterThan>
```

If the cookie's value is greater than the **value** attribute's value, the content between the starting and ending **greaterThan** tags will be processed. Otherwise, it will be ignored.

The second way to use the **greaterThan** tag is shown here:

```
<logic:greaterThan header="Content-Length" value="100000">
Page has large amount of content.
</logic:greaterThan>
```

This example compares the incoming request's Content-Length header against the **value** attribute to determine whether the content length is greater than 100,000. If so, the content between the starting and ending **greaterThan** tags will be processed.

The following is the third way to use the **greaterThan** tag:

```
<logic:greaterThan parameter="catId" value="10">
Category Id is greater than 10.
</logic:greaterThan>
```

This example compares a request parameter from the incoming request against the value of the **value** attribute. If the parameter is greater than the value, the content between the starting and ending **greaterThan** tags will be processed.

The fourth way to use the **greaterThan** tag is shown here:

```
<logic:greaterThan name="resultCount" value="1">
Search returned more than 1 result.
</logic:greaterThan>
```

This example compares the value of the **resultCount** object against the value of the **value** attribute. If the **resultCount** object's value is greater than the value of the **value** attribute, the content between the starting and ending **greaterThan** tags will be processed. Remember that you can explicitly specify the scope of the **resultCount** object with the **scope** attribute.

The following is the fifth and final way to use the **greaterThan** tag:

```
<logic:greaterThan name="employee" property="age" value="20">
Employee is old enough to drink.
</logic:greaterThan>
```

In this example, the **name** and **property** attributes are used in tandem to specify the name of an object and its field whose getter method will be called to return an object whose value will be compared against that of the **value** attribute. Again, you can explicitly specify the scope of the object with the **scope** attribute.

The iterate Tag

The **iterate** tag is used to wrap content that is repeated for each element of a specified collection. The collection can be any of the following:

- An array of Java objects or primitives (e.g., int, long, and so on)
- An implementation of **java.util.Collection**
- An implementation of **java.util.Enumeration**
- An implementation of **java.util.Iterator**
- An implementation of **java.util.Map**

Additionally, this tag sets two JSP variables on each iteration through the specified collection's elements. The first variable, whose name is specified by the **id** attribute, stores a reference to the current element of the collection. The second variable, whose name is specified by the **indexId** attribute, stores the numeric index for the current element. Note that each element will be stored as type **Object** unless specified otherwise with use of the **type** attribute. Also note that **java.util.Map**-based collections house **java.util.Map.Entry** elements, which contain the key and value for the given element.

There are three ways you can specify which collection to iterate over, as listed here and shown later in the section "Example Usage":

- You can use the **collection** attribute to specify an expression that evaluates to a collection object.
- You can use the **name** attribute to specify the name of a collection object that can be in any scope or limited to a specific scope with the **scope** attribute.
- You can use the **name** and **property** attributes in tandem to specify the name of an object and its field whose getter method will be called to return a collection object. Again, the object specified by the **name** attribute can be in any scope or limited to a specific scope with the **scope** attribute.

Note that if none of the aforementioned ways is used to specify the collection that should be iterated over, a **JspException** will be thrown by this tag at run time.

Also note that if the collection you are iterating over can contain **null** values, the loop will still be performed but no page scope attribute will be stored for elements that are **null**.

Attributes

Attribute	Description	Accepts JSP Expression	Required
collection	Specifies an expression that evaluates to an array, **java.util.Collection**, **java.util.Enumeration**, **java.util.Iterator**, or **java.util.Map**.	Yes	No
id	Specifies the name for the page-scoped JSP variable that will hold a reference to the current element of the collection on each iteration.	No	Yes
indexed	Specifies the name for the page-scoped JSP variable that will hold the current index of the collection on each iteration.	No	No
length	Specifies the maximum number of entries from the collection that will be iterated over. If not specified, all entries in the collection will be iterated over. This attribute can specify an integer value or the name of an **Integer** object (in any scope).	Yes	No

Attribute	Description	Accepts JSP Expression	Required
name	Specifies the name of the object that contains the collection that will be iterated over. If the **property** attribute is also specified, one of the fields of the object defined by this attribute will have its getter method called to return the collection that will be iterated over.	Yes	No
offset	Specifies the zero-relative index to start the collection iteration at. If not specified, iteration will start at 0 (the beginning). This attribute can specify an integer value or the name of an **Integer** object (in any scope).	Yes	No
property	Specifies the field of the object specified by the **name** attribute whose getter method will be called to return the collection that will be iterated over.	Yes	No
scope	Specifies the scope (application, page, request, or session) to look in for the object specified by the **name** attribute. If not specified, each scope will be searched, in this order: page, request, session, and then application.	Yes	No
type	Specifies the fully qualified class type (e.g., **java.lang.Integer**) to expose each collection element as, with the **id** attribute. A **ClassCastException** will be thrown at run time if any of the collection's elements are not assignment compatible with this type. If not specified, no type conversions will be performed and each element will be exposed as type **Object**.	Yes	No

Example Usage

As mentioned, there are three basic ways you can use the **iterate** tag. The first way, shown here, uses the **collection** attribute to specify the collection to iterate over:

```
<logic:iterate id="result" collection="<%=results%>">
Result: <%=result%><br>
</logic:iterate>
```

This example assumes you have defined a collection named "results" and then iterates over each result, printing it. Notice that the **collection** attribute was specified with an expression. This attribute only accepts expressions. Anything else will result in a **JspException** being thrown at run time.

The second way to use the **iterate** tag is shown here:

```
<logic:iterate id="result" name="results">
Result: <bean:write name="result"/><br>
</logic:iterate>
```

This example is similar to the first example; however, it differs in that the collection to be iterated over is specified with the **name** attribute. Remember that you can explicitly specify the scope of the object, defined by the **name** attribute, with the **scope** attribute.

The following is the third and final way to use the **iterate** tag:

```
<logic:iterate id="result" name="searchObj" property="results">
Result: <bean:write name="result"/><br>
</logic:iterate>
```

In this example, the **name** and **property** attributes are used in tandem to specify the name of an object and its field whose getter method will be called to return a collection to be iterated over. Again, you can explicitly specify the scope of the object with the **scope** attribute.

The lessEqual Tag

The **lessEqual** tag is used to wrap content that is conditionally processed based on whether a specified object's value is less than or equal to a specified constant value. This tag works for both numeric and string comparisons.

There are five ways you can use the **lessEqual** tag, as listed here and shown later in the section "Example Usage":

- You can use the **cookie** attribute to specify the name of an HTTP cookie from the incoming request whose value will be used for the comparison.
- You can use the **header** attribute to specify the name of an HTTP header from the incoming request whose value will be used for the comparison.
- You can use the **parameter** attribute to specify the name of a parameter from the incoming request whose value will be used for the comparison.
- You can use the **name** attribute to specify the name of an object whose value will be used for the comparison. This object can be in any scope or limited to a specific scope with the **scope** attribute.
- You can use the **name** and **property** attributes in tandem to specify the name of an object and its field whose getter method will be called to return an object whose value will be used for the comparison. Again, the object specified by the **name** attribute can be in any scope or limited to a specific scope with the **scope** attribute.

Attributes

Attribute	Description	Accepts JSP Expression	Required
cookie	Specifies the name of the HTTP cookie from the incoming request whose value is used for comparison.	Yes	No
header	Specifies the name of the HTTP header from the incoming request whose value is used for comparison.	Yes	No

Attribute	Description	Accepts JSP Expression	Required
name	Specifies the name of an object whose value is used for comparison. If the **property** attribute is also specified, one of the fields of the object defined by this attribute will have its getter method called to return an object whose value is used for comparison.	Yes	No
parameter	Specifies the name of the parameter from the incoming request whose value is used for comparison.	Yes	No
property	Specifies the field of the object specified by the **name** attribute whose getter method will be called to return an object whose value is used for comparison.	Yes	No
scope	Specifies the scope (application, page, request, or session) to look in for the object specified by the **name** attribute. If not specified, each scope will be searched, in this order: page, request, session, and then application.	Yes	No
value	Specifies the constant value to which the value, specified by other attributes of this tag, will be compared.	Yes	Yes

Example Usage

As mentioned, there are five ways you can use the **lessEqual** tag. The first way, shown here, uses the **cookie** attribute to specify the name of an HTTP cookie from the incoming request whose value is compared against the value specified with the **value** attribute:

```
<logic:lessEqual cookie="size" value="0">
Size is invalid.
</logic:lessEqual>
```

If the cookie's value is less than or equal to the **value** attribute's value, the content between the starting and ending **lessEqual** tags will be processed. Otherwise, it will be ignored.

The following is the second way to use the **lessEqual** tag:

```
<logic:lessEqual header="Content-Length" value="500">
Page has small amount of content.
</logic:lessEqual>
```

This example compares the incoming request's Content-Length header against the **value** attribute to determine whether the content length is less than or equal to 500. If so, the content between the starting and ending **lessEqual** tags will be processed.

The third way to use the **lessEqual** tag is shown here:

```
<logic:lessEqual parameter="catId" value="10">
Category Id is less than or equal to 10.
</logic:lessEqual>
```

This example compares a request parameter from the incoming request against the value of the **value** attribute. If the parameter is less than or equal to the value, the content between the starting and ending **lessEqual** tags will be processed.

The fourth way to use the **lessEqual** tag is shown here:

```
<logic:lessEqual name="resultCount" value="19">
Search returned less than 20 results.
</logic:lessEqual>
```

This example compares the value of the **resultCount** object against the value of the **value** attribute. If the **resultCount** object's value is less than or equal to the value of the **value** attribute, the content between the starting and ending **lessEqual** tags will be processed. Remember that you can explicitly specify the scope of the **resultCount** object with the **scope** attribute.

The following is the fifth and final way to use the **lessEqual** tag:

```
<logic:lessEqual name="employee" property="age" value="20">
Employee is not old enough to drink.
</logic:lessEqual>
```

In this example, the **name** and **property** attributes are used in tandem to specify the name of an object and its field whose getter method will be called to return an object whose value will be compared against that of the **value** attribute. Again, you can explicitly specify the scope of the object with the **scope** attribute.

The lessThan Tag

The **lessThan** tag is used to wrap content that is conditionally processed based on whether a specified object's value is less than a specified constant value. This tag works for both numeric and string comparisons.

There are five ways you can use the **lessThan** tag, as listed here and shown later in the section "Example Usage":

- You can use the **cookie** attribute to specify the name of an HTTP cookie from the incoming request whose value will be used for the comparison.
- You can use the **header** attribute to specify the name of an HTTP header from the incoming request whose value will be used for the comparison.
- You can use the **parameter** attribute to specify the name of a parameter from the incoming request whose value will be used for the comparison.
- You can use the **name** attribute to specify the name of an object whose value will be used for the comparison. This object can be in any scope or limited to a specific scope with the **scope** attribute.
- You can use the **name** and **property** attributes in tandem to specify the name of an object and its field whose getter method will be called to return an object whose value will be used for the comparison. Again, the object specified by the **name** attribute can be in any scope or limited to a specific scope with the **scope** attribute.

Attributes

Attribute	Description	Accepts JSP Expression	Required
cookie	Specifies the name of the HTTP cookie from the incoming request whose value is used for comparison.	Yes	No
header	Specifies the name of the HTTP header from the incoming request whose value is used for comparison.	Yes	No
name	Specifies the name of an object whose value is used for comparison. If the **property** attribute is also specified, one of the fields of the object defined by this attribute will have its getter method called to return an object whose value is used for comparison.	Yes	No
parameter	Specifies the name of the parameter from the incoming request whose value is used for comparison.	Yes	No
property	Specifies the field of the object specified by the **name** attribute whose getter method will be called to return an object whose value is used for comparison.	Yes	No
scope	Specifies the scope (application, page, request, or session) to look in for the object specified by the **name** attribute. If not specified, each scope will be searched, in this order: page, request, session, and then application.	Yes	No
value	Specifies the constant value to which the value, specified by other attributes of this tag, will be compared.	Yes	Yes

PART III

Example Usage

As mentioned, there are five ways you can use the **lessThan** tag. The first way, shown here, uses the **cookie** attribute to specify the name of an HTTP cookie from the incoming request whose value is compared against the value specified with the **value** attribute:

```
<logic:lessThan cookie="size" value="1">
Size is invalid.
</logic:lessThan>
```

If the cookie's value is less than the **value** attribute's value, the content between the starting and ending **lessThan** tags will be processed. Otherwise, it will be ignored.

The second way to use the **lessThan** tag is shown here:

```
<logic:lessThan header="Content-Length" value="500">
Page has small amount of content.
</logic:lessThan>
```

This example compares the incoming request's Content-Length header against the **value** attribute to determine whether the content length is less than 500. If so, the content between the starting and ending **lessThan** tags will be processed.

The following is the third way to use the **lessThan** tag:

```
<logic:lessThan parameter="catId" value="10">
Category Id is less than 10.
</logic:lessThan>
```

This example compares a request parameter from the incoming request against the value of the **value** attribute. If the parameter is less than the value, the content between the starting and ending **lessThan** tags will be processed.

The following is the fourth way to use the **lessThan** tag:

```
<logic:lessThan name="resultCount" value="1">
Search returned no results.
</logic:lessThan>
```

This example compares the value of the **resultCount** object against the value of the **value** attribute. If the **resultCount** object's value is less than the value of the **value** attribute, the content between the starting and ending **lessThan** tags will be processed. Remember that you can explicitly specify the scope of the **resultCount** object with the **scope** attribute.

The fifth and final way to use the **lessThan** tag is shown here:

```
<logic:lessThan name="employee" property="age" value="21">
Employee is not old enough to drink.
</logic:lessThan>
```

In this example, the **name** and **property** attributes are used in tandem to specify the name of an object and its field whose getter method will be called to return an object whose value will be compared against that of the **value** attribute. Again, you can explicitly specify the scope of the object with the **scope** attribute.

The match Tag

The **match** tag is used to wrap content that is conditionally processed based on whether a specified object's value contains, starts with, or ends with a specified constant value. This tag essentially provides a convenient interface to the **String** object's **indexOf( )**, **startsWith( )**, and **endsWith( )** methods. If the **location** attribute of this tag is not specified, an **indexOf( )** match will be performed to see if the specified object's value contains the value specified by the **value** attribute. If the **location** attribute is specified as "start", a **startsWith( )** match will be performed to see if the specified object's value starts with the value specified by the **value** attribute. Finally, if the **location** attribute is specified as "end", an **endsWith( )** match will be performed to see if the specified object's value ends with the value specified by the **value** attribute. Note that all of the matches are case sensitive.

There are five ways you can use the **match** tag, as listed here and shown later in the section "Example Usage":

- You can use the **cookie** attribute to specify the name of an HTTP cookie from the incoming request whose value will be used to match against.

- You can use the **header** attribute to specify the name of an HTTP header from the incoming request whose value will be used to match against.
- You can use the **parameter** attribute to specify the name of a parameter from the incoming request whose value will be used to match against.
- You can use the **name** attribute to specify the name of an object whose value will be used to match against. This object can be in any scope or limited to a specific scope with the **scope** attribute.
- You can use the **name** and **property** attributes in tandem to specify the name of an object and its field whose getter method will be called to return an object whose value will be used to match against. Again, the object specified by the **name** attribute can be in any scope or limited to a specific scope with the **scope** attribute.

Attributes

Attribute	Description	Accepts JSP Expression	Required
cookie	Specifies the name of the HTTP cookie from the incoming request whose value is matched against.	Yes	No
header	Specifies the name of the HTTP header from the incoming request whose value is matched against.	Yes	No
location	Accepts *start* or *end* to specify where the match should occur. If not specified, the match can occur at any location.	Yes	No
name	Specifies the name of an object whose value is matched against. If the **property** attribute is also specified, one of the fields of the object defined by this attribute will have its getter method called to return an object whose value is matched against.	Yes	No
parameter	Specifies the name of the parameter from the incoming request whose value is matched against.	Yes	No
property	Specifies the field of the object specified by the **name** attribute whose getter method will be called to return an object whose value is matched against.	Yes	No
scope	Specifies the scope (application, page, request, or session) to look in for the object specified by the **name** attribute. If not specified, each scope will be searched, in this order: page, request, session, and then application.	Yes	No

Attribute	Description	Accepts JSP Expression	Required
value	Specifies the constant value that other attributes of this tag should contain, start with, or end with.	Yes	Yes

Example Usage

As mentioned, there are five ways you can use the **match** tag. The first way, shown here, uses the **cookie** attribute to specify the name of an HTTP cookie from the incoming request whose value is used to match the value specified with the **value** attribute:

```
<logic:match cookie="roles" value="Manager">
User is a Manager.
</logic:match>
```

If the cookie's value contains the value specified by the **value** attribute, the content between the starting and ending **match** tags will be processed. Otherwise, it will be ignored.

The second way to use the **match** tag is shown here:

```
<logic:match header="User-Agent" location="end" value="Windows NT 5.1)">
Browser is Windows-based.
</logic:match>
```

This example checks to see if the incoming request's User-Agent header ends with the value specified by the **value** attribute. If so, the content between the starting and ending **match** tags will be processed.

The third way to use the **match** tag is shown here:

```
<logic:match parameter="category" location="start" value="Cloth">
Category is Clothes.
</logic:match>
```

This example checks to see if the parameter from the incoming request starts with the value of the **value** attribute. If so, the content between the starting and ending **match** tags will be processed.

The following is the fourth way to use the **match** tag:

```
<logic:match name="lastName" location="start" value="H">
Last name starts with "H".
</logic:match>
```

This example checks to see if the value of the **lastName** object starts with the value of the **value** attribute. If so, the content between the starting and ending **match** tags will be processed. Remember that you can explicitly specify the scope of the **lastName** object with the **scope** attribute.

The fifth and final way to use the **match** tag is shown here:

```
<logic:match name="employee"
             property="lastName"
             location="start"
```

```
              value="H">
Last name starts with "H".
</logic:match>
```

In this example, the **name** and **property** attributes are used in tandem to specify the name of an object and its field whose getter method will be called to return an object whose value will be used to match that of the **value** attribute. Again, you can explicitly specify the scope of the object with the **scope** attribute.

The messagesNotPresent Tag

The **messagesNotPresent** tag is used to wrap content that is conditionally processed based on whether Struts' **org.apache.struts.action.ActionErrors** or **org.apache.struts.action.ActionMessages** objects do *not* have any errors or messages in them, respectively. Additionally, you can optionally specify a particular property to check for the presence of errors or messages with the **property** attribute.

Attributes

Attribute	Description	Accepts JSP Expression	Required
message	Accepts *true* or *false* to specify whether the presence of messages is checked for. If set to *false*, the presence of errors will be checked for. Note that if this attribute is set to *true*, the **name** attribute will be ignored. Defaults to *false*.	Yes	No
name	Specifies the key to use to look up an **org.apache.struts.action.ActionErrors** or **org.apache.struts.action.ActionMessages** object that will be checked for the presence of errors or messages, respectively.	Yes	No
property	Specifies the name of a particular property to check for the presence of errors or messages. If not specified, the presence of any messages or errors will be checked for.	Yes	No

Example Usage

The following example illustrates the basic usage of the **messagesNotPresent** tag:

```
<logic:messagesNotPresent>
No errors are present.
</logic:messagesNotPresent>
```

This example simply checks if no errors are present. The following example checks if no errors are present for a specific property named "username":

```
<logic:messagesNotPresent property="username">
No errors are present for username property.
</logic:messagesNotPresent>
```

PART III

The messagesPresent Tag

The **messagesPresent** tag is used to wrap content that is conditionally processed based on whether Struts' **org.apache.struts.action.ActionErrors** or **org.apache.struts.action.ActionMessages** object has any errors or messages in it, respectively. Additionally, you can optionally specify a particular property to check for the presence of errors or messages with the **property** attribute.

Attributes

Attribute	Description	Accepts JSP Expression	Required
message	Accepts *true* to *false* to specify whether the presence of messages is checked for. If set to *false*, the presence of errors will be checked for. Note that if this attribute it set to *true*, the **name** attribute will be ignored. Defaults to *false*.	Yes	No
name	Specifies the key to use to look up an **org.apache.struts.action.ActionErrors** or **org.apache.struts.action.ActionMessages** object that will be checked for the presence of errors or messages, respectively.	Yes	No
property	Specifies the name of a particular property to check for the presence of errors or messages. If not specified, the presence of any messages or errors will be checked for.	Yes	No

Example Usage

The following example illustrates the basic usage of the **messagesPresent** tag:

```
<logic:messagesPresent>
Errors are present.
</logic:messagesPresent>
```

This example simply checks if any errors are present. The following example checks if there are any errors present for a specific property named "username":

```
<logic:messagesPresent property="username">
Errors are present for username property.
</logic:messagesPresent>
```

The notEmpty Tag

The **notEmpty** tag is used to wrap content that is conditionally processed based on whether the specified object is non-**null** and does *not* contain an empty (zero-length) **String**. Additionally, if the object specified implements **java.util.Collection** or **java.util.Map**, this tag will call the object's **isEmpty( )** method to determine if the object is not empty. If the object is not empty, then the wrapped content will be processed.

Attributes

Attribute	Description	Accepts JSP Expression	Required
name	Specifies the name of an object to check as being not empty. If the **property** attribute is also specified, one of the fields of the object defined by this attribute will have its getter method called to return an object to check as being not empty.	Yes	No
property	Specifies the field of the object specified by the **name** attribute whose getter method will be called to return an object to check as being not empty.	Yes	No
scope	Specifies the scope (application, page, request, or session) to look in for the object specified by the **name** attribute. If not specified, each scope will be searched, in this order: page, request, session, and then application.	Yes	No

Example Usage

There are two ways you can use the **notEmpty** tag. The first way, shown here, uses the **name** attribute to specify the name of an object to check as being not empty:

```
<logic:notEmpty name="results">
Your search returned results!
</logic:notEmpty>
```

If the **results** object is non-**null**, does not contain a zero-length string, and does not contain a **Collection** or **Map** with zero elements, then the content between the starting and ending **empty** tags will be processed. Remember that you can explicitly specify the scope of the object with the **scope** attribute.

The second way to use the **notEmpty** tag is shown here:

```
<logic:notEmpty name="bizObj" property="results">
Your search returned results!
</logic:empty>
```

In this example, the **name** and **property** attributes are used in tandem to specify the name of an object and its field whose getter method will be called to return an object to check as being not empty. Again, you can explicitly specify the scope of the object with the **scope** attribute.

The notEqual Tag

The **notEqual** tag is used to wrap content that is conditionally processed based on whether a specified object's value is *not* equal to a specified constant value. This tag works for both numeric and string comparisons.

There are five ways you can use the **notEqual** tag, as listed here and shown later in the section "Example Usage":

- You can use the **cookie** attribute to specify the name of an HTTP cookie from the incoming request whose value will be used for the comparison.
- You can use the **header** attribute to specify the name of an HTTP header from the incoming request whose value will be used for the comparison.
- You can use the **parameter** attribute to specify the name of a parameter from the incoming request whose value will be used for the comparison.
- You can use the **name** attribute to specify the name of an object whose value will be used for the comparison. This object can be in any scope or limited to a specific scope with the **scope** attribute.
- You can use the **name** and **property** attributes in tandem to specify the name of an object and its field whose getter method will be called to return an object whose value will be used for the comparison. Again, the object specified by the **name** attribute can be in any scope or limited to a specific scope with the **scope** attribute.

Attributes

Attribute	Description	Accepts JSP Expression	Required
cookie	Specifies the name of the HTTP cookie from the incoming request whose value is used for comparison.	Yes	No
header	Specifies the name of the HTTP header from the incoming request whose value is used for comparison.	Yes	No
name	Specifies the name of an object whose value is used for comparison. If the **property** attribute is also specified, one of the fields of the object defined by this attribute will have its getter method called to return an object whose value is used for comparison.	Yes	No
parameter	Specifies the name of the parameter from the incoming request whose value is used for comparison.	Yes	No
property	Specifies the field of the object specified by the **name** attribute whose getter method will be called to return an object whose value is used for comparison.	Yes	No
scope	Specifies the scope (application, page, request, or session) to look in for the object specified by the **name** attribute. If not specified, each scope will be searched, in this order: page, request, session, and then application.	Yes	No
value	Specifies the constant value that will be compared.	Yes	Yes

Example Usage

As mentioned, there are five ways you can use the **notEqual** tag. The first way, shown here, uses the **cookie** attribute to specify the name of an HTTP cookie from the incoming request whose value is compared against the value specified with the **value** attribute:

```
<logic:notEqual cookie="role" value="Manager">
User is NOT a Manager.
</logic:notEqual>
```

If the cookie's value and the **value** attribute's value are not equal, the content between the starting and ending **notEqual** tags will be processed. Otherwise, it will be ignored.

The following is the second way to use the **notEqual** tag:

```
<logic:notEqual header="Content-Length" value="1000">
Content length is not 1,000.
</logic:notEqual>
```

This example compares the incoming request's Content-Length header against the **value** attribute to determine whether they are equal. If they are not equal, the content between the starting and ending **notEqual** tags will be processed.

The third way to use the **notEqual** tag is shown here:

```
<logic:notEqual parameter="catId" value="10">
Category Id is NOT 10.
</logic:notEqual>
```

This example compares a request parameter from the incoming request against the value of the **value** attribute. If the two values are not equal, the content between the starting and ending **notEqual** tags will be processed.

The following is the fourth way to use the **notEqual** tag:

```
<logic:notEqual name="resultCount" value="0">
Search returned results.
</logic:notEqual>
```

This example compares the value of the **resultCount** object against the value of the **value** attribute. If the two values are not equal, the content between the starting and ending **notEqual** tags will be processed. Remember that you can explicitly specify the scope of the **resultCount** object with the **scope** attribute.

The fifth and final way to use the **notEqual** tag is shown here:

```
<logic:notEqual name="employee" property="gender" value="male">
Employee is a female.
</logic:notEqual>
```

In this example, the **name** and **property** attributes are used in tandem to specify the name of an object and its field whose getter method will be called to return an object whose value will be compared against that of the **value** attribute. Again, you can explicitly specify the scope of the object with the **scope** attribute.

The notMatch Tag

The **notMatch** tag is used to wrap content that is conditionally processed based on whether a specified object's value does *not* contain, start with, or end with a specified constant value. This tag essentially provides a convenient interface to the **String** object's **indexOf( )**, **startsWith( )**, and **endsWith( )** methods. If the **location** attribute of this tag is not specified, an **indexOf( )** match will be performed to see if the specified object's value does not contain the value specified by the **value** attribute. If the **location** attribute is specified as "start", a **startsWith( )** match will be performed to see if the specified object's value does not start with the value specified by the **value** attribute. Finally, if the **location** attribute is specified as "end", an **endsWith( )** match will be performed to see if the specified object's value does not end with the value specified by the **value** attribute. Note that all of the matches are case sensitive.

There are five ways you can use the **notMatch** tag, as listed here and shown later in the section "Example Usage":

- You can use the **cookie** attribute to specify the name of an HTTP cookie from the incoming request whose value will be used to match against.
- You can use the **header** attribute to specify the name of an HTTP header from the incoming request whose value will be used to match against.
- You can use the **parameter** attribute to specify the name of a parameter from the incoming request whose value will be used to match against.
- You can use the **name** attribute to specify the name of an object whose value will be used to match against. This object can be in any scope or limited to a specific scope with the **scope** attribute.
- You can use the **name** and **property** attributes in tandem to specify the name of an object and its field whose getter method will be called to return an object whose value will be used to match against. Again, the object specified by the **name** attribute can be in any scope or limited to a specific scope with the **scope** attribute.

Attributes

Attribute	Description	Accepts JSP Expression	Required
cookie	Specifies the name of the HTTP cookie from the incoming request whose value is matched against.	Yes	No
header	Specifies the name of the HTTP header from the incoming request whose value is matched against.	Yes	No
location	Accepts *start* or *end* to specify where the match should occur. If not specified, the match can occur at any location.	Yes	No

Attribute	Description	Accepts JSP Expression	Required
name	Specifies the name of an object whose value is matched against. If the **property** attribute is also specified, one of the fields of the object defined by this attribute will have its getter method called to return an object whose value is matched against.	Yes	No
parameter	Specifies the name of the parameter from the incoming request whose value is matched against.	Yes	No
property	Specifies the field of the object specified by the **name** attribute whose getter method will be called to return an object whose value is matched against.	Yes	No
scope	Specifies the scope (application, page, request, or session) to look in for the object specified by the **name** attribute. If not specified, each scope will be searched, in this order: page, request, session, and then application.	Yes	No
value	Specifies the constant value that attributes of this tag should contain, start with, or end with.	Yes	Yes

Example Usage

As mentioned, there are five ways you can use the **notMatch** tag. The first way, shown here, uses the **cookie** attribute to specify the name of an HTTP cookie from the incoming request whose value is used to match the value specified with the **value** attribute:

```
<logic:notMatch cookie="roles" value="Manager">
User is not a Manager.
</logic:notMatch>
```

If the cookie's value does not contain the value specified by the **value** attribute, the content between the starting and ending **notMatch** tags will be processed. Otherwise, it will be ignored.

The second way to use the **notMatch** tag is shown here:

```
<logic:notMatch header="User-Agent" location="end" value=""Windows NT
5.1)">
Browser is not Windows XP-based.
</logic:notMatch>
```

This example checks to see if the incoming request's User-Agent header does not end with the value specified by the **value** attribute. If so, the content between the starting and ending **notMatch** tags will be processed.

The following is the third way to use the **notMatch** tag:

```
<logic:notMatch parameter="category" location="start" value="Cloth">
Category is not Clothes.
</logic:notMatch>
```

This example checks to see if the parameter from the incoming request does not start with the value of the **value** attribute. If so, the content between the starting and ending **notMatch** tags will be processed.

The following is the fourth way to use the **notMatch** tag:

```
<logic:notMatch name="lastName" location="start" value="H">
Last name does not start with "H".
</logic:notMatch>
```

This example checks to see if the value of the **lastName** object does not start with the value of the **value** attribute. If so, the content between the starting and ending **notMatch** tags will be processed. Remember that you can explicitly specify the scope of the **lastName** object with the **scope** attribute.

The fifth and final way to use the **notMatch** tag is shown here:

```
<logic:notMatch name="employee"
                property="lastName"
                location="start"
                value="H">
Last name starts with "H".
</logic:notMatch>
```

In this example, the **name** and **property** attributes are used in tandem to specify the name of an object and its field whose getter method will be called to return an object whose value will be used to match that of the **value** attribute. Again, you can explicitly specify the scope of the object with the **scope** attribute.

The notPresent Tag

The **notPresent** tag is used to wrap content that is conditionally processed based on whether a specified object does *not* exist. That is, this tag looks up the specified object, and if it is not found, the wrapped content will be processed. If the specified object is found, the content will be skipped.

In addition to the standard existence checks this tag offers, it provides a mechanism for interacting with the J2EE security system to determine if there is an authenticated user with a given name or role. For more information on security in Struts applications, refer to Chapter 19.

There are seven ways you can use the **notPresent** tag, as listed here and shown later in the section "Example Usage":

- You can use the **cookie** attribute to specify the name of an HTTP cookie from the incoming request whose existence will be checked for.
- You can use the **header** attribute to specify the name of an HTTP header from the incoming request whose existence will be checked for.

- You can use the **parameter** attribute to specify the name of a parameter from the incoming request whose existence will be checked for.
- You can use the **name** attribute to specify the name of an object whose existence will be checked for. This object can be in any scope or limited to a specific scope with the **scope** attribute.
- You can use the **name** and **property** attributes in tandem to specify the name of an object and one of its fields whose existence will be checked for. Again, the object specified by the **name** attribute can be in any scope or limited to a specific scope with the **scope** attribute.
- You can use the **role** attribute to specify a list of roles to check the currently authenticated user against. If the current user is in one of the roles, the existence check passes.
- You can use the **user** attribute to specify a name to compare against the currently authenticated user. If the name matches the user, the existence check passes.

Attributes

Attribute	Description	Accepts JSP Expression	Required
cookie	Specifies the name of the HTTP cookie from the incoming request whose existence is checked for.	Yes	No
header	Specifies the name of the HTTP header from the incoming request whose existence is checked for.	Yes	No
name	Specifies the name of an object whose existence is checked for. If the **property** attribute is also specified, one of the fields of the object defined by this attribute will have its existence checked for.	Yes	No
parameter	Specifies the name of the parameter from the incoming request whose existence is checked for.	Yes	No
property	Specifies the field of the object specified by the **name** attribute whose existence is checked for.	Yes	No
role	Specifies the list of roles to check the currently authenticated user against. Multiple roles are delimited by commas (i.e., "role1,role2,role3").	Yes	No
scope	Specifies the scope (application, page, request, or session) to look in for the object specified by the **name** attribute. If not specified, each scope will be searched, in this order: page, request, session, and then application.	Yes	No
user	Specifies a name to compare against the currently authenticated user.	Yes	No

Example Usage

As mentioned, there are seven ways you can use the **notPresent** tag. The first way, shown here, uses the **cookie** attribute to specify the name of an HTTP cookie from the incoming request whose existence is checked for:

```
<logic:notPresent cookie="role">
No role cookie exists.
</logic:notPresent>
```

If the incoming request does not have a cookie named "role" in it, the content between the starting and ending **notPresent** tags will be processed. Otherwise, it will be ignored.

The second way to use the **notPresent** tag is shown here:

```
<logic:notPresent header="Host">
Host header was not specified.
</logic:notPresent>
```

This example checks the incoming request for a header named "Host". If the header does not exist, the content between the starting and ending **notPresent** tags will be processed.

The following is the third way to use the **notPresent** tag:

```
<logic:notPresent parameter="catId">
Category Id was not specified.
</logic:notPresent>
```

This example checks the incoming request for a parameter name "catId". If the parameter does not exist, the content between the starting and ending **notPresent** tags will be processed.

The fourth way to use the **notPresent** tag is shown here:

```
<logic:notPresent name="results">
Results object exists.
</logic:notPresent>
```

This example looks up an object named "results" to see if it exists. If it does not, the content between the starting and ending **notPresent** tags will be processed. Remember that you can explicitly specify the scope of the **results** object with the **scope** attribute.

The following is the fifth way to use the **notPresent** tag:

```
<logic:notPresent name="employee" property="name">
Employee object does not have a name field.
</logic:notPresent>
```

In this example, the **name** and **property** attributes are used in tandem to specify the name of an object and one of its fields that is checked for existence. Again, you can explicitly specify the scope of the object with the **scope** attribute.

The following is the sixth way to use the **notPresent** tag:

```
<logic:notPresent role="manager">
James is not part of the manager group.
</logic:notPresent>
```

This example checks if the currently authenticated user is associated with the "manager" role. If not, the content between the starting and ending **notPresent** tags will be processed.

The seventh and final way to use the **notPresent** tag is shown here:

```
<logic:notPresent user="jholmes">
James Holmes is not currently logged in.
</logic:notPresent>
```

This example checks if there is currently an authenticated user and if that user's name is "jholmes." If not, the content between the starting and ending **notPresent** tags will be processed. Otherwise, the content will be skipped.

The present Tag

The **present** tag is used to wrap content that is conditionally processed based on whether a specified object exists. That is, this tag looks up the specified object, and if it is found (regardless of its value), the wrapped content will be processed. If the specified object is not found, the content will be skipped.

In addition to the standard existence checks this tag offers, it provides a mechanism for interacting with the J2EE security system to determine if there is an authenticated user with a given name or role. For more information on security in Struts applications, refer to Chapter 19.

There are seven ways you can use the **present** tag, as listed here and shown later in the section "Example Usage":

- You can use the **cookie** attribute to specify the name of an HTTP cookie from the incoming request whose existence will be checked for.
- You can use the **header** attribute to specify the name of an HTTP header from the incoming request whose existence will be checked for.
- You can use the **parameter** attribute to specify the name of a parameter from the incoming request whose existence will be checked for.
- You can use the **name** attribute to specify the name of an object whose existence will be checked for. This object can be in any scope or limited to a specific scope with the **scope** attribute.
- You can use the **name** and **property** attributes in tandem to specify the name of an object and one of its fields whose existence will be checked for. Again, the object specified by the **name** attribute can be in any scope or limited to a specific scope with the **scope** attribute.
- You can use the **role** attribute to specify a list of roles to check the currently authenticated user against. If the current user is in one of the roles, the existence check passes.
- You can use the **user** attribute to specify a name to compare against the currently authenticated user. If the name matches the user, the existence check passes.

Attributes

Attribute	Description	Accepts JSP Expression	Required
cookie	Specifies the name of the HTTP cookie from the incoming request whose existence is checked for.	Yes	No
header	Specifies the name of the HTTP header from the incoming request whose existence is checked for.	Yes	No
name	Specifies the name of an object whose existence is checked for. If the **property** attribute is also specified, one of the fields of the object defined by this attribute will have its existence checked for.	Yes	No
parameter	Specifies the name of the parameter from the incoming request whose existence is checked for.	Yes	No
property	Specifies the field of the object specified by the **name** attribute whose existence is checked for.	Yes	No
role	Specifies the list of roles to check the currently authenticated user against. Multiple roles are delimited by commas (i.e., "role1,role2,role3").	Yes	No
scope	Specifies the scope (application, page, request, or session) to look in for the object specified by the **name** attribute. If not specified, each scope will be searched, in this order: page, request, session, and then application.	Yes	No
user	Specifies a name to compare against the currently authenticated user.	Yes	No

Example Usage

As mentioned, there are seven ways you can use the **present** tag. The first way, shown here, uses the **cookie** attribute to specify the name of an HTTP cookie from the incoming request whose existence is checked for:

```
<logic:present cookie="role">
Role cookie exists.
</logic:present>
```

If the incoming request has a cookie named "role" in it, the content between the starting and ending **present** tags will be processed. Otherwise, it will be ignored.

The following is the second way to use the **present** tag:

```
<logic:present header="Host">
Host header was specified.
</logic:present>
```

This example checks the incoming request for a header named "Host". If the header exists, the content between the starting and ending **present** tags will be processed.

The third way to use the **present** tag is shown here:

```
<logic:present parameter="catId">
Category Id was specified.
</logic:present>
```

This example checks the incoming request for a parameter name "catId". If the parameter exists, the content between the starting and ending **present** tags will be processed.

The following is the fourth way to use the **present** tag:

```
<logic:present name="results">
Results object exists.
</logic:present>
```

This example looks up an object named "results" to see if it exists. If it does, the content between the starting and ending **present** tags will be processed. Remember that you can explicitly specify the scope of the **results** object with the **scope** attribute.

The fifth way to use the **present** tag is shown here:

```
<logic:present name="employee" property="name">
Employee object has a name field.
</logic:present>
```

In this example, the **name** and **property** attributes are used in tandem to specify the name of an object and one of its fields that is checked for existence. Again, you can explicitly specify the scope of the object with the **scope** attribute.

The sixth way to use the **present** tag is shown here:

```
<logic:present role="manager">
James is part of the manager group.
</logic:present>
```

This example checks if the currently authenticated user is associated with the "manager" role. If so, the content between the starting and ending **present** tags will be processed.

The seventh and final way to use the **present** tag is shown here:

```
<logic:present user="jholmes">
James Holmes is currently logged in.
</logic:present>
```

This example checks if there is currently an authenticated user and if that user's name is "jholmes." If so, the content between the starting and ending **present** tags will be processed. Otherwise, the content will be skipped.

The redirect Tag

The **redirect** tag is used to compose a URL to another page and then redirect to it. The URL is composed by specifying a base URL and optionally specifying an anchor and/or query string parameters to add to the URL.

There are four ways to specify the base URL:

- You can use the **action** attribute to specify the name of an action from the Struts configuration file whose URL will be used.
- You can use the **forward** attribute to specify the name of a forward from the Struts configuration file whose URL will be used.
- You can use the **href** attribute to specify an absolute URL, including protocol (e.g., http://www.yahoo.com/).
- You can use the **page** attribute to specify an application-relative URL.

In addition to specifying the base URL, you have two options for specifying query string parameters to add to the base URL:

- You can use the **paramId** attribute in conjunction with the **paramName** attribute, and optionally the **paramProperty** attribute, to specify a single parameter.
- You can use the **name** attribute, either alone or in tandem with the **property** attribute, to specify a **java.util.Map** object that will be used to add several parameters.

Attributes

Attribute	Description	Accepts JSP Expression	Required
action	Specifies the name of an action from the Action Mappings Configuration section of the Struts configuration file, which contains the URL that will be used as the base of the URL generated by this tag.	Yes	No
anchor	Specifies the anchor (e.g., "#bottom") to be added to the URL generated by this tag. This value should be specified without the leading hash (#) character.	Yes	No
forward	Specifies the name of a forward, from the Global Forwards Configuration section of the Struts configuration file, which contains the URL that will be used as the base of the URL generated by this tag.	Yes	No
href	Specifies the absolute URL (including protocol, such as http://) that will be used as the base of the URL generated by this tag.	Yes	No

Attribute	Description	Accepts JSP Expression	Required
name	Specifies the name of the **java.util.Map** object whose elements are added as query string parameters to the URL generated by this tag. If the **property** attribute is also specified, one of the fields of the object defined by this attribute will have its getter method called to return the **java.util.Map** object whose elements are added as query string parameters to the URL generated by this tag.	Yes	No
page	Specifies the application-relative URL (starts with a leading slash, /) that will be used as the base of the URL generated by this tag.	Yes	No
paramId	Specifies the name of a single parameter to add to the URL generated by this tag.	Yes	No
paramName	Specifies the name of an object whose value will be used as the value for the parameter specified with the **paramId** attribute. If the **property** attribute is also specified, one of the fields of the object defined by this attribute will have its getter method called to return an object whose value will be used as the value for the parameter specified with the **paramId** attribute.	Yes	No
paramProperty	Specifies the field of the object specified by the **name** attribute whose getter method will be called to return an object whose value will be used as the value for the parameter specified with the **paramId** attribute.	Yes	No
paramScope	Specifies the scope (application, page, request, or session) to look in for the object specified by the **paramName** attribute. If not specified, each scope will be searched, in this order: page, request, session, and then application.	Yes	No

Attribute	Description	Accepts JSP Expression	Required
property	Specifies the field of the object specified by the **name** attribute whose getter method will be called to return the **java.util.Map** object whose elements are added as query string parameters to the URL generated by this tag.	Yes	No
scope	Specifies the scope (application, page, request, or session) to look in for the object specified by the **name** attribute. If not specified, each scope will be searched, in this order: page, request, session, and then application.	Yes	No
transaction	Accepts *true* or *false* to specify whether the current transaction token will be included in the URL generated by this tag. Defaults to *false.*	Yes	No
useLocalEncoding	Accepts *true* or *false* to specify whether the character encoding of the URL parameters should be performed using the encoding type of the HTTP response object. If this attribute is set to *false,* the encoding type defaults to UTF-8. Defaults to *false.*	Yes	No

Example Usage

There are a few different ways to use the **redirect** tag. The first way, shown here, uses the **href** attribute to specify an absolute URL to redirect to:

```
<logic:redirect href="http://www.yahoo.com/"/>
```

Upon this tag's execution, an HTTP redirect response will be sent to the requesting browser. The browser will then request the specified URL.

The following example adds to the first example by specifying a single query string parameter to add to the base URL specified by the **href** attribute:

```
<logic:redirect href="http://www.yahoo.com/"
                paramId="query"
                paramName="queryObj"/>
```

This example takes the base URL specified by the **href** attribute and appends the query string parameter specified by the **paramId** and **paramName** attributes and composes a URL that the tag then redirects to.

Another way to use the **redirect** tag is shown here:

```
<logic:redirect page="/search.jsp" name="params"/>
```

This example uses the **page** attribute to specify an application-relative base URL and the **name** attribute to specify a **java.util.Map** object whose entries are added to the URL as query string parameters.

16

CHAPTER

The Nested Tag Library

In addition to Struts' core JSP tag libraries—Bean, HTML, and Logic—Struts provides an advanced tag library called Nested that can be used to enhance and simplify JSP development. The Nested Tag Library extends several tags from the Bean, HTML, and Logic Tag Libraries, giving them the ability to work in a nested context. The Nested Tag Library was initially created by Arron Bates as an extension to Struts to fill what he saw as a void in the way many of the tags worked in the existing libraries. As his library became popular, it was later integrated into the core Struts framework during the 1.1 release cycle.

Understanding Object Nesting in Struts

The best way to understand the importance of the Nested Tag Library is to begin by reviewing the way nested objects work without it. By default, each of the tags (hereafter referred to as the *base tags*) extended by the Nested Tag Library supports the notion of objects nested within other objects. That is, the base tags can access properties of one object nested inside another to any arbitrary level. For example, an **Employee** object might have a nested **Address** object, and the **Address** object may have several fields, such as **Line 1**, **Line 2**, **City**, **State**, and **Zip**. To access an **Employee** object named "employee" with a nested **Address** object named "address" whose **State** field is named "state" with the base Struts tags, you would specify the field as "employee.address.state", as shown in the following example:

```
<html:text property="employee.address.state"/>
```

Struts uses reflection to access the state field. Each level of the nested hierarchy is traversed by calling a getter method for that level's field; thus, in the preceding example, Struts uses reflection to call **getAddress( )** on the employee object and **getState( )** on the address object.

Although the default method of specifying nested references for fields is very useful and greatly simplifies JSP development, it can be problematic for two reasons:

- If an object in a nested hierarchy has its name changed, each nested reference has to be updated. For example, if an **Employee** object had a nested **Address** object named "address" that later becomes "homeAddress", every nested reference that refers to fields in the **Address** object has to be updated to access the fields as "employee .homeAddress.state" instead of "employee.address.state". This is not a huge problem, but it is both time-consuming and error-prone.

- When you are working with a nested object that has several fields, you have to type out the entire nested hierarchy for each field over and over. For example, you have to type "employee.address.line1", "employee.address.line2", "employee.address .city", and so on. Again, this is not a major problem, but it is tedious and is a potential source of errors.

Fortunately, the Nested Tag Library eliminates both problems associated with the default approach to nested tags. The Nested Tag Library allows you to define logical nesting levels and then associate objects with them so that all tags nested inside a level are relative to that level. Therefore, instead of fully qualifying a nested reference within each level of the object hierarchy, you can use the Nested Tag Library's **nest** tag to define each level of the hierarchy. Within each level, you specify the property that you're interested in along with any other tags you need. Here is an example:

```
<nested:nest property="employee">
  <nested:nest property="address">
    Line 1: <nested:text property="line1"/>
    Line 2: <nested:text property="line2"/>
    City: <nested:text property="city"/>
    State: <nested:text property="state"/>
    Zip: <nested:text property="zip"/>
  </nested:nest>
</nested:nest>
```

Notice that the Nested Tag Library's **text** tag was used instead of the HTML Tag Library's **text** tag. The reason is that the base tags are not designed to work with the Nested Tag Library's nesting features. Instead, you must use the Nested Tag Library's extensions to the base tags.

To best understand the benefits of the Nested Tag Library, here is the same example coded without use of the Nested Tag Library:

```
Line 1: <html:text property="employee.address.line1"/>
Line 2: <html:text property="employee.address.line2"/>
City: <html:text property="employee.address.city"/>
State: <html:text property="employee.address.state"/>
Zip: <html:text property="employee.address.zip"/>
```

As you can see, specifying nested properties without the Nested Tag Library results in more verbose JSP code, which increases the chance for error and the potential for a great deal of maintenance work should the nesting hierarchy change.

Using the Nested Tag Library

To use the Nested Tag Library in a Struts application, your application's JSPs must declare their use of the library with a JSP **taglib** directive:

```
<%@ taglib uri="http://struts.apache.org/tags-nested" prefix="nested" %>
```

Notice that the **prefix** attribute is set to "nested." This attribute can be set to whatever you want; however, "nested" is the accepted default for the Nested Tag Library. The **prefix** attribute declares the prefix that each tag must have when it is used in the JSP, as shown here:

```
<nested:nest property="results">
```

Because "nested" was defined as the prefix, the **nest** tag was used as shown. However, if you choose to use a prefix of "strutsnest", the tag would be used as follows:

```
<strutsnest:nest property="results">
```

NOTE *Modern application servers use the* **uri** *attribute of the* **taglib** *directive to automatically resolve the location of the tag library descriptor file. Older application servers that support only JSP version 1.1 and/or version 1.0 require that tag libraries be registered in the* **web.xml** *file so that they can be resolved, as shown here:*

```
<taglib>
  <taglib-uri>http://struts.apache.org/tags-nested</taglib-uri>
  <taglib-location>/WEB-INF/tlds/struts-nested.tld</taglib-location>
</taglib>
```

PART III

The Nested Tag Library Tags

The following table lists each of the tags in the Nested Tag Library and provides a short description of each tag's purpose.

Tag	Description
checkbox	Nesting-enabled version of the HTML Tag Library's **checkbox** tag.
define	Nesting-enabled version of the Bean Tag Library's **define** tag.
empty	Nesting-enabled version of the Logic Tag Library's **empty** tag.
equal	Nesting-enabled version of the Logic Tag Library's **equal** tag.
errors	Nesting-enabled version of the HTML Tag Library's **errors** tag.
file	Nesting-enabled version of the HTML Tag Library's **file** tag.
form	Nesting-enabled version of the HTML Tag Library's **form** tag.
greaterEqual	Nesting-enabled version of the Logic Tag Library's **greaterEqual** tag.
greaterThan	Nesting-enabled version of the Logic Tag Library's **greaterThan** tag.
hidden	Nesting-enabled version of the HTML Tag Library's **hidden** tag.
image	Nesting-enabled version of the HTML Tag Library's **image** tag.
img	Nesting-enabled version of the HTML Tag Library's **img** tag.
iterate	Nesting-enabled version of the Logic Tag Library's **iterate** tag.

Tag	Description
lessEqual	Nesting-enabled version of the Logic Tag Library's **lessEqual** tag.
lessThan	Nesting-enabled version of the Logic Tag Library's **lessThan** tag.
link	Nesting-enabled version of the HTML Tag Library's **link** tag.
match	Nesting-enabled version of the Logic Tag Library's **match** tag.
message	Nesting-enabled version of the Bean Tag Library's **message** tag.
messages	Nesting-enabled version of the HTML Tag Library's **messages** tag.
messagesNotPresent	Nesting-enabled version of the Logic Tag Library's **messagesNotPresent** tag.
messagesPresent	Nesting-enabled version of the Logic Tag Library's **messagesPresent** tag.
multibox	Nesting-enabled version of the HTML Tag Library's **multibox** tag.
nest	Defines a logical level in a nesting hierarchy and associates an object with it that all of its nested tags will be relative to.
notEmpty	Nesting-enabled version of the Logic Tag Library's **notEmpty** tag.
notEqual	Nesting-enabled version of the Logic Tag Library's **notEqual** tag.
notMatch	Nesting-enabled version of the Logic Tag Library's **notMatch** tag.
notPresent	Nesting-enabled version of the Logic Tag Library's **notPresent** tag.
options	Nesting-enabled version of the HTML Tag Library's **options** tag.
optionsCollection	Nesting-enabled version of the HTML Tag Library's **optionsCollection** tag.
password	Nesting-enabled version of the HTML Tag Library's **password** tag.
present	Nesting-enabled version of the Logic Tag Library's **present** tag.
radio	Nesting-enabled version of the HTML Tag Library's **radio** tag.
root	Defines the root object of a nested hierarchy of objects.
select	Nesting-enabled version of the HTML Tag Library's **select** tag.
size	Nesting-enabled version of the Bean Tag Library's **size** tag.
submit	Nesting-enabled version of the HTML Tag Library's **submit** tag.
text	Nesting-enabled version of the HTML Tag Library's **text** tag.
textarea	Nesting-enabled version of the HTML Tag Library's **textarea** tag.
write	Nesting-enabled version of the Bean Tag Library's **write** tag.
writeNesting	Renders or creates a JSP scripting variable for a string representation of the object related to the current nesting level.

As mentioned, the majority of the tags in the Nested Tag Library are simply tags from the Bean, HTML, and Logic Tag Libraries to which support for nesting has been added. Thus, they are not individually covered in detail here. Instead, the basic concepts of nesting are discussed because they apply to all the extended tags in the same way. For nonnesting-related information on each of the extended tags, see the descriptions of their base tags in their respective chapters.

The remainder of this section discusses in detail each of the tags that are specific to the Nesting Tag Library, including a complete description of the tag, a table listing each of the tag's attributes, and a usage example for the tag. In the tables that describe each tag's attributes, pay special attention to the Required and Accepts JSP Expression columns.

The Required column simply denotes whether the given attribute is required when using the tag. In addition to the required column denoting whether an attribute is required, the rows for required attributes are highlighted in gray so that you can determine at a glance which attributes are required.

If an attribute is required and you do not specify it when using the tag, the tag will throw a **javax.servlet.jsp.JspException** at run time. Note that you can declare an error page in your JSP with a **page** directive to capture any **JspException**s that might be thrown, as shown here:

```
<%@ page errorPage="error.jsp" %>
```

If an exception occurs, the page specified by the **errorPage** attribute will be internally redirected to display an error page.

The Accepts JSP Expression column denotes whether the given attribute's value can be specified with a JSP expression. If a JSP expression is used to specify an attribute value, the expression must comprise the complete value, quote (") to quote ("), as shown here.
Correct:

```
<nested:nest property="<%=result%>">
```

Incorrect:

```
<nested:nest property="<%=result%>-result">
```

Notice in the incorrect example that "-result" is used as part of the value for the **property** attribute following the expression. This is invalid because there are extra characters between the end of the expression and the ending quote.

A corrected version of the incorrect example follows:

```
<nested:nest property="<%=result + "-result"%>"/>
```

The concatenation of "-result" is now part of the expression, and the expression comprises the complete value for the attribute.

The nest Tag

The **nest** tag is used to define a logical level in a nesting hierarchy and associate an object with it that all of its nested tags are relative to.

Attribute

Attribute	Description	Accepts JSP Expression	Required
property	Specifies the name of the object (in any scope) to associate with this logical nesting level.	Yes	No

Example Usage

The following example illustrates how to use the **nest** tag:

```
<nested:nest property="address">
  Line 1: <nested:text property="line1"/>
  Line 2: <nested:text property="line2"/>
  City: <nested:text property="city"/>
  State: <nested:text property="state"/>
  Zip: <nested:text property="zip"/>
</nested:nest>
```

Because the **nest** tag specifies the object that all of its nested tags are relative to, the nested tags only have to specify properties of the nested object.

The equivalent without the Nested Tag Library is shown here:

```
Line 1: <html:text property="address.line1"/>
Line 2: <html:text property="address.line2"/>
City: <html:text property="address.city"/>
State: <html:text property="address.state"/>
Zip: <html:text property="address.zip"/>
```

As you can see, nesting simplifies JSP development for even this short example; however, the real benefit comes when you have several layers of nesting to handle.

The root Tag

The **root** tag is used to define the root object of a nested hierarchy of objects. Typically, tags from this tag library and the HTML Tag Library are nested inside the HTML Tag Library's **form** tag and use the form's Form Bean object as the root of the nested hierarchy. However, the **root** tag can be used to explicitly set the hierarchy's root object, effectively overriding the Form Bean object.

Attribute

Attribute	Description	Accepts JSP Expression	Required
name	Specifies the name of an object (in any scope) to set as the root of a nested hierarchy.	Yes	No

Example Usage

The following example illustrates how to use the **root** tag:

```
<nested:root name="employee">
  <nested:nest property="address">
    Line 1: <nested:text property="line1"/>
    Line 2: <nested:text property="line2"/>
    City: <nested:text property="city"/>
    State: <nested:text property="state"/>
    Zip: <nested:text property="zip"/>
  </nested:nest>
</nested:root>
```

All tags nested inside the **root** tag will use its associated object as the root object for a nested hierarchy. Thus, in the example, the nested **text** tags will actually be accessing "employee.address.line1" even though they only specify "line1".

The writeNesting Tag

The **writeNesting** tag is used to render or create a JSP scripting variable for a string representation of the object related to the current nesting level.

Attributes

Attribute	Description	Accepts JSP Expression	Required
filter	Accepts *true* or *false* to specify whether HTML-sensitive characters should be converted to their entity equivalents. For example, if this attribute is enabled, the less-than sign (<) would get converted to < before it is rendered. Defaults to *true.*	Yes	No
id	Specifies the name of the JSP variable that will hold a reference to the object related to the current nesting level.	Yes	No
property	Specifies the name of a property of the current nesting level's object.	Yes	No

Example Usage

The following snippet shows the basic usage of the **writeNesting** tag:

```
<nested:nest property="address">
  Line 1: <nested:writeNesting property="line1"/>
</nested:nest>
```

This example will generate the following output:

```
Line 1: address.line1
```

Essentially, this tag generates the fully qualified nested reference for the given property.

17

CHAPTER

Using JSTL with Struts

A key advantage of working with Struts is its support for the View layer of MVC applications. At the foundation of this support is its JSP tag libraries. As you've seen in the previous four chapters, the tag libraries greatly simplify JSP development and reduce the need to use JSP scriptlets. At the time of their creation, the Struts tag libraries filled a void in JSP functionality. They provided a simple and convenient interface for getting and setting data on Java beans, implementing simple conditional logic, and accessing Web application attributes. Although an important part of Struts, today large portions of the Struts tag libraries have been superseded by the JSP Standard Tag Library (JSTL). Here's why.

Like Struts, many other frameworks and development teams implemented a set of tag libraries to accomplish basic Java bean manipulation and conditional logic functionality inside JSPs. Although several of those implementations are quite similar, each is a little different in the scope of what it can do and each uses different names for its tags and attributes. Because of the duplication of effort across multiple projects, the need arose for a common, standardized set of tag libraries that could be used universally. Having a standardized set of tags would eliminate the need to learn the details of several different tag libraries as well as curtail the duplication of effort across projects. To meet this need, the JSP Standard Tag Library was created. JSTL is an extension to JSP technology that provides a set of standardized tag libraries and a simple expression language (EL) for accessing objects in JSPs.

Because JSTL offers a standardized set of tags, it is now the preferred approach for JSP development with Struts. Thus, applications should use the JSTL tag libraries and expression language instead of the Struts tags wherever possible. This chapter provides a brief introduction to JSTL, a list of the Struts tags that can be replaced by JSTL, and information on the Struts EL tag libraries that support the JSTL expression language.

JSTL Overview

JSTL can be broken into two functional areas: a set of tag libraries and an expression language. The tag libraries provide a set of tags that implement general-purpose functionality for iteration and conditional processing, data formatting and localization, XML manipulation, and database access. The expression language simplifies access to Java language constructs within JSPs. Together, the two make up a powerful set of functionality for developing applications with JSPs.

JSTL arose out of the Java Community Process (JCP) and thus had the input and forethought of many high-profile organizations and influential individuals in the industry. In June 2000, the first JSTL specification was finalized and targeted to work with the JSP 1.2 and Servlet 2.3 specifications. Since then, a maintenance release (JSTL 1.1) became available in January 2004. With JSP 1.2, JSTL expressions can only be used as an attribute value with Tag Library tags that support them. However, with JSP 2.0 expressions are supported throughout JSPs. This means that the expressions are usable anywhere inside the JSP and are not limited to just JSTL-enabled tags as they are with JSP 1.2.

You can download JSTL from Sun's Web site at **http://java.sun.com/products/jsp/jstl/**.

The JSTL Expression Language

JSTL's greatest strength lies in its expression language. The expression language simplifies access to Java language constructs from within JSPs and provides the foundation for the JSTL tag libraries' usefulness. With the expression language, you create simple expressions that return a value. For example, one expression might retrieve the value of a request parameter. Another might evaluate a conditional expression that returns a **boolean** result. This latter use is extremely helpful when conditionally processing portions of a JSP.

JSTL expressions are surrounded by an opening **${** and a closing **}**, as shown in the following snippet:

```
<c:out value="${userObj}"/>
```

Everything between the opening **${** and closing **}** constitutes the expression. Expressions can contain references to JSP page-scoped objects and implicit objects and can use operators to traverse the objects and manipulate them. The following sections describe the details of the expression language.

Accessing Objects

The JSTL expression language provides a simple mechanism for accessing objects and their properties. The dot (**.**) operator is used to traverse object hierarchies and access properties. The following snippet illustrates a basic example of the dot operator's usage:

```
<c:out value="${customer.address.city}"/>
```

In this example, the dot operator is used to access the **customer** object's **address** property and then the **address** object's **city** property. Each instance of the dot operator in the expression evaluates to a getter method call for the property on the left of the operator. Thus, the first dot will call a **getAddress( )** method on the **customer** object. The second dot will then call a **getCity( )** method on the object returned from the **getAddress( )** call. In order for the dot operator to work, the object on the right of the operator must have a getter method for the property on the left of the operator. Otherwise, the operator will fail.

As you can see, this method of traversing object hierarchies is quick and simple. Without JSTL, you'd have to use a JSP expression similar to the following to access properties down a hierarchy:

```
<%= customer.getAddress().getCity() %>
```

The dot operator is great for accessing simple properties; however, it doesn't allow you to access elements of arrays or collections. For that, JSTL has the brackets (**[ ]**) operator. The brackets operator allows you to specify the index of an element you want to access, as shown next:

```
<c:set var="highBid" value="${bids[0]}"/>
```

This approach works for arrays and list-based collections. For map-based collections, you specify the key for the element you want to access, as shown next:

```
<c:set var="color" value="${param['color']}"/>
```

Implicit Objects

JSTL makes several objects available to the expression language as *implicit objects.* The implicit objects are built in and can be used by any expression without having to be initialized or otherwise set up. They are available by default. Utilizing an implicit object is as simple as referencing its name in an expression, as shown here:

```
<c:out value="${header['User-Agent']}"/>
```

In this example, the Core Tag Library's **out** tag is used to output the value of the "User-Agent" HTTP header. The **header** implicit object is a **java.util.Map** instance containing the incoming request's HTTP headers.

The following table lists and describes each of the JSTL implicit objects.

Category	Implicit Object	Description
Cookies	cookie	A **java.util.Map** instance containing the current request's cookies.
Initialization parameters	initParam	A **java.util.Map** instance containing the Web application's context initialization parameters specified in **web.xml**.
JSP	pageContext	A **javax.servlet.jsp.PageContext** instance for the current page.
Request headers	header	A **java.util.Map** instance containing the primary values for the current request's HTTP headers.
	headerValues	A **java.util.Map** instance containing all the values for the current request's HTTP headers.
Request parameters	param	A **java.util.Map** instance containing the primary values for the current request's parameters.
	paramValues	A **java.util.Map** instance containing all the values for the current request's parameters.
Scopes	applicationScope	A **java.util.Map** instance containing application-scoped attributes.
	pageScope	A **java.util.Map** instance containing page-scoped attributes.
	requestScope	A **java.util.Map** instance containing request-scoped attributes.
	sessionScope	A **java.util.Map** instance containing session-scoped attributes.

Using Operators

The JSTL expression language supports several operators for comparing and manipulating data in expressions. When expressions contain operators, the operators are applied to the operands and the resulting value is used as the expression's value. Take for example the following snippet:

```
<c:set var="sqrFt" value="${width * length}"/>
```

This example uses the asterisk (*) multiplication operator to multiply a **width** variable times a **length** variable and stores the result in a JSP scripting variable.

Operators can also be combined to create complex expressions, as shown next:

```
<c:set var="halfSqrFt" value="${(width * length) / 2}"/>
```

Here, **width** and **length** are multiplied and then divided and the resulting value is stored.

Logical and relational operators work the same; however, their results are often used with conditional tags, as shown here:

```
<c:if test="${count == 5}">
Count equals 5.
</c:if>
```

This example compares the value of the **count** object to 5 to see if they match. If they do, the text enclosed between the opening and closing **if** tags is processed. Otherwise, it is skipped.

The following table lists each of the JSTL expression language operators.

<table>
<tr><th>Category</th><th>Operators</th></tr>
<tr><td>Arithmetic</td><td>+, –, *, / (or div), % (or mod)</td></tr>
<tr><td>Logical</td><td>&& (or and), || (or or), ! (or not)</td></tr>
<tr><td>Relational</td><td><b>==</b> (or <b>eq</b>), <b>!=</b> (or <b>ne</b>), <b><</b> (or <b>lt</b>), <b>></b> (or <b>gt</b>), <b><=</b> (or <b>le</b>), <b>>=</b> (or <b>ge</b>)</td></tr>
<tr><td>Validation</td><td>empty</td></tr>
</table>

As mentioned, multiple operators can be used together in a single expression. The following lists the order of precedence of operators:

- []
- ( )
- unary –, not, !, empty
- *, /, div, %, mod
- +, binary –
- <, >, <=, >=, lt, gt, le, ge
- ==, !=, eq, ne
- &&, and
- ||, or

The JSTL Tag Libraries

JSTL's tag libraries provide a common thread for JSP applications to be sewn from, offering the base functionality needed by most applications. The JSTL tag libraries work like any other JSP tag libraries with the added functionality of supporting JSTL expressions for tag attribute values. The following table lists each of the JSTL tag libraries. The following sections describe the tags in each library.

Library	Taglib Prefix	Description
Core	c	Provides tags for conditional logic, loops, output, variable creation, text imports, and URL manipulation.
Format	fmt	Provides tags for formatting dates and numbers and for localizing text messages.
SQL	sql	Provides tags for making SQL queries to databases.
XML	x	Provides tags for parsing of XML documents, selection of XML fragments, flow control based on XML, and XSLT transformations.

The Core Tag Library Tags

The following table lists each of the tags in the Core Tag Library and provides a short description of each tag's purpose.

Tag	Description
catch	Catches and optionally exposes any exception (i.e., anything derived from **java.lang.Throwable**) that may be thrown from nested instances of other tags in this library.
choose	Establishes a context for mutually exclusive conditional operations, marked by nested **when** and **otherwise** tags.
forEach	Iterates over each element in a collection.
forTokens	Iterates over tokens, separated by the supplied delimiters.
if	Evaluates its body if the supplied condition is true and optionally exposes a **java.lang.Boolean** scripting variable representing the evaluation of this condition.
import	Retrieves an absolute or relative URL and exposes its contents to the page, a **String** specified by its **var** attribute, or a **Reader** specified by its **varReader** attribute.
out	Outputs JSTL expressions. Equivalent to JSP's **<%= ... >** for JSTL expressions.
otherwise	Subtag of **choose** that follows **when** tags and runs only if all of the prior conditions evaluate to false.
param	Adds a parameter to a containing **import** tag's URL.
redirect	Redirects to a new URL.
remove	Removes a scoped variable (from a particular scope, if specified).
set	Sets the result of an expression evaluation in a scope.

PART III

Tag	Description
url	Creates a URL with optional query parameters.
when	Subtag of **choose** that includes its body if its condition evaluates to true.

The Format Tag Library Tags

The following table lists each of the tags in the Format Tag Library and provides a short description of each tag's purpose.

Tag	Description
bundle	Loads a resource bundle to be used by nested instances of other tags in this library.
formatDate	Formats a date and/or time using the supplied styles and pattern.
formatNumber	Formats a numeric value as a number, currency, or percentage.
message	Specifies a localized message from the current bundle and performs parametric replacement on it and then outputs it.
param	Supplies an argument for parametric replacement to a containing **message** tag.
parseDate	Parses the string representation of a date and/or time.
parseNumber	Parses the string representation of a number, currency, or percentage.
requestEncoding	Sets the request character encoding.
setBundle	Loads a resource bundle and stores it in the named scoped variable or the bundle configuration variable.
setLocale	Stores the given locale in the locale configuration variable.
setTimeZone	Stores the given time zone in the time zone configuration variable.
timeZone	Specifies the time zone for any time formatting or parsing tags nested in its body.

The SQL Tag Library Tags

The following table lists each of the tags in the SQL Tag Library and provides a short description of each tag's purpose.

Tag	Description
dateParam	Sets a parameter in an SQL statement to the specified **java.util.Date** value.
param	Sets a parameter in an SQL statement to the specified value.
query	Executes the SQL query defined in its body or through its **sql** attribute.
setDataSource	Specifies a JDBC data source for which nested instances of other tags in this library will use when to execute SQL statements.
transaction	Provides nested instances of other tags in this library with a shared connection, set up to execute all statements as one transaction.
update	Executes the SQL update defined in its body or through its **sql** attribute.

The XML Tag Library Tags

The following table lists each of the tags in the XML Tag Library and provides a short description of each tag's purpose.

Tag	Description
choose	Establishes a context for mutually exclusive conditional operations, marked by **when** and **otherwise**.
forEach	Iterates over a collection of XML tags.
if	Evaluates its body if the supplied XPath expression evaluates to true.
otherwise	Subtag of **choose** that follows **when** tags and runs only if all of the prior conditions evaluated to false.
out	Outputs XPath (XML Path) expressions. Equivalent to JSP's **<%= ... >** for XPath expressions. XPath is a set of syntax rules for defining parts of an XML document.
param	Adds a parameter to a containing **transform** tag.
parse	Parses XML content from a specified **source** attribute or from body content.
set	Saves the result of an XPath expression evaluation in a scope.
transform	Conducts a transformation given a source XML document and an XSLT stylesheet.
when	Subtag of **choose** that includes its body if its expression evaluates to true.

Using JSTL with Struts

Using JSTL with Struts is as simple as adding the JSTL **.jar** files (**jstl.jar** and **standard.jar**) to your Web application's library directory (**/WEB-INF/lib**) and then referencing the Tag Library Descriptors (**.tld**s) from your JSPs. There are two ways that you can reference JSTL **.tld**s in your JSPs. First, you can use an absolute URI, as shown next:

```
<%@ taglib prefix="c" uri="http://java.sun.com/jstl/core" %>
```

Second, you can make an entry in the **web.xml** file and then the URI assigned in the **web.xml** file is used by JSPs. This approach is not necessary or recommended; however, if you choose to take this route, you must copy the JSTL **.tld** files into your Web application's **WEB-INF** directory so that you can reference them.

The following table lists the absolute URI for each of the libraries, should you choose to reference the **.tld**s in that way.

Library	Prefix	URL
Core	c	http://java.sun.com/jstl/core
Format	fmt	http://java.sun.com/jstl/fmt
XML	x	http://java.sun.com/jstl/xml

Struts EL

As previously mentioned, with the advent of JSTL, the Struts tag library tags should now be used only when there is not a JSTL equivalent tag to replace them. This ensures that JSPs are as portable as possible and shields your application from being too heavily tied to Struts-specific facilities. The following table lists each of the Struts tag library tags that can be replaced by JSTL tags and their corresponding replacements.

Struts Tag Library	Tag	JSTL Replacement
Bean	cookie	c:set
Bean	define	c:set
Bean	header	c:set
Bean	include	c:import
Bean	parameter	c:set
Bean	write	c:out
Logic	empty	c:if, c:when
Logic	equal	c:if, c:when
Logic	greaterEqual	c:if, c:when
Logic	greaterThan	c:if, c:when
Logic	iterate	c:forEach
Logic	lessEqual	c:if, c:when
Logic	lessThan	c:if, c:when
Logic	notEmpty	c:if, c:when
Logic	notEqual	c:if, c:when

As you can see, JSTL can be used in lieu of many of the Struts tag library tags. However, you may have noticed that none of the tags from the Struts HTML Tag Library has an equivalent JSTL tag. JSTL does not have a tag library for rendering HTML form elements, thus the absence of Struts tag replacements. For the HTML tags and all the tags in the Bean and Logic tag libraries that do not have JSTL replacements, a project called Struts EL was created. Struts EL was created by David Karr and is distributed with Struts.

The Struts EL project is an extension to Struts that provides a JSTL expression language–enabled version of each Struts tag for which no JSTL replacement exists. Most of the base Struts tag library tags' attributes accept values represented as JSP expressions. This allows the tags to have dynamic attribute values. For example, the Bean Tag Library's **message** tag accepts expressions for its **key** attribute, as shown here:

```
<bean:message key="<%=messageKey%>"/>
```

This example uses the value of the **messageKey** JSP scripting variable as the value for the **message** tag's **key** attribute. Notice that the JSP scripting variable had to be specified within the JSP expression identifiers **<%=** and **%>**.

The following example shows the Struts EL equivalent of the previous example using a JSTL expression to specify a dynamic value for the **key** attribute:

```
<bean:message key="${messageKey}"/>
```

As you can see, the JSTL expression syntax is a little shorter and is cleaner looking.

As mentioned, the basic concepts of using JSTL expressions apply to all the Struts EL tags in the same way. Any tag attribute that accepts a JSP expression with the base tags will accept a JSTL expression with the Struts EL tags.

JSTL Replacement Examples

The following sections provide examples for replacing Struts tag library tags with their JSTL equivalents. Remember that not all the Bean, HTML, and Logic tags can be replaced by JSTL tags.

bean:cookie Replacement Example

The following snippet shows the basic usage of the **cookie** tag from the Bean Tag Library:

```
<bean:cookie id="category" name="cat"/>
```

The JSTL equivalent is as follows:

```
<c:set var="category" value="${cookie['cat'].value}"/>
```

This example accesses the **cat** cookie with a JSTL expression that makes use of the JSTL implicit **cookie** object.

bean:define Replacement Example

The following snippet shows the basic usage of the **define** tag from the Bean Tag Library:

```
<bean:define id="name" name="nameObj"/>
```

The JSTL equivalent is as follows:

```
<c:set var="name" value="${nameObj}"/>
```

bean:header Replacement Example

The following snippet shows the basic usage of the **header** tag from the Bean Tag Library:

```
<bean:header id="browser" name="User-Agent"/>
```

The JSTL equivalent is as follows:

```
<c:set var="browser" value="${header['User-Agent']}"/>
```

This example accesses the "User-Agent" header with a JSTL expression that makes use of the JSTL implicit **header** object.

bean:include Replacement Example

The following snippet shows the basic usage of the **include** tag from the Bean Tag Library:

```
<bean:include id="yahooContents" href="http://www.yahoo.com/"/>
```

The JSTL equivalent is as follows:

```
<c:import var="yahooContents" url=" http://www.yahoo.com/"/>
```

bean:parameter Replacement Example

The following snippet shows the basic usage of the **parameter** tag from the Bean Tag Library:

```
<bean:parameter id="color" name="clr"/>
```

The JSTL equivalent is as follows:

```
<c:set var="color" value="${param['clr']}"/>
```

This example accesses the **clr** parameter with a JSTL expression that makes use of the JSTL implicit **param** object.

bean:write Replacement Example

The following snippet shows the basic usage of the **write** tag from the Bean Tag Library:

```
<bean:write name="bizObj"/>
```

The JSTL equivalent is as follows:

```
<c:out value="${bizObj}" />
```

logic:empty Replacement Example

The following snippet shows the basic usage of the **empty** tag from the Logic Tag Library:

```
<logic:empty name="results">
Your search yielded no results.
</logic:empty>
```

The JSTL equivalent is as follows:

```
<c:if test="${empty results}">
Your search yielded no results.
</c:if>
```

logic:equal Replacement Example

The following snippet shows the basic usage of the **equal** tag from the Logic Tag Library:

```
<logic:equal name="count" value="0">
Count is zero.
</logic:equal>
```

The JSTL equivalent is as follows:

```
<c:if test="${count == 0}">
Count is zero.
</c:if>
```

bean:greaterEqual Replacement Example

The following snippet shows the basic usage of the **greaterEqual** tag from the Logic Tag Library:

```
<logic:greaterEqual name="count" value="5">
Count is greater than or equal to five.
</logic:greaterEqual>
```

The JSTL equivalent is as follows:

```
<c:if test="${count >= 5}">
Count is greater than or equal to five.
</c:if>
```

logic:greaterThan Replacement Example

The following snippet shows the basic usage of the **greaterThan** tag from the Logic Tag Library:

```
<logic:greaterThan name="count" value="5">
Count is greater than five.
</logic:greaterThan>
```

The JSTL equivalent is as follows:

```
<c:if test="${count > 5}">
Count is greater than five.
</c:if>
```

logic:iterate Replacement Example

The following snippet shows the basic usage of the **iterate** tag from the Logic Tag Library:

```
<logic:iterate id="result" collection="<%=results%>">
Result: <%=result%><br>
</logic:iterate>
```

The JSTL equivalent is as follows:

```
<c:forEach var="result" items="${results}">
Result: <c:out value="${result}"/>
</c:forEach>
```

logic:lessEqual Replacement Example

The following snippet shows the basic usage of the **lessEqual** tag from the Logic Tag Library:

```
<logic:lessEqual name="count" value="5">
Count is less than or equal to five.
</logic:lessEqual>
```

The JSTL equivalent is as follows:

```
<c:if test="${count <= 5}">
```

```
Count is less than or equal to five.
</c:if>
```

logic:lessThan Replacement Example

The following snippet shows the basic usage of the **lessThan** tag from the Logic Tag Library:

```
<logic:lessThan name="count" value="5">
Count is less than five.
</logic:lessThan>
```

The JSTL equivalent is as follows:

```
<c:if test="${count < 5}">
Count is less than five.
</c:if>
```

logic:notEmpty Replacement Example

The following snippet shows the basic usage of the **notEmpty** tag from the Logic Tag Library:

```
<logic:notEmpty name="results">
Your search returned results!
</logic:notEmpty>
```

The JSTL equivalent is as follows:

```
<c:if test="${!empty results}">
Your search returned results!
</c:if>
```

logic:notEqual Replacement Example

The following snippet shows the basic usage of the **notEqual** tag from the Logic Tag Library:

```
<logic:notEqual name="count" value="0">
Count is not equal to zero.
</logic:notEqual>
```

The JSTL equivalent is as follows:

```
<c:if test="${count != 0}">
Count is not equal to zero.
</c:if>
```

Using the Struts EL Tag Libraries

To use the Struts EL tag libraries in a Struts application, your application's JSPs must declare their use of the libraries with JSP **taglib** directives:

```
<%@ taglib uri="http://struts.apache.org/tags-bean-el" prefix="bean" %>
<%@ taglib uri="http://struts.apache.org/tags-html-el" prefix="html" %>
<%@ taglib uri="http://struts.apache.org/tags-logic-el" prefix="logic" %>
```

Notice that the **prefix** attributes are set to "bean", "html", and "logic", respectively. These attributes can be set to whatever you want; however, "bean", "html", and "logic" are the accepted defaults for the Struts EL tag libraries. Using the same prefix for the Struts EL tag libraries as the base Struts tag libraries allows applications to easily transition to JSP 2.0.

The **prefix** attribute declares the prefix that each tag must have when it is used in a JSP, as shown here:

```
<bean:message key="label.search.name">
```

Because "bean" was defined as the prefix, the **message** tag was used as shown. However, if you chose to use a prefix of "strutsbean", the tag would be used in the following way:

```
<strutsbean:message key="label.search.name">
```

PART III

NOTE *Modern application servers use the* **uri** *attribute of the* **taglib** *directive to automatically resolve the location of the tag library descriptor file. Older application servers that support only JSP version 1.1 and/or version 1.0 require that tag libraries be registered in the* **web.xml** *file so that they can be resolved, as shown here:*

```
<taglib>
  <taglib-uri>http://struts.apache.org/tags-bean-el</taglib-uri>
  <taglib-location>/WEB-INF/struts-bean-el.tld</taglib-location>
</taglib>
<taglib>
  <taglib-uri>http://struts.apache.org/tags-html-el</taglib-uri>
  <taglib-location>/WEB-INF/struts-html-el.tld</taglib-location>
</taglib>
<taglib>
  <taglib-uri>http://struts.apache.org/tags-logic-el</taglib-uri>
  <taglib-location>/WEB-INF/struts-logic-el.tld</taglib-location>
</taglib>
```

The Struts EL Tag Library Tags

As mentioned, each of the tags in the Struts EL tag libraries is simply a tag from the Bean, HTML, Logic, or Tiles tag libraries to which support for JSTL expressions has been added. Thus, they are not individually covered in detail here. Instead, the basic concepts of using JSTL expressions with the tags were discussed because they apply to all the extended tags in the same way. For non–Struts EL–related information on each of the extended tags, see the descriptions of their base tags in their respective chapters.

The remainder of this section lists each Struts EL library-specific tag and the base tag from which it has been extended. Remember that not all of the Bean, HTML, Logic, and Tiles tags have been extended to support JSTL expressions. Only those tags whose functionality cannot be wholly replaced by a JSTL tag have been extended.

The Struts EL Bean Tag Library Tags

The following table lists each of the tags in the Struts EL Bean Tag Library and provides a short description of each tag's purpose.

Tag	Description
include	Expression language–enabled version of the Bean Tag Library's **include** tag.
message	Expression language–enabled version of the Bean Tag Library's **message** tag.
page	Expression language–enabled version of the Bean Tag Library's **page** tag.
resource	Expression language–enabled version of the Bean Tag Library's **resource** tag.
size	Expression language–enabled version of the Bean Tag Library's **size** tag.
struts	Expression language–enabled version of the Bean Tag Library's **struts** tag.

The Struts EL HTML Tag Library Tags

The following table lists each of the tags in the Struts EL HTML Tag Library and provides a short description of each tag's purpose.

Tag	Description
base	Expression language–enabled version of the HTML Tag Library's **base** tag.
button	Expression language–enabled version of the HTML Tag Library's **button** tag.
cancel	Expression language–enabled version of the HTML Tag Library's **cancel** tag.
checkbox	Expression language–enabled version of the HTML Tag Library's **checkbox** tag.
errors	Expression language–enabled version of the HTML Tag Library's **errors** tag.
file	Expression language–enabled version of the HTML Tag Library's **file** tag.
form	Expression language–enabled version of the HTML Tag Library's **form** tag.
frame	Expression language–enabled version of the HTML Tag Library's **frame** tag.
hidden	Expression language–enabled version of the HTML Tag Library's **hidden** tag.
html	Expression language–enabled version of the HTML Tag Library's **html** tag.
image	Expression language–enabled version of the HTML Tag Library's **image** tag.
img	Expression language–enabled version of the HTML Tag Library's **img** tag.

Tag	Description
javascript	Expression language–enabled version of the HTML Tag Library's **javascript** tag.
link	Expression language–enabled version of the HTML Tag Library's **link** tag.
messages	Expression language–enabled version of the HTML Tag Library's **messages** tag.
multibox	Expression language–enabled version of the HTML Tag Library's **multibox** tag.
option	Expression language–enabled version of the HTML Tag Library's **option** tag.
options	Expression language–enabled version of the HTML Tag Library's **options** tag.
optionsCollection	Expression language–enabled version of the HTML Tag Library's **optionsCollection** tag.
password	Expression language–enabled version of the HTML Tag Library's **password** tag.
radio	Expression language–enabled version of the HTML Tag Library's **radio** tag.
reset	Expression language–enabled version of the HTML Tag Library's **reset** tag.
rewrite	Expression language–enabled version of the HTML Tag Library's **rewrite** tag.
select	Expression language–enabled version of the HTML Tag Library's **select** tag.
submit	Expression language–enabled version of the HTML Tag Library's **submit** tag.
text	Expression language–enabled version of the HTML Tag Library's **text** tag.
textarea	Expression language–enabled version of the HTML Tag Library's **textarea** tag.
xhtml	Expression language–enabled version of the HTML Tag Library's **xhtml** tag.

The Struts EL Logic Tag Library Tags

The following table lists each of the tags in the Struts EL Logic Tag Library and provides a short description of each tag's purpose.

Tag	Description
forward	Expression language–enabled version of the Logic Tag Library's **forward** tag.
iterate	Expression language–enabled version of the Logic Tag Library's **iterate** tag.
match	Expression language–enabled version of the Logic Tag Library's **match** tag.
messagesNotPresent	Expression language–enabled version of the Logic Tag Library's **messagesNotPresent** tag.

Tag	Description
messagesPresent	Expression language–enabled version of the Logic Tag Library's **messagesPresent** tag.
notMatch	Expression language–enabled version of the Logic Tag Library's **notMatch** tag.
notPresent	Expression language–enabled version of the Logic Tag Library's **notPresent** tag.
present	Expression language–enabled version of the Logic Tag Library's **present** tag.
redirect	Expression language–enabled version of the Logic Tag Library's **redirect** tag.

The Struts EL Tiles Tag Library Tags

The following table lists each of the tags in the Struts EL Tiles Tag Library and provides a short description of each tag's purpose.

Tag	Description
add	Expression language–enabled version of the Tiles Tag Library's **add** tag.
definition	Expression language–enabled version of the Tiles Tag Library's **definition** tag.
get	Expression language–enabled version of the Tiles Tag Library's **get** tag.
getAsString	Expression language–enabled version of the Tiles Tag Library's **getAsString** tag.
importAttribute	Expression language–enabled version of the Tiles Tag Library's **importAttribute** tag.
initComponentDefinitions	Expression language–enabled version of the Tiles Tag Library's **initComponentDefinitions** tag.
insert	Expression language–enabled version of the Tiles Tag Library's **insert** tag.
put	Expression language–enabled version of the Tiles Tag Library's **put** tag.
putList	Expression language–enabled version of the Tiles Tag Library's **putList** tag.
useAttribute	Expression language–enabled version of the Tiles Tag Library's **useAttribute** tag.

IV

PART

Struts Configuration Files

Chapter 18
The Struts Configuration File

Chapter 19
The Tiles Configuration File

Chapter 20
The Validator Configuration File

18

CHAPTER

The Struts Configuration File

One of the core benefits to using the Struts framework is that a great deal of your application's configuration can be specified declaratively in an external configuration file instead of being hard-coded into the application. This greatly simplifies development because many changes can be made to the application without having to recompile any code. Upon application startup, Struts loads its configuration file(s) and creates a series of configuration objects that correspond to the settings in the file. Struts then uses those configuration objects to guide its behavior.

The Struts configuration file is XML-based, and its format is governed by a Document Type Definition (DTD) file that specifies how the configuration tags must be ordered in the file, what settings are required, and so on. Each Struts configuration file declares its conformance to the DTD by having the following DOCTYPE definition at the top of the file:

```
<!DOCTYPE struts-config PUBLIC
  "-//Apache Software Foundation//DTD Struts Configuration 1.3//EN"
  "http://struts.apache.org/dtds/struts-config_1_3.dtd">
```

When Struts reads the configuration file, its XML parser uses the DOCTYPE definition to determine the DTD that the XML file must conform to. If configured to do so, the XML parser will validate the XML file's conformance to the DTD.

Understanding XML DTDs

Because DTD conformance is important for Struts tags, a brief overview of how XML DTDs work is given here. DTDs specify a set of tags and attributes that make up a specific XML document type. DTDs also specify the order in which tags must be placed in the file, and the relationship between tags. For example, a tag definition defines what other tags can be nested inside of it, how many occurrences can be nested, and in what order the nesting can occur. Additionally, DTDs define which tag attributes are required and which are optional.

Each tag described in this chapter has a DTD Definition section that lists the tag's definition in the Struts configuration file DTD. The definitions will be similar to the one shown in the following snippet:

```
<!ELEMENT form-bean (icon?, display-name?, description?, set-property*, form-
property*)>
```

This example defines a **form-bean** tag and the tags that can be nested inside of it. According to the definition, the tag can have nested **icon**, **display-name**, **description**, **set-property**, and **form-property** tags. The question mark (?) and asterisk (*) characters following the nested tags' names indicate the number of times the nested tag can be nested. The question mark character indicates that the tag can be nested zero or one time. The asterisk character indicates that the tag can be nested zero or more (unlimited) times. A plus (+) character indicates that the tag must be nested at least once and as many times as you'd like. The lack of a trailing character means that the tag must be nested exactly once and no more. If no tags can be nested inside the defined tag, EMPTY will be used to denote that:

```
<!ELEMENT set-property EMPTY>
```

Configuring the web.xml Deployment Descriptor

As explained in Chapter 2, Struts configuration files are specified inside in the **web.xml** deployment descriptor file when defining the use of the Struts **ActionServlet**, as shown here:

```
<!DOCTYPE web-app
  PUBLIC "-//Sun Microsystems, Inc.//DTD Web Application 2.3//EN"
  "http://java.sun.com/dtd/web-app_2_3.dtd">

<web-app>
  <servlet>
    <servlet-name>action</servlet-name>
    <servlet-class>org.apache.struts.action.ActionServlet</servlet-class>
    <init-param>
      <param-name>config</param-name>
      <param-value>/WEB-INF/struts-config.xml</param-value>
    </init-param>
    <load-on-startup>1</load-on-startup>
  </servlet>

  ...

</web-app>
```

The Struts configuration file is specified by declaring a servlet initialization parameter named **config**. The **config** parameter must be set to the Web application-relative path of your configuration file, which will be underneath the protected **/WEB-INF/** directory so that it can be accessed only from server-side applications.

As of version 1.1, Struts supports the use of multiple configuration files. This way, configuration settings can be broken down into separate files, which allows teams of developers to work on an application in parallel without having the configuration file be a point of contention. To specify multiple configuration files, simply list each configuration file delimited by commas, as shown here:

```
<init-param>
  <param-name>config</param-name>
  <param-value>
    /WEB-INF/struts-config.xml,
    /WEB-INF/struts-config2.xml,
```

```
    /WEB-INF/struts-config3.xml,
  </param-value>
</init-param>
```

When Struts loads the configuration files, if there is any overlap among the files' settings, Struts will use the last settings specified. For example, if configuration file A specifies a setting and then configuration file B specifies the same setting with a different value, the setting in configuration file B will override the one in configuration file A, provided that file B is loaded after file A.

In addition to support for multiple configuration files, Struts version 1.1 added support for application modules. The module feature allows applications to be broken down into discrete chunks and can be thought of as being almost a mini-application inside of a large application. Using modules requires you to create a separate configuration file for each module, as shown here:

```
<servlet>
  <servlet-name>action</servlet-name>
  <servlet-class>org.apache.struts.action.ActionServlet</servlet-class>
  <init-param>
    <param-name>config</param-name>
    <param-value>/WEB-INF/struts-config.xml</param-value>
  </init-param>
  <init-param>
    <param-name>config/ModuleA</param-name>
    <param-value>/WEB-INF/struts-config-moduleB.xml</param-value>
  </init-param>
  <init-param>
    <param-name>config/ModuleB</param-name>
    <param-value>/WEB-INF/struts-config-moduleA.xml</param-value>
  </init-param>
  <load-on-startup>1</load-on-startup>
</servlet>
```

Notice that the second and third **init-param** definitions specify parameters named **config/moduleA** and **config/ModuleB**, respectively. Struts uses the part of the name following the slash (/) as the logical name for the module and loads and associates the specified configuration file with that module. Thus, for a parameter named **config/ModuleA**, the module's name is **ModuleA**. For module configuration files, parameter names must begin with **config/** in order for Struts to recognize them. When using modules, you still need to define a default configuration file for your application with the **config** parameter, as you would with a nonmodular application.

NOTE *For more information on using Struts modules, refer to Chapter 9.*

The Struts Configuration File Tags

Table 18-1 lists and describes each of the tags used to configure the Struts configuration file.

The remainder of this chapter discusses each tag in detail, including a complete description of the tag, the tag's DTD definition, a table that lists each of the tag's attributes (if the tag has attributes), and a usage example for the tag. In the tables that describe each

Tag	Description
action	Maps an application URL either to an **Action** object that will be executed when the specified URL is requested or to another URL that will be forwarded to.
action-mappings	Encapsulates the set of actions the application will have.
controller	Defines several global configuration settings for a Struts application.
exception	Defines an exception handler to process a specific exception thrown by an **Action**.
form-bean	Defines a Form Bean and assigns a logical name to it.
form-beans	Encapsulates the set of Form Beans the application will have.
form-property	Defines a form property for dynamic Form Beans.
forward	Defines a logical name for a URL, thus allowing code to reference the logical name and not the URL itself.
global-exceptions	Encapsulates a set of exception handlers, defined by **exception** tags, which are global to the application.
global-forwards	Encapsulates a set of forwards, defined by **forward** tags, which are global to the application.
message-resources	Defines a resource bundle that Struts will use when looking up externalized strings, messages, and labels.
plug-in	Defines a plugin that Struts loads at application startup and unloads at application shutdown.
set-property	Defines a property and its value.
struts-config	Is the root tag for the Struts configuration file and thus encapsulates all other tags in the file.

TABLE 18-1 Struts Configuration File Tags

tag's attributes, pay special attention to the Required column, which denotes whether the given attribute is required when using the tag. In addition to the required column denoting whether an attribute is required, the rows for required attributes are highlighted in gray so that you can determine at a glance which attributes are required. If an attribute is required and you do not specify it when using the tag, the Struts framework will not be properly configured and, consequently, will not function properly.

The action Tag

The **action** tag is used to map an application URL to an **Action** object that will be executed when the specified URL is requested or to map the URL to another URL to forward the request to.

There are three ways you can use the **action** tag, as listed here and shown later in the "Example Usage" section.

- You can use the **type** attribute to map an **org.apache.struts.action.Action** subclass to the application URL specified by the **path** attribute.

- You can use the **forward** attribute to specify a URL to forward to with a call to **RequestDispatcher.forward( )** when the URL specified by the **path** attribute is matched.
- You can use the **include** attribute to specify a URL to forward to with a call to **RequestDispatcher.include( )** when the URL specified by the **path** attribute is matched.

DTD Definition

Following is the definition for the **action** tag from the Struts configuration file DTD:

```
<!ELEMENT action (icon?, display-name?, description?, set-property*, exception*,
forward*)>
```

Attributes

Attribute	Description	Required
attribute	Specifies the name of the request- or session-scope attribute under which the Form Bean associated with this action is stored. Normally the name specified with the **name** attribute is used to look up the Form Bean; however, if this attribute is used, it will be used instead. This attribute is only valid if the **name** attribute is specified.	No
cancellable	Accepts *true* or *false* to specify whether the action can be canceled. If the action is canceled and this attribute is *not* set to *true*, an **org.apache.struts.action.InvalidCancelException** will be thrown. Defaults to *false*.	No
catalog	Specifies the Commons Chain catalog in which the command specified with the **command** attribute will be looked up. This attribute is only applicable when the **command** attribute is specified. If not specified, the default catalog is used.	No
className	Specifies the fully qualified class name of the configuration object to instantiate for this **Action** definition. Defaults to **org.apache.struts.config.ActionConfig**. The DTD comments say the default is o.a.s.action.ActionMapping	No
command	Specifies the Commons Chain command that will be executed before this action (if any) is executed.	No
extends	Specifies the path of another action mapping that this mapping will inherit configuration information from.	No
forward	Specifies a module-relative URL to forward to when this **Action** mapping's path is matched. Uses **RequestDispatcher.forward( )** to perform forward. Only this attribute or one of the **include** or **type** attributes can be specified at a time.	No
include	Specifies a module-relative URL to forward to when this **Action** mappings path is matched. Uses **RequestDispatcher.include( )** to perform forward. Only this attribute or one of the **forward** or **type** attributes can be specified at a time.	No
input	Specifies a module-relative URL to which control will be forwarded if the Form Bean associated with this **Action** is set to be validated and the validation process fails. This attribute is only valid if the **name** attribute is specified.	No

Attribute	Description	Required
name	Specifies the logical name of a Form Bean, defined with a **form-bean** tag, which will be associated with this action.	No
parameter	Specifies a value that will be passed as a general-purpose configuration parameter to the **Action** object defined by the **type** attribute upon each execution of the action.	No
path	Specifies the module-relative URL to map to.	Yes
prefix	Specifies the prefix to add to request parameter names when populating this **Action**'s associated Form Bean. Thus, a request parameter named "username" coupled with this attribute set to "search" would try to call a method called **setSearchUsername( )** on the Form Bean. This attribute is only valid if the **name** attribute is specified.	No
roles	Specifies a comma-delimited list of security roles that are allowed to access this **Action**.	No
scope	Specifies the scope (*request* or *session*) that will be used to access the Form Bean associated with this action with the **name** attribute. This attribute is only valid if the **name** attribute is specified. Defaults to *session*.	No
suffix	Specifies the suffix to add to request parameter names when populating this **Action**'s associated Form Bean. Thus, a request parameter named "username" coupled with this attribute set to "search" would try to call a method called **setUsernameSearch( )** on the Form Bean. This attribute is only valid if the **name** attribute is specified.	No
type	Specifies the fully qualified class name for the **org.apache.struts.action.Action** subclass to associate with this **Action** mapping. Only this attribute or one of the **forward** or **include** attributes can be specified at a time.	No
unknown	Accepts *true* or *false* to specify whether this action will be set as the default action for the application. If set to *true*, any application URLs that don't match another mapping will be handled by this action definition. Only one **action** definition per module configuration should have this attribute set to *true*. Defaults to *false*.	No
validate	Accepts *true* or *false* to specify whether the Form Bean specified by the **name** attribute will have its **validate( )** method invoked before this **Action** is executed. This attribute is only valid if the **name** attribute is specified. Defaults to *true*.	No

Example Usage

As mentioned, there are three ways you can use the **action** tag. The first way, shown here, defines a global exception handler:

```
<action-mappings>
  <action path="/search"
          type="com.xyzcorp.app.SearchAction"/>
</action-mappings>
```

This example uses the **type** attribute to specify an **Action** object that will be executed when the specified path is matched.

The second way to use the **action** tag is shown here:

```
<action-mappings>
  <action path="/search"
       forward="/search.jsp"/>
</action-mappings>
```

This example uses the **forward** attribute to specify that the "/search.jsp" URL will be forwarded by using **RequestDispatcher.forward( )** when the specified path is matched.

The following snippet shows the third general way to use the **action** tag:

```
<action-mappings>
  <action path="/search"
       include="/search.jsp"/>
</action-mappings>
```

This example uses the **include** attribute to specify that the "/search.jsp" URL will be forwarded by using **RequestDispatcher.include( )** when the specified path is matched.

The action-mappings Tag

The **action-mappings** tag is used to encapsulate the set of actions the application will have. This tag is simply a container for **action** tags.

DTD Definition

Following is the definition for the **action-mappings** tag from the Struts configuration file DTD:

```
<!ELEMENT action-mappings (action*)>
```

Attribute

Attribute	Description	Required
type	Deprecated. Use the **action** tag's **className** attribute instead.	No

Example Usage

The following example illustrates how to use the **action-mappings** tag:

```
<action-mappings>
  <action path="/search"
          type="com.xyzcorp.app.SearchAction"/>
</action-mappings>
```

The controller Tag

The **controller** tag is used to define several global configuration settings for your Struts application. In earlier versions of Struts, many of these settings were configured via the Web deployment descriptor **web.xml** by specifying initialization parameters for the Struts **ActionServlet**. However, when Struts added support for application modules in version 1.1,

PART IV

these settings were moved to the Struts configuration file so that they could be configured on a per-module basis.

DTD Definition

Following is the definition for the **controller** tag from the Struts configuration file DTD:

```
<!ELEMENT controller (set-property*)>
```

Attributes

Attribute	Description	Required
bufferSize	Specifies the input buffer size that will be used for file uploads. Defaults to 4096 bytes.	No
catalog	Specifies the Commons Chain catalog to use when processing requests for the application (or individual module if using modules). Defaults to *struts*.	No
className	Specifies the fully qualified class name of the configuration object to instantiate for this controller definition. Defaults to **org.apache.struts.config.ControllerConfig**.	No
command	Specifies the Commons Chain command that will be executed to process requests for the application (or individual module if using modules). Defaults to *servlet-standard*.	No
contentType	Specifies the content type (and optional character encoding) that will be set on each HTTP response. Note that this setting can be overridden by an **Action**, JSP, or similar resource that a request is forwarded to. Defaults to *text/html*.	No
forwardPattern	Specifies the pattern for how the **path** attribute of **forward** tags is mapped to URLs. *$M* – Replaced by this module's prefix. *$P* – Replaced by the **path** attribute of the selected forward. *$$* – Causes a literal dollar sign ($) to be used. All other *$x* variables, where *x* is variable, are reserved for future use and will be silently ignored. Defaults to *MP*.	No
inputForward	Accepts *true* or *false* to specify whether the **action** tag's **input** attribute will be treated as the name of a forward whose path will be used. If set to *false* (the default), the **action** tag's **input** attribute will be taken as the literal path. Defaults to *false*.	No
locale	Accepts *true* or *false* to denote whether or not a **java.util. Locale** object will be stored in user sessions. Defaults to *true*.	No

Attribute	Description	Required
maxFileSize	Specifies the maximum size, in bytes, for file uploads. Alternatively, if you add "K", "M", or "G" to the end of the value, it will be interpreted as kilobytes, megabytes, or gigabytes, respectively. Defaults to *250M*.	No
memFileSize	Specifies the maximum size in bytes for file uploads that will be kept in memory. Alternatively, if you add "K", "M", or "G" to the end of the value, it will be interpreted as kilobytes, megabytes, or gigabytes, respectively. Files larger than this threshold will be written to disk. Defaults to *256K*.	No
multipartClass	Specifies the fully qualified class name of the object to use for handling file uploads. Defaults to **org.apache.struts.upload.CommonsMultipartRequestHandler**.	No
nocache	Accepts *true* or *false* to specify whether HTTP headers will be added to each response to disable browser caching. Defaults to *false*.	No
pagePattern	Specifies the pattern for how the **page** attribute of Struts' tag library tags is mapped to URLs. *$M* – Replaced by this module's prefix. *$P* – Replaced by the **page** attribute of the selected tag. *$$* – Causes a literal dollar sign ($) to be used. All other *$x* variables, where *x* is variable, are reserved for future use and will be silently ignored. Defaults to *MP*.	No
processorClass	Specifies the fully qualified class name for the **RequestProcessor** subclass that will be used for this module. Defaults to **org.apache.struts.chain.ComposableRequestProcessor**.	No
tempDir	Specifies a temporary directory to use to store data during file uploads.	No

Example Usage

There are many different ways that the **controller** tag can be used because it has several attributes, all of which are optional. Following is an example usage that specifies the maximum file size for file uploads:

```
<controller maxFileSize="3M"/>
```

This example sets the maximum size for file uploads to three megabytes.

PART IV

The exception Tag

The **exception** tag is used to define an exception handler to process a specific exception thrown by an **Action**. This feature allows you to assign a different handler to each type of exception that is thrown by actions.

There are two ways you can use the **exception** tag, as listed here and shown later in the "Example Usage" section:

- You can define global exception handlers by placing the **exception** tags inside the **global-exceptions** tag. Global exception handlers apply to all actions.
- You can define action-specific exception handlers by nesting **exception** tags underneath an **action** tag. Action-specific exception handlers can only be "seen" by the enclosing action and will override any global exception handlers with the same target exception.

DTD Definition

Following is the definition for the **exception** tag from the Struts configuration file DTD:

```
<!ELEMENT exception (icon?, display-name?, description?, set-property*)>
```

Attributes

Attribute	Description	Required
bundle	Specifies the servlet context attribute key for a resource bundle, defined with the **message-resources** tag, which will be used to retrieve the message for the key specified by the **key** attribute.	No
className	Specifies the fully qualified class name for the configuration object to instantiate for this exception definition. Defaults to **org.apache.struts.config.ExceptionConfig**.	No
extends	Specifies the name (specified with the **handler** attribute) of another exception handler that this handler will inherit configuration information from.	No
handler	Specifies the fully qualified class name for this exception handler.	No
key	Specifies the resource bundle message key to use with this handler.	No
path	Specifies the module-relative URL to redirect to if this exception handler is triggered.	No
scope	Specifies the scope (*request* or *session*) that will be used to access the **org.apache.struts.action.ActionError** object for this exception.	No
type	Specifies the fully qualified class name of the exception class that this handler is for.	Yes

Example Usage

As mentioned, there are two ways you can use the **exception** tag. The first way, shown here, defines a global exception handler:

```
<global-exceptions>
  <exception type="com.xyzcorp.app.DateFormatException"
             key="errors.date.format"
            path="/error.jsp"/>
</global-exceptions>
```

The following is the second way to use the **exception** tag:

```
<action-mappings>
  <action path="/search"
          type="com.xyzcorp.app.SearchAction">
    <exception type="com.xyzcorp.app.DateFormatException"
               key="errors.date.format"
              path="/searchError.jsp"/>
  </action>
</action-mappings>
```

This example defines an action-specific exception handler. Only the enclosing action can "see" this exception handler and it will override a global exception handler targeted at the same exception.

The form-bean Tag

The **form-bean** tag is used to define a Form Bean and assign a logical name to it. Struts uses Form Beans to capture form data when a form is submitted and to populate forms before being displayed.

There are two ways you can use the **form-bean** tag, as listed here and shown later, in the section "Example Usage":

- You can define a concrete Form Bean by specifying its concrete class with the **type** attribute. This requires creating a class that subclasses **org.apache.struts.action .ActionForm** and creating all the getter and setter methods.
- You can define a dynamic Form Bean by using the **type** attribute to specify that its type is **org.apache.struts.action.DynaActionForm** or a subclass thereof. With this approach, you specify each of the Form Bean's fields in the configuration file with **form-property** tags.

PART IV

DTD Definition

Following is the definition for the **form-bean** tag from the Struts configuration file DTD:

```
<!ELEMENT form-bean (icon?, display-name?, description?, set-property*, form-
property*)>
```

Attributes

Attribute	Description	Required
className	Specifies the fully qualified class name of the configuration object to instantiate for this Form Bean definition. Defaults to **org.apache.struts.config.FormBeanConfig**.	No
enhanced	This attribute is not currently used and is simply a placeholder for future use.	No

Attribute	Description	Required
extends	Specifies the name of another Form Bean that this Form Bean will inherit configuration information from.	No
name	Specifies the logical name for the Form Bean.	Yes
type	Specifies the fully qualified class name for the Form Bean class.	Yes

Example Usage

As mentioned, there are two ways you can use the **form-bean** tag. The first way, shown here, defines a concrete Form Bean:

```
<form-beans>
  <form-bean name="logonForm"
             type="com.xyzcorp.app.LogonForm"/>
</form-beans>
```

The following is the second way to use the **form-bean** tag:

```
<form-beans>
  <form-bean name="logonForm"
             type="org.apache.struts.action.DynaActionForm">
    <form-property name="username"
                   type="java.lang.String"/>
    <form-property name="password"
                   type="java.lang.String"/>
  </form-bean>
</form-beans>
```

This example defines a dynamic Form Bean whose properties are specified with the nested **form-property** tags. Notice that the **type** attribute is set to **org.apache.struts.action.DynaActionForm**. This informs Struts that the Form Bean's properties are defined in the configuration file.

The form-beans Tag

The **form-beans** tag is used to encapsulate the set of Form Beans the application will have. This tag is simply a container for **form-bean** tags.

DTD Definition

Following is the definition for the **form-beans** tag from the Struts configuration file DTD:

```
<!ELEMENT form-beans (form-bean*)>
```

Attribute

Attribute	Description	Required
type	Deprecated.Use the **form-bean** tag's **className** attribute instead.	No

Example Usage

The following example illustrates how to use the **form-beans** tag:

```
<form-beans>
  <form-bean name="searchForm"
             type="com.xyzcorp.app.SearchForm"/>
</form-beans>
```

The form-property Tag

The **form-property** tag is used to define form properties for dynamic Form Beans. Dynamic Form Beans allow you to define a form's properties in the Struts configuration file instead of in a concrete class. Use of this tag will be ignored if the enclosing **form-bean** tag's **type** attribute is not **org.apache.struts.action.DynaActionForm** or a subclass of it.

DTD Definition

Following is the definition for the **form-property** tag from the Struts configuration file DTD:

```
<!ELEMENT form-property (set-property*)>
```

Attributes

Attribute	Description	Required
className	Specifies the fully qualified class name of the **FormPropertyConfig** subclass to use for this property. Defaults to **org.apache.struts.config.FormPropertyConfig**.	No
initial	Specifies the initial value of the property. If not specified, primitives will be initialized to 0 and objects will be initialized with their default constructor (thus, **String**s will be initialized to "").	No
name	Specifies the name of the property.	Yes
size	Specifies the size of the array to create if the **type** attribute specifies an array and the **initial** attribute is omitted.	No
type	Specifies the fully qualified class name for the property's underlying field. Optionally, [] can be appended to the type declaration to denote that the field is indexed (e.g., **java.lang.String[]**).	Yes

Example Usage

The following example illustrates the basic usage of the **form-property** tag:

```
<form-beans>
  <form-bean name="logonForm"
             type="org.apache.struts.action.DynaActionForm">
    <form-property name="username"
                   type="java.lang.String"/>
    <form-property name="password"
                   type="java.lang.String"/>
  </form-bean>
</form-beans>
```

Instead of specifying a concrete class for your Form Bean definition, you set its type to **org.apache.struts.action.DynaActionForm** or a subclass and then list each of its properties with the **form-property** tag.

The forward Tag

The **forward** tag is used to define a logical name for a URL, thus allowing code and so on to reference the logical name and not the URL itself.

There are two ways you can use the **forward** tag, as listed here and shown later, in the section "Example Usage":

- You can define global forwards by placing the **forward** tags inside the **global-forwards** tag. Global forwards are accessible by any action.
- You can define action-specific forwards by nesting **forward** tags underneath an **action** tag. Action-specific forwards can only be "seen" by the enclosing action and will override any global forwards with the same logical name.

DTD Definition

Following is the definition for the **forward** tag from the Struts configuration file DTD:

```
<!ELEMENT forward (icon?, display-name?, description?, set-property*)>
```

Attributes

Attribute	Description	Required
catalog	Specifies the Commons Chain catalog in which the command specified with the **command** attribute will be looked up. This attribute is only applicable when the **command** attribute is specified.	No
className	Specifies the fully qualified class name for the configuration object to instantiate for this forward definition. Defaults to **org.apache.struts.config.ForwardConfig**.	No
command	Specifies the Commons Chain command that will be executed before this forward (if any) is executed.	No
extends	Specifies the path of another action mapping that this mapping will inherit configuration information from.	No
module	Specifies a module prefix, including the leading slash (/) (e.g., /moduleA), that will be prefixed to the forward's path.	No
name	Specifies the logical name for the forward.	Yes
path	Specifies the URL for this forward.	No
redirect	Accepts *true* or *false* to denote whether or not an HTTP redirect will be executed for this forward's URL. Defaults to *false*.	No

Example Usage

As stated, there are two ways you can use the **forward** tag. The first way, shown here, defines a global forward:

```
<global-forwards>
  <forward name="success"
           path="/success.jsp"/>
</global-forwards>
```

```
The second way to use the forward tag is shown here:
<action-mappings>
  <action path="/search"
          type="com.xyzcorp.app.SearchAction">
    <forward name="success"
             path="/results.jsp"/>
  </action>
</action-mappings>
```

This example defines an action-specific forward. Only the enclosing action can "see" this forward, and it will override a global forward with the same logical name if present.

The global-exceptions Tag

The **global-exceptions** tag is used to encapsulate a set of exception handlers, defined by **exception** tags, which are global to the application. This set of global exception handlers will be used to handle any exceptions being thrown from actions unless an action's corresponding **action** tag overrides one or more of the global exception handlers by nesting **exception** tags underneath it.

DTD Definition

Following is the definition for the **global-exceptions** tag from the Struts configuration file DTD:

```
<!ELEMENT global-exceptions (exception*)>
Example Usage
```

The following example illustrates how to use the **global-exceptions** tag:

```
<global-exceptions>
  <exception type="com.xyzcorp.app.DateFormatException"
             key="errors.date.format"
             path="/error.jsp"/>
</global-exceptions>
```

This tag simply encapsulates the set of exception handlers that are global to the application.

PART IV

The global-forwards Tag

The **global-forwards** tag is used to encapsulate a set of forwards, defined by **forward** tags, which are global to the application. Unless an action defines a forward with a nested **forward** tag that overrides one or more of these global forwards, the global forward will be used to determine where to forward when an action finishes executing.

DTD Definition

Following is the definition for the **global-forwards** tag from the Struts configuration file DTD:

```
<!ELEMENT global-forwards (forward*)>
```

Attribute

Attribute	Description	Required
type	Deprecated. Use the **forward** tag's **className** attribute instead.	No

Example Usage

The following example illustrates the basic usage of the **global-forwards** tag:

```
<global-forwards>
  <forward name="success" path="/success.jsp"/>
  <forward name="failure" path="/failure.jsp"/>
</global-forwards>
```

This tag simply encapsulates the set of forwards that will be global to the application.

The message-resources Tag

The **message-resources** tag is used to define a resource bundle that Struts will use when looking up externalized strings, messages, and labels.

DTD Definition

Following is the definition for the **message-resources** tag from the Struts configuration file DTD:

```
<!ELEMENT message-resources (set-property*)>
```

Attributes

Attribute	Description	Required
className	Specifies the fully qualified class name of the configuration object to instantiate for this message resource's definition. Defaults to **org.apache.struts.config.MessageResourcesConfig**.	No
factory	Specifies the fully qualified class name of the **MessagesResourcesFactory** subclass that will be used to create this message resource instance. Defaults to **org.apache.struts.util.PropertyMessageResources Factory**.	No
key	Specifies the servlet context attribute key under which this message resource instance will be stored. If using application modules, the module prefix will be appended to the key (e.g., "${key}${prefix}"). Defaults to the value specified by the constant **org.apache .struts.Globals.MESSAGES_KEY**.	No
null	Accepts *true* or *false* to specify whether missing messages should return null. Defaults to *true*.	No
parameter	Specifies a configuration parameter value that will be passed to the **createResources( )** method of the factory object specified by the **factory** attribute.	Yes

Example Usage

The following example illustrates the basic usage of the **message-resources** tag:

```
<message-resources
  parameter="com.xyzcorp.app.MessageResources"/>
```

This example specifies that Struts should use a file called **MessageResources .properties** from the **com.xyzcorp.app** package as its resource bundle. Notice that the ".properties" portion of the filename is not specified with the tag; Struts automatically appends that to the name of the file that you specify with the **parameter** attribute.

Sometimes it's useful or necessary to have more than one resource bundle. You can accomplish that by using multiple **message-resources** tags in your configuration file, as shown here:

```
<message-resources
  parameter="com.xyzcorp.app.MessageResources"/>

<message-resources
  parameter="com.xyzcorp.app.AlternateMessageResources"
        key="alternate"/>
```

Each instance of the **message-resources** tag must specify a unique key with the **key** attribute to identify it, unless it's for the default resource bundle, which does not require an explicit key.

The plug-in Tag

The **plug-in** tag is used to define a plugin that Struts loads at application startup and unloads at application shutdown. Among other things, plugins are useful for loading persistent resources at application startup. Each plugin class must implement Struts' **org.apache.struts.action.PlugIn** interface. Upon application startup, the plugin's **init( )** method will be called. Upon application shutdown, the plugin's **destroy( )** method will be called.

DTD Definition

Following is the definition for the **plug-in** tag from the Struts configuration file DTD:

```
<!ELEMENT plug-in (set-property*)>
```

Attribute

Attribute	Description	Required
className	Specifies the fully qualified class name for the plugin. This class must implement the **org.apache.struts.action.PlugIn** interface.	Yes

Example Usage

The following example illustrates the usage of the **plug-in** tag:

```
<plug-in className="org.apache.struts.validator.ValidatorPlugIn">
  <set-property property="pathnames"
                   value="/WEB-INF/validator-rules.xml,
                          /WEB-INF/validation.xml"/>
</plug-in>
```

The **plug-in** tag is quite simple because it has only one attribute. In most cases, there will be nested **set-property** tags to dynamically configure the plugin. Each plugin defines its own set of properties that can be configured via **set-property** tags.

PART IV

The set-property Tag

The **set-property** tag is used to define a property and its value. Several of the other Struts configuration file tags allow instances of this tag to be nested inside them to specify properties that will be set when the tags' corresponding configuration objects are instantiated. Struts uses reflection to look up and invoke a setter method (e.g., **setMyProp( )** for a property called **myProp**) on the configuration object based on the name specified with this tag's **property** attribute. In Struts version 1.3, a new attribute, **key**, was added that allows arbitrary properties to be set on a configuration object independent of whether a property with the specified name exists or not (i.e., whether or not there is a **setMyProp()** method). Either the **key** or **property** attribute must be specified; they are mutually exclusive.

DTD Definition

Following is the definition for the **set-property** tag from the Struts configuration file DTD:

```
<!ELEMENT set-property EMPTY>
```

Attributes

Attribute	Description	Required
key	Specifies the name of an arbitrary property to set the value for.	No
property	Specifies the name of an existing property to set the value for.	No
value	Specifies the value of the property.	Yes

Example Usage

The following example illustrates the basic usage of the **set-property** tag:

```
<plug-in className="org.apache.struts.tiles.TilesPlugin">
  <set-property property="definitions-config"
                   value="/WEB-INF/tiles-defs.xml"/>
  <set-property property="moduleAware" value="true"/>
</plug-in>
```

At run time, when Struts parses a configuration file with a definition similar to this, it will use reflection to look up and invoke the **setDefinitionsConfig( )** and **setModuleAware( )** methods of the class specified by the **plug-in** tag's **className** attribute, passing them the defined values.

The struts-config Tag

The **struts-config** tag is the root tag for the Struts configuration file and thus encapsulates all other tags in the file. This tag has no other use than to denote the beginning and end of configuration data.

DTD Definition

Following is the definition for the **struts-config** tag from the Struts configuration file DTD:

```
<!ELEMENT struts-config (display-name?, description?, form-beans?, global-
exceptions?, global-forwards?, action-mappings?, controller?, message-resources*,
plug-in*)>
```

Example Usage

The following snippet illustrates how to use the **struts-config** tag:

```
<struts-config>
  <form-beans>
    ...
  </form-beans>
  <action-mappings>
    ...
  </action-mappings>
</struts-config>
```

Metadata Tags

Several of the tags for the Struts configuration file give you the option to nest metadata tags. The metadata tags exist solely for adding extra information to the configuration file that will show up in GUI tools and the like; Struts itself ignores the metadata tags. None of the metadata tags has any attributes; thus, you just add text between opening and closing tags to specify their value, as shown here:

```
<action path="/search"
        type="com.xyzcorp.app.SearchAction">
  <icon>
    <small-icon>small.gif</small-icon>
    <large-icon>large.gif</large-icon>
  </icon>
  <display-name>Search Action</display-name>
  <description>Search Action searches for employees.</description>
</action>
```

The following table lists and describes each of the metadata tags.

Tag	Description
description	Defines descriptive text for the enclosing tag.
display-name	Defines a short description (or name) for the enclosing tag.
icon	Encapsulates an instance of the **large-icon** and the **small-icon** tags.
large-icon	Defines the location for a large (32×32 pixel) icon to associate to the enclosing tag.
small-icon	Defines the location for a small (16×16 pixel) icon to associate to the enclosing tag.

Editing Struts Configuration Files with Struts Console

As you can imagine, trying to remember every tag's list of attributes as well as its proper order inside the configuration file can be cumbersome. If you make a mistake in typing any of the tag's or attribute's names, your Struts application will not be configured properly. To simplify the creation and modification of Struts configuration files, you can use a GUI tool called Struts Console. Struts Console is a stand-alone Java Swing application that provides a graphical editor for Struts configuration files. Additionally, Struts Console can be used as a plugin with several major Java IDEs, providing a seamless Struts development experience.

Struts Console is free software and can be downloaded from

http://www.jamesholmes.com/struts/

which has all the information you need to configure Struts Console to work with your favorite Java IDE. In addition, this book's appendix provides a Struts Console quick reference.

Figure 18-1 shows Struts Console running as a stand-alone application.

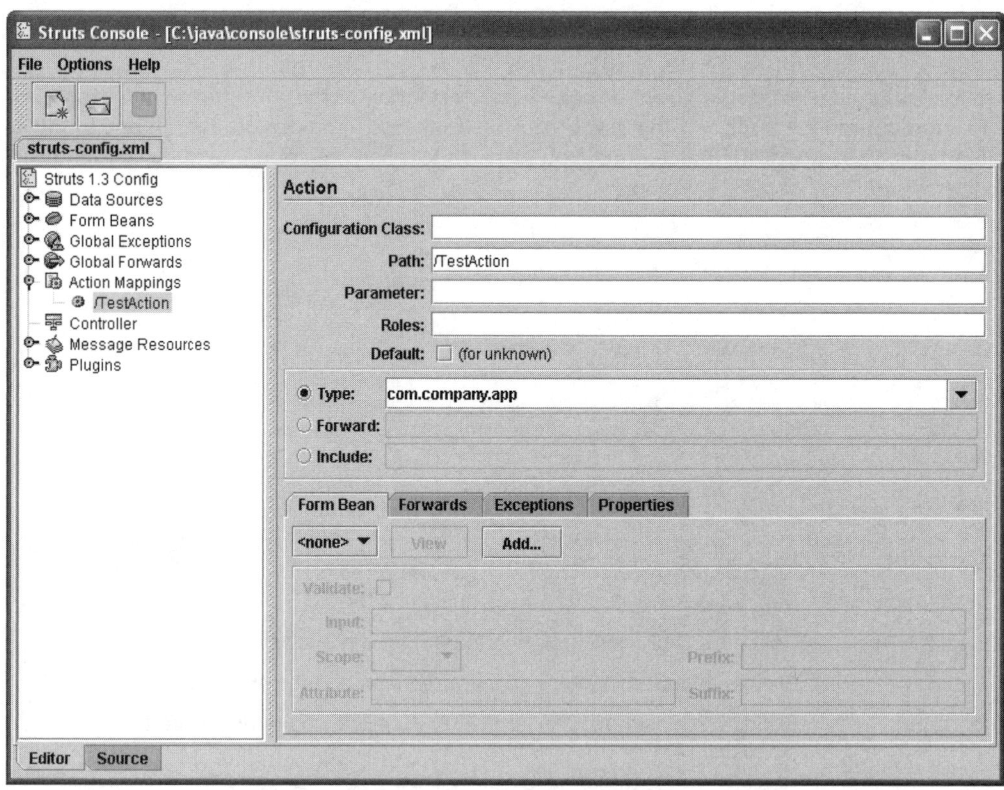

FIGURE 18-1 Struts Console running as a stand-alone application

19

CHAPTER

The Tiles Configuration File

The Tiles framework, which supports the creation of regions within a page, provides a rich JSP templating system that extends beyond JSP's built-in include mechanism. Like the include mechanism, Tiles templates can be defined and accessed via JSP Tag Library tags. However, Tiles takes it one step further by allowing your application's configuration to be specified declaratively in an external configuration file instead of being hard-coded into JSPs. This greatly simplifies development because many changes can be made to the application without having to recompile any code.

The Tiles configuration file is XML-based, and its format is governed by a Document Type Definition (DTD) file that specifies how the configuration tags must be ordered in the file, what settings are required, and so on. Each Tiles configuration file declares its conformance to the DTD by having the following DOCTYPE definition at the top of the file:

```
<!DOCTYPE tiles-definitions PUBLIC
  "-//Apache Software Foundation//DTD Tiles Configuration 1.3//EN"
  "http://struts.apache.org/dtds/tiles-config_1_3.dtd">
```

When Tiles reads the configuration file, its XML parser uses the DOCTYPE definition to determine to which DTD the XML file must conform. If configured to do so, the XML parser will validate the XML file's conformance to the DTD.

NOTE *An in-depth discussion of the Tiles framework is found in Chapter 7.*

Understanding XML DTDs

Because DTD conformance is important for Tiles tags, a brief overview of how XML DTDs work is given here. DTDs specify a set of tags and attributes that make up a specific XML document type. DTDs also specify the order in which tags must be placed in the file, and the relationship between tags. For example, a tag definition defines what other tags can be nested inside of it, how many occurrences can be nested, and in what order the nesting can occur. Additionally, DTDs define which tag attributes are required and which are optional.

Each tag described in this chapter has a DTD Definition section that lists the tag's definition in the Tiles configuration file DTD. The definitions will be similar to the one shown in the following snippet:

```
<!ELEMENT definition (icon?,display-name?,description?,put*,putList*)>
```

This example defines a **definition** tag and the tags that can be nested inside of it. According to the definition, the tag can have nested **icon**, **display-name**, **description**, **put**, and **putList** tags. The question mark (?) and asterisk (*) characters following the nested tags' names indicate the number of times the nested tag can be nested. The ? character indicates that the tag can be nested zero or one time. The * character indicates that the tag can be nested zero or more (unlimited) times. A plus (+) character indicates that the tag must be nested at least once and as many times as you'd like. No trailing character means that the tag must be nested exactly once and no more. If no tags can be nested inside the defined tag, EMPTY is used to denote that, as shown next:

```
<!ELEMENT set-property EMPTY>
```

Enabling the Tiles Plugin

Although the Tiles framework comes packaged with Struts, by default Tiles is not enabled. In order to enable and use Tiles, you have to add the Tiles **.jar** file (e.g., **struts-tiles-1.3.5.jar**) to your application's **WEB-INF/lib** directory. Additionally, the following **<plug-in>** definition must be added to your application's Struts configuration file:

NOTE *As of Struts 1.3, the Struts distribution was broken down into several* **.jar** *files in order to modularize the framework so that it could be used piece by piece as needed. Thus the need to include the Tiles* **.jar** *file when using Tiles. Prior versions of Struts were packaged as one monolithic* **.jar** *file* (**struts.jar**) *and did not require you to include additional* **.jar** *files for certain features.*

```
<!-- Tiles Configuration -->
<plug-in className="org.apache.struts.tiles.TilesPlugin">
  <set-property property="definitions-config"
                   value="/WEB-INF/tiles-defs.xml"/>
</plug-in>
```

This definition causes Struts to load and initialize the Tiles plugin for your application. Upon initialization, the plugin loads the comma-delimited list of Tiles configuration files specified by the **definitions-config** property. Each configuration file's path must be specified using a Web application–relative path, as shown in the preceding example.

In version 1.3 Struts moved away from using the **RequestProcessor** for customized request processing to using a Jakarta Commons Chain–based solution. As a result of this change, Tiles no longer extends the base Struts **RequestProcessor** to implement its functionality. Instead Tiles now uses a custom chain command and custom chain configuration file with the custom command enabled to handle its processing. For Struts versions 1.3 and later, you must configure the Struts **ActionServlet** definition in the **web.xml** file to use a Tiles-specific chain configuration file. Following is an example of the necessary servlet configuration with the additional configuration details in bold:

```
<servlet>
  <servlet-name>action</servlet-name>
  <servlet-class>org.apache.struts.action.ActionServlet</servlet-class>
  <init-param>
    <param-name>config</param-name>
```

```
    <param-value>/WEB-INF/struts-config.xml</param-value>
  </init-param>
  <init-param>
    <param-name>chainConfig</param-name>
    <param-value>org/apache/struts/tiles/chain-config.xml</param-value>
  </init-param>
  <load-on-startup>1</load-on-startup>
</servlet>
```

This will cause Struts to load the Tiles-specific **chain-config.xml** file from the Tiles **struts-tiles.jar** file.

Note that your application's Struts configuration file must conform to the Struts configuration file DTD, which specifies the order in which elements are to appear in the file. Because of this, you must place the Tiles **<plug-in>** definition in the proper place in the file. The easiest way to ensure that you are properly ordering elements in the file is to use a tool, such as Struts Console, that automatically formats your configuration file so that it conforms to the DTD.

Table 19-1 lists each of the tags used to configure the Tiles configuration file and provides a short description of each tag's purpose.

The Tiles Configuration File Tags

The remainder of this chapter discusses each tag in detail, including a complete description of the tag, the tag's DTD definition, a table that lists each of the tag's attributes (if the tag has attributes), and a usage example for the tag. In the tables that describe each tag's attributes, pay special attention to the Required column, which denotes whether the given attribute is required when using the tag. In addition to the required column denoting whether an attribute is required, the rows for required attributes are highlighted in gray so that you can determine at a glance which attributes are required. If an attribute is required and you do not specify it when using the tag, the Tiles framework will not be properly configured and, consequently, will not function properly.

PART IV

Tag	Description
add	Defines an entry for a list created with the **putList** tag.
bean	Defines an entry (of the specified type) for a list created with the **putList** tag.
definition	Defines a "tile" and assigns a logical name to it.
item	Defines a **MenuItem** entry for a list created with the **putList** tag.
put	Defines an attribute for a definition.
putList	Defines a list attribute (of **java.util.List** type) containing an ordered collection of individual attributes.
set-property	Defines a property and its value for a bean defined with the **bean** tag.
tiles-definitions	Is the root tag for the Tiles configuration file and thus encapsulates all other tags in the file.

TABLE 19-1 Tiles Configuration File Tags

The add Tag

The **add** tag is used to define an entry for a list created with the **putList** tag. There are two ways that the value for the entry can be specified. The value can be specified with the **value** attribute, or the value can be placed between opening and closing **add** tags, as shown next:

```
<add>value goes here</add>
```

DTD Definition

Following is the definition for the **add** tag from the Tiles configuration file DTD:

```
<!ELEMENT add (#PCDATA)>
```

Attributes

Attribute	Description	Required
content	Deprecated. Originally for compatibility with the now-defunct Template Tag Library. Use the **value** attribute instead.	No
direct	Deprecated. Originally for compatibility with the now-defunct Template Tag Library. Use the **type** attribute set to *string* instead.	No
type	Specifies the type (*string*, *page*, or *definition*) of the value. If present, it indicates how the value specified with the **value** attribute is treated.	No
value	Specifies the value for this entry.	No

Example Usage

The following example illustrates the basic usage of the **add** tag:

```
<definition name="mainLayout"
            path="/layouts/main.jsp">
  <putList name="urls">
    <add value="http://www.google.com/"/>
    <add value="http://www.yahoo.com/"/>
  </putList>
</definition>
```

Each **add** definition is added to the enclosing list in the order specified.

The bean Tag

The **bean** tag is used to define an entry (of the specified type) for a list created with the **putList** tag.

DTD Definition

Following is the definition for the **bean** tag from the Tiles configuration file DTD:

```
<!ELEMENT bean (set-property*)>
```

Attribute

Attribute	Description	Required
classtype	Specifies the fully qualified class name for the bean.	Yes

Example Usage

The following snippet illustrates how to use the **bean** tag:

```
<definition name="mainLayout"
            path="/layouts/main.jsp">
  <putList name="items">
    <bean classtype="org.apache.struts.tiles.beans.SimpleMenuItem">
      <set-property property="link" value="aLink1"/>
      <set-property property="value" value="aValue1"/>
    </bean>
  </putList>
</definition>
```

Beans defined with the **bean** tag can have their properties initialized at creation by nesting **set-property** tags with the name of the property and the value to be initialized.

The definition Tag

The **definition** tag is used to define a tile (which is a region within a page) and assign a logical name to it.

DTD Definition

Following is the definition for the **definition** tag from the Tiles configuration file DTD:

```
<!ELEMENT definition (icon?, display-name?, description?, put*, putList*)>
```

Attributes

Attribute	Description	Required
controllerClass	Specifies the fully qualified class name of a controller object that is executed before this definition is inserted.	No
controllerUrl	Specifies the URL for a controller that is executed before this definition is inserted.	No
extends	Specifies the name of another definition that this definition is to extend.	No
name	Specifies the logical name for the definition.	Yes
page	Deprecated. Use the **path** attribute instead.	No
path	Specifies the URL for the tile.	No
role	Specifies a role to check against the currently authenticated user. If the user is not in the specified role, this definition will not be inserted.	No

Attribute	Description	Required
template	Deprecated. Originally for compatibility with the now-defunct Template Tag Library. Use the **path** attribute instead.	No

Example Usage

The following example illustrates the basic usage of the **definition** tag:

```
<definition name="mainLayout"
            path="/layouts/main.jsp">
  <put name="header" value="/layouts/header.jsp"/>
  <put name="footer" value="/layouts/footer.jsp"/>
</definition>
```

Each of the attributes nested underneath the **definition** tag can be accessed by the JSP specified with the **path** attribute.

The item Tag

The **item** tag is used to define a **MenuItem** entry for a list created with the **putList** tag.

DTD Definition

Following is the definition for the **item** tag from the Tiles configuration file DTD:

```
<!ELEMENT item (#PCDATA)>
```

Attributes

Attribute	Description	Required
classtype	Specifies the fully qualified class name of the item. If specified, it must be a subclass of **org.apache.struts.tiles.beans.MenuItem**.	No
icon	Specifies the value to set the bean's **icon** property to.	No
link	Specifies the value to set the bean's **link** property to.	Yes
tooltip	Specifies the value to set the bean's **tooltip** property to.	No
value	Specifies the value to set the bean's **value** property to.	Yes

Example Usage

The following example illustrates the basic usage of the **item** tag:

```
<definition name="mainLayout"
            path="/layouts/main.jsp">
  <putList name="items">
    <item value="Home" link="/index.jsp"/>
    <item value="Search" link="/search.jsp"/>
  </putList>
</definition>
```

The values specified with the **value** and **link** attributes are used to initialize the corresponding properties on the **MenuItem** object.

The put Tag

The **put** tag is used to define an attribute for a definition. There are two ways that the value for the attribute can be specified. The value can be specified with the **value** attribute, or the value can be placed between opening and closing **put** tags, as shown next:

```
<put name="header">value goes here</put>
```

DTD Definition

Following is the definition for the **put** tag from the Tiles configuration file DTD:

```
<!ELEMENT put (#PCDATA)>
```

Attributes

Attribute	Description	Required
content	Deprecated. Originally for compatibility with the now-defunct Template Tag Library. Use the **value** attribute instead.	No
direct	Deprecated. Originally for compatibility with the now-defunct Template Tag Library. Use the **type** attribute set to *string* instead.	No
name	Specifies the name for the attribute.	Yes
type	Specifies the type (*string*, *page*, or *definition*) of the value. If present, it indicates how the value specified with the **value** attribute is treated.	No
value	Specifies the value for the attribute.	No

Example Usage

The following example illustrates the basic usage of the **put** tag:

```
<definition name="mainLayout"
            path="/layouts/main.jsp">
  <put name="header" value="/layouts/header.jsp"/>
  <put name="footer" value="/layouts/footer.jsp"/>
</definition>
```

Defining attributes with the **put** tag is as simple as specifying their names and values.

The putList Tag

The **putList** tag is used to define a list attribute (of **java.util.List** type) containing an ordered collection of individual attributes. The list can be populated with **add**, **item**, or **bean** definitions or any combination thereof.

DTD Definition

Following is the definition for the **putList** tag from the Tiles configuration file DTD:

```
<!ELEMENT putList ((add*|item*|bean*|putList*)+)>
```

Attribute

Attribute	Description	Required
name	Specifies the name of the list.	Yes

Example Usage

The following example illustrates the basic usage of the **putList** tag:

```
<definition name="mainLayout"
            path="/layouts/main.jsp">
  <putList name="urls">
    <add value="http://www.google.com/"/>
    <add value="http://www.yahoo.com/"/>
  </putList>
</definition>
```

Each tag nested between opening and closing **putList** tags will be added to the backing **java.util.List** instance in the order specified.

The set-property Tag

The **set-property** tag is used to define a property and its value for a bean defined with the **bean** tag. The Tiles framework uses reflection to look up and invoke a setter method (e.g., **setMyProp( )** for a property called **myProp**) on the enclosing bean based on the name specified with this tag's **property** attribute.

DTD Definition

Following is the definition for the **set-property** tag from the Tiles configuration file DTD:

```
<!ELEMENT set-property EMPTY>
```

Attributes

Attribute	Description	Required
property	Specifies the name of the property.	Yes
value	Specifies the value of the property.	Yes

Example Usage

The following example illustrates the basic usage of the **set-property** tag:

```
<definition name="mainLayout"
            path="/layouts/main.jsp">
  <putList name="items">
    <bean classtype="org.apache.struts.tiles.beans.SimpleMenuItem">
      <set-property property="link" value="aLink1"/>
      <set-property property="value" value="aValue1"/>
    </bean>
  </putList>
</definition>
```

At run time, when the Tiles framework parses a configuration file with a definition similar to this, it will use reflection to look up and invoke the **setLink( )** and **setValue( )** methods of the class specified by the **bean** tag's **classtype** attribute, passing them the defined values.

The tiles-definitions Tag

The **tiles-definitions** tag is the root tag for the Tiles configuration file and thus encapsulates all other tags in the file. This tag has no other use than to denote the beginning and end of configuration data.

DTD Definition

Following is the definition for the **tiles-definitions** tag from the Tiles configuration file DTD:

```
<!ELEMENT tiles-definitions (definition+)>
```

Example Usage

The following snippet illustrates how to use the **tiles-definitions** tag:

```
<tiles-definitions>
  <definition .../>
  <definition .../>
  ...
</tiles-definitions>
```

Metadata Tags

Several of the tags for the Tiles configuration file give you the option to nest metadata tags. The metadata tags exist solely for adding extra information to the configuration file that will show up in GUI tools and the like; the Tiles framework, itself, ignores the metadata tags. None of the metadata tags has any attributes; thus you just add text between opening and closing tags to specify their value, as shown here:

```
<action path="/search"
        type="com.jamesholmes.minihr.SearchAction">
  <icon>
    <small-icon>small.gif</small-icon>
    <large-icon>large.gif</large-icon>
  </icon>
  <display-name>Search Action</display-name>
  <description>Search Action searches for employees.</description>
</action>
```

The following table lists each of the metadata tags and its description.

Tag	Description
description	Defines descriptive text for the enclosing tag.
display-name	Defines a short description (or name) for the enclosing tag.
icon	Encapsulates an instance of the **large-icon** and **small-icon** tags.
large-icon	Defines the location for a large (32×32 pixel) icon to associate to the enclosing tag.
small-icon	Defines the location for a small (16×16 pixel) icon to associate to the enclosing tag.

Editing Tiles Configuration Files with Struts Console

As you can imagine, trying to remember every tag's list of attributes as well as its proper order inside the configuration file can be cumbersome. If you make a mistake in typing any of the tag's or attribute's names, your Struts application will not be configured properly. To simplify the creation and modification of Tiles configuration files, you can use a GUI tool called Struts Console. Struts Console is a stand-alone Java Swing application that provides a graphical editor for Tiles configuration files. Additionally, Struts Console can be used as a plugin with several major Java IDEs, providing a seamless Struts development experience.

Struts Console is free software and can be downloaded from http://www.jamesholmes.com/struts/. This Web site has all the information for configuring Struts Console to work with your favorite Java IDE. In addition, this book's appendix provides a Struts Console quick reference. Figure 19-1 shows Struts Console running as a stand-alone application.

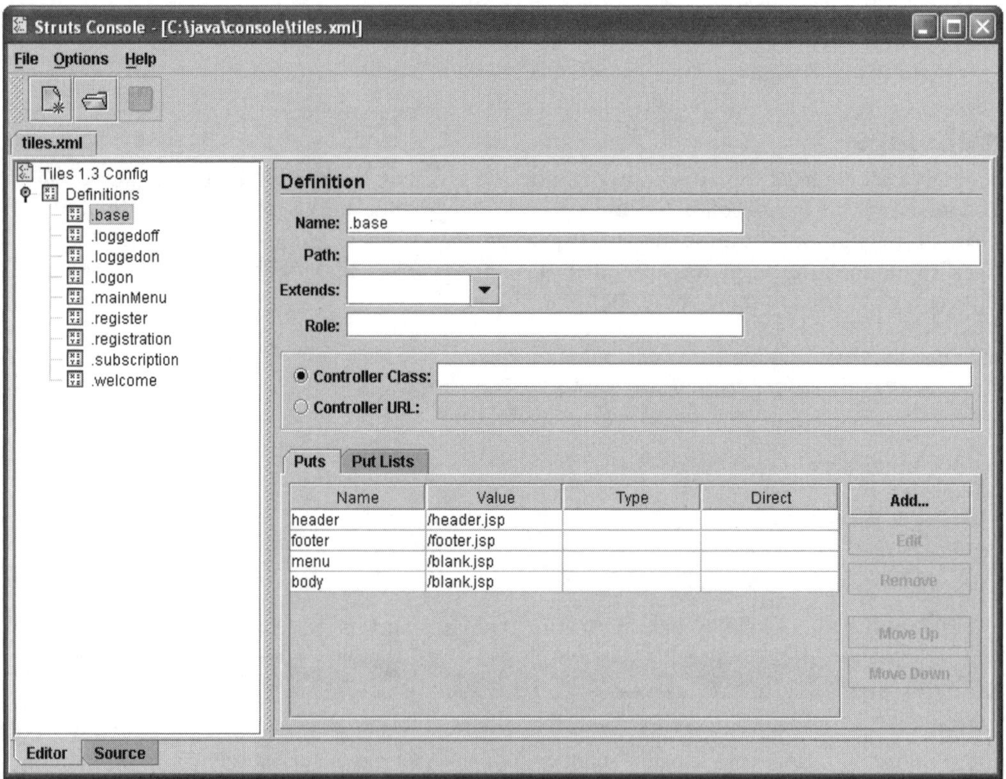

FIGURE 19-1 Struts Console running as a stand-alone application

CHAPTER 20

The Validator Configuration Files

The Validator framework is designed to enable you to specify validations declaratively in external configuration files instead of having to hard-code validation logic into the application. This simplifies development because validations can be changed, added, or removed as necessary without having to recompile any code. Using configuration files also enables a significant amount of code reuse for the validation routines.

The Validator configuration files are XML-based and their formats are governed by a Document Type Definition (DTD) file that specifies how the configuration tags must be ordered in each file, what settings are required, and so on. Each Validator configuration file declares its conformance to the DTD by having the following DOCTYPE definition at the top of the file:

```
<!DOCTYPE form-validation PUBLIC
  "-//Apache Software Foundation//DTD Commons
   Validator Rules Configuration 1.3.0//EN"
  "http://jakarta.apache.org/commons/dtds/validator_1_3_0.dtd">
```

When Validator reads the configuration file, its XML parser uses the DOCTYPE definition to determine the DTD that the XML file must conform to. If configured to do so, the XML parser will validate the XML file's conformance to the DTD.

NOTE *An in-depth discussion of using the Validator framework is found in Chapter 6.*

Two Configuration Files

In general, Validator uses two XML configuration files to tell it which validation routines should be "installed" and how they should be applied for a given application, respectively. The first configuration file, typically named **validator-rules.xml**, declares the validation routines that are plugged into the framework and assigns logical names to each of the validations. Additionally, the **validator-rules.xml** file is used to define client-side JavaScript code for each validation routine. If configured to do so, Validator will emit this JavaScript code to the browser so that validations are performed on the client side as well as the server side. The second configuration file, typically named **validation.xml**, defines which validation routines are applied to which Form Beans. The definitions in this file use the logical names of Form Beans from the Struts configuration file along with the logical names of validation routines from the **validator-rules.xml** file to tie the two together.

Although it is standard to use two configuration files for Validator, it is not technically required. Both configuration files must conform to the same DTD and thus could be combined into one large file that specifies both the validation routines and their use with forms. However, it's advantageous to have the individual files because you can reuse the **validation-rules.xml** file in multiple applications. Similarly, if your application uses the Struts module feature, then you will likely have a **validation.xml** file for each module. Embedding the contents of **validator-rules.xml** in **validation.xml** would result in a great deal of redundancy in this scenario.

Understanding XML DTDs

Because DTD conformance is important for Validator tags, a brief overview of how XML DTDs work is given here. DTDs specify a set of tags and attributes that make up a specific XML document type. DTDs also specify the order in which tags must be placed in the file, and the relationship between tags. For example, a tag definition defines what other tags can be nested inside of it, how many occurrences can be nested, and in what order the nesting can occur. Additionally, DTDs define which tag attributes are required and which are optional.

Each tag described in this chapter has a DTD Definition section that lists the tag's definition in the Struts configuration file DTD. The definitions will be similar to the one shown in the following snippet:

```
<!ELEMENT form-set (constant*, form+)>
```

This example defines a **form-set** tag and the tags that can be nested inside of it. According to the definition, the tag can have nested **constant** and **form** tags. The asterisk (*) and plus (+) characters following the nested tags' names indicate the number of times the nested tag can be nested. The * character indicates that the tag can be nested zero or more (unlimited) times. The + character indicates that the tag must be nested at least once and as many times as you'd like. A question mark (?) character indicates that the tag can be nested zero or one time. No trailing character means that the tag must be nested exactly once and no more. If no tags can be nested inside the defined tag, EMPTY is used to denote that, as shown next:

```
<!ELEMENT arg EMPTY>
```

Enabling the Validator Plugin

Although the Validator framework comes packaged with Struts, by default Validator is not enabled. In order to enable and use Validator, you have to add the following **<plug-in>** definition to your application's Struts configuration file:

```
<!-- Validator Configuration -->
<plug-in className="org.apache.struts.validator.ValidatorPlugIn">
  <set-property property="pathnames"
                   value="/org/apache/struts/validator/validator-rules.xml,
                          /WEB-INF/validation.xml"/>
</plug-in>
```

This definition causes Struts to load and initialize the Validator plugin for your application. Upon initialization, the plugin loads the comma-delimited list of Validator configuration files specified by the **pathnames** property. Each configuration file's path must be specified using a Web application–relative path or using a path to a file on the classpath of the server, as shown in the preceding example. The **validator-rules.xml** file shown in the preceding example happens to be stored in the core Struts **.jar** file and thus it is accessible via the classpath.

Note that your application's Struts configuration file must conform to the Struts configuration file DTD, which specifies the order in which elements are to appear in the file. Because of this, you must place the Validator **<plug-in>** definition in the proper place in the file. The easiest way to ensure that you are properly ordering elements in the file is to use a tool, such as Struts Console, that automatically formats your configuration file so that it conforms to the DTD.

The Validator Configuration File Tags

Table 20-1 lists each of the tags used to configure the Validator configuration file and provides a short description of each tag's purpose.

Tag	Description
arg	Defines a parametric replacement value (e.g., **{0}**, **{1}**, **{2}**, and so on) for a validation's error message.
constant	Defines a named value that can be used as a replacement parameter within the **field** tag's nested tags.
constant-name	Defines the **constant** tag's constant name.
constant-value	Defines the **constant** tag's constant value.
field	Defines the set of validations that will be applied to a form's field.
form	Defines a Form Bean whose set of fields will be validated based on rules defined by nested **field** tags.
form-validation	Is the root tag for the Validator configuration file and thus encapsulates all other tags in the file.
formset	Defines validations for a set of forms.
global	Encapsulates the set of validations and the set of constants that Validator will use.
javascript	Defines client-side JavaScript code for a validation.
msg	Defines an error message that will override a validation's default message.
validator	Defines a validation routine and assigns it a logical name.
var	Defines a variable that will be passed to each of a field's validators at run time.
var-jstype	Defines the **var** tag's JavaScript type.
var-name	Defines the **var** tag's variable name.
var-value	Defines the **var** tag's variable value.

Table 20-1 Validator Configuration File Tags

The remainder of this chapter discusses each tag in detail, including a complete description of the tag, the tag's DTD definition, a table that lists each of the tag's attributes (if the tag has attributes), and a usage example for the tag. In the tables that describe a tag's attributes, pay special attention to the Required column, which denotes whether the given attribute is required when using the tag. In addition to the required column denoting whether an attribute is required, the rows for required attributes are highlighted in gray so that you can determine at a glance which attributes are required. If an attribute is required and you do not specify it when using the tag, the Validator framework will not be properly configured and, consequently, will not function properly.

The arg Tag

The **arg** tag is used to define a parametric replacement value (e.g., **{0}**, **{1}**, **{2}**, and so on) for a validation's error message. Before the specified validation's error message is generated, it is parsed and any {*N*} reference is replaced with the message specified by the corresponding tag. Following is an example resource bundle message that contains a **{0}** reference:

```
errors.required={0} is a required field
```

At run time, when Validator uses this error message, it will attempt to replace any parametric references with the values specified by the **arg** tag. Thus, if "Username" was specified with the **arg** tag, the preceding message would be turned into the following message:

```
Username is a required field
```

NOTE *In previous versions of Validator there were multiple* **arg** *tags (i.e.,* **arg0–arg3***) that were used to specify the parametric replacement values. The multiple tags were deprecated and eventually removed in favor of having a single* **arg** *tag with a* **position** *attribute so that an endless number of parametric values could be specified. Before only replacement values 0–3 could be specified.*

DTD Definition

Following is the definition for the **arg** tag from the Validator configuration file DTD:

```
<!ELEMENT arg EMPTY>
```

Attributes

Attribute	Description	Required
bundle	Specifies the logical name of a resource bundle that will be used when looking up the message key specified by the **key** attribute.	No
key	Specifies a key for a resource bundle message that will be used as the replacement value.	Yes
name	Specifies the logical name of the validation that this tag will be applied to.	No
position	Specifies the position of the parametric replacement value (e.g., 0, 1, 2, etc.).	No
resource	Accepts *true* or *false* to specify whether the **key** attribute's value will *not* be taken as a literal value rather than a message key. Defaults to *true*.	*No*

Example Usage

The following example illustrates the basic usage of the **arg** tag:

```
<field property="zipCode"
       depends="required,mask">
  <arg position="0" key="prompt.zipCode"/>
  <var>
    <var-name>mask</var-name>
    <var-value>\>^\d{5}\d*$</var-value>
  </var>
</field>
```

This example specifies the **{0}** replacement value to use for each of the validations specified by the **field** tag's **depends** attribute. Alternatively, the **arg** tag can be configured to apply to only a specific validation's error message by using the **name** attribute, as shown next:

```
<arg position="0" name="required" key="prompt.zipCode"/>
```

In this example, the replacement value will be applied only to the **required** validation's error message.

The constant Tag

The **constant** tag is used to define a named value that can be used as a replacement parameter within the **field** tag's nested tags. For example, a constant can be used to define an often-used regular expression for the configurable **mask** validation, as shown here:

```
<constant>
  <constant-name>zip</constant-name>
  <constant-value>^\d{5}\d*$</constant-value>
</constant>
```

Each time a ZIP code needs to be validated with the **mask** validation, the constant can be used to specify the regular expression to use, instead of having to specify the regular expression itself, as shown next:

```
<field property="zipCode"
       depends="required,mask">
  <var>
    <var-name>mask</var-name>
    <var-value>${zip}</var-value>
  </var>
</field>
```

To use constants, you simply enclose the constant name with an opening **${** and a closing **}**.

DTD Definition

Following is the definition for the **constant** tag from the Validator configuration file DTD:

```
<!ELEMENT constant (constant-name, constant-value)>
```

Example Usage

The following snippet illustrates how to use the **constant** tag:

```
<global>
  <constant>
```

PART IV

```
    <constant-name>zip</constant-name>
    <constant-value>^\d{5}\d*$</constant-value>
  </constant>
</global>
```

The **constant** tag can be used an unlimited number of times. Each use of the **constant** tag must have nested **constant-name** and **constant-value** tags.

The constant-name Tag

The **constant-name** tag is used to define the **constant** tag's constant name. This tag must be nested exactly once underneath the **constant** tag.

DTD Definition

Following is the definition for the **constant-name** tag from the Validator configuration file DTD:

```
<!ELEMENT constant-name (#PCDATA)>
```

Example Usage

The following snippet illustrates how to use the **constant-name** tag:

```
<global>
  <constant>
    <constant-name>zip</constant-name>
    <constant-value>^\d{5}\d*$</constant-value>
  </constant>
</global>
```

The constant-value Tag

The **constant-value** tag is used to define the **constant** tag's constant value. This tag must be nested exactly once underneath the **constant** tag.

DTD Definition

Following is the definition for the **constant-value** tag from the Validator configuration file DTD:

```
<!ELEMENT constant-value (#PCDATA)>
```

Example Usage

The following snippet illustrates how to use the **constant-value** tag:

```
<global>
  <constant>
    <constant-name>zip</constant-name>
    <constant-value>^\d{5}\d*$</constant-value>
  </constant>
</global>
```

The field Tag

The **field** tag is used to define the set of validations that will be applied to a form's field.

DTD Definition

Following is the definition for the **field** tag from the Validator configuration file DTD:

```
<!ELEMENT field (msg|arg|var)*>
```

Attributes

Attribute	Description	Required
depends	Specifies the comma-delimited list of validations that will be applied to this field.	No
indexedListProperty	Specifies the name of a collection field whose elements will be validated. If this attribute is specified, the value specified with the **property** attribute will be used as the name of the property that will be validated on each object in the collection.	No
page	Specifies a value that will be compared against the enclosing Form Bean's **page** property if it has one. If the value if less than or equal to the Form Bean's **page** property, then this field definition's validations will be applied. If not, they will be bypassed. This feature is useful for wizard-style forms where fields need to be conditionally validated based on which page the wizard is on currently.	No
property	Specifies the name of the form field.	Yes

Example Usage

The following example illustrates the basic usage of the **field** tag:

```
<field property="zipCode"
       depends="required,mask">
  <arg position="0" key="prompt.zipCode"/>
  <var>
    <var-name>mask</var-name>
    <var-value>^\d{5}\d*$</var-value>
  </var>
</field>
```

Each validation specified with the **depends** attribute will be executed in order. Consequently, if a validation fails, the remaining validations will be skipped. Additionally, each validation can be globally or individually customized with nested **arg**, **msg**, and **var** tags.

The form Tag

The **form** tag is used to define a Form Bean whose set of fields will be validated based on rules defined by nested **field** tags.

DTD Definition

Following is the definition for the **form** tag from the Validator configuration file DTD:

```
<!ELEMENT form (field*)>
```

Attributes

Attribute	Description	Required
extends	Specifies the name of another form that this form extends.	No
name	Specifies the name of the form.	Yes

Example Usage

The following snippet illustrates how to use the **form** tag:

```
<form name="logonForm">
  <field property="username" depends="required">
    <arg position="0" key="prompt.username"/>
  </field>
  <field property="password" depends="required">
    <arg position="0" key="prompt.password"/>
  </field>
</form>
```

The name specified with the **name** attribute must match the logical name of a Form Bean from the Struts configuration file. Similarly, each of the form's nested **field** tags must match a property of the Form Bean.

The form-validation Tag

The **form-validation** tag is the root tag for the Validator configuration file and thus encapsulates all other tags in the file. This tag has no other use than to denote the beginning and end of configuration data.

DTD Definition

Following is the definition for the **form-validation** tag from the Validator configuration file DTD:

```
<!ELEMENT form-validation (global*, formset*)>
```

Example Usage

The following snippet illustrates how to use the **form-validation** tag:

```
<form-validation>
  <global>
    ...
  </global>
  <formset>
    ...
  </formset>
</form-validation>
```

The formset Tag

The **formset** tag is used to define validations for a set of forms. By default, the validations are applied to the enclosing forms for users within any locale. However, you can optionally use the **country**, **language**, and **variant** attributes to tailor a set of validations to a specific locale. The **formset** definition without a **country**, **language**, or **variant** attribute specified is considered the default set of validations. Any other **formset** definitions with one or multiple of the locale-narrowing attributes will override any overlapping forms. That is, if the default (or master) form set defines three forms and a locale-specific form set overrides one of the forms for French users, only the one form will be overridden for French users—not every form defined by the default form set.

DTD Definition

Following is the definition for the **formset** tag from the Validator configuration file DTD:

```
<!ELEMENT formset (constant*, form+)>
```

Attributes

Attribute	Description	Required
country	Specifies the locale country code that this form set's definitions will be applied to.	No
language	Specifies the locale language code that this form set's definitions will be applied to.	No
variant	Specifies the locale variant that this form set's definitions will be applied to.	No

Example Usage

The following example illustrates the basic usage of the **formset** tag:

```
<formset>
  <form name="logonForm">
    ...
  </form>
  <form name="searchForm">
    ...
  </form>
</formset>
```

Because this example omits the **country**, **language**, and **variant** attributes, the enclosed validations will be applied to users within any locale unless specifically overridden with other **formset** definitions.

If desired, one or more forms' validations can be overridden by specifying additional form sets for specific locales, as shown next:

```
<formset language="fr">
  <form name="logonForm">
    ...
  </form>
</formset>
```

This example provides validation settings for all users whose locale has French as its language. The **country**, **language**, and **variant** attributes can be used together or individually based on how specific or broad the validation settings will be.

The global Tag

The **global** tag is used to encapsulate the set of validations and the set of constants that Validator will use. This tag is simply a container for **validator** and **constant** tags.

DTD Definition

Following is the definition for the **global** tag from the Validator configuration file DTD:

```
<!ELEMENT global (validator*, constant*)>
```

Example Usage

The following example illustrates the basic usage of the **global** tag:

```
<global>
  <constant>
    <constant-name>zip</constant-name>
    <constant-value>^\d{5}\d*$</constant-value>
  </constant>
</global>
```

The javascript Tag

The **javascript** tag is used to define client-side JavaScript code for a validation. The code placed between opening and closing **javascript** tags will be used to perform a preliminary client-side (browser) validation if Validator is configured to do so.

DTD Definition

Following is the definition for the **javascript** tag from the Validator configuration file DTD:

```
<!ELEMENT javascript (#PCDATA)>
```

Example Usage

The following example illustrates how to use the **javascript** tag:

```
<validator name="minlength"
      classname="org.apache.struts.validator.FieldChecks"
         method="validateMinLength"
   methodParams="java.lang.Object,
                 org.apache.commons.validator.ValidatorAction,
                 org.apache.commons.validator.Field,
                 org.apache.struts.action.ActionMessages,
                 org.apache.commons.validator.Validator,
                 javax.servlet.http.HttpServletRequest"
            msg="errors.minlength">
  <javascript>
    <![CDATA[
      function validateMinLength(form) {
        var isValid = true;
        var focusField = null;
        var i = 0;
        var fields = new Array();
        oMinLength = new minlength();
        for (x in oMinLength) {
```

```
          var field = form[oMinLength[x][0]];
          if (field.type == 'text' ||
              field.type == 'textarea') {
            var iMin = parseInt(oMinLength[x][2]("minlength"));
            if ((trim(field.value).length > 0) &&
                (field.value.length < iMin)) {
              if (i == 0) {
                focusField = field;
              }
              fields[i++] = oMinLength[x][1];
              isValid = false;
            }
          }
        }
        if (fields.length > 0) {
          focusField.focus();
          alert(fields.join('\n'));
        }
        return isValid;
      }
    ]]>
  </javascript>
</validator>
```

Notice that the JavaScript code is enclosed in a **<![CDATA[ ]]>** tag. This is an XML facility that is used to notify XML parsers that the enclosed text should be taken as is and should not be parsed. Normally, parsers would parse the text for other tags or XML entities; however, sometimes it's necessary to specify text that has XML-like references in it, but that should not be parsed. The **<![CDATA[ ]]>** tag makes that possible.

NOTE *This example of using the* **<javascript>** *tag is for illustration purposes and does not exactly match the actual definition for the* **minlength** *validation. In the latest versions of Validator, all of the JavaScript code has been removed from the* **validator-rules.xml** *file and moved into separate* **.js** *files (e.g.,* **validateMinLength.js***). The file the JavaScript version of a routine is stored in is specified with the* **jsFunction** *attribute of the* **<validator>** *tag using a fully qualified path to the file. However, if you want to override the default JavaScript code provided by a validation routine or are adding your own validation routine with associated JavaScript code, you can use the* **<javascript>** *tag as shown.*

The msg Tag

The **msg** tag is used to define an error message that will override a validation's default message. When validations are defined with the **validator** tag, they define a resource bundle message key for an error message that will be used when the validation fails. Sometimes, however, it's necessary to use an error message other than the default for a validation. The **msg** tag makes this possible by allowing for an alternative message to be set for a specific use of the validation.

DTD Definition

Following is the definition for the **msg** tag from the Validator configuration file DTD:

```
<!ELEMENT msg EMPTY>
```

Attributes

Attribute	Description	Required
bundle	Specifies the logical name of a resource bundle that will be used when looking up the message key specified by the **key** attribute.	No
key	Specifies a resource bundle message key that the specified validation will use for its error message instead of its default message.	Yes
name	Specifies the logical name of the validation whose error message will be overridden.	No
resource	Accepts *true* or *false* to specify whether the **key** attribute's value will *not* be taken as a literal value rather than a message key. Defaults to *true*.	*No*

Example Usage

The following example illustrates the basic usage of the **msg** tag:

```
<field property="ssNum"
        depends="required,mask">
  <msg name="mask" key="errors.ssNum"/>
  <arg position="0" key="ssNum.prompt"/>
  <var>
    <var-name>mask</var-name>
    <var-value></var-value>
  </var>
</field>
```

In this example, the **mask** validation is overridden to use the **errors.ssNum** message key instead of the one defined by the validation. As you can see, the **msg** tag is useful for specifying custom error messages for validations.

The validator Tag

The **validator** tag is used to define a validation routine and assign it a logical name. Each definition specifies the Java class, method, and method arguments for the validation routine. Once defined, the validation routine can be applied to form fields using its logical name.

DTD Definition

Following is the definition for the **validator** tag from the Validator configuration file DTD:

```
<!ELEMENT validator (javascript?)>
```

Attributes

Attribute	Description	Required
classname	Specifies the name of the class that houses the validation routine.	Yes
depends	Specifies a comma-delimited list of other validations defined by the **validator** tag that must pass before this validation is executed.	No

Attribute	Description	Required
jsFunction	Specifies the JavaScript method name for this validation routine.	No
jsFunctionName	Specifies an alternate method name to use for the JavaScript code generated by this tag if client-side validation is enabled.	No
method	Specifies the name of the validation routine's method in the class specified by the **classname** attribute.	Yes
methodParams	Specifies the comma-delimited list (in order) of the validation routine's arguments.	Yes
msg	Specifies a resource bundle message key for the error message that will be generated if this validation fails.	Yes
name	Specifies the logical name for the validation.	Yes

Example Usage

The following example illustrates the basic usage of the **validator** tag:

```
<validator name="minlength"
      classname="org.apache.struts.validator.FieldChecks"
         method="validateMinLength"
   methodParams="java.lang.Object,
                 org.apache.commons.validator.ValidatorAction,
                 org.apache.commons.validator.Field,
                 org.apache.struts.action.ActionMessages,
                 org.apache.commons.validator.Validator,
                 javax.servlet.http.HttpServletRequest"
            msg="errors.minlength"/>
```

Each validation definition specifies the Java class, method, and method arguments for the validation. Validator uses reflection to instantiate and invoke the validation at run time.

PART IV

The var Tag

The **var** tag is used to define a variable that will be passed to each of a field's validations at run time. This allows validations to be configurable. For example, the maximum length validation has a variable that specifies its maximum length that must be set using this tag. Additionally, variables defined with the **var** tag can be used by the **arg** and **msg** tags, as shown here:

```
<arg position="0" name="maxlength" key="${var:maxlength}" resource="false"/>
```

To reference variables defined by the **var** tag from other tags, you must use this form: **${var:varName}** (where **varName** is the name of the defined variable).

The variable's name, value, and JavaScript type are defined with nested **var-name**, **var-value**, and **var-jstype** tags, respectively.

DTD Definition

Following is the definition for the **var** tag from the Validator configuration file DTD:

```
<!ELEMENT var (var-name,var-value,var-jstype?)>
```

Example Usage

The following snippet illustrates how to use the **var** tag:

```
<field property="username"
       depends="required,maxlength">
  <arg position="0" key="prompt.username"/>
  <var>
    <var-name>maxlength</var-name>
    <var-value>16</var-value>
  </var>
</field>
```

The **var** tag can be nested underneath the **field** tag an unlimited number of times. Each use of the **var** tag must have nested **var-name** and **var-value** tags.

The var-jstype Tag

The **var-jstype** tag is used to define the **var** tag's JavaScript type. This tag must be nested exactly once underneath the **var** tag or not at all. The JavaScript type specifies the data type of the variable that will be created in the client-side JavaScript version of the validation routine. There are three acceptable values for the type: *int, string,* and *regexp.*

DTD Definition

Following is the definition for the **var-jstype** tag from the Validator configuration file DTD:

```
<!ELEMENT var-jstype (#PCDATA)>
```

Example Usage

The following snippet illustrates how to use the **var-jstype** tag:

```
<field property="username"
       depends="required,maxlength">
  <arg position="0" key="prompt.username"/>
  <var>
    <var-name>maxlength</var-name>
    <var-value>16</var-value>
    <var-jstype>int</var-jstype>
  </var>
</field>
```

The var-name Tag

The **var-name** tag is used to define the **var** tag's variable name. This tag must be nested exactly once underneath the **var** tag.

DTD Definition

Following is the definition for the **var-name** tag from the Validator configuration file DTD:

```
<!ELEMENT var-name (#PCDATA)>
```

Example Usage

The following snippet illustrates how to use the **var-name** tag:

```
<field property="username"
       depends="required,maxlength">
  <arg position="0" key="prompt.username"/>
  <var>
    <var-name>maxlength</var-name>
    <var-value>16</var-value>
  </var>
</field>
```

The var-value Tag

The **var-value** tag is used to define the **var** tag's variable value. This tag must be nested exactly once underneath the **var** tag.

DTD Definition

Following is the definition for the **var-value** tag from the Validator configuration file DTD:

```
<!ELEMENT var-value (#PCDATA)>
```

Example Usage

The following snippet illustrates how to use the **var-value** tag:

```
<field property="username"
       depends="required,maxlength">
  <arg position="0" key="prompt.username"/>
  <var>
    <var-name>maxlength</var-name>
    <var-value>16</var-value>
  </var>
</field>
```


Editing Validator Configuration Files with Struts Console

As you can imagine, trying to remember every tag's list of attributes as well as its proper order inside the configuration file can be cumbersome. If you make a mistake in typing any of the tag's or attribute's names, your Struts application will not be configured properly. To simplify the creation and modification of Validator configuration files, you can use a GUI tool called Struts Console. Struts Console is a stand-alone Java Swing application that provides a graphical editor for Validator configuration files. Additionally, Struts Console can be used as a plugin with several major Java IDEs, providing a seamless Struts development experience.

Struts Console is free software and can be downloaded from http://www.jamesholmes.com/struts/. This Web site has all the information for configuring Struts Console to work with your favorite Java IDE. In addition, this book's appendix provides a Struts Console quick reference. Figure 20-1 shows Struts Console running as a stand-alone application.

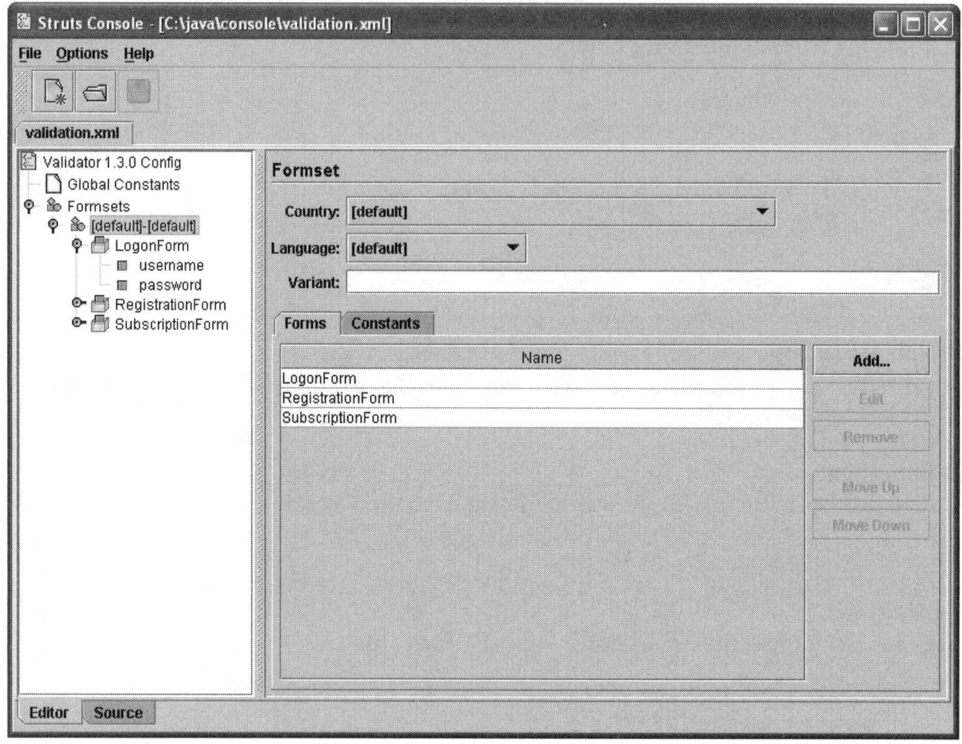

FIGURE 20-1 Struts Console running as a stand-alone application

V

PART

Struts Extensions

CHAPTER 21
Struts Scripting

CHAPTER 22
The Struts-Faces Integration Library

CHAPTER 23
Using AJAX with Struts

21

CHAPTER

Struts Scripting

Developing Web applications in Java can be tedious and time consuming. Most servlet containers require a Web application to be reloaded every time one of the application's Java classes is modified and recompiled or when a resource file such as **web.xml** is modified. While Struts greatly enhances basic JSP and servlet Web application development by providing a robust framework to leverage, it is not immune to these inefficiencies—Struts suffers from the same time consuming constraint of application reloads. Each time a Struts Action class, Form Bean, Struts configuration file, or resource bundle file is modified, the application must be reloaded. To get around this limitation and to speed up development time, Don Brown created *Struts Scripting*. Struts Scripting was originally a third-party extension to Struts but was later incorporated into the core Struts codebase.

Struts Scripting is an extension to Struts that leverages the Jakarta Bean Scripting Framework (BSF) (**http://jakarta.apache.org/bsf/**) to create scripting language–based actions. Because scripting languages are interpreted at run time, Scripting language–based actions have the advantage of not requiring Web application reloads. Although changes to Form Beans, the Struts configuration file, or the resource bundle file still require application reloads, Struts Scripting provides a huge advantage and greatly reduces development time.

Bean Scripting Framework Overview

Before getting into the details of using Struts Scripting, it's necessary to give a brief overview of BSF. BSF is a scripting framework that allows scripting languages to be leveraged by Java applications. As part of this, BSF allows scripting languages to access Java objects and methods. BSF by default supports many popular scripting languages. The following table lists the default scripting languages supported by BSF along with their associated file extension(s).

Language	File Extension(s)
beanbasic	bb
beanshell	bsh
bml	bml
jacl	jacl
java	java
javaclass	class

Language	File Extension(s)
javascript	js
jpython	py
jscript	jss
judoscript	jud, judo
jython	py
lotusscript	lss
netrexx	nrx
perl	pl
perlscript	pls
pnuts	pnut
ruby	rb
vbscript	vbs
xslt	xslt

Languages not supported by default by BSF can be plugged into BSF by providing a BSF engine for the given language. For more details on BSF, see the BSF Web site: **http://jakarta.apache.org/bsf/**.

Struts Scripting Overview

Struts Scripting essentially provides a wrapper around BSF for creating Struts Actions. Instead of writing standard actions in Java, you can write actions in any BSF-supported scripting language of your choice. The main benefit to writing actions in a scripting language (instead of using the traditional approach of coding them in Java) is that the development cycle can be sped up. Writing actions in Java requires action code to be edited and compiled and for the application to be reloaded in the servlet container the code is running on. Struts Scripting, however, significantly reduces development time by allowing the actions to be written in a scripting language that does not need to be recompiled and does not require the application to be reloaded in the servlet container.

To fully understand how Struts Scripting works, a brief architectural overview is in order. Struts Scripting provides a built-in **Action** subclass (**org.apache.struts.scripting.ScriptAction**) that is used to execute script-based actions. **ScriptAction** is configured in the Struts configuration file like any other action but with one additional parameter: the script to execute for the given action mapping. When executed, **ScriptAction** uses BSF to map the specified script's file extension to a particular language. Next, BSF uses the mapped language to execute the specified script. Each time the script is executed, it is re-read. That is the mechanism that allows actions to be modified without requiring the Web application to be reloaded in the servlet container it is running on.

Using Struts Scripting

Using Struts Scripting involves these three steps:

1. Add the Struts Scripting **.jar** files and properties file to the application.
2. Create script-based actions.
3. Configure script-based actions in the application's Struts configuration file.

The following sections describe these steps in detail.

Adding the Struts Scripting .jar Files and Properties File to the Application

A few **.jar** files must be added to the application in order to use Struts Scripting functionality. Each required **.jar** file should be copied to the application's **WEB-INF\lib** directory (or added to the classpath of the server[s] on which the application runs). First, add the Struts Scripting **.jar** file (e.g., **c:\java\struts-1.3.5\lib\struts-scripting-1.3.5.jar**) from the Struts distribution to the application if it is not already present. Next, add the BSF **.jar** file (e.g., **c:\java\struts-1.3.5\lib\bsf-2.3.0.jar**) from the Struts distribution to the application if it is not already present. Finally, scripting language **.jar** files must be added to the application.

Each scripting language has a set of **.jar** files that it needs in order to run. For detailed instructions on which **.jar** files are required for a given scripting language, visit that language's Web site. To give an example of what is involved in adding required scripting language **.jar** files to an application, take Groovy (**http://groovy.codehaus.org/**). First, download Groovy. Next, copy the Groovy **.jar** file (e.g., **c:\java\groovy-1.0-JSR-06\embeddable\groovy-all-1.0-JSR-06.jar**) to the application's **WEB-INF\lib** directory. That's it.

After adding the required **.jar** files to the application, a Struts Scripting properties file must be added to the application for BSF non-default scripting languages. As stated earlier, BSF supports many languages by default without any special configuration; however, any language not supported by default by BSF must be configured in a Struts Scripting properties file. The Struts Scripting properties file specifies the BSF non-default scripting languages being used and their associated script file extensions (e.g., **.groovy** for Groovy scripts, **.jruby** for JRuby scripts, and so on). This file must be named **struts-scripting.properties** and be accessible from the application's classloader (i.e., be placed on the classpath of the server[s] the application runs on). Typically the file is placed in the application's **WEB-INF\classes** directory. The following code shows an example properties file's content:

```
struts-scripting.engine.groovy.class=org.codehaus.groovy.bsf.GroovyEngine
struts-scripting.engine.groovy.extensions=gv,groovy
struts-scripting.engine.jruby.class=org.jruby.javasupport.bsf.JRubyEngine
struts-scripting.engine.jruby.extensions=rb,jruby
```

PART V

There is no limit to the number of scripting languages that can be in use at one time. The preceding example properties file shows how to enable two scripting languages at once: Groovy and JRuby.

Each BSF non-default scripting language is defined using two properties: **struts-scripting.engine.*LANGUAGE_NAME*.class** and **struts-scripting.engine.*LANGUAGE_NAME*.extensions**, where *LANGUAGE_NAME* is an *arbitrary* name assigned to the scripting language. The **struts-scripting.engine.*LANGUAGE_NAME*.class** property specifies the fully qualified class name of the language's BSF engine. The **struts-scripting.engine.*LANGUAGE_NAME*.extensions** property specifies the file extensions that will be mapped to the language. Any number of file extensions can be specified using commas to delimit them.

Creating Script-Based Actions

Creating a script-based action is very similar to creating a standard Java-based action; however, instead of writing the action in Java, you write it in the scripting language of your choice. The scripting language being used determines the specific details of how the action is written, but all script-based actions follow the same general pattern and have the same general operating facilities as Java-based actions. Like Java-based actions, script-based actions can access details of the action mapping, the Form Bean, the HTTP request object, and the HTTP response object. Also like Java-based actions, script-based actions typically specify a forward to inform Struts of how to proceed with navigation at the end of executing the action.

Unlike Java-based actions, script-based actions do not extend **org.apache.struts.action.Action** and do not operate inside of an **execute( )** method. Instead, script-based actions are written like a basic linear script. Script-based actions access the action mapping, the Form Bean, the HTTP request object, and the HTTP response object via implicit predefined variables. Forwards are specified using the predefined **struts** variable and setting either **struts.forwardName** to the logical name of a forward or **struts.forward** to an actual **org.apache.struts.action.ActionForward** object. Following is an example Groovy script–based action that illustrates the basic concepts of creating a script-based action:

```
// Access the Form Bean associated with this Action.
loginForm = struts.form;

// Access Form Bean fields.
username = loginForm.username;
password = loginForm.password;

// Perform processing of data here.
// ...

// Forward to a Forward named "success".
struts.setForwardName("success");
```

As stated, each scripting language has its particular nuances, but in general this is how script-based actions are written. Changes can be quickly made to script-based actions without the need for recompilation or servlet container restarts—simply reload the page that executes the action. For more information on the implicit predefined variables made available to script-based actions, see the section "Predefined Scripting Variables."

Configuring Script-Based Actions in the Application's Struts Configuration File

After creating script-based actions, they must be configured in your application's Struts configuration file. Script-based actions are configured differently than standard Struts actions that subclass **Action**. Instead of specifying the fully qualified class name of an action with the **action** tag's **type** attribute, the **type** attribute is set to the standard Struts Scripting action: **org.apache.struts.scripting.ScriptAction**. **ScriptAction** will execute the script-based action specified with the **action** tag's **parameter** attribute. Following is an example of how to configure a script-based action in the Struts configuration file:

```
<!-- Action Mappings Configuration -->
<action-mappings>
  <action path="/search"
          type="org.apache.struts.scripting.ScriptAction"
```

```
            parameter="/WEB-INF/scripts/Search.groovy"
            name="searchForm"
            scope="request"
            validate="true"
            input="/search.jsp">
    </action>
</action-mappings>
```

As stated, the **type** attribute of the **action** tag must specify that **org.apache.struts.scripting.ScriptAction**. **ScriptAction** executes the script at the location specified by the **parameter** attribute. The remaining **action** tag attributes are the same as would be used with any other action definition.

Predefined Scripting Variables

Struts Scripting makes a set of predefined variables available to scripts. The predefined variables can be used without any special setup or definition; they are simply available. The following table lists the name, type, and description of each predefined variable.

Name	Type	Description
application	javax.servlet.ServletContext	The servlet context object for the Web application.
log	org.apache.commons.logging.Log	A Commons Logging log object for logging.
request	javax.servlet.http.HttpServletRequest	The HTTP request object.
response	javax.servlet.http.HttpServletResponse	The HTTP response object.
session	javax.servlet.http.HttpSession	The HTTP session object.
struts	org.apache.struts.scripting.StrutsInfo	The Struts information container object for accessing Struts objects.

Predefined variables are accessed by name as shown next in the example Groovy script snippet:

```
// Retrieve User object from session using pre-defined "session" variable.
user = session.getAttribute("user");
```

As stated, no setup is required to use the predefined variables.

In addition to the predefined variables provided by Struts Scripting, custom predefined variables can be configured that will be made available to scripts. There are two ways to configure predefined variables: by specifying them in script-based action definitions in the Struts configuration file and/or by creating a **BSFManagerFilter** implementation. The two approaches have one major distinction: Struts configuration file–based custom variables are specific to an action definition, and **BSFManagerFilter** implementation–based custom variables are made available to all scripts. Each of these methods is described in detail in the following sections.

Struts Configuration File-Based Custom Variables

Custom predefined variables can be configured that will be made available only to specific actions by specifying them in the script-based action definitions in the Struts configuration file. This technique for defining custom variables is useful for creating **DispatchAction**-like script-based actions. The following code shows an example of two action-specific custom predefined variables:

```
<!-- Action Mappings Configuration -->
<action-mappings>
  <action path="/search"
          type="org.apache.struts.scripting.ScriptAction"
          parameter="/WEB-INF/scripts/Search.groovy?prop1=val1&amp;prop2=val2"
          name="searchForm"
          scope="request"
          validate="true"
          input="/search.jsp">
  </action>
</action-mappings>
```

The custom variables are specified by appending name-value pairs to the script path specified with the **action** tag's **parameter** attribute using URL query string-style syntax. The syntax for specifying custom variables is shown next:

```
?PARAM_NAME=PARAM_VALUE&amp;PARAM_NAME=PARAM_VALUE
```

Like URL query strings, the custom variables are prefixed with a question mark (?) and then each variable is specified as *PARAM_NAME=PARAM_VALUE*, where *PARAM_NAME* is the name of the custom variable and *PARAM_VALUE* is the custom variable value. Multiple custom variables are separated by "&".

Note that as of Struts 1.3, action-specific custom variables can be specified using nested **set-property** tags inside script-based action definitions instead of using the query string–style syntax with the **parameter** attribute. The following example illustrates this technique:

```
<!-- Action Mappings Configuration -->
<action-mappings>
  <action path="/search"
          type="org.apache.struts.scripting.ScriptAction"
          parameter="/WEB-INF/scripts/Search.groovy"
          name="searchForm"
          scope="request"
          validate="true"
          input="/search.jsp">
    <set-property key="prop1" value="val1"/>
    <set-property key="prop2" value="val2"/>
  </action>
</action-mappings>
```

BSFManagerFilter Implementation-Based Custom Variables

Custom predefined variables can be configured that will be made available to *all* scripts by creating an implementation of **org.apache.struts.scripting.BSFManagerFilter** and configuring it in the **struts-scripting.properties** file. The following code shows an example **BSFManagerFilter** instance:

```
import java.util.Properties;

import org.apache.bsf.BSFException;
import org.apache.bsf.BSFManager;
```

```
import org.apache.struts.scripting.BSFManagerFilter;

public class ExampleScriptingFilter implements BSFManagerFilter
{
  private String prop1;
  private String prop2;

  public void init(String name, Properties props) {
    // Utilize initialization parameters here.
    prop1 = props.getProperty("prop1");
    prop2 = props.getProperty("prop2");
  }

  public BSFManager apply(BSFManager mgr) {
    try {
      mgr.declareBean("prop1", prop1, String.class);
      mgr.declareBean("prop2", prop2, String.class);
    } catch (BSFException e) {
      // Handle exception here.
    }

    return mgr;
  }
}
```

Inside the filter instance custom variables are registered with calls to the **declareBean( )** method of BSF's **org.apache.bsf.BSFManager** class.

After creating the **BSFManagerFilter** instance, it must be configured in the **struts-scripting.properties** file as shown next in bold:

```
struts-scripting.engine.groovy.class=org.codehaus.groovy.bsf.GroovyEngine
struts-scripting.engine.groovy.extensions=gv,groovy
struts-scripting.filters.example.class=com.jamesholmes.minihr.ExampleScriptingFilter
struts-scripting.filters.example.prop1=val1
struts-scripting.filters.example.prop2=val2
```

The filter instance is specified using a property named **struts-scripting.filters.*FILTER_NAME*.class**, where *FILTER_NAME* is an arbitrary name assigned to the filter. The value specified for the property is the fully qualified class name for the filter instance. In addition to specifying the class name of the filter instance, filter initialization parameters can be specified using properties named **struts-scripting.filters.*FILTER_NAME.PARAM_NAME*=*PARAM_VALUE***, where *FILTER_NAME* is the name of the instance, *PARAM_NAME* is the name of the initialization parameter, and *PARAM_VALUE* is the initialization parameter value. Initialization parameters are packaged in a **java.util.Properties** instance and passed to the filter instance's **init( )** method.

Using Struts Scripting with the Mini HR Application

Now that you've seen the details of using Struts Scripting, you are ready to update the Mini HR application to use it. Following is the list of steps that you follow to use Struts Scripting with the Mini HR application:

1. Add the Struts Scripting **.jar** files and properties file to the application.

2. Convert **SearchAction** to a Groovy script.
3. Configure Struts to use the new Groovy script–based action instead of the existing **SearchAction** in the **struts-config.xml** file.
4. Repackage and run the updated application.

The following sections walk you through each step of the process in detail.

Add the Struts Scripting .jar Files and Properties File to the Application

The Struts Scripting **.jar** file must be added to the application in order to use Struts Scripting. Additionally, the BSF **.jar** file and the **.jar** file required for the Groovy scripting language must be added to the application. Finally, a Struts Scripting properties file must be added to the application. The properties file specifies any BSF non-default scripting languages being used and their associated script file extensions; in this case, Groovy.

The Struts Scripting and BSF **.jar** files must be copied from the Struts distribution (e.g., **c:\java\struts-1.3.5\lib\struts-scripting-1.3.5.jar** & **c:\java\struts-1.3.5\lib\bsf-2.3.0.jar**) to Mini HR's **WEB-INF\lib** directory. Next, download Groovy (**http://groovy.codehaus.org/**) if you haven't already and copy the Groovy **.jar** file (e.g., **c:\java\groovy-1.0-JSR-06\embeddable\groovy-all-1.0-JSR-06.jar**) to Mini HR's **WEB-INF\lib** directory. The Struts Scripting properties file must be named **struts-scripting.properties** and be accessible from the application's classloader (i.e., be placed on the application classpath). This file should be placed in Mini HR's **WEB-INF\classes** directory. The following code shows the properties file's content in its entirety.

```
struts-scripting.engine.groovy.class=org.codehaus.groovy.bsf.GroovyEngine
struts-scripting.engine.groovy.extensions=gv,groovy
```

Convert SearchAction to a Groovy Script

The next step in using Struts Scripting with Mini HR is to replace the current Java-based **SearchAction** class with a Groovy script. Groovy is the scripting language used in this example because its syntax is very similar to Java. First, create a **scripts** directory underneath Mini HR's **WEB-INF** directory (i.e., **WEB-INF\scripts**). Placing the **scripts** directory under **WEB-INF** will protect scripts from being read directly from browsers. Next, create a file named **Search.groovy** with the contents shown next and place it in the newly created **scripts** directory.

```
import com.jamesholmes.minihr.EmployeeSearchService;

service = new EmployeeSearchService();
searchForm = struts.form;

// Perform employee search based on what criteria was entered.
name = searchForm.name;
if (name != null && name.trim().length() > 0) {
  results = service.searchByName(name);
} else {
  results = service.searchBySsNum(searchForm.ssNum.trim());
}

// Place search results in SearchForm for access by JSP.
```

```
searchForm.setResults(results);

// Forward control to this Action's input page.
struts.setForward(struts.mapping.inputForward);
```

This Groovy script is essentially the same as the original **SearchAction** class but with some small abbreviations that the Groovy language enables. Note that the existing **SearchAction** class does not need to be removed from the application in order for Struts Scripting to work. It simply won't be referenced anymore now that there is a Groovy script replacement.

Configure the struts-config.xml File

After creating the Groovy script replacement for **SearchAction**, you must configure Struts to use it by updating Mini HR's Struts configuration file: **struts-config.xml**. The following snippet configures Struts to use the new Groovy script–based action:

```
<!-- Action Mappings Configuration -->
<action-mappings>
  <action path="/search"
          type="org.apache.struts.scripting.ScriptAction"
          parameter="/WEB-INF/scripts/Search.groovy"
          name="searchForm"
          scope="request"
          validate="true"
          input="/search.jsp">
  </action>
</action-mappings>
```

Notice that the **type** attribute of the **action** tag now specifies **org.apache.struts.scripting.ScriptAction**. **ScriptAction** is used to execute the script specified by the **parameter** attribute. The remaining attributes are unchanged from the original action definition used by Mini HR.

The following code shows the updated Struts configuration file for Mini HR in its entirety. The sections that have changed or that have been added are shown in bold.

```
<?xml version="1.0"?>

<!DOCTYPE struts-config PUBLIC
  "-//Apache Software Foundation//DTD Struts Configuration 1.3//EN"
  "http://struts.apache.org/dtds/struts-config_1_3.dtd">

<struts-config>

  <!-- Form Beans Configuration -->
  <form-beans>
    <form-bean name="searchForm"
               type="com.jamesholmes.minihr.SearchForm"/>
  </form-beans>

  <!-- Global Forwards Configuration -->
  <global-forwards>
    <forward name="search" path="/search.jsp"/>
  </global-forwards>
```

```
  <!-- Action Mappings Configuration -->
  <action-mappings>
    <action path="/search"
            type="org.apache.struts.scripting.ScriptAction"
            parameter="/WEB-INF/scripts/Search.groovy"
            name="searchForm"
            scope="request"
            validate="true"
            input="/search.jsp">
    </action>
  </action-mappings>

  <!-- Message Resources Configuration -->
  <message-resources
    parameter="com.jamesholmes.minihr.MessageResources"/>

</struts-config>
```

Repackage and Run the Updated Application

Because no Java code was modified during this process, it's not necessary to recompile the Mini HR application. However, a file has been added and a file has been modified, so the application needs to be repackaged and redeployed before it is run. Assuming you've made modifications to the original Mini HR application and it was set up in the **c:\java\MiniHR** directory (as described in Chapter 2), the following command line will repackage the application when run from **c:\java\MiniHR**:

```
jar cf MiniHR.war *
```

Similar to the way you ran Mini HR the first time, you now need to place the new **MiniHR.war** file that you just created into Tomcat's **webapps** directory, delete the **webapps/MiniHR** directory, and start Tomcat. As before, to access the Mini HR application, point your browser to **http://localhost:8080/MiniHR/**. Once you have the updated Mini HR running, everything should work as it did before. However, now you can develop actions much faster and easier by using script-based actions that don't require compilation or server restarts.

CHAPTER 22

The Struts-Faces Integration Library

The popularity of Struts has given rise to a number of competing Java Web application frameworks over the past several years. One that stands out is JavaServer Faces (JSF). JSF is especially important because it was developed via the Java Community Process (JCP) with input from several leading companies and developers in the Java industry. Additionally, JSF is being positioned as the Java EE standard Web framework. Craig McClanahan, the original creator of Struts and an employee of Sun Microsystems, was the initial Java Specification Request (JSR) lead for JSF. In an effort to promote the use of JSF, Craig created the Struts-Faces Integration Library that enables Struts applications to make use of JSF user interface components for creating the View layer of a Struts application. Essentially, the Struts-Faces integration library provides a mechanism that enables existing Struts applications to leverage JSF technology instead of being redeveloped from scratch using JSF. The Struts-Faces library also provides a migration path for application's transitioning from Struts to JSF.

JSF Overview

Before getting into the details of using the Struts-Faces library, it's necessary to give a brief overview of JSF. JSF is an application framework for creating Web-based interfaces. Similar to Struts, JSF is based on the MVC design pattern and provides a controller servlet that manages the lifecycle of application requests. In addition to that, and in contrast to Struts, JSF provides a robust user interface component model that includes support for the rendering of components and event handling. The component model enables Web application user interfaces to be easily assembled and linked to back-end business logic components. This easy-to-use component model is the main selling point behind JSF and is not offered by other frameworks. A complete review of JSF is outside the scope of this book, but is covered in the *JavaServer Faces: The Complete Reference* book that I co-authored.

Struts-Faces Library Overview

While Struts and JSF are competing frameworks for developing Web applications in Java, they can also be used together via the Struts-Faces integration library. As JSF technology is more widely adopted, it is likely that many companies will have both Struts- and JSF-based applications in their environment. Companies adopting JSF will probably not rewrite existing Struts applications simply for the sake of using a new technology. However, those companies may decide that all new development will be done using JSF. The Struts-Faces integration library packaged with Struts provides an easy to use "adapter" for using the two technologies together, whether it be to enhance an existing application with JSF's rich UI components or to provide a migration path from Struts to JSF for applications.

The Struts-Faces library is basically an integration layer that allows an application to have a JSF-based user interface that interfaces with a Struts back end. That is, with Struts-Faces, JSF-based user interfaces can be created that utilize Struts back-end code instead of back-end code created using JSF technology. As you know, a typical Struts application uses JSPs and Struts tag libraries to create the user interface. Furthermore, actions and Form Beans are used by the Struts controller servlet to process requests from the user interface. JSF works similarly in that (typically) JSPs are used in conjunction with JSF component tag libraries to create user interfaces that communicate with the JSF controller servlet. The controller servlet uses managed beans along with actions and action listeners to process requests. With Struts-Faces, JSF is used to create the user interface and Struts-Faces ties the JSF-based user interface to a Struts back end consisting of the typical actions and Form Beans managed by the Struts controller servlet.

Struts-Faces ties the two frameworks together by having a custom Struts request processor that integrates with the JSF request processing lifecycle. Additionally, Struts-Faces provides a JSP tag library that integrates the two frameworks. The Struts-Faces tag library has a few tags that take the place of some JSF tags, providing a Struts-based equivalent, and a few other tags that replace some Struts tags with JSF-specific tie-ins.

Supported Versions of Struts

The Struts-Faces library is designed to work with Struts versions 1.2 and later. Previous versions of Struts are not compatible with this library.

Supported Versions of JSF

The Struts-Faces library is designed to work with any implementation of JavaServer Faces version 1.0 or later. Note, however, that the Struts-Faces library has primarily been tested only with version 1.1 of the JavaServer Faces reference implementation from Sun.

Using the Struts-Faces Library

Using the Struts-Faces library involves these five steps:

1. Add the required **.jar** files to the application.
2. Add a servlet definition for the JSF controller servlet to the **web.xml** file.
3. Configure Struts to use a custom Struts-Faces request processor.
4. Use the Struts-Faces and JSF tag library tags to create JSF-based user interfaces.
5. Configure forward and action definitions in the application's Struts configuration file.

The following sections explain how to set up and use the Struts-Faces library in detail.

Adding the Required .jar Files to the Application

Several **.jar** files must be added to the application in order to use JSF and Struts-Faces functionality. Each required **.jar** file should be copied to the application's **WEB-INF\lib** directory (or added to the classpath of the server[s] the application runs on). First, add the Struts-Faces **.jar** file (e.g., **c:\java\struts-1.3.5\lib\struts-faces-1.3.5.jar**) from the Struts distribution to the application if it is not already present. Next, add the JSTL **.jar** files (e.g., **c:\java\struts-1.3.5\lib\jstl-1.0.2.jar** and **c:\java\struts-1.3.5\lib\standard-1.0.2.jar**) from the Struts distribution to the application if they are not already present. Finally, a JSF implementation's **.jar** files must be added to the application. Any JSF implementation that has been certified to be compatible with the JSF specification will work, such as the reference implementation from Sun or the Apache MyFaces implementation. Assuming, you're using the reference implementation from Sun, you must copy the **jsf-api.jar** and **jsf-impl.jar** files from the reference implementation's lib directory (e.g., **c:\java\jsf-1_1_01\lib**) to the application.

Adding a Servlet Definition for the JSF Controller Servlet to the web.xml File

Similar to the setup for the Struts controller servlet, a servlet definition and related configuration details must be added to the **web.xml** file for the JSF controller servlet. The following snippet shows an example:

```
<!-- JSF Servlet Configuration -->
<servlet>
  <servlet-name>faces</servlet-name>
  <servlet-class>javax.faces.webapp.FacesServlet</servlet-class>
  <load-on-startup>1</load-on-startup>
</servlet>

<!-- JSF Servlet Mapping -->
<servlet-mapping>
  <servlet-name>faces</servlet-name>
  <url-pattern>*.faces</url-pattern>
</servlet-mapping>
```

Generally, the JSF controller servlet is mapped to URI's using extension mapping (e.g., *.faces) as shown in the preceding configuration snippet. However, path mapping (e.g., /faces/*) can be used as well, as shown next.

```
<!-- JSF Servlet Mapping -->
<servlet-mapping>
  <servlet-name>faces</servlet-name>
  <url-pattern>/faces/*</url-pattern>
</servlet-mapping>
```

In addition to adding the JSF controller servlet configuration details to the **web.xml** file, the Struts servlet configuration details must be modified so that the JSF controller servlet is initialized before the Struts controller servlet. Recall that the order in which servlets are initialized is controlled by the **<load-on-startup>** tag. The **<load-on-startup>** tag specifies a priority value for the order in which servlets are loaded; servlets with a higher priority (lower value) are loaded first. The JSF controller servlet priority is set to *1*, so the Struts controller servlet must be updated to a priority of 2 so that it loads after the JSF controller servlet, as shown here:

```
<!-- Action Servlet Configuration -->
<servlet>
  <servlet-name>action</servlet-name>
  <servlet-class>org.apache.struts.action.ActionServlet</servlet-class>
  <init-param>
    <param-name>config</param-name>
    <param-value>/WEB-INF/struts-config.xml</param-value>
  </init-param>
  <load-on-startup>2</load-on-startup>
</servlet>
```

Configuring Struts to Use a Custom Struts-Faces Request Processor

Struts must be configured to use a custom Struts-Faces request processor in order to recognize requests for pages utilizing JSF and to handle them appropriately. There are two custom request processors provided by Struts-Faces that can be used:

- org.apache.struts.faces.application.FacesRequestProcessor
- org.apache.struts.faces.application.FacesTilesRequestProcessor

FacesRequestProcessor is for standard Struts applications not using Tiles and **FacesTilesRequestProcessor** is for Struts applications making use of Tiles. To configure Struts to use a custom request processor, you must update your application's Struts configuration file (e.g., **struts-config.xml**). The following snippet configures Struts to use the basic non-Tiles Struts-Faces request processor:

```
<!-- Controller Configuration -->
<controller>
  <set-property property="processorClass"
    value="org.apache.struts.faces.application.FacesRequestProcessor"/>
</controller>
```

NOTE *Although Struts versions 1.3 and later use Commons Chain for request processing, at the time of this writing Struts-Faces still relies on the outdated method of extending the* **RequestProcessor** *class to modify the behavior of the request processing engine.*

Using the Struts-Faces and JSF Tag Library Tags to Create JSF-Based User Interfaces

The main task in using the Struts-Faces library is to create JSPs that use (or update JSPs to use) the Struts-Faces and JSF tag library tags to build a user interface. As in any Struts or JSF application, first you must declare the tag libraries that will be used by the JSP. The following JSF tag library declarations must be added to the JSP:

```
<%@ taglib uri="http://java.sun.com/jsf/core" prefix="f" %>
<%@ taglib uri="http://java.sun.com/jsf/html" prefix="h" %>
```

Additionally, the declaration shown next must be added to the JSP for the Struts-Faces tag library.

```
<%@ taglib uri="http://struts.apache.org/tags-faces" prefix="s" %>
```

After declaring the tag libraries, user interfaces can be created using the JSF and Struts-Faces tag libraries. The interface is created just as it would be in a JSF application with a few exceptions where Struts-Faces tags are used instead of JSF tags.

Whereas in a JSF application the JSF Html Tag Library **form** tag (i.e., **<h:form>**) is used to encapsulate a form, with Struts-Faces the Struts-Faces **form** tag (i.e., **<s:form>**) must be used. The Struts-Faces **form** tag behaves the same as the JSF form tag except that it interfaces with the Struts controller servlet for processing the request. Similarly, Struts-Faces requires that its **commandLink** tag be used instead of the JSF **commandLink** tag so that form submissions are processed properly. The Struts-Faces library also provides other tags such as the **message** and **write** tags that make integrating with Struts easy. The **message** and **write** tags essentially mirror those from the Struts Bean Tag Library. The Struts-Faces tag library also has several other tags that ease the integration of Struts and JSF (or transition from Struts to JSF as the case may be).

Configuring Forward and Action Definitions in the Application's Struts Configuration File

Once application JSPs have been created or updated to use Struts-Faces and JSF Tag Library tags, you must create or update each of the forward and action definitions in the Struts configuration file that point to those JSPs. Without Struts-Faces, forward and action definitions usually point directly to JSPs. With Struts-Faces, however, the definitions must point to URIs that map to the JSF controller servlet, either by extension (e.g., *.faces) or by path (e.g., /faces/*). For example, the following forward definition points directly to **search.jsp**.

```
<!-- Global Forwards Configuration -->
<global-forwards>
  <forward name="search" path="/search.jsp"/>
</global-forwards>
```

With Struts-Faces, the forward must point to the search page's JSF URI, as shown here:

```
<!-- Global Forwards Configuration -->
<global-forwards>
  <forward name="search" path="/search.faces"/>
</global-forwards>
```

At run time, the Struts-Faces library will determine whether a forward or action definition points to the path of a JSF URI or directly to a JSP. If a JSF URI is specified, then Struts-Faces will process the page accordingly; otherwise, normal Struts processing will take place.

PART V

Known Limitations

At the time of this writing the Struts-Faces library has a few documented limitations. Each limitation is listed next with details about its impact.

- The Struts modules feature is not yet supported by Struts-Faces. Additionally, as a result of that, the **forwardPattern** and **pagePattern** attributes of the **<controller>** tag in the Struts configuration file are not supported by Struts-Faces. A servlet filter can be used to get around this limitation; however, such a filter is not provided by Struts-Faces.
- The Struts Nested and Struts-EL tag libraries are not supported by Struts-Faces. Because many of the tags in the Struts tag libraries have JSTL equivalent replacements, JSTL should be used instead.

- The **forward** attribute of the **<action>** tag in the Struts configuration file cannot be used to forward to a JSF page.
- Custom request processors cannot be used unless they extend one of the Struts-Faces custom request processors. Because Struts-Faces does not yet support the more modern Commons Chain-based request processing approach, each layer of customization to the request processing engine requires an extension of another request processing class. This makes it difficult to use multiple features that each extend the engine.

The Struts-Faces Tag Library Tags

The following table lists each of the tags in the Struts-Faces Tag Library and provides a short description of each tag's purpose.

Tag	Description
base	Renders an HTML **<base>** tag with a reference pointing to the absolute location of the enclosing page.
commandLink	Creates an HTML hyperlink that submits the current form.
errors	Displays the set of Struts and JSF error messages generated by the application during data validation.
form	Renders an HTML **<form>** tag tied to a Struts action and its corresponding form bean from the Struts configuration file (e.g., **struts-config.xml**).
html	Renders an HTML **<html>** tag with language attributes set to the current user's locale.
javascript	Generates client-side JavaScript validation code for validations defined in the Jakarta Commons Validator framework's configuration file (e.g., **validation.xml**).
loadMessages	Exposes a Struts application resource bundle as a **java.util.Map** instance with request scope so that the messages can be referenced in JSF value binding expressions (and JSP 2.0 EL expressions).
message	Retrieves an internationalized message from the application resource bundle (e.g., **MessageResources.properties)** and renders it to a JSP's output stream.
stylesheet	Renders an HTML **<link>** tag with a reference to a Cascading Style Sheet (CSS) at the specified context-relative path.
write	Renders a literal value or the value of a JSF value binding expression to a JSP's output stream.

The remainder of this section discusses each tag in detail, including a complete description of the tag, a table listing each of the tag's attributes, and a usage example for the tag. In the tables that describe each tag's attributes, pay special attention to the Accepts JSP Expression and Required columns.

The Required column simply denotes whether the given attribute is required when using the tag. In addition to the required column denoting whether an attribute is required, the rows for required attributes are highlighted in gray so that you can determine at a glance which attributes are required.

If an attribute is required and you do not specify it when using the tag, the tag will throw a **javax.servlet.jsp.JspException** at run time. Note that you can declare an error page in your JSP with a **page** directive to capture any **JspExceptions** that might be thrown, as shown here:

```
<%@ page errorPage="error.jsp" %>
```

If an exception occurs, the page specified by the **errorPage** attribute will be internally redirected to display an error page.

The Accepts JSP Expression column denotes whether or not the given attribute's value can be specified with a JSP expression. If a JSP expression is used to specify an attribute value, the expression must comprise the complete value, quote (") to quote ("), as shown here. Correct:

```
<s:javascript formName="<%=searchForm%>"/>
```

Incorrect:

```
<s:javascript formName="<%=searchForm%>-name"/>
```

Notice in the incorrect example that "-name" is used as part of the value for the **formName** attribute following the expression. This is invalid because there are extra characters between the end of the expression and the ending quote.

A corrected version of the incorrect example follows:

```
<s:javascript formName="<%=searchForm + "-name"%>"/>
```

The concatenation of "-name" is now part of the expression, and the expression comprises the complete value for the attribute.

The base Tag

The **base** tag is used to render an HTML **<base>** tag with a reference pointing to the absolute location of the enclosing page. The HTML **<base>** tag defines the page's base URL for resolving relative URLs contained in the page. That said, the **base** tag is useful for scenarios where relative URLs should be based on the URL of the enclosing page instead of the URL to which the last form submission took place. Following is an example of the output generated by this tag:

```
<base href="http://www.abc.com/sfapp/myPage.jsp"/>
```

NOTE *The* **base** *tag must be nested inside an HTML* **<head>** *tag.*

Attributes

Attribute	Description	Accepts JSP Expression	Required
binding	Specifies the JSF value binding expression that will bind this component to a backing bean property.	No	No
id	Specifies the JSF component ID for this component.	No	No

Attribute	Description	Accepts JSP Expression	Required
rendered	Accepts *true* or *false* to specify whether this JSF component will be rendered. Defaults to *true*.	*No*	*No*
target	Specifies the name of the target frame in which all links in the page will be rendered. By default all links will be rendered in the same frame as this tag's enclosing page; however, this attribute allows for other frames to be targeted.	No	No

Example Usage

The following example illustrates the basic usage of the **base** tag.

```
<html>
<head>
  <s:base/>
</head>
```

Assuming the URL of the enclosing page is: **http://www.abc.com/sfapp/myPage.jsp**, the output generated from the example usage will be:

```
<base href="http://www.abc.com/sfapp/myPage.jsp"/>
```

The commandLink Tag

The **commandLink** tag is used to create an HTML hyperlink that submits the current form. This tag mirrors the **commandLink** tag in the JSF Core Tag Library. The difference, however, between the JSF Core **commandLink** tag and the Struts-Faces **commandLink** tag is that the Struts-Faces version is designed to work with the other tags in the Struts-Faces Tag Library. Unfortunately, the tags in different libraries don't intermix and the Struts-Faces version of the tag is required.

Attributes

Attribute	Description	Accepts JSP Expression	Required
accesskey	Same as the corresponding HTML tag's attribute with the same name. Specifies the keyboard key that causes the link to immediately receive focus when the key is pressed.	No	No
action	Specifies the JSF method binding expression that references a method that will be invoked when the link is selected.	No	No
actionListener	Specifies the JSF method binding expression that references a method that will be invoked with action event notifications when the link is selected.	No	No

Attribute	Description	Accepts JSP Expression	Required
charset	Same as the corresponding HTML tag's attribute with the same name. Specifies the character encoding for the link.	No	No
dir	Same as the corresponding HTML tag's attribute with the same name. Specifies the directionality of the link's text.	No	No
hreflang	Same as the corresponding HTML tag's attribute with the same name. Specifies the language for the link.	No	No
id	Specifies the JSF component ID for this component.	No	No
immediate	Accepts *true* or *false* to specify whether this JSF component will have its action listener invoked immediately. That is, if *true,* the action listener will be invoked during the Apply Request Values phase of the JSF request processing lifecycle rather than during the Invoke Application phase. Defaults to *true.*	No	No
lang	Same as the corresponding HTML tag's attribute with the same name. Specifies the language for the link's text.	No	No
onblur	Same as the corresponding HTML tag's attribute with the same name. Specifies the JavaScript code to execute when the link loses input focus.	No	No
onclick	Same as the corresponding HTML tag's attribute with the same name. Specifies the JavaScript code to execute when the link receives a mouse click.	No	No
ondblclick	Same as the corresponding HTML tag's attribute with the same name. Specifies the JavaScript code to execute when the link receives a mouse double-click.	No	No
onfocus	Same as the corresponding HTML tag's attribute with the same name. Specifies the JavaScript code to execute when the link receives input focus.	No	No
onkeydown	Same as the corresponding HTML tag's attribute with the same name.Specifies the JavaScript code to execute when the link has focus and a key is pressed.	No	No

Attribute	Description	Accepts JSP Expression	Required
onkeypress	Same as the corresponding HTML tag's attribute with the same name. Specifies the JavaScript code to execute when the link has focus and a key is pressed and released.	No	No
onkeyup	Same as the corresponding HTML tag's attribute with the same name. Specifies the JavaScript code to execute when the link has focus and a key is released.	No	No
onmousedown	Same as the corresponding HTML tag's attribute with the same name. Specifies the JavaScript code to execute when the link is under the mouse pointer and a mouse button is pressed.	No	No
onmousemove	Same as the corresponding HTML tag's attribute with the same name. Specifies the JavaScript code to execute when the link is under the mouse pointer and the mouse is moved.	No	No
onmouseout	Same as the corresponding HTML tag's attribute with the same name. Specifies the JavaScript code to execute when the link is under the mouse pointer and is then moved away from the link.	No	No
onmouseover	Same as the corresponding HTML tag's attribute with the same name. Specifies the JavaScript code to execute when the link is not under the mouse pointer and is then moved to the link.	No	No
onmouseup	Same as the corresponding HTML tag's attribute with the same name. Specifies the JavaScript code to execute when the link is under the mouse pointer and a mouse button is released.	No	No
rel	Same as the corresponding HTML tag's attribute with the same name. Specifies the relationship from the current page to the page specified with the link.	No	No

Attribute	Description	Accepts JSP Expression	Required
rendered	Accepts *true* or *false* to specify whether this JSF component will be rendered. Defaults to *true*.	No	No
rev	Same as the corresponding HTML tag's attribute with the same name. Specifies the relationship from the page specified with the link to the current page.	No	No
style	Specifies the CSS style to be applied to this JSF component.	No	No
styleClass	Specifies the CSS style class to be applied to this JSF component.	No	No
tabindex	Same as the corresponding HTML tag's attribute with the same name. Specifies the tab order for the link.	No	No
target	Same as the corresponding HTML tag's attribute with the same name. Specifies the frame or window target in which the link will be displayed.	No	No
title	Same as the corresponding HTML tag's attribute with the same name. Specifies the title for the link.	No	No
type	Same as the corresponding HTML tag's attribute with the same name. Specifies the content type for the link.	No	No
value	Specifies the text for the link.	No	No

Example Usage

The following example illustrates the basic usage of the **commandLink** tag.

```
<s:commandLink actionListener="#{searchAction.search}">
  <h:outputText value="Search Employees"/>
</s:commandLink>
```

The Struts-Faces **commandLink** tag is used exactly the same way as the **commandLink** tag from the JSF Core Tag Library is used.

PART V

The errors Tag

The **errors** tag is used to display the set of Struts and JSF error messages generated by the application during data validation. This tag will take the stored error messages and iterate over them, displaying them in succession. The following table lists a set of keys from the application resource bundle file (e.g., **MessageResources.properties)** that will be used to format the messages for display.

Key	Purpose
errors.header	Text that will be output before the list of error messages.
errors.footer	Text that will be output after the list of error messages.
errors.prefix	Text that will be output before each error message.
errors.suffix	Text that will be output after each error message.

Attributes

Attribute	Description	Accepts JSP Expression	Required
binding	Specifies the JSF value binding expression that will bind this component to a backing bean property.	No	No
bundle	Specifies the logical name of a resource bundle that will be used when looking up message keys. The referenced resource bundle must be defined in the application's Struts configuration file.	No	No
id	Specifies the JSF component ID for this component.	No	No
property	Specifies the field for which messages will be displayed. If not specified, all messages, regardless of property, will be displayed.		No
rendered	Accepts *true* or *false* to specify whether this JSF component will be rendered. Defaults to *true*.	No	No

Example Usage

The following snippet illustrates the basic usage of the **errors** tag:

```
<s:errors/>
```

This example will display all the errors currently stored. If you want to limit the errors that are displayed to a specific property, you can specify that property when using the **errors** tag, as shown here:

```
<s:errors property="username"/>
```

In this case, only the errors associated with the property specified by the **property** attribute will be displayed. Additionally, you can specify the resource bundle from which error messages will be retrieved using the **bundle** attribute:

```
<s:errors bundle="CustomBundleName"/>
```

The bundle specified with the **bundle** attribute must be configured in the Struts configuration file.

The form Tag

The **form** tag is used to render an HTML **<form>** tag tied to a Struts action and its corresponding form bean from the Struts configuration file (e.g., **struts-config.xml**). The action's form bean will be used by JSF components to populate themselves with data when they are nested inside this tag. This tag differs from the **form** tag in the JSF HTML Tag Library in that it interfaces with Struts actions and form beans instead of JSF managed beans.

Attributes

Attribute	Description	Accepts JSP Expression	Required
action	Specifies the logical name of an action, defined in the Struts configuration file, to which the form will be submitted.	No	Yes
binding	Specifies the JSF value binding expression that will bind this component to a backing bean property.	No	No
enctype	Same as the corresponding HTML tag's attribute with the same name. Specifies the encoding type that will be used if the form is submitted using the POST method. This attribute must be set to *multipart/form-data* if the form includes a file upload field.	No	No
focus	Specifies the name of a field inside the form that initial focus will be assigned to using JavaScript once the page has been rendered.	No	No
focusIndex	Specifies an index to be used if the field specified with the **focus** attribute is a field array such as a radio button group.	No	No
id	Specifies the JSF component ID for this component.	No	No
onreset	Same as the corresponding HTML tag's attribute with the same name. Specifies the JavaScript code to execute when the form is reset.	No	No
onsubmit	Same as the corresponding HTML tag's attribute with the same name. Specifies the JavaScript code to execute when the form is submitted.	No	No
rendered	Accepts *true* or *false* to specify whether this JSF component will be rendered. Defaults to *true*.	No	No
style	Specifies the CSS style to be applied to this JSF component.	No	No
styleClass	Specifies the CSS style class to be applied to this JSF component.	No	No

Attribute	Description	Accepts JSP Expression	Required
target	Same as the corresponding HTML tag's attribute with the same name. Specifies the name of the target frame in which the form will be submitted. By default the form will be submitted in the same frame as this tag's enclosing page; however, this attribute allows for other frames to be targeted.	No	No

Example Usage

The following snippet illustrates the basic usage of the **form** tag:

```
<s:form id="search" action="/search">
Name: <h:inputText id="name" value="#{searchForm.name}"/><br>
Social Security Number: <h:inputText id="ssNum" value="#{searchForm.ssNum}"/><br>
<h:commandButton id="submit" value="Search"/>
</s:form>
```

The Form Bean associated with the action specified by the **action** attribute will be used for populating the nested JSF components inside the opening and closing **form** tags.

The html Tag

The **html** tag is used to render an HTML **<html>** tag with language attributes set to the current user's locale. Additionally, you can use this tag to instruct nested tags from the Struts HTML Tag Library to generate their output as XHTML instead of HTML. More information on XHTML can be found at **http://www.xhtml.org/**.

Attributes

Attribute	Description	Accepts JSP Expression	Required
binding	Specifies the JSF value binding expression that will bind this component to a backing bean property.	No	No
id	Specifies the JSF component ID for this component.	No	No
locale	Accepts *true* or *false* to specify whether a **java.util.Locale** object, set to the current request's **AcceptLanguage** HTTP header, will be placed into the session. If a session does not exist, one will be created when this tag stores the **Locale** object. Defaults to *false*.	No	No
rendered	Accepts *true* or *false* to specify whether this JSF component will be rendered. Defaults to *true*.	No	No

Attribute	Description	Accepts JSP Expression	Required
xhtml	Accepts *true* or *false* to specify whether nested tags from the Struts HTML Tag Library will generate their output as XHTML instead of HTML. Note that enabling this feature will not cause JSF components to render their output as XHTML. Defaults to *false*.	No	No

Example Usage

The following snippet shows the basic usage of the **html** tag:

```
<f:view>
<s:html>
<body>
...
</body>
</s:html>
</f:view>
```

If you want nested tags from the Struts HTML Tag Library to generate XHTML instead of HTML, use the **html** tag as shown here:

```
<f:view>
<s:html xhtml="true">
<body>
...
</body>
</s:html>
</f:view>
```

The javascript Tag

The **javascript** tag is used to generate client-side JavaScript validation code for validations defined in the Jakarta Commons Validator framework's configuration file (e.g., **validation .xml**). The JavaScript code generated by the **javascript** tag can be broken down into two pieces: static code and dynamic code. The static piece is composed of all the generic validation routine methods. The dynamic piece is composed of the code that is specific to a particular HTML form and that calls the static validation methods. Because the static piece of code is typically very large and is often repeated across several pages, it is advantageous to break that piece out and store it in its own file. That way, it can simply be referenced by each page that makes use of it. The **javascript** tag allows you to break up the two pieces of code by specifying which code it generates with the **dynamicJavascript** and **staticJavascript** attributes.

PART V

NOTE *Unlike the other tags in the Struts Faces Tag Library, the* **javascript** *tag is not tied to a JSF component and is simply a replication of the functionality provided by the Struts HTML Tag Library's* **javascript** *tag.*

Attributes

Attribute	Description	Accepts JSP Expression	Required
cdata	Accepts *true* or *false* to specify whether the generated JavaScript code will be enclosed in XML CDATA tags (i.e., **<![CDATA[ ]]>**). CDATA tags are necessary to prevent JavaScript code from being parsed when used in conjunction with XHTML. Defaults to *true.*	*Yes*	*No*
dynamicJavascript	Accepts *true* or *false* to specify whether dynamic JavaScript will be generated. Defaults to *true.*	*No*	*No*
formName	Specifies the logical name of a form whose validation rules will be used to generate JavaScript validation code. The name specified with this attribute must match the named specified in a **<form>** definition in the Validator configuration file.	Yes	No
htmlComment	Accepts *true* or *false* to specify whether the generated JavaScript code will be enclosed in HTML comment tags (i.e., **<!– –>**). Note that this attribute will be ignored when operating in XHTML mode. Defaults to *true.*	*Yes*	*No*
method	Specifies an alternate JavaScript method name to be used by the client-side Validator code instead of the default method name. The default method name is generated based on the form name by prefixing the form name with "validate" (e.g., a form name of "logonForm" would have a validate method of "validateLogonForm").	Yes	No
page	Specifies the logical name of a page to use to filter which validations for the specified form will be generated. This logical name matches the logical name that can be applied to individual fields in the Validator configuration file.	Yes	No
src	Same as the corresponding JavaScript tag's attribute with the same name. Specifies the URL to a static JavaScript file to be included.	Yes	No
staticJavascript	Accepts *true* or *false* to specify whether static JavaScript will be generated. Defaults to *true.*	No	No

Example Usage

The following snippet illustrates the basic usage of the **javascript** tag:

```
<s:javascript formName="logonForm"/>
```

This example will generate JavaScript code for all of the validation rules in the Validator configuration file that are tied to the form specified by the **formName** attribute.

If you want to separate the dynamic and static pieces of the generated JavaScript code, you can use the **javascript** tag as shown next:

```
<s:javascript formName="logonForm"
      staticJavascript="false"
                 src="staticJavascript.jsp"/>
```

This usage only generates the dynamic JavaScript for the specified form. The following example generates the generic static JavaScript code:

```
<s:javascript formName="logonForm" dynamicJavascript="false"/>
```

This snippet must be placed into a separate file named **staticJavascript.jsp** to match the file name specified by the **src** attribute of the previous example.

The loadMessages Tag

The **loadMessages** tag is used to expose a Struts application resource bundle as a **java.util .Map** instance with request scope so that the messages can be referenced in JSF value binding expressions (and JSP 2.0 EL expressions).

Attributes

Attribute	Description	Accepts JSP Expression	Required
messages	Specifies the logical name of a resource bundle that will be exposed. The referenced resource bundle must be defined in the application's Struts configuration file.	No	No
var	Specifies the request scope key that the map will be stored under.	No	Yes

Example Usage

The following example illustrates the basic usage of the **loadMessages** tag.

```
<s:loadMessages var="messages"/>
```

The preceding example exposes the default Struts application resource bundle. The following example exposes an alternate application resource bundle with the "alternateBundle" logical name:

```
<s:loadMessages messages="alternateBundle" var="messages"/>
```

Once the resource bundle has been exposed via the **loadMessages** tag, its messages can be referenced using the variable name defined with the **var** attribute, as shown here:

```
<h:outputText value="#{messages['label.search.ssNum']}"/>
```

The exposed variable containing the messages is a **Map** instance that has request scope.

The message Tag

The **message** tag is used to retrieve an internationalized message from the application resource bundle (e.g., **MessageResources.properties)** and render it to a JSP's output stream. Recall that resource bundle files in Struts applications are based on Java's Resource Bundle functionality for externalizing and internationalizing application strings, messages, and labels. Following is a sample resource bundle properties file:

```
# Label Resources
label.search.name=Name
label.search.ssNum=Social Security Number

# Error Resources
error.search.criteria.missing=Search Criteria Missing
error.search.ssNum.invalid=Invalid Social Security Number
errors.header=<font color="red"><cTypeface:Bold>Validation Error(s)</b></font><ul>
errors.footer=</ul><hr width="100%" size="1" noshade="true">
errors.prefix=<li>
errors.suffix=</li>
```

As you can see, the file is made up of key/value pairs. The **message** tag simply looks up a message with a given key and returns its matching value.

NOTE *The resource bundle file must be configured in your application's Struts configuration file before it can be accessed via the* **message** *tag. See Chapter 18 for more information on the Struts configuration file.*

The **message** tag also allows you to insert content into messages at run time before they are rendered using *parametric replacement,* which is the substitution of an argument for a placeholder parameter at run time. Following is an example message that uses parametric replacement:

```
missing.field=The {0} field is missing.
```

Notice the {0} reference in the message. At run time, the {0} parameter will be dynamically replaced with another value. The **message** tag allows you to specify what the replacement values are by nesting instances of the JSF HTML Tag Library's **parameter** tag.

Attributes

Attribute	Description	Accepts JSP Expression	Required
binding	Specifies the JSF value binding expression that will bind this component to a backing bean property.	No	No
bundle	Specifies the logical name of a resource bundle that will be used when looking up message keys. The referenced resource bundle must be defined in the application's Struts configuration file.	No	No

Attribute	Description	Accepts JSP Expression	Required
filter	Accepts *true* or *false* to specify whether this component's output will be filtered for sensitive HTML characters (e.g., > and <). Filtered characters are replaced with their HTML entity equivalent (e.g., ">" replaced with ">" and so on). Defaults to *true.*	No	No
id	Specifies the JSF component ID for this component.	No	No
key	Specifies the name of the application resource bundle key whose corresponding value will be rendered. This attribute and the **value** attribute are mutually exclusive—one or the other must be specified.	No	No
rendered	Accepts *true* or *false* to specify whether this JSF component will be rendered. Defaults to *true.*	No	No
style	Specifies the CSS style to be applied to this JSF component.	No	No
styleClass	Specifies the CSS style class to be applied to this JSF component.	No	No
value	Specifies a JSF value binding expression that evaluates to the name of the application resource bundle key whose corresponding value will be rendered. This attribute and the **key** attribute are mutually exclusive—one or the other must be specified.	No	No

Example Usage

Generally speaking, there are two ways that the **message** tag can be used. The first way, shown here, uses the **key** attribute to specify the name of a resource bundle key whose value will be rendered:

```
<s:message key="label.search.ssNum"/>
```

The second way to use the **message** tag is shown here:

```
<s:message value="#{errors.missingField}">
  <f:param value="Social Security Number"/>
</s:message>
```

In this example, the **value** attribute is used to specify a JSF value binding expression that evaluates to the name of a resource bundle key whose value will be rendered. The nested **parameter** tags specify the parametric replacement values for the resource bundle message.

The stylesheet Tag

The **stylesheet** tag is used to render an HTML **<link>** tag with a reference to a Cascading Style Sheet (CSS) at the specified context-relative path. Following is an example of the output generated by this tag:

```
<link rel="stylesheet" href="/myWebApp/site.css" type="text/css"/>
```

The output of this tag is the same as would be coded by hand when referencing a style sheet. The **stylesheet** tag simplifies the creation of the HTML **<link>** tag, though, by allowing the path to the style sheet to be specified relative to the Web application. That way, Web application names are not hard-coded into your JSPs, thus allowing seamless application renaming and so on.

To determine the context path to prefix to the style sheet path, the **stylesheet** tag makes a call to **javax.faces.context.FacesContext.getExternalContext( ).getRequestContextPath( )** which ultimately calls **javax.servlet.http.HttpServletRequest.getContextPath( )** for servlets or **javax.portlet.PortletRequest.getContextPath( )** for portlets.

Attributes

Attribute	Description	Accepts JSP Expression	Required
binding	Specifies the JSF value binding expression that will bind this component to a backing bean property.	No	No
id	Specifies the JSF component ID for this component.	No	No
path	Specifies the context-relative path to the style sheet.	No	Yes
rendered	Accepts *true* or *false* to specify whether this JSF component will be rendered. Defaults to *true*.	No	No

Example Usage

The following example illustrates the basic usage of the **stylesheet** tag.

```
<s:stylsheet path="/site.css"/>
```

Assuming a context path of **/sfapp**, the output generated from this example usage will be:

```
<link rel="stylesheet" href="/sfapp/site.css" type="text/css"/>
```

The path specified with the **path** attribute is simply appended to the context path to form the complete path to the style sheet.

The write Tag

The **write** tag is used to render a literal value or the value of a JSF value binding expression to a JSP's output stream.

Attributes

Attribute	Description	Accepts JSP Expression	Required
binding	Specifies the JSF value binding expression that will bind this component to a backing bean property.	No	No
filter	Accepts *true* or *false* to specify whether this component's output will be filtered for sensitive HTML characters (e.g., > and <). Filtered characters are replaced with their HTML entity equivalent (e.g., ">" replaced with ">" and so on). Defaults to *true.*	No	No
id	Specifies the JSF component ID for this component.	No	No
rendered	Accepts *true* or *false* to specify whether this JSF component will be rendered. Defaults to *true.*	No	No
style	Specifies the CSS style to be applied to this JSF component.	No	No
styleClass	Specifies the CSS style class to be applied to this JSF component.	No	No
value	Specifies the literal value to be rendered or a JSF value binding expression that evaluates to the value to be rendered.	No	No

Example Usage

The following example illustrates the basic usage of the **write** tag.

```
<s:write value="text to render"/>
```

The preceding example simply outputs the literal text to the JSP. The real benefit in using the **write** tag, however, is in using it to render the value of a JSF value binding expression, as shown here:

```
<s:write value="#{regForm.employee.firstName}"/>
```

The **write** tag will evaluate the expression and render its value.

Using the Struts-Faces Library with the Mini HR Application

Now that you've seen the details of using the Struts-Faces library, you are ready to update the Mini HR application to use the library. Following is the list of steps that you follow to use the Struts-Faces library with the Mini HR application:

1. Add a JSF implementation's and JSTL **.jar** files to the application.
2. Add a servlet definition for the JSF controller servlet to the **web.xml** file.

3. Configure Struts to use a custom Struts-Faces request processor in the **struts-config.xml** file. Also, update forward definitions in the **struts-config.xml** file.
4. Update existing JSPs to use the Struts-Faces and JSF tag library tags.
5. Repackage and run the updated application.

The following sections walk you through each step of the process in detail.

Add a JSF Implementation's and JSTL .jar Files to the Application

A JSF implementation's **.jar** files must be added to the application in order to use JSF functionality. Any JSF implementation that has been certified to be compatible with the JSF specification will work, such as the reference implementation from Sun or the Apache MyFaces implementation. Additionally, JSTL **.jar** files must be added to the application for Struts-Faces to function.

Assuming you're using the reference implementation from Sun, you must copy the **jsf-api.jar** and **jsf-impl.jar** files from the reference implementation's lib directory (e.g., **c:\java\jsf-1_1_01\lib**) to Mini HR's **WEB-INF\lib** directory. Next, copy the JSTL **.jar** files packaged with the Struts distribution (e.g., **c:\java\struts-1.3.5\lib\jstl-1.0.2.jar** & **c:\java\struts-1.3.5\lib\standard-1.0.2.jar**) to Mini HR's **WEB-INF\lib** directory.

Add a Servlet Definition for the JSF Controller Servlet to the web.xml File

Similar to the setup for the Struts controller servlet, a servlet definition and related configuration details must be added to the **web.xml** file for the JSF controller servlet. The following snippet shows the configuration details that must be added to the **web.xml** file:

```
<!-- JSF Servlet Configuration -->
<servlet>
  <servlet-name>faces</servlet-name>
  <servlet-class>javax.faces.webapp.FacesServlet</servlet-class>
  <load-on-startup>1</load-on-startup>
</servlet>

<!-- JSF Servlet Mapping -->
<servlet-mapping>
  <servlet-name>faces</servlet-name>
  <url-pattern>*.faces</url-pattern>
</servlet-mapping>
```

In addition to adding the JSF controller servlet configuration details to the **web.xml** file, the Struts servlet configuration details must be modified so that the JSF controller servlet is initialized before the Struts controller servlet. Recall that the order in which servlets are initialized is controlled by the **<load-on-startup>** tag. The **<load-on-startup>** tag specifies a priority value for the order in which servlets are loaded. Servlets with a higher priority (lower value) are loaded first. The JSF controller servlet priority is set to *1*, so the Struts controller servlet must be updated to a priority of 2 so that it loads after the JSF controller servlet, as shown here:

```
<!-- Action Servlet Configuration -->
<servlet>
  <servlet-name>action</servlet-name>
  <servlet-class>org.apache.struts.action.ActionServlet</servlet-class>
```

```
  <init-param>
    <param-name>config</param-name>
    <param-value>/WEB-INF/struts-config.xml</param-value>
  </init-param>
  <load-on-startup>2</load-on-startup>
</servlet>
```

The following code shows the updated **web.xml** file for Mini HR in its entirety. The sections that have changed or that have been added are shown in bold.

```
<?xml version="1.0"?>

<!DOCTYPE web-app PUBLIC
  "-//Sun Microsystems, Inc.//DTD Web Application 2.3//EN"
  "http://java.sun.com/dtd/web-app_2_3.dtd">

<web-app>

  <!-- Action Servlet Configuration -->
  <servlet>
    <servlet-name>action</servlet-name>
    <servlet-class>org.apache.struts.action.ActionServlet</servlet-class>
    <init-param>
      <param-name>config</param-name>
      <param-value>/WEB-INF/struts-config.xml</param-value>
    </init-param>
    <load-on-startup>2</load-on-startup>
  </servlet>

  <!-- Action Servlet Mapping -->
  <servlet-mapping>
    <servlet-name>action</servlet-name>
    <url-pattern>*.do</url-pattern>
  </servlet-mapping>

  <!-- JSF Servlet Configuration -->
  <servlet>
    <servlet-name>faces</servlet-name>
    <servlet-class>javax.faces.webapp.FacesServlet</servlet-class>
    <load-on-startup>1</load-on-startup>
  </servlet>

  <!-- JSF Servlet Mapping -->
  <servlet-mapping>
    <servlet-name>faces</servlet-name>
    <url-pattern>*.faces</url-pattern>
  </servlet-mapping>

  <!-- The Welcome File List -->
  <welcome-file-list>
    <welcome-file>/index.jsp</welcome-file>
  </welcome-file-list>

</web-app>
```

Configure the struts-config.xml File

After you have updated the **web.xml** file, you must configure Struts to use a custom Struts-Faces request processor by updating Mini HR's Struts configuration file: **struts-config.xml**. The following snippet configures Struts to use a Struts-Faces request processor:

```
<!-- Controller Configuration -->
<controller>
  <set-property property="processorClass"
    value="org.apache.struts.faces.application.FacesRequestProcessor"/>
</controller>
```

Using the Struts-Faces request processor causes Struts to recognize requests for pages utilizing JSF and to handle them appropriately.

In addition to configuring the Struts-Faces request processor, you must update each of the forward and action definitions in the Struts configuration file that point to JSPs that make use of JSF components. Without Struts-Faces, forward and action definitions point directly to JSPs. With Struts-Faces, they point to the page's JSF URI. For example, before, the **search** action pointed directly to **search.jsp**, as shown here:

```
<action path="/search"
        type="com.jamesholmes.minihr.SearchAction"
        name="searchForm"
       scope="request"
    validate="true"
       input="/search.jsp"/>
```

However, now the action will point to the search page's JSF URI, as shown here:

```
<action path="/search"
        type="com.jamesholmes.minihr.SearchAction"
        name="searchForm"
       scope="request"
    validate="true"
       input="search.faces"/>
```

At run time, the Struts-Faces library will determine if a specified page is the path of a JSF URI or an actual path to a page. If a JSF URI is specified, then Struts-Faces will process the page accordingly; otherwise, normal Struts processing will take place.

The following code shows the updated Struts configuration file for Mini HR in its entirety. The sections that have changed or that have been added are shown in bold.

```
<?xml version="1.0"?>

<!DOCTYPE struts-config PUBLIC
  "-//Apache Software Foundation//DTD Struts Configuration 1.3//EN"
  "http://struts.apache.org/dtds/struts-config_1_3.dtd">

<struts-config>

  <!-- Form Beans Configuration -->
  <form-beans>
```

```
    <form-bean name="searchForm"
               type="com.jamesholmes.minihr.SearchForm"/>
  </form-beans>

  <!-- Global Forwards Configuration -->
  <global-forwards>
    <forward name="search" path="/search.faces"/>
  </global-forwards>

  <!-- Action Mappings Configuration -->
  <action-mappings>
    <action path="/search"
            type="com.jamesholmes.minihr.SearchAction"
            name="searchForm"
            scope="request"
            validate="true"
            input="/search.faces">
    </action>
  </action-mappings>

  <!-- Controller Configuration -->
  <controller>
    <set-property property="processorClass"
      value="org.apache.struts.faces.application.FacesRequestProcessor"/>
  </controller>

  <!-- Message Resources Configuration -->
  <message-resources
    parameter="com.jamesholmes.minihr.MessageResources"/>

</struts-config>
```

Update Existing JSPs to Use the Struts-Faces and JSF Tag Library Tags

The next step is to update the application's original JSPs to use Struts-Faces and JSF Tag Library tags instead of the Struts Tag Library tags. To do this, you must replace each of the Struts tags that have JSF replacements in the original page. Following is the updated **search.jsp** page using the JSF tags. Each section of the file that is new or has been changed is shown in bold.

```
<%@ taglib uri="http://struts.apache.org/tags-bean" prefix="bean" %>
<%@ taglib uri="http://struts.apache.org/tags-html" prefix="html" %>
<%@ taglib uri="http://struts.apache.org/tags-logic" prefix="logic" %>

<%@ taglib uri="http://java.sun.com/jsf/html" prefix="h" %>
<%@ taglib uri="http://java.sun.com/jsf/core" prefix="f" %>

<%@ taglib uri="http://struts.apache.org/tags-faces" prefix="s" %>

<f:view>

<html>
<head>
<title>ABC, Inc. Human Resources Portal - Employee Search</title>
```

```
</head>
<body>

<font size="+1">
ABC, Inc. Human Resources Portal - Employee Search
</font><br>
<hr width="100%" noshade="true">

<s:errors/>

<s:form id="search" action="/search">

<table>
<tr>
<td align="right"><s:message key="label.search.name"/>:</td>
<td><h:inputText id="name" value="#{searchForm.name}"/></td>
</tr>
<tr>
<td></td>
<td>-- or --</td>
</tr>
<tr>
<td align="right"><s:message key="label.search.ssNum"/>:</td>
<td><h:inputText id="ssNum" value="#{searchForm.ssNum}"/> (xxx-xx-xxxx)</td>
</tr>
<tr>
<td></td>
<td><h:commandButton value="Submit"/></td>
</tr>
</table>

</s:form>

<logic:present name="searchForm" property="results">

<hr width="100%" size="1" noshade="true">

<bean:size id="size" name="searchForm" property="results"/>
<logic:equal name="size" value="0">
<center><font color="red"><cTypeface:Bold>No Employees Found</b></font></center>
</logic:equal>

<logic:greaterThan name="size" value="0">
<table border="1">
<tr>
<th>Name</th>
<th>Social Security Number</th>
</tr>
<logic:iterate id="result" name="searchForm" property="results">
<tr>
<td><bean:write name="result" property="name"/></td>
<td><bean:write name="result" property="ssNum"/></td>
</tr>
</logic:iterate>
</table>
</logic:greaterThan>
```

```
</logic:present>

</body>
<html>

</f:view>
```

As you can see, the Struts Tag Library tags were replaced with Struts-Faces and JSF tags. The Struts-Faces tags enable the rest of your Struts application to stay unchanged and continue to work as it did before.

Repackage and Run the Updated Application

Because no Java code was modified during this process, it's not necessary to recompile the Mini HR application. However, several files have been modified, so the application needs to be repackaged and redeployed before it is run. Assuming you've made modifications to the original Mini HR application and it was set up in the **c:\java\MiniHR** directory (as described in Chapter 2), the following command line will repackage the application when run from **c:\java\MiniHR**:

```
jar cf MiniHR.war *
```

Similar to the way you ran Mini HR the first time, you now need to place the new **MiniHR.war** file that you just created into Tomcat's **webapps** directory, delete the **webapps/MiniHR** directory, and start Tomcat. As before, to access the Mini HR application, point your browser to **http://localhost:8080/MiniHR/**. Once you have the updated Mini HR running, everything should work as it did before. However, now you can use JSF to create advanced component-based user interfaces.

CHAPTER 23

Using AJAX with Struts

Traditionally Web application interfaces have been static in nature, lacking the high level of interactivity features commonly found in desktop applications. Web application interfaces have been limited in this regard because round-trips to the server and complete page refreshes were needed to update the state of the application. However, Web application development has been evolving significantly over the past few years, and one of the technologies that stands out most in the sea of innovation is AJAX. *AJAX,* or Asynchronous JavaScript and XML (the less commonly known basis for the acronym), is the name given to a technique used to develop dynamic Web application interfaces. AJAX introduces the ability to update the state of a Web application without requiring complete page refreshes. Instead of refreshing the entire page, AJAX allows discrete portions of a page to be updated asynchronously, thus enabling a Web application to look and behave very similar to traditional desktop applications.

This chapter provides a brief overview of AJAX that introduces the technologies and concepts behind it. Because there are so many approaches to implementing AJAX techniques in Web applications, a comprehensive review of AJAX is outside the scope of this book. Instead this chapter will highlight a very basic approach for using AJAX by integrating AJAX into the Mini HR application. Although quite simple, this example provides insight into the foundation that all AJAX-based frameworks use, such as the popular DWR (http://getahead.ltd.uk/dwr/) and Dojo (http://dojotoolkit.org/) frameworks.

As a point of interest, there are two Struts AJAX extensions available on the http://struts.sf.net/ site, AjaxTags and AjaxChat, which are useful for developing Struts applications that leverage AJAX.

AJAX Overview

To integrate AJAX with Struts applications, it's necessary to understand in a general way how AJAX works. As stated, AJAX is an acronym that stands for Asynchronous JavaScript and XML. AJAX is not a technology itself, but rather a composite of technologies that are used to perform updates to a web page without requiring the page to be refreshed entirely. The core technologies used to accomplish the updates are JavaScript and XML, thus the acronym (which was coined by Jesse James Garrett).

Architecturally, AJAX is straightforward. JavaScript is used to asynchronously (that is, without refreshing the entire page) make an HTTP request to a server and retrieve data.

Typically the data is in XML format, but it can be in any format such as HTML or even plain text. After retrieving the data from the server, JavaScript code then updates a portion of the page it resides in. Thus, this mechanism avoids refreshing the entire page when only a portion of it changes. As a result, more responsive Web-based applications can be built.

Integrating AJAX with the Mini HR Application

Following is the list of steps that you follow to integrate AJAX with the Mini HR application:

1. Add a method called **getEmployeeCount()** to the **EmployeeSearchService** class. This method will get the current employee count.
2. Create a **CountAction** class.
3. Configure the **CountAction** class in the **struts-config.xml** file.
4. Update **search.jsp** to use AJAX to retrieve the current employee count and display it.
5. Recompile, repackage, and run the updated application.

The following sections walk you through each step of the process in detail.

Add getEmployeeCount( ) to EmployeeSearchService

The first step in updating the Mini HR application to use AJAX is to add a new method to the **EmployeeSearchService** class for obtaining the current employee count. This new method, **getEmployeeCount( )**, will become part of the existing Model layer of the application and be called by an action. The new **getEmployeeCount( )** method is shown next:

```
// Calculate count of employees.
public int getEmployeeCount() {
  return employees.length;
}
```

As you can see, the method is very simple. If **EmployeeSearchService** were a more sophisticated implementation that interfaced with a dynamic data source, the **getEmployeeCount()** method would make a query to obtain the count instead of returning the static count in the current implementation.

Following is the updated **EmployeeSearchService** class in its entirety; the new method is shown in bold:

```
package com.jamesholmes.minihr;

import java.util.ArrayList;

public class EmployeeSearchService
{
  /* Hard-coded sample data. Normally this would come from a real data
     source such as a database. */
  private static Employee[] employees =
  {
    new Employee("Bob Davidson", "123-45-6789"),
    new Employee("Mary Williams", "987-65-4321"),
    new Employee("Jim Smith", "111-11-1111"),
    new Employee("Beverly Harris", "222-22-2222"),
```

```
    new Employee("Thomas Frank", "333-33-3333"),
    new Employee("Jim Davidson", "444-44-4444")
  };

  // Search for employees by name.
  public ArrayList searchByName(String name) {
    ArrayList resultList = new ArrayList();

    for (int i = 0; i < employees.length; i++) {
      if (employees[i].getName().toUpperCase().indexOf(name.toUpperCase()) != -1)
      {
        resultList.add(employees[i]);
      }
    }

    return resultList;
  }

  // Search for employee by social security number.
  public ArrayList searchBySsNum(String ssNum) {
    ArrayList resultList = new ArrayList();

    for (int i = 0; i < employees.length; i++) {
      if (employees[i].getSsNum().equals(ssNum)) {
        resultList.add(employees[i]);
      }
    }

    return resultList;
  }

  // Calculate count of employees.
  public int getEmployeeCount() {
    return employees.length;
  }
}
```

Create a CountAction Class

Now that the new **getEmployeeCount()** method has been added to **EmployeeSearchService**, a **CountAction** class must be created for calling the new method and returning its output to a browser via an AJAX call. **CountAction** is like any other action in that it subclasses the Struts **Action** class and provides an implementation for the **execute()** method. It differs, however, in an important way. Instead of returning an **ActionForward** from the **execute()** method, it returns **null** and a response is written directly to the HTTP response stream. The **CountAction** class is shown next:

```
package com.jamesholmes.minihr;

import java.io.PrintWriter;

import java.util.ArrayList;

import javax.servlet.http.HttpServletRequest;
import javax.servlet.http.HttpServletResponse;
```

```
import org.apache.struts.action.Action;
import org.apache.struts.action.ActionForm;
import org.apache.struts.action.ActionForward;
import org.apache.struts.action.ActionMapping;

public final class CountAction extends Action
{
  public ActionForward execute(ActionMapping mapping,
    ActionForm form,
    HttpServletRequest request,
    HttpServletResponse response)
    throws Exception
  {
    EmployeeSearchService service = new EmployeeSearchService();

    // Retrieve employee count.
    int employeeCount = service.getEmployeeCount();

    // Write employee count to HTTP response.
    PrintWriter out = response.getWriter();
    out.print(employeeCount);

    // Return null to inform the controller servlet
    // that the HTTP response has been handled.
    return null;
  }
}
```

As you can see, this action is straightforward; it instantiates the **EmployeeSearchService** service and retrieves the current employee count. The count is then written directly to the HTTP response so that it can be read by an AJAX call. Finally, **null** is returned to indicate to the Struts controller servlet that the response has been generated and no further processing is required.

Configure the CountAction Class in the struts-config.xml File

After you have created the new **CountAction** class, you must configure an action mapping for it in Mini HR's Struts configuration file, **struts-config.xml**, as shown here:

```
<action path="/count"
        type="com.jamesholmes.minihr.CountAction">
</action>
```

You'll notice that this action mapping is less detailed than the mapping for **SearchAction**. Because no Form Bean is required or used, none of the **action** tag's attributes for configuring a Form Bean are specified.

The following code shows the updated Struts configuration file for Mini HR in its entirety. The section that has changed is shown in bold.

```
<?xml version="1.0"?>

<!DOCTYPE struts-config PUBLIC
  "-//Apache Software Foundation//DTD Struts Configuration 1.3//EN"
  "http://struts.apache.org/dtds/struts-config_1_3.dtd">
```

```
<struts-config>

  <!-- Form Beans Configuration -->
  <form-beans>
    <form-bean name="searchForm"
               type="com.jamesholmes.minihr.SearchForm"/>
  </form-beans>

  <!-- Global Forwards Configuration -->
  <global-forwards>
    <forward name="search" path="/search.jsp"/>
  </global-forwards>

  <!-- Action Mappings Configuration -->
  <action-mappings>
    <action path="/search"
            type="com.jamesholmes.minihr.SearchAction"
            name="searchForm"
            scope="request"
            validate="true"
            input="/search.jsp">
    </action>
    <action path="/count"
            type="com.jamesholmes.minihr.CountAction">
    </action>
  </action-mappings>

  <!-- Message Resources Configuration -->
  <message-resources
    parameter="com.jamesholmes.minihr.MessageResources"/>

</struts-config>
```

Update search.jsp to Use AJAX

The next step is to update the application's original **search.jsp** file to use AJAX for retrieving a current employee count and displaying the count. There are a few changes that have to be made in order to do this. The following list outlines each of the changes.

- Add JavaScript for performing the AJAX call to the **CountAction** and for updating the page's HTML.
- Add a section of HTML inside a **<span>** tag that will be updated by the JavaScript.
- Add an HTML button that invokes the JavaScript that makes the AJAX call and updates the page's HTML.

Following is the updated **search.jsp** page. Each section of the file that is new or has been changed is shown in bold.

```
<%@ taglib uri="http://struts.apache.org/tags-bean" prefix="bean" %>
<%@ taglib uri="http://struts.apache.org/tags-html" prefix="html" %>
<%@ taglib uri="http://struts.apache.org/tags-logic" prefix="logic" %>

<html>
```

```
<head>
<title>ABC, Inc. Human Resources Portal - Employee Search</title>
<script language="JavaScript">
  var request;

  function getCount() {
    var url = "/MiniHr/count.do";

    // Perform the AJAX request using a non-IE browser.
    if (window.XMLHttpRequest) {
      request = new XMLHttpRequest();

      // Register callback function that will be called when
      // the response is generated from the server.
      request.onreadystatechange = updateCount;

      try {
          request.open("GET", url, true);
      } catch (e) {
         alert("Unable to connect to server to retrieve count.");
      }

      request.send(null);
    // Perform the AJAX request using an IE browser.
    } else if (window.ActiveXObject) {
      request = new ActiveXObject("Microsoft.XMLHTTP");

      if (request) {
        // Register callback function that will be called when
        // the response is generated from the server.
        request.onreadystatechange = updateCount;

        request.open("GET", url, true);
        request.send();
      }
    }
  }

  // Callback function to update page with count retrieved from server.
  function updateCount() {
    if (request.readyState == 4) {
      if (request.status == 200) {
        var count = request.responseText;

        document.getElementById('employeeCount').innerHTML = count;
      } else {
        alert("Unable to retrieve count from server.");
      }
    }
  }
</script>
</head>
<body>
```

```
<font size="+1">
ABC, Inc. Human Resources Portal - Employee Search
</font><br>
<hr width="100%" noshade="true">

<html:errors/>

<html:form action="/search">

<table>
<tr>
<td align="right">Current Employee Count:</td>
<td>
  <i><span id="employeeCount">?</span></i>
  <input type="button" value="Get Count" onclick="getCount();">
</td>
</tr>
<tr>
<td colspan="2"><br></td>
</tr>
<tr>
<td align="right"><bean:message key="label.search.name"/>:</td>
<td><html:text property="name"/></td>
</tr>
<tr>
<td></td>
<td>-- or --</td>
</tr>
<tr>
<td align="right"><bean:message key="label.search.ssNum"/>:</td>
<td><html:text property="ssNum"/> (xxx-xx-xxxx)</td>
</tr>
<tr>
<td></td>
<td><html:submit/></td>
</tr>
</table>

</html:form>

<logic:present name="searchForm" property="results">

<hr width="100%" size="1" noshade="true">

<bean:size id="size" name="searchForm" property="results"/>
<logic:equal name="size" value="0">
<center><font color="red"><b>No Employees Found</b></font></center>
</logic:equal>

<logic:greaterThan name="size" value="0">
<table border="1">
<tr>
<th>Name</th>
```

```
<th>Social Security Number</th>
</tr>
<logic:iterate id="result" name="searchForm" property="results">
<tr>
<td><bean:write name="result" property="name"/></td>
<td><bean:write name="result" property="ssNum"/></td>
</tr>
</logic:iterate>
</table>
</logic:greaterThan>

</logic:present>

</body>
<html>
```

As you can see, there are two new sections of code in the JSP. The first section contains the JavaScript code that performs the AJAX request to **CountAction**. **CountAction** returns a count of the current number of employees directly to the HTTP response stream, which is read by the JavaScript code. The JavaScript code then updates the count section of the page with the value returned from **CountAction**. The second new section of code added to the JSP is the section that displays the current employee count. Notice that **<span>** tags are used to encapsulate the count value. When using AJAX, **<span>** tags are used to mark specific sections of content for easy updating. The JavaScript code that updates the page will reference the encapsulated content by the name specified with the surrounding **<span>** tags.

Recompile, Repackage, and Run the Updated Application

Because you added the **getEmployeeCount( )** method to **EmployeeSearchService** and created the **CountAction** class, you need to recompile and repackage the Mini HR application before you run it. Assuming that you've made modifications to the original Mini HR application and it was set up in the **c:\java\MiniHR** directory (as described in Chapter 2), you can run the **build.bat** batch file or the **build.xml** Ant script file to recompile the application.

After recompiling Mini HR, you need to repackage it using the following command line:

```
jar cf MiniHR.war *
```

This command should also be run from the directory where you have set up the Mini HR application (e.g., **c:\java\MiniHR**).

Similar to the way you ran Mini HR the first time, you now need to place the new **MiniHR.war** file that you just created into Tomcat's **webapps** directory, delete the **webapps/MiniHR** directory, and start Tomcat. As before, to access the Mini HR application, point your browser to **http://localhost:8080/MiniHR/**. Once you have the updated Mini HR running, you will see the new "Current Employee Count" section on the search page as illustrated in Figure 23-1. Try clicking the "Get Count" button. You will notice that the count on the page updated without the entire page refreshing as illustrated in Figure 23-2. This is a basic usage of AJAX, but it illustrates the core steps involved in using this powerful technique.

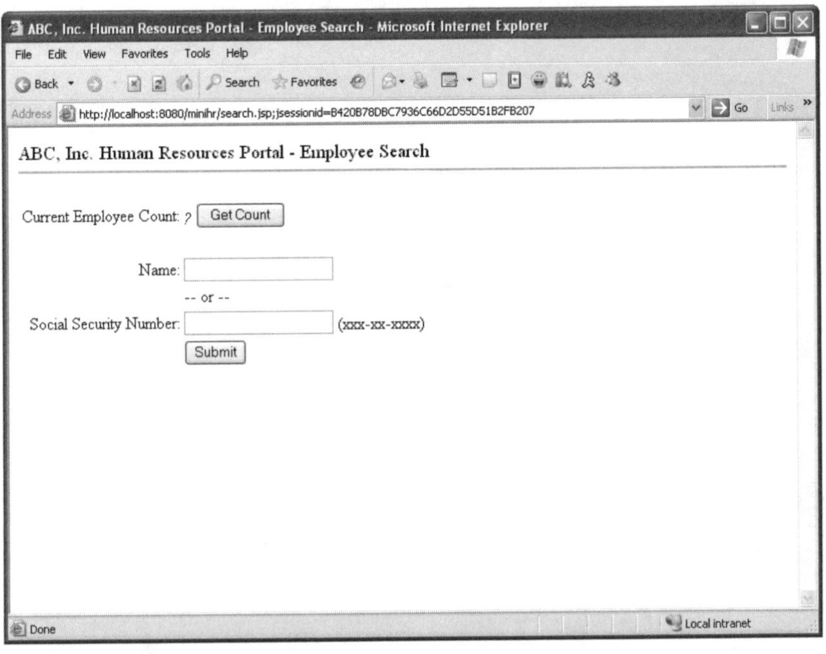

FIGURE 23-1 The Current Employee Count section on the Employee Search page

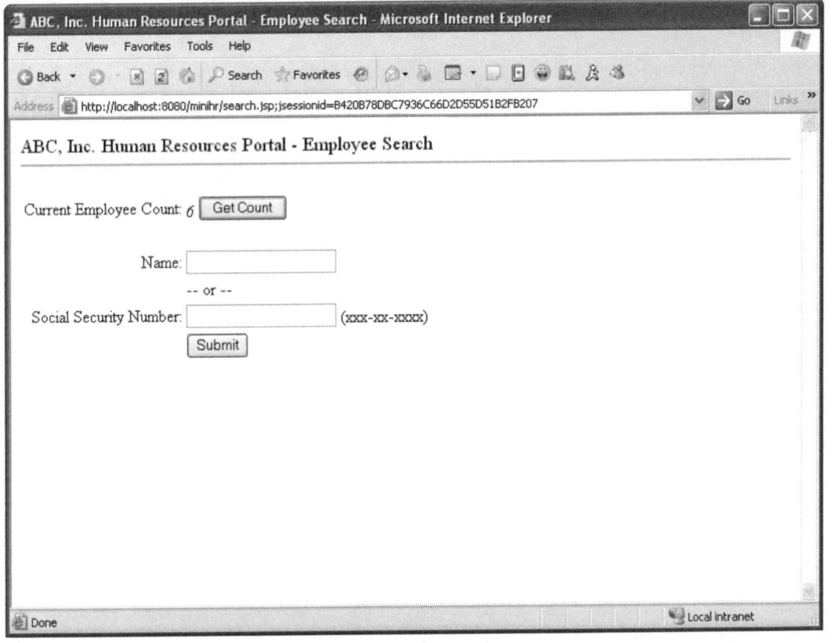

FIGURE 23-2 Updated Employee Count on the Employee Search page

PART VI

Appendixes

Appendix A
Struts Console Quick Reference

Appendix B
Third-Party Struts Extensions

APPENDIX A

Struts Console Quick Reference

A fundamental advantage of using the Struts framework for Java Web application development is its declarative nature. Instead of binding components of an application together in code, Struts applications use a centralized XML configuration file to declaratively connect components together. Unfortunately, modifying Struts configuration files by hand can be tedious and error prone. If you mistakenly leave off a closing bracket for a tag or misspell a tag or attribute name, Struts is unable to parse the configuration file and thus does not function properly. Trying to correct errors like these for a typical application, whose configuration file is usually quite long, can be time-consuming because of the many details involved. For this reason, I created the Struts Console GUI tool to simplify the creation and maintenance of the Struts configuration file. Struts Console provides a simple and intuitive graphical interface with which to edit Struts configuration files.

Struts Console has evolved significantly since its initial release and continues to evolve today. Originally, Struts Console supported editing of only Struts configuration files. Since then Struts Console has been updated to support editing of Tiles and Validator configuration files as well as JSP Tag Library Descriptor (**.tld**) files. Struts Console is written in Java and thus can be run on any platform that supports Java GUI applications (e.g., Microsoft Windows, Macintosh, Linux, and so on). In its original release, Struts Console could be run only as a stand-alone application. Subsequently, Struts Console has been updated to support being run as a plugin in most of the major Java IDEs. Following is the list of IDEs that Struts Console can be used with:

- Borland JBuilder (versions 4.0 and later)
- Eclipse (versions 1.0 and later)
- IBM Rational Application Developer for WebSphere (previously known as WebSphere Studio Application Developer [WSAD]) (versions 4.0.3 and later)
- IntelliJ IDEA (versions 3.0 build 668 and later)

- NetBeans (versions 3.2 and later)
- Oracle JDeveloper (versions 9*i* and later)
- Sun Java Studio (previously known as Forte or Sun ONE Studio) (versions 3.0 and later)

The following sections explain how to acquire, install, and use Struts Console, both as a stand-alone application and as a plugin inside all the supported IDEs. Because IDEs are continually evolving, some of the instructions for using Struts Console inside the IDEs may change over time. If any of the instructions found in this appendix do not work for you, visit my Web site at **http://www.jamesholmes.com/struts/** for the most up-to-date instructions.

Supported Configuration Files

As explained, the current version of Struts Console supports editing not only Struts configuration files, but also Tiles and Validator configuration files, plus the JSP Tag Library Descriptor (**.tld**) files. All of these files are XML-based. In order for Struts Console to distinguish these files from any random XML file, they must have a proper XML **<!DOCTYPE>** declaration. The **<!DOCTYPE>** declaration specifies the Document Type Definition (DTD) to which the file must conform. Following is a list of the configuration files supported by Struts Console and their **<!DOCTYPE>** definitions.

The Struts 1.3 Configuration File

```
<!DOCTYPE struts-config PUBLIC
  "-//Apache Software Foundation//DTD Struts Configuration 1.3//EN"
  "http://struts.apache.org/dtds/struts-config_1_3.dtd">
```

The Struts 1.2 Configuration File

```
<!DOCTYPE struts-config PUBLIC
  "-//Apache Software Foundation//DTD Struts Configuration 1.2//EN"
  "http://jakarta.apache.org/struts/dtds/struts-config_1_2.dtd">
```

The Struts 1.1 Configuration File

```
<!DOCTYPE struts-config PUBLIC
  "-//Apache Software Foundation//DTD Struts Configuration 1.1//EN"
  "http://jakarta.apache.org/struts/dtds/struts-config_1_1.dtd">
```

The Struts 1.0 Configuration File

```
<!DOCTYPE struts-config PUBLIC
  "-//Apache Software Foundation//DTD Struts Configuration 1.0//EN"
  "http://jakarta.apache.org/struts/dtds/struts-config_1_0.dtd">
```

The Tiles 1.3 Configuration File

```
<!DOCTYPE tiles-definitions PUBLIC
  "-//Apache Software Foundation//DTD Tiles Configuration 1.3//EN"
  "http://struts.apache.org/dtds/tiles-config_1_3.dtd">
```

The Tiles 1.1 Configuration File

```
<!DOCTYPE tiles-definitions PUBLIC
  "-//Apache Software Foundation//DTD Tiles Configuration 1.1//EN"
  "http://jakarta.apache.org/struts/dtds/tiles-config_1_1.dtd">
```

The Validator 1.3.0 Configuration File

```
<!DOCTYPE form-validation PUBLIC
   "-//Apache Software Foundation//DTD Commons
    Validator Rules Configuration 1.3.0//EN"
   "http://jakarta.apache.org/commons/dtds/validator_1_3_0.dtd">
```

The Validator 1.1 Configuration File

```
<!DOCTYPE form-validation PUBLIC
   "-//Apache Software Foundation//DTD Commons
    Validator Rules Configuration 1.1//EN"
   "http://jakarta.apache.org/commons/dtds/validator_1_1.dtd">
```

The Validator 1.0 Configuration File

```
<!DOCTYPE form-validation PUBLIC
   "-//Apache Software Foundation//DTD Commons
    Validator Rules Configuration 1.0//EN"
   "http://jakarta.apache.org/commons/dtds/validator_1_0.dtd">
```

The JSP Tag Library 1.2 File

```
<!DOCTYPE taglib PUBLIC
  "-//Sun Microsystems, Inc.//DTD JSP Tag Library 1.2//EN"
  "http://java.sun.com/dtd/web-jsptaglibrary_1_2.dtd">
```

The JSP Tag Library 1.1 File

```
<!DOCTYPE taglib PUBLIC
  "-//Sun Microsystems, Inc.//DTD JSP Tag Library 1.1//EN"
  "http://java.sun.com/j2ee/dtds/web-jsptaglibrary_1_1.dtd">
```

NOTE *Your configuration file must contain one of the preceding* **<!DOCTYPE>** *declarations; otherwise, Struts Console will be unable to load your configuration file.*

Acquiring and Installing Struts Console

Struts Console is free software and can be used both noncommercially and commercially free of charge. However, Struts Console is not open-source software like Struts itself. Struts Console can be acquired from my Web site at **http://www.jamesholmes.com/struts/**.

Struts Console comes packaged as both a Zip file (**.zip**) and a Gzipped Tar file (**.tar.gz**). Select your desired packaging and download the file. Once you have downloaded Struts Console, installing it is straightforward. Because Struts Console is simply packaged in an archive file and not as an executable installation program, all you have to do is unpack the archive file into your desired installation directory. All the files inside the archive file are beneath a version-specific directory (e.g., **struts-console-5.0**); thus when you unpack them into your desired directory, they will all be beneath the version-specific directory. For example, if you were to download version 5.0 of Struts Console and unpack its archive to **c:\java**, the Struts Console files would all be located at **c:\java\struts-console-5.0**. That's all you have to do to install Struts Console.

NOTE *Because Struts Console does not use an installer to place any special files into system directories, multiple versions of Struts Console can be installed on the same machine if necessary or desired.*

Using Struts Console as a Stand-Alone Application

Most often, Struts Console is used as an IDE plugin because of the convenience of working seamlessly inside one tool. However, Struts Console can just as easily be run as a stand-alone application. Before running Struts Console as a stand-alone application, though, you must set the **JAVA_HOME** environmental variable. Many Java development kit (JDK) distributions set this for you when you install them; however, if it is not set on your machine, you must set it before you run Struts Console. The **JAVA_HOME** variable must be set to the directory where you have your JDK installed. For example, if you have JDK 1.5.0_07 installed at **c:\java\jdk1.5.0_07**, your **JAVA_HOME** variable should be set to **c:\java\ jdk1.5.0_07**.

Once you have set the **JAVA_HOME** environmental variable, you are ready to run Struts Console. Simply navigate to the directory where you installed Struts Console (e.g., **c:\java\struts-console-5.0**) and then navigate into the **bin** directory. The **bin** directory contains two files: **console.bat** and **console.sh**. If you are on a Microsoft Windows machine, run **console.bat**. However, if you are on Linux, Unix, or Macintosh, run **console.sh**.

NOTE *On Linux, Unix, and Macintosh you have to set the executable flag on the* **console.sh** *file before it can be executed.*

Once Struts Console is up and running, you can open an existing configuration file or create a new configuration file for editing. Figure A-1 shows Struts Console in action as a stand-alone application. Notice that open files have an Editor and a Source tab at the bottom. The Source tab shows you the source XML for the configuration file. Unlike many of the Struts Console IDE plugins, you cannot edit the XML source directly. This, however, may be a new feature in the future.

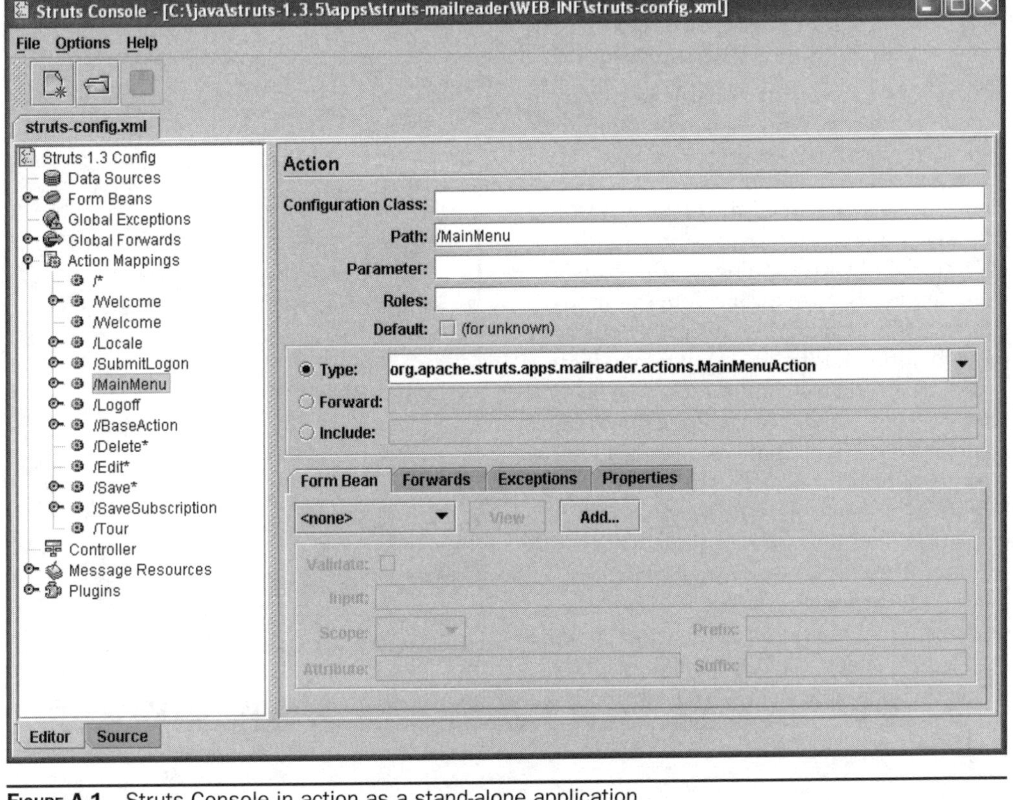

FIGURE A-1 Struts Console in action as a stand-alone application

Using Struts Console Inside Borland JBuilder

Struts Console can be run as a plugin inside Borland JBuilder versions 4.0 and later. To do so, you first must install the Struts Console JBuilder plugin. Following is the list of steps for installing the Struts Console JBuilder plugin:

1. Shut down JBuilder if it is currently running.
2. Navigate to the directory in which you have JBuilder installed (e.g., **c:\Program Files\JBuilder**) and then navigate into the **lib** directory.
3. In another window, navigate to the directory in which you installed Struts Console (e.g., **c:\java\struts-console-5.0**) and then navigate into the **com.jamesholmes.console.struts** directory and then into the **lib** directory.
4. Copy the **xerces.jar** file from the Struts Console **lib** directory (e.g., **c:\java\struts-console-4.4\lib**) into the JBuilder **lib** directory (e.g., **c:\Program Files\JBuilder\lib**), *if and only if* ***xerces.jar*** does not already exist in the JBuilder **lib** directory.

NOTE *Step 4 should only be necessary for JBuilder version 4.*

5. Navigate into the **ext** directory (e.g., **c:\Program Files\JBuilder\lib\ext**) from the JBuilder **lib** directory.
6. Copy the **struts-console.jar** file from the Struts Console **lib** directory into the JBuilder **ext** directory.

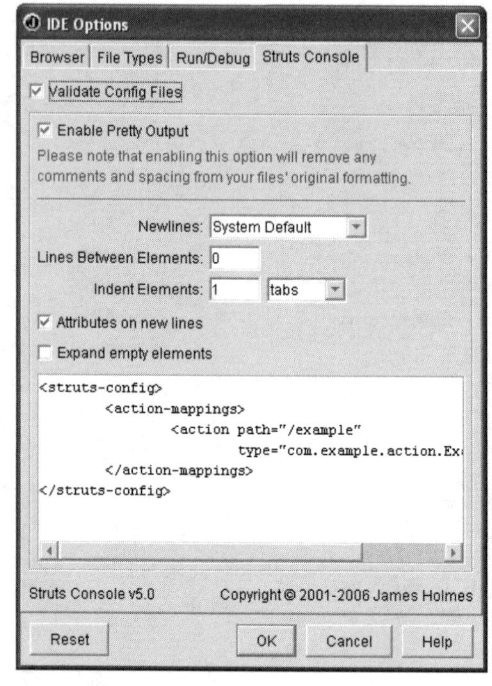

After you have installed the Struts Console JBuilder plugin, you must restart JBuilder.

Once JBuilder is running, to use Struts Console, simply open a valid configuration file supported by Struts Console. Struts Console will be a tab option for the file, as shown in Figure A-2. You can edit the configuration file using Struts Console, or you can edit the file by hand from the Source tab. Changes made in either tab are automatically reflected in the other tab.

Struts Console also allows you to modify some of its configuration settings from inside JBuilder. To access the Struts Console configuration settings, select Tools | IDE Options. The illustration to the right shows the Struts Console IDE Options dialog box.

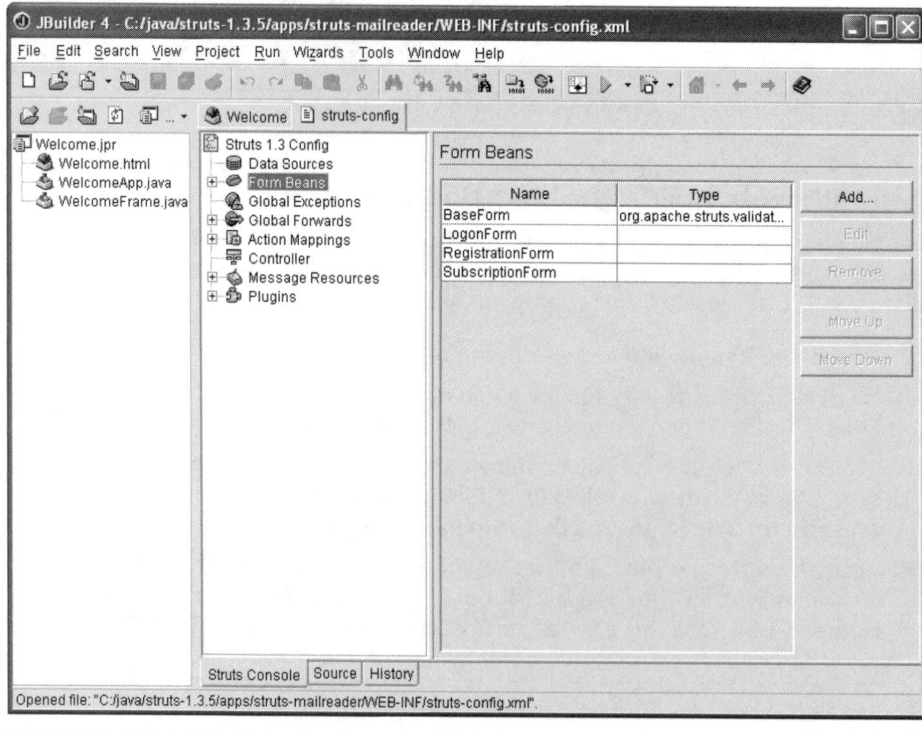

FIGURE A-2 Struts Console inside JBuilder

For more information on these configuration settings, see the section "Configuring the Struts Console Output Options" later in this appendix.

Using Struts Console Inside Eclipse

Struts Console can be run as a plugin inside Eclipse versions 1.0 and later. To do so, you first have to install the Struts Console Eclipse plugin. Following is the list of steps for installing the Struts Console Eclipse plugin:

1. Shut down Eclipse if it is currently running.
2. Navigate to the directory in which you have Eclipse installed (e.g., **c:\Program Files\eclipse**) and then navigate into the **plugins** directory.
3. In another window, navigate to the directory in which you installed Struts Console (e.g., **c:\java\struts-console-5.0**).
4. Copy the **com.jamesholmes.console.struts** directory from the Struts Console installation directory into the Eclipse **plugins** directory.
5. *If and only if you are running Eclipse versions 3.0m6 or earlier,* rename the **plugin.xml** file beneath the Eclipse **plugins** directory to **plugin.xml.bak**. Next, rename **plugin-old.xml** to **plugin.xml**. This step is necessary because there are two Struts Console Eclipse plugins, one for Eclipse versions 3.0m7 and later and one for earlier versions of Eclipse.

After you have installed the Struts Console Eclipse plugin, you must restart Eclipse.

Once Eclipse is running, to use Struts Console, simply right-click a valid configuration file and select Open With | Struts Console, as shown here:

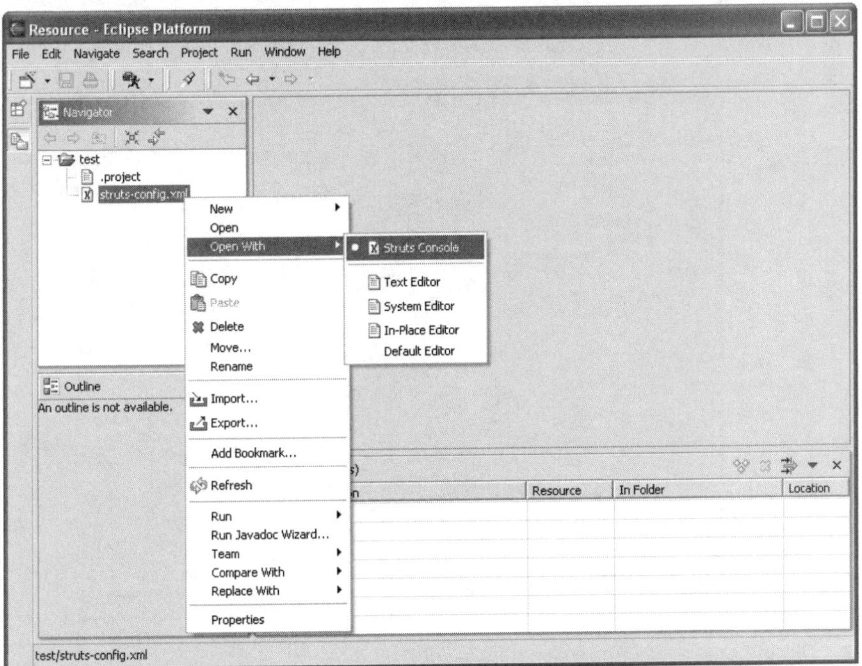

PART VI

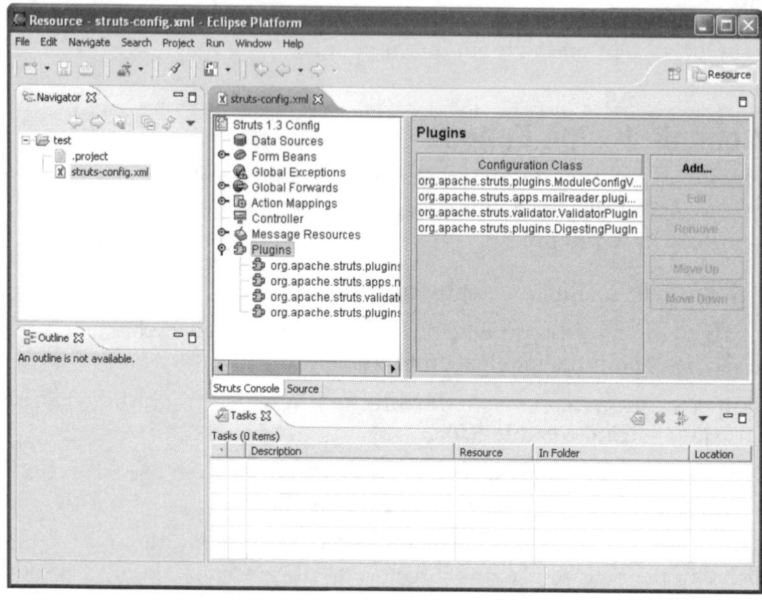

FIGURE A-3 Struts Console editor inside Eclipse

For Eclipse versions 3.0m7 and later, after you have opened the file, it will load into the Struts Console editor inside of Eclipse, as shown in Figure A-3. You can edit the configuration file using Struts Console, or you can edit the file by hand from the Source tab. Changes made in either tab are automatically reflected in the other tab. For versions of Eclipse prior to 3.0m7, the file will load into a separate Struts Console window, as shown in Figure A-4.

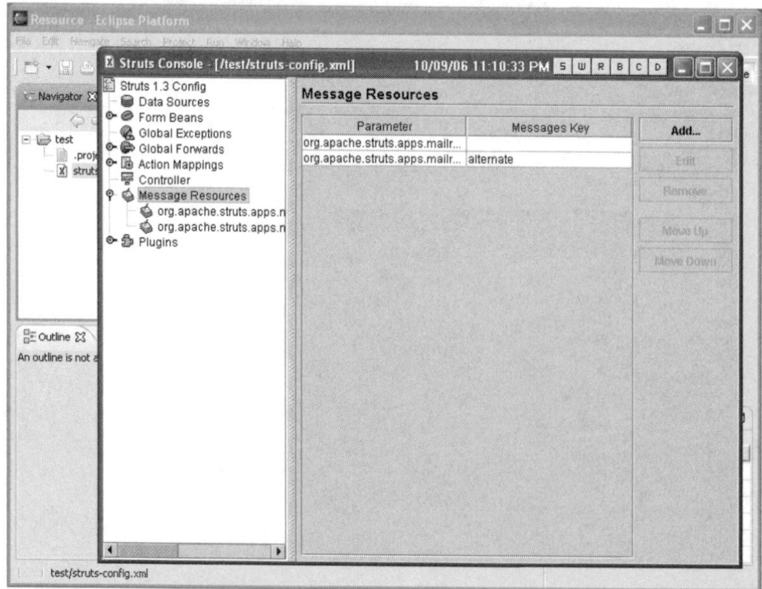

FIGURE A-4 Struts Console editor in a separate window

NOTE *The Struts Console Eclipse plugin requires that your configuration files have specific filenames in order for the plugin to recognize them. Struts configuration files must be named* **struts-config.xml**; *Tiles configuration files must be named* **tiles.xml**; *and Validator configuration files must be named* **validation.xml**. *JSP TLD files only need to have a file extension of* **.tld**.

Struts Console also allows you to modify some of its configuration settings from inside Eclipse. To access the Struts Console configuration settings, select Window | Preferences. The following illustration shows the Struts Console Preferences dialog box.

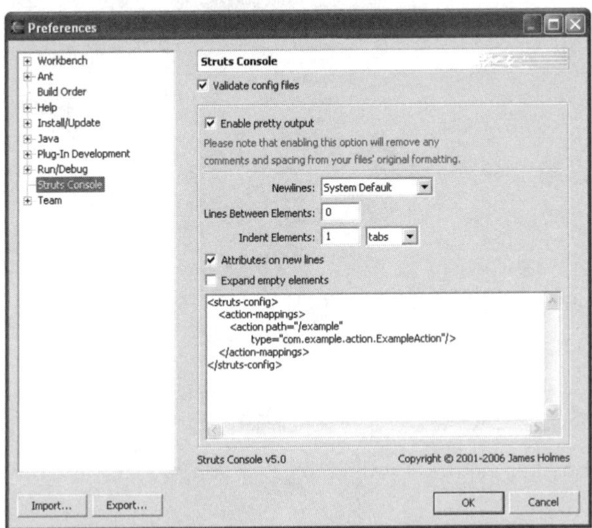

For more information on these configuration settings, see the section "Configuring the Struts Console Output Options" later in this appendix.

Using Struts Console Inside IBM Rational Application Developer for WebSphere

Struts Console can be run as a plugin inside IBM Rational Application Developer for WebSphere (RAD) (previously known as WebSphere Studio Application Developer [WSAD]) versions 4.0.3 and later. To do so, you first have to install the Struts Console Eclipse plugin. Following is the list of steps for installing the Struts Console RAD plugin:

1. Shut down RAD if it is currently running.
2. Navigate to the directory in which you have RAD installed (e.g., **c:\Program Files\IBM\WebSphere Studio**) and then navigate into the **eclipse** directory and then into the **plugins** directory.
3. In another window, navigate to the directory in which you installed Struts Console (e.g., **c:\java\struts-console-5.0**).
4. Copy the **com.jamesholmes.console.struts** directory from the Struts Console installation directory into the RAD **plugins** directory.

After you have installed the Struts Console RAD plugin, you must restart RAD.

Once RAD is running, to use Struts Console, simply right-click a valid configuration file and select Open With | Struts Console, as shown here:

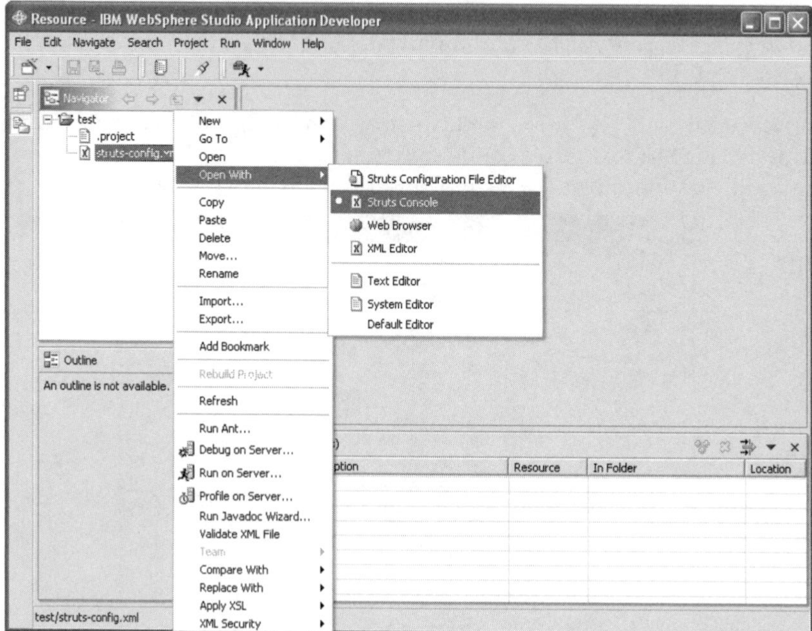

After you have opened the file, it will load into a separate Struts Console window, as shown in Figure A-5.

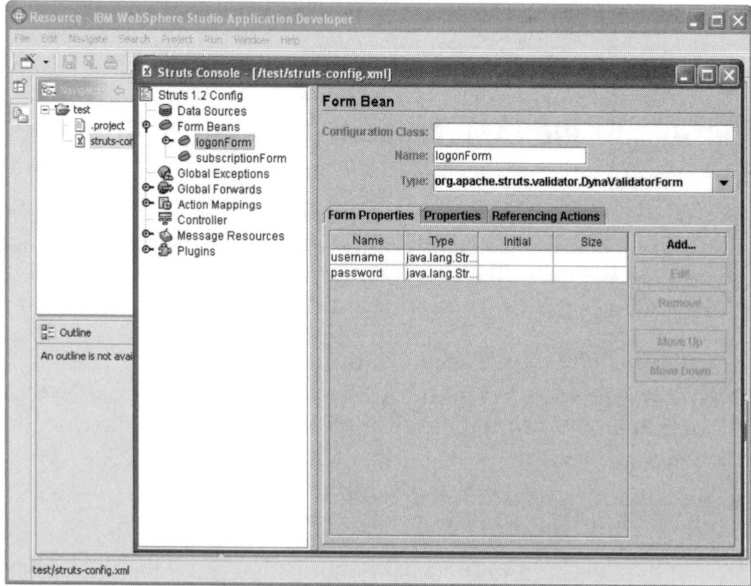

FIGURE A-5 Struts Console editor in a separate window

NOTE *The Struts Console RAD plugin requires that your configuration files have specific filenames in order for the plugin to recognize them. Struts configuration files must be named* **struts-config.xml**; *Tiles configuration files must be named* **tiles.xml**; *and Validator configuration files must be named* **validation.xml**. *JSP TLD files only need to have a file extension of* **.tld**.

Struts Console also allows you to modify some of its configuration settings from inside RAD. To access the Struts Console configuration settings, select Window | Preferences. The following illustration shows the Struts Console Preferences dialog box.

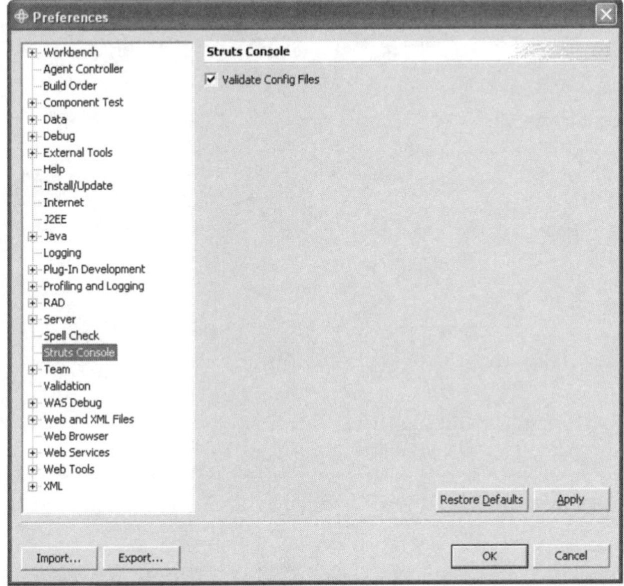

For more information on these configuration settings, see the section "Configuring the Struts Console Output Options" later in this appendix.

Using Struts Console Inside IntelliJ IDEA

Struts Console can be run as a plugin inside JetBrains' IntelliJ IDEA versions 3.0 build 668 and later. To do so, you first have to install the Struts Console IDEA plugin. Following is the list of steps for installing the Struts Console IntelliJ IDEA plugin:

1. Shut down IntelliJ IDEA if it is currently running.
2. Navigate to the directory in which you have IntelliJ IDEA installed (e.g., **c:\Program Files\IntelliJ-IDEA-4.0**) and then navigate into the **plugins** directory.
3. In another window, navigate to the directory in which you installed Struts Console (e.g., **c:\java\struts-console-5.0**) and then navigate into the **com.jamesholmes.console.struts** directory and then into the **lib** directory.
4. Copy the **struts-console.jar** file from the Struts Console **lib** directory into the IDEA **plugins** directory.

After you have installed the Struts Console IDEA plugin, you must restart IDEA.

PART VI

Once IDEA is running, to use Struts Console, simply right-click a valid configuration file and select Edit With Struts Console, as shown here:

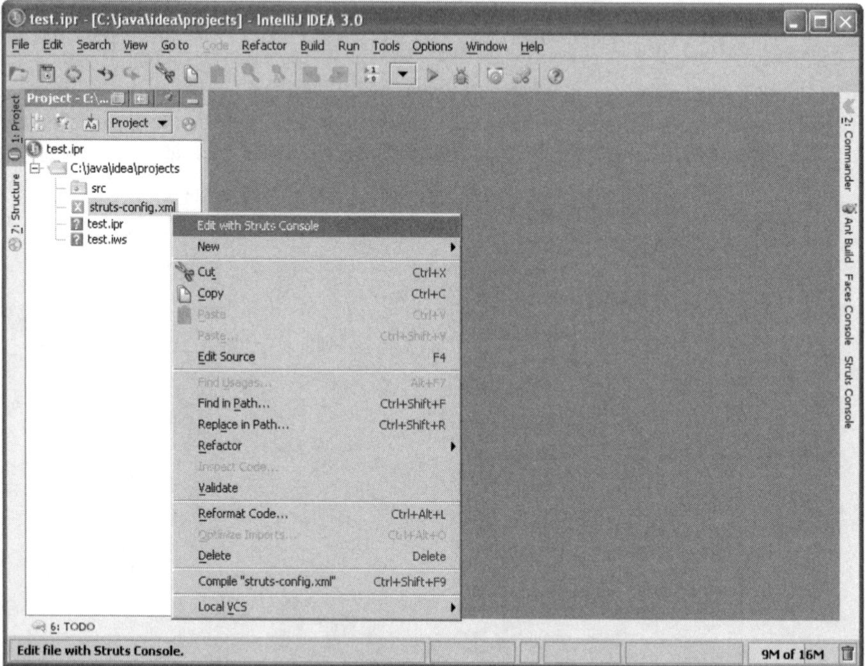

After you have opened the file, it will load into the Struts Console editor, as shown in Figure A-6.

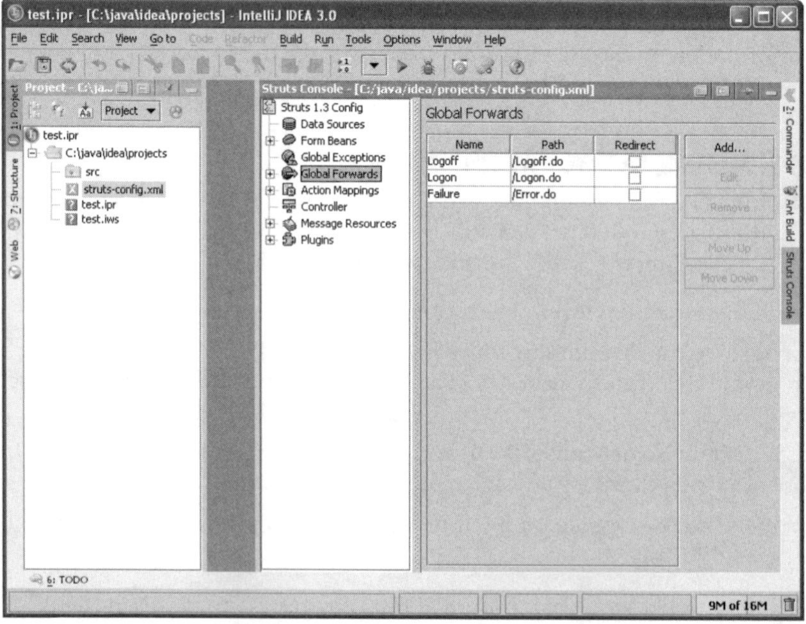

FIGURE A-6 Struts Console editor inside IDEA

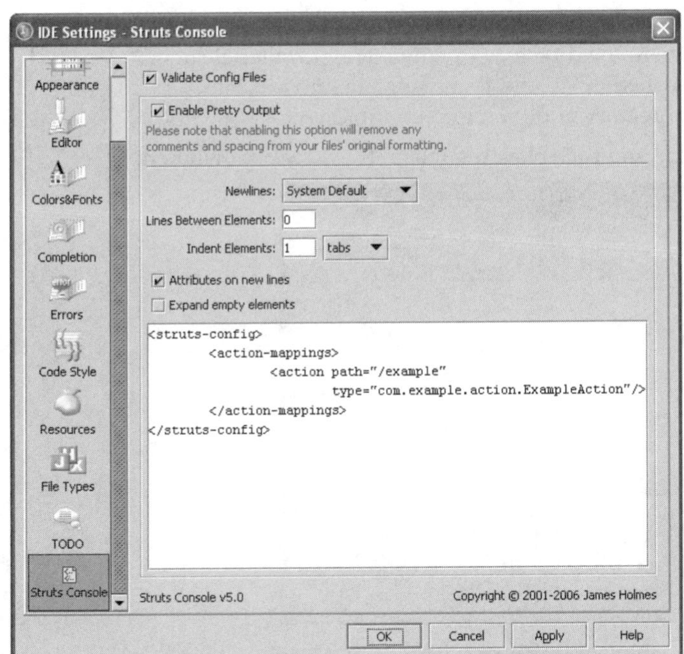

Struts Console also allows you to modify some of its configuration settings from inside IDEA. To access the Struts Console configuration settings, select Options | IDE Settings. Here is the Struts Console IDE Settings dialog box.

For more information on these configuration settings, see the "Configuring the Struts Console Output Options" section later in this appendix.

Using Struts Console Inside NetBeans and Sun Java Studio

Struts Console can be run as a plugin inside NetBeans versions 3.2 and later and inside Sun Java Studio versions 3.0 and later. To do so, you first have to install the Struts Console NetBeans plugin. Following is the list of steps for installing the Struts Console NetBeans plugin:

1. Start up NetBeans if it is not currently running.
2. Select Tools | Options. In the Options dialog box, navigate to the Options | IDE Configuration | System | Modules node in the tree on the left and then right-click it and select Add | Module, as shown here:

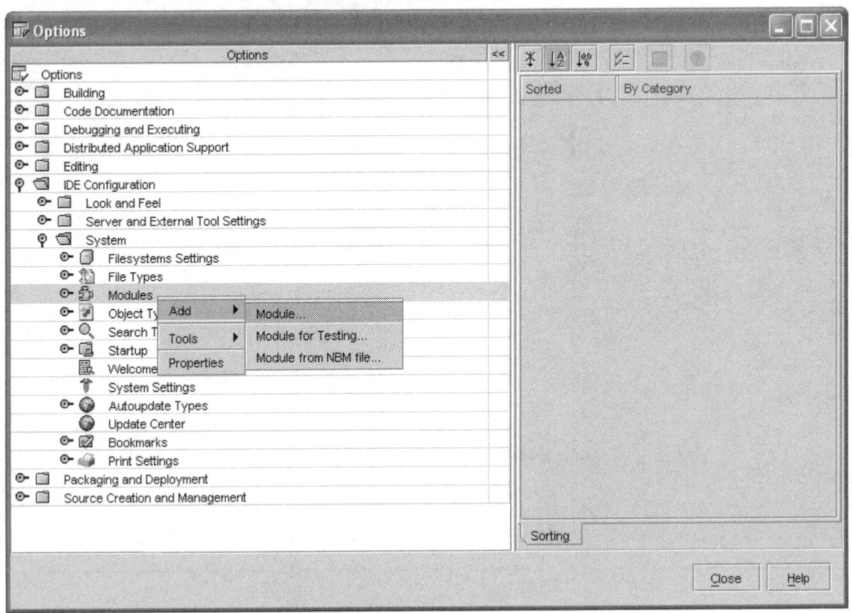

3. Using the file chooser, navigate to the directory in which you installed Struts Console (e.g., **c:\java\struts-console-5.0**) and then navigate into the **com.jamesholmes.console.struts** directory and then into the **lib** directory.
4. Select the **struts-console.jar** file and then click the Install button, as shown here.

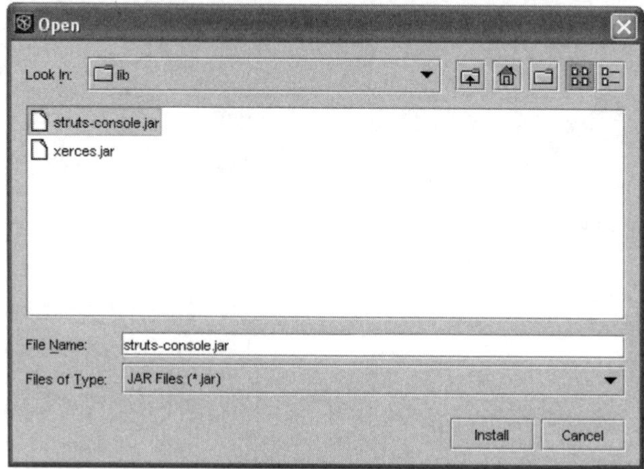

After you have installed the Struts Console NetBeans plugin, you must restart NetBeans.

Once NetBeans is running, to use Struts Console, simply open a valid configuration file supported by Struts Console. The file will load into the Struts Console editor inside of NetBeans, as shown in Figure A-7.

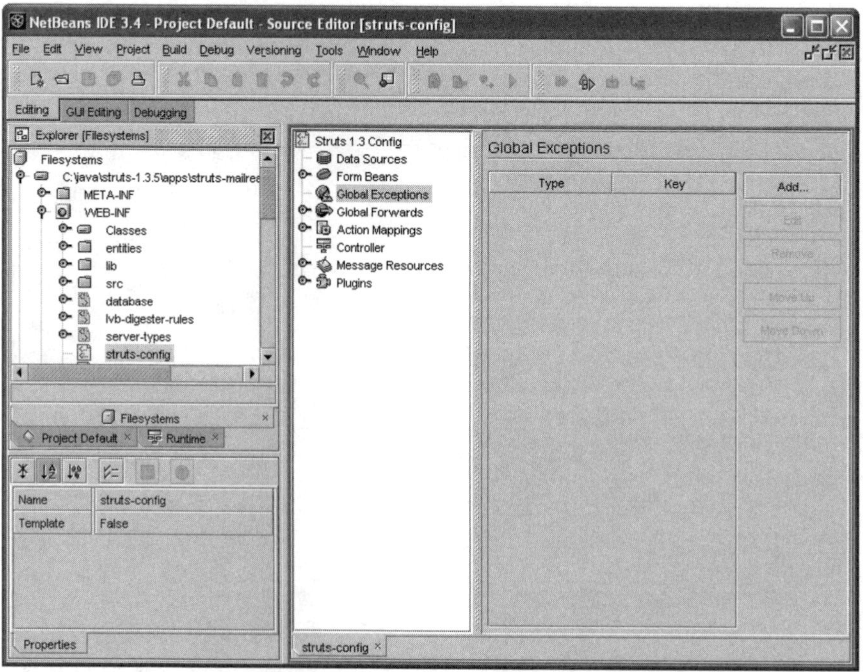

FIGURE A-7 Struts Console inside NetBeans

Using Struts Console Inside Oracle JDeveloper

Struts Console can be run as a plugin inside Oracle JDeveloper versions 9*i* and later. To do so, you first have to install the Struts Console JDeveloper plugin. Following is the list of steps for installing the Struts Console JDeveloper plugin:

1. Shut down JDeveloper if it is currently running.
2. Navigate to the directory in which you have JDeveloper installed (e.g., **c:\Program Files\JDeveloper**) and then navigate into the **jdev** directory and then into the **lib** directory and then into the **ext** directory.
3. In another window, navigate to the directory in which you installed Struts Console (e.g., **c:\java\struts-console-5.0**) and then navigate into the **com.jamesholmes.console.struts** directory and then into the **lib** directory.
4. Copy the **struts-console.jar** file from the Struts Console **lib** directory into the JDeveloper **ext** directory.

After you have installed the Struts Console JDeveloper plugin, you must restart JDeveloper.

Once JDeveloper is running, to use Struts Console, simply right-click a valid configuration file and select Struts Console Editor, as shown here:

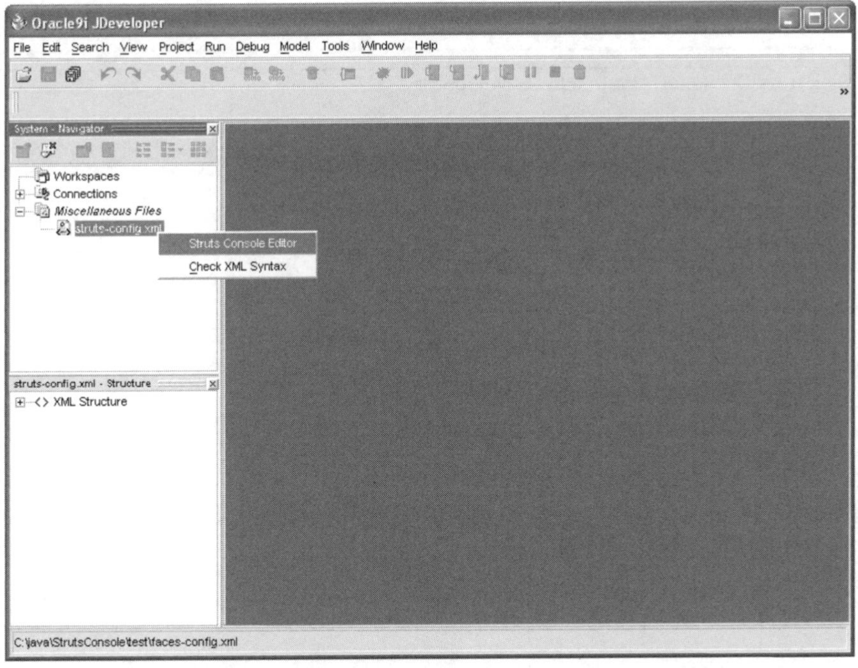

After you have opened the file, it will load into the Struts Console editor inside of JDeveloper, as shown in Figure A-8.

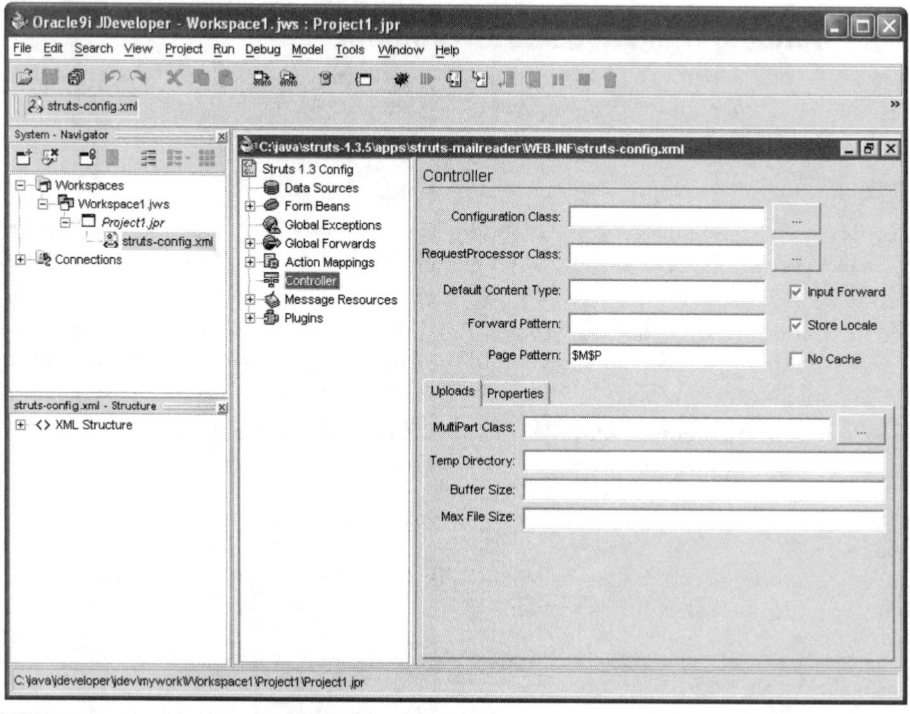

FIGURE A-8 Struts Console editor inside JDeveloper

Struts Console also allows you to modify some of its configuration settings from inside JDeveloper. To access the Struts Console configuration settings, select Tools | Preferences. Here is the Struts Console Preferences dialog box.

For more information on these configuration settings, see the next section, "Configuring the Struts Console Output Options."

Configuring the Struts Console Output Options

Struts Console uses an XML parser to read in XML configuration files, and then it manipulates the files in memory. Because XML parsers do not retain all of a file's original formatting when the file is parsed, the files are often poorly formatted when they are saved. By default, Struts Console simply preserves the in-memory representation of configuration files, which results in poorly formatted XML files. To get around the limitation of XML parsers not retaining complete formatting information, Struts Console has a feature called Pretty Output that allows the format configuration of an XML file to be saved.

The Pretty Output options can be configured in the stand-alone version of Struts Console as well as from inside IDEs that Struts Console plugs into. (For information on how to access the configuration settings for the Pretty Output options in a supported IDE, see that IDE's section in this appendix.) To configure the Pretty Output options in the stand-alone version of Struts Console, select Options | Output. This opens the dialog box shown here with options for specifying the details of how XML files should be formatted when they are saved.

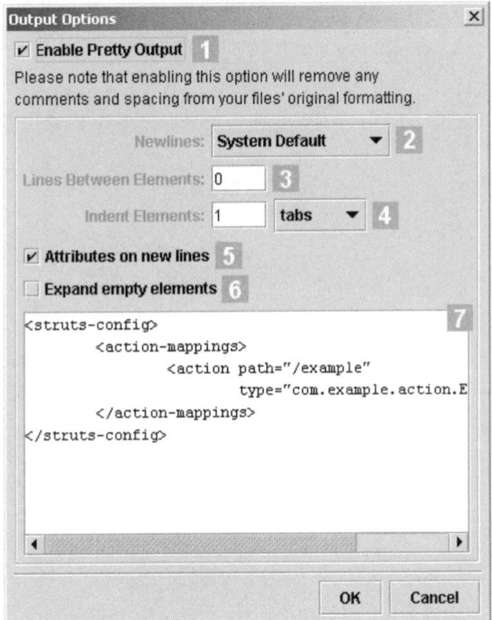

Following is an explanation of each of the output options:

- **Enable Pretty Output** Enables and disables the use of Pretty Output options.
- **Newlines** Specifies the type of newline character to use. System Default is the default and recommended setting. System Default defaults to the newline character for the given system on which the application is running. For example, if run on Windows, System Default uses Windows-style newline characters.
- **Lines Between Elements** Specifies the number of new lines to place in between tags.

- **Indent Elements** Specifies the number and type of indenting to use. Indenting is used for tags and is hierarchical. Each level in the tag hierarchy is a level of indenting.
- **Attributes on New Lines** Specifies whether a tag's attributes should each be placed on a new line or if each should be placed on the same line as the tag.
- **Expand Empty Elements** Specifies whether or not empty tags (that is, tags without nested tags) should be expanded (e.g., **<tag/>** versus **<tag></tag>**).
- **Bottom pane** Shows an example of how the output will look with the current output options applied. This changes as you change the output options.

NOTE *Enabling Pretty Output removes any XML comments (e.g.,* **<!-- -->***) and formatting from your original configuration files.*

Third-Party Struts Extensions

One of Struts' most important selling points has been the large number of third-party extensions available for the framework. If there is a feature that Struts doesn't offer itself, it's likely that someone has developed an extension that supplies that feature and made it available for the community to use. Simply put, the third-party extensions have contributed greatly to the growth and popularity of Struts over the past several years because they have significantly expanded the richness of the Struts development environment.

As developers have adopted Struts and added functionality for their specific needs, they have contributed a significant amount of that code back to the Struts project itself (e.g., Tiles, Validator, Declarative Exception Handling, Nested Tag Library, etc.). Several third-party extension projects have been created as well. This appendix provides a brief introduction to some of the more popular third-party extensions available for Struts. In addition to the extensions highlighted in this appendix, there is a Struts project hosted at SourceForge (**http://struts.sourceforge.net/**) that serves as a general repository for Struts extensions.

For a comprehensive list of all of the extensions available for Struts, you can visit the Struts Central Web site at **http://www.StrutsCentral.net/**. Additionally, the Planet Struts website at **http://www.PlanetStruts.org/** provides an archive of all of the latest news about Struts and extensions to the framework.

Strecks

Strecks, the Struts Extension Framework for Java 5, provides a suite of enhancements to Struts based on Java 5. Enhancements include the ability to use annotations, thus reducing the need for some configuration code via XML, the ability to use Plain Old Java Objects (POJOs) to reduce framework dependencies, the ability to create action interceptors, and much more.

See **http://strecks.sourceforge.net/**.

SSLEXT

SSLEXT, the Struts SSL Extension, provides a convenient mechanism for switching between the HTTP and HTTPS protocols in a Struts application. SSLEXT helps to greatly reduce the overhead incurred by placing of all of your Struts application behind the HTTPS protocol.

See **http://sslext.sourceforge.net/**.

Note *SSLEXT is covered further, along with Struts security in general, in Chapter 11.*

Struts Menu

The *Struts Menu* extension provides a rich library for creating application menus. Struts Menu has options for several types of menus, including DHTML drop-down style, tree style, tab style, and more. Additionally Struts Menu supports creating role-based menus and database-driven menus.

See **http://struts-menu.sourceforge.net/**.

displaytag

displaytag is an advanced library for displaying tables of data in an HTML page. It takes care of the implementation for paging, sorting, cropping, grouping, and the display of data in tables. Additionally, displaytag has built-in options for exporting table data to popular formats such as CSV, Excel, PDF, and XML.

See **http://displaytag.sourceforge.net/**.

stxx

stxx, the Struts for Transforming XML with XSL extension, provides a set of tools for generating XML from **Action** classes and applying XSL to the generated XML. It removes the need to use JSP for the View layer of Struts applications. Additionally, stxx provides a path for migrating the View layer to the Cocoon framework.

See **http://stxx.sourceforge.net/**.

formdef

The *formdef* extension provides a convenient mechanism for reusing Model layer business objects in the View layer of your Struts application. Instead of creating Form Beans, you can use formdef to generate Dynamic Form Bean definitions based on your business objects. It also provides formatting and conversion methods for moving data between forms and business objects.

See **http://formdef.dev.java.net/**.

Struts Layout

The *Struts Layout* extension provides an easy-to-use JSP tag library that simplifies and speeds up development of JSPs in a Struts application. Struts Layout provides tags for creating display panels, input fields, tables, trees, sortable lists, popups, calendars, and more.

See **http://struts.application-servers.com/**.

Struts Console

Struts Console provides a simple and intuitive graphical interface with which to edit Struts configuration files. Struts Console also supports editing of Tiles and Validator configuration files as well as JSP Tag Library Descriptor (**.tld**) files.

See **http://www.jamesholmes.com/struts/**.

NOTE *Struts Console is covered further in Appendix A.*

Index

A

Action class, 71
- customizing the response from, 73
- retrieving values from Form Beans, 71–72
- *See also* built-in actions

Action subclasses, 24
action tag, 402–405
ActionForward class, 85–86
action-mappings tag, 405
ActionServlet class, 65, 66–67
add tag, 145–146, 422
AJAX
- extensions, 485
- integrating with the Mini HR application, 486–493
- overview, 485–486
- updating search.jsp to use, 489–492

AjaxChat, 485
AjaxTags, 485
Ant, 34–35
Apache Ant, 34–35
Apache JMeter, 246–248
Apache Software Foundation (ASF), 7
application performance, testing, 245–248
application-managed security, 211
- vs. container-managed security, 202–204
- creating a security service, 211–221
- extending Struts' request processing engine, 215–217
- integrating Struts with SSL, 221–223
- page/action-level security checks, 215
- SSLEXT, 222–223
- using cookies, 220–221
- using servlet filters for security, 217–220

arg tag, 432–433
assertions, 226
Asynchronous JavaScript and XML. *See* AJAX
authentication, 202
authorization, 202

B

base tag, 255, 463–464
Bean Scripting Framework (BSF), 447–448
bean tag, 422–423
Bean Tag Library, 18, 19
- cookie tag, 314–316
- define tag, 316–318
- header tag, 318–320
- include tag, 320–321
- message tag, 321–323
- overview, 311, 312–314
- page tag, 323–324

parameter tag, 324–326
resource tag, 326–327
size tag, 327–329
Struts EL Bean Tag Library tags, 394
struts tag, 329–331
variables and scope, 311–312
write tag, 331–332
BeanUtils, using to transfer data to Model classes, 42–44
Beck, Kent, 226
Borland JBuilder. *See* JBuilder
Brown, Don, 447
BSF. *See* Bean Scripting Framework (BSF)
built-in actions, 73, 74
DispatchAction class, 73–75
DownloadAction class, 76
EventDispatchAction class, 76–78
ForwardAction class, 78–79
IncludeAction class, 79
LocaleAction class, 79–80
LookupDispatchAction class, 80–82
MappingDispatchAction class, 82–84
SwitchAction class, 84–85
button tag, 256–257
byte validation, 103–104
byteLocale validation, 104

C

Cactus project, 225
using for integration unit testing, 233–236
using StrutsTestCase with, 236–238
cancel tag, 257–258
Canoo WebTest, 242–245
CGI. *See* Common Gateway Interface (CGI)
chain of responsibility (COR)-based request processing engine, 7, 68–69
checkbox tag, 259–260
client-side validation, 116–119
code logic testing, 225
commandLink tag, 464–467
committers, 8
Common Gateway Interface (CGI), 4
Commons Chain-based request processing, 68–69
compiling, Mini HR sample application, 33–35
configuration file tags, 401–402
action tag, 402–405
action-mappings tag, 405
controller tag, 405–407
exception tag, 408–409
form-bean tag, 409–410
form-beans tag, 410–411
form-property tag, 411
forward tag, 412–413
global-exceptions tag, 413
global-forwards tag, 413–414
message-resources tag, 414–415
plug-in tag, 415
set-property tag, 416
struts-config tag, 416–417
configuration files, 399
configuring the web.xml deployment descriptor, 400–401
editing with Struts Console, 417–418
metadata tags, 417
support for multiple configuration files, 173–174
supported by Struts Console, 498–499
Tiles configuration files, 419–428
XML DTDs, 399–400
Console. *See* Struts Console
constant tag, 433–434
constant-name tag, 434
constant-value tag, 434
container-managed security
vs. application-managed security, 202–204
BASIC login, 206–208
FORM-based login, 209–210
login configurations, 205–206
overview, 204–205
transport-level security, 210–211
URL patterns, 205

Controller layer
- Action class, 71–85
- ActionForward class, 85–86
- ActionServlet class, 65, 66–67
- built-in actions, 73–85
- Commons Chain-based request processing, 68–69
- of the Mini HR sample application, 86–87
- request processing engine, 67–70
- RequestProcessor class-based processing, 69–70
- Struts and, 65–66

controller tag, 405–407
cookie tag, 314–316
cookies, 220–221
CountAction class, 487–488
creditCard validation, 104
custom validations, 119–124

D

date validation, 104–105
declarative exception handling
- adding new exception-handler definitions to the application's Struts configuration file, 166
- adding to the Mini HR application, 166–171
- for committed responses, 162–163
- configuring the declarative exception handler, 161–162
- creating a custom exception handler, 163–166
- creating a new exception-handler class, 164–166

default mapping, 205
define tag, 316–318
definition tag, 146–147, 423–424
DispatchAction class, 73–75
displaytag, 516
Document Type Definitions (DTDs), 399–400, 419–420, 430
Dojo, 485
double validation, 105–106
doubleRange validation, 106
DownloadAction class, 76
downloading Struts, 10
Dumoulin, Cedric, 131
DWR, 485
dynamic content, 3
Dynamic Form Beans, 54–55, 92
- *See also* Form Beans

E

Eclipse, using Struts Console inside of, 503–505
email validation, 106–107
Employee.java, 27
EmployeeSearchService.java, 25–27
empty tag, 337–338
equal tag, 338–340
errors tag, 260–262, 467–468
EventDispatchAction class, 76–78
exception handling
- adding new exception-handler definitions to the application's Struts configuration file, 166
- adding to the Mini HR application, 166–171
- for committed responses, 162–163
- configuring the application resource bundle file, 161–162
- creating a custom exception handler, 163–166
- creating a new exception-handler class, 164–166

exception tag, 408–409
execute( ) method, 164–165
explicit mapping, 205
extension mapping, 205
- and modules, 176

extensions
- AJAX, 485
- third-party, 515–516

F

field tag, 434–435
file tag, 262–264
float validation, 107
floatLocale validation, 107
floatRange validation, 108
Form Beans
- configuring, 50
- creating with Validator, 91–94
- Dynamic Form Beans, 54–55
- indexed and mapped properties, 55–57
- Lazy DynaBeans, 55
- lifecycle, 53–54
- overview, 48–50
- and the reset() method, 50–51
- retrieving values from, 71–72
- and the validate() method, 51–53

form tag, 264–266, 435–436, 469–470
form-bean tag, 409–410
form-beans tag, 410–411
formdef, 516
form-property tag, 411
formset tag, 436–437
form-validation tag, 436
forward definitions, 14, 85
forward tag, 340–341, 412–413
ForwardAction class, 78–79
frame tag, 266–270
framework, 9
functional testing, 226
functional unit testing, 226

G

Gamma, Erich, 226
Garrett, Jesse James, 485
Geary, David, 131
getEmployeeCount(), 486–487
global tag, 438
global-exceptions tag, 413
global-forwards tag, 413–414
greaterEqual tag, 341–343
greaterThan tag, 343–345

H

header tag, 318–320
hidden tag, 270–271
html tag, 271–272, 470–471
HTML Tag Library
- base tag, 255
- button tag, 256–257
- cancel tag, 257–258
- checkbox tag, 259–260
- common tag attributes, 307–309
- errors tag, 260–262
- file tag, 262–264
- form tag, 264–266
- frame tag, 266–270
- hidden tag, 270–271
- html tag, 271–272
- image tag, 272–274
- img tag, 274–277
- javascript tag, 278–279
- link tag, 280–283
- messages tag, 283–285
- multibox tag, 285–286
- option tag, 287
- options tag, 287–289
- optionsCollection tag, 289–290
- overview, 251, 252–255
- password tag, 290–292
- radio tag, 292–294
- reset tag, 294–296
- rewrite tag, 296–298
- select tag, 299–301
- Struts EL HTML Tag Library tags, 394–395
- submit tag, 301–302
- text tag, 302–304
- textarea tag, 304–306
- variables and scope, 251–252
- xhtml tag, 307

HTTPS, 201–202, 210–211

I

I18N. *See* internationalization
IBM Rational Application Developer for WebSphere. *See* RAD
image tag, 272–274
img tag, 274–277
implicit objects, 383
importAttribute tag, 147–148
include tag, 320–321
IncludeAction class, 79
includes, 131
indexed properties, 55–57
  creating validations for, 100
index.jsp, 13–15
initComponentDefinitions tag, 148
insert tag, 148–150
integer validation, 108
integerLocale validation, 109
integration unit testing, 225, 233–236
IntelliJ IDEA, using Struts Console inside of, 507–509
internationalization, 19, 185, 190–191
  java.text.MessageFormat class, 190
  java.util.Locale class, 188–189, 191
  java.util.ResourceBundle class, 189
  message resources, 191–193
  of the Mini HR sample application, 194–200
  tag library support for, 193–194
  of Tiles, 140–143
  of validations, 124–126
intRange validation, 109–110
item tag, 424
iterate tag, 345–348

J

Jakarta Bean Scripting Framework (BSF), 447–448
Jakarta project, 7
JAVA_HOME environmental variable, 500
javascript tag, 278–279, 438–439, 471–473
JavaServer Faces (JSF), 457
JavaServer Pages (JSP), 4
  development models, 5–6
  includes, 131
  Model-View-Controller (MVC) architecture, 5–6
  tag libraries, 9
  variables and scope, 251–252, 311–312, 333–334
  and the View layer, 48
  See also JSP tag libraries
java.text.MessageFormat class, 190
java.util.Locale class, 188–189, 191
java.util.ResourceBundle class, 189
JBuilder, using Struts Console inside of, 501–503
JDeveloper, using Struts Console inside of, 511–512
JMeter, 246–248
JSF. *See* JavaServer Faces (JSF)
JSP. *See* JavaServer Pages (JSP)
JSP Standard Tag Library. *See* JSTL
JSP tag libraries, 57–58
JSTL
  absolute URIs, 387
  accessing objects, 382–383
  brackets operator, 383
  Core Tag Library, 385–386
  dot operator, 382
  expression language, 382–384
  Format Tag Library, 386
  implicit objects, 383
  operators, 384
  overview, 381–382
  replacement examples, 389–392
  SQL Tag Library, 386
  Struts EL, 388–389
  Struts EL tag libraries, 392–396
  tag libraries, 385–387
  XML Tag Library, 387
JUnit, 226
  StrutsTestCase, 231–233, 236–238
  See also unit testing
JUnitPerf, 245–246

L

layouts, 132
    See also Tiles
Lazy DynaBeans, 55, 72
lessEqual tag, 348–350
lessThan tag, 350–352
link tag, 14, 280–283
loadMessage tag, 473
Locale class, 188–189, 191
LocaleAction class, 79–80
Logic Tag Library, 18, 20
    empty tag, 337–338
    equal tag, 338–340
    forward tag, 340–341
    greaterEqual tag, 341–343
    greaterThan tag, 343–345
    iterate tag, 345–348
    lessEqual tag, 348–350
    lessThan tag, 350–352
    match tag, 352–355
    messagesNotPresent tag, 355
    messagesPresent tag, 356
    notEmpty tag, 356–357
    notEqual tag, 357–359
    notMatch tag, 360–362
    notPresent tag, 362–365
    overview, 333, 334–337
    present tag, 365–367
    redirect tag, 367–371
    Struts EL Logic Tag Library tags, 395–396
    variables and scope, 333–334
long validation, 110
longLocale validation, 110
longRange validation, 110–111
LookupDispatchAction class, 80–82

M

mapped properties, 57
MappingDispatchAction class, 82–84
mask validation, 111–112
match tag, 352–355
maxlength validation, 112
McClanahan, Craig R., 7, 8
message resources, 191–193
message tag, 321–323, 474–475
MessageFormat class, 190
message-resources tag, 414–415
MessageResources.properties, 32
messages tag, 283–285
messagesNotPresent tag, 355
messagesPresent tag, 356
metadata tags, 417, 427
Mini HR sample application
    adding declarative exception handling to, 166–171
    adding Tiles to, 153–160
    adding Validator to, 126–129
    application files, 11–13
    compiling, 33–35
    Controller layer, 86–87
    converting to use modules, 178–184
    Employee.java, 27
    EmployeeSearchService.java, 25–27
    flow of execution, 38–39
    index.jsp, 13–15
    integrating AJAX with, 486–493
    internationalizing, 194–200
    MessageResources.properties, 32
    Model layer, 44–46
    overview, 11
    packaging, 35
    recompiling, repackaging, and running with AJAX, 492–493
    running, 35–37
    SearchAction.java, 23–25
    SearchForm.java, 21–23
    search.jsp, 15–20, 489–492
    struts-config.xml, 29–32, 488–489
    using Struts Scripting with, 453–456
    using the Struts-Faces Integration Library with, 477–483
    View layer, 60–64
    web.xml, 28–29
    Welcome File list, 29

minlength validation, 112–113
Model layer
  of the Mini HR sample application, 44–46
  overview, 41
  and Struts, 42–44
  sublayers, 41–42
  using BeanUtils to transfer data to Model classes, 42–44
Model-View-Controller architecture. *See* MVC architecture
modules
  configuring links to access module-specific JSPs, 176–177
  configuring the web.xml deployment descriptor, 175–176
  converting the Mini HR application to use modules, 178–184
  creating a Struts configuration file for each module, 180–181
  creating Struts configuration files for, 174–175
  overview, 173–174
  setting up module directories and files, 179–180
  updating the index.jsp file to link to each module, 183
  using Tiles with, 177–178
  using Validator with, 177
msg tag, 439–440
multibox tag, 285–286
multiple configuration files, support for, 173–174
MVC architecture
  controller components, 6
  Controller layer, 65–87
  model components, 6
  Model layer, 41–46
  overview, 5–6
  view components, 6
  View layer, 47–64

N

nest tag, 377–378
nested properties, 49
Nested Tag Library
  nest tag, 377–378
  object nesting, 373–374
  overview, 373, 374–377
  root tag, 378–379
  writeNesting tag, 379–380
NetBeans, using Struts Console inside of, 509–510
notEmpty tag, 356–357
notEqual tag, 357–359
notMatch tag, 360–362
notPresent tag, 362–365

O

object nesting, 373–374
  See also Nested Tag Library
option tag, 287
options tag, 287–289
optionsCollection tag, 289–290
Oracle JDeveloper. *See* JDeveloper

P

packaging, Mini HR sample application, 35
page tag, 323–324
parameter tag, 324–326
parametric replacement, 96, 321–322
password tag, 290–292
path mapping, and modules, 176
path prefix mapping, 205
performance testing, 245–248
plug-in tag, 415
plugins. *See* Eclipse; IntelliJ IDEA; JBuilder; JDeveloper; NetBeans; RAD; Tiles; Validator
present tag, 365–367
Pretty Output, 513–514
put tag, 150–151, 425
putList tag, 151–152, 425–426

R

RAD, using Struts Console inside of, 505–507
radio tag, 292–294
RBAC. *See* role-based access control (RBAC)
redirect tag, 367–371
request processing engine, 67–70
  extending, 215–217
RequestProcessor class-based processing, 69–70
required validation, 113
reset( ) method, 50–51, 94
reset tag, 294–296
resource bundles, 58–59
  configuring the application resource bundle file with Validator, 95–97
resource tag, 326–327
ResourceBundle class, 189
reuse, 131
rewrite tag, 296–298
role-based access control (RBAC), 202
root tag, 378–379
running, Mini HR sample application, 35–37

S

sample application (Mini HR)
  adding declarative exception handling to, 166–171
  adding Tiles to, 153–160
  adding Validator to, 126–129
  application files, 11–13
  compiling, 33–35
  Controller layer, 86–87
  converting to use modules, 178–184
  Employee.java, 27
  EmployeeSearchService.java, 25–27
  flow of execution, 38–39
  index.jsp, 13–15
  integrating AJAX with, 486–493
  internationalizing, 194–200
  MessageResources.properties, 32
  Model layer, 44–46
  overview, 11
  packaging, 35
  recompiling, repackaging, and running with AJAX, 492–493
  running, 35–37
  SearchAction.java, 23–25
  SearchForm.java, 21–23
  search.jsp, 15–20, 489–492
  struts-config.xml, 29–32, 488–489
  using Struts Scripting with, 453–456
  using the Struts-Faces Integration Library with, 477–483
  View layer, 60–64
  web.xml, 28–29
  Welcome File list, 29
scope, 251–252, 311–312, 333–334
scripting. *See* Struts Scripting
SearchAction.java, 23–25
SearchForm.java, 21–23
search.jsp, 15–20
  updating to use AJAX, 489–492
security
  application-managed, 202–204, 211–223
  authentication and authorization, 202
  container-managed, 202–204, 204–211
  HTTPS, 201–202
  overview, 201
  role-based access control (RBAC), 202
select tag, 299–301
separations of concerns, 131
servlet filters, using for security, 217–220
servlets, 4
set-property tag, 416, 426
short validation, 113–114
shortLocale validation, 114
size tag, 327–329
SSL, integrating Struts with, 221–223

SSL Extension to Struts. *See* SSLEXT
SSLEXT, 222–223, 515
Strecks, 515
Struts, 9
 base framework, 9
 binary distribution, 10
 downloading, 10, 33
 evolution of, 7–8
 JSP tag libraries, 9
 as open source software, 8
 overview, 7
 Sandbox, 9
 source distribution, 10
 support for, 8
 See also Tiles; Validator
Struts Console
 acquiring and installing, 500
 editing Struts configuration files, 417–418
 editing Tiles configuration files, 428
 editing Validator configuration files, 443–444
 output options, 513–514
 overview, 498–498, 516
 supported configuration files, 498–499
 using as a stand-alone application, 500–501
 using inside Borland JBuilder, 501–503
 using inside Eclipse, 503–505
 using inside IBM Rational Application Developer for WebSphere, 505–507
 using inside IntelliJ IDEA, 507–509
 using inside NetBeans, 509–510
 using inside Oracle JDeveloper, 511–512
Struts EL tag libraries, 392–396
Struts Layout, 516
Struts Menu, 516
Struts Scripting
 adding .jar files and properties file to the application, 449
 BSFManagerFilter implementation-based custom variables, 452–453
 configuring script-based actions in the application's Struts configuration file, 450–451
 creating script-based actions, 450
 overview, 447, 448
 predefined scripting variables, 451
 Struts configuration file-based custom variables, 451–452
 using with Mini HR application, 453–456
struts tag, 329–331
struts-config tag, 416–417
struts-config.xml, 29–32, 158–160, 488–489
 adding the Validator plugin to, 128
Struts-Faces Integration Library
 adding a servlet definition for the JSF controller servlet to the web.xml file, 459–460
 adding required .jar files to the application, 459
 base tag, 463–464
 commandLink tag, 464–467
 configuring forward and action definitions in the application's Struts configuration file, 461
 configuring Struts to use a custom Struts-Faces request processor, 460
 creating JSF-based user interfaces with Struts-Faces and JSF Tag Library tags, 460–461
 errors tag, 467–468
 form tag, 469–470
 html tag, 470–471
 javascript tag, 471–473
 limitations, 461–462
 loadMessage tag, 473
 message tag, 474–475
 overview, 457–458
 stylesheet tag, 476

supported versions of JSF, 458
supported versions of Struts, 458
tags, 462–463
using with the Mini HR application, 477–483
write tag, 476–477
StrutsTestCase, 231–233
using with Cactus, 236–238
stxx, 516
stylesheet tag, 476
submit tag, 301–302
SwitchAction class, 84–85, 176–177
system testing, 226

T

tag libraries, 9
support for internationalization, 193–194
See also Bean Tag Library; HTML Tag Library; JSTL; Logic Tag Library; Nested Tag Library
Template Tag Library, 131
templates, 132
testing
application performance, 245–248
code logic testing, 225
functional testing, 226
functional unit testing, 226
integration unit testing, 225, 233–236
system testing, 226
unit testing, 225–226, 226–240
use-case-driven, 240–245
See also Apache JMeter; Canoo WebTest; JUnit; JUnitPerf
text tag, 302–304
textarea tag, 304–306
third-party extensions, 515–516
Tiles, 9, 131–132
add tag, 145–146
adding to the Mini HR application, 153–160
attributes, 133
creating content JSPs, 138
creating layout JSPs, 138, 153–155
definition tag, 146–147
definitions, 133, 134–138
enabling, 133–134, 420–421
extending definitions, 135–137
handling relative URLs with, 140
importAttribute tag, 147–148
initComponentDefinitions tag, 148
insert tag, 148–150
internationalizing, 140–143
JSP-based definitions and attributes, 135
overview, 133
put tag, 150–151
putList tag, 151–152
struts-config.xml configuration file, 158–160
Tiles Tag Library, 138, 143–145
tiles-defs.xml configuration file, 157–158
useAttribute tag, 152–153
using definitions as attribute values, 137–138
using existing JSPs to work with layouts, 155–157
using Tiles definitions, 139
using with modules, 177–178
XML configuration file-based definitions and attributes, 134–135
Tiles configuration file, overview, 419
Tiles configuration files, 419
add tag, 422
bean tag, 422–423
definition tag, 423–424
editing with Struts Console, 428
item tag, 424
metadata tags, 427
put tag, 425
putList tag, 425–426
set-property tag, 426
tags, 421

tiles-definitions tag, 427
XML DTDs, 419–420
Tiles Tag Library, 138, 143–145
Struts EL Tiles Tag Library tags, 396
tiles-definitions tag, 427
Tomcat, 32
downloading, 33

U

unit testing, 225–226
assertions, 226
integration unit testing, 233–236
JUnit, 226
the model, 227–230
testing controller behavior, 230–238
testing the view, 238–240
using StrutsTestCase, 231–233
url validation, 114–115
useAttribute tag, 152–153
use-case-driven testing, 240
creating test cases, 241–242
using Canoo WebTest, 242–245

V

validate( ) method, 51–53, 94
Validator, 9
adding messages to the MessageResources.properties file, 124, 129
adding new validation definitions, 123–124
adding new validation rules, 121–123
adding to the Mini HR application, 126–129
byte validation, 103–104
byteLocale validation, 104
configurable validations, 98–99
configuring the application resource bundle file, 95–97
configuring validation.xml, 97–101
configuring validator-rules.xml, 94–95
creating Form Beans, 91–94
creating validation methods, 119–121
creating validations for indexed properties, 100
creditCard validation, 104
custom validations, 119–124
date validation, 104–105
double validation, 105–106
doubleRange validation, 106
email validation, 106–107
enabling, 90–91, 430–431
enabling client-side validations, 116–119
extending a set of validations, 99–100
float validation, 107
floatLocale validation, 107
floatRange validation, 108
included validations, 102–116
integer validation, 108
integerLocale validation, 109
internationalizing validations, 124–126
intRange validation, 109–110
long validation, 110
longLocale validation, 110
longRange validation, 110–111
mask validation, 111–112
maxlength validation, 112
minlength validation, 112–113
overview, 89–90
required validation, 113
short validation, 113–114
shortLocale validation, 114
url validation, 114–115
using with modules, 177
using with the Form Bean's reset( ) and validate( ) methods, 94

validations spanning multiple pages, 100–101
validwhen validation, 115–116
Validator configuration files
arg tag, 432–433
constant tag, 433–434
constant-name tag, 434
constant-value tag, 434
editing with Struts Console, 443–444
field tag, 434–435
form tag, 435–436
formset tag, 436–437
form-validation tag, 436
global tag, 438
javascript tag, 438–439
msg tag, 439–440
overview, 429–430
tags, 431–432
validation.xml, 430
validator tag, 440–441
validator-rules.xml, 429–430
var tag, 441–442
var-jstype tag, 442
var-name tag, 442–443
var-value tag, 443
XML DTDs, 430
validator tag, 440–441
validwhen validation, 115–116
var tag, 441–442
variables, 251–252, 311–312, 333–334
var-jstype tag, 442
var-name tag, 442–443
var-value tag, 443
View layer
alternative technologies, 64
Form Beans, 48–57
JSP pages, 48
JSP tag libraries, 57–58
of the Mini HR sample application, 60–64
resource bundles, 58–59
Struts and, 47–48

W

web application development, history of, 3–4
Web conversation, 238
web.xml, 28–29, 400–401
Welcome File list, 29
write tag, 331–332, 476–477
writeNesting tag, 379–380

X

xhtml tag, 307
XML DTDs, 399–400, 419–420, 430